Prose Models

NINTH EDITION

Gerald Levin

PROFESSOR EMERITUS
University of Akron

Harcourt Brace College Publishers

Fort Worth   Philadelphia   San Diego   New York   Orlando   Austin   San Antonio
Toronto   Montreal   London   Sydney   Tokyo

Editor in Chief	Ted Buchholz
Executive Editor	Bill McLane
Acquisitions Editor	Stephen T. Jordan
Developmental Editor	Sarah Helyar Smith
Project Editor	Kelly Riche
Production Manager	Erin Gregg
Book Designer	Burl Sloan

Address for Editorial Correspondence
Harcourt Brace College Publishers, 301 Commerce Street, Suite 3700, Fort Worth, TX 76102

Address for Orders
Harcourt Brace & Company, 6277 Sea Harbor Drive, Orlando, FL 32887
1-800-782-4479, or 1-800-433-0001 (in Florida)

ISBN: 0-15-500174-4
Library of Congress Catalog Card Number: 92-71196
Printed in the United States of America
3 4 5 6 7 8 9 0 1 2 016 9 8 7 6 5 4 3 2

PREFACE

❦ ❦ ❦

Prose Models offers the student models for composition drawn from contemporary and older writers. The book contains numerous and varied examples of the personal, the expository, and the persuasive essay, as well as detailed discussions of the sentence, the paragraph, and elements of the essay. The book introduces inductive and deductive reasoning through interesting and accessible paragraphs and essays.

The Ninth Edition contains 60 complete essays and self-contained sections of essays and chapters and 37 single-paragraph and multiparagraph excerpts. Twenty-five of the readings are new to the book. Essays by the following writers appear for the first time: Diane Ackerman, Jane Adams, Wendell Berry, Bruno Bettelheim, Paul Brodeur, Annie Dillard, Robert C. Ellickson, Antonia Fraser, Herbert J. Gans, Jane Goodall, David H. Hackworth, Amy Jo Keifer, Garrison Keillor, Elaine Tyler May, Mark H. Moore, Anna Quindlen, John Richards, Phyllis Rose, Peter H. Rossi, Richard Selzer, Edward Tenner, Alice Walker, Donovan Webster, Eudora Welty, and Nancy Wood.

Part I of the Ninth Edition addresses matters of organization in the paragraph and essay. Part II demonstrates methods of exposition in the paragraph and essay: example, classification and division, definition, comparison and contrast, analogy, process, and cause and effect. Part II also contains sections on description and narration. Part III presents argument and persuasion; the four documented essays in this part of the book illustrate some uses of primary and secondary sources in historical writing and in the social sciences. Part IV explains usage, tone, imagery, and other matters of diction. Part V illustrates sentence style. Part VI concludes the book with a series of essays on writing.

Each of the 97 readings contains a headnote giving a few details about the author and the context of the essay or excerpt. Questions and suggestions for writing follow all selections except the supplementary essays on writing. Vocabulary studies following some of the readings invite the student to look up unfamiliar words and to find the exact meaning of familiar ones.

To quote James Sledd, "Nobody ever learned to write without

reading." In his essay on composition, Mark Twain refers to the "model-chamber" or store of effective sentences gathered by the writer from many kinds of reading. These statements express the philosophy of this book. Student writers need to understand the methods of prose composition and to see these methods in practice. Discussion of the writing process and exercises in invention enhance writing skills, but analysis and discussion of a wide selection of readings are also essential.

In choosing the readings, I have looked for writing models that students will find both intriguing and challenging. Composition students may vary in writing ability, but all possess wider interests and a greater capacity to think abstractly than is sometimes assumed. They are eager to think about and write about important issues. Many recognize the importance of learning to write about these issues effectively and cogently.

I have sought readings that meet these interests and that connect in theme in various ways. For example, the contrasting readings by Norman Mailer and Norman Cousins examine from different perspectives the death of Benny Paret in the boxing ring. The essays of John Holt, Kenneth B. Clark, Liane Ellison Norman, and William Zinsser (on "the right to fail") present very different views on the purpose of education. Essays on homelessness in America and on women in combat take different approaches to issues of current interest. The thematic table of contents suggests similarities in topics, and the Instructor's Guide suggests other connections.

I wish to express my gratitude to Thomas Dukes of the University of Akron and to Donald G. Anderson of Bemidji State University for their helpful recommendations. I owe a debt again to William Francis, Alan Hart, Bruce Holland, Robert Holland, Alice MacDonald, Sally K. Slocum, and Linda Weiner, all of the University of Akron, who made suggestions for previous editions and gave me their advice and support over many years. I thank my acquisitions editor, Stephen T. Jordan, and my developmental editor, Sarah Helyar Smith, for useful suggestions for this edition. Eleanor Garner was again indispensable in securing permissions. I owe thanks also to project editor Kelly Riche, designer Burl Sloan, and production manager Erin Gregg. I thank again my wife, Lillian Levin, for her continuing support and help with the book over many editions. Elizabeth and Bill Ziegler and Sylvia and David Rubin were always in mind.

Gerald Levin

PREFACE TO THE STUDENT: HOW TO USE THIS BOOK

❦ ❦ ❦

Part I of *Prose Models* discusses matters common to various kinds of writing. These include stating and highlighting your central idea or thesis, organizing your ideas and supporting details, and showing how these ideas and details connect. Part II deals with ways of developing ideas in expository essays—those whose purpose is to explain ideas and processes. Parts I and II, in addition, illustrate how to organize and develop paragraphs—the basic units of the essay. Part III deals with various kinds of arguments and their use in persuasive writing; Parts IV and V, with choosing effective diction and building sentences in effective ways. Part VI concludes the book with a series of essays on the art of composition.

In your reading, you probably have noticed that a particular writer often favors similar kinds of sentences and certain expressions and ways of phrasing ideas, or builds paragraphs and essays in similar ways. The word *style* describes these recurrent patterns in a writer. Though still connected for many people with what is "correct" or "proper" in writing (style for the eighteenth-century writer Jonathan Swift was "proper words in proper places"), style refers commonly to individual choices in diction and sentence construction as well as in organization. It is in this sense that people refer to a "Hemingway style" in fiction.

However, much of what we describe as style in speaking and writing is probably not a matter of choice at all. Your writing is governed strongly by habits that develop without your being aware of them. One writer may favor long, heavily coordinated sentences, as in the speech of a nonstop talker. Another person, used to speaking in clipped sentences, may write in very short sentences or very short paragraphs. Habits of speech strongly influence how you write, though written communication requires more attention to such matters as sentence structure, punctuation, the organization of the whole essay.

You do have control, then, over your writing. Though you will continue to speak and write in ways natural to you, you can make your writing more expressive and effective. The more writing you do, the more aware you will become of your own habitual choices. As your awareness increases, you will have the opportunity to experiment with new ways of writing—as college gives you the opportunity to think about new ideas in new ways. The discovery and mastery of your own style of writing and thinking is one important purpose of this book.

The readings in this book are examples of effective writing by mostly contemporary American and British authors. They show how various writers choose to organize and develop their impressions and ideas. The readings do not, however, represent every kind of effective writing, nor are they "models" in the sense of representing the best and only ways to write sentences, paragraphs, and essays. They illustrate, rather, some choices possible in writing; they are models in being effective solutions to problems you will face in the course of writing your own essays. The readings have also been selected to help you draw on your own experiences and observations in writing your own essays. You will discover that many of the selections connect in theme or point of view. The expository and argumentative essays—many dealing with important issues of our time—offer an opportunity for you to work out your own ideas and bring your experience to bear on the issue under discussion. Essays that interest or move you can serve as resources to which you will return for inspiration and help in planning and revising your own.

The readings constitute in this way a repertory of choices available in practicing and refining your writing skills. The study and discussion of paragraphs and essays is only one part of the process of writing, but it is an indispensable part. For you learn to write as you learn to speak—by reading and listening to the words of others. Thus, in planning, drafting, and revising your own essays, you will have many opportunities to return to your reading and perhaps discover new ways to build and develop your ideas.

You will discover that principles of organization and development in paragraphs and sentences occur also in the whole essay; thus the topic sentence of the paragraph bears a close relationship to the main clause that organizes a sentence and to the thesis that organizes the essay. You will have an opportunity, then, to reconsider topics of organization and development in the smaller and larger units of the essay. Though each reading illustrates a particular way of organizing ideas or developing them, each also employs other methods discussed in the book. The questions often call attention to these, and your instructor may use a reading to focus discussion on another topic.

A final word on the vocabulary list that follows many of the readings: These lists contain unfamiliar words as well as many you use everyday. The familiar words are singled out because the author of the reading uses them in a special or unusual way. Often you will recognize the general meaning of a word, but you will need your dictionary to discover a subtle meaning that the author has in mind. In preparing for class discussion of these essays, you will gain the most from the reading if you keep a dictionary at hand and check the meanings of these words and others about whose meaning you are doubtful. A log of words and their definitions can be of immense help in your reading for composition and other courses.

Contents

❦ ❦ ❦

---

* Complete section, chapter, or essay

PART III: ARGUMENT AND PERSUASION   233

THEMATIC TABLE OF CONTENTS

❧ ❧ ❧

People

Places

Childhood and Adolescence

Education

Urban and Rural Life

Values

Native Americans, African Americans, Hispanic Americans

Nature

Language and Media

Social and Political Issues

Hunger, Poverty, Homelessness

Women and Society

Technology and Its Effects

Work

The Environment

War

Reading and Writing

PART
I

ORGANIZING
THE ESSAY

INTRODUCTION: THE ESSAY AND THE PARAGRAPH

The Nature of the Essay. If asked what an essay is, many would say that it is a piece of writing that states one or more ideas or impressions, develops these fully, and has a clearly marked beginning, middle, and end. The essay may be addressed to a single reader—perhaps in the form of a letter—or to a general audience, the readers of a newspaper or magazine, or a special audience, the readers of a technical journal. Many essays today— those written by newspaper and magazine columnists, television commentators, scholars, students—meet this definition.

But many essays in newspapers, magazines, and journals do not work out ideas completely; the essayist may do no more than explore an idea or an impression of a person or place briefly. The etymology of the word indeed suggests that an essay was for many writers of the past a trying-out or weighing of an idea, a first attempt at expression that might be followed by a second or third attempt. The essayist might put words on paper and not revise them; or might rephrase ideas, introduce new ideas and details, or recast the whole essay or parts of it. One of the creators of the modern essay, the sixteenth-century French writer Michel de Montaigne, states that some of his late essays added to "other parts of my portrait." "I add, but I do not correct," he writes in the third book of his essays, though he did make corrections later. It would be better to restate his ideas in new essays. Montaigne adds that he fears

> to lose by the change; my understanding does not always advance, it also goes backwards. I do not distrust my thoughts less because they are the second or third, than because they are the first, or my present less than my past thoughts. Besides, we often correct ourselves as foolishly as we correct others.—"Of Vanity," *Essays*

For Montaigne and for the British essayist and novelist Virginia Woolf, the essay is first of all an expression of personal ideas:

> A very wide definition obviously must be that which will include all the varieties of thought which are suitably enshrined in essays. . . . Almost all essays begin with a capital I—"I think," "I feel"—and when you have said that, it is clear that you are not writing history or philosophy or biography or anything but an essay, which may be brilliant or profound, which may deal with the immortality of the soul, or the rheumatism in your left shoulder, but is primarily an expression of personal opinion.—"The Decay of Essay-Writing"

3

Since Montaigne's day, the essay has broadened to include "all the varieties of thought," as Woolf states. The contemporary essay sometimes expresses personal opinion and feelings and as such sometimes seems extemporaneous and unfinished. But the contemporary essay may at other times be entirely objective in tone and approach to the subject, omitting personal opinions and feelings.

Organizing and Developing the Essay. The contemporary essay may narrate experiences, describe persons and places, explain an idea or a process, give the history of an event, or argue a point and seek to persuade us to accept it. Essays indeed have been traditionally classified as narrative, descriptive, expository, and argumentative, depending on the chief method used to organize and develop the essay. We commonly refer to novels as narratives, word pictures as descriptions, sets of directions as expositions, and defenses of opinion as arguments. This traditional classification does not, however, tell us why the essayist chooses to narrate or describe, explain or argue. We need to know the purpose that the writer has in doing so.

Thus an autobiographical essay or memoir like Sally Carrighar's recollection of her father (p. 40) may use narrative and description to express the writer's sense of the past or help us to understand it. Narratives in the form of short stories and novels may entertain us, or, like John Steinbeck's *The Grapes of Wrath*, seek to move us or persuade us to take action. An explanatory essay helps us to understand a process or, as in Florence H. Pettit's essay on how to sharpen a knife (p. 207), teaches us to perform it. Usually argument is used as a means to persuasion. Though essays may depend on a single method of development, most depend upon more than one method. Description usually gives support to narrative. And exposition often aids in expressing feelings and attitudes, as in Anna Quindlen's essay on privacy (p. 56), and often joins with argument, as in an advertisement that explains how a product works and gives us reasons for buying it.

The Nature of the Paragraph. In this section and those following in Parts One and Two, we will see how individual paragraphs and complete essays illustrate a principle of organization and development of ideas. In looking at paragraphs, we need to remember that they form complete essays and do not stand alone, except where the essay consists of a single paragraph, as in E. B. White's "In an Elevator" (p. 52).

Some paragraphs develop a single impression or idea; some develop related impressions or ideas. The paragraphs that follow in this and later sections are of this type. Other paragraphs, it should be noted, are transitional, marking a turn to a new idea, as in the following paragraph that introduces a discussion of the word *Chicano*, and some are summary paragraphs—stating or reiterating the central idea or thesis, without developing it:

> [*Transitional*] It can be safely said that no one knows for certain the origin of the word. Various theories do exist; of those suggested, scholars and students of Mexican-American life and literature generally accept one of two. Each is plausible, but neither has been proved.—Edward Simmen, "Chicano: Origin and Meaning"

> [*Summary*] Yet even as the word is being used, the meaning is changing; amelioration is taking place as more Mexican-Americans in responsible educational, governmental, and professional positions begin to refer to themselves as *Chicanos*. We may assume that as more and more of these individuals use the term, the word will be defined as follows: "An American of Mexican descent who attempts through peaceful, reasonable, and responsible means to correct the image of the Mexican-American and to improve the position of this minority in the American social structure.—Edward Simmen

The essays and paragraphs that follow by no means show all possible ways of organizing and developing ideas. But the methods illustrated are common ones that all writers draw upon.

Topic Sentence, Thesis, and Unity
❦ ❦ ❦

Topic Sentence and Unity in the Paragraph

In reading an essay, we depend on the opening sentence of each paragraph to direct us from one idea to the next. As in the following paragraph from Eric Sevareid's essay describing his hometown in North Dakota (p. 27), the opening sentence (italicized here) sometimes directs us through a topic sentence or statement of the central idea:

> *Sights have changed:* there is a new precision about street and home, a clearing away of chicken yards, cow barns, pigeon-crested cupolas, weed lots and coulees, the dim and secret adult-free rendezvous of boys. An intricate metal "jungle gym" is a common backyard sight, the sack swing uncommon. . . .—"Velva, North Dakota"

Not all opening sentences state the central idea fully. Some state only the subject or topic of the paragraph—occasionally through a single word, as in another paragraph of Sevareid's:

> *Consolidation.* The nearby hamlets of Sawyer and Logan and Voltaire had their own separate banks and papers and schools in my days of dusty buggies and Model Ts marooned in the snowdrifts. Now these hamlets are dying. . . . [italics added]

The subject or topic may also be introduced through a question that the remainder of the paragraph answers:

> *But now I must ask myself: Are they nearer to one another?* And the answer is no; yet I am certain that this is good. The shrinking of time and distance has made contrast and relief available to their daily lives. They do not know one another quite so well because they are not so much obliged to. . . .—Sevareid [italics added]

In paragraphs that open with a statement of the subject or topic, the central or topic idea may follow immediately, as in the paragraph just cited. In other paragraphs, details and explanatory statements may build to the central idea. Paragraphs of this kind sometimes generate suspense or a sense of climax, for the reader must wait for the central statement in order to gain the full impact of the paragraph. When the details alone make the point, the paragraph is said to have an implied topic sentence, the central idea or generalization remaining unstated.

The topic sentence helps in unifying the paragraph. A unified paragraph not only develops one idea at a time but also makes each idea and detail relevant to the topic idea. In a unified paragraph, the reader sees the relation of ideas and details. A disunified paragraph, by contrast, seems disconnected, its ideas and details introduced without transition or apparent reason.

EUDORA WELTY

One of America's most distinguished writers of fiction, Eudora Welty was born and raised in Jackson, Mississippi. After college she worked at a number of jobs before beginning her career as a photographer and writer about Mississippi life. She is the author of numerous short stories, novels, and essays; her novel The Optimist's Daughter *won the Pulitzer Prize for fiction in 1973. Her description of her family house in Jackson reveals what novelist Katherine Anne Porter finds in Welty's stories, "an eye and an ear sharp, shrewd and true as a tuning fork."*

In Our House on North Congress Street

In our house on North Congress Street in Jackson, Mississippi, where I was born, the oldest of three children, in 1909, we grew up to the striking of clocks. There was a mission-style oak grandfather clock standing in the hall, which sent its gong-like strokes through the livingroom, diningroom, kitchen, and pantry, and up the sounding board of the stairwell. Through the night, it could find its way into our ears; sometimes, even on the sleeping porch, midnight could wake us up. My parents' bedroom had a smaller striking clock that answered it. Though the kitchen clock did nothing but show the time, the diningroom clock was a cuckoo clock with weights on long chains, on one of which my baby brother, after climbing on a chair to the top of the china closet, once succeeded in suspending the cat for a moment. I don't know whether or not my father's Ohio family, in having been Swiss back in the 1700s before the first three Welty brothers came to America, had anything to do with this; but we all of us have been time-minded all our lives. This was good at least for a future fiction writer, being able to learn so penetratingly, and almost first of all, about chronology. It was one of a good many things I learned almost without knowing it; it would be there when I needed it.

My father loved all instruments that would instruct and   2
fascinate. His place to keep things was the drawer in the "library table" where lying on top of his folded maps was a telescope with brass extensions, to find the moon and the Big Dipper after supper in our front yard, and to keep appointments with eclipses. There was a folding Kodak that was brought out for Christmas, birthdays, and trips. In the back of the drawer you could find a magnifying glass, a kaleidoscope, and a gyroscope kept in a black buckram box, which he would set dancing for us on a string pulled tight. He had also supplied himself with an assortment of puzzles composed of metal rings and intersecting links and keys chained together, impossible for the rest of us, however patiently shown, to take apart; he had an almost childlike love of the ingenious.

QUESTIONS

1. Welty states the topic idea of paragraph 1 in her opening sentence. How does she illustrate this idea, and in what order does she present her examples?

2. Having illustrated her topic idea, Welty reflects on it in the remainder of paragraph 1. How does the reflection on her father's Ohio and Swiss background lead to the reflections that follow?

3. What is the topic sentence of paragraph 2, and how does it organize the paragraph? What additional comment does Welty make about her father?

SUGGESTIONS FOR WRITING

1. Rewrite paragraph 1, opening with the idea that learning about chronology was one of the important things "I learned almost without knowing it . . ." Include all of the ideas and details of the paragraph.
2. Write a paragraph of your own on a significant feature of your household in growing up. Like Welty, be specific in your details, letting your reader experience what you did.
3. The newspaper columnist Dave Barry develops his topic idea through a humorous definition and series of examples:

> Local TV news programs have given a whole new definition to the word *news*. To most people, *news* means *information about events that affect a lot of people.* On local TV news shows, *news* means *anything that you can take a picture of, especially if a local TV News Personality can stand in front of it.* This is why they are so fond of car accidents, burning buildings, and crowds: these are good for standing in front of. On the other hand, local TV news shows tend to avoid stories about things that local TV News Personalities cannot stand in front of, such as budgets and taxes and the economy. If you want to get a local TV news show to do a story on the budget, your best bet is to involve it in a car crash.—*Bad Habits*

In a paragraph of your own, illustrate an idea relating to national television news programs. State your subject or topic in your opening sentence as Barry does, or state your topic idea fully.

JAMES STEVENSON

JAMES STEVENSON *has written a series of articles and profiles for* The New Yorker *magazine. His description of a steep road in Los Angeles—from one of these profiles—introduces the reader to a contemporary director of horror films, John Carpenter. Notice how Stevenson creates a feeling of suspense in his selection of details and building of the paragraph.*

Loma Vista Drive

Partway down the long, very steep slope of Loma Vista Drive, descending through Beverly Hills, with the city of Los Angeles spread out far below the houses of sparkling opulence on either side, there is a sign warning "Use Lowest Gear" and, shortly after that, a sign that says "Runaway Vehicle Escape Lane 600 Feet Ahead." Just before Loma Vista crosses Doheny Road, it expands on the right into a third lane, composed of a succession of low, uneven piles of loose gravel nestled against cement block set in an embankment. The operator of a runaway vehicle is apparently expected to steer his car into this soft and receptive lane and come to a halt like a baseball player sliding into third. It seems a perfectly reasonable solution; the unsettling aspect is the underlying assumption that automobiles will so frequently go berserk hereabouts that some accommodation must be made for them. Similarly, along the heavily populated canyon roads of Beverly Hills there are signs forbidding cigarettes and matches: these dry hills may burst into flame at any time. The houses above Sunset Boulevard are stuck in the nearly vertical slopes like cloves in a ham; how they stay there is mysterious. It seems likely that, if they do not catch fire first, a good rain will send them tumbling down the mountain; already, earth has slid out from under retaining walls, terraces, swimming pools, driveways, even roads. In some places, tons of concrete have been poured like icing over a section of hillside to hold it back—and the concrete has even been painted green—but the earth has begun to slip away beneath that, too, leaving edges of concrete sticking out against the sky. In addition, of course, the entire area sits close to the quiescent but menacing San Andreas Fault. Gazing up the perilous roads at the plucky, high-risk homes perched in the tinderlike hills near the great rift, a visitor feels that this may be a community where desire and imagination automatically take precedence over danger, and even over reality.

QUESTIONS

1. Stevenson builds up to his central idea instead of starting the paragraph with it. How does the opening sentence introduce the topic or subject of the paragraph and prepare the reader for the details that follow?

2. How do the details develop the central idea, stated in the final sentence?

3. Did Stevenson need to state the central idea, or could he have depended on the details to state it implicitly?

4. How is the paragraph appropriate as an introduction to a man who makes horror films?

SUGGESTIONS FOR WRITING

1. In a paragraph of your own, give an account of a drive down an unusual street. Describe the street for someone who has not seen it—building through a series of details to a central idea as Stevenson does.

2. Write a second paragraph describing the street from the point of view of a person seeing it for the first time. Let your details develop an idea; do not state it explicitly. Your details should be vivid enough and well enough organized to make the idea clear to your reader.

Thesis and Unity in the Essay

The thesis of an essay is its central or controlling idea, the proposition or chief argument—the point of the essay. The topic sentence of a paragraph may be either a full or a partial statement of the controlling idea: the thesis is always a full statement of it.

Where the thesis appears depends largely on the audience. If we believe that the audience requires no introduction to the thesis— no background or explanation of the issue or important terms—we may state it in the first sentence. Many newspaper editorials begin with a statement of the thesis—a practice consistent with that of putting the important information in the opening sentences of a news story. Most essayists, by contrast, prefer to build to the thesis—stating it partially or fully in the introductory paragraphs, in company with an explanation of important terms and the issues to be discussed. George Orwell gives such an explanation in the opening paragraph of "Politics and the English Language" (p. 476):

> Most people who bother with the matter at all would admit that the English language is in a bad way, but it is generally assumed that we cannot by conscious action do anything about it. Our civilization is decadent and our language—so the argument runs—must inevitably share in the general collapse. It follows that any struggle against the abuse of language is a sentimental archaism, like preferring candles to electric light or hansom cabs to airplanes. Underneath this lies the half-conscious belief that language is a natural growth and not an instrument which we shape for our own purposes.

Orwell has built to a partial statement of his thesis in his concluding sentence: language, he will show, is an instrument that we shape to our purposes. And in the opening sentence of his second paragraph he expands this statement to cover the specific concern of the essay—the political uses of language:

> Now, it is clear that the decline of a language must ultimately have political and economic causes. . . .

In later paragraphs he restates his thesis as he presents various pieces of evidence in support of it:

> In our time it is broadly true that political writing is bad writing.
>
> In our time, political speech and writing are largely the defense of the indefensible.
>
> But if thought corrupts language, language can also corrupt thought.

Orwell introduces his thesis early in "Politics and the English Language" and restates it throughout. If the thesis needs extensive background and discussion to be understood or perhaps is so controversial that we will win our audience by building to it slowly, we may put it at the end of the essay. In some essays we may not wish to state the thesis at all, but rather let the reader draw conclusions from the details or facts we provide. In this case the thesis is said to be *implied*.

GEORGE ORWELL

GEORGE ORWELL (1903–50) *was the pseudonym of the English novelist and essayist Eric Hugh Blair. Orwell was born in India, where his father was a customs official in the British colonial government; at the age of eight, he was sent to school in England. At the end of his schooling, instead of entering a university, Orwell returned to India, taking a job with the Imperial Police. "Shooting an Elephant" describes one of his experiences as a police officer in Burma, where he served from 1922 to 1927. On leaving the police service, Orwell returned to Europe where he began his career as journalist and novelist. The rise of totalitarianism in Europe led Orwell to write increasingly about its causes—in essays like "Politics and the English Language" (p. 476) and in his most famous novels,* Animal Farm *(1945) and* Nineteen Eighty-Four *(1949).*

In "Shooting an Elephant," Orwell skillfully combines his description of a small Burmese town and British colonial officials with a narrative of what happened to him when summoned to deal with a temporarily crazed elephant. In narrating this incident, Orwell is arguing a thesis in a special way—through an episode typical of a situation faced by colonial powers. More than this, Orwell has something important to say about human nature. Great Britain no longer governs India or Burma, yet Orwell's ideas still are pertinent to current political issues.

Shooting an Elephant

In Moulmein, in lower Burma, I was hated by large numbers   1
of people—the only time in my life that I have been important
enough for this to happen to me. I was subdivisional police

officer of the town, and in an aimless, petty kind of way anti-European feeling was very bitter. No one had the guts to raise a riot, but if a European woman went through the bazaars alone somebody would probably spit betel juice over her dress. As a police officer, I was an obvious target and was baited whenever it seemed safe to do so. When a nimble Burman tripped me up on the football field and the referee (another Burman) looked the other way, the crowd yelled with hideous laughter. This happened more than once. In the end the sneering yellow faces of young men that met me everywhere, the insults hooted after me when I was at a safe distance, got badly on my nerves. The young Buddhist priests were the worst of all. There were several thousands of them in the town and none of them seemed to have anything to do except stand on street corners and jeer at Europeans.

All this was perplexing and upsetting. For at that time I had already made up my mind that imperialism was an evil thing and the sooner I chucked up my job and got out of it the better. Theoretically—and secretly, of course—I was all for the Burmese and all against their oppressors, the British. As for the job I was doing, I hated it more bitterly than I can perhaps make clear. In a job like that you see the dirty work of Empire at close quarters. The wretched prisoners huddling in the stinking cages of the lock-ups, the gray, cowed faces of the long-term convicts, the scarred buttocks of the men who had been flogged with bamboos—all these oppressed me with an intolerable sense of guilt. But I could get nothing into perspective. I was young and ill educated and I had had to think out my problems in the utter silence that is imposed on every Englishman in the East. I did not even know that the British Empire is dying, still less did I know know that it is a great deal better than the younger empires that are going to supplant it. All I knew was that I was stuck between my hatred of the empire I served and my rage against the evil-spirited little beasts who tried to make my job impossible. With one part of my mind I thought of the British Raj as an unbreakable tyranny, as something clamped down, in *saecula saeculorum,* upon the will of prostrate peoples; with another part I thought that the greatest joy in the world would be to drive a bayonet into a Buddhist priest's guts.

Feelings like these are the normal by-products of imperialism; ask any Anglo-Indian official, if you can catch him off duty.

One day something happened which in a roundabout 3 way was enlightening. It was a tiny incident in itself, but it gave me a better glimpse than I had had before of the real nature of imperialism—the real motives for which despotic governments act. Early one morning the sub-inspector at a police station the other end of the town rang me up on the 'phone and said that an elephant was ravaging the bazaar. Would I please come and do something about it? I did not know what I could do, but I wanted to see what was happening and I got on to a pony and started out. I took my rifle, an old .44 Winchester and much too small to kill an elephant, but I thought the noise might be useful in *terrorem*. Various Burmans stopped me on the way and told me about the elephant's doings. It was not, of course, a wild elephant, but a tame one which had gone "must." It had been chained up, as tame elephants always are when their attack of "must" is due, but on the previous night it had broken its chain and escaped. Its mahout, the only person who could manage it when it was in that state, had set out in pursuit, but had taken the wrong direction and was now twelve hours' journey away, and in the morning the elephant had suddenly reappeared in the town. The Burmese population had no weapons and were quite helpless against it. It had already destroyed somebody's bamboo hut, killed a cow and raided some fruit-stalls and devoured the stock; also it had met the municipal rubbish van and, when the driver jumped out and took to his heels, had turned the van over and inflicted violences upon it.

The Burmese sub-inspector and some Indian constables 4 were waiting for me in the quarter where the elephant had been seen. It was a very poor quarter, a labyrinth of squalid bamboo huts, thatched with palm-leaf winding all over a steep hillside. I remember that it was a cloudy, stuffy morning at the beginning of the rains. We began questioning the people as to where the elephant had gone and, as usual, failed to get any definite information. That is invariably the case in the East; a story always sounds clear enough at a distance, but the nearer you get to the scene of events the vaguer it becomes. Some of the people said that the elephant had gone in one direction, some said that he had gone in another, some professed not even to have heard of any elephant. I had almost made up my mind that the whole story was a pack of lies, when we heard yells a little distance away. There was a loud, scandalized cry of "Go away, child! Go away this instant!" and an old woman with a switch in her hand came round the corner of a hut, violently shooing away a crowd of naked children. Some more women followed, clicking their tongues and exclaiming; evidently there was something that the children ought not to have seen. I rounded the hut and saw a man's dead body sprawling in the mud. He was an Indian, a black Dravidian coolie, almost naked, and he could not have been dead many minutes. The people said that the elephant had come suddenly upon him round the corner of the hut, caught him with its trunk, put its foot on his back and ground him into the earth. This was the rainy season and the ground was soft, and his face had scored a trench a foot deep and a couple of yards long. He was lying on his belly with arms crucified and head sharply twisted to one side. His face was coated with mud, the eyes wide open, the teeth bared and grinning with an expression of unendurable agony. (Never tell me, by the way, that the dead look peaceful. Most of the corpses I have seen looked devilish.) The friction of the great beast's foot had stripped the skin from his back as neatly as one skins a rabbit. As soon as I saw the dead man I sent an orderly to a friend's house nearby to borrow an elephant rifle. I had already sent back the pony, not wanting it to go mad with fright and throw me if it smelt the elephant.

The orderly came back in a few minutes with a rifle and five cartridges, and meanwhile some Burmans had arrived and told us that the elephant was in the paddy fields below, only a few hundred yards away. As I started forward practically the whole population of the quarter flocked out of the houses and followed me. They had seen the rifle and were all shouting excitedly that I was going to shoot the elephant. They had not shown much interest in the elephant when he was merely ravaging their homes, but it was different now that he was going to be shot. It was a bit of fun to them, as it would be to an English crowd; besides they wanted the meat. It made me vaguely uneasy. I had no intention of shooting the elephant—I had merely sent for the rifle to defend myself if necessary—and it is always unnerving to have a crowd following you. I marched down the hill, looking and feeling a fool, with the rifle over my shoulder and an ever-growing army of people jostling at my heels. At the bottom, when you got away from the huts, there was a metalled road and beyond that a miry waste of paddy fields a thousand yards across, not yet ploughed but soggy from the first rains and dotted with coarse grass. The elephant was standing eight yards from the road, his left side toward us. He took not the slightest notice of the crowd's approach. He was tearing up bunches of grass, beating them against his knees to clean them, and stuffing them into his mouth.

I had halted on the road. As soon as I saw the elephant 6 I knew with perfect certainty that I ought not to shoot him. It is a serious matter to shoot a working elephant—it is comparable to destroying a huge and costly piece of machinery—and obviously one ought not to do it if it can possibly be avoided. And at that distance, peacefully eating, the elephant looked no more dangerous than a cow. I thought then and I think now that his attack of "must" was already passing off; in which case he would merely wander harmlessly about until the mahout came back and caught him. Moreover, I did not in the least want to shoot him. I decided that I would watch him for a little while to make sure that he did not turn savage again, and then go home.

But at that moment I glanced round at the crowd that 7 had followed me. It was an immense crowd, two thousand at the least and growing every minute. It blocked the road for a long distance on either side. I looked at the sea of yellow faces above the garish clothes—faces all happy and excited over this bit of fun, all certain that the elephant was going to be shot. They were watching me as they would watch a conjurer about to perform a trick. They did not like me, but with the magical rifle in my hands I was momentarily worth watching. And suddenly I realized that I should have to shoot the elephant after all. The people expected it of me and I had got to do it; I could feel their two thousand wills pressing me forward, irresistibly. And it was at this moment, as I stood there with the rifle in my hands, that I first grasped the hollowness, the futility of the white man's dominion in the East. Here was I, the white man with his gun, standing in front of the unarmed native crowd—seemingly the leading actor of the piece; but in reality I was only an absurd puppet pushed to and fro by the will of those yellow faces behind. I perceived in this moment that when the white man turns tyrant it is his own freedom that he destroys. He becomes a sort of hollow, posing dummy, the conventionalized figure of a sahib. For it is the condition of his rule that he shall spend his life in trying to impress the "natives," and so in every crisis he has got to do what the "natives" expect of him. He wears a mask, and his face grows to fit it. I had got to shoot the elephant. I had committed myself to doing it when I sent for the rifle. A sahib has got to act like a sahib; he has got to appear resolute, to know his own mind and do definite things. To come all that way, rifle in hand, with two thousand people marching at my heels, and then to trail feebly away, having done nothing—no, that was impossible. The crowd would laugh at me. And my whole life, every white man's life in the East, was one long struggle not to be laughed at.

But I did not want to shoot the elephant. I watched him 8 beating his bunch of grass against his knees with that preoccupied grandmotherly air that elephants have. It seemed to me that it would be murder to shoot him. At that age I was not squeamish about killing animals, but I had never shot an elephant and never wanted to. (Somehow it always seems worse to kill a *large* animal.) Besides, there was the beast's owner to be considered. Alive, the elephant was worth at least a hundred pounds; dead, he would only be worth the value of his tusks, five pounds, possibly. But I had got to act quickly. I turned to some experienced-looking Burmans who had been there when we arrived, and asked them how the elephant had been behaving. They all said the same thing: he took no notice of you if you left him alone, but he might charge if you went too close to him.

It was perfectly clear to me what I ought to do. I ought 9 to walk up to within, say, twenty-five yards of the elephant and test his behavior. If he charged, I could shoot; if he took no notice of me, it would be safe to leave him until the mahout came back. But also I knew that I was going to do no such thing. I was a poor shot with a rifle and the ground was soft mud into which one would sink at every step. If the elephant charged and I missed him, I should have about as much chance as a toad under a steam-roller. But even then I was not thinking particularly of my own skin, only of the watchful yellow faces behind. For at that moment, with the crowd watching me, I was not afraid in the ordinary sense, as I would have been if I had been alone. A white man mustn't be frightened in front of "natives"; and so, in general, he isn't frightened. The sole thought in my mind was that if anything went wrong those two thousand Burmans would see me pursued, caught, trampled on, and reduced to a grinning corpse like that Indian up the hill. And if that happened it was quite probable that some of them would laugh. That would never do. There was only one alternative. I shoved the cartridges into the magazine and lay down on the road to get a better aim.

The crowd grew very still, and a deep, low, happy sigh, 10 as of people who see the theater curtain go up at last, breathed from innumerable throats. They were going to have their bit of fun after all. The rifle was a beautiful German thing with crosshair sights. I did not then know that in shooting an elephant one would shoot to cut an imaginary bar running from ear-hole to ear-hole. I ought, therefore, as the elephant was sideways on, to have aimed straight at his ear-hole; actually I aimed several inches in front of this, thinking the brain would be further forward.

When I pulled the trigger I did not hear the bang or feel 11 the kick—one never does when a shot goes home—but I heard the devilish roar of glee that went up from the crowd. In that instant, in too short a time, one would have thought, even for the bullet to get there, a mysterious, terrible change had come over the elephant. He neither stirred nor fell, but every line of his body had altered. He looked suddenly stricken, shrunken, immensely old, as though the frightful impact of the bullet had paralyzed him without knocking him down. At last, after what seemed a long time—it might have been five seconds, I dare say—he sagged flabbily to his knees. His mouth slobbered. An enormous senility seemed to have settled upon him. One could have imagined him thousands of years old. I fired again into the same spot. At the second shot he did not collapse but climbed with desperate slowness to his feet and stood weakly upright, with legs sagging and head drooping. I fired a third time. That was the shot that did for him. You could see the agony of it jolt his whole body and knock the last remnant of strength from his legs. But in falling he seemed for a moment to rise, for as his hind legs collapsed beneath him he seemed to tower upward like a huge rock toppling, his trunk reaching skyward like a tree. He trumpeted, for the first and only time. And then down he came, his belly toward me, with a crash that seemed to shake the ground even where I lay.

I got up. The Burmans were already racing past me 12 across the mud. It was obvious that the elephant would never rise again, but he was not dead. He was breathing very rhythmically with long rattling gasps, his great mound of a side painfully rising and falling. His mouth was wide open—I could see far down into caverns of pale pink throat. I waited a long time for him to die, but his breathing did not weaken. Finally I fired my two remaining shots into the spot where I thought his heart must be. The thick blood welled out of him like red velvet, but still he did not die. His body did not even jerk when the shots hit him, the tortured breathing continued without a pause. He was dying, very slowly and in great agony, but in some world remote from me where not even a bullet could damage him further. I felt that I had got to put an end to that dreadful noise. It seemed dreadful to see the great beast lying there, powerless to move and yet powerless to die, and not even to be able to finish him. I sent back for my small rifle and poured shot after shot into his heart and down his throat. They seemed to make no impression. The tortured gasps continued as steadily as the ticking of a clock.

In the end I could not stand it any longer and went 13 away. I heard later that it took him half an hour to die. Burmans were bringing dahs and baskets even before I left, and I was told they had stripped his body almost to the bones by the afternoon.

Afterward, of course, there were endless discussions 14 about the shooting of the elephant. The owner was furious, but he was only an Indian and could do nothing. Besides, legally I had done the right thing, for a mad elephant has to be killed, like a mad dog, if its owner fails to control it. Among the Europeans opinion was divided. The older men said I was right, the younger men said it was a damn shame to shoot an elephant for killing a coolie, because an elephant was worth more than any damn Coringhee coolie. And afterward I was very glad that the coolie had been killed; it put me legally in the right and it gave me a sufficient pretext for shooting the elephant. I often wondered whether any of the others grasped that I had done it solely to avoid looking a fool.

VOCABULARY

paragraph 2: imperialism, supplant, prostrate

paragraph 3: must

paragraph 4: Dravidian

paragraph 6: mahout

paragraph 7: dominion, sahib

paragraph 8: squeamish

paragraph 11: glee, sagged, slobbered, senility

paragraph 13: dahs

paragraph 14: pretext

QUESTIONS

1. Orwell states in paragraph 3: "One day something happened which in a roundabout way was enlightening. It was a tiny incident in itself, but it gave me a better glimpse than I had had before of the real nature of imperialism—the real motives for which despotic governments act." The incident, in its details, reveals the psychology of the imperialist ruler. What effects do the stuffy, cloudy weather and the behavior of the Burmese and their attitude toward the elephant have on this psychology? Why is the dead coolie described in detail in paragraph 4? Why is the shooting of the elephant described in detail in paragraph 11? In general, how does the incident reveal the motives Orwell mentions?

2. The incident reveals more than just the motives of the imperi-

alist ruler: what does it reveal about mob and crisis psychology and the man in the middle?

3. Where in the essay is the thesis stated, and how do you account for its placement? Does Orwell restate it?

4. The exact diction contributes greatly to the development of the thesis, for Orwell does not merely *tell us*, he makes us see. In paragraph 11, for example, he states: ". . . I heard the devilish roar of *glee* that went up from the crowd." He might have chosen *laughter, hilarity,* or *mirth* to describe the behavior of the crowd, but *glee* is the exact word because it connotes something that the other three words do not—malice. And the elephant "*sagged* flabbily to his knees," not *dropped* or *sank*, because *sagged* connotes weight and, in the context of the passage, age. What does Orwell mean in the same paragraph by "His mouth slobbered" and "An enormous senility seemed to have settled upon him"? In paragraph 12 why "*caverns* of pale pink throat" rather than *depths*? In paragraph 4 why is the corpse *grinning* rather than *smiling*? (Consult the synonym listings in your dictionary, or compare definitions.)

SUGGESTIONS FOR WRITING

1. Illustrate the last sentence of the essay from your own experience. Build the essay to the moment when you acted to avoid looking like a fool. Make your reader see and feel what you saw and felt.

2. Orwell states: "And my whole life, every white man's life in the East, was one long struggle not to be laughed at." Drawing on your experience and observation, discuss what you see as the feelings and motives of people charged with enforcing rules of some sort—perhaps hall monitors in high school, or lifeguards at a swimming pool, or supervisors at a playground, or babysitters. Use your discussion to draw a conclusion, as Orwell does.

PEGGY AND PIERRE STREIT

PEGGY and PIERRE STREIT collaborated on numerous articles on life in the Middle East and Asia. Pierre Streit also produced documentaries for television and business corporations. In a

recent article, Barbara Crossette writes that the thousands
of subcastes in the Hindu caste system fall into major divi-
sions or varnas *in a descending hierarchy—the learned and*
warrior castes, followed by the merchant, laboring, servant,
and other castes: "Under them all are the outcastes, people
considered impure and therefore untouchable, who do the
lowliest jobs" (New York Times Magazine, *May 19, 1991).*
Today 600,000 Indian families perform the same work as
Shanti and other menial jobs. Through the influence of the
great Hindu political leader Mahatma Gandhi, the untouchable
caste is now called Harijan—meaning "Child of God." In 1949
the Indian government outlawed discrimination against Har-
ijans, but as the Streits show in their 1959 article, traditional
attitudes remain powerful.

A Well in India

The hot dry season in India. . . . A corrosive wind drives 1
rivulets of sand across the land; torpid animals stand at the
edge of dried-up water holes. The earth is cracked and in the
rivers the sluggish, falling waters have exposed the sludge of
the mud flats. Throughout the land the thoughts of men turn
to water. And in the village of Rampura these thoughts are
focused on the village well.

It is a simple concrete affair, built upon the hard earth 2
worn by the feet of five hundred villagers. It is surmounted
by a wooden structure over which ropes, tied to buckets, are
lowered to the black, placid depths twenty feet below.
Fanning out from the well are the huts of the villagers—their
walls white from sun, their thatched roofs thick with dust
blown in from the fields.

At the edge of the well is a semi-circle of earthen pots 3
and, crouched at some distance behind them, a woman. She
is an untouchable—a sweeper in Indian parlance—a scaven-
ger of the village. She cleans latrines, disposes of dead
animals and washes drains. She also delivers village babies,
for this—like all her work—is considered unclean by most of
village India.

Her work—indeed, her very presence—is considered 4
polluting, and since there is no well for untouchables in

Rampura, her water jars must be filled by upper-caste villagers.

There are dark shadows under her eyes and the flesh 5 has fallen away from her neck, for she, like her fellow outcastes, is at the end of a bitter struggle. And if, in her narrow world, shackled by tradition and hemmed in by poverty, she had been unaware of the power of the water of the well at whose edge she waits—she knows it now.

Shanti, 30 years old, has been deserted by her husband, 6 and supports her three children. Like her ancestors almost as far back as history records, she has cleaned the refuse from village huts and lanes. Hers is a life of inherited duties as well as inherited rights. She serves, and her work calls for payment of one chapatty—a thin wafer of unleavened bread—a day from each of the thirty families she cares for.

But this is the hiatus between harvests; the oppressive 7 lull before the burst of monsoon rains; the season of flies and dust, heat and disease, querulous voices and frayed tempers—and the season of want. There is little food in Rampura for anyone, and though Shanti's chores have continued as before, she has received only six chapatties a day for her family—starvation wages.

Ten days ago she revolted. Driven by desperation, she 8 defied an elemental law of village India. She refused to make her sweeper's rounds—refused to do the work tradition and religion had assigned her. Shocked at her audacity, but united in desperation, the village's six other sweeper families joined in her protest.

Word of her action spread quickly across the invisible 9 line that separates the untouchables' huts from the rest of the village. As the day wore on and the men returned from the fields, they gathered at the well—the heart of the village— and their voices rose, shrill with outrage: a *sweeper* defying them all! Shanti, a sweeper *and* a woman challenging a system that had prevailed unquestioned for centuries! Their indignation spilled over. It was true, perhaps, that the sweepers had not had their due. But that was no fault of the upper caste. No fault of theirs that sun and earth and water had failed to produce the food by which they could fulfill their obligations. So, to bring the insurgents to heel, they employed their ultimate weapon; the earthen water jars of the village untouchables would remain empty until they returned to work. For the sweepers of Rampura the well had run dry.

No water; thirst, in the heat, went unslaked. The embers 10 of the hearth were dead, for there was no water for cooking. The crumbling walls of outcaste huts went untended, for there was no water for repairs. There was no fuel, for the fires of the village were fed with dung mixed with water and dried. The dust and the sweat and the filth of their lives congealed on their skins and there it stayed, while life in the rest of the village—within sight of the sweepers—flowed on.

The day began and ended at the well. The men, their 11 dhotis wrapped about their loins, congregated at the water's edge in the hushed post-dawn, their small brass water jugs in hand, their voices mingling in quiet conversation as they rinsed their bodies and brushed their teeth. The buffaloes were watered, their soft muzzles lingering in the buckets before they were driven off to the fields. Then came the women, their brass pots atop their heads, to begin the ritual of water drawing: the careful lowering of the bucket in the well, lest it come loose from the rope; the gratifying splash as it touched the water; the maneuvering to make it sink; the squeal of rope against wooden pulley as it ascended. The sun rose higher. Clothes were beaten clean on the rocks surrounding the well as the women gossiped. A traveler from a near-by road quenched his thirst from a villager's urn. Two little boys, hot and bored, dropped pebbles into the water and waited for their hollow splash, far below.

As the afternoon wore on and the sun turned orange 12 through the dust, the men came back from the fields. They doused the parched, cracked hides of their water buffaloes and murmured contentedly, themselves, as the water coursed over their own shoulders and arms. And finally, as twilight closed in, came the evening procession of women, stately, graceful, their bare feet moving smoothly over the earth, their full skirts swinging about their ankles, the heavy brass pots once again balanced on their heads.

The day was ended and life was as it always was— 13 almost. Only the fetid odor of accumulated refuse and the assertive buzz of flies attested to strife in the village. For, while tradition and religion decreed that sweepers must clean, it also ordained that the socially blessed must not. Refuse lay where it fell and rotted.

The strain of the water boycott was beginning to tell on the untouchables. For days they had held their own. But on the third their thin reserve of flesh had fallen away. Movements were slower; voices softer; minds dull. More and more the desultory conversation turned to the ordinary: the delicious memory of sliding from the back of a wallowing buffalo into a pond; the feel of bare feet in wet mud; the touch of fresh water on parched lips; the anticipation of monsoon rains. 14

One by one the few tools they owned were sold for food. A week passed, and on the ninth day two sweeper children were down with fever. On the tenth day Shanti crossed the path that separated outcaste from upper caste and walked through familiar, winding alleyways to one of the huts she served. 15

"Your time is near," she told the young, expectant mother. "Tell your man to leave his sickle home when he goes to the fields. I've had to sell mine." (It is the field sickle that cuts the cord of newborn babies in much of village India.) Shanti, the instigator of the insurrection, had resumed her ancestral duties; the strike was broken. Next morning, as ever, she waited at the well. Silently, the procession of upper-caste women approached. They filled their jars to the brim and without a word they filled hers. 16

She lifted the urns to her head, steadied them, and started back to her quarters—back to a life ruled by the powers that still rule most of the world: not the power of atoms or electricity, nor the power of alliances or power blocs, but the elemental powers of hunger, of disease, of tradition—and of water. 17

VOCABULARY

paragraph 1: corrosive, rivulets
paragraph 3: untouchable, parlance
paragraph 4: upper-caste
paragraph 7: hiatus, monsoon

paragraph 9: insurgents
paragraph 10: unslaked, congealed
paragraph 13: fetid

QUESTIONS

1. The Streits build to a statement of their thesis at the end of paragraph 5. Why is it necessary to portray the world of the untouchable before stating the thesis?
2. Where in the essay is the thesis restated? Is the restatement more informative or detailed than the original statement of it?
3. What is the attitude of the authors toward the world they portray and the fate of Shanti? Do they seem to be taking sides?
4. Is it important to the thesis that Shanti is a woman? Are the authors concerned with her as a woman, in addition to their concern for her as an untouchable?
5. Is the concern of the essay equally with the power of water and the power of tradition? Or are these considerations subordinate to the portrayal of the untouchable and the courage shown?
6. Are we given a motive directly for what Shanti does—or is the motive implied?

SUGGESTIONS FOR WRITING

1. Develop an idea relating to the power of tradition and illustrate it from personal experience and observation. Provide enough background so that your reader understands why the tradition is important to the people who observe it.
2. Describe a conflict between you and your parents or school officials or between a person and a group of some sort. Explain how the conflict arises from a basic difference in attitude, ideas, or feelings—a difference that reveals something important about you and the other people involved.

ERIC SEVAREID

Born in 1912 in Velva, North Dakota, ERIC SEVAREID graduated from the University of Minnesota in 1935 and immediately began his career as a journalist with the

Minneapolis Journal. *He later reported for the Paris edition of* The New York Herald Tribune. *In 1939 Sevareid began his long association with the Columbia Broadcasting Company as a war correspondent in Europe. From 1964 to 1977 he delivered his commentary on the CBS Evening News. His books include* Small Sounds in the Night *(1956) and an autobiography,* Not So Wild a Dream *(1976). Like Orwell in "Shooting an Elephant," Sevareid builds through a careful presentation of detail to increasingly broad truths about the world of his youth and human nature generally.*

Velva, North Dakota

My home town has changed in these thirty years of the   1
American story. It is changing now, will go on changing as
America changes. Its biography, I suspect, would read much
the same as that of all other home towns. Depression and
war and prosperity have all left their marks; modern science,
modern tastes, manners, philosophies, fears and ambitions
have touched my town as indelibly as they have touched
New York or Panama City.

Sights have changed: there is a new precision about   2
street and home, a clearing away of chicken yards, cow
barns, pigeon-crested cupolas, weed lots and coulees, the
dim and secret adult-free rendezvous of boys. An intricate
metal "jungle gym" is a common backyard sight, the sack
swing uncommon. There are wide expanses of clear windows designed to let in the parlor light, fewer ornamental
windows of colored glass designed to keep it out. Attic and
screen porch are slowly vanishing and lovely shades of
pastel are painted upon new houses, tints that once would
have embarrassed farmer and merchant alike.

Sounds have changed; I heard not once the clopping of   3
a horse's hoofs, nor the mourn of a coyote. I heard instead
the shriek of brakes, the heavy throbbing of the once-a-day
Braniff airliner into Minot, the shattering sirens born of war,
the honk of a diesel locomotive which surely cannot call to
faraway places the heart of a wakeful boy like the old steam
whistle in the night. You can walk down the streets of my
town now and hear from open windows the intimate voices

of the Washington commentators in casual converse on the great affairs of state; but you cannot hear on Sunday morning the singing in Norwegian of the Lutheran hymns; the old country seems now part of a world left long behind and the old-country accents grow fainter in the speech of my Velva neighbors.

The people have not changed, but the *kinds of* people 4 have changed; there is no longer an official, certified town drunk, no longer a "Crazy John," spitting his worst epithet, "rotten chicken legs," as you hurriedly passed him by. People so sick are now sent to places of proper care. No longer is there an official town joker, like the druggist MacKnight, who would spot a customer in the front of the store, have him called to the phone, then slip to the phone behind the prescription case, and imitate the man's wife to perfection with orders to bring home more bread and sausage and Cream of Wheat. No longer anyone like the early attorney, J. L. Lee, who sent fabulous dispatches to that fabulous tabloid, the *Chicago Blade,* such as his story of the wild man captured on the prairie and chained to the wall in the drugstore basement. (This, surely, was Velva's first notoriety; inquiries came from anthropologists all over the world.)

No, the "characters" are vanishing in Velva, just as they 5 are vanishing in our cities, in business, in politics. The "well-rounded, socially integrated" personality that the progressive schoolteachers are so obsessed with is increasing rapidly, and I am not at all sure that this is good. Maybe we need more personalities with knobs and handles and rugged lumps of individuality. They may not make life more smooth; more interesting they surely make it.

They eat differently in Velva now; there are frozen fruits 6 and sea food and exotic delicacies we only read about in novels in those meat-and-potato days. They dress differently. The hard white collars of the businessmen are gone with the shiny alpaca coats. There are comfortable tweeds now, and casual blazers with a touch in their colors of California, which seems so close in time and distance.

It is distance and time that have changed the most and 7 worked the deepest changes in Velva's life. The telephone, the car, the smooth highway, radio and television are consolidating the entities of our country. The county seat of Towner now seems no closer than the state capital of Bismarck; the voices and concerns of Presidents, French premiers and Moroccan pashas are no farther away than the portable radio on Aunt Jessey's kitchen table. The national news magazines are stacked each week in Harold Anderson's drugstore beside the new soda fountain, and the excellent *Minot Daily News* smells hot from the press each afternoon.

Consolidation. The nearby hamlets of Sawyer and Lo- 8 gan and Voltaire had their own separate banks and papers and schools in my days of dusty buggies and Model T's marooned in the snowdrifts. Now these hamlets are dying. A bright yellow bus takes the Voltaire kids to Velva each day for high school. Velva has grown—from 800 to 1,300— because the miners from the Truax coal mine can commute to their labors each morning and the nearby farmers can live in town if they choose. Minot has tripled in size to 30,000. Once the "Magic City" was a distant and splendid Baghdad, visited on special occasions long prepared for. Now it is a twenty-five minute commuter's jump away. So P. W. Miller and Jay Louis Monicken run their businesses in Minot but live on in their old family homes in Velva. So Ray Michelson's two girls on his farm to the west drive up each morning to their jobs as maids in Minot homes. Aunt Jessey said, "Why, Saturday night I counted sixty-five cars just between here and Sawyer, all going up to the show in Minot."

The hills are prison battlements no longer; the prairies 9 no heart-sinking barrier, but a passageway free as the swelling ocean, inviting you to sail home and away at your whim and your leisure. (John and Helen made an easy little jaunt of 700 miles that week-end to see their eldest daughter in Wyoming.)

Consolidation. Art Kumm's bank serves a big region 10 now; its assets are $2,000,000 to $3,000,000 instead of the $200,000 or $300,000 in my father's day. Eighteen farms near Velva are under three ownerships now. They calculate in sections; "acres" is an almost forgotten term. Aunt Jessey owns a couple of farms, and she knows they are much better run. "It's no longer all take out and no put in," she said. "Folks strip farm now; they know all about fertilizers. They care for it and they'll hand on the land in good shape." The farmers gripe about their cash income, and not without reason at the moment, but they will admit that life is good compared with those days of drought and foreclosure, manure banked against the house for warmth, the hand pump frozen at 30 below and the fitful kerosene lamp on the kitchen table. Electrification has done much of this, eased back-breaking chores that made their wives old as parchment at forty, brought life and music and the sound of human voices into their parlors at night.

11 And light upon the prairie. "From the hilltop," said Aunt Jessey, "the farms look like stars at night."

12 Many politicians deplore the passing of the old family-size farm, but I am not so sure. I saw around Velva a release from what was like slavery to the tyrannical soil, release from the ignorance that darkens the soul and from the loneliness that corrodes it. In this generation my Velva friends have rejoined the general American society that their pioneering fathers left behind when they first made the barren trek in the days of the wheat rush. As I sit here in Washington writing this, I can feel their nearness. I never felt it before save in my dreams.

13 But now I must ask myself: Are they nearer to one another? And the answer is no; yet I am certain that this is good. The shrinking of time and distance has made contrast and relief available to their daily lives. They do not know one another quite so well because they are not so much obliged to. I know that democracy rests upon social discipline, which in turn rests upon personal discipline; passions checked, hard words withheld, civic tasks accepted, work well done, accountings honestly rendered. The old-fashioned small town was this discipline in its starkest, most primitive form; without this discipline the small town would have blown itself apart.

14 For personal and social neuroses festered under this hard scab of conformity. There was no place to go, no place to let off steam; few dared to voice unorthodox ideas, read strange books, admire esoteric art or publicly write or speak of their dreams and their soul's longings. The world was not "too much with us," the world was too little with us and we were too much with one another.

The door to the world stands open now, inviting them 15
to leave anytime they wish. It is the simple fact of the open
door that makes all the difference; with its opening the stale
air rushed out. So, of course, the people themselves do not
have to leave, because, as the stale air went out, the fresh air
came in.

Human nature is everywhere the same. He who is not 16
forced to help his neighbor for his own existence will not
only give him help, but his true good will as well. Minot and
its hospital are now close at hand, but the people of Velva
put their purses together, built their own clinic and homes
for the two young doctors they persuaded to come and live
among them. Velva has no organized charity, but when a
farmer falls ill, his neighbors get in his crop; if a townsman
has a financial catastrophe his personal friends raise a fund
to help him out. When Bill's wife, Ethel, lay dying so long in
the Minot hospital and nurses were not available, Helen and
others took their turns driving up there just to sit with her so
she would know in her gathering dark that friends were at
hand.

It is personal freedom that makes us better persons, 17
and they are freer in Velva now. There is no real freedom
without privacy, and a resident of my home town can be a
private person much more than he could before. People are
able to draw at least a little apart from one another. In
drawing apart, they gave their best human instincts room for
expansion.

VOCABULARY

paragraph 1: indelibly
paragraph 4: certified, epithet, tabloid, notoriety, anthropologists
paragraph 5: progressive
paragraph 6: alpaca, blazers
paragraph 7: pashas
paragraph 8: consolidation, commute
paragraph 9: battlements, whim, jaunt
paragraph 10: foreclosure

paragraph 12: deplore, corrodes, trek

paragraph 13: starkest

paragraph 14: neuroses, scab, unorthodox, esoteric

QUESTIONS

1. Where does Sevareid indicate his attitude toward his hometown? What is his thesis?

2. What details in the whole essay support the dominating impression Sevareid creates of the town in his opening paragraph? Is any of this detail unrelated to this impression?

3. What is the tone of or attitude expressed in the comment on the story of the wild man, and how is the comment related to the thesis?

4. What are the causes of the change in life in Velva? Does Sevareid indicate a main cause?

5. What does Sevareid mean by *discipline* in the statement in paragraph 13, "without this discipline the small town would have blown itself apart"?

6. Sevareid points up a series of paradoxes toward the end. What are these, and what do they contribute to the tone of the conclusion?

SUGGESTIONS FOR WRITING

1. Analyze how Eric Sevareid introduces his thesis and keeps it before the reader. Then discuss another way he might have organized the essay.

2. Describe the changes that have occurred in the neighborhood in which you grew up and discuss the reasons for these. Use these changes to develop a thesis of your own.

Main and Subordinate Ideas

❦ ❦ ❦

The Paragraph

An author may develop the main or central idea of a paragraph through a series of subordinate ideas. Consider the opening sentences of the following paragraph on country superstitions.

> In the folklore of the country, numerous superstitions relate to winter weather. Back-country farmers examine their corn husks—the thicker the husk, the colder the winter. They watch the acorn crop—the more acorns, the more severe the season. They observe where white-faced hornets place their paper nests—the higher they are, the deeper will be the snow. They examine the size and shape and color of the spleens of butchered hogs for clues to the severity of the season. They keep track of the blooming of dogwood in the spring—the more abundant the blooms, the more bitter the cold in January. When chipmunks carry their tails high and squirrels have heavier fur and mice come into country houses early in the fall, the superstitious gird themselves for a long, hard winter. Without any scientific basis, a wider-than-usual black band on a woolly-bear caterpillar is accepted as a sign that winter will arrive early and stay late. Even the way a cat sits beside the stove carries its message to the credulous. According to a belief once widely held in the Ozarks, a cat sitting with its tail to the fire indicates very cold weather is on the way.—Edwin Way Teale, *Wandering through Winter*

The first sentence is the main idea; the second sentence, a subordinate idea that develops it through illustration:

> In the folklore of the country, numerous superstitions relate to
> winter weather.
>> Back-country farmers examine their corn husks—
>> the thicker the husk, the colder the winter.

We have indented to show the levels of subordination in these sentences. Notice that the third sentence has the same importance as the second in developing the main idea:

> They watch the acorn crop—
>   the more acorns, the more severe the season.

Of course, in writing paragraphs you do not indent in this way to show the relative importance of your ideas. But you do in writing essays: the break for a new paragraph—through an indentation—tells the reader that you are introducing a new or related idea or topic. Within the paragraph you need ways of substituting for the indentations shown above. One of these ways is the use of parallel phrasing to show that ideas have the same importance:

> They watch the acorn crop . . .
> They observe . . .
> They examine . . .

We will consider later in this section other devices that show the relative importance of ideas—among them transitional words and phrases (for example, the phrase *of equal importance*).

In longer paragraphs, you can distinguish the main idea by repeating or restating it at the end. We will see later in the book that the beginning and ending are usually the most emphatic parts of sentences because of their prominence. The same is true of paragraphs and essays.

LYTTON STRACHEY

LYTTON STRACHEY *(1890–1932), one of England's great biographers, was particularly interested in revered figures of the nineteenth century, and earlier English history, whose human qualities he wanted to discover. In his biographies, Strachey looks at the strengths and failings of his subjects, joining fact with the imagined creation of their inner life. We see this method in his portrait of Queen Victoria. Born in 1819, Victoria became queen in 1837 at the age of eighteen, and in 1840 married a first cousin her own age, the German prince Albert of Saxe-Coburg. When Albert died of a sudden illness in 1861, at the age of 42, she entered a long period of private mourning—for the remainder of her life preserving her physical surroundings as they had existed in his lifetime. Strachey shows how little the author needs to say when the right details are chosen and organized carefully.*

Queen Victoria at the End of Her Life

[1]She gave orders that nothing should be thrown away—and nothing was. [2]There, in drawer after drawer, in wardrobe after wardrobe, reposed the dresses of seventy years. [3]But not only the dresses—the furs and the mantles and subsidiary frills and the muffs and the parasols and the bonnets—all were ranged in chronological order, dated and complete. [4]A great cupboard was devoted to the dolls; in the china room at Windsor a special table held the mugs of her childhood, and her children's mugs as well. [5]Mementoes of the past surrounded her in serried accumulations. [6]In every room the tables were powdered thick with the photographs of relatives; their portraits, revealing them at all ages, covered the walls; their figures, in solid marble, rose up from pedestals, or gleamed from brackets in the form of gold and silver statuettes. [7]The dead, in every shape—in miniatures, in porcelain, in enormous life-size oil-paintings—were perpetually about her. [8]John Brown stood upon her writing table in solid gold.* [9]Her favorite horses and dogs, endowed with a new durability, crowded round her footsteps. [10]Sharp, in silver gilt, dominated the dinner table; Boy and Boz lay together among unfading flowers in bronze. [11]And it was not enough that each particle of the past should be given the stability of metal or of marble: the whole collection, in its arrangement, no less than its entity, should be immutably fixed. [12]There might be additions, but there might never be alterations. [13]No chintz might change, no carpet, no curtain, be replaced by another; or, if long use at last made it necessary, the stuffs and the patterns must be so identically reproduced that the keenest eye might not detect the difference. [14]No new picture could be hung upon the walls at Windsor, for those already there had been put in their places by Albert, whose decisions were eternal. [15]So, indeed, were Victoria's. [16]To ensure that they should be the aid of the camera was called in. [17]Every single article in the Queen's possession was photographed from several points of view.

---

* John Brown (1826–1883) was the Scottish attendant to Victoria's husband, Prince Albert, and after the death of the Prince in 1861, to the Queen herself.—Ed.

[18]These photographs were submitted to Her Majesty, and when, after careful inspection, she had approved of them, they were placed in a series of albums, richly bound. [19]Then, opposite each photograph, an entry was made, indicating the number of the article, the number of the room in which it was kept, its exact position in the room and all its principal characteristics. [20]The fate of every object which had undergone this process was henceforth irrevocably sealed. [21]The whole multitude, once and for all, took up its steadfast station. [22]And Victoria, with a gigantic volume or two of the endless catalogue always beside her, to look through, to ponder upon, to expatiate over, could feel, with a double contentment, that the transitoriness of this world had been arrested by the amplitude of her might.

QUESTIONS

1. In his portrait of Victoria in her old age, Strachey develops and illustrates several major ideas that build to his central or topic idea. What are these ideas?

2. Strachey states in sentence 2 that Victoria saved the dresses of seventy years; in sentence 3, that she saved her furs and bonnets, as well as other articles of clothing—and arranged and dated them chronologically. How does the formal transition between these sentences help to show that Strachey is moving from one surprising, even astonishing, fact to an even more surprising one?

3. Compare sentences 11 and 12 with those that follow. How does Strachey indicate that he is building the paragraph to even more surprising details?

4. What contributes to the climactic effect of the final sentence of the paragraph?

5. Has Strachey made Queen Victoria human to you? Or is she merely an eccentric?

SUGGESTIONS FOR WRITING

1. Write a character sketch of an unusual friend or teacher, centering on a dominant trait and presenting related traits as

Strachey does. Present these related traits in the order of rising importance—as illustrations of the dominant trait.

2. Rewrite Strachey's paragraph, beginning with his concluding sentence and achieving a sense of climax in your reordering of ideas and details.

The Essay

The thesis is the most important idea in an essay. When an essay builds to its thesis through a series of subordinate ideas and details, we may sense a rising importance of ideas in it, even perhaps a sense of climax. As in the paragraph, it is important that we sense the relative importance of these ideas and details. An essay in which all of these seem to have the same importance would be extremely hard to read.

We can sense this relative importance of ideas even in the topic sentences, as in these sentences that open the first seven paragraphs of Sevareid's essay on Velva, North Dakota. The different indentations show the relative weight of each idea:

> My home town has changed in these thirty years. . . .
>> Sights have changed. . . .
>> Sounds have changed. . . .
>> The people have not changed, but the *kinds* of people have changed.
>>> No, the "characters" are vanishing in Velva. . . .
>> They eat differently in Velva now. . . .
> It is distance and time that have changed the most and worked the deepest changes in Velva's life.

Sevareid builds to his thesis through a series of increasingly broad generalizations. Here are the opening sentences of the last six paragraphs:

> Many politicians deplore the passing of the old family-size farm, but I am not so sure.
> But now I must ask myself: Are they nearer to one another?
> For personal and social neuroses festered under this hard scab of conformity.
> The door to the world stands open now. . . .
> Human nature is everywhere the same.
> It is personal freedom that makes us better persons, and they are freer in Velva now [*thesis*].

Sevareid's sentences show that we do not always need formal transitions to tell us which ideas are main and which are subordinate. The clear, logical relationship of Sevareid's ideas shows their relative importance. But, as in the paragraph, formal transitions are sometimes needed. Having a sense of the relative importance of our ideas and details is important as we write.

SALLY CARRIGHAR

The writer and naturalist SALLY CARRIGHAR *was born in Cleveland, Ohio, the scene of the introduction to her autobiography,* Home to the Wilderness *(1973), reprinted here. After graduation from Wellesley College Carrighar discovered an interest in birds and animals, and she decided to become a nature writer: "There could be no finer subject than woods and fields, streams, lakes, and mountainsides and the creatures who live in that world. It would be a subject of inexhaustible interest, a supreme joy to be learning to tell it all straight and truthfully," she writes. For nine years she lived in an isolated Alaskan village, studying Eskimo life and the animals of the Arctic region. She has written about this experience and about wildlife generally in* Icebound Summer *(1953),* Wild Voice of the North *(1959),* Wild Heritage *(1965), and other books. In the passage that follows, she describes experiences and people that awakened her imagination and curiosity about life.*

The Blast Furnace

We were a father and his first-born, a four-year-old girl, set- 1
ting out every Sunday afternoon to see the industrial marvels of Cleveland, Ohio. The young man had grown up in a smaller Canadian town and he was delighted with Cleveland, which hummed and clanged with the vast new developments steel had made possible. In temperament he was anything but an engineer; here however he was excited to feel that he had jumped into the very heart of the torrent of progress.

Most often we walked on the banks of the Cuyahoga 2
River to see the drawbridge come apart and rise up, like giant black jaws taking a bite of the sky, so that boats could go through: the long freighters that brought iron ore from Lake Superior, other large and small freighters, fishing boats, passenger steamers. My father's eyes never tired of watching them make their smooth way up and down the river. His father, born in Amsterdam of a seagoing family, had been a skipper on the Great Lakes. Perhaps my father too should have been a sailor, but he was something nearly as satisfying—he worked for a railroad.

And so we went to the roundhouse where the steam 3
engines stood when they were not pulling trains. They had
all entered through the same door but inside their tracks
spread apart, as gracefully as the ribs of a lady's fan. My
father knew a great deal about engines, he knew the names
of some of these and he walked among them with pride.

On our way to the roundhouse we passed through the 4
freight yards where long trains of boxcars lay on their
sidings. My father said that the cars belonged to different
railroads and came from various parts of the country, being
coupled together here because all those in one train were
bound for the same destination. This was getting too complicated but there was nothing complicated about my father's
emotion when he said, "Working for a railroad is like living
everywhere in the country at once!" A characteristic enchantment came into his eyes and voice, a contagious exhilaration
which meant that anything it attached to was good. Living
everywhere was something that even a child could grasp
vaguely and pleasantly.

My father and I made other trips and best were the ones 5
to the blast furnaces. He explained how the iron ore from the
boats was mixed with coal and carried in little cars to the top
of the chimney above the furnace. It was dumped in, and as
it fell down "a special kind of very hot air" was blown into it.
The coal and iron ore caught fire, and below they fell into
great tubs as melting metal, a pinkish gold liquid, incandescent as the sun is when it is starting to set. The man and child
were allowed to go rather near the vats, to feel the scorching
heat and to drown their gaze in the glowing boil. All the rest
of the building was dark; the silhouettes of the men who
worked at the vats were black shadows. Wearing long leather
aprons, they moved about the vats ladling off the slag. That
was very skilled work, my father said; the men had to know
just how much of the worthless slag to remove. For years
afterwards, when we could no longer spend Sunday afternoons on these expeditions, we used to go out of our house
at night to see the pink reflections from the blast furnaces
on the clouds over Cleveland. We could remember that we
had watched the vatfuls of heavily moving gold, and those
events from the past were an unspoken bond between us.

Someone once said, "Your father must have been trying 6

to turn you into a boy. He'd probably wanted his first child to be a son." Perhaps; but it was not strange to him to show a girl the achievements of men. He thought of women as human beings and assumed that they, even one very young, would be interested in anything that was interesting to him. He had absorbed that attitude from the women he'd grown up with, his mother and her four sisters, all of whom led adventurous lives. His favorite Aunt Chris had married a clipper captain and sailed with him all her life. When they retired, having seen the entire world, they chose to settle in Burma. Another aunt married one of the Morgan family, who established the famous breed of Morgan horses, and took up a homestead in Manitoba. Aunt Mary, a physician's wife, went with him out to San Francisco during the Gold Rush and stayed there. The fourth aunt had married the inspector of ships' chronometers at Quebec; and my father's mother, of course, had married her skipper from Holland. In the winter when he was not on his ship he ran a factory for making barrel staves that he had established in western Kentucky—all this and the fathering of five children by the time he was twenty-eight, when he lost his life in a notorious Lake Erie storm. His wife, a musician, brought up her five without complaint, just as her mother, also an early widow, had reared her five gallant girls. With his memories of women like these it was not surprising that my father would wish, even somewhat prematurely, to show his daughter the things that were thrilling to him. I did not comprehend all his family history at four, but I did absorb the impression that girls and women reached out for life eagerly and that it was natural for them to be interested in absolutely everything.

QUESTIONS

1. In paragraph 1 Carrighar develops her opening sentence—the main idea of the paragraph—with specific detail about her father. What is the main idea of paragraph 2, and how does she use the detail of the paragraph to develop it?

2. Paragraph 4 moves from specific detail to the main idea. What is that idea, and how does the author give it prominence?

3. Which of the subordinate ideas in paragraph 5 are in turn illustrated or developed?

4. Paragraphs 1–5 are subordinate to paragraph 6, which draws a conclusion from the experiences described and develops it through details of a different sort. What is this conclusion, and what new details develop it? How is this conclusion—the main idea of the paragraph—restated later in the paragraph and made prominent?

SUGGESTIONS FOR WRITING

1. Write several paragraphs describing childhood experiences that taught you something about the adult world and about yourself, or perhaps led to a conflict in values or ideas. Begin with these truths, or build the paragraphs to them, as Carrighar does.

2. Write several paragraphs about information you received or impressions you developed about women in your family. If you wish, contrast these impressions with those you received about boys and men. Use these impressions to develop a thesis.

DAVID HOLAHAN

DAVID HOLAHAN *attended Yale University, graduating in 1971. He published two Connecticut weekly newspapers until their sale in 1982, and since then has written for numerous magazines and newspapers throughout the United States. Holahan's essay is original and interesting because he writes about his football experiences from an unusual point of view. He makes the subject his own through concrete details that give insight into college football and the attitudes and feelings of the players.*

Why Did I Ever Play Football?

Coach kept running the halfback sweep through the projec-   1
tor, clicking the stop, rewind and forward buttons as he dwelled on each "individual breakdown" by our defense. Princeton had gained 20 yards on the play and our individual

mistakes added up to a "total Yale breakdown." Gallagher and I sat with the other sophomores, savoring the embarrassment of the first-stringers.

The last individual to break down on the play was the 2 defensive safety who started ahead of me. Yale's sports publicity department was touting him as a "pro prospect," but during the 11th screening of his mistake, he protested that he was not sure how to defense a sweep. After three years on the varsity, our NFL-bound star didn't know how to play your everyday end run.

"The first rule," Gallagher said as loudly as he could, "is 3 don't get hurt." Suppressed laughter spread through the room. Everyone knew "the films don't lie" and that "newspaper clippings don't make tackles"; that "you have to want it," even in the Ivy League.

I'm not entirely sure why I played football; it might have 4 been because of those great clichés. I certainly didn't enjoy hitting people the way Gallagher did. He liked to bury his helmet into a quarterback's ribs and drive him into the turf. As he returned to the huddle, there would be a strange expression on his face, somewhere between a grimace and a smile. After a game he would be sore, bruised and bloodied, like the other linemen and linebackers, while I would feel about the same as I did after an uneventful mixer at Vassar.

Defensive safeties are not supposed to make a lot of 5 tackles, especially when the people up front are good, which ours were, and that was just fine with me. Still, some of my most vivid memories are of moments of intense pain. Once in junior year I found myself in a dreaded position: one-on-one with a fullback charging as swiftly as his bulky legs would carry him. He was 10 yards away and closing fast. He was also growling. "His S.A.T. scores must be beauts," flashed through my mind and the urge to flee became acute. Thousands of eyes were watching—including Coach's camera. If I blew it I would have to see the replay at least a dozen times.

Suddenly I was moving sideways through the air, pain 6 jolting my body, the fullback forgotten. I hit the ground writhing, clutching my side and pulling my knees up to my chest. There was no air in my lungs. For a moment the world stopped at my skin. I wanted to stay crumpled up on the ground, but one of our linemen pulled me to my feet with one hand and half-carried me to the huddle. It must have been their end who hit me. I had seen him split out wide, then I forgot about him. He weighed over 200 pounds; I went about 160. What was I thinking of, playing football? I didn't hear our captain call the defensive signals, but fear slowly returned as the pain subsided. If that quarterback were smart he would try a pass in my zone. The pass never came. Thank God we were playing Harvard.

Continuing to play football was not a particularly rational thing for me to do. In sixth grade I was as big and strong and fast as anyone our six-man team faced. And jocks were popular then. By college virtually everyone I played against was bigger and stronger, and the consensus on campus in the late 1960s was that we were a bunch of neofascists, at best. So much for "Boola, Boola." And when it wasn't a physically grinding ordeal, practice, too, could be as boring as Archeology 101. 7

Saturday's approach would turn my insides to mush, but the day I dreaded most was Sunday, film day. "Now I want everyone to watch the tackling technique on this play," Coach would say. "Holahan, I hope you squeeze your dates harder than this." Gallagher laughed the loudest. 8

Oh, I had my moments, usually when the people up front either played badly or were overmatched. Then I got a workout and there was no place to hide. Against Dartmouth, senior year, I turned positively vicious after watching their halfback gloat over one of our players lying injured on the field. I started burying my helmet into people even if they didn't have the ball. Once I made that halfback groan in pain. I also said some ugly things about his mother. I intercepted two passes. And the next day brought sweet soreness; so that's how Gallagher felt after every game. 9

There were other players who must have had a tougher time figuring out why they were playing football; high-school hotshots who couldn't crack the second string, but who hung on. Some who didn't play in games, never expected to, maybe never even wanted to, for blocking and tackling are clearly unpleasant experiences. A few were not in the least bit athletic. Who knows, they may have been doing it for their résumés, but I suppose they had their 10 moments too, when things would happen that could never take place in Archeology 101. For me, Coach's films had something to do with why I continued to play.

Sunday afternoon was both a social and a moral occa- 11 sion—funny, embarrassing, depressing or happy, depending on how the team had done and how each player had performed. Every fall Sabbath was a new Judgment Day. What was shown on the screen was often harsh, but always just. I could fool professors and pass courses without working very hard, but no one could slip anything past that camera. If I played well Saturday, I knew it; still, the camera confirmed it. There was no place to hide in that room, no big linemen up front to take the heat. Film immortalized shirking efforts.

I have often thought of driving 40 minutes to New 12 Haven and digging up that old Dartmouth game, going back 14 years to see a younger, stronger, less cautious me. The temptation seems to grow each year, but I will never do it. It would be cheating the camera to look only at that one film.

VOCABULARY

paragraph 1: savoring, first-stringers
paragraph 2: touting, varsity
paragraph 4: clichés, grimace
paragraph 7: virtually, neofascists
paragraph 10: résumés
paragraph 11: shirking

QUESTIONS

1. Holahan might have opened the essay with the question asked in the title instead of building to it through the details of paragraphs 1–3. What does he gain through this buildup of details?

2. In paragraphs 5–6 Holahan describes an experience as a defensive safety in a college game with Harvard. Why does he present this experience before turning to earlier experiences as a football player?

3. Holahan builds to general conclusions through his experiences with football. How does he show that these conclusions are the main ideas of his essay?

4. What is the answer to the question that Holahan asks in the title of the essay and in paragraph 4, and where in the final paragraphs does he answer the question? What does Holahan gain in not answering the question earlier in the essay?

SUGGESTIONS FOR WRITING

1. Illustrate your reasons for playing a sport or a musical instrument or for performing a similar activity. Don't state the reasons directly. Let your reader discover them through the details of your essay.

2. Write an essay on one of the following topics or on one of your own choosing. Give your thesis emphasis by introducing it in a prominent place in the essay—perhaps at the end of the opening paragraph, or in the final paragraph. If you begin the essay with your thesis, you can give it emphasis by repeating or restating it at key points:

   a. the art of keeping friends

   b. on not giving advice

   c. the art of persuading children

   d. on living away from home

   e. on waiting in line

ORDER OF IDEAS

❦ ❦ ❦

The Paragraph

A unified paragraph develops one idea at a time and makes each idea relevant to the topic idea. You will keep a paragraph unified if, as you write and revise, you consider the order in which you want to present your ideas and details. This order is sometimes determined by the subject of the paragraph and sometimes by the audience you have in mind—and sometimes by both. For example, in describing parallel parking for people learning to drive, you probably would present each step as it occurs. But in describing the same process to driving instructors, you might present these steps in the order of their difficulty, to single out those steps needing most practice.

An account of a process, or a narrative, is usually chronological. A description of a scene is generally spatial in organization—the details are presented as the eye sees them, moving from one part of what is seen to another. The details or ideas can also be ordered in other ways. For example, you can write them

- from the easy to the difficult, as in the paragraph written for driving instructors
- from the less to the more important
- from the less to the more interesting or exciting
- from the general to the specific—for example, from the theory of combustion to the details of the process
- from the specific to the general—for example, from simple effects of gravity, like falling off a bike, to a definition of gravity or comment on these effects.

When ideas move from the less to the more important, the sense of importance is sometimes our own. We need to show this to the reader, perhaps through a simple transition like the words *more importantly* (p. 81). We can dispense with such transitions when the sense of rising importance is expressed directly, as in the famous statement of Julius Caesar—"I came, I saw, I conquered"—or in the details themselves:

> A furious gale attacks him like a personal enemy, tries to grasp his limbs, fastens upon his mind, seeks to rout his very spirit out of him.—Joseph Conrad, *Typhoon*

As in this sentence, we can achieve climax by making one idea seem to anticipate another and by giving weight to the final idea (in Conrad's sentence, through the word *very*). The terminal position in a sentence or paragraph is a position of natural emphasis because of its prominence—a fact that we can take advantage of in giving weight to ideas or details.

A paragraph may combine two or more orders of ideas. For instance, a paragraph written for driving instructors may move from the easy to the difficult steps of parallel parking, and at the same time from the less to the more important or even interesting.

MARY McCARTHY

> *"I was born in Seattle in 1912, the first of four children,"* the novelist and essayist **MARY McCARTHY** *tells us in her autobiography,* Memories of a Catholic Girlhood. *Following the death of her parents in the influenza epidemic of 1918, she and her three young brothers lived for five years in Minneapolis with a great-aunt and her new husband, Uncle Myers, "a fat man of forty-two"—hired by her father's parents to take care of the children. Later the children lived with other relatives. "The idea that anybody could have entered the McCarthy orbit and failed to take notice of Uncle Myers was clearly fantastic," McCarthy writes. We discover why in this amazing description of an eccentric man.*

Uncle Myers

And here was another strange thing about Myers. He not only did nothing for a living but he appeared to have no history. He came from Elkhart, Indiana, but beyond this fact nobody seemed to know anything about him—not even how he had met my aunt Margaret. Reconstructed from his conversation, a picture of Elkhart emerged for us that showed it as a flat place consisting chiefly of ball parks, poolrooms, and hardware stores. Aunt Margaret came from Chicago, which consisted of the Loop, Marshall Field's, assorted priests and monsignors, and the black-and-white problem. How had these two worlds impinged? Where our family spoke freely of its relations, real and imaginary, Myers spoke of no one, not even a parent. At the very beginning, when my father's old touring car, which had been shipped on, still remained in our garage, Myers had certain seedy cronies whom he took riding in it or who simply sat in it in our driveway, as if anchored in a houseboat; but when the car went, they went or were banished. Uncle Myers and Aunt Margaret had no friends, no couples with whom they exchanged visits—only a middle-aged, black-haired, small, emaciated woman with a German name and a yellowed skin whom we were taken to see one afternoon because she was dying of cancer. This protracted death had the aspect of a public execution, which was doubtless why Myers took us to it; that is, it was a spectacle and it was free, and it inspired restlessness and depression. Myers was the perfect type of rootless munici-palized man who finds his pleasures in the handouts or overflow of an industrial civilization. He enjoyed standing on a curbstone, watching parades, the more nondescript the better, the Labor Day parade being his favorite, and next to that a military parade, followed by the commercial parades with floats and girls dressed in costumes; he would even go to Lake Calhoun or Lake Harriet for doll-carriage parades and competitions of children dressed as Indians. He liked bandstands, band concerts, public parks devoid of grass; sky writing attracted him; he was quick to hear of a department-store demonstration where colored bubbles were blown, advertising a soap, to the tune of "I'm Forever Blowing Bubbles," sung by a mellifluous soprano. He collected cou-pons and tinfoil, bundles of newspaper for the old rag-and-bone man (thus interfering seriously with our school paper drives), free samples of cheese at Donaldson's, free tickets given out by a neighborhood movie house to the first installment of a serial—in all the years we lived with him, we never saw a full-length movie but only those truncated beginnings. He was also fond of streetcar rides (could the system have been municipally owned?), soldiers' monuments, cemeteries, big, coarse flowers like cannas and cockscombs set in beds by city gardeners. Museums did not appeal to him, though we did go one night with a large crowd to see Marshal Foch on the steps of the Art Institute. He was always weighing himself on penny weighing machines. He seldom left the house except on one of these purposeless errands, or else to go to a ball game, by himself. In the winter, he spent the days at home in the den, or in the kitchen, making candy. He often had enormous tin trays of decorated fondants cooling in the cellar, which leads my brother Kevin to think today that at one time in Myers' life he must have been a pastry cook or a confectioner. He also liked to fashion those little figures made of pipe cleaners that were just then coming in as favors in the better candy shops, but Myers used *old* pipe cleaners, stained yellow and brown. The bonbons, with their pecan or almond topping, that he laid out in such perfect rows were for his own use; we were permitted to watch him set them out, but never—and my brother Kevin confirms this—did we taste a single one.

QUESTIONS

1. At the beginning of the paragraph Mary McCarthy discusses Uncle Myers' history and proceeds to his friendships and interests. What are these interests?

2. Why does she save the information about the pipe cleaners and the candy for the end of the paragraph? How would the impression of Uncle Myers have changed if the paragraph ended with the details of his cronies and his collections?

3. The paragraph is unified because McCarthy discusses one thing at a time, without returning haphazardly to earlier considerations. What is the order of details in the whole paragraph? What does she gain by not dividing the paragraph into several short ones?

4. Does McCarthy directly state her attitude toward Uncle Myers, or does she let it emerge through what she shows about him? What is that attitude?

5. How else might McCarthy have organized the paragraph to develop a different idea or impression?

6. Does Uncle Myers seem monstrous to you, or does McCarthy show his human side or give some explanation for his character?

SUGGESTIONS FOR WRITING

1. Build a paragraph around a central impression of an unusual person, selecting details from different areas of experience. Do not state your attitude toward the person; let your details reveal it.

2. Rewrite the paragraph on Uncle Myers, presenting the details in a different order and providing a new topic sentence. In a short second paragraph explain your reasons for organizing the new paragraph as you did.

E. B. WHITE

> E. B. WHITE (*1899–1985*) *was one of America's most distinguished writers—an essayist, a poet, a writer of books for children. His long association with* The New Yorker *magazine began in 1926. The columns that appeared in* Harper's *magazine under the title "One Man's Meat" were collected in 1942 in a book of the same name. Other essays are found in* The Second Tree From the Corner (*1954*), The Points of My Compass (*1962*), *and* Essays of E. B. White (*1977*). *In all of these books there is much about Maine, where White lived for many years. But the city of New York was never far from his thoughts, as you can see in his profile of the city later in this book (p. 132).*

In an Elevator

In an elevator, ascending with strangers to familiar heights, the breath congeals, the body stiffens, the spirit marks time. These brief vertical journeys that we make in a common lift, from street level to office level, past the missing thirteenth floor—they afford moments of suspended animation, unique and probably beneficial. Passengers in an elevator, whether wedged tight or scattered with room to spare, achieve in their perpendicular passage a trancelike state: each person adhering to the unwritten code, a man descending at five in the afternoon with his nose buried in a strange woman's back hair, reducing his breath to an absolute minimum necessary to sustain life, willing to suffocate rather than allow a suggestion of his physical presence to impinge; a man coming home at one A.M. ascending with only one other occupant of the car, carefully avoiding any slight recognition of joint occupancy. What is there about elevator travel that induces this painstaking catalepsy? A sudden solemnity, perhaps, which seizes people when they feel gravity being tampered with—they hope successfully. Sometimes it seems to us as though everyone in the car were in silent prayer.

QUESTIONS

1. What kind of tensions build in elevator rides, according to White?
2. How does White suggest this buildup of tension through the details of various rides?
3. Why do you think he concluded his description of elevator rides with a ride at one A.M.?
4. To what idea or reflection does White build the paragraph? Would the paragraph have the same effect if White had begun with this idea?
5. How well does White describe your own feelings riding an elevator?

SUGGESTIONS FOR WRITING

1. White asks the following question:

   What is there about elevator travel that induces this painstaking catalepsy?

Write your own answer to this question or another suggested by an elevator ride you have taken recently.

2. Describe an experience similar to those described by White, and build the details to a climax as he does. Conclude with your own comment or reflection on the experience as White does.

The Essay

The subject of a paragraph or essay often suggests how to organize it, as in the step-by-step, chronological description of a process. So does the intended audience. If the audience is unfamiliar with the subject, it may be preferable to build from simple to more difficult steps, details, and ideas, instead of presenting these chronologically. In a persuasive essay, for example, you might introduce the thesis at the beginning if you believe the audience will understand it without explanation; if the thesis requires explanation or is controversial, you might build to it through explanatory details and ideas.

The essay of personal experience usually follows a freer course than a formal essay of ideas. In her book *Pilgrim at Tinker Creek*, a description of her life in the Blue Ridge Mountains of Virginia, Annie Dillard (p. 521) divides an essay on winter into sections, each presenting diverse experiences and reflections that capture feelings of the moment inspired by the season. Here are sentences that introduce the opening sections:

> It is the first of February, and everyone is talking about starlings.
> It is winter proper; the cold weather, such as it is, has come to stay.
> Some weather's coming; you can taste on the sides of your tongue a quince tang in the air.
> This is the sort of stuff I read all winter.

By contrast, an expository or persuasive essay will show the logical relationships of ideas, as these opening sentences of Margaret Mead and Rhoda Metraux's essay on discipline (p. 137) show:

> In the matter of childhood discipline there is no absolute standard.
> The Mundugumor, a New Guinea people, trained their children to be tough and self-reliant.
> The Arapesh, another New Guinea people, had a very different view of life and personality.
> Even very inconsistent discipline may fit a child to live in an inconsistent world.
> There are also forms of discipline that may be self-defeating.

The order of ideas in an essay may reveal a writer's characteristic way of expressing ideas. Other of Annie Dillard's essays reveal the same free exploration of feelings and ideas. Expository and argumentative essays, too, may reveal an organization of ideas favored by a writer—perhaps a characteristic building to the thesis.

ANNA QUINDLEN

ANNA QUINDLEN *grew up in a large Philadelphia family of Irish and Italian descent. She attended Barnard College and after graduation worked as a reporter on the* New York Post, *then later as a columnist for* The New York Times. *In her column "About New York" and the later "Life in the 30's," Quindlen described daily life in New York City. She now writes biweekly on political and social issues for the* Times. *"Alone at Last" appears in* Living Out Loud *(1988), a collection of her essays. Quindlen is also the author of a novel,* Object Lessons *(1991). In 1992 she received the Pulitzer Prize for commentary.*

Alone at Last

I got in a lot of trouble when I was a kid for not getting 1 enough fresh air. There was a big chair in our living room, overstuffed and worn, and even on the nicest day of the year I could be found there, my legs draped over one arm of the chair, reading. I read a great deal, with no particular sense of originality or discernment. I read the Hardy Boys and Nancy Drew, C. S. Lewis and Robert Louis Stevenson, *A Little Princess* and *A Wrinkle in Time.* I read pretty awful stuff, like teen magazines, and I read pretty adult stuff, like *Wuthering Heights.* I still remember reading *Ulysses* when I was thirteen and thinking "What a weird book."

My mother was thinking "What a weird child." When 2 the sun was shining and the neighborhood kids were playing Monkey in the Middle, my mother was always yelling at me to go outside and get some fresh air. She did not think it was healthy to stay inside and read so much. One summer, to force me into the great outdoors, I was sent to camp in the mountains. Thinking of it even today is, as Evelyn Waugh's Bright Young Things say, "too, too sick-making." All those people and all that activity all the time: my God, I'll never forget it.

I still read constantly: if my kids ever go into analysis, 3 I'm sure they will say they don't really remember my face because it was always hidden by a book. Obviously this is in part because I like books. But another reason is that I like to be alone. I like to go deep inside myself and not be accompanied there by anyone else. But I am the oldest of five children, and when I was young I had about as much chance of being alone as I did of being a lion tamer. Reading was for me then a way of lifting myself out of a crowded environment into a place where I could be by myself. No wonder my mother was concerned. Being by yourself was considered, at my age and in my family, an aberrant behavior. Camp was normal. Camp was fun. Camp was crowded. Camp was horrible.

We pay lip service to a notion that privacy is important, 4 but I don't really think we believe it much. When anyone lives alone we have a tendency to think they are just waiting to meet the right roommate; we have an impulse to pair our friends off or introduce them to others. Single people eating in restaurants are assumed to be there for lack of a companion, not because they like their own company. It is difficult for us to accept that a great many gregarious people are often, also, quite private inside, that they have a chocolate-covered almond kind of character. This happens to be the case with me, although societal conditioning has made me think about these two parts of myself as a little like the geography of the state of Michigan. I am so gregarious that I once went to an Irish wake and was the perfect mourner, even though I realized when I approached the casket that I was in the wrong viewing room. And I love solitude so much that easily one of my favorite parts of the week is when I have somehow finished my work before the sitter is due to leave and I can hide out in my room for half an hour and read a Lord Peter Wimsey mystery.

Actually when I lived alone I was lonely a fair amount of 5 the time, but it felt somehow restorative. Perhaps I was making up for all those years of living in a crowded house, and all the years to come when, I suspected, I would live in one again. Because of youth or duty or love I have most often lived in crowded houses, in which a book was partly an excuse for staring into the middle distance, zoning out, being inside your own skin. I have cultivated pastimes that make this kind of behavior socially acceptable. I do needlework, watch television, and, yes, read—all excuses for chewing the cud, ruminating over whatever crosses my mental screen.

Or, like a narcoleptic, I can simply lapse into my middle distance attitude. My eyes unfocus and my mouth drops open just a bit. I look like a fish who has just been sideswiped by the *QE II* and never knew what hit it. My family calls this my "zone look." It means *do not disturb.*

I wonder if this is hereditary, or whether I simply belong to a family made up of essentially solitary people placed by fate within large and voluble groups. My father, for example, fishes; it is a pursuit some people don't understand, luring a stupid cold-blooded animal to its death on the end of a piece of string. But fishing has very little to do with fish, at least the way my dad practices it. It has to do with sinking within yourself, charting your course. And I'm all for that. 6

I also have a child who habitually lapses into the zone look, although at his age I cannot imagine what he is thinking. Friends have started to ask me when he will begin lessons: swimming, piano, art, and the like. I want him to have the best of everything, but the best of everything for me was often staring off into the middle distance. I want him to have lots of time for that. If I were asked what I am most afraid of his missing in life, I think I would answer "Solitude." I would say the same for me. 7

VOCABULARY

paragraph 1: discernment
paragraph 3: aberrant
paragraph 4: gregarious
paragraph 5: ruminating, narcoleptic
paragraph 6: hereditary, voluble
paragraph 7: lapses

QUESTIONS

1. What is the central topic of the essay, and how does Quindlen introduce it through the details in paragraphs 1–3?
2. Quindlen states that "we pay lip service to a notion that privacy is important, but I don't think we believe it much" (paragraph 4). How is this point related to the information about herself and her family in paragraphs 4–6?

3. In the course of the essay, in what order does Quindlen present her personal experiences with privacy?

4. Is Quindlen's purpose in the whole essay chiefly to express personal attitudes, interests, or habits? Or is it to define or explain the nature of privacy, or to argue for the right of solitude or privacy? How do you know?

SUGGESTIONS FOR WRITING

1. Quindlen describes the effects of growing up in a large family. Discuss the effect that the size of your family has had on your own interests, habits, and attitudes. Present these in the order of their importance or seriousness or some other order of ideas and details.

2. Present your own experiences and observations to support or challenge Quindlen's statement that "we pay lip service to a notion that privacy is important, but I don't really think we believe it much." Organize your experiences and observations clearly and consistently.

JOAN DIDION

JOAN DIDION *established her reputation as a magazine columnist and editor and later as a short story and screen writer and novelist. After graduating from the University of California, Berkeley, in 1956, she was an associate editor of* Vogue, *and later a columnist for* The Saturday Evening Post *and contributing editor to the* National Review. *Her nonfictional writings include* Salvador *(1983), a report on the Central American country, and* Miami *(1988), a report on the Cuban-American community. Her essays are collected in* Slouching towards Bethlehem *(1968) and* The White Album *(1979). In her novels* Play It As It Lays *(1970) and* The Book of Common Prayer *(1977) and in her many essays Didion depicts personal and social values often imperceptible to the people who live by them. She explores such values in her ironic essay on the marriage business in Las Vegas.*

Marrying Absurd

To be married in Las Vegas, Clark County, Nevada, a bride   1
must swear that she is eighteen or has parental permission
and a bridegroom that he is twenty-one or has parental
permission. Someone must put up five dollars for the
license. (On Sundays and holidays, fifteen dollars. The Clark
County Courthouse issues marriage licenses at any time of
the day or night except between noon and one in the
afternoon, between eight and nine in the evening, and
between four and five in the morning.) Nothing else is
required. The State of Nevada, alone among these United
States, demands neither a premarital blood test nor a waiting
period before or after the issuance of a marriage license.
Driving in across the Mojave from Los Angeles, one sees the
signs way out on the desert, looming up from the moonscape
of rattlesnakes and mesquite, even before the Las Vegas
lights appear like a mirage on the horizon: "GETTING
MARRIED? Free License Information First Strip Exit." Perhaps
the Las Vegas wedding industry achieved its peak opera-
tional efficiency between 9:00 P.M. and midnight of August
26, 1965, an otherwise unremarkable Thursday which happened to be, by Presidential order, the last day on which
anyone could improve his draft status merely by getting
married. One hundred and seventy-one couples were pronounced man and wife in the name of Clark County and the
State of Nevada that night, sixty-seven of them by a single
justice of the peace, Mr. James A. Brennan. Mr. Brennan did
one wedding at the Dunes and the other sixty-six in his
office, and charged each couple eight dollars. One bride lent
her veil to six others. "I got it down from five to three
minutes," Mr. Brennan said later of his feat. "I could've
married them *en masse,* but they're people, not cattle. People
expect more when they get married."

What people who get married in Las Vegas actually do   2
expect—what, in the largest sense, their "expectations"
are—strikes one as a curious and self-contradictory business.
Las Vegas is the most extreme and allegorical of American
settlements, bizarre and beautiful in its venality and in its
devotion to immediate gratification, a place the tone of
which is set by mobsters and call girls and ladies' room

attendants with amyl nitrite poppers in their uniform pockets. Almost everyone notes that there is no "time" in Las Vegas, no night and no day and no past and no future (no Las Vegas casino, however, has taken the obliteration of the ordinary time sense quite so far as Harold's Club in Reno, which for a while issued, at odd intervals in the day and night, mimeographed "bulletins" carrying news from the world outside); neither is there any logical sense of where one is. One is standing on a highway in the middle of a vast hostile desert looking at an eighty-foot sign which blinks "STARDUST" or "CAESAR'S PALACE." Yes, but what does that explain? This geographical implausibility reinforces the sense that what happens there has no connection with "real" life; Nevada cities like Reno and Carson are ranch towns, Western towns, places behind which there is some historical imperative. But Las Vegas seems to exist only in the eye of the beholder. All of which makes it an extraordinarily stimulating and interesting place, but an odd one in which to want to wear a candlelight satin Priscilla of Boston wedding dress with Chantilly lace insets, tapered sleeves and a detachable modified train.

And yet the Las Vegas wedding business seems to 3 appeal to precisely that impulse. "Sincere and Dignified Since 1954," one wedding chapel advertises. There are nineteen such wedding chapels in Las Vegas, intensely competitive, each offering better, faster, and, by implication, more sincere services than the next: Our Photos Best Anywhere, Your Wedding on A Phonograph Record, Candlelight with Your Ceremony, Honeymoon Accommodations, Free Transportation from Your Motel to Courthouse to Chapel and Return to Motel, Religious or Civil Ceremonies, Dressing Rooms, Flowers, Rings, Announcements, Witnesses Available, and Ample Parking. All of these services, like most others in Las Vegas (sauna baths, payroll-check cashing, chinchilla coats for sale or rent) are offered twenty-four hours a day, seven days a week, presumably on the premise that marriage, like craps, is a game to be played when the table seems hot.

But what strikes one most about the Strip chapels, with 4 their wishing wells and stained-glass paper windows and their artificial bouvardia, is that so much of their business is by no means a matter of simple convenience, of late-night liaisons between show girls and baby Crosbys. Of course there is some of that. (One night about eleven o'clock in Las Vegas I watched a bride in an orange minidress and masses of flame-colored hair stumble from a Strip chapel on the arm of her bridegroom, who looked the part of the expendable nephew in movies like *Miami Syndicate*. "I gotta get the kids," the bride whimpered. "I gotta pick up the sitter, I gotta get to the midnight show." "What you gotta get," the bridegroom said, opening the door of a Cadillac Coupe de Ville and watching her crumple on the seat, "is sober.") But Las Vegas seems to offer something other than "convenience"; it is merchandising "niceness," the facsimile of proper ritual, to children who do not know how else to find it, how to make the arrangements, how to do it "right." All day and evening long on the Strip, one sees actual wedding parties, waiting under the harsh lights at a crosswalk, standing uneasily in the parking lot of the Frontier while the photographer hired by The Little Church of the West ("Wedding Place of the Stars") certifies the occasion, takes the picture: the bride in a veil and white satin pumps, the bridegroom usually in a white dinner jacket, and even an attendant or two, a sister or a best friend in hot-pink *peau de soie*, a flirtation veil, a carnation nosegay. "When I Fall in Love It Will Be Forever," the organist plays, and then a few bars of Lohengrin. The mother cries; the stepfather, awkward in his role, invites the chapel hostess to join them for a drink at the Sands. The hostess declines with a professional smile; she has already transferred her interest to the group waiting outside. One bride out, another in, and again the sign goes up on the chapel door: "One moment please— Wedding."

I sat next to one such wedding party in a Strip restaurant   5
the last time I was in Las Vegas. The marriage had just taken place; the bride still wore her dress, the mother her corsage. A bored waiter poured out a few swallows of pink champagne ("on the house") for everyone but the bride, who was too young to be served. "You'll need something with more kick than that," the bride's father said with heavy jocularity to his new son-in-law; the ritual jokes about the wedding night had a certain Panglossian character, since the bride

was clearly seven months pregnant. Another round of pink champagne, this time not on the house, and the bride began to cry. "It was just as nice," she sobbed, "as I hoped and dreamed it would be."

VOCABULARY

paragraph 1: mesquite

paragraph 2: allegorical, bizarre, venality, implausibility

paragraph 4: bouvardia, liaisons, expendable, facsimile, nosegay

paragraph 5: jocularity

QUESTIONS

1. One principle of order in Didion's essay is spatial: we see Las Vegas as a visitor would see it from the highway. From what other viewpoints do we see Las Vegas?

2. At the same time, the essay moves to increasingly bizarre episodes, culminating in the wedding party of the final paragraph. What is bizarre about the episode? What sentences indicate this organization?

3. In Voltaire's satirical novel *Candide* the philosopher Pangloss explains the evils and imperfections of the world in the statement, "All is for the best in the best of all possible worlds." Does Didion agree? What is her attitude to the world she describes? What is the dominant tone of or attitude expressed by the essay, and how does Didion establish it?

4. Does Didion state a thesis, or is she concerned only with giving a picture of Las Vegas and the people who marry there? Does Didion imply ideas or attitudes rather than state them?

SUGGESTIONS FOR WRITING

1. Compare Didion's way of revealing her attitude toward Las Vegas with James Stevenson's way of revealing his attitude toward Los Angeles (p. 10) or Donovan Webster's way of revealing his attitude toward the Mississippi River delta (p. 105)?

2. Characterize another city through an activity typical of its way of life and values. Let your details reveal this way of life and these values.

Beginning, Middle, and Ending

❦ ❦ ❦

To make your ideas convincing, you need to capture the attention of your readers and hold it. You will lose their attention if, in beginning the essay, you describe in too much detail how you intend to proceed. Sometimes you need to indicate a point of view and suggest how you will develop the essay. The following is an ineffective way of doing so:

> I am going to describe my home town as I saw it on a recent visit. I will illustrate the changes and discuss their causes.

Compare these sentences with the opening paragraph of Eric Sevareid's essay on Velva, North Dakota. Sevareid states his subject and suggests how he will develop his essay without directly stating his purpose:

> My home town has changed in these thirty years of the American story. It is changing now, will go on changing as America changes. Its biography, I suspect, would read much the same as that of all other home towns. Depression and war and prosperity have all left their marks; modern science, modern tastes, manners, philosophies, fears and ambitions have touched my town as indelibly as they have touched New York or Panama City.

If you do need to state your purpose and outline the discussion to follow, you can do so with a minimum of personal reference and without sounding stuffy. Here is a paragraph that states the purpose of the author and outlines the book introduced by the paragraph:

> The aim of this book is to delineate two types of clever schoolboy: the converger and the diverger. The earlier chapters offer a fairly detailed description of the intellectual abilities, attitudes and personalities of a few hundred such boys. In the later chapters, this description is then used as the basis for a more speculative discussion—of the nature of intelligence and originality and of the ways in which intellectual and personal qualities interact. Although the first half of

the book rests heavily on the results of psychological tests, and the last two chapters involve psychoanalytic theory, I have done my best to be intelligible, and, wherever possible, interesting to everyone interested in clever schoolboys: parents, school-teachers, dons, psychologists, administrators, clever schoolboys.—Liam Hudson, *Contrary Imaginations*

This author directly challenges the interest of his reader. The bonus, this introductory paragraph promises, will be the wit of the author, evident in the humorous announcement of a seemingly dry subject.

By contrast, the author of the following paragraph eases his readers into the subject without an immediate statement of purpose. But he does make an immediate appeal to an important concern of his readers—the problem of how to deal with their own failures and those of friends and family members:

The administration of criminal justice and the extent of individual moral responsibility are among the crucial problems of a civilized society. They are indissolubly linked, and together they involve our deepest emotions. We often find it hard to forgive ourselves for our own moral failures. All of us, at some time or other, have faced the painful dilemma of when to punish and when to forgive those we love—our children, our friends. How much harder it is, then, to deal with the stranger who transgresses.—David L. Bazelon, "The Awesome Decision"

Notice that personal references are not out of place in an opening paragraph—or anywhere else in an essay. The risk of such references is that they can divert the reader from the subject of the essay to the author. For this reason they should be kept to a minimum.

The opening paragraphs build the expectations of the reader. The middle paragraphs develop ideas introduced at the beginning. They ought not to introduce new ideas without preparing the reader for a new turn of thought, as Eric Sevareid does:

The people have not changed, but the *kinds* of people have changed. . . .
They eat differently in Velva now. . . .

An effective ending will not let the discussion drop: the reader should not finish the essay with a sense of loose ends, of lines of thought left uncompleted. In the formal essay, the ending may restate the thesis or perhaps even state it for the first time—if you build to the thesis through explanation and details. One of the most effective conclusions, the reference back to ideas that opened the essay, gives the reader a sense of completion:

It is personal freedom that makes us better persons, and they are freer in Velva now. There is no real freedom without privacy, and a resident of my home town can be a private person much more than he could before. People are able to draw at least a little apart from one another. In drawing apart, they gave their best human instincts room for expansion.—Eric Sevareid

---

RACHEL CARSON

The American naturalist and conservationist RACHEL CAR-SON *(1907–1964) worked as a biologist at the Marine Biological Laboratory at Woods Hole, Massachusetts, and as editor-in-chief for the U.S. Fish and Wildlife Service. Carson wrote several books about the natural life of the Atlantic coast and waters, including* Under the Sea-Wind *(1941),* The Sea Around Us *(1951) (given the National Book Award the same year), and* The Edge of the Sea *(1955). In 1962 she published* Silent Spring, *which warned of the pollution of the environment by insecticides and chemicals.* Silent Spring *is probably the most influential book written in the United States on environmental issues. The following paragraph from* The Edge of the Sea *describing the birth of a volcano begins with the topic idea and develops it thoroughly.*

The Birth of an Island

The birth of a volcanic island is an event marked by prolonged and violent travail: the forces of the earth striving to create, and all the forces of the sea opposing. The sea floor, where an island begins, is probably nowhere more than about fifty miles thick—a thin covering over the vast bulk of the earth. In it are deep cracks and fissures, the results of unequal cooling and shrinkage in past ages. Along such lines of weakness the molten lava from the earth's interior presses up and finally bursts forth into the sea. But a submarine volcano is different from a terrestrial eruption, where the lava, molten rocks, gases, and other ejecta are hurled into the air through an open crater. Here on the bottom of the ocean the volcano has resisting it all the weight of the ocean water above it. Despite the immense pressure of, it may be, two or three miles of sea water, the new volcanic cone builds upward toward the surface, in flow after flow of lava. Once within reach of the waves, its soft ash and tuff are violently attacked, and for a long period the potential island may remain a shoal, unable to emerge. But, eventually, in new eruptions, the cone is pushed up into the air and a rampart against the attacks of the waves is built of hardened lava.

QUESTIONS

1. Paragraphs, like the whole essay, have a beginning, a middle, and an end. What point about the birth of the island does the opening sentence make?
2. How does the paragraph develop this point? What is the principle of order in the whole paragraph?
3. Is the comparison with a terrestrial eruption a parenthetical idea, or is it essential to the explanation?
4. How do we know that Carson has completed her explanation?

SUGGESTIONS FOR WRITING

Use one of the following statements or an idea of your own to develop a paragraph. Draw on your personal experience and observations. You might begin the paragraph with the statement, or build the paragraph to it:

a. "Seeing is of course very much a matter of verbalization. Unless I call my attention to what passes before my eyes, I simply won't see it."—Annie Dillard, *Pilgrim at Tinker Creek*

b. "The simple words 'I was born' have somehow a charm beside which all the splendors of romance and fairy-tale turn to moonshine and tinsel."—Virginia Woolf, "The Personal Essay"

c. "[A newspaper] cannot be used as if all its parts had equal value or authenticity."—Allan Nevins, "The Newspaper"

ELIZABETH A. BROWN

After graduating from Harvard University in 1983, Eliza-
beth A. Brown worked for Vogue *magazine in New York*
and later traveled in China, Tibet, and Japan. She taught
Western literature in rural China and worked as an English
tutor in Kyoto, Japan, and as a model in nearby Osaka. Her
essay on jogging along the Kamo Gawa River in Kyoto first
appeared in The Christian Science Monitor. *Brown uses a*
familiar pastime to describe a distant place and culture.

Jogging in Japan

It's another scorching day in Kyoto—so hot I don't need an   1
alarm clock. By 6 a.m. the sun is streaming through the
shoji—sliding doors of opaque glass—filling my small room
with sunshine, spilling onto my bed on the floor. Quickly I
dress for my morning jog along the river.

As an American living and working in this fast-paced   2
country, I value this time to be alone with my thoughts and
the peaceful surroundings. Keeps my soul toned, and my
body trim for modeling assignments.

Since it hasn't rained for days, the river is calm. The air   3
is clean and only early-morning humid. It smells of little fish
and tall trees. Rhythmically the gravel scrunches beneath my
feet. All is quiet except for the few cars and Japanese-sized
trucks on their way to work.

I jog past a couple of elderly gentlemen—one in a white   4
sweat suit, being towed briskly by his dog, another in a
traditional robe of dark brown linen, moving slowly, bent
over his knobby walking stick. After the second bridge I pass
the old man who does *tai chi*—Chinese exercise, a sort of
slow kung fu—every morning on the riverbank. His slow,
controlled movements remind me of early mornings in
China—my home before Japan—where old people rise at
dawn to stretch their limbs and soothe their minds before the
day's work begins. I feel a kinship with folks who share the
secrets of morning serenity.

A few fishermen dot the riverbank; the rhythm of the   5
gravel is broken as I leap over scattered bamboo fishing poles

and rusty pails. The sun is hot on my back as I continue along the river's path. Only the *tsuru*—white cranes—have commenced communal activity, but quietly. They soar. They wade. They dive for fish. Even the pigeons are listless in this heat, except when they waddle aside to let me pass.

At the northern tip of my loop I am in the country, surrounded by rice and vegetable fields. On spring and fall mornings, when I run later, I see groups of school-children—in uniforms, caps, and knapsacks—playing on their way to school. They stare and giggle awkwardly when I run by; if I speak to them they laugh and run for cover. But this morning it's too early to see them. 6

Now I come to my favorite spot: the horse barn. I jog across the road, into the barn, and greet the horses—in Japanese. Would they understand English? I inhale deeply, eyes closed; for a moment I am back home in my father's horse barn. Summer is my favorite time on the farm in Michigan, but I haven't been there for two years. 7

Second half of the loop, sun in my face. 8

"*Ohayo gozaimasu,*" pants a familiar voice. She smiles— we're friends without names—and nods her visor. Maybe she's a housewife—as most women are—who returns home to prepare her husband for work and her children for school. Yet she is an unusual sight—a middle-aged woman jogging alone every morning, rain or shine (and at a faster clip than I!). I wonder why she jogs so diligently. Is it to keep fit? 9

A thin breeze rustles the grass along the path. The old women who tend the riverbank are ready to start working. Chattering, they assemble, carrying trowels, rakes, and towels. They're dressed in traditional blue cotton pants and little jackets, with white hand towels resting on the tops of their heads. A funny sight, I think. But perhaps they find my wide-soled shoes, sweat-soaked tank top, and punky sun-glasses just as silly. Whatever, we always exchange greet-ings—bows and smiles—as I jog by. 10

It's hot, and my 10 kilometers are finished. Stopping by a place with easy access to the river, I look around to make sure no one is watching, take off my shoes and socks, and wade to my knees in the icy river. Ah, heaven. 11

On the way back to my room, I stop by the neighbor's abundant flower bed for a whiff of some new blossoms. The 12 flowers come and go so quickly in the summer. The earth feels cold under my feet, but I must be careful that no one sees my delight; the Japanese do *not* approve of bare feet outdoors.

By now my room smells of tatami—the straw matting 13 used for floors in traditional Japanese homes. The smell reminds me of summer haymows back home. But here we live, work, and sleep on the plant. I'm glad the mats in my room are still fresh.

I turn on the floor fan and begin my morning chores: 14 fold the sheets, hang the *futon*, or cotton mattress, on the railing outside my window, vacuum the floor, dust the table in my room, and turn on the TV for my morning French lesson in Japanese.

I wander outside and bring in laundry from my little 15 clothesline. Already my landlady is in the garden pulling weeds from around the rocks. I think that's her serenity before the day. When she sees me watching, she smiles, stands to straighten her apron, and giggles with her hand covering her mouth. *"Ohayo gozaimasu, Riza-san,"* she says with a bowing nod.

"Ohayo gozaimasu, Ueda-san," I return, with a quick bow. 16 We talk about the weather and the garden—all in Japanese. How I wish I could talk about more personal things—ask her what it's like to be a single woman raising teen-age sons in modern Japan, or what she thinks about when she's pulling weeds. Sometimes when I see her watching TV by herself or sitting alone at the kitchen table, she seems lonely. This morning she looks happy.

Towel and toiletries container in hand, I walk across the 17 garden to her house, where I use the *ofuro*—Japanese bath. I stop to look at the *koi*—big carp, once I heard one speak— when splash! the frog jumps in. Happens every morning.

QUESTIONS

1. How do paragraphs 1 and 2 and the title of the essay prepare the reader for what is to follow? Do they state or imply a central theme or idea that Brown will explore or develop?

2. How are these expectations realized in the remainder of the essay? Is Brown only describing the experience of jogging in

Japan, or is she also making a point about herself or Japan through that experience or something in addition?

3. Does Brown refer to or hint at one or more similarities or differences between Japanese and American behavior and customs? Or are similarities or differences incidental or of no concern in the essay?

4. Why does Brown conclude with the experience at the bath? Is she making a point or expressing a momentary feeling?

SUGGESTIONS FOR WRITING

1. Write an essay describing a similar experience of your own—for example, bicycling in an unfamiliar neighborhood. Your opening paragraphs should establish a point of view and indicate your subject and your purpose in writing. You may wish to give an impression of a place or to reveal feelings and thoughts of the moment. Or you may wish to make a point about the experience.

2. Rewrite one or two paragraphs of your essay for another purpose and perhaps another audience. In an additional paragraph, explain why you made changes in details, point of view, or focus.

AMY JO KEIFER

> AMY JO KEIFER *majored in international relations at American University, in Washington, D.C. Keifer grew up on a farm in Eastern Pennsylvania; in "The Death of a Farm," which appeared in the* New York Times *on June 30, 1991, she gives the history of the farm and traces its gradual deterioration. In the essay that follows, John L. Moore describes a different threat to the farmer—that of drought.*

The Death of a Farm

I am a farmer's daughter. I am also a 4-H member, breeder   1
and showman of sheep and showman of cattle. My family's
farm is dying and I have watched it, and my family, suffer.

Our eastern Pennsylvania farm is a mere sixty acres. The [2] green rolling hills and forested land are worth a minimum of $300,000 to developers, but no longer provide my family with the means to survive. It's a condition called asset rich and cash poor, and it's a hard way of life.

My grandfather bought our farm when he and my [3] grandmother were first married. He raised dairy cattle and harvested the land full time for more than twenty years. When he died, my father took over and changed the farm to beef cattle, horses and pigs, and kept the crops. But it wasn't enough to provide for a young family, so he took on a full time job, too.

I can remember, when I was young, sitting on the fence [4] with my sister and picking out a name for each calf. My sister's favorite cow was named Flower, and so we named her calves Buttercup, Daisy, Rose and Violet. Flower was the leader of a herd of more than twenty. The only cattle left on our farm now are my younger sister's and brother's 4-H projects.

I can remember a huge tractor-trailer backed into the [5] loading chute of our barn on days when more than two hundred pigs had to be taken to market. That was before the prices went down and my father let the barn go empty rather than take on more debt.

I can remember my father riding on the tractor, larger [6] than life, baling hay or planting corn. When prices started dropping, we began to rent some land to other farmers, so they could harvest from it. But prices have dropped so low this year there are no takers. The land will go unused; the tractor and the equipment have long since been sold off.

I don't remember the horses. I've seen a few pictures in [7] which my father, slim and dark, is holding his newborn daughter on horseback amid a small herd. And I've heard stories of his delivering hay to farms all over the state, but I can't ever remember his loading up a truck to do it.

Piece by piece, our farm has deteriorated. We started [8] breeding sheep and now have about twenty-five head, but they yield little revenue. My mother, who works as a registered nurse, once said something that will remain with me forever: "Your father works full time to support the farm. I work full time to support the family."

I've seen movies like "The River" and "Places in the 9
Heart." They tell the real struggle. But people can leave a
movie theater, and there's a happy ending for them. There
aren't many happy endings in a real farmer's life. I was
reared hearing that hard work paid off, while seeing that it
didn't. My younger brother would like to take over the farm
some day, but I'm not sure it will hold on much longer. Its
final breath is near.

QUESTIONS

1. What does Keifer tell us about herself in her opening paragraph?
   How does she use this information to introduce the subject of
   her essay?

2. In what order does she present additional information about
   herself and her family and farm in paragraphs 2–7? How do
   these details lead us to her statement in paragraph 8, "Piece by
   piece, our farm has deteriorated"?

3. Is Keifer making a point about the deterioration of the farm or
   developing a thesis?

4. What parts of the essay are informative or expository, and what
   parts are expressive of a feeling or attitude? Is the essay chiefly
   expository, or is it chiefly expressive or persuasive?

SUGGESTIONS FOR WRITING

1. Keifer suggests that film depictions of farm life are not always
   true to reality. Discuss the extent to which a recent movie or
   television drama fails to describe an aspect of your own world or
   experience.

2. Keifer says the following in her concluding paragraph: "I was
   reared hearing that hard work paid off, while seeing that it
   didn't." Discuss a similar truth that you discovered while
   growing up. Describe the circumstances of your discovery, then
   discuss its effects on your view of people and your life.

JOHN L. MOORE

JOHN L. MOORE *runs a cattle ranch in Miles City, in southeastern Montana. The severe drought of 1988, following years of low rainfall, brought farmers and ranchers in western and other states to economic ruin. Thousands in the 1980s lost their land and livestock through foreclosure. In his article, published in the* New York Times Magazine *on August 14, 1988, Moore describes the effect of drought on his own ranch and family.*

Bad Days at "Big Dry"

I turned the horses out again tonight. 1

The saddle horses come into the corral early every 2
morning for feed. I pour a bucket of "cake"—pellets of
compressed alfalfa and grain—into their troughs and close
the gate behind them. They're locked up in case I need to
ride. Or want to.

I used to look for reasons to ride, especially on a cool 3
Montana evening when I had a young horse that needed the
work. Nothing felt as good as the smooth leather of a latigo
sliding through my fingers, or the slight jingle of my spurs as
I led my horses to the pickup and trailer. But I turned the
horses out because now I don't care to ride.

There is nothing out there. There are no green coulees to 4
ride through, no little badland creeks trickling with water the
color and thickness of creamed coffee. There are only the
haunted looks of sad-eyed cows and the constant reminder
that decisions—difficult, painful decisions—need to be
made. Before, I could ride around my cattle, watching the
calves grow fat and shiny, seeing the contentedness of
mother cows grazing green creek bottoms. I kept an eye
open for an eagle on the wing or the mossy horns of a mule
deer buck in velvet.

But this is the seventh year that drought has gripped 5
this eastern Montana landscape—seven out of the last nine,
and this one is by far the worst.

This stretch of terrain, east of Billings and west of the 6

Dakotas, is naturally arid. The frontier photographer L. A. Huffman labeled it the "Big Dry." When the homesteaders arrived in the early 1920's, several wet years lay back-to-back. This land, they thought, was surely as fertile as Ohio. They filed claims and took out loans to buy seed, teams, even steam-engined tractors. They experienced a good year or two, then the Dirty Thirties came. Like a young bride with a sinister secret, the land revealed herself as she truly was, harsh, cruel, unrelenting, a land of meager, self-sacrificing survival.

The homesteaders left in droves. They left their little tarpaper shacks. They left their big black steam-engined tractors rusting in the fields. They turned their horses out. 7

A few homesteaders remained, surviving either on the little scratch of desert they called their claim or by herding sheep or working in town. They are today's old-timers. They stand and talk quietly on the shaded corners of the main streets of our communities. They visit sale barns and watch as the cattle are sold. 8

"Yes, this is bad," they said during the drought of 1979 and '80, "but it ain't as bad as '31. God, how the wind blew, and the mormon crickets—they ate everything in sight." During the drought of '84 and '85, when countless ranchers and farmers were foreclosed on and the Governor announced "our state literally is on fire" from lightning strikes, they said: "It ain't nothin' compared to '34 and '36. Never did rain then." 9

But the old-timers have shut up. There has never been a summer like the summer of 1988. 10

I returned to the ranch in 1979. I came out of a dead-end position in the Air Force to help my recently widowed mother. I remember sitting in base supply in Great Falls, Montana, two meager stripes on my sleeve, noticing that no one cared about the weather. To the urban person, weather was simply a matter of convenience. Snow made it hard to get to work in the morning. Rain prevented recreation on weekends. I would love to be back on the ranch, I told myself. I would love to again be dependent on the environment. 11

We returned in the spring of 1979, my wife, two little 12
children and I. Those first few years were terribly dry, but
we were young, full of hope and naïve.

When my mother passed away in 1982, I inherited a 13
small herd of cattle and a ten-year lease on the family ranch.
It is a small ranch, but with our shares in the larger corporate
ranch owned mainly by two of my surviving uncles, an
economic base is possible. The whole is a "cowboy" kind of
outfit. We don't own any tractors, no motorcycles, no
snowmobiles. We depend on battered old four-wheel-drive
pickups and good horseflesh to find our way around some
40,000 acres of badlands and prairie.

In 1984, I had to sell most of my cows. There was little 14
grass, no water. We put them on trucks and shipped them to
the auction barn in town. I didn't watch them sell, but I
made another mistake. After they were sold, I walked the
alleys in the back lot of the sales yard and saw my cows
penned, waiting for the trucks that would take them to
slaughter. And they recognized me. I could see the recognition in their eyes; and I didn't dare speak because they knew
my voice better than my appearance, so many winter days
they had heard me calling them to the pickup, where I fed
the tamer ones cake pellets from my hand. I wondered that
day if maybe I was too sentimental to be a good rancher.

But we started building our herd again. We kept as 15
many heifer calves as we could, and we did without things,
such as new pickups, or fresh linoleum for the kitchen floor.

Last year was a good year. It rained. The market 16
improved. Things were looking up. There was hope. But if I
had ridden out tonight, I would have seen what is left of last
year's brittle grass and I would have worried about the stale
water the cows sip through the mud and moss of the
reservoirs.

I remember May, and how the ranchers met in the cafes 17
over coffee to predict when it would rain. I remember the big
storm that rolled across the state on Memorial Day weekend,
the heavy, black clouds, the thunder, but no rain.

Then came June, traditionally our wettest—and 18
greenest—month in a calendar year that rarely gives us more
than eleven inches of moisture. But the skies paled to a hazy
white. The winds blew. The temperature climbed to 102, 105,

108 and, finally, 112. Thunderstorms tried to form but had no moisture, just noise and flash. One night I took my children—ages ten and eleven—to the top of a hill and pointed toward the Powder River country south of town. We counted the black, billowing smoke of three separate range fires burning uncontrolled. "Remember this day," I told them. "This is something you will someday tell your children about."

I remember setting the alarm clock for 3:30 A.M. to ride 19 out to the bogs and move cattle away from reservoirs that were becoming muddy deathtraps.

I remember trying to keep bulls with little bunches of 20 cows, hoping against hope that they were in good enough condition to have their estrous cycle.

But much of June I do not remember. The days merely 21 melted, one into another, then dried to dust and blew away.

In mid-July, we sold my uncle's sheep. I do not remem- 22 ber my uncle's ever being without sheep. He has herded sheep from Greybull, Wyoming, to the Canadian line. He has walked most of eastern Montana caring for the woollies. I remember as a child thinking I was alone in the hills, just me and my horse, and then I would feel a presence. There he would be, a distant, dark specter walking the land.

He cared little for being on horseback. When we trailed 23 cows, he would dismount and lead his horse. My father was a cowboy; he liked his horses fast and wild. But sheepherders want their horses to be slow and lazy and stay close to camp. My uncle never cared to drive, either. It has been more than fifty years since he drove a vehicle on a public highway. And he never married. He was, whether he would admit it or not, married to the sheep.

My uncle survived June. He followed the sheep every 24 morning as they left his cluttered yard and headed up Sunday Creek in search of something to eat. By eleven o'clock, the sun would force them to seek shade. They would crowd into an abandoned airplane hangar on the edge of a crested wheat-grass field. He would come home, lie on his couch and listen to market reports on the radio.

Just before dark, he would go back out to get them. The 25 coyotes are thick here, so the sheep have to be brought in at night. The first lamb the coyotes killed was the largest in the herd. They got him in broad daylight, during the few minutes my uncle left the herd to feed his bums—the motherless lambs that are fed on a bottle. When the coyotes got the second lamb, I think something snapped inside him. The ewes were old. It was too hot. Too dry. It was time to sell the sheep. We loaded them into trailers and took them to town.

My uncle pretends he was mad at the sheep—for 26 making it so much work to keep them bunched, for letting themselves be killed by coyotes. I know he is just a mile up the road from my house, lying on his couch, reading newspapers or playing with the little button that controls his satellite television. But it is hard for me to imagine him without his sheep.

One day in late July, I went up to Deadman Creek to 27 check on my cows. I drove my pickup and parked at one of the last reservoirs that still had a little water. I found a dead turtle on the bank. I don't know why he died. Maybe it was boredom.

I felt guilty as I walked past the first little bunch of cows. 28 They looked at me, curious, hungry. I did not like to look back; they looked worse than I had ever seen. I know each one, her personality, her ancestry. I may have assisted in bringing her into the world, and probably assisted in the birthing of her first calf. As I walked by them, they looked at me as if I had let them down. It is not for lack of land; in this pasture, each cow and calf have almost 300 acres. It is the heat, the lack of grass, the sour, muddy water.

We are conservative ranchers. We don't believe in 29 dryland farming this fragile ground. The Government for years paid some of our neighbors to plant their pastures to wheat. Now it is paying them to plant them back to grass. We have never been paid for mistakes. We don't expect to be.

I do not own this land. I am only its present steward. 30 Perhaps it is my time to move on. Should the last reservoir go dry, I will go somewhere with my cattle. But where do I go? To the sales ring? To distant grass, paying someone else to feed and care for them?

I would like to be able to keep my cows until October. By 31 then, the calves will be old enough to wean and sell. The market has dropped because of the drought in the Midwest— the forced sale of cattle has depressed prices for now—but I hope to get enough for the calves to meet expenses. By October, I will be able to pregnancy test my cows. I would like to keep the ones that are pregnant. My biggest fear now is how many that will be.

I have checked with the local Agricultural Stabilization 32 and Conservation Service office on the emergency feed program. It could make the difference in whether I can keep my cows. The man in the office said we're lucky it's an election year.

The national press is acting as if it has just discovered 33 drought. As a society, we are so far removed from the land we do not know where our food comes from. It simply has always been there, in neat rows on the grocery shelves, and all we have cared about is the price.

Meanwhile, the local paper says the onslaught of prairie 34 and timber fires is actually helping Miles City's economy. Several hundred firefighters are camped at the fairgrounds, sleeping in tents and barn stalls. How ironic! The economy here has been so bad for so long that businesses have burned down regularly. Arson has been confirmed in several cases. Now a reprieve has been granted. The economy has been temporarily saved by an invasion of tired, hungry firefighters.

But there is no rain in the forecast. In the last eleven 35 months we have received only two inches of moisture. I can look at the reservoirs and count the days before they will be finished.

I went out today to feel the pulse of the land. I felt none. 36
There is only one more thing to do. 37
I am going to turn the horses out. 38

VOCABULARY

paragraph 3: latigo
paragraph 4: coulees
paragraph 15: heifer calves
paragraph 20: estrous cycle

paragraph 22: specter
paragraph 25: ewes
paragraph 29: dryland farming

QUESTIONS

1. Why does Moore open with the statement, "I turned the horses out again tonight?" Why does he repeat this statement at the end of the essay? How does the statement widen in meaning as the essay progresses? What is the effect of beginning and ending the essay with the same statement?

2. Why does Moore begin by describing eastern Montana in the summer of 1988 and then turn to the past? Would the essay be different in its effect if the narrative were entirely chronological? What was that effect on your first reading?

3. Why does Moore give more details about his uncle than about his mother or others who lived through the drought of the 1930s?

4. Is Moore writing only to express his sense of place and time? Or is his purpose also persuasive—to urge a change in governmental policy and law, or encourage a change in how his readers think about farmers and ranchers? Does Moore state his purpose directly, or do you discover it indirectly, in his narrative and his comments?

SUGGESTIONS FOR WRITING

1. Moore suggests that the circumstances of our life determine how we look at people and issues—at farmers, ranchers, mortgage foreclosures, the price of food. Discuss how circumstances shape your view of farmers and farm issues or shape your view of people in another occupation or society and related issues.

2. Describe the effects of drought, or the effects of another natural disaster, on your own life. Your purpose in writing may be to express your feelings and thoughts about the experience. Your purpose may also be persuasive—perhaps to attack a stereotype or change the thinking of your readers on a public issue and urge them to take action of some kind.

TRANSITIONS

❦ ❦ ❦

Transitional words and phrases help us connect ideas and details in our paragraphs and essays. We especially need them when we change the subject or course of discussion, as in the following sentence by James Stevenson:

> In some places, tons of concrete have been poured like icing over a section of hillside to hold it back—and the concrete has even been painted green—but the earth has begun to slip away beneath that, too, leaving edges of concrete sticking out against the sky.

The transitional words *even* and *too* show the course of Stevenson's thinking in the sentence: *even* tells us he is adding a detail to intensify his description of the street; *too* shows he is comparing the slipping earth to other sections of the road.

Words like *after* and *since* express relationships of time; words like *above* and *below*, relationships of space. Here are some important transitions that show the relationship of ideas:

- qualification: *but, however, nevertheless, nonetheless*
- illustration and explanation: *for example, for instance, so, thus*
- comparison: *similarly, in the same way, by comparison, likewise*
- contrast: *by contrast, on the one hand, on the other hand*
- consequence: *thus, so, as a result, consequently, therefore*
- concession: *but, admittedly, nevertheless, however*
- amplification: *and, moreover, furthermore, also, in addition, indeed*
- summation: *in conclusion, to sum up, all in all, finally*

Punctuation also shows us how ideas are related. A colon tells us that an expansion, explanation, or illustration follows; a semicolon, that the ideas joined are closely related or of the same importance.

RENÉ DUBOS

René Dubos (1901–1982), one of the world's leading bacteriologists, was associated most of his life with Rockefeller University for Medical Research in New York City and made important contributions to the treatment of tuberculosis and the development of commercial antibiotics. In later years, he wrote much about the environment and the social consequences of advances in medicine and technology. His many books include Only One Earth (1972), written with Barbara Ward, and So Human an Animal (1968)—awarded the Pulitzer Prize in 1969. In his book Man Adapting, Dubos argues that advances in medical care have led people to neglect one important means of dealing with the world, "adaptive resources," illustrated in the passage reprinted here. But he warns that this adaptability can be dangerous because "it implies so often a passive acceptance of conditions which really are not desirable for mankind. The lowest common denominators of existence tend to become the accepted criteria, merely for the sake of gray and anonymous peace or tranquillity."

Fitness in the Modern World

[1]There is no such thing as fitness per se with regard to military service, because fitness must always be defined in terms of a particular combat situation. [2]In consequence, the armed forces find it necessary to revise the physical standards of health at frequent intervals, in order to keep them in tune with the changing requirements of military service. [3]With propeller-driven aircraft, for example, there were many situations in which survival depended on strength of arm and limb. [4]Moreover, the pilot of a fighter airplane in World War II had to watch for enemies in the sky by direct visual perception. [5]His head swiveled from side to side looking to the rear, and for this reason calisthenics to develop neck muscles were part of training.

[6]Today, power controls have lessened physical requirements of the aircraft operator, and with electronic vision the fighter pilot never needs to look to the rear. [7]In any case, direct vision would be of little help in modern air combat because of the terrific speeds at which aircraft approach each

other. [8]At 600 miles per hour, and this is now moderate speed, half a mile means little more than a second, clearly not enough time for the pilot to see, to react, and to change the direction of his aircraft. [9]As a result, keenness of distant vision no longer means the difference between life and death for the fighter pilot; this attribute has been superseded by keenness in ability to detect slight changes on electronic dials and gauges. [10]More generally, strenuous physical conditioning programs are no longer as directly relevant to performance in the armed forces as they used to be. [11]And in fact, recent tests indicate that pilots at the peak of physical form do not score any better in difficult operations than do those of comparable groups who are less well endowed physically.

[12]The changes in relevance of physical prowess to military performance have many counterparts in civilian life. [13]Effectiveness in modern technology depends to a large extent on dial-watching and on reading printed matter. [14]Whereas physical stamina and distant vision were once extremely important, muscles are now called into play chiefly during leisure time, and nearsightedness has become almost an asset in several professions. [15]The present trends of life seem to provide justification for the child who does not want to walk because he considers it old-fashioned and for his mother who dissuades him from engaging in physical exertion or exposing himself to inclemencies because modern existence is and will increasingly become air-conditioned and effortless. [16]And yet this attitude may have unfavorable consequences in the long run. [17]A state of adaptedness to the conditions of today is no guarantee of adaptability to the challenges of tomorrow.

QUESTIONS

1. What transitional words and phrases do you find in sentences 2–4? What relationships do these establish?
2. What relationships do the transitions in the second paragraph express? Could any of these transitions be omitted without loss of coherence or clarity?
3. What other transitions might the author have substituted for those in sentences 2, 4, 9, and 11?

4. How does the whole discussion illustrate sentence 17—the thesis statement or main idea of the three paragraphs?

5. What physical skills does a competent bicyclist need? Does a competent driver require the same skills or different ones?

SUGGESTIONS FOR WRITING

1. Write a paragraph from your own experience that develops one of the following ideas or another of your choosing. Restate the idea, qualifying or disagreeing with it, if you wish. Use transitional words and phrases where appropriate.

   a. What we learn in school often is obsolete by the time we are ready to use it.

   b. Using household appliances often requires special skills.

2. Illustrate sentence 17 from your own experience. You might show how physical capabilities once important in childhood are no longer important to you. Use transitional words and phrases where needed for coherence.

MARY E. MEBANE

> *Born in 1933 in Durham, North Carolina, MARY E. MEBANE grew up on a farm—the world she describes in her autobiography,* Mary *(1981), and in* Mary, Wayfarer *(1983). Following her graduation from college in Durham, she taught in public schools and took graduate degrees at the University of North Carolina. She has taught at various schools, including the University of South Carolina and the University of Wisconsin at Milwaukee. Like Sally Carrighar, Eudora Welty, and Mary McCarthy, Mebane immerses us in the sights, sounds, and smells of childhood in this portrait of her mother and in the experience with segregation she describes later in this book (p.123).*

Nonnie

Nonnie led a structured, orderly existence. Before six o'clock 1
in the morning, she was up, starting her day. First she
turned on WPTF and listened to the news and the weather

and the music. Later, when WDNC in Durham hired Nor-
fleet Whitted, the first black announcer in the area, she
listened first to one station, then to the other. Some mornings
it would be "They Traced Her Little Footprints in the Snow,"
and other mornings it would be black gospel-singing and
rhythm-and-blues. Then she would make a fire in the wood
stove and start her breakfast. She prepared some meat—
fried liver pudding or fatback, or a streak-of-fat streak-of-
lean—and made a hoecake of bread on top of the stove,
which she ate with either Karo syrup or homemade black-
berry preserves, occasionally with store-bought strawberry
preserves, or sometimes with homemade watermelon-rind
preserves that she had canned in the summer. Then she
would drink her coffee, call me to get up, and leave the
house in her blue uniform, blue apron, and blue cap—it
would still be dark when she left on winter mornings—and
go to catch her ride to the tobacco factory (with Mr. Ralph
Baldwin at first, and then, when he retired, with Mr. James
Yergan). When Miss Delilah still lived in Wildwood, before
she and Mr. Leroy separated, she would come by and call
from the road and the two of them would walk together to
the end of the road near the highway and wait for Mr. Ralph
there.

My job after she left was to see that the fire didn't go out   2
in the wood stove, to see that the pots sitting on the back
didn't burn—for in them was our supper, often pinto beans
or black-eyed peas or collard greens or turnip salad. Occasionally there was kale or mustard greens or cressy salad.
The other pot would have the meat, which most often was
neck bones or pig feet or pig ears, and sometimes spareribs.
These would cook until it was time for me to go to school;
then I would let the fire die down, only to relight it when I
came home to let the pots finish cooking.

After Nonnie left, I also had the task of getting Ruf   3
Junior up so that he could get to school on time. This
presented no problem to me until Ruf Junior was in high
school and started playing basketball. Often he would travel
with the team to schools in distant towns, sometimes getting
home after midnight, and the next morning he would be
tired and sleepy and wouldn't want to get up. I sympathized,
but I had my job to do. If I let him oversleep, I knew that

Nonnie would fuss when she got home. But on the other hand, no matter how often I called to him, he would murmur sleepily, "All right, all right," then go back to sleep. I solved this problem one bitter-cold winter morning. I jerked all the covers off his bed and ran. I knew that the only place he could get warm again would be in the kitchen. (The only fire was in the wood stove.) The fire was already out, so he'd have to make one. After that, I didn't have such a hard time getting him up.

My mother worked as a cutter, clipping the hard ends of 4 each bundle of tobacco before it was shredded to make cigarettes. At noon she ate the lunch she had brought from home in a brown paper bag: a biscuit with meat in it and a sweet potato or a piece of pie or cake. Some of the women ate in the cafeteria, but in her thirty years at the Liggett and Myers factory, she never once did. She always took her lunch. Then she worked on until closing time, caught her ride back to Wildwood, and started on the evening's activities. First she had supper, which I had finished preparing from the morning. After I got older we sometimes had meat other than what had to be prepared in a "pot." It would be my duty to fry chicken or prepare ham bits and gravy.

After supper, she'd read the Durham *Sun* and see to it 5 that we did the chores if we hadn't done them already: slop the hogs, feed the chickens, get in the wood for the next day. Then we were free. She'd get her blue uniform ready for the next day, then listen to the radio. No later than nine o'clock, she would be in bed. In the morning she would get up, turn on the radio, and start frying some fatback. Another day would have started.

Saturdays were work days, too, the time for washing, 6 ironing, going to the garden, preparing Sunday dinner (no one was supposed to work on the Sabbath, so we ran the chicken down in the yard and Nonnie wrung its neck or chopped its head off with the ax). Sometimes we went to town on Saturday but not often, for Nonnie went to town every day. Sometimes, at lunchtime, she'd go down to Belk's, and always on Friday she went to the A&P on Mangum Street and bought her groceries; then she'd stop at the Big Star in Little Five Points if she had heard that there was a particularly good buy on something. So the Saturday-in-town ritual that is so much a part of the lives of most country children was not mine at all. I myself sometimes went to Brookstown several times a week when my father was alive, because that is where he went to get trash, sell vegetables, and visit his relatives.

Sunday afternoons she would go to see her friends or 7 they would come to see her. She would say, "I believe I'll go up to Miss Angeline's a little while." Or it would be Miss Pauline's or Claudia's. And she would stay until about dusk and come home, listen to the radio, then go to bed, ready to start Monday morning again.

In the spring and summer after work, my mother would 8 plant in her garden: tomatoes, string beans, okra, and she'd sow a turnip patch. Then, every day after work, she'd go over to the garden on the hill to see how it was doing. On Saturdays she'd get her buckets if it was time for us to go berrypicking. And on hot summer evenings, if the peaches man had been around, she'd can them after work because they wouldn't keep until Saturday, the day she did most of her canning.

This was her routine—fixed, without change, unvary- 9 ing. And she accepted it. She more than accepted it, she embraced it; it gave meaning to her life, it was what she had been put here on this earth to do. It was not to be questioned.

To Nonnie this life was ideal; she saw nothing wrong 10 with it. And she wondered in baffled rage why her daughter didn't value it but rather sought something else, some other rhythm, a more meaningful pattern to human life.

Nonnie Mebane was not political. However, a special 11 awe would come into her voice when she said, "And Lee *surrendered*." She was from Virginia, and I realize now that she probably would have been imbued with Virginia history in her eight years of schooling there. I myself never heard Robert E. Lee's name mentioned in any class at Wildwood School. But my mother loved to say, "And Lee *surrendered*." She also liked to say sometimes that the Yankee soldiers rode up and said, "Come on out. Ya'll are free this morning."

The way she said it, I could see the men on horseback— 12 the Yankees—coming around to the fields and to the cabins and saying to the blacks who had been slaves for centuries, "Come on out. Ya'll are free this morning." That was a magical moment. I used to get cold chills when she said it, for, I now realize, in her voice I heard the voice of my mother's mother as she told Nonnie and her other children how the Yankees came early one morning and what they had said. My mother's grandmother had heard them.

Nonnie was a good plain cook, but she couldn't sew 13 very well, couldn't fix hair—her own or her daughter's—and, though dutiful, was an indifferent housekeeper. She was thrifty and paid all of her bills on time. Work at the tobacco factory was her life.

QUESTIONS

1. How does the opening sentence—"Nonnie led a structured, orderly existence"—organize the paragraphs that follow?

2. Many of the transitional words are chronological, showing how the events of the day were connected in time. What examples of such transitions do you find in paragraphs 1, 4, and 8?

3. What transitional ideas do *often, but,* and *on the other hand* express in paragraph 3? What about *too* and *so* in paragraph 6, *however* in paragraph 11, and *for* in paragraph 12? Might Mebane have omitted any of these without loss of coherence—that is, without losing the sense of connection between ideas?

4. Does Mebane imply more about her mother's life than she states? What does she reveal about her own feelings or attitudes?

SUGGESTIONS FOR WRITING

1. Mebane describes the work she performed as a member of the family. Describe jobs that you similarly performed, and use this description to say something about the general attitude in your family toward everyday life or the role of children in the family.

2. Mebane refers in paragraph 10 to "some other rhythm, a more meaningful pattern to human life." She is suggesting here the values that children sometimes discover they possess. Discuss a conflict in values between yourself and another member of your family and the origin of this conflict as you see it.

ALICE WALKER

ALICE WALKER, *the youngest of eight children in a family of Georgia sharecroppers, was educated at Spelman College and Sarah Lawrence College. She is best known for her novel about the life of a black Georgia woman,* The Color Purple (1982), *which received the Pulitzer Prize and the American Book Award in 1983. Walker's other writings include the novels* Meridian (1976) *and* The Temple of My Familiar (1989), *and several collections of stories and essays, including* In Search of Our Mothers' Gardens (1983) *and* Living by the Word (1988).

In Search of Our Mothers' Gardens

> I described her own nature and temperament. Told how they needed a larger life for their expression. . . . I pointed out that in lieu of proper channels, her emotions had overflowed into paths that dissipated them. I talked, beautifully I thought, about an art that would be born, an art that would open the way for women the likes of her. I asked her to hope, and build up an inner life against the coming of that day. . . . I sang, with a strange quiver in my voice, a promise song.—
> Jean Toomer, "Avey," *Cane*

The poet speaking to a prostitute who falls asleep while he's talking— 1

When the poet Jean Toomer walked through the South in the early twenties, he discovered a curious thing: black women whose spirituality was so intense, so deep, so *unconscious*, that they were themselves unaware of the richness they held. They stumbled blindly through their lives: creatures so abused and mutilated in body, so dimmed and confused by pain, that they considered themselves unworthy even of hope. In the selfless abstractions their bodies became to the men who used them, they became more than "sexual objects," more even than mere women: they became "Saints." Instead of being perceived as whole persons, their bodies became shrines: what was thought to be their minds became temples suitable for worship. These crazy Saints 2 stared out at the world, wildly, like lunatics—or quietly, like suicides; and the "God" that was in their gaze was as mute as a great stone.

Who were these Saints? These crazy, loony, pitiful 3 women?

Some of them, without a doubt, were our mothers and 4 grandmothers.

In the still heat of the post-Reconstruction South, this is 5 how they seemed to Jean Toomer: exquisite butterflies trapped in an evil honey, toiling away their lives in an era, a century, that did not acknowledge them, except as "the *mule of the world.*" They dreamed dreams that no one knew—not even themselves, in any coherent fashion—and saw visions no one could understand. They wandered or sat about the countryside crooning lullabies to ghosts, and drawing the mother of Christ in charcoal on courthouse walls.

They forced their minds to desert their bodies and their 6 striving spirits sought to rise, like frail whirlwinds from the hard red clay. And when those frail whirlwinds fell, in scattered particles, upon the ground, no one mourned. Instead, men lit candles to celebrate the emptiness that remained, as people do who enter a beautiful but vacant space to resurrect a God.

Our mothers and grandmothers, some of them: moving 7 to music not yet written. And they waited.

They waited for a day when the unknown thing that 8 was in them would be made known; but guessed, somehow in their darkness, that on the day of their revelation they would be long dead. Therefore to Toomer they walked, and even ran, in slow motion. For they were going nowhere immediate, and the future was not yet within their grasp. And men took our mothers and grandmothers, "but got no pleasure from it." So complex was their passion and their calm.

To Toomer, they lay vacant and fallow as autumn fields, 9 with harvest time never in sight: and he saw them enter loveless marriages, without joy; and become prostitutes, without resistance; and become mothers of children, without fulfillment.

For these grandmothers and mothers of ours were not 10

Saints, but Artists; driven to a numb and bleeding madness by the springs of creativity in them for which there was no release. They were Creators, who lived lives of spiritual waste, because they were so rich in spirituality—which is the basis of Art—that the strain of enduring their unused and unwanted talent drove them insane. Throwing away this spirituality was their pathetic attempt to lighten the soul to a weight their work-worn, sexually abused bodies could bear.

What did it mean for a black woman to be an artist in our 11 grandmothers' time? In our great-grandmothers' day? It is a question with an answer cruel enough to stop the blood.

Did you have a genius of a great-great-grandmother 12 who died under some ignorant and depraved white overseer's lash? Or was she required to bake biscuits for a lazy backwater tramp, when she cried out in her soul to paint watercolors of sunsets, or the rain falling on the green and peaceful pasturelands? Or was her body broken and forced to bear children (who were more often than not sold away from her)—eight, ten, fifteen, twenty children—when her one joy was the thought of modeling heroic figures of rebellion, in stone or clay?

How was the creativity of the black woman kept alive, 13 year after year and century after century, when for most of the years black people have been in America, it was a punishable crime for a black person to read or write? And the freedom to paint, to sculpt, to expand the mind with action did not exist. Consider, if you can bear to imagine it, what might have been the result if singing, too, had been forbidden by law. Listen to the voices of Bessie Smith, Billie Holiday, Nina Simone, Roberta Flack, and Aretha Franklin, among others, and imagine those voices muzzled for life. Then you may begin to comprehend the lives of our "crazy," "Sainted" mothers and grandmothers. The agony of the lives of women who might have been Poets, Novelists, Essayists, and Short-Story Writers (over a period of centuries), who died with their real gifts stifled within them.

And, if this were the end of the story, we would have 14 cause to cry out in my paraphrase of Okot p'Bitek's great poem:

O, my clanswomen
Let us all cry together!
Come,
Let us mourn the death of our mother,
The death of a Queen
The ash that was produced
By a great fire!
O, this homestead is utterly dead
Close the gates
With *lacari* thorns,
For our mother
The creator of the Stool is lost!
And all the young women
Have perished in the wilderness!

But this is not the end of the story, for all the young 15
women—our mothers and grandmothers, *ourselves*—have
not perished in the wilderness. And if we ask ourselves why,
and search for and find the answer, we will know beyond all
efforts to erase it from our minds, just exactly who, and of
what, we black American women are.

One example, perhaps the most pathetic, most misun- 16
derstood one, can provide a backdrop for our mothers' work:
Phillis Wheatley, a slave in the 1700s.

Virginia Woolf, in her book *A Room of One's Own*, wrote 17
that in order for a woman to write fiction she must have two
things, certainly: a room of her own (with key and lock) and
enough money to support herself.

What then are we to make of Phillis Wheatley, a slave, 18
who owned not even herself? This sickly, frail black girl who
required a servant of her own at times—her health was so
precarious—and who, had she been white, would have been
easily considered the intellectual superior of all the women
and most of the men in the society of her day.

Virginia Woolf wrote further, speaking of course not of 19
our Phillis, that "any woman born with a great gift in the
sixteenth century [insert "eighteenth century," insert "black
woman," insert "born or made a slave"] would certainly
have gone crazed, shot herself, or ended her days in some
lonely cottage outside the village, half witch, half wizard
[insert "Saint"], feared and mocked at. For it needs little skill
and psychology to be sure that a highly gifted girl who had

tried to use her gift for poetry would have been so thwarted and hindered by contrary instincts [add "chains, guns, the lash, the ownership of one's body by someone else, submission to an alien religion"], that she must have lost her health and sanity to a certainty."

The key words, as they relate to Phillis, are "contrary 20 instincts." For when we read the poetry of Phillis Wheatley—as when we read the novels of Nella Larsen or the oddly false-sounding autobiography of that freest of all black women writers, Zora Hurston—evidence of "contrary instincts" is everywhere. Her loyalties were completely divided, as was, without question, her mind.

But how could this be otherwise? Captured at seven, a 21 slave of wealthy, doting whites who instilled in her the "savagery" of the Africa they "rescued" her from . . . one wonders if she was even able to remember her homeland as she had known it, or as it really was.

Yet, because she did try to use her gift for poetry in a 22 world that made her a slave, she was "so thwarted and hindered by . . . contrary instincts, that she . . . lost her health. . . ." In the last years of her life, burdened not only with the need to express her gift but also with a penniless, friendless "freedom" and several small children for whom she was forced to do strenuous work to feed, she lost her health, certainly. Suffering from malnutrition and neglect and who knows what mental agonies, Phillis Wheatley died.

So torn by "contrary instincts" was black, kidnapped, 23 enslaved Phillis that her description of "the Goddess"—as she poetically called the Liberty she did not have—is ironically, cruelly humorous. And, in fact, has held Phillis up to ridicule for more than a century. It is usually read prior to hanging Phillis's memory as that of a fool. She wrote:

The Goddess comes, she moves divinely fair,
Olive and laurel binds her *golden* hair.
Wherever shines this native of the skies,
Unnumber'd charms and recent graces rise. [italics added]

It is obvious that Phillis, the slave, combed the "God- 24 dess's" hair every morning; prior, perhaps, to bringing in the milk, or fixing her mistress's lunch. She took her imagery from the one thing she saw elevated above all others.

With the benefit of hindsight we ask, "How could she?" 25

But at last, Phillis, we understand. No more snickering 26 when your stiff, struggling, ambivalent lines are forced on us. We know now that you were not an idiot or a traitor; only a sickly little black girl, snatched from your home and country and made a slave; a woman who still struggled to sing the song that was your gift, although in a land of barbarians who praised you for your bewildered tongue. It is not so much what you sang, as that you kept alive, in so many of our ancestors, *the notion of song.*

Black women are called, in the folklore that so aptly 27 identifies one's status in society, "the *mule* of the world," because we have been handed the burdens that everyone else—*everyone* else—refused to carry. We have also been called "Matriarchs," "Superwomen," and "Mean and Evil Bitches." Not to mention "Castraters" and "Sapphire's Mama." When we have pleaded for understanding, our character has been distorted; when we have asked for simple caring, we have been handed empty inspirational appellations, then stuck in the farthest corner. When we have asked for love, we have been given children. In short, even our plainer gifts, our labors of fidelity and love, have been knocked down our throats. To be an artist and a black woman, even today, lowers our status in many respects, rather than raises it: and yet, artists we will be.

Therefore we must fearlessly pull out of ourselves and 28 look at and identify with our lives the living creativity some of our great-grandmothers were not allowed to know. I stress *some* of them because it is well known that the majority of our great-grandmothers knew, even without "knowing" it, the reality of their spirituality, even if they didn't recognize it beyond what happened in the singing at church—and they never had any intention of giving it up.

How they did it—those millions of black women who 29 were not Phillis Wheatley, or Lucy Terry or Frances Harper or Zora Hurston or Nella Larsen or Bessie Smith; or Elizabeth Catlett, or Katherine Dunham, either—brings me to the title of this essay, "In Search of Our Mothers' Gardens," which is a personal account that is yet shared, in its theme and its meaning, by all of us. I found, while thinking about the far-reaching world of the creative black woman, that often the truest answer to a question that really matters can be found very close.

    In the late 1920s my mother ran away from home to 30 marry my father. Marriage, if not running away, was expected of seventeen-year-old girls. By the time she was twenty, she had two children and was pregnant with a third. Five children later, I was born. And this is how I came to know my mother: she seemed a large, soft, loving-eyed woman who was rarely impatient in our home. Her quick, violent temper was on view only a few times a year, when she battled with the white landlord who had the misfortune to suggest to her that her children did not need to go to school.

    She made all the clothes we wore, even my brothers' 31 overalls. She made all the towels and sheets we used. She spent the summers canning vegetables and fruits. She spent the winter evenings making quilts enough to cover all our beds.

    During the "working" day, she labored beside—not 32 behind—my father in the fields. Her day began before sunup, and did not end until late at night. There was never a moment for her to sit down, undisturbed, to unravel her own private thoughts; never a time free from interruption—by work or the noisy inquiries of her many children. And yet, it is to my mother—and all our mothers who were not famous—that I went in search of the secret of what has fed that muzzled and often mutilated, but vibrant, creative spirit that the black woman has inherited, and that pops out in wild and unlikely places to this day.

    But when, you will ask, did my overworked mother 33 have time to know or care about feeding the creative spirit?

    The answer is so simple that many of us have spent 34 years discovering it. We have constantly looked high, when we should have looked high—and low.

    For example: in the Smithsonian Institution in Wash- 35 ington, D.C., there hangs a quilt unlike any other in the world. In fanciful, inspired, and yet simple and identifiable figures, it portrays the story of the Crucifixion. It is considered rare, beyond price. Though it follows no known pattern of quilt-making, and though it is made of bits and pieces of worthless rags, it is obviously the work of a person of powerful imagination and deep spiritual feeling. Below this quilt I saw a note that says it was made by "an anonymous Black woman in Alabama, a hundred years ago."

If we could locate this "anonymous" black woman from Alabama, she would turn out to be one of our grandmothers—an artist who left her mark in the only materials she could afford, and in the only medium her position in society allowed her to use. 36

As Virginia Woolf wrote further, in *A Room of One's Own:* 37

> Yet genius of a sort must have existed among women as it must have existed among the working class. [Change this to "slaves" and "the wives and daughters of sharecroppers."] Now and again an Emily Brontë or a Robert Burns [change this to "a Zora Hurston or a Richard Wright"] blazes out and proves its presence. But certainly it never got itself on to paper. When, however, one reads of a witch being ducked, of a woman possessed by devils [or "Sainthood"], of a wise woman selling herbs [our root workers], or even a very remarkable man who had a mother, then I think we are on the track of a lost novelist, a suppressed poet, of some mute and inglorious Jane Austen. . . . Indeed, I would venture to guess that Anon, who wrote so many poems without signing them, was often a woman. . . .

And so our mothers and grandmothers have, more often than not anonymously, handed on the creative spark, the seed of the flower they themselves never hoped to see: or like a sealed letter they could not plainly read. 38

And so it is, certainly, with my own mother. Unlike "Ma" Rainey's songs, which retained their creator's name even while blasting forth from Bessie Smith's mouth, no song or poem will bear my mother's name. Yet so many of the stories that I write, that we all write, are my mother's stories. Only recently did I fully realize this: that through years of listening to my mother's stories of her life, I have absorbed not only the stories themselves, but something of the manner in which she spoke, something of the urgency that involves the knowledge that her stories—like her life— 39 must be recorded. It is probably for this reason that so much of what I have written is about characters whose counterparts in real life are so much older than I am.

But the telling of these stories, which came from my 40 mother's lips as naturally as breathing, was not the only way my mother showed herself as an artist. For stories, too, were subject to being distracted, to dying without conclusion. Dinners must be started, and cotton must be gathered before the big rains. The artist that was and is my mother showed itself to me only after many years. This is what I finally noticed:

Like Mem, a character in *The Third Life of Grange Cope-* 41 *land*, my mother adorned with flowers whatever shabby house we were forced to live in. And not just your typical straggly country stand of zinnias, either. She planted ambitious gardens—and still does—with over fifty different varieties of plants that bloom profusely from early March until late November. Before she left home for the fields, she watered her flowers, chopped up the grass, and laid out new beds. When she returned from the fields she might divide clumps of bulbs, dig a cold pit, uproot and replant roses, or prune branches from her taller bushes or trees—until night came and it was too dark to see.

Whatever she planted grew as if by magic, and her fame 42 as a grower of flowers spread over three counties. Because of her creativity with her flowers, even my memories of poverty are seen through a screen of blooms—sunflowers, petunias, roses, dahlias, forsythia, spirea, delphiniums, verbena . . . and on and on.

And I remember people coming to my mother's yard to 43 be given cuttings from her flowers; I hear again the praise showered on her because whatever rocky soil she landed on, she turned into a garden. A garden so brilliant with colors, so original in its design, so magnificent with life and creativity, that to this day people drive by our house in Georgia— perfect strangers and imperfect strangers—and ask to stand or walk among my mother's art.

I notice that it is only when my mother is working in her 44 flowers that she is radiant, almost to the point of being invisible—except as Creator: hand and eye. She is involved in work her soul must have. Ordering the universe in the image of her personal conception of Beauty.

Her face, as she prepares the Art that is her gift, is a   45
legacy of respect she leaves to me, for all that illuminates and
cherishes life. She has handed down respect for the possibilities—and the will to grasp them.

For her, so hindered and intruded upon in so many   46
ways, being an artist has still been a daily part of her life.
This ability to hold on, even in very simple ways, is work
black women have done for a very long time.

This poem is not enough, but it is something, for the   47
woman who literally covered the holes in our walls with
sunflowers:

> They were women then
> My mama's generation
> Husky of voice—Stout of
> Step
> With fists as well as
> Hands
> How they battered down
> Doors
> And ironed
> Starched white
> Shirts
> How they led
> Armies
> Headragged Generals
> Across mined
> Fields
> Booby-trapped
> Kitchens
> To discover books
> Desks
> A place for us
> How they knew what we
> *Must* know
> Without knowing a page
> Of it
> Themselves.

Guided by my heritage of a love of beauty and a respect   48
for strength—in search of my mother's garden, I found my
own.

And perhaps in Africa over two hundred years ago,   49
there was just such a mother; perhaps she painted vivid and

daring decorations in oranges and yellows and greens on the walls of her hut; perhaps she sang—in a voice like Roberta Flack's—*sweetly* over the compounds of her village; perhaps she wove the most stunning mats or told the most ingenious stories of all the village storytellers. Perhaps she was herself a poet—though only her daughter's name is signed to the poems that we know.

Perhaps Phillis Wheatley's mother was also an artist. 50

Perhaps in more than Phillis Wheatley's biological life is 51 her mother's signature made clear.

VOCABULARY

paragraph 2: selfless abstractions, mute

paragraph 5: post-Reconstruction South, coherent

paragraph 6: resurrect

paragraph 14: paraphrase

paragraph 21: doting

paragraph 22: thwarted

paragraph 23: ironically

paragraph 26: snickering, ambivalent

paragraph 27: matriarchs, appellations

paragraph 32: muzzled, mutilated

paragraph 39: counterparts

QUESTIONS

1. What is the main topic of the essay, and how does Walker present it in the epigraph (the opening statement of Jean Toomer) and in her opening paragraphs?
2. Walker marks major divisions or subtopics by spacing between paragraphs. What are these subtopics, and how does each lead into the next?
3. Many of Walker's paragraphs consist of one or two sentences. Which of these paragraphs are transitional, marking turns in the discussion and introducing new topics? Which of these paragraphs are used to emphasize key ideas or conclusions?
4. In what ways did Afro-American mothers and grandmothers

express their lives? How does Walker help the reader experience these lives?

5. What are the "contrary instincts" that Walker stresses in paragraph 20? What point is she making about these instincts?

6. Does Walker agree with Virginia Woolf that a successful woman writer must have "a room of her own" and sufficient money? Is she saying that Phillis Wheatley requires a qualification of Woolf's statement?

7. What effect did the discoveries Walker made about her mother and other Afro-American women have on her life?

8. What is Walker's thesis, and where does she first state it? How does she restate it in the course of the essay?

SUGGESTIONS FOR WRITING

1. Walker shows how she made discoveries about her mother and other Afro-American women and how these affected her life. Discuss a discovery you made about a member of your family and the effect of this discovery on your own life.

2. Walker shows that artistic expression can take many forms. Illustrate this idea from your own experience and observation. Like Walker, be specific in your detail.

3. Listen to the songs of one of the singers named in paragraph 13. Then discuss what recurrent feelings, attitudes, and ideas you find expressed in these songs.

EXPOSITION

INTRODUCTION: EXPOSITION

In exposition, we explain ideas and processes through various methods, including example, comparison and contrast, analogy, classification and division, definition, process, and cause and effect. In explaining how to repair a car engine, you might define key terms, trace the process, make comparisons with other kinds of engine repair, and discuss the causes of engine failure, to cite a few kinds of explanation. Description and narration also serve exposition in important ways, as in John L. Moore's account of the hazards of ranching in a time of drought, and they are included in this part of the book for this reason.

The methods named are not used just in exposition: they also occur in persuasive and other kinds of writing, as some of the following readings show. The more explanation your essay requires, the more attention you must give to organization and transitions. The reader should understand at every point in the essay what particular method you are using and why. Keep in mind that you know more about the subject than do your readers: you are illustrating and analyzing ideas and processes for their clarification. Obviously the kind and number of examples and other methods you choose depend on how much help your readers need. How you organize the essay depends, too, on the reader. Some expository essays, like an essay on the causes of a war, contain a thesis; others, like an essay on repairing an engine, do not. If the essay contains a thesis, where it is placed may depend on how much information readers need to understand it. Where the thesis is placed in the persuasive essay depends on how disposed readers are to accept it.

DESCRIPTION

❦ ❦ ❦

In describing a person, an object, or a place, we create a picture. George Orwell does so in describing a quarter of the Burmese town where as a police officer he had been called to deal with an elephant:

> It was a very poor quarter, a labyrinth of squalid bamboo huts, thatched with palm-leaf winding all over a steep hillside.— "Shooting an Elephant"

How much detail the writer gives depends on the purpose of the description. Orwell might have given more details of the town quarter. But additional details would have diverted us from the purpose of the description—to show that the impoverished life of the townspeople made them want to see the elephant shot.

In a descriptive paragraph or essay, the spatial arrangement of details must be clear, the physical point of view obvious and consistent. The writer must be careful to specify the place from which the observation is made. Orwell is careful to do so in describing the shooting of the elephant, and so is James Stevenson in describing a steep road:

> Part way down the long, very steep slope of Loma Vista Drive, descending through Beverly Hills, with the city of Los Angeles spread out far below the houses of sparkling opulence on either side, there is a sign warning "Use Lowest Gear" and, shortly after that, a sign that says "Runaway Vehicle Escape Lane 600 Feet Ahead."—"Loma Vista Drive"

Something more than the physical point of view is suggested in this opening sentence: we discover a dominant mood or attitude. This psychological point of view may be stated directly or conveyed by the details of the description. Orwell does both in describing the crowd of excited spectators:

> But at that moment I glanced round at the crowd that had followed me. It was an immense crowd, two thousand at the least and growing every minute. It blocked the road for a long distance on

either side. . . . And suddenly I realized that I should have to shoot the elephant after all. The people expected it of me and I had got to do it; I could feel their two thousand wills pressing me forward, irresistibly.

If the writer fails to clarify the point of view or changes it without preparing the reader, details will seem blurred. Abrupt or unexpected shifts in mood or attitude can also be confusing. Brief transitions that bridge these changes are the remedy.

DONOVAN WEBSTER

In the opening paragraphs of his report on crop dusting in the Mississippi River Delta for The New Yorker *magazine,* DONOVAN WEBSTER *describes the extreme threat of insects to crops in the rich delta farmland. His description of the delta reprinted here allows us to visualize the area and also explains its remarkable fertility. In the remainder of his report, Webster describes the operations of a crop-dusting company in West Helena, Arkansas. About seven thousand agricultural pilots are at work in the United States, Webster tells us, but their number is declining.*

The Mississippi River Delta

The Mississippi River Delta is a roughly triangular floodplain   1
that stretches away—east and west—from each bank of the mighty brown river itself. Though the state of Mississippi has claimed the Delta as its own, the region's topographic and agricultural character actually extends to Cairo, Illinois, where the Ohio River joins the Mississippi. From there, the Delta traces a constantly broadening path south, always keeping the river roughly at its center. Through the bootheel of Missouri, across western Tennessee, past Memphis and into the Cotton Belt, the Delta encompasses much of the western half of the state of Mississippi, the eastern half of Arkansas, and most of Louisiana as it makes its cross-bayou splay for the Gulf of Mexico.

Through the millennia, as the Mississippi has moved 2 south, it has also etched a switchback east-west course over hundreds of miles—an apparently random path that has widened its floodplain considerably and has left behind a layer of fertile topsoil sediment, which, in some places, is more than forty feet thick. At its widest, the Delta spans more than five hundred ballroom-floor-flat miles (its topographic influences can be seen as far west as Houston), and over its entire length it contains nearly three hundred thousand square miles of Delta-grade silt, a loosely packed dirt as rich as any potting soil you could buy at the local garden nursery.

If you take the time to drive across the Delta in winter, 3 its sky and earth and seemingly abandoned shotgun shacks all assume the same shade of gray. It's a world of three-hundred-and-sixty-degree horizon—a damp, windy, desolate place, where daytime temperatures hover just above freezing, and where dormant fields stretch away forever, snagged only occasionally by a brake of cypress trees, a planter's shack, or a boxy, whitewashed, single-story Baptist church. In the cold months, wintering red-tailed hawks rest on top of telephone poles and fence posts, and stringy trails of cotton blow across the farm roads. Road-killed armadillos and hounds lie along the highways like mile markers. And, all season long, there are vast flocks of ducks and geese overhead, moving south and, later, back north along the Mississippi River flyway. The birds often stop to rest, and they can be seen by the million in the flooded river bottoms, gorging themselves in the drained rice fields. They are a squawking, honking, cacophonous lot, and their noise is the soundtrack of Delta winters.

Then comes the explosion of spring and summer: the 4 verdant pastels of young rice fields, the deep green of cotton plants, the thick growths of soybeans. And above it all lies the flat and pale-blue sky, where monstrous thunderheads form every afternoon at about three-thirty. During the hot months, weeds sprout in every sidewalk crack, and the air is thick with the smell of flowers and drying mud and dirt-road dust. The sun crushes down at midday, washing the color from everything and adding its own shimmery silver patina. And then there's the animal life: the deer hiding in the swamp brakes; the snakes crossing the two-lanes like dark, slippery lengths of rope; the buzzards riding afternoon thermals in the sky; and, of course, the flying insects, which swarm there in infuriating, mind-numbing density. You drive through the Mississippi River Delta during summer, and, day or night, insects clatter constantly against your car's windshield.

VOCABULARY

paragraph 1: floodplain, topographic, bootheel, encompasses
paragraph 2: millennia, etched, switchback, sediment, potting soil
paragraph 3: dormant, brake, armadillos, gorging, cacophonous
paragraph 4: verdant, pastels, patina, thermals

QUESTIONS

1. How broad is the picture of the Mississippi River Delta in paragraph 1? From what physical point of view does Webster show the Delta?
2. How do the details of paragraph 2 enhance your view of the Delta and help you understand the meaning of the word?
3. From what vantage points does Webster show the Delta in paragraphs 3 and 4? How are these views different from the view presented in paragraph 1?
4. What do the views in paragraphs 3 and 4 add to your understanding of the world of the Delta? Does it matter that Webster first describes the Delta in winter, then in spring and summer?
5. Does Webster establish a dominant impression of the Delta, perhaps stressing an important physical feature or quality of life?

SUGGESTIONS FOR WRITING

1. Describe your neighborhood, city, town, or region from several physical vantage points to give the reader a sense of its size. You might describe the place from a high building or a bridge, then from a moving vehicle.

2. Add to your description a view of the place at one or more times
   of day or seasons of the year. Choose details that distinguish it.
   You may wish to create a dominant impression.

NANCY WOOD

A poet, novelist, and photographer, NANCY WOOD *writes
about the Ute and the Taos Pueblo Indians of the Southwest in*
When Buffalo Free the Mountains *(1980) and other books.
The Utes, who once inhabited large areas of Colorado, Utah,
and New Mexico, today live on several small reservations in
southwestern Colorado and in Utah. In the late nineteenth
century, the Southern Utes adopted the Sun Dance performed
by the Sioux and other Plains Indians. The ceremony varied.
"For the Utes," Wood states, "it was enough to fast and dance
for three days and three nights, when the moon was fullest and
the sun was hottest. During that time, the men of the tribe
danced to gain power to cure through being cured themselves;
they danced after they had had a vision and related it to the Sun
Dance chief or shaman, the holiest of their holy men." The
federal government banned the Sun Dance in 1904, but some
tribes continued the dance in other forms; the Southern Utes
continued until the death of their Sun Dance chief in 1941. In
1954 Eddie Box, a member of the tribe, revived the ceremony.
Today the Dance is performed by the Shoshone Indians, the
Sioux, and a few Southern Ute families. The excerpt reprinted
here describes part of the first day of a Southern Ute Sun Dance
in southwestern Colorado in 1978.*

The Sun Dance

There was only a dim smudge of light to the west now; the   1
moon was a quarter full and hung low, cupping the clouds
that raced toward it. All at once a single drum sounded,
muffled and forlorn; the whistle blew again, and voices
spoke in Ute. Then without warning the dancers emerged
from their camps and walked quickly toward the lodge in

groups of two and three; they were wrapped entirely from head to toe in white sheets, ghostly in the pale moonlight. As they neared the sacred circle, Eddie Box cried out to them in Ute.

Fifteen dancers wrapped in sheets, caught in the stunning lights of the cars and pickups, moved like mummies single file after Eddie Box, his solemn face upturned toward the nighttime sky as he blew on his eagle-bone whistle, making a noise that the Indians believe is always heard by the Great Spirit. The Sun Dance chief marched triumphantly, his shoulders thrown back, the edge of his sheet dragging the ground. Each dancer blew on an eagle-bone whistle; each held a sacred plume in either hand as they circled the Sun Dance lodge four times, once for each day they were going to dance. The ghostly parade, on completion of its final circle, turned and went through the opening of the lodge, which faced east; across its wide entrance was bunched a huge, heavy piece of canvas on a wire. On the cool night air rose the strains of a Ute prayer, uttered by someone in the circle.

The dancers went inside, one man at a time, moving quietly in the darkness to their chosen places against the back of the lodge, pressed against fresh branches of cottonwood and cedar. By the pale gleam of moonlight the gigantic buffalo head on top of the center pole seemed ominous and from another time entirely. It loomed stark and eerie against the inky blue sky, dotted now with stars and the neat, clean quarter slice of moon. An ancient ritual of purification had begun; between dancers and buffalo there already seemed a strange, unearthly power.

Half of the circle was occupied by the dancers; the other half was for the people and for the singers who were seated around an enormous drum. It played softly as the Indians filed slowly in, spreading blankets on the ground. Insistently, the drum beat the same note again and again, regular as a heartbeat; the sound filled the enclosure and quietly and demandingly awakened the earth.

In the dimness the people sat, some covered with shawls and blankets, others in heavy jackets; even in July the nights were always cool at an altitude of six thousand feet. Outlined in the gloom was a pile of sticks in the shape of a tepee placed at the entrance to the circle; one man stepped out of the shadows, bent, and struck a match. In the sudden illumination the buffalo head came to life, glassy-eyed and gaping down at the dancers from its perch on top of the center pole, a sacred cottonwood called the Tree of Life. Stripped of its bark and embedded in the sacred earth of the sacred circle, the tree was tall and straight, chosen for its symmetry and for the fork at the top, on which the head and some of the hide of the buffalo rested. The back of the carcass was stuffed with sweet grass as an offering to assure the animals abundant grass the following year; on either side of it, attached to the fork of the tree, were ribbons of the four sacred colors of the Sun Dance—red, white, black, and yellow, one for each of the races, Eddie Box once said. These colors were always together to show that all men are brothers underneath, he claimed. But traditional Indians insisted that the sacred colors were nothing of the sort. Red always meant earth; white was for purity, yellow stood for enlightenment, and black was the unknown night. The base of the tree was painted red and black and around it were placed offerings of tobacco and sage, left there by the families of the dancers for the spirits in order that some special favor be granted.

The dancers, illuminated by the light from the fire, were 6 naked to the waist. Some wore beads, others were painted with the sacred colors of the ceremonial, all were dressed in colorful long skirts with beaded waistbands; their feet were bare, as is the custom, for they must always be in contact with the sacred earth. The fifteen men stood motionless; their torsos, some hard, some flabby, gleamed in the firelight. They waited expectantly as Eddie Box paused at his spot in the middle of his dancers; to his left was tribal chairman Leonard Burch, suddenly more Indian than he had ever appeared in his office. Near him was Harold Silva, a twenty-nine-year-old Southern Ute, participating in his second Sun Dance.

Eddie Box stepped to the center pole and told everyone 7 to sit on the ground, to "come in contact with Mother Earth." Then he sang four sacred songs, the ones, according to one of the dancers, that the men sing to themselves while dancing. It had never been done in front of people until that night, but few seemed to understand what had happened except for two dancers who suddenly tensed as though shot.

The songs finished, Eddie Box stood reverently beneath the beady gaze of the buffalo, staring up at it as though he could hear it speak, blowing the eagle-bone whistle, an eagle feather in either hand. Because he is the Sun Dance chief, he was the first to move forward in a kind of strut, up to the pole and back, his eyes always on the buffalo, his movements slow and deliberate. When he was back against the boughs, another dancer moved out in the same way, then another and another. Some shuffled clumsily, others moved lightly on their toes; some bent their shoulders toward the pole, others were ramrod straight. All of them held their heads high; their eyes never wandered from the darkly brooding buffalo head. After a while they appeared hypnotized as they moved steadily back and forth, their legs like pistons, their arms waving, their faces with the most profound expressions of humility and frenzy. 8

The drumming and singing became furious; the sticks of the drummers lashed the hide of the drum, and the energy of the dance exploded, the energy entered the dancers and enriched the breath that escaped through their whistles. All was energy, for all was power. All was continuous, in the sacred circle of the dance and the sacred circle of the drum; all was continuous in the circle above the sky and the circle below the earth. 9

The moon rested at last in the fork of the tree on the buffalo's horns. With the moon in this position, the first group of singers left and another took its place. The canvas curtain was drawn across the opening, sealing in the feeble warmth of the fire smoldering at its edge; the fire cast a glow around the circle, infusing it with importance and mystery. The old ritual, older than the oldest man, older than the town, the treaties, and perhaps even older than the tribe, took root in that circle, blessed by fire and moonlight. 10

The singing and dancing lasted almost all night. Most of the people eventually left; others, the families of the dancers, dozed on the ground next to the singers, curled up on blankets and sleeping bags. As the singers urged them up, the dancers, tense, particular, stately, rose and began their 11 shuffle back and forth, confined to the narrow path between their positions and the tree, a path eventually to be worn into a rut before the dance was through. Every movement of hand and foot had some significance and there was a prayer in the action itself, understood by the dancers' women, who sat on the ground all night and did not sleep. When a song was finished and the drum rested, the women sang a sort of "amen" together, a personal offering of encouragement and salutation in the night.

There was sleep but it was wakeful sleep, with the 12 drumming and singing lasting until long after the moon had set. By four o'clock in the morning the world was silent except for the lowing of a cow, the chirp of crickets, and within the circle, a Ute who had remembered his prayers. In the gray light of predawn, the drum began again, softly at first, then in the earth language that it possesses.

The sacred fire had burned all night, and before dawn, 13 the ashes were carefully gathered and the canvas curtain was pulled back. Around the circle, the people who had spent the night were stirring sleepily, hurrying to rise and walk through the lingering coolness of the night. The crickets still sang, small bats scurried against the approaching light, and a chorus of frogs still croaked in the nearby marsh along the river. As the night watchers left, others came silently, reverently through the opening facing east, to the sacred circle, and stood there shivering, faces turned toward the flaming horizon. The dancers, asleep for several hours, got up from their sleeping bags and huddled beneath the Tree of Life. Their whistles became a shrill, insistent greeting to the sun about to begin its journey into the sky. The drum was a crescendo, the heart of the earth bursting toward the sun, to be consumed and purified. Earth to sun. Sun to earth. People to sun. Sun to people. We welcome you, the giver of all life, the power behind all growth, the father of the universe. In joy and expectation, in thanksgiving and reverence, we greet you, mighty sun. We ask your blessing, your goodness to shine upon us and all our people now born and those who are yet to come. Hear us!

The power that came from its night in the Lower World 14 was now ready to possess the Upper World. The power was manifest in the thin arc of brilliance lying on top of the mountains to the east, the thin arc expanding to the incessant din of the whistles until it became whole. The dancers and the people stared steadily at the sun until it had popped all the way up in the sky, a giant, blinding ball of fire. By then the whistles were so shrill, so filled with the joyousness of the new day, so intense with the efforts of the dancers emptying themselves of passion that the sacred circle vibrated and was lifted by the relentless pounding of the drum out of the earth circle into the sky circle, where it joined the sun.

The people, wrapped in blankets, and the dancers, wrapped in sheets, parted their cocoons in one great encompassing gesture, arms extended toward the sun. The warmth, power, and mystery of the sun were contained within those arms, drawn back against the body; the sun washed over the face and the beating heart. The people helped themselves. The generosity of the sun was theirs for this day; they walked in grace for they had remembered to greet the sun at dawn, as they had always done in the old days and now did but once a year.

VOCABULARY

paragraph 1: smudge, forlorn
paragraph 3: ominous, stark, eerie
paragraph 5: tepee, symmetry, enlightenment
paragraph 8: ramrod, brooding
paragraph 9: continuous
paragraph 10: smoldering
paragraph 11: shuffle
paragraph 14: arc, incessant

QUESTIONS

1. What details in paragraphs 1 and 2 establish the time and place of the Sun Dance? What details in later paragraphs give additional information about the setting? How does the setting help you to understand the purpose of the ceremony?

2. What details of the buffalo head and the center pole does Wood

stress? How do these details add to your understanding of the dance?

3. What features of the dancers and the dance does Wood stress? Do these add to your understanding?

4. What does the greeting of the sun, in paragraphs 13–15, further reveal about the purpose of the dance?

5. How does Wood organized the description? Does she give details of the setting, the dancers, and the dance from a single vantage point or physical point of view?

6. Does Wood state or imply an attitude toward the Sun Dance? Is she making a point through her description?

SUGGESTIONS FOR WRITING

1. Describe a dance that you have witnessed or performed. Give details of the setting, the dancers, and the dance itself, stressing those features that help to explain the feelings or intentions of the dancers.

2. Describe a social or religious ceremony—perhaps a holiday celebration, a wedding, a memorial service, or a funeral—that you have participated in and that gives insight into the beliefs and values of the group of people who perform it. Give details of the setting, the participants, and the ceremony itself.

NARRATION

❦ ❦ ❦

Description shows a person, an object, or a place at a particular time; the ordering of details is spatial—proceeding from left to right or top to bottom or in some other way. The order of details in narration is temporal. Narration shows the person, object, or place undergoing change; a series of events, personal experiences, and the like are presented chronologically, sometimes supported with descriptive details:

> I marched down the hill, looking and feeling a fool, with the rifle over my shoulder and an ever-growing army of people jostling at my heels. At the bottom, when you got away from the huts, there was a metalled road and beyond that a miry waste of paddy fields a thousand yards across, not yet ploughed but soggy from the first rains and dotted with coarse grass. The elephant was standing eight yards from the road, his left side toward us. He took not the slightest notice of the crowd's approach. He was tearing up bunches of grass, beating them against his knees to clean them, and stuffing them into his mouth.—George Orwell, "Shooting an Elephant"

Narration is often found in exposition. In explaining why the Spanish Armada came to defeat or why England survived heavy bombing at the beginning of World War Two, the writer may give an account of a decisive event—the wind that blew the Armada off course, the discovery of radar—and subsequent events. Though narration is usually chronological, the writer may have reason to present events in a different order. Transitions are essential in preparing the reader for this change.

NORMAN MAILER

NORMAN MAILER *attended Harvard University, where he made the decision to become a writer. After serving in the Pacific in World War Two, he wrote* The Naked and the

Dead (1948), *the novel that established his reputation as an important American writer. Mailer has maintained that reputation through a series of controversial novels about postwar America, and also through his journalism on a wide range of topics—from boxing to "hip" culture, lunar exploration, and American politics. A remarkable example is his eyewitness account of the knockout of Benny Paret in the twelfth round of a world championship welterweight bout at Madison Square Garden on March 25, 1962. Paret died on April 3, at the age of 24. Norman Cousins, later in this book, discusses the cause of Paret's death. Mailer's account is excerpted from* The Presidential Papers *(1963).*

The Death of Benny Paret

[1]Paret was a Cuban, a proud club fighter who had become welterweight champion because of his unusual ability to take a punch. [2]His style of fighting was to take three punches to the head in order to give back two. [3]At the end of ten rounds, he would still be bouncing, his opponent would have a headache. [4]But in the last two years, over the fifteen-round fights, he had started to take some bad maulings.

[5]This fight had its turns. [6]Griffith won most of the early rounds, but Paret knocked Griffith down in the sixth. [7]Griffith had trouble getting up, but made it, came alive and was dominating Paret again before the round was over. [8]Then Paret began to wilt. [9]In the middle of the eighth round, after a clubbing punch had turned his back to Griffith, Paret walked three disgusted steps away, showing his hindquarters. [10]For a champion, he took much too long to turn back around. [11]It was the first hint of weakness Paret had ever shown, and it must have inspired a particular shame, because he fought the rest of the fight as if he were seeking to demonstrate that he could take more punishment than any man alive. [12]In the twelfth, Griffith caught him. [13]Paret got trapped in a corner. [14]Trying to duck away, his left arm and his head became tangled on the wrong side of the top rope. [15]Griffith was in like a cat ready to rip the life out of a huge boxed rat. [16]He hit him eighteen right hands in a row, an act which took perhaps three or four seconds, Griffith making a pent-up whimpering sound all the while

he attacked, the right hand whipping like a piston rod which has broken through the crankcase, or like a baseball bat demolishing a pumpkin. [17]I was sitting in the second row of that corner—they were not ten feet away from me, and like everybody else, I was hypnotized. [18]I had never seen one man hit another so hard and so many times. [19]Over the referee's face came a look of woe as if some spasm had passed its way through him, and then he leaped on Griffith to pull him away. [20]It was the act of a brave man. [21]Griffith was uncontrollable. [22]His trainer leaped into the ring, his manager, his cut man, there were four people holding Griffith, but he was off on an orgy, he had left the Garden, he was back on a hoodlum's street. [23]If he had been able to break loose from his handlers and the referee, he would have jumped Paret to the floor and whaled on him there.

[24]And Paret? [25]Paret died on his feet. [26]As he took those eighteen punches something happened to everyone who was in psychic range of the event. [27]Some part of his death reached out to us. [28]One felt it hover in the air. [29]He was still standing in the ropes, trapped as he had been before, he gave some little half-smile of regret, as if he were saying, "I didn't know I was going to die just yet," and then, his head leaning back but still erect, his death came to breathe about him. [30]He began to pass away. [31]As he passed, so his limbs descended beneath him, and he sank slowly to the floor. [32]He went down more slowly than any fighter had ever gone down, he went down like a large ship which turns on end and slides second by second into its grave. [33]As he went down, the sound of Griffith's punches echoed in the mind like a heavy ax in the distance chopping into a wet log.

QUESTIONS

1. At what points in the narrative does Mailer comment on the action? Do these comments interrupt the narrative, diverting the reader from the action and blurring the focus?

2. How does Mailer establish a physical point of view—the angle from which he views the action? How does he establish a psychological point of view—a mood or attitude toward the action?

3. Is Mailer concerned only with Paret, or is he making a statement about boxing as a sport?

4. Does sentence 29 describe a continuous action? Would the mood of the paragraph be changed if Mailer broke the sentence into segments or punctuated it differently? How does sentence 22 convey the jarring confusion of the moment?

SUGGESTIONS FOR WRITING

1. Discuss the implications of the passage, including what it tells you about Mailer's attitude toward the death of Paret. Explain how Mailer conveys these ideas and attitudes.

2. Narrate a sporting or other event that revealed something unexpected about the participants or spectators. Let your details show why the event surprised you.

JANE ADAMS

A writer who lives in Seattle, Washington, JANE ADAMS *gives an account of her first experience in scuba diving. Adams gives us enough details about herself to help us understand the difficulties faced by a first-time diver as well as her feelings during the course of the dive. Too much detail about herself or any aspect of scuba diving would have directed our attention from the central experience; Adams keeps that experience in focus by giving a sufficient amount of detail and making that detail pertinent to it.*

Into the Void, and Back

No one had a camera, but the picture is etched in my mind. 1
I am preparing for my first open-water dive, hung about with hoses, mask and snorkel, bent double from the weight of the cylinder of compressed air on my back. I have somehow twisted my instrument console and extra regulator together and buckled my buoyancy compensator and weight

belt over them both, which necessitates taking off everything except my bathing suit and beginning the whole clumsy and confusing process of gearing up all over again.

I am not usually tempted by gear or gadgets. I don't 2 trust anything that comes with directions, even if they're written in German. Yet I am putting my faith—not to mention my life—in this bewildering array of equipment whose functions I apprehend somewhat dimly and whose functioning I understand hardly at all. I am that way about cars, cameras and computers, too, but if they fail to work I have my legs, my eyes and my brain. This time, if the more sophisticated technology fails, I will have to trust the strength of my body, the speed of my reflexes and the capacity of my lungs, all of which are showing the evidence of middle age.

My life, for the most part, has been devoted to cerebral 3 rather than physical pursuits, except for swimming, which I do daily. I swim to take my mind off my mind; I do not know where it goes when it leaves, but when it returns, it is rested and refreshed, and so am I. For scuba diving, though, I need my mind, need all those logical left-brain skills, need directions. And I have them right here, on this white plastic slate that dangles by a rubber loop from a grommet on my inflatable vest. Attached to it is a pen that's guaranteed to write underwater. This gizmo was one of the few items in the dive shop whose function I understood. I chose it rather than a stainless steel knife in a lethal-looking black sheath. It made me feel slightly more secure, although I harbored no illusions that even underwater the pen really would prove mightier than the sword.

I was afraid I'd forget my directions, the barely deci- 4 pherable notes I'd distilled from the manual: *"Dnt hld brth cmng up / rmbr to =ize ear prshr gng dwn / dump air lst."* I didn't need crib notes the only other time I tried this; I held on to my instructor's wrists every second of those twenty minutes in freezing, frightening Puget Sound. I just did exactly what he did, and somehow I managed to pass the final test for scuba certification.

Taking the test in the first place had been a struggle of 5 mind over body, will over fear. Friends with whom I regularly traveled had taken up the sport; they were no longer interested in picturesque South American villages, exotic jungle temples or lively foreign capitals. They talked instead of barren islands in the middle of nowhere, wreck diving in Truk and coral gardens off the African coast. I would have to find new friends or learn to dive myself.

The whole idea was terrifying. When I was twenty I raced sports cars and jumped out of airplanes—once, anyway. But when you are twenty you think you'll live forever. In middle age you know better, and in the years between then and now I had arranged my life in such a way as to minimize at least the predictable perils. Diving into the unknown appealed to me only in the metaphorical sense— the abyss is a central image in the midlife journey, and I thought, finally, that by plunging into it I might banish my fear of it.

Even after three weeks of lectures and pool practice, my checkout dive had been, from start to finish, a terrifying experience. I concentrated only on surviving, and having done so, I was more than relieved—I was exhilarated. My reward—a little blue plastic certification card—meant more to me than all my degrees, diplomas and awards.

But I was not particularly eager to dive again. So for the first few days of a vacation in the Cayman Islands, six months after completing the scuba course, I concentrated on what I could see from the surface. I snorkeled while my companions dived, until one morning when I swam after a flashing, preening trigger fish, only to lose it once it swam too far beneath the surface for me to follow. And so, the next day, I donned the clumsy gear, read and reread my scuba manual, and made crib notes on my dive slate until my buddy unclipped it deftly from my vest and tossed it, with the manual, into the cabin of the boat. "Up here you read and write," she said. "Down there you breathe."

It sounded easy, but down there was the Wall, the awesome shelf of coral plunging sheer down to the Caribbean's unfathomable bottom that accounts for Cayman's reputation as one of the finest dive destinations in the world. The Wall off Cayman Brac begins at a depth of around 75 feet. I decided to skip the Wall dive that morning, as I did for most of the week, thus increasing my terror with every passing day. I managed the shallow dives, though, at the relatively comfortable depth of 40 feet—from which, in the event technology failed, my buddies assured me, there would be sufficient air even in my middle-aged lungs to get me back to the surface safely. So I fastened my slate securely to my vest and jumped in.

My skills improved with every dive, and my terror 10 subsided somewhat. I discovered that hovering motionless over a reef and waiting patiently for it to reveal its secrets concentrates the mind on the present moment just as meditation does, or the long slow unfolding of a sunset. I found a world undersea so extraordinary and fantastical that I could never have imagined it. It seemed like another planet, and in the sensuous pleasure of tumbling weightless over the tickle of another diver's bubbles, I felt like a day tripper in deep space. Swooping down into a stand of elkhorn coral and drifting up again was like flying; finning along in the midst of a school of gaily colored parrotfish to the bubbly music of my own breathing like joining a street parade of costumed conga dancers during Carnival. But as the days went on, the abyss beckoned.

Finally, the day before my departure, I summoned my 11 courage and resolved to dive the Wall. I followed the other divers down, deeper than I had ever dived before. At first it was not that different from my previous dives. We followed along the top of a reef like many others I had seen, a few feet above the huge, neon-colored basket corals and delicate peach-hued anenomes that were guarded by striped, silly looking clown fish. A school of deadly-looking silvery barracuda brought us to a respectful halt; once the formation finned past, we continued.

My gauge read 75 feet, but the Wall I had pictured in my 12 mind was nowhere in sight. Then I looked down—and there was nothing beneath me. Below was a dark, shadowy emptiness that seemed to go on forever, the abyss of my imagination, the void of my dreams. I inhaled sharply and bobbed 10 feet up before I could control my breathing. Then I turned around and swam quickly back to the Wall itself. I anchored myself securely to a coral outcropping where the reef became the top of the Wall and stared out at the darkness that had nearly claimed me. My terror was gone; in its place was excitement. The void seemed to beckon me, so I swam out to it. I floated in it, watching the other divers exploring the Wall's caves and contours.

For a long, numinous, trancelike time, I tumbled in the 13 void—inhaled it, exhaled it, did somersaults and back flips in it. When my gauges registered the numbers that meant my time and air were nearly up, I swam back to the Wall, across the reef and to the surface. And when I unclipped my slate from my vest, I saw that I had written all over it without realizing I had done so—the mathematical sign for infinity, repeated again and again.

I have dived other walls since that one, although I 14 hardly ever venture more than a few feet from the edge. The void has no interest anymore, the abyss no allure. But when friends my own age take up flying, or climbing, or diving—activities I once thought suited only to the young, the strong or the foolish—I hardly ever ask them anymore if they wouldn't rather go to Puerto Vallarta, or even Paris, instead.

VOCABULARY

paragraph 1: snorkel, console, regulator, buoyancy compensator
paragraph 3: cerebral, lethal
paragraph 4: decipherable
paragraph 6: metaphorical, abyss
paragraph 8: preening
paragraph 10: sensuous, finning
paragraph 11: anemones, barracuda
paragraph 12: contours
paragraph 13: numinous

QUESTIONS

1. What details of the preparation for the open-water dive does Adams stress in paragraphs 1–8? What personal details does she also give? What is her purpose in describing this preparation, and how do these details serve it?
2. What details of her first few days does Adams give in para-

graphs 9 and 10? What does she omit? Does she give special attention to the physical act of diving or the experience itself or her feelings about it in later paragraphs, or instead give equal attention to all of these?

3. Adams describes the experience of "the void" in paragraphs 11–14. What details help you understand this word?

4. Is Adams merely narrating her experience, or is she also making a point about it? If she is making a point, where does she state it?

SUGGESTIONS FOR WRITING

1. Narrate your own first experience with a sport, explaining how you trained for it, what happened in first performing it, and what you felt in doing so. Like Adams, you might discuss a discovery you made about yourself or about the place where you trained and performed the sport.

2. Narrate an experience about traveling in which you made an unexpected discovery about yourself, about a place, or about people you were traveling with. You need not give the full details of the trip to share your experience.

MARY E. MEBANE

This book contains MARY E. MEBANE's *portrait of her mother, from her autobiography* Mary *(1980). In this chapter of the autobiography, Mebane narrates a childhood experience that gives us insight into the segregated world of blacks and whites in the South. The experience suggests the complexities of a segregated world—complexities both practical and psychological.*

Living with Segregation

Historically, my lifetime is important because I was part of 1 the last generation born into a world of total legal segregation in the Southern United States. When the Supreme Court

outlawed segregation in the public schools in 1954, I was
twenty-one. When Congress passed the Civil Rights Act of
1964, permitting blacks free access to public places, I was
thirty-one. The world I was born into had been segregated
for a long time—so long, in fact, that I never met anyone
who had lived during the time when restrictive laws were
not in existence, although some people spoke of parents and
others who had lived during the "free" time. As far as
anyone knew, the laws as they then existed would stand
forever. They were meant to—and did—create a world that
fixed black people at the bottom of society in all aspects of
human life. It was a world without options.

Most Americans have never had to live with terror. I had
had to live with it all my life—the psychological terror of
segregation, in which there was a special set of laws governing your movements. You violated them at your peril, for
you knew that if you broke one of them, knowingly or not,
physical terror was just around the corner, in the form of
policemen and jails, and in some cases and places white
vigilante mobs formed for the exclusive purpose of keeping
blacks in line.

It was Saturday morning, like any Saturday morning in
dozens of Southern towns.

The town had a washed look. The street sweepers had
been busy since six o'clock. Now, at eight, they were still
slowly moving down the streets, white trucks with clouds of
water coming from underneath the swelled tubular sides.
Unwary motorists sometimes got a windowful of water as a
truck passed by. As it moved on, it left in its wake a clear
stream running in the gutters or splashed on the wheels of
parked cars.

Homeowners, bent over industriously in the morning
sun, were out pushing lawn mowers. The sun was bright,
but it wasn't too hot. It was morning and it was May. Most
of the mowers were glad that it was finally getting warm
enough to go outside.

Traffic was brisk. Country people were coming into
town early with their produce; clerks and service workers
were getting to the job before the stores opened at ten
o'clock. Though the big stores would not be open for another
hour or so, the grocery stores, banks, open-air markets,

dinettes, were already open and filling with staff and customers.

Everybody was moving toward the heart of Durham's 7 downtown, which waited to receive them rather complacently, little knowing that in a decade the shopping centers far from the center of downtown Durham would create a ghost town in the midst of the busiest blocks on Main Street.

Some moved by car, and some moved by bus. The more 8 affluent used cars, leaving the buses mainly to the poor, black and white, though there were some businesspeople who avoided the trouble of trying to find a parking place downtown by riding the bus.

I didn't mind taking the bus on Saturday. It wasn't so 9 crowded. At night or on Saturday or Sunday was the best time. If there were plenty of seats, the blacks didn't have to worry about being asked to move so that a white person could sit down. And the knot of hatred and fear didn't come into my stomach.

I knew the stop that was the safety point, both going 10 and coming. Leaving town, it was the Little Five Points, about five or six blocks north of the main downtown section. That was the last stop at which four or five people might get on. After that stop, the driver could sometimes pass two or three stops without taking on or letting off a passenger. So the number of seats on the bus usually remained constant on the trip from town to Braggtown. The nearer the bus got to the end of the line, the more I relaxed. For if a white passenger got on near the end of the line, often to catch the return trip back and avoid having to stand in the sun at the bus stop until the bus turned around, he or she would usually stand if there were not seats in the white section, and the driver would say nothing, knowing that the end of the line was near and that the standee would get a seat in a few minutes.

On the trip to town, the Magnum Street A&P was the 11 last point at which the driver picked up more passengers than he let off. These people, though they were just a few blocks from the downtown section, preferred to ride the bus downtown. Those getting on at the A&P were usually on their way to work at the Duke University Hospital—past the downtown section, through a residential neighborhood, and then past the university, before they got to Duke Hospital.

So whether the driver discharged more passengers than he took on near the A&P on Mangum was of great importance. For if he took on more passengers than got off, it meant that some of the newcomers would have to stand. And if they were white, the driver was going to have to ask a black passenger to move so that a white passenger could sit down. Most of the drivers had a rule of thumb, though. By custom the seats behind the exit door had become "colored" seats, and no matter how many whites stood up, anyone sitting behind the exit door knew that he or she wouldn't have to move.

The disputed seat, though, was the one directly opposite the exit door. It was "no-man's land." White people sat there, and black people sat there. It all depended on whose section was fuller. If the back section was full, the next black passenger who got on sat in the no-man's-land seat; but if the white section filled up, a white person would take the seat. Another thing about the white people: they could sit anywhere they chose, even in the "colored" section. Only the black passengers had to obey segregation laws.

On this Saturday morning Esther and I set out for town for our music lesson. We were going on our weekly big adventure, all the way across town, through the white downtown, then across the railroad tracks, then through the "colored" downtown, a section of run-down dingy shops, through some fading high-class black neighborhoods, past North Carolina College, to Mrs. Shearin's house.

We walked the two miles from Wildwood to the bus line. Though it was a warm day, in the early morning there was dew on the grass and the air still had the night's softness. So we walked along and talked and looked back constantly, hoping someone we knew would stop and pick us up.

I looked back furtively, for in one of the few instances that I remembered my father criticizing me severely, it was for looking back. One day when I was walking from town he had passed in his old truck. I had been looking back and had seen him. "Don't look back," he had said. "People will think that you want them to pick you up." Though he said "people," I knew he meant men—not the men he knew, who lived in the black community, but the black men who were not part of the community, and all of the white men. To be picked up meant that something bad would happen to me. Still, two miles is a long walk and I occasionally joined Esther in looking back to see if anyone we knew was coming.

Esther and I got to the bus and sat on one of the long 17 seats at the back that faced each other. There were three such long seats—one on each side of the bus and a third long seat at the very back that faced the front. I liked to sit on a long seat facing the side because then I didn't have to look at the expressions on the faces of the whites when they put their tokens in and looked at the blacks sitting in the back of the bus. Often I studied my music, looking down and practicing the fingering. I looked up at each stop to see who was getting on and to check on the seating pattern. The seating pattern didn't really bother me that day until the bus started to get unusually full for a Saturday morning. I wondered what was happening, where all these people were coming from. They got on and got on until the white section was almost full and the black section was full.

There was a black man in a blue windbreaker and a gray 18 porkpie hat sitting in no-man's land, and my stomach tightened. I wondered what would happen. I had never been on a bus on which a black person was asked to give a seat to a white person when there was no other seat empty. Usually, though, I had seen a black person automatically get up and move to an empty seat farther back. But this morning the only empty seat was beside a black person sitting in no-man's land.

The bus stopped at Little Five Points and one black got 19 off. A young white man was getting on. I tensed. What would happen now? Would the driver ask the black man to get up and move to the empty seat farther back? The white man had a businessman's air about him: suit, shirt, tie, polished brown shoes. He saw the empty seat in the "colored" section and after just a little hesitation went to it, put his briefcase down, and sat with his feet crossed. I relaxed a little when the bus pulled off without the driver saying anything. Evidently he hadn't seen what had happened, or since he was just a few stops from Main Street, he figured the mass exodus there would solve all the problems. Still, I was afraid of a scene.

The next stop was an open-air fruit stand just after Little Five Points, and here another white man got on. Where would he sit? The only available seat was beside the black man. Would he stand the few stops to Main Street or would the driver make the black man move? The whole colored section tensed, but nobody said anything. I looked at Esther, who looked apprehensive. I looked at the other men and women, who studiously avoided my eyes and everybody else's as well, as they maintained a steady gaze at a far-distant land. 20

Just one woman caught my eye; I had noticed her before, and I had been ashamed of her. She was a stringy little black woman. She could have been forty; she could have been fifty. She looked as if she were a hard drinker. Flat black face with tight features. She was dressed with great insouciance in a tight boy's sweater with horizontal lines running across her flat chest. It pulled down over a nondescript skirt. Laced-up shoes, socks, and a head rag completed her outfit. She looked tense. 21

The white man who had just gotten on the bus walked to the seat in no-man's-land and stood there. He wouldn't sit down, just stood there. Two adult males, living in the most highly industrialized, most technologically advanced nation in the world, a nation that had devastated two other industrial giants in World War II and had flirted with taking on China in Korea. Both these men, either of whom could have fought for the United States in Germany or Korea, faced each other in mutual rage and hostility. The white one wanted to sit down, but he was going to exert his authority and force the black one to get up first. I watched the driver in the rearview mirror. He was about the same age as the antagonists. The driver wasn't looking for trouble, either. 22

"Say there, buddy, how about moving back," the driver said, meanwhile driving his bus just as fast as he could. The whole bus froze—whites at the front, blacks at the rear. They didn't want to believe what was happening was really happening. 23

The seated black man said nothing. The standing white man said nothing. 24

"Say, buddy, did you hear me? What about moving on 25 back." The driver was scared to death. I could tell that.

"These is the niggers' seats!" the little lady in the 26 strange outfit started screaming. I jumped. I had to shift my attention from the driver to the frieze of the black man seated and white man standing to the articulate little woman who had joined in the fray.

"The government gave us these seats! These is the 27 niggers' seats." I was startled at her statement and her tone. "The president said that these are the niggers' seats!" I expected her to start fighting at any moment.

Evidently the bus driver did, too, because he was 28 driving faster and faster. I believe that he forgot he was driving a bus and wanted desperately to pull to the side of the street and get out and run.

"I'm going to take you down to the station, buddy," the 29 driver said.

The white man with the briefcase and the polished 30 brown shoes who had taken a seat in the "colored" section looked as though he might die of embarrassment at any moment.

As scared and upset as I was, I didn't miss a thing. 31

By that time we had come to the stop before Main Street, 32 and the black passenger rose to get off.

"You're not getting off, buddy. I'm going to take you 33 downtown." The driver kept driving as he talked and seemed to be trying to get downtown as fast as he could.

"These are the niggers' seats! The government plainly 34 said these are the niggers' seats!" screamed the little woman in rage.

I was embarrassed at the use of the word "nigger" but I 35 was proud of the lady. I was also proud of the man who wouldn't get up.

The bus driver was afraid, trying to hold on to his job 36 but plainly not willing to get into a row with the blacks.

The bus seemed to be going a hundred miles an hour 37 and everybody was anxious to get off, though only the lady and the driver were saying anything.

The black man stood at the exit door; the driver drove 38 right past the A&P stop. I was terrified. I was sure that the bus was going to the police station to put the black man in jail. The little woman had her hands on her hips and she never stopped yelling. The bus driver kept driving as fast as he could.

Then, somewhere in the back of his mind, he decided to 39 forget the whole thing. The next stop was Main Street, and when he got there, in what seemed to be a flash of lightning, he flung both doors open wide. He and his black antagonist looked at each other in the rearview mirror; in a second the windbreaker and porkpie hat were gone. The little woman was standing, preaching to the whole bus about the government's gift of these seats to the blacks; the man with the brown shoes practically fell out of the door in his hurry; and Esther and I followed the hurrying footsteps.

We walked about three doors down the block, then 40 caught a bus to the black neighborhood. Here we sat on one of the two long seats facing each other, directly behind the driver. It was the custom. Since this bus had a route from a black neighborhood to the downtown section and back, passing through no white residential areas, blacks could sit where they chose. One minute we had been on a bus in which violence was threatened over a seat near the exit door; the next minute we were sitting in the very front behind the driver.

The people who devised this system thought that it was 41 going to last forever.

VOCABULARY

paragraph 2: vigilante
paragraph 4: tubular
paragraph 8: affluent
paragraph 16: furtively
paragraph 19: exodus
paragraph 21: insouciance, nondescript
paragraph 22: antagonists
paragraph 26: frieze

QUESTIONS

1. Is Mebane writing for a special audience familiar with the practices of segregation, or for a general audience, some of who know the facts and some of who do not?
2. What does the behavior of the bus driver show? What is his motive in ordering the black man to the back of the bus?
3. What other details show that the system of bus segregation was breaking down in Durham and elsewhere?
4. How does Mebane convey the dilemma created for the black by segregation? Does Mebane comment on this dilemma or merely illustrate it?
5. How many points is Mebane making about segregation in the essay? Does she state a thesis?
6. How effective do you find her narrative of the experience?

SUGGESTIONS FOR WRITING

1. Narrate an experience that illustrates the injustice or the contradictions or pointlessness of a social code or rule of etiquette or behavior in our society. Let the details of your narrative make your point. Do not state it explicitly.
2. Narrate an experience that supports your belief that an existing law needs to be repealed or that a law not in existence needs to be enacted. Choose details that will best persuade your readers.

Example

❦ ❦ ❦

The word *example* originally referred to a sample or a typical instance. The word still has this meaning, and for many writers it is an outstanding instance—even one essential to the idea under discussion, as in the following explanation of right- and left-handedness in the world:

> The world is full of things whose right-hand version is different from the left-hand version: a right-handed corkscrew as against a left-handed, a right snail as against a left one. Above all, the two hands; they can be mirrored one in the other, but they cannot be turned in such a way that the right hand and the left hand become interchangeable. That was known in Pasteur's time to be true also of some crystals, whose facets are so arranged that there are right-hand versions and left-hand versions.—J. Bronowski, *The Ascent of Man*

When we are presenting ideas, examples are essential. Those that seem clear to us may not be clear to our readers. Concrete instances will help to make our ideas understood.

E. B. WHITE

In this excerpt from a profile of New York City, first published in Holiday Magazine, *E. B. White (p. 52) writes from the point of view of an inhabitant who knows the city well. White conveys the special excitement of the city through a series of examples. Compare this general characterization of New York with the specific picture of a New York street presented by Jane Jacobs (p. 503).*

New York

It is a miracle that New York works at all. The whole thing is implausible. Every time the residents brush their teeth, millions of gallons of water must be drawn from the Catskills

EXAMPLE **133**

and the hills of Westchester. When a young man in Manhattan writes a letter to his girl in Brooklyn, the love message gets blown to her through a pneumatic tube—*pfft*—just like that. The subterranean system of telephone cables, power lines, steam pipes, gas mains and sewer pipes is reason enough to abandon the island to the gods and the weevils. Every time an incision is made in the pavement, the noisy surgeons expose ganglia that are tangled beyond belief. By rights New York should have destroyed itself long ago, from panic or fire or rioting or failure of some vital supply line in its circulatory system or from some deep labyrinthine short circuit. Long ago the city should have experienced an insoluble traffic snarl at some impossible bottleneck. It should have perished of hunger when food lines failed for a few days. It should have been wiped out by a plague starting in its slums or carried in by ships' rats. It should have been overwhelmed by the sea that licks at it on every side. The workers in its myriad cells should have succumbed to nerves, from the fearful pall of smoke-fog that drifts over every few days from Jersey, blotting out all light at noon and leaving the high offices suspended, men groping and depressed, and the sense of world's end. It should have been touched in the head by the August heat and gone off its rocker.

QUESTIONS

1. What examples does White give to show that "the whole thing is implausible"?
2. White explicitly compares New York City to a human being. What are the similarities, and how does the comparison help to emphasize the "miracle" he is describing?
3. What is the tone or attitude expressed, and how does White convey it?

SUGGESTIONS FOR WRITING

1. In a well-developed paragraph state an idea about your hometown or city and develop it by a series of short examples. Make your examples vivid and lively.

2. Develop one of the following statements by example:

   a. "The insupportable labor of doing nothing."—Sir Richard Steele

   b. "The first blow is half the battle."—Oliver Goldsmith

   c. "Ask yourself whether you are happy, and you cease to be so."—John Stuart Mill

   d. "Parentage is a very important profession; but no test of fitness for it is ever imposed in the interest of the children."—George Bernard Shaw

---

TOM WOLFE

> Tom Wolfe *has written much about American life in the 1960s and 1970s, particularly about the "youth culture" of this period. Wolfe has documented this world in a large number of articles published in* New York Magazine *and other periodicals. These have been collected in a number of books, including* The Electric Kool-Aid Acid Test *(1968),* The Pump House Gang *(1968), and* The Kandy-Kolored Tangerine-Flake Streamline Baby *(1965), from which the following excerpt is taken. Wolfe's ironic view of urban life is nowhere better illustrated than in his portrait of New York teenagers at a subway station at rush hour. Wolfe here develops one of his favorite themes, the "generation gap," and says something about New York life generally.*

Thursday Morning in a New York Subway Station

Love! Attar of libido in the air! It is 8:45 A.M. Thursday morning in the IRT subway station at 50th Street and Broadway and already two kids are hung up in a kind of herringbone weave of arms and legs, which proves, one has to admit, that love is not *confined* to Sunday in New York. Still, the odds! All the faces come popping in clots out of the Seventh Avenue local, past the King Size Ice Cream machine, and the turnstiles start whacking away as if the world were

EXAMPLE **135**

breaking up on the reefs. Four steps past the turnstiles everybody is already backed up haunch to paunch for the climb up the ramp and the stairs to the surface, a great funnel of flesh, wool, felt, leather, rubber and steaming alumicron, with the blood squeezing through everybody's old sclerotic arteries in hopped-up spurts from too much coffee and the effort of surfacing from the subway at the rush hour. Yet there on the landing are a boy and a girl, both about eighteen, in one of those utter, My Sin, backbreaking embraces.

He envelops her not only with his arms but with his 2 chest, which has the American teen-ager concave shape to it. She has her head cocked at a 90-degree angle and they both have their eyes pressed shut for all they are worth and some incredibly feverish action going with each other's mouths. All round them, ten, scores, it seems like hundreds, of faces and bodies are perspiring, trooping and bellying up the stairs with arteriosclerotic grimaces past a showcase full of such novel items as Joy Buzzers, Squirting Nickels, Finger Rats, Scary Tarantulas and spoons with realistic dead flies on them, past Fred's barbershop, which is just off the landing and has glossy photographs of young men with the kind of baroque haircuts one can get in there, and up onto 50th Street into a madhouse of traffic and shops with weird lingerie and gray hair-dyeing displays in the windows, signs for free teacup readings and a pool-playing match between the Playboy Bunnies and Downey's Showgirls, and then everybody pounds on toward the Time-Life Building, the Brill Building or NBC.

The boy and the girl just keep on writhing in their 3 embroilment. Her hand is sliding up the back of his neck, which he turns when her fingers wander into the intricate formal gardens of his Chicago Boxcar hairdo at the base of the skull. The turn causes his face to start to mash in the ciliated hull of her beehive hairdo, and so she rolls her head 180 degrees to the other side, using their mouths for the pivot. But aside from good hair grooming, they are oblivious to everything but each other. Everybody gives them a once-over. Disgusting! Amusing! How touching! A few kids pass by and say things like "Swing it, baby." But the great majority in that heaving funnel up the stairs seem to be as much astounded as anything else. The vision of love at rush hour cannot strike anyone exactly as romance. It is a feat, like a fat man crossing the English Channel in a barrel. It is an earnest accomplishment against the tide. It is a piece of slightly gross heroics, after the manner of those knobby, varicose old men who come out from some place in baggy shorts every year and run through the streets of Boston in the Marathon race. And somehow that is the gaffe against love all week long in New York, for everybody, not just two kids writhing under their coiffures in the 50th Street subway station; too hurried, too crowded, too hard, and no time for dalliance.

QUESTIONS

1. Wolfe illustrates "the gaffe against love all week long in New York." What precisely is the "gaffe"? What do the details suggest about the Thursday morning mood of New Yorkers?
2. What does the description of the showcase and of 50th Street imply about the world of the lovers? Would they stand out in any setting? Does Wolfe find the lovers comical, or is he sympathetic and admiring?
3. How similar is Wolfe's view of New York to White's, in the quality of life or its pace?

SUGGESTIONS FOR WRITING

1. Every piece of writing suggests something about the personality, interests, and ideas of the author, even when he or she speaks to us through a narrator. Discuss the impression you receive of the author of this selection.
2. Describe one or two people in a situation made comical by the setting. Allow your reader to visualize the setting as well as the situation through your choice of examples.

EXAMPLE **137**

MARGARET MEAD AND RHODA METRAUX

MARGARET MEAD (1901–1978) *was for more than forty years an ethnologist at the Museum of Natural History in New York City. She taught at numerous universities, mostly at Columbia, and wrote some of the most influential books in the field of social anthropology—including* Coming of Age in Samoa *(1928),* Growing Up in New Guinea *(1930), and* Male and Female *(1949).* RHODA METRAUX, *an anthropologist also associated with the Museum of Natural History, collaborated with Mead on the writing of several books and a series of magazine essays, later collected in the books* A Way of Seeing *(1970) and* Aspects of the Present *(1980). Mead and Metraux look at parents and children from the point of view of the anthropologist. Their ideas on how children can be encouraged to develop an independent judgment might be compared with those of John Holt in the following section.*

Discipline—To What End?

In the matter of childhood discipline there is no absolute 1 standard. The question is one of appropriateness to a style of living. What is the intended outcome? Are the methods of discipline effective in preparing the child to live in the adult world into which he is growing? The means of discipline that are very effective in rearing children to become headhunters and cannibals would be most ineffective in preparing them to become peaceful shepherds.

The Mundugumor, a New Guinea people, trained their 2 children to be tough and self-reliant. Among these headhunters, when one village was preparing to attack another and wanted to guard itself against attack by a third village, the first village sent its children to the third to be held as hostages. The children knew that they faced death if their own people broke this temporary truce. Mundugumor methods of child-rearing were harsh but efficient. An infant sleeping in a basket hung on the wall was not taken out and held when it wakened and cried. Instead, someone scratched on the outside of the basket, making a screeching sound like the squeak of chalk on a blackboard. And a child that cried with fright was not given the mother's breast. It was simply lifted and held off the ground. Mundugumor children learned to live in a tough world, unfearful of hostility. When they lived among strangers as hostages, they watched and listened, gathering the information they would need someday for a successful raid on this village.

The Arapesh, another New Guinea people, had a very 3 different view of life and human personality. They expected their children to grow up in a fairly peaceful world, and their methods of caring for children reflected their belief that both men and women were gentle and nurturing in their intimate personal relations. Parents responded to an infant's least cry, held him and comforted him. And far from using punishment as a discipline, adults sometimes stood helplessly by while a child pitched precious firewood over a cliff.

Even very inconsistent discipline may fit a child to live in 4 an inconsistent world. A Balinese mother would play on her child's fright by shouting warnings against nonexistent dangers: "Look out! Fire! . . . Snake! . . . Tiger!" The Balinese system required people to avoid strange places without inquiring why. And the Balinese child learned simply to be afraid of strangeness. He never learned that there are no bears under the stairs, as American children do. We want our children to test reality. We teach our children to believe in Santa Claus and later, without bitter disappointment, to give up that belief. We want them to be open to change, and as they grow older, to put childhood fears and rewards aside and be ready for new kinds of reality.

There are also forms of discipline that may be self- 5 defeating. Training for bravery, for example, may be so rigorous that some children give up in despair. Some Plains Indians put boys through such severe and frightening experiences in preparing them for their young manhood as warriors that some boys gave up entirely and dressed instead as women.

In a society in which many people are socially mobile 6 and may live as adults in a social or cultural environment very different from the one in which they grew up, old forms of discipline may be wholly unsuited to new situations. A father whose family lived according to a rigid, severe set of standards, and who was beaten in his boyhood for lying or

EXAMPLE **139**

stealing, may still think of beatings as an appropriate method of disciplining his son. Though he now lives as a middle-class professional man in a suburb, he may punish his son roughly for not doing well in school. It is not the harshness as such that then may discourage the boy even more, but his bewilderment. Living in a milieu in which parents and teachers reward children by praise and presents for doing well in school—a milieu in which beating is not connected with competence in schoolwork—the boy may not be able to make much sense of the treatment he receives.

There is still another consideration in this question 7 about discipline. Through studies of children as they grow up in different cultures we are coming to understand more about the supportive and the maiming effects of various forms of discipline. Extreme harshness or insensitivity to the child may prepare him to survive in a harsh environment. But it also may cripple the child's ability to meet changing situations. And today we cannot know the kind of world the children we are rearing will live in as adults. For us, therefore, the most important question to ask about any method of discipline is: How will it affect the child's capacity to face change? Will it give the child the kind of strength necessary to live under new and unpredictable conditions?

An unyielding conscience may be a good guide to 8 successful living in a narrow and predictable environment. But it may become a heavy burden and a cruel scourge in a world in which strength depends on flexibility. Similarly, the kind of discipline that makes a child tractable, easy to bring up and easy to teach in a highly structured milieu, may fail to give the child the independence, courage and curiosity he will need to meet the challenges in a continually changing situation. At the same time, the absence of forms of discipline that give a child a sense of living in an ordered world in which it is rewarding to learn the rules, whatever they may be, also may be maiming. A belief in one's own accuracy and a dependable sense of how to find the patterning in one's environment are necessary parts of mature adaptation to new styles of living.

There is, in fact, no single answer to the problem of 9 childhood discipline. But there is always the central question: For what future?

VOCABULARY

paragraph 1: appropriateness
paragraph 3: nurturing
paragraph 6: mobile, environment, milieu
paragraph 8: scourge, maiming

QUESTIONS

1. Do Mead and Metraux give examples of childhood discipline that works well? Or are all of the kinds of discipline discussed effective?
2. What thesis do their examples support, and where do Mead and Metraux first state it? Where do they restate it?
3. How do the examples in paragraph 6 help us to understand the kind of society that is "socially mobile"?
4. Would the exposition be as clear if Mead and Metraux had discussed the Arapesh of New Guinea before discussing the Mundugumor? Or does the order of discussion not matter?
5. How do the opening sentences of the nine paragraphs state the relationship of ideas in the whole essay?

SUGGESTION FOR WRITING

State why you agree or disagree with one of the following statements, supporting your ideas with examples from your own experience and observation:
a. "Even very inconsistent discipline may fit a child to live in an inconsistent world."
b. "There are also forms of discipline that may be self-defeating."
c. "In a society in which many people are socially mobile and may live as adults in a social or cultural environment very different from the one in which they grew up, old forms of discipline may be wholly unsuited to new situations."
d. "Extreme harshness or insensitivity to the child may prepare him to survive in a harsh environment. But it also may cripple the child's ability to meet changing situations."
e. "At the same time, the absence of forms of discipline that give a child a sense of living in an ordered world in which it is rewarding to learn the rules, whatever they may be, also may be maiming."

CLASSIFICATION AND DIVISION

❧ ❧ ❧

There are times when you want to show what various objects have in common. To do so, you engage in the process of classification—grouping objects, persons, or ideas that share significant qualities. To show the range of cars manufactured in the United States, you might classify Chevrolets, Dodges, and Fords with other American cars. To illustrate the importance of General Motors in the manufacture of cars, you can classify Chevrolets with Buicks, Oldsmobiles, and other GM cars. The number of classes to which an object can be fitted is obviously wide.

The process of division begins with a class and shows its subclassifications or divisions. The class may be a broad one, as in the following division of American cars according to manufacturer:

By manufacturer: GM cars, Chrysler cars, Ford cars, etc.

The same class of American cars may be divided in another way:

By transmission: cars with manual transmission, cars with automatic transmission

Any one of the subclasses or divisions may be divided by the same or by another principle—GM cars may be subdivided according to size, engine, color, or place of manufacture, to cite only a few ways:

By size: small, compact, medium, large GM cars

By engine: (GM cars with) four-cylinder, six-cylinder, eight-cylinder engines

Again the basis or principle of division you choose depends on the purpose of the analysis.

Here is an example of division in a scientific discussion of meteorites:

purpose of analysis

For the investigator of meteorites, the basic challenge is deducing the history of the *meteorites* from a bewildering abundance of evidence. The richness of the problem is indicated by the sheer variety of *types* of meteorite. The two main classes are the *stony meteorites* and the *iron meteorites*.

class: *meteorites*

division or subclassification according to constituent material

first type: *stony*

second type: *iron*

The stony meteorites consist mainly of silicates, with an a mix ture if nickel and iron. The iron meteorites consist mainly of nickel and iron in various proportions. A smaller class is the *stony-iron meteorites*, which are intermediate in composition between the other two.

third type: *stony-iron*

subdivision of stony meteorites according to presence or absence of chondrules

Stony meteorites are in turn divided into two groups: the chrondites and the achrondites, according to whether or not they contain chondrules, spherical aggregates of magnesium silicate. With each group there are further subdivisions based on mineralogical and chemical composition.

further subdivisions

—I. R. Cameron, "Meteorites and Cosmic Radiation" [italics added]

JOHN HOLT

JOHN HOLT (1923–1985) *widely influenced ideas on the teaching of children in the 1960s and 1970s—through such books as* How Children Fail (1964), How Children Learn (1967), Escape from Childhood (1974), *and* Freedom from Beyond (1972), *based on his experience as a high school teacher in Colorado and Massachusetts. Holt believes that teachers do their job best when they help students teach themselves. His discussion of the various disciplines that guide our learning reveals other assumptions and beliefs.*

Kinds of Discipline

A child, in growing up, may meet and learn from three 1
different kinds of disciplines. The first and most important is
what we might call the Discipline of Nature or of Reality.
When he is trying to do something real, if he does the wrong
thing or doesn't do the right one, he doesn't get the result he
wants. If he doesn't pile one block right on top of another, or
tries to build on a slanting surface, his tower falls down. If he
hits the wrong key, he hears the wrong note. If he doesn't hit
the nail squarely on the head, it bends, and he has to pull it
out and start with another. If he doesn't measure properly
what he is trying to build, it won't open, close, fit, stand up,
fly, float, whistle, or do whatever he wants it to do. If he
closes his eyes when he swings, he doesn't hit the ball. A
child meets this kind of discipline every time he tries to *do*
something, which is why it is so important in school to give
children more chances to do things, instead of just reading or
listening to someone talk (or pretending to). This discipline
is a great teacher. The learner never has to wait long for his
answer; it usually comes quickly, often instantly. Also it is
clear, and very often points toward the needed correction;
from what happened he can not only see that what he did
was wrong, but also why, and what he needs to do instead.
Finally, and most important, the giver of the answer, call it
Nature, is impersonal, impartial, and indifferent. She does
not give opinions, or make judgments; she cannot be whee-
dled, bullied, or fooled; she does not get angry or disap-
pointed; she does not praise or blame; she does not
remember past failures or hold grudges; with her one always
gets a fresh start, this time is the one that counts.

The next discipline we might call the Discipline of 2
Culture, of Society, of What People Really Do. Man is a
social, a cultural animal. Children sense around them this
culture, this network of agreements, customs, habits, and
rules binding the adults together. They want to understand
it and be a part of it. They watch very carefully what people
around them are doing and want to do the same. They want
to do right, unless they become convinced they can't do
right. Thus children rarely misbehave seriously in church,
but sit as quietly as they can. The example of all those

grownups is contagious. Some mysterious ritual is going on, and children, who like rituals, want to be part of it. In the same way, the little children that I see at concerts or operas, though they may fidget a little, or perhaps take a nap now and then, rarely make any disturbance. With all those grownups sitting there, neither moving nor talking, it is the most natural thing in the world to imitate them. Children who live among adults who are habitually courteous to each other, and to them, will soon learn to be courteous. Children who live surrounded by people who speak a certain way will speak that way, however much we may try to tell them that speaking that way is bad or wrong.

The third discipline is the one most people mean when they speak of discipline—the Discipline of Superior Force, of sergeant to private, of "you do what I tell you or I'll make you wish you had." There is bound to be some of this in a child's life. Living as we do surrounded by things that can hurt children, or that children can hurt, we cannot avoid it. We can't afford to let a small child find out from experience the danger of playing in a busy street, or of fooling with the pots on the top of a stove, or of eating up the pills in the medicine cabinet. So, along with other precautions, we say to him, "Don't play in the street, or touch things on the stove, or go into the medicine cabinet, or I'll punish you." Between him and the danger too great for him to imagine we put a lesser danger, but one he can imagine and maybe therefore want to avoid. He can have no idea of what it would be like to be hit by a car, but he can imagine being shouted at, or spanked, or sent to his room. He avoids these substitutes for the greater danger until he can understand it and avoid it for its own sake. But we ought to use this discipline only when it is necessary to protect the life, health, safety, or well-being of people or other living creatures, or to prevent destruction of things that people care about. We ought not to assume too long, as we usually do, that a child cannot understand the real nature of the danger from which we want to protect him. The sooner he avoids the danger, not to escape our punishment, but as a matter of good sense, the better. He can learn that faster than we think. In Mexico, for example, where people drive their cars with a good deal of spirit, I saw many children no older than five or four walking unattended on the streets. They understood about cars, they knew what to do. A child whose life is full of the threat and fear of punishment is locked into babyhood. There is no way for him to grow up, to learn to take responsibility for his life and acts. Most important of all, we should not assume that having to yield to the threat of our superior force is good for the child's character. It is never good for *anyone's* character. To bow to superior force makes us feel impotent and cowardly for not having had the strength or courage to resist. Worse, it makes us resentful and vengeful. We can hardly wait to make someone pay for our humiliation, yield to us as we were once made to yield. No, if we cannot always avoid using the Discipline of Superior Force, we should at least use it as seldom as we can.

There are places where all three disciplines overlap. Any 4 very demanding human activity combines in it the disciplines of Superior Force, of Culture, and of Nature. The novice will be told, "Do it this way, never mind asking why, just do it that way, that is the way we always do it." But it probably *is* just the way they always do it, and usually for the very good reason that it is a way that has been found to work. Think, for example, of ballet training. The student in a class is told to do this exercise, or that; to stand so; to do this or that with his head, arms, shoulders, abdomen, hips, legs, feet. He is constantly corrected. There is no argument. But behind these seemingly autocratic demands by the teacher lie many decades of custom and tradition, and behind that, the necessities of dancing itself. You cannot make the moves of classical ballet unless over many years you have acquired, and renewed every day, the needed strength and suppleness in scores of muscles and joints. Nor can you do the difficult motions, making them look easy, unless you have learned hundreds of easier ones first. Dance teachers may not always agree on all the details of teaching these strengths and skills. But no novice could learn them all by himself. You could not go for a night or two to watch the ballet and then, without any other knowledge at all, teach yourself how to do it. In the same way, you would be unlikely to learn any complicated and difficult human activity without drawing heavily on the experience of those who know it better. But the point is that the authority of these experts or teachers stems from, grows out of, their greater competence and experience, the fact that what they do *works*, not the fact that they happen to be the teacher and as such have the power to kick a student out of the class. And the further point is that children are always and everywhere attracted to that competence, and ready and eager to submit themselves to a discipline that grows out of it. We hear constantly that children will never do anything unless compelled to by bribes or threats. But in their private lives, or in extracurricular activities in school, in sports, music, drama, art, running a newspaper, and so on, they often submit themselves willingly and wholeheartedly to very intense disciplines, simply because they want to learn to do a given thing well. Our Little-Napoleon football coaches, of whom we have too many and hear far too much, blind us to the fact that millions of children work hard every year getting better at sports and games without coaches barking and yelling at them.

QUESTIONS

1. Does Holt divide discipline according to source or to the uses of discipline in education—or according to some other principle? Is Holt's division exhaustive?

2. Holt states in paragraph 4 that the kinds of discipline distinguished overlap. How do they?

3. Holt's principle of division might have been the effects of discipline on the personality of the young person. Is Holt concerned with effects in the course of his discussion?

4. How else might discipline be analyzed in a discussion of it, and to what purpose?

5. Do you agree with Holt that people learn best when they are not coerced? Do you agree with him about coercive sports coaches?

SUGGESTIONS FOR WRITING

1. Divide discipline according to a principle different from Holt's. Make your divisions exclusive of one another and indicate how exhaustive you think they are.

2. Write an essay on jobs or hobbies, developing the topic by

division. If you divide by more than one principle, keep each breakdown and discussion separate and consistent.

3. Discuss why you think Holt would agree or disagree with Margaret Mead and Rhoda Metraux on effective and ineffective kinds of discipline (p. 137). Analyze key statements in the two essays to support your answer.

ALLAN NEVINS

One of America's most important historians, ALLAN NEVINS *(1890–1971) taught at Columbia and was associated with the Huntington Library in California for many years. Nevins wrote important biographies of many famous Americans, including John D. Rockefeller and Henry Ford, and won Pulitzer Prizes in 1933 and 1937 for his lives of Grover Cleveland and Hamilton Fish. His discussion of newspapers shows one important use of division in exposition and also tells us something important about the interpretation of evidence—a subject we will consider later in this book.*

The Newspaper

Obviously, it is futile to talk of accuracy or inaccuracy, authority or lack of authority, with reference to the newspaper as a whole. The newspaper cannot be dismissed with either a blanket endorsement or a blanket condemnation. It cannot be used as if all its parts had equal value or authenticity. The first duty of the historical student of the newspaper is to discriminate. He must weigh every separate department, every article, every writer, for what the department or article or writer seems to be worth. Clearly, a great part of what is printed in every newspaper is from official sources, and hence may be relied upon to be perfectly accurate. The weather report is accurate; so are court notices, election notices, building permits, lists of marriage licenses, bankruptcy lists. Though unofficial, other classes of news are almost totally free from error. The most complete precautions are taken to keep the stock market quotations minutely accurate, both by stock exchange authorities and by the newspaper staffs. An error in stock quotations may have the most disastrous consequences, and mistakes are hence excluded by every means within human power. So with shipping news, news of deaths, and a considerable body of similar matter—sports records, registers of Congressional or legislative votes, and so on.

Thus one great division of material in newspapers can   2 be treated as completely authentic. There is another large division which may in general be treated as trustworthy and authoritative. This is the news which is prepared by experts under conditions exempt from hurry and favorable to the gathering of all the significant facts. The weekly review of a real estate expert is a case in point. The sporting news of the best newspapers, prepared by experts under conditions which make for accuracy, is singularly uniform, and this uniformity is the best evidence that it is truthful and well proportioned. Society news, industrial news, and similar intelligence, especially when it appears in the form of weekly surveys written by known specialists, is worthy of the utmost reliance.

But in dealing with news which contains a large subjec-   3 tive element, and which is prepared under conditions of hurry and strain, the critical faculty must be kept constantly alert. Every conscientious correspondent at an inauguration, or a battle, or a political rally, or in an interview, tries to report the facts. But not one of them can help reporting, in addition to the facts, the impression that he has personally received of them. The most honest and careful observer ordinarily sees a little of what he wishes to see. It is through failure to make critical allowance for this fact that the historical student of newspapers is most likely to be led astray. Beveridge in his life of Lincoln remarks upon the striking difference between the Democratic reports and the Republican reports of the Lincoln-Douglas debates. At Ottawa, Illinois, for example, these two great leaders held their first joint debate on August 21, 1858. Lincoln came on a special train of fourteen cars crowded with shouting Republicans. It arrived at Ottawa at noon and, according to the Republican papers, when Lincoln alighted a shout went up from a dense and enthusiastic crowd which made the bluffs of the Illinois River and the woods along it ring and ring again. Lincoln entered a carriage; according to the *Chicago Tribune* men with evergreens, mottoes, fair young ladies, bands of music, military companies, and a dense mass of cheering humanity followed him through the streets in a scene of tumultuous excitement. But according to the *Philadelphia Press* and other Douglas papers, Lincoln had only a chilly and lackadaisical reception. "As his procession passed," stated the *Philadelphia Press*, "scarcely a cheer went up. They marched along silently and sorrowfully, as if it were a funeral cortege following him to the grave." On the other hand, the Democratic papers declared that the reception of Douglas was perfectly tremendous; the cheers were so thundering, said the *Philadelphia Press*, that they seemed to rend the very air. But the *Chicago Tribune* said that Douglas had no reception of consequence; that the only cheers he got came from the Irish Catholics. Yet both reporters were probably fairly honest. They saw what they wished to see.

QUESTIONS

1. On what basis does Nevins divide his paragraphs on material in newspapers? What are the three divisions he distinguishes?

2. What point is he making through these divisions?

3. In referring to the "large subjective element" of certain newspaper accounts, is Nevins referring to bias or prejudice in the reporters? What does his example of the Lincoln–Douglas debates show?

4. What is the order of ideas in the three paragraphs? Why does Nevins save "news which contains a large subjective element" for last?

5. How many classes can you think of for newspapers? What purposes might these classifications serve?

SUGGESTIONS FOR WRITING

1. In one or two paragraphs of your own, divide materials in newspapers by another principle of division and use your division to make a point, as Nevins does.

2. Analyze the front-page stories of an issue of a newspaper according to the degree of their reliability. Discuss the "subjective element" of one of the stories, as Nevins discusses the account of the Lincoln–Douglas debates.

GARRISON KEILLOR

Born in Anoka, Minnesota, the humorist and essayist GARRISON KEILLOR *worked as a radio announcer following graduation from the University of Minnesota in 1966. In his radio program,* Prairie Home Companion, *begun in 1974, Keillor made famous a fictional midwestern town he called Lake Wobegon. Keillor has collected his sketches and essays in* Lake Wobegon Days *(1985),* Leaving Home *(1987), and* We Are Still Married *(1989), in which his essay "Hoppers" appears. Keillor received the George Foster Peabody Broadcasting Award in 1980, and in 1985 the Edward R. Murrow Award of the Corporation for Public Broadcasting for service to public radio. In "Hoppers" Keillor uses both classification and division in describing people on a New York City street.*

Hoppers

A hydrant was open on Seventh Avenue above 23rd Street last Friday morning, and I stopped on my way east and watched people hop over the water. It was a brilliant spring day. The water was a nice clear creek about three feet wide and ran along the gutter around the northwest corner of the intersection. A gaggle of pedestrians crossing 23rd went *hop hop hop hop hop* over the creek as a few soloists jaywalking Seventh performed at right angles to them, and I got engrossed in the dance. Three feet isn't a long leap for most people, and the ease of it permits a wide range of expression. Some hoppers went a good deal higher than necessary.

Long, lanky men don't hop, as a rule. The ones I saw hardly paused at the water's edge, just lengthened one stride and trucked on across—a rather flatfooted approach that showed no recognition of the space or occasion. Tall men typically suffer from an excess of cool, but I kept hoping for one of them to get off the ground. Most of the tall men wore topcoats and carried briefcases, so perhaps their balance was thrown off. One tall man in a brown coat didn't notice the water and stepped off the curb into the fast-flowing Hydrant Creek and made a painful hop, like a wounded heron: a brown heron with a limp wing attached to a briefcase bulging full of dead fish. He crossed 23rd looking as though his day had been pretty much shot to pieces.

Short, fat men were superb: I could have watched them 3 all morning. A typical fat man crossing the street would quicken his step when he saw the creek and, on his approach, do a little shuffle, arms out to the sides, and suddenly and with great concentration *spring*—a nimble step all the more graceful for the springer's bulk. Three fairly fat men jiggled and shambled across 23rd together, and then one poked another and they saw the water. They stepped forward, studying the angle, and just before the point man jumped for the curb his pals said something, undoubtedly discouraging, and he threw back his head and laughed over his shoulder and threw himself lightly, boyishly, across the water, followed—*boing boing*—by the others.

The women who hopped the water tended to stop and 4 study the creek and find its narrows and measure the distance and then lurch across. They seemed dismayed that the creek was there at all, and one, in a beige suit, put her hands on her hips and glared upstream, as if to say, "Whose water *is* this? This is utterly unacceptable. I am *not* about to jump over this." But then she made a good jump after all. She put her left toe on the edge of the curb, leaned forward with right arm outstretched—for a second, she looked as if she might take off and zoom up toward the Flatiron Building—and pushed off, landing easily on her right toe, her right arm raised. The longest leap was made by a young woman in a blue raincoat carrying a plastic Macy's bag and crossing west on Seventh. She gathered herself up in three long, accelerating strides and sailed, her coat billowing out behind her, over the water and five feet beyond, almost creaming a guy coming out of Radio Shack. He shrank back as she loped past, her long black hair and snow-white hands and face right *there*, then gone, vanished in the crowd.

And then it was my turn. I waited for the green light,   5 crossed 23rd, stopped by the creek flowing around the bend of curb and heard faint voices of old schoolmates ahead in the woods, and jumped heavily across and marched after them.

VOCABULARY

paragraph 1: gaggle
paragraph 3: jiggle, shamble
paragraph 4: lurch, billowing, creaming, lope

QUESTIONS

1. By what principle does Keillor divide the class *male hoppers*? How do the characteristics shared by "long, lanky men" influence the way they cross the water? How do the characteristics of "short, fat men" influence the way they do?
2. How do most of the women differ from men in how they cross the water?
3. In what class does Keillor put himself in paragraph 5? How does this class differ from the other classes described?
4. Is Keillor making a point or developing a thesis in the essay? Or is his essay descriptive only?

SUGGESTIONS FOR WRITING

1. Like Keillor, identify classes of people on the basis of how they act on the street or at home—for example, how they cross a busy intersection, get up in the morning, or prepare for bed.
2. Like Keillor, who divides the men hopping the stream, divide one of the classes identified according to a single principle. And, like Keillor, put yourself in a separate class or, if appropriate, in one of the classes you identify. If you wish, use your classification to make a point, perhaps an observation about human nature or differences in age groups or genders.

DEFINITION

❦ ❦ ❦

There are many ways of defining something, and the way we choose depends on our purpose and audience. If we are in a store that advertises "Hero Sandwiches" and a visitor asks what these are, we can point to one on the counter. But pointing may not be enough: we may have to "denote" what a hero sandwich is—that is, distinguish the "hero" from all other things like it. In a denotative definition we can start with a classification of things like food and single the hero out from all other kinds. But since the visitor knows a hero is something to eat, we can narrow our class to sandwiches.

A dictionary definition usually gives us a denotative definition of this sort—identifying first the class or genus of objects to which the word belongs and then distinguishing the word by its specific difference. As we noted, the class or genus may be broad (*food*) or it may be narrow (*sandwich*). The following dictionary definition of *hero* chooses a narrow genus:

> *hero* U.S. A sandwich [*genus*] made with a loaf of bread cut lengthwise [*specific difference*].—*Standard College Dictionary*

Sometimes we want to do more than merely name or identify an object: we want to present ideas and impressions, the emotional aura we associate with it. The word *rose* has a precise denotation—a particular flower with describable properties. It also has a range of connotations or associations. Thus roses are often associated with success or happiness, and we recognize this association in the popular expression "a rosy future." Connotations may be positive in their implication, or negative. Though the words *inexpensive* and *cheap* both mean low in price, *cheap* usually carries the connotation of poor quality or of something contemptible. *Inexpensive* is an emotionally neutral word; *cheap* is not.

Denotative and connotative definitions tell us how words are used currently. Sometimes we find it helpful to give the original meaning, or etymology, to clarify the current meaning—for example, to explain that the word *gravity* comes from the Latin *gravitas* meaning weight or heaviness. But we must be careful not to assume that a current word possesses, or should be limited to, its original meaning. We would certainly be misunderstood if we used *sinister*, a word of French derivation originally meaning *left* and *left-handed*, to refer to a left-handed person.

We can also use definition to fix words that have become indefinite or confused in popular usage. We sometimes call this kind of definition *precising*. Judicial decisions are often of this kind, as in decisions that define obscenity in books and films. Another use of definition is to stipulate or propose a name or term for a newly discovered phenomenon so that we can refer to it. An example is the term *quasar,* proposed in the 1960s for newly discovered "quasi-stellar" sources of light in the sky that seem not to be stars. *Stipulative* definitions are proposed with the understanding that the term may change later as more is discovered. By contrast, *theoretical* definitions propose an explanation or theory of the phenomenon: they do not merely propose a term for discussion and further research. Most textbook definitions of democracy and similar ideas are theoretical. In giving definitions, we should be clear about the use we are making of them. It will matter to the reader whether we are trying to make a commonly used word more exact in its usage or proposing a definition without claiming to know the whole truth about it.

PAUL BRODEUR

A native of Boston, Massachusetts, Paul Brodeur *graduated from Harvard University in 1953; in 1958 he began his association with* The New Yorker *magazine as a staff writer. His* New Yorker *reports on asbestos and other environmental hazards are the basis of* Outrageous Misconduct *(1985),* Currents of Death *(1989), and other books. His introductory definition of asbestos in* Outrageous Misconduct, *reprinted here, uses etymological definition to illuminate the present meaning of the word.*

Asbestos

The adverse biological effects of asbestos, a word that comes   1
from a Greek adjective meaning inextinguishable, were observed as early as the first century by the Greek geographer

Strabo and by the Roman naturalist Pliny the Elder, both of whom mentioned in passing a sickness of the lungs in slaves whose task was to weave asbestos into cloth. Strabo and Pliny were calling attention for the first time to the disease from which Claude Tomplait* would be diagnosed as suffering nearly two thousand years later, but the ancients were much too awed by the unique and astonishing physical properties of asbestos, which they called "the magic mineral," to be concerned with the possibility that it might constitute a health hazard. Indeed, their attitude toward asbestos—a broad term embracing a number of silicate minerals, whose delicate fibers not only can withstand the fiercest heat but are so soft and flexible that they can be spun and woven as easily as fibers of cotton or flax—sometimes bordered on veneration. Strabo and Plutarch noted that the "perpetual" wicks used in the sacred lamps of the vestal virgins were made of asbestos, and Pliny described asbestos cloth, which had been used for centuries in cremations, as the rare and costly "funeral dress of kings." The Romans were especially impressed by the fact that when cloth made of asbestos was exposed to flame it always came out whiter than before—hence the Latin word for asbestos, *amiantus*, meaning unpolluted or undefiled—and they are said to have cleaned asbestos napkins by tossing them into the fire. During the Dark Ages, the use of asbestos in Europe appears to have diminished greatly, although it is said that the Emperor Charlemagne convinced some warrior guests from a rival kingdom that he possessed magical powers by throwing an asbestos tablecloth into the fire and then withdrawing it, unscathed, from the flames. In the latter part of the thirteenth century, when the indefatigable Venetian traveler Marco Polo was traversing a part of Siberia then known as the Great Empire of Tartary, he was shown some cloth that would not burn, and was told by his Tartar hosts that it was made from salamander's wool. Too wily to be taken in by a story like that, Polo examined the material carefully and, after making inquiries, learned that there was a mineral in the mountains of the district that contained threads like

---

*An East Texas asbestos insulator diagnosed with pulmonary fibrosis in 1961; a plaintiff in a landmark product-liability suit. [Ed.]

those of wool. After a long period of eclipse, the astonishing properties of asbestos were rediscovered in the Western world, with the advent of the industrial revolution in the eighteenth century, and by the late 1800s the incombustible mineral began to be used extensively to insulate boilers, steam pipes, turbines, ovens, kilns, and other high-temperature equipment. As a result, the fact that asbestos could produce lung disease, which had been forgotten since Strabo and Pliny first recorded it around the time of Christ, soon manifested itself again.

VOCABULARY

paragraph 1: inextinguishable, silicate, veneration, vestal virgin, unpolluted, undefiled, unscathed, indefatigable, salamander, advent

QUESTIONS

1. What denotative definition does Brodeur give of *asbestos*? Is the definition more or less detailed than the definition in your college dictionary?
2. What is the topic idea of the paragraph, and how does this denotative definition help Brodeur develop it?
3. What etymological definitions does Brodeur provide, and how do these help to develop the topic idea?
4. How does Brodeur organize the details of the paragraph?
5. What may be the significance of the fact that adverse effects of asbestos have long been observed?

SUGGESTION FOR WRITING

Use the *Oxford English Dictionary* and other reference books to discover the etymology and distinguishing properties of one of the following objects or substances, or another of your choosing. Look also for information on its history and effects. Organize your information into a single well-organized paragraph.

a. aspirin
b. DDT

c. insulin
d. nitroglycerin
e. radar

PHILIP HAMBURGER

A native of Wheeling, West Virginia, PHILIP HAMBURGER *has been a staff member of* The New Yorker *magazine since 1939, except for two years of government service during World War Two in the Office of Facts and Figures (later the Office of War Information). On his return to* The New Yorker *in 1943, he served as a war correspondent in Europe for the magazine. Hamburger has written for most sections of* The New Yorker. *His many contributions include pieces in "Talk of the Town" and "Notes and Comments," "Reporter at Large" articles, film and music criticism, and columns on television. His "Notes for a Gazetteer," a series of profiles of American cities, were collected in* An American Notebook *(1965). His most recent book is* Curious World: A New Yorker at Large *(1987). In* An American Notebook *he shows a particular city through the eyes of its inhabitants; this excerpt is taken from his profile of Oklahoma City.*

The Sooners

No higher compliment can be paid to an Oklahoma City man these days than to call him a Sooner. Call an Oklahoma City man a Sooner, and his chest puffs out and his eyes light up. It means that you appreciate the chap—his vigor, his vitality, his civic pride, his alliance with the tall white buildings that, first glimpsed from miles away and across long stretches of land, appear to be a mirage but turn out, upon a closer approach, to be Oklahoma City. Call a man a Sooner, and you identify him with, among other things, the University of Oklahoma football team—the Sooners—and what man could ask for more? Oklahoma City's most fashionable hotel, the Skirvin (Perle Mesta owns part of the Skirvin; her daddy was a Skirvin), has a Sooner Room, which constitutes semi-official recognition that the word "Sooner" has reached an impeccable social plateau. The use of "Sooner" as an accolade represents a mellowing process. Up to seventy years ago, to call a man a Sooner was to risk being hit over the head with the spare wheel of a covered wagon, kicked in the stomach, or worse. It all goes back to April 22, 1889, the day of The Run, when the Oklahoma Territory (then called the Indian Territory) was opened to settlers, and when the settlers, poised and in natural Technicolor, awaited the sound of the gun that would permit them to race pell-mell for new land and new homes. There is many a man in Oklahoma City today who remembers The Run, and millions of moviegoers feel that they, too, made The Run, as a result of the numerous cinema epics that have glorified it. When dawn broke on that April 22nd, what was to become Oklahoma City was a sleepy little railroad stop sitting out on the lonely grass. Nothing much to be said about it, really—a few wooden houses, a water tower, some railroad tracks, the usual complement of early-rising roosters, perhaps a barefoot boy with a can of worms, and the West stretching as far as the eye could see. There were also on hand some people called Sooners. These were people who had shown up too soon—who weren't taking any chances on losing out in the race for land, and who had crossed the line before the starting gun. To the thousands of law-abiding citizens who waited patiently behind the line, the Sooners were beneath contempt. "They were chisellers, that's what they were," an old-time Oklahoma City resident said not long ago. He was in the Sooner Room at the time, sipping a brandy. "The organized Sooners, who were sooner than the Sooners, were known as Boomers, and it is hard to say which were worse. They were all mean, dirty, low-life chisellers." By nightfall, after the gun had gone off and The Run had been accomplished, Oklahoma City was a city of ten thousand souls, many of them out looking for the Sooners and the Boomers. Time heals many wounds.

QUESTIONS

1. What is the denotative definition of *Sooner*, and where in the paragraph does Hamburger present it?

2. What positive and negative connotations does the word *Sooner* have? Why does Hamburger give us information about the Boomers?

3. What do these connotations tell you about Oklahomans and changes in Oklahoma life since 1889?

4. What is the tone of the paragraph—the voice of the writer that you hear in reading it? Specifically, is the tone admiring or sarcastic or amused? Or does Hamburger express no attitude toward the people and the world he describes?

SUGGESTIONS FOR WRITING

1. First give the denotative meaning of a name like the one Hamburger describes—perhaps the name associated with your city or town or with your high school and its teams. Then give its connotations and, if you can, explain their origin. Use your definition to make a point.

2. Advertisers depend on connotative meanings to sell their products. Discuss differences in the connotations of similar products—for example, automobiles with names like "Cougar" and "Charger." Use your discussion to make a point.

CASEY MILLER AND KATE SWIFT

> CASEY MILLER *has worked in publishing and as a free-lance writer and editor.* KATE SWIFT *is also a free-lance writer and editor and has been a science writer for the American Museum of Natural History and a news director for the Yale School of Medicine. The discussion reprinted here is taken from* Words and Women *(1976)—a book concerned with the influence of language on the lives of women.*

"Manly" and "Womanly"

Webster's Third New International Dictionary (1966) defines 1 *manly* as "having qualities appropriate to a man: not effeminate or timorous; bold, resolute, open in conduct or bearing." The definition goes on to include "belonging or appropriate in character to a man" (illustrated by "manly sports" and "beer is a manly drink"), "of undaunted courage: gallant, brave." The same dictionary's definition of *womanly* is less specific, relying heavily on phrases like "marked by qualities characteristic of a woman"; "possessed of the character or behavior befitting a grown woman"; "characteristic of, belonging to, or suitable to a woman's nature and attitudes rather than to a man's." Two of the examples provided are more informative: "convinced that drawing was a waste of time, if not downright womanly . . ." and "her usual womanly volubility."

In its definition of *manly* the *Random House Dictionary of the English Language* (1967) supplies the words "strong, brave, honorable, resolute, virile" as "qualities usually considered desirable in a man" and cites "feminine; weak, cowardly," as antonyms. Its definitions of *womanly* are "like or befitting a woman; feminine; not masculine or girlish" and "in the manner of, or befitting, a woman." The same dictionary's synonym essays for these words are worth quoting in full because of the contrasts they provide: 2

> Manly, Manful, Mannish mean possessing the qualities of a man. Manly implies possession of the most valuable or desirable qualities a man can have, as dignity, honesty, directness, etc., in opposition to servility, insincerity, underhandedness, etc.: *A manly foe is better than a weak friend.* It also connotes courage, strength, and fortitude: *manly determination to face what comes.* Manful stresses the reference to courage, strength, and industry: *manful resistance.* Mannish applies to that which resembles man: *a boy with a mannish voice.* Applied to a woman, the term is derogatory, suggesting the aberrant possession of masculine characteristics: *a mannish girl; a mannish stride.*
>
> Womanly, womanlike, womanish, mean resembling a woman. Womanly implies resemblance in appropriate, fitting ways: *womanly decorum, modesty.* Womanlike, a neutral synonym, may suggest mild disapproval or, more rarely, disgust: *Womanlike, she (he) burst into tears.* Womanish usually implies an inappropriate resemblance and suggests weakness or effeminacy; *womanish petulance.*

What are these parallel essays saying? That we perceive males in terms of human qualities, females in terms of 3 qualities—often negative—assigned to them as females. The qualities males possess may be good or bad, but those that come to mind when we consider what makes "a man" are positive. Women are defined circularly, through characteristics seen to be appropriate or inappropriate to women—not to human beings. In fact, when women exhibit positive attributes considered typical of men—dignity, honesty, courage, strength, or fortitude—they are thought of as aberrant. A person who is "womanlike" may (although the term is said to be "neutral") prompt a feeling of disgust.

The broad range of positive characteristics used to define males could be used to define females too, of course, but they are not. The characteristics of women—weakness is among the most frequently cited—are something apart. At its entry for *woman Webster's Third* provides this list of "qualities considered distinctive of womanhood": "Gentleness, affection, and domesticity or on the other hand fickleness, superficiality, and folly." Among the "qualities considered distinctive of manhood" listed in the entry for *man,* no negative attributes detract from the "courage, strength, and vigor" the definers associate with males. According to this dictionary, *womanish* means "unsuitable to a man or to a strong character of either sex." 4

Lexicographers do not make up definitions out of thin air. Their task is to record how words are used, it is not to say how they should be used. The examples they choose to illustrate meanings can therefore be especially revealing of cultural expectations. The *American Heritage Dictionary* (1969), which provides "manly courage" and "masculine charm," also gives us "Woman is fickle," "brought out the woman in him," "womanly virtue," "feminine allure," "feminine wiles," and "womanish tears." The same dictionary defines *effeminate,* which comes from the Latin *effeminare,* meaning "to make a woman out of," as "having the qualities associated with women; not characteristic of a man; unmanly" and "characterized by softness, weakness, or lack of force; not dynamic or vigorous." For synonyms one is referred to *feminine.* 5

Brother and *sister* and their derivatives have acquired similar features. A columnist who wrote that "the political operatives known as 'Kennedy men' and 'Nixon men' have 6 been sisters under their skins" could not possibly have called those adversaries "brothers," with all the mutual respect and loyalty that word implies. As the writer explained, "Like the colonel's lady and Judy O'Grady, their styles were different but their unwavering determination to win was strikingly similar." Other kinds of sisters for whom no comparable male siblings exist include the sob sister, the weak sister, and the plain ordinary sissy, whose counterpart in the brotherhood is the buddy, a real pal. Like *effeminate*, these female-related words and phrases are applied to males when a cutting insult is intended.

Masculine, manly, manlike, and other male-associated words used to compliment men are frequently also considered complimentary when applied to women: thus a woman may be said to have manly determination, to have a masculine mind, to take adversity like a man, or to struggle manfully against overwhelming odds. The one male-associated word sometimes used to insult her is mannish, which may suggest she is too strong or aggressive to be a true woman, or that she is homosexually oriented, in which case mannish can become a code word. 7

Female-associated words, on the other hand, must be hedged, as in "He has almost feminine intuition," if they are used to describe a man without insulting him. He may be praised for admirable qualities defined as peculiar to women, but he cannot be said to have womanly compassion or womanlike tenderness. In exceptions to this rule—for example, when a medic on the battlefield or a sports figure in some postgame situation of unusual drama is said to be "as gentle as a woman"—the life-and-death quality of the circumstances makes its own ironic and terrible commentary on the standards of "masculinity" ordinarily expected of men. 8

The role expectations compressed into our male-positive-important and female-negative-trivial words are extremely damaging, as we are beginning to find out. The female stereotypes they convey are obvious, but the harm doesn't stop there. The inflexible demands made on males, which allow neither for variation nor for human frailty, are dehumanizing. They put a premium on a kind of perfection that can be achieved only through strength, courage, industry, and fortitude. These are admirable qualities, but if they 9 are associated only with males, and their opposites are associated only with females, they become sex-related demands that few individuals can fulfill.

VOCABULARY

paragraph 1: effeminate, timorous, undaunted, volubility

paragraph 2: virile, antonym, servility, derogatory, aberrant, decorum, synonym, petulance

paragraph 4: fickleness, superficiality

paragraph 5: lexicographer, wiles

paragraph 6: sibling

paragraph 8: intuition

paragraph 9: stereotype, dehumanizing, fortitude

QUESTIONS

1. The Random House Dictionary shows that the words *manly* and *womanly* connote or suggest certain ideas and attitudes. Why are connotative meanings of *manly* distinguished from other meanings? Does the dictionary distinguish meanings of *womanly* in the same way?

2. Miller and Swift state that "Women are defined circularly, through characteristics seen to be appropriate or inappropriate to women—not to human beings." How is the definition of women circular?

3. What attitudes toward men and women underline the dictionary definition—and current uses—of *manly* and *womanly*? What change in attitude toward men and women do Miller and Swift favor? Do they say what change they favor, or do you infer their beliefs from their analysis?

4. To what extent do Miller and Swift describe your own use of *manly* and *womanly* and your conceptions of manhood and womanhood?

SUGGESTIONS FOR WRITING

1. Miller and Swift state that language today makes "sex-related demands that few individuals can fulfill." Explain what they mean. Then state your reasons for agreeing or disagreeing with them.

2. Analyze your own conception of manliness and womanliness, comparing your use of *manly* and *womanly* with those discussed by Miller and Swift.

HERBERT J. GANS

HERBERT J. GANS *is Robert S. Lynd Professor of Sociology at Columbia University in New York City. In his article on the word "underclass" published in* The Washington Post *September 10, 1990, Gans shows how a widely accepted word can create an unfair stereotype and influence thinking on issues of welfare and poverty. In exploring the connotations of the term, Gans is also considering the implications of what is for journalists and sociologists a theoretical definition.*

The Underclass

Sticks and stones may break my bones, but names can never hurt me goes the old proverb. But like many old proverbs, this one is patent nonsense, as anyone knows who has ever been hurt by ethnic, racist or sexist insults and stereotypes.

The most frequent victims of insults and stereotypes have been the poor, especially those thought to be undeserving of help because someone decided—justifiably or not—that they had not acted properly. America has a long history of insults for the "undeserving" poor. In the past they were bums, hoboes, vagrants and paupers; more recently they have been culturally deprived and the hard-core poor. Now they are "the underclass."

Underclass was originally a 19th-century Swedish term for the poor. In the early 1960s, the Swedish economist Gunnar Myrdal revived it to describe the unemployed and unemployables being created by the modern economy, people who, he predicted, would soon be driven out of that economy unless it was reformed. Twenty years later, in

Ronald Reagan's America, the word sprang to life again, this time not only to describe but also to condemn. Those normally consigned to the underclass include: women who start their families before marriage and before the end of adolescence, youngsters who fail to finish high school or find work, and welfare "dependents"—whether or not the behavior of any of these people is their own fault. The term is also applied to low-income delinquents and criminals—but not to affluent ones.

"Underclass" has become popular because it seems to 4 grab people's attention. What grabs is the image of a growing horde of beggars, muggers, robbers and lazy people who do not carry their part of the economic load, all of them threatening nonpoor Americans and the stability of American society. The image may be inaccurate, but then insults and pejoratives don't have to be accurate. Moreover, underclass sounds technical, academic, and not overtly pejorative, so it can be used without anyone's biases showing. Since it is now increasingly applied to blacks and Hispanics, it is also a respectable substitute word with which to condemn them.

There are other things wrong with the word underclass. 5 For one, it lumps together in a single term very diverse poor people with diverse problems. Imagine all children's illnesses being described with the same word, and the difficulties doctors would have in curing them.

For example, a welfare recipient often requires little 6 more than a decent paying job—and a male breadwinner who also has such a job—to make a normal go of it, while a high school dropout usually needs both a better-equipped school, better teachers and fellow students—and a rationale for going to school when he or she has no assurance that a decent job will follow upon graduation. Neither the welfare recipient nor the high school dropout deserves to be grouped with, or described by, the same word as muggers or drug dealers.

Labeling poor people as underclass is to blame them for 7 their poverty, which enables the blamers to blow off the steam of self-righteousness. That steam does not, however, reduce their poverty. Unfortunately, underclass, like other buzzwords for calling the poor undeserving, is being used to avoid starting up needed antipoverty programs and other economic reforms.

Still, the greatest danger of all lies not in the label itself 8 but in the possibility that the underclass is a symptom of a possible, and dark, American future: that we are moving toward a "post-post-industrial" economy in which there may not be enough decent jobs for all. Either too many more jobs will move to Third World countries where wages are far lower or they will be performed by ever more efficient computers and other machines.

If this happens, the underclass label may turn out to be 9 a signal that the American economy, and our language, are preparing to get ready for a future in which some people are going to be more or less permanently jobless—and will be blamed for their joblessness to boot.

Needless to say, an American economy with a perma- 10 nently jobless population would be socially dangerous, for all of the country's current social problems, from crime and addiction to mental illness would be sure to increase considerably. America would then also become politically more dangerous, for various kinds of new protests have to be expected, not to mention the rise of quasi-facist movements. Such movements can already be found in France and other European countries.

Presumably, Americans—the citizenry and elected offi- 11 cials both—will not let any of this happen here and will find new sources of decent jobs, as they have done in past generations, even if today this requires a new kind of New Deal. Perhaps there will be another instance of what always saved America in the past: new sources of economic growth that cannot even be imagined now.

The only problem is that in the past, America ruled the 12 world economically, and now it does not—and it shows in our lack of economic growth. Consequently, the term underclass could become a permanent entry in the dictionary of American pejoratives.

VOCABULARY

paragraph 1: stereotype
paragraph 2: hoboes, vagrants, paupers
paragraph 4: pejoratives
paragraph 6: rationale
paragraph 8: symptom
paragraph 10: quasi-facist

QUESTIONS

1. Gans shows that the economist Gunnar Myrdal introduced a precising definition for the nineteenth-century Swedish word *underclass*. What was the original meaning of the word, and how did Mydral make the meaning precise?
2. To what extent has Myrdal's meaning been adopted by Americans, according to Gans? What additional meanings has the word acquired since the early 1960s?
3. Why does Gans consider *underclass* an inaccurate term or label for the poor? What additional danger does he see in the widespread acceptance of the term?
4. Does Gans believe that poverty is irremediable? Or does he believe that remedies exist in America today?

SUGGESTIONS FOR WRITING

1. Define one of the following words or another word descriptive of an attitude or behavior by stating what it is and what it is not. Comment on the significance of its etymology.
   a. gluttony
   b. greed
   c. intolerance
   d. laziness
   e. stinginess
2. Discuss the various meanings of a descriptive term like *cool* or *tacky*, illustrating these meanings by your use of them.

EDWARD SIMMEN

EDWARD SIMMEN, *who teaches at the Universidad de las Américés, in Puebla, Mexico, wrote this definition of the word* Chicano *in 1972, at a time when Mexican-Americans were gaining recognition and asking for understanding of their needs and culture. Etymological and connotative definition are essential to Simmen's definition, for he is concerned with origins, attitudes, and feelings. The anonymous Chicano whose essay appears later in this book (p. 401) writes about his origins and culture in a much different way.*

Chicano: Origin and Meaning

Another minority group—the Mexican-American—is presently being heard on campuses in the Southwest and West. Following the blacks, this new voice—the Chicano—is now asking for special ethnic study programs. Surprising to many, he is receiving not only serious administrative attention, but action. And with it all, a new word has come into the printed English vocabulary—*Chicano*. Most often it is seen in the headlines of daily newspapers or national magazines leading to reports of incidents involving the actions of Mexican-Americans, such as those demonstrations that occurred in September 1970 in the streets of Los Angeles and at a school-board meeting in Houston.

However, the word, while freely used nationally by journalists, has little meaning for the general public who live outside the Southwest. Even those who live in the areas populated by the ten million Mexican-Americans in the United States do not fully understand the word.

Especially elusive are the origin and meaning of *Chicano*. Dictionaries are of no help; the word does not appear in even the most recently published English dictionaries. And as far as is known, its first appearance in print is the use of the term by Mario Suárez, a Mexican writer from Arizona, in a sketch entitled "El Hoyo," published in the *Arizona Quarterly*, Summer, 1947, to describe a barrio (a Mexican-American ghetto) in Tucson, whose inhabitants he refers to as "*chicanos* who raise hell on Saturday night, listen to Padre Estanislao

on Sunday morning and then raise hell on Sunday night."
But Suárez does not attempt to explain the origin of the word
except to say that "the term *chicano* is a short way of saying
Mexicano."

It can be safely said that no one knows for certain the 4
origin of the word. Various theories do exist; of those
suggested, scholars and students of Mexican-American life
and literature generally accept one of two. Each is plausible,
but neither has been proved.

According to Professor Philip D. Ortego of the Univer- 5
sity of Texas at El Paso, one theory "ascribes the word to
Nahuatl origin, suggesting that Indians pronounce Mexicano
as 'Me-shi-ca-noh' " (letter dated October 6, 1970). If such is
the case, the first syllable was in time dropped and the soft
"shi" was replaced with the hard "ch," and the word as it is
known became commonly used in speech by Mexican-
Americans within the barrios. The word then was merely a
term of ethnic identification and not meant in any way to
demean. More recently, however, *Chicano* has been used by
other Mexican-Americans of a "lower" class who identify
more with the Mexican-Indian culture than with the
Mexican-Spanish culture.

Another theory asserts that the word was conventionally 6
formed by suffixing *ano* to *chico* (a young boy), exactly as one
would form, for example, Mexicano from Mexico. Thus, the
word was used in the barrio for emphasis, to place in a
special category an individual so called. A Chicano, then,
would have been any Mexican-American who acted as a
"young boy." Perhaps, in this sense, *Chicano* is related to
chicazo, meaning "a poorly educated young man who aim-
lessly, as a vagabond, roams the streets."

Other problems arise with regard to meaning. Today, 7
who is a Chicano? Certainly, the word is no longer used
exclusively in speech by Mexican-Americans as an uncom-
plimentary term of address. In addition to newspapers and
magazines, it is often seen in *El Grito,* a journal from the
newly formed publishing house Quinto Sol Publications,
Inc., of Berkeley, California. Chicano also is the title of a
novel written by Richard Vásquez, published in 1970. *El
Chicano* is a barrio newspaper published in the slums of San
Bernardino, California.

To assist in understanding one popular meaning of Chicano, Professor Ortego has offered the following series of equivalents: "Negro/Mexican; Afro-American/Mexican-American; Black/Chicano" (letter dated May 26, 1970). In this sense, then, it describes the more radical and youthful Mexican-Americans whose controversial actions and statements often make the headlines. For example, in the June 4, 1969, issue of *The National Catholic Reporter*, an article on Mexican-American activities by Kathy Mulherin was headlined: CHICANOS TURN TO BROWN POWER: FIVE YEARS BEHIND THE BLACKS, BUT WE'LL CATCH UP VERY FAST. A year later, in an article entitled "Chicano Power: Militance Among the Mexican-Americans" (*The New Republic*, June 20, 1970), Stan Steiner wrote of the increasing "political revolt of the Chicanos, as the young Mexican Americans call themselves throughout the Southwest." He quoted Bexar County (San Antonio) Commissioner Albert Pena on the subject: "These young people are the wave of the future. If things are going to change in Texas, they are going to do it. The Chicano is more determined and more militant. He is no longer asking, he is demanding." On October 5, 1970, the Houston *Chronicle* reported such an event which had occurred in a small Texas city on the Rio Grande. The headline read: CHICANOS HOLD PROTEST AT MC ALLEN. The Associated Press coverage began: "Some 250 young Mexican-Americans chanting 'Kill the Gringos' staged a protest rally and march here."

But many Mexican-Americans who would never be considered by the general public as lawless or irresponsible political activists are in increasing numbers calling themselves Chicanos, such as those individuals who attended a conference on Mexican-American studies at the University of Texas at Austin in November 1970. The participants, who came not only from inside the academic community but from outside as well, used the terms *Mexican-American* and *Chicano* interchangeably, with the emphasis on *Chicano*. Such individuals are attempting to discard a variety of other labels such as Latin, Latin-American, Spanish-American, and even Mexican-American and to replace them with one term— *Chicano*—to apply to all Americans of Mexican descent, regardless of profession, education, or political persuasion.

Nevertheless, Mexican-Americans who would define

Chicano in this way are presently in the minority. The vast majority of Americans, influenced by the press, believe that while all Chicanos are Mexican-Americans, not *all* Mexican-Americans are Chicanos. The term, for most Americans who hear and read it, seems to possess pejorative connotations. Today, the noun *Chicano* could well be defined: "A dissatisfied American of Mexican descent whose ideas regarding his position in the social or economic order are, in general, considered to be liberal or radical and whose statements and actions are often extreme and sometimes violent."

Yet even as the word is being used, the meaning is 11 changing; amelioration is taking place as more Mexican-Americans in responsible educational, governmental, and professional positions begin to refer to themselves as *Chicanos*. We may assume that as more and more of these individuals use the term, the word will be defined as follows: "An American of Mexican descent who attempts through peaceful, reasonable, and responsible means to correct the image of the Mexican-American and to improve the position of this minority in the American social structure."

VOCABULARY

paragraph 3: elusive
paragraph 4: plausible
paragraph 5: ethnic
paragraph 6: suffixing
paragraph 10: pejorative
paragraph 11: amelioration

QUESTIONS

1. Simmen opens the essay by identifying the term *Chicano* with Mexican-Americans. Is Simmen saying that all Mexican-Americans are Chicanos?
2. Is Simmen giving a denotative definition in the final paragraph, or is his definition theoretical or stipulative (p. 154)?
3. What are the possible etymologies of *Chicano,* and why are these important to understanding the various connotations?

4. What are the connotations of *Chicano?* Which are positive and which are negative? Why is it important to distinguish between the two kinds?

5. What does the comparison of terms in paragraph 8 contribute to your understanding of the term *Chicano?*

6. What is the purpose of the analysis, and how do you discover it in reading the essay?

SUGGESTION FOR WRITING

Use the *Oxford English Dictionary* or the *Dictionary of American English* and other reference books in your college library to trace the history of one of the following terms. In a concluding paragraph, suggest one or more uses to which this history of the term might be put:

a. anarchist
b. communist
c. creole
d. democrat
e. fascist

f. mugwump
g. republican
h. socialist
i. tory
j. Yankee

COMPARISON AND CONTRAST
❦ ❦ ❦

Comparison shows the similarities between people, things, or ideas; contrast shows the differences. The word *comparison* sometimes refers to both kinds of analysis, as in this block comparison of President Franklin Roosevelt with Great Britain's wartime prime minister, Winston S. Churchill:

> Roosevelt, as a public personality, was a spontaneous, optimistic, pleasure-loving ruler who dismayed his assistants by the gay and apparently heedless abandon with which he seemed to delight in pursuing two or more totally incompatible policies, and astonished them even more by the swiftness and ease with which he managed to throw off the cares of office during the darkest and most dangerous moments. Churchill too loves pleasure, and he too lacks neither gaiety nor a capacity for exuberant self-expression, together with the habit of blithely cutting Gordian knots in a manner which often upset his experts; but he is not a frivolous man. His nature possesses a dimension of depth—and a corresponding sense of tragic possibilities—which Roosevelt's light-hearted genius instinctively passed by.—Sir Isaiah Berlin, "Mr. Churchill"

Block comparisons present the details of the first subject as a whole and then the details of the second. But the author may choose to develop the comparison point by point, as in this second paragraph on Roosevelt and Churchill:

> Roosevelt played the game of politics with virtuosity, and both his successes and his failures were carried off in splendid style; his performance seemed to flow with effortless skill. Churchill is acquainted with darkness as well as light. Like all inhabitants and even transient visitors of inner worlds, he gives evidence of seasons of agonized brooding and slow recovery. Roosevelt might have spoken of sweat and blood, but when Churchill offered his people tears, he spoke a word which might have been uttered by Lincoln or Mazzini or Cromwell, but not Roosevelt, great-hearted, generous and perceptive as he was.

Both paragraphs build from similarities to differences. Were the similarities more important, the author would probably have built to them instead. Notice also that the purpose of the comparison is to arrive at a relative estimate of the two men as leaders. We discover the qualities of Roosevelt through Churchill, and those of Churchill through Roosevelt.

Relative estimates aid in explaining something strange or new, as in the following extended comparison of a concentration-camp inmate of Nazi Germany or the Soviet Union with other kinds of prisoners:

> Forced labor as a punishment is limited as to time and intensity. The convict retains his rights over his body; he is not absolutely tortured and he is not absolutely dominated. Banishment banishes only from one part of the world to another part of the world, also inhabited by human beings; it does not exclude from the human world altogether. Throughout history slavery has been an institution within a social order; slaves were not, like concentration-camp inmates, withdrawn from the sight and hence the protection of their fellow-men; as instruments of labor they had a definite price and as property a definite value. The concentration-camp inmate has no price, because he can always be replaced; nobody knows to whom he belongs, because he is never seen. From the point of view of normal society he is absolutely superfluous, although in times of acute labor shortage, as in Russia and in Germany during the war, he is used for work.—Hannah Arendt, *The Origins of Totalitarianism*

Though the author is concerned with defining the status of the concentration-camp inmate, she does so through a relative estimate that illuminates the special situation of each kind of prisoner or captive. Only through comparison to other kinds of imprisonment will we understand this new form.

MARIE WINN

MARIE WINN *is the author of numerous articles and books on parents and children—including* Children Without Childhood *(1983) and* Unplugging the Plug-In Drug *(1987). Her book on children and television,* The Plug-In Drug *(1977), is based on interviews with parents and children, social workers, teachers, and child psychologists in Denver and New York City. Winn is concerned about our experience with television and about what happens to children when it takes the place of reading. She believes that "a disposition toward 'openness,' " acquired through years of television viewing "has influenced adversely viewers' ability to concentrate, to read, to write clearly—in short, to demonstrate any of the verbal skills a literate society requires." Her comparison between reading and television viewing tells us why.*

Reading and Television

A comparison between reading and viewing may be made in respect to the pace of each experience, and the relative control a person has over that pace, for the pace may influence the ways one uses the material received in each experience. In addition, the pace of each experience may determine how much it intrudes upon other aspects of one's life. 1

The pace of reading, clearly, depends entirely upon the reader. He may read as slowly or as rapidly as he can or wishes to read. If he does not understand something, he may stop and reread it, or go in search of elucidation before continuing. The reader can accelerate his pace when the material is easy or less than interesting, and slow down when it is difficult or enthralling. If what he reads is moving, he can put down the book for a few moments and cope with his emotions without fear of losing anything. 2

The pace of the television experience cannot be controlled by the viewer; only its beginning and end are within his control as he clicks the knob on and off. He cannot slow down a delightful program or speed up a dreary one. He cannot "turn back" if a word or phrase is not understood. The program moves inexorably forward, and what is lost or misunderstood remains so. 3

Nor can the television viewer readily transform the material he receives into a form that might suit his particular emotional needs, as he invariably does with material he reads. The images move too quickly. He cannot use his own imagination to invest the people and events portrayed on television with the personal meanings that would help him understand and resolve relationships and conflicts in his own life; he is under the power of the imagination of the show's creators. In the television experience the eyes and ears are overwhelmed with the immediacy of sights and 4 sounds. They flash from the television set just fast enough for the eyes and ears to take them in before moving on quickly to the new pictures and sounds . . . so as *not to lose the thread.*

Not to lose the thread . . . it is this need, occasioned by the irreversible direction and relentless velocity of the television experience, that not only limits the workings of the viewer's imagination, but also causes television to intrude into human affairs far more than reading experiences can ever do. If someone enters the room while one is watching television—a friend, a relative, a child, someone, perhaps, one has not seen for some time—one must continue to watch or one will lose the thread. The greetings must wait, for the television program will not. A book, of course, can be set aside, with a pang of regret, perhaps, but with no sense of permanent loss.

QUESTIONS

1. What is the purpose of the comparison, according to paragraph 1?
2. What are the differences? In what order does Winn present them?
3. Does Winn say that we should give up television, or is she making no recommendation?
4. Do you agree with her description of reading and watching television? Is reading ever as compelling an experience as television for you?
5. Is the experience of watching a sports event on television much the same as reading about the event? If not, what are the differences? Do these similarities give support to Winn, or do they provide contrary evidence?

SUGGESTIONS FOR WRITING

1. In a few well-developed paragraphs, develop a comparison between one of the following pairs. State the purpose of your comparison somewhere in your essay, and draw conclusions as you discuss the similarities or differences.
   a. playing baseball (or another sport) and watching baseball
   b. listening to a particular kind of music and dancing to it

   c. reading a book and seeing the movie made from it

   d. riding a bicycle and driving a car on a busy highway

2. Compare the experience of reading a newspaper or newsmagazine with that of reading a novel or a textbook. Draw conclusions from your comparison at the end of your discussion.

3. The following activities require similar skills. First discuss these similarities, and then discuss the different skills also required:

   a. parallel parking and backing into a garage

   b. pruning a hedge and pruning a tree

   c. learning to ride a bike and learning to drive

   d. painting a chair and painting a room

J. BRONOWSKI

A mathematician, scientist, and writer, J. BRONOWSKI *(1908–1974) was born in Poland and educated in England. Coming to the United States in 1964, he taught at various universities and did scientific research at the Salk Institute of Biological Studies in San Diego. "We are a scientific civilization," he states in his book (and television series)* The Ascent of Man; *"that means, a civilization in which knowledge and its integrity are crucial. Science is only a Latin word for knowledge." Bronowski argues that we cannot afford to be ignorant or unconcerned about the values of science: "Knowledge is not a loose-leaf notebook of facts. Above all, it is a responsibility for the integrity of what we are, primarily of what we are as ethical creatures." Bronowski's comparison of the athlete and the gazelle, in* The Ascent of Man, *illustrates how facts of nature can help us understand ourselves as human beings.*

The Athlete and the Gazelle

Every human action goes back in some part to our animal   1 origins; we should be cold and lonely creatures if we were cut off from that blood-stream of life. Nevertheless, it is right to ask for a distinction: What are the physical gifts that man must share with the animals, and what are the gifts that make him different? Consider any example, the more straightforward the better—say, the simple action of an athlete when running or jumping. When he hears the gun, the starting response of the runner is the same as the flight response of the gazelle. He seems all animal in action. The heartbeat goes up; when he sprints at top speed the heart is pumping five times as much blood as normal, and ninety per cent of it is for the muscles. He needs twenty gallons of air a minute now to aerate his blood with the oxygen that it must carry to the muscles.

The violent coursing of the blood and intake of air can be   2
made visible, for they show up as heat on infra-red films which are sensitive to such radiation. (The blue or light zones are hottest; the red or dark zones are cooler.) The flush that we see and that the infra-red camera analyzes is a by-product that signals the limit of muscular action. For the main chemical action is to get energy for the muscles by burning sugar there; but three-quarters of that is lost as heat. And there is another limit, on the runner and the gazelle equally, which is more severe. At this speed, the chemical burn-up in the muscles is too fast to be complete. The waste products of incomplete burning, chiefly lactic acid, now foul up the blood. This is what causes fatigue, and blocks the muscle action until the blood can be cleansed with fresh oxygen.

So far, there is nothing to distinguish the athlete from   3
the gazelle—all that, in one way or another, is the normal metabolism of an animal in flight. But there is a cardinal difference: the runner was not in flight. The shot that set him off was the starter's pistol, and what he was experiencing, deliberately, was not fear but exaltation. The runner is like a child at play; his actions are an adventure in freedom, and the only purpose of his breathless chemistry was to explore the limits of his own strength.

Naturally there are physical differences between man   4
and the other animals, even between man and the apes. In the act of vaulting, the athlete grasps his pole, for example, with an exact grip that no ape can quite match. Yet such differences are secondary by comparison with the overriding

difference, which is that the athlete is an adult whose behavior is not driven by his immediate environment, as animal actions are. In themselves, his actions make no practical sense at all; they are an exercise that is not directed to the present. The athlete's mind is fixed ahead of him, building up his skill; and he vaults in imagination into the future.

Poised for that leap, the pole-vaulter is a capsule of 5 human abilities: the grasp of the hand, the arch of the foot, the muscles of the shoulder and pelvis—the pole itself, in which energy is stored and released like a bow firing an arrow. The radical character in that complex is the sense of foresight, that is, the ability to fix an objective ahead and rigorously hold his attention on it. The athlete's performance unfolds a continued plan; from one extreme to the other, it is the invention of the pole, the concentration of the mind at the moment before leaping, which give it the stamp of humanity.

QUESTIONS

1. What similarities between humans and animals does Bronowski develop through his example?
2. What are the differences between the pole vaulter and the gazelle and other animals discussed in these paragraphs?
3. In general, what are the physical traits that humans share with animals, and what gifts make humans different?
4. What other comparison between humans and animals could Bronowski have used to distinguish human from animal qualities?

SUGGESTIONS FOR WRITING

1. Compare and contrast one of the following pairs of activities, or a similar pair, to arrive at a relative estimate of them and to make a point:
   a. softball and hardball
   b. football and touch football
   c. jogging and running

    d. tennis and badminton

    e. checkers and chess

2. Do the same for one of the following pairs, or a similar pair, of activities:

    a. studying for examinations in different subjects

    b. repairing or changing an automobile tire and a bicycle tire

    c. driving in a small town and in a large city

BARRY LOPEZ

Barry Lopez, a writer and photographer, has written about the world of nature in numerous articles and books. These include Desert Notes *(1976),* Arctic Dreams *(1986), and* Crossing Open Ground *(1988). In 1986 he received the Award in Literature of the American Academy of Arts and Letters. The following excerpt is from* Of Wolves and Men, *which received the American Book Award for nonfiction in 1986. With his wife, Lopez raised two hybrid wolves at his Oregon home. On the basis of this and other experiences, Lopez disputes some recent conclusions of biologists. Wolves do kill healthy animals, sometimes beyond their needs, and they do on occasions kill people and one another: "Everything we have been told about wolves in the past should have been said, I think, with more care, with the preface that it is only a perception in a particular set of circumstances, that in the end it is only an opinion."*

The Indian and the Wolf

One of the problems that comes with trying to take a wider view of animals is that most of us have cut ourselves off from them conceptually. We do not think of ourselves as part of the animal kingdom. Indians did. They thought of themselves as The People (that is the translation from the native tongue of most tribal names) and of animals as The Wolves, The Bears, The Mice, and so forth. From here on in this chapter, the line between Indians and wolves may fade, not because Indians did not perceive the differences but because they were preoccupied with the similarities. They were inclined to compare and contrast their way of living with, say, the weasel's way or the eagle's way. They would say, "We are like wolves in that we . . ." They were anthropomorphic—and animistic. Highly so. We aren't talking, really, about our wolf anymore. We are talking about their wolf. We are, in a sense, in a foreign country.

The question the old Nunamiut man answered was an 2 eminently sensible one in his view. The caribou-hunting tactics of wolves in the Brooks Range and those of the Nunamiut *were* similar. And similarity in hunting technique in the same geographical area was found elsewhere. Wolves and Cree Indians in Alberta maneuvered buffalo out onto lake ice, where the big animals lost their footing and were more easily killed. Pueblo Indians and wolves in Arizona ran deer to exhaustion, though it might have taken the Pueblos a day to do it. Wolf and Shoshoni Indian lay flat on the prairie grass of Wyoming and slowly waved—the one its tail, the other a strip of hide—to attract curious but elusive antelope close enough to kill. And if we have made the right assumptions at Paleolithic sites in North America such as Folsom, early man killed mammoths in the same mobbing way wolves did, because men did not yet have extensions of themselves like the bow and arrow. They had to get in close with a spear and stab the animal to death.

The correspondence in life-styles, however, goes deeper 3 than this. Wolves ate grass, possibly as a scour against intestinal parasites; Indians ate wild plants for medicinal reasons. Both held and used hunting territories. Both were strongly familial and social in organization. To some extent both went to specific areas to hunt certain types of game. (Two or three wolf packs today come to hunt sheep at a place called Okokmilaga on the North Slope of Alaska's Brooks Range. Various tribes, Ponca and Sioux among them, traveled to the same leks in South Dakota to hunt sage grouse.) Both wolf and Indian had a sign language. The tribe, like the pack, broke up at certain times of the year, and joined together later to hunt more efficiently. In times of scarcity, Indian hunters ate first; this also seems to be the case with wolves.

Highly intriguing is the fact that white-tailed deer in 4 Minnesota sought security from Indian hunters by moving into the border area between warring tribes, where hunters were least likely to show up, and the fact that deer do the same with respect to wolves—seek security along the border zones between wolf territories, where wolves spend the least time hunting.

The most interesting correspondence between wolf and 5 Indian, however, may be that involving the perception of territory.

When Indians left their own country and entered that of 6 another tribe—a group of young Assiniboin warriors, for example, sneaking off on foot into the country of the Gros Ventre to steal horses—they moved like wolves: in small packs; at night and during the crepuscular hours; taking advantage of ground contours to observe but remain hidden; moving in and out of the foreign territory quickly. Often on foot and in unfamiliar surroundings, they had to remain invisible to the inhabitants. Elusiveness, therefore, was a quality Indians cultivated and admired. It served them as well as it served the wolf who, in a hard winter, trespasses into neighboring packs' territories to look for food, to make a kill, and to go home before anyone knows he's been there.

The definition and defense of home range was as 7 important to the Indian as it seems to be to the wolf. The defense was mostly of food resources in general and of the physical area adjacent to the village in particular; under certain circumstances trespassers were killed. If a party of Flathead warriors was surprised in northern Idaho by a party of resident Kutenai, the Flatheads might be attacked and killed to a man. If it was bitter cold and storming, they might signal each other that it was too cold to fight (wolves probably wouldn't). If the Flathead party was reduced to one man who fought bravely and was thought, therefore, to have strong medicine, he might be let go. Fatal encounters and nonfatal encounters between trespassing and resident wolves bear a striking similarity. In Minnesota, for example, in 1975, a small pack of wolves moving through the territory of a much larger pack was suddenly surprised by the larger pack. One animal in the small pack was killed, two ran off, and the fourth, a female, held ten or eleven wolves to a standoff in a river before they all withdrew and left her.

Some tribes were stricter about boundaries and more 8 bellicose about trespassing incidents than others, as are some wolf packs. The boundaries of most Indian territories, like those of wolves, were fluid; they changed with the movement of the game herds, the size of the tribe, the evolution of tribal divisions, and the time of year. For both wolf and Indian, where the principal game animal was nonmigratory, as deer and moose are, territorial boundaries were more important than they were in areas where principal game species were migratory, like caribou. There are instances where neighboring wolf packs have fought each other and then joined territories, just as some tribes established alliances—the five nations of the Iroquois, for example. And I mentioned earlier that the Pawnee and Omaha, traditional enemies, had an agreement whereby each could enter the other's territory to hunt buffalo.

The Indian practice of passing family hunting territories 9 on to succeeding generations throws even more light on this interesting correspondence of territorial spacing, hunting rights, and trespassing. Family hunting territories were most important, again, where food could be found in the same place all the time. The salmon-eating tribes on the northwest coast and the Algonkian deer eaters in the northeastern woodlands both had appropriate family and clan hunting territories that were passed from one generation to the next. Among the Tlingit, a northwest coast tribe, each family had its own place on the rivers where it fished and an area where it gathered berries. No one else would fish or berry there unless invited to do so. In the eastern woodlands, especially in northeastern Minnesota, resident wolves seem to have a strong sense of territory as defined by the major food source (white-tailed deer), at least as strong as the family hunting territories that existed in that same country when the Chippewa lived there.

Which leads to another thought, more abstract, about 10 trespassing. It was often assumed that Plains Indians went out intending to kill their rivals. This was not true. They went out to deliberately face rivals in a very dangerous game. The danger itself, the threat of death, was the thrill, not killing; and to engage in it repeatedly was recognized as a way to prove strength of character. Analogously, it might be valuable to consider the encounters of rival wolves as a similar kind of deadly recreation. Just as intriguing is the idea that some game animals assent to a chase-without-death with wolves. Caribou and yearling wolves, for example, are often seen in harmless chases getting a taste of death. Building spirit. Training. Wolf *and* caribou.

That wolves and Neolithic hunting people in North America resembled each other as predators was not the result of conscious imitation. It was convergent evolution, the most successful way for meat eaters to live. Conscious *identification* with the wolf, on the other hand, especially among Indians on the Great Plains, was a mystical experience based on a penetrating perception of the wolf's lifeway, its gestalt. And it could, on occasion, become conscious imitation. 11

Native American perceptions of the wolf varied largely according to whether or not a tribe was agricultural. It was naturally among the hunting tribes that the wolf played the greater mythic-religious role because the wolf himself was a great hunter, not a great farmer. He was retained for a while in the mythology of agricultural tribes and regarded by them as an animal of great power and mystery, but his place there was slowly eclipsed by anthropomorphic gods of the harvest. 12

In the native American cosmology, insofar as it can be regarded as the same from tribe to tribe, the universe was perceived in six directions: the space above; that below; and the four cardinal divisions of the world horizon. Frequently on the plains the bear represented the west, the mountain lion the north, the wolf the east, and the wildcat the south. They were regarded as the creatures with the greatest power and influence in the spirit world. 13

It should be understood, however, that the Indian did not rank-order animals. Each creature, from deer mouse to meadowlark, was respected for the qualities it best seemed to epitomize; when those particular qualities were desired by someone, that animal was approached as one who knew much about that thing. The animals assigned the greatest cosmological significance—the bear, lion, wolf, cat, and 14 eagle—were not regarded as the "best" animals. They were chosen primarily because they were the great hunters. The stealth of the cats, the endurance of the wolf, the strength of the bear, the vision of the eagle—these were the qualities held in high esteem by human hunters.

The Pawnee of present-day Nebraska and Kansas dif- 15 fered from most other tribes in that they divided their world horizon into four semicardinal points, assigning the wolf to the southeast. In the Pawnee cosmogony the wolf was also set in the sky as a star, along with the bear and the two cats, to guard the primal female presence, the Evening Star. The Wolf Star was red—the color associated with the wolf by virtually every tribe (red did not signify blood; it was simply an esteemed color).

In time, the wolf became associated among the four 16 seasons with summer, among the trees on the plains with the willow, among the great natural forces with clouds (the others being wind, thunder, and lightning).

Like the Nunamiut, most Indians respected the wolf's 17 prowess as a hunter, especially his ability to always secure game, his stamina, the way he moved smoothly and silently across the landscape. They were moved by his howling, which they sometimes regarded as talking with the spirit world. The wolf appears in many of their legends as a messenger in fact, a great long-distance traveler, a guide for anyone seeking the spirit world. Blind Bull, for example, a Cheyenne shaman, was highly respected among his people before his death in 1885 as one who had learned about things from the comings and goings of wolves, from listening to their howls. The wolves, for their part, took Blind Bull's messages to various places in the real and spiritual world. The wolf as oracle, as interlocutor with the dead, is an old idea.

The wolf was also held in high regard because, though 18 he was a fiercely loyal familial animal, he was also one who took the role of provider for the larger community (for carrion eaters like the fox and raven). This was something that tribal Indians understood very well, for in difficult times a man had the dual responsibility of feeding his own family as well as others. An Hidatsa man named Bear in the Flat acknowledged this lifeway of the wolf when he took as one of his sacred medicine songs the "Invitation Song" of the wolf—the howl the wolf used to call coyotes, foxes, and magpies to the remains of his kill. (The situation is neatly imitated among Bella Coola hunters, who sing a song to call the wolf to one of *their* kills—a bear. They would take a bear's hide but believed bears did not wish to be eaten by humans.)

The interrelationships between one's allegiance to self 19 and household on the one hand and one's duty to the larger community on the other cannot be overemphasized; it was a primal, efficient system of survival that held both man and wolf in a similar mesh.

Consider again the Indian's perception. 20

Each of the animals—mosquitoes, elk, mice—belonged 21 to a separate tribe. Each had special powers, but each was dependent on the others for certain services. When, for example, the Indian left his buffalo kill, he called out to the magpies and others to come and eat. The dead buffalo nourished the grasses; the grasses in turn fed the elk and provided the mouse with straw for a nest; the mouse, for his part, instructed the Indian in magic; and the Indian called on his magic to kill buffalo.

With such a strong sense of the interdependence among 22 all creatures and an acute awareness of the ways in which his own life resembled the wolf's (hunting for himself, hunting for his family, defending his tribe against enemy attack as the wolf protected the den against the grizzly), the Indian naturally turned to the wolf as a paradigm—a mirror reflection. He wished directly for that power ("Hear me, Great Spirit! I wish to be like the wolf'"); and he imitated him homeopathically by wearing his skin. He wished always to be as well integrated in his environment as he could *see* the wolf was in the universe. Imagine him saying: "Help me to fit, to be valuable in the world, like the wolf."

To fit into the universe, the Indian had to do two things 23 simultaneously: be strong as an individual, and submerge his personal feelings for the good of the tribe. In the eyes of many native Americans, no other animal did this as well as the wolf.

The wolf fulfilled two roles for the Indian: he was a 24 powerful and mysterious animal, and so perceived by most tribes; and he was a medicine animal, identified with a particular individual, tribe, or clan. In the first role he was simply an object of interest, for reasons already given. He might be marginally so in the eyes of some (most California tribes, where there were no wolves, thought little of the wolf) or of major importance to others (Cheyenne, Sioux, Pawnee).

At a *tribal* level, the attraction of the wolf was strong 25 because the wolf lived in a way that made the tribe strong: he provided food that all, even the sick and old, could eat; he saw to the education of his children; he defended his territory against other wolves. At a *personal* level, those for whom the wolf was a medicine animal or personal totem understood the qualities that made the wolf stand out as an individual; for example, his stamina and ability to track well and go without food for long periods.

That each perception contributed to and reinforced the 26 other—as the individual grows stronger, the tribe grows stronger, and vice versa—is what made the wolf such a significant animal in the eyes of hunting peoples. The inclination of white men to regard individual and social motivations in themselves as separate led them to misunderstand the Indian. The Indian was so well integrated in his environment that his motivation was almost hidden; his lifeway was as mysterious to white men as the wolf's.

This is obviously a complex thought, but in the light of 27 it, the Indian's preoccupation with wolves becomes more than quaint. The wolf was the one animal that, again, did two things at once year after year: remained distinct and exemplary as an individual, yet served the tribe. There are no stories among Indians of lone wolves.

This association with, and imitation of, the wolf among 28 American Indians was absolutely pervasive. The two great clan divisions of the northwest coast tribes were the wolf and the raven. One of the three divisions of the southern Arapaho were *Haqihana*, the wolves; one of the ten Caddo bands were *Tasha*, the wolf. A Cherokee setting out in winter on a long journey rubbed his feet with ashes and, singing a wolf song, moved a few steps in imitation of the wolf, whose feet he knew were protected from frostbite, as he wished his to be. Nez Perce warriors wore a wolf tooth pushed through the septum of their noses. Cheyenne medicine men wrapped wolf fur around the sacred arrows used to motion antelope into a trap. Arikara men wove wolf hair and buffalo hair together in small sacred blankets. Bella Coola mothers painted a wolf's gallbladder on a young child's back so he would grow up to perform religious ceremonies without making mistakes as a hunter. An Hidatsa woman experiencing a difficult birth might call on the familial power of the wolf by rubbing her belly with a wolf skin cap.

VOCABULARY

paragraph 1: anthropomorphic, animistic
paragraph 2: elusive, Paleolithic, mammoths
paragraph 6: crepuscular
paragraph 8: bellicose, migratory
paragraph 10: abstract
paragraph 11: Neolithic, convergent evolution, gestalt
paragraph 14: cosmological, stealth
paragraph 15: semicardinal, cosmogony
paragraph 19: mesh
paragraph 22: paradigm, homeopathically

QUESTIONS

1. What reason does Lopez give for stressing the similarities between Indians and wolves rather than the differences?
2. Lopez begins his comparison in paragraph 2 with the similarity in hunting tactics. Why does he consider this similarity less important than the similarities he focuses on in the paragraphs that follow?
3. To which similarities does he give the most attention, and how does he explain these similarities in paragraph 11 and the paragraphs following?
4. What special qualities does the Indian attribute to the wolf in contrast to other animals? Why does Lopez stress these differences?
5. Is he developing a relative estimate of Indians *and* wolves, or is his main concern with one of these? What do the concluding paragraphs show to be the purpose of the comparison?

SUGGESTIONS FOR WRITING

1. Lopez shows us the attitude of North American Indians toward wolves. Each of us develops attitudes toward particular animals in the course of growing up. Discuss how your family or school or the media shaped your attitude toward a species like dogs or cats or wolves or snakes or perhaps toward animals in general. If your attitudes are conflicting ones, try to account for the conflict.

2. We make discoveries about ourselves and about animals in raising or caring for a pet animal. Discuss a particular experience in raising or caring for an animal and the personal discovery that resulted.

EDWARD T. HALL

EDWARD T. HALL, *professor of anthropology at Northwestern University from 1967 to 1977, has studied the cultures of many peoples of the world, especially the culture of the Pueblo Indians of the Southwest. His books include* The Silent Language *(1959) and* Beyond Culture *(1976). In* The Hidden Dimension *(1966) Hall states a major theme of his many writings on culture and the nonverbal forms of language: "Contrary to common belief, the many diverse groups that make up our country have proved to be surprisingly persistent in maintaining their separate identities. Superficially, these groups may all look alike and sound somewhat alike but beneath the surface there lie manifold unstated, unformulated differences in the structuring of time, space, materials, and relationships. It is these very things that, though they give significance to our lives, so often result in the distortion of meaning regardless of good intentions when peoples of different cultures interact." In this section Hall combines contrast with other methods of analysis in discussing how people perceive space in different ways. The word* proxemics *is a term coined by Hall for "the interrelated observations and theories of man's use of space as a specialized elaboration of culture."*

The English and the Americans

It has been said that the English and the Americans are two 1
great people separated by one language. The differences for
which language gets blamed may not be due so much to
words as to communications on other levels beginning with
English intonation (which sounds affected to many Americans) and continuing to ego-linked ways of handling time,
space, and materials. If there ever were two cultures in
which differences of the proxemic details are marked it is in
the educated (public school) English and the middle-class
Americans. One of the basic reasons for this wide disparity is
that in the United States we use space as a way of classifying
people and activities, whereas in England it is the social
system that determines who you are. In the United States,
your address is an important cue to status (this applies not
only to one's home but to the business address as well). The
Joneses from Brooklyn and Miami are not as "in" as the
Joneses from Newport and Palm Beach. Greenwich and
Cape Code are worlds apart from Newark and Miami.
Businesses located on Madison and Park avenues have more
tone than those on Seventh and Eighth avenues. A corner
office is more prestigious than one next to the elevator or at
the end of a long hall. The Englishman, however, is born and
brought up in a social system. He is still Lord—no matter
where you find him, even if it is behind the counter in a
fishmonger's stall. In addition to class distinctions, there are
differences between the English and ourselves in how space
is allotted.

The middle-class American growing up in the United 2
States feels he has a right to have his own room, or at least
part of a room. My American subjects, when asked to draw
an ideal room or office, invariably drew it for themselves and
no one else. When asked to draw their present room or
office, they drew only their own part of a shared room and
then drew a line down the middle. Both male and female
subjects identified the kitchen and the master bedroom as
belonging to the mother or the wife, whereas Father's
territory was a study or a den, if one was available; otherwise, it was "the shop," "the basement," or sometimes only
a workbench or the garage. American women who want to

be alone can go to the bedroom and close the door. The closed door is the sign meaning "Do not disturb" or "I'm angry." An American is available if his door is open at home or at his office. He is expected not to shut himself off but to maintain himself in a state of constant readiness to answer the demands of others. Closed doors are for conferences, private conversations, and business, work that requires concentration, study, resting, sleeping, dressing, and sex.

The middle- and upper-class Englishman, on the other 3 hand, is brought up in a nursery shared with brothers and sisters. The oldest occupies a room by himself which he vacates when he leaves for boarding school, possibly even at the age of nine or ten. The difference between a room of one's own and early conditioning to shared space, while seeming inconsequential, has an important effect on the Englishman's attitude toward his own space. He may never have a permanent "room of his own" and seldom expects one or feels he is entitled to one. Even Members of Parliament have no offices and often conduct their business on the terrace overlooking the Thames. As a consequence, the English are puzzled by the American need for a secure place in which to work, an office. Americans working in England may become annoyed if they are not provided with what they consider appropriate enclosed work space. In regard to the need for walls as a screen for the ego, this places the Americans somewhere between the Germans and the English.

The contrasting English and American patterns have 4 some remarkable implications, particularly if we assume that man, like other animals, has a built-in need to shut himself off from others from time to time. An English student in one of my seminars typified what happens when hidden patterns clash. He was quite obviously experiencing strain in his relationships with Americans. Nothing seemed to go right and it was quite clear from his remarks that we did not know how to behave. An analysis of his complaints showed that a major source of irritation was that no American seemed to be able to pick up the subtle clues that there were times when he didn't want his thoughts intruded on. As he stated it, "I'm walking around the apartment and it seems that whenever I want to be alone my roommate starts talking to me.

Pretty soon he's asking 'What's the matter?' and wants to know if I'm angry. By then I am angry and say something."

It took some time but finally we were able to identify most of the contrasting features of the American and British problems that were in conflict in this case. When the American wants to be alone he goes into a room and shuts the door—he depends on architectural features for screening. For an American to refuse to talk to someone else present in the same room, to give them the "silent treatment," is the ultimate form of rejection and a sure sign of great displeasure. The English, on the other hand, lacking rooms of their own since childhood, never developed the practice of using space as a refuge from others. They have in effect internalized a set of barriers, which they erect and which others are supposed to recognize. Therefore, the more the Englishman shuts himself off when he is with an American the more likely the American is to break in to assure himself that all is well. Tension lasts until the two get to know each other. The important point is that the spatial and architectural needs of each are not the same at all.

VOCABULARY

paragraph 1: intonation, ego-linked, fishmonger

QUESTIONS

1. What is Hall's thesis, and where does he first state it? Where does he restate it later in the essay?
2. How does he organize the contrast between the English and the Americans? Does he contrast the English and American patterns point by point or in blocks? Or does he mix these methods of organization?
3. How does he illustrate these patterns? Does he illustrate all of them?
4. Hall traces cause-and-effect relations through contrast of living patterns. What are the chief relations he traces?
5. How do the examples explain the phrase *internalized a set of barriers,* in the concluding paragraph? What does Hall mean by *screening?*

6. What use does he make of classification in the whole essay? On what basis does he divide the English and the Americans?

7. To what extent does Hall clarify a misunderstanding you have had with a roommate or friend?

SUGGESTIONS FOR WRITING

1. Discuss the extent to which your study habits fit the English or the American pattern. Use your analysis to comment on the accuracy of Hall's thesis.

2. Contrast two of your friends or relatives on the basis of their attitudes toward space and architecture or toward privacy. State the similarities before commenting on the differences. Notice that the differences may be slight ones, and even slight differences may be revealing of people.

RICHARD SELZER

For many years a surgeon and member of the faculty of the Yale School of Medicine, RICHARD SELZER *has written on medicine and the art of surgery in* Mortal Lessons (*1976*), Letters to a Young Doctor (*1982*), Confessions of a Knife (*1986*), *and* Taking the World in for Repairs (*1986*). *He is also the author of a collection of stories,* Rituals of Surgery (*1974*). *In the following essay, published in* The New York Times Magazine *August 21, 1988, Selzer describes his two vocations of writing and medicine.*

The Pen and the Scalpel

I had been a general surgeon for 15 years when, at the age of 40, the psychic energy for writing inexplicably appeared. It was an appearance that was to knock over my life. For 15 years I had studied, practiced and taught surgery at the Yale School of Medicine, all the while enjoying the usefulness and the *handsomeness* of the craft. For the next 16 years, until my recent retirement, I would practice both surgery and writing. But where to fit in the writing when all of my days and half of my nights were fully engaged? Certainly not evenings. In the evening, one visits with one's next-of-kin; in the evening one helps with homework; in the evening, if one is so inclined, one has a martini. Instead, I became the first adult in the state of Connecticut to go to bed in the evening. Having slept from 8:30 P.M. to 1 in the morning, I rose, went down to the kitchen, put on a pot of tea and wrote in longhand (a typewriter would disturb the household) until precisely 3 o'clock. Then it was back upstairs and to sleep until 6 in the morning, when I began the day's doctoring. Plenty of sleep, only divided by two hours, when I was alone with my pen, and all the light in the world gathered upon a sheet of paper. In this way, I wrote three collections of stories, essays and memoirs.

Time was when in the professions—medicine and law—to patronize the arts was respectable; to practice them was not. For a surgeon it was even more questionable. Who wants to know, after all, what a surgeon does in his spare time? When it became known how I was spending my wild nights, my colleagues at the hospital were distressed. "Come, come" they coaxed in (more or less) the words of the poet Richard Wilbur, "Forsake those roses of the mind, and tend the true, the moral flower." But because the subject of my writings was my work as a doctor, the two seemed inseparable. The one fertilized the other. Why, I wondered, doesn't every surgeon write? A doctor walks in and out of a dozen short stories a day. It is irresistible to write them down. When, at last, the time came to make a choice between my two passions, it had already been made for me. Listen:

In the operating room, the patient must be anesthetized in order that he feel no pain. The surgeon too must be "anesthetized" in order to remain at some distance from the event: when he cuts the patient, his own flesh must not bleed. It is this seeming lack of feeling that gives the surgeon the image of someone who is out of touch with his humanity, a person wanting only to cut, to perform. I assure you that it is the image only. A measure of insulation against the laying open of the bodies of his fellow human beings is necessary for the well-being of both patient and doctor. In surgery, if nowhere else, dispassion is an attribute. But the surgeon-writer is not anesthetized. He remains awake; sees everything; censors nothing. It is his dual role to open and repair the body of his patient and to report back to the waiting world in the keenest language he can find. By becoming a writer, I had stripped off the protective carapace. It was time to go. A surgeon can unmake himself; a writer cannot.

A Faustian bargain, you say? Perhaps, but, truth to tell, 4 New Haven had begun to seem rather like the Beast With a Thousand Gallbladders. And where is it graven in stone that, once having been ordained, a surgeon must remain at the operating table until the scalpel slips from his lifeless fingers? Nor had I any wish to become like the old lion whose claws are long since blunt but not the desire to use them. Still, one does not walk away from the workbench of one's life with a cheery wave of the hand. In the beginning, I felt a strange sense of dislocation. As though I were standing near a river whose banks were flowing while the stream itself stood still. Only now, after two years, have I ceased to have attacks of longing for the labor that so satisfied and uplifted my spirit. Then, too, there was the risk that by withdrawing from the hospital, with its rich cargo of patients and those who tend them, I would be punished as a writer, suffer from impotence of the pen. A writer turns his back upon his native land at his own peril. Besides, to begin the life of a writer at the age of 56 is to toil under the very dart of death. As did another doctor-writer, John Keats, I too "have fears that I may cease to be before my pen has gleaned my teeming brain."

In medicine, there is a procedure called transillumina- 5 tion. If, in a darkened room, a doctor holds a bright light against a hollow part of the body, he will see through the outer tissues to the structures within that cavity—arteries, veins, projecting shelves of bone. In such a ruby gloom he can distinguish among a hernia, a hydrocele of the scrotum and tumor of the testicle. Or he can light up a sinus behind the brow. Unlike surgery, which opens the body to direct examination, transillumination gives an indirect vision, calling into play the simplest perceptions of the doctor. To write about a patient is like transillumination. You hold the lamp of language against his body and gaze through the covering layers at the truths within.

At first glance, it would appear that surgery and writing 6 have little in common, but I think that is not so. For one thing, they are both sub-celestial arts; as far as I know, the angels disdain to perform either one. In each of them you hold a slender instrument that leaves a trail wherever it is applied. In one, there is the shedding of blood; in the other it is ink that is spilled upon a page. In one, the scalpel is restrained; in the other, the pen is given rein. The surgeon sutures together the tissues of the body to make whole what is sick or injured; the writer sews words into sentences to fashion a new version of human experience. A surgical operation is rather like a short story. You make the incision, rummage around inside for a bit, then stitch up. It has a beginning, a middle and an end. If I were to choose a medical specialist to write a novel, it would be a psychiatrist. They tend to go on and on. And on.

Despite that I did not begin to write until the middle of 7 my life, I think I must always have been a writer. Like my father who was a general practitioner during the Depression in Troy, N.Y., and who wrote a novel. It was all about a prostitute with a heart of gold (her name was Goldie!) and the doctor who first saves her life, then falls in love with her. Mother read it and told him: "Keep it away from the children."

Father's office was on the ground floor of an old 8 brownstone, and we lived upstairs. At night, after office hours, my brother Billy and I (we were 10 and 9 years old) would sneak downstairs to Father's darkened consultation room and there, shamefaced, by the light of a candle stub, we would take down from the shelves his medical textbooks. Our favorite was "The Textbook of Obstetrics and Gynecology."

It was there that I first became aware of the rich 9 language of medicine. Some of the best words began with the letter C. *Carcinoma*, I read, and thought it was that aria from "Rigoletto" that mother used to sing while she washed and dried the dishes. *Cerebellum*. I said the word aloud, letting it drip off the end of my tongue like melted chocolate. And I read *choledochojejunostomy*, which I later was to learn was the name of an operation. All those syllables marching off in my mind to that terminal *y*! If that was the way surgeons talked, I thought, I would be one of them, and live forever in a state of mellifluous rapture. I do not use these words in my writing, but I do try to use the language that evokes the sounds of the body—the *lub-dup, lub-dup* of the garrulous heart, the gasp and wheeze of hard breathing, all the murmur and splash of anatomy and physiology. And I have tried to make use of the poetic potential in scientific language. Here, from my diary, this specimen:

How gentle the countryside near Troy, with much 10 farming everywhere. Farming gives a sense of health to the land. It is replenishing to watch at dusk as a herd of cattle flows like a giant amoeba toward the barn. First one cow advances. She pauses. Another pseudopodium is thrust ahead, pulling the others behind it until all of the cytoplasm, trailing milk, is inside the barn. All along the banks of the Hudson River, oak, elm and locust trees have grown very tall. The bark of the locust is thrown into deep folds coated with lichen and moss. So old are these trees that, without the least wind, one will drop off a quite large branch as if to shed a part of its burden. This letting-fall doesn't seem to do the tree any harm. It is more an anatomical relinquishment of a part so that the whole might remain healthy. Much as a diabetic will accept amputation of a gangrenous toe in order that he might once again walk on his foot. How clever of these locust trees to require no surgeon for their trimmage, only their own corporeal wisdom.

VOCABULARY

paragraph 1: psychic, inexplicably

paragraph 2: patronize

paragraph 3: insulation, dispassion, attribute, carapace

paragraph 4: Faustian, ordained, blunt, dislocation

paragraph 5: hernia, hydrocele

paragraph 6: sub-celestial, suture

paragraph 8: obstetrics, gynecology

paragraph 9: mellifluous, evoke, garrulous, specimen

paragraph 10: replenishing, amoeba, pseudopodium, cytoplasm, relinquishment, gangrenous, corporeal

QUESTIONS

1. How did his work as a surgeon prepare Selzer to become a writer?
2. Does Selzer compare surgery and writing in blocks or point by point? How many similarities and differences does Selzer discuss?
3. In what sense of the word must the surgeon be "anesthetized"? Why must the surgeon-writer not be anesthetized?
4. Is the reader referring to surgery or writing in asking about a "Faustian bargain" in paragraph 4?
5. What is transillumination, and how is writing similar to it? Why does Selzer introduce this comparison in paragraph 5?
6. How did childhood experiences prepare Selzer to become a writer? Why does Selzer conclude the essay with these experiences, instead of opening the essay with them?
7. What does the sample from Selzer's diary show?

SUGGESTIONS FOR WRITING

1. Discuss experiences in your own childhood or adolescence that generated interest in a type of work or career. Discuss later decisions and acts that resulted from these experiences.
2. Selzer discusses two different occupations, surgery and writing, each of which nurtured the other. Discuss two interests or occupations with which you have had a similar experience. In the course of your discussion, cite similarities as well as differences, developing your comparision in blocks or point by point.

ANALOGY

❧ ❧ ❧

Illustrative *analogy* is a special kind of example, a comparison, usually point by point, between two quite different things or activities for the purpose of explanation—a child growing like a tender plant and needing sun, water, and a receptive soil as well as proper care from a skilled gardener. But there are differences also, and if there is danger of the analogy being carried too far (children are not so tender that they need as much protection as plants from the hazards of living), the writer may state these differences to limit the inferences readers may draw. The writer has chosen the analogy for the sake of vivid illustration and nothing more. We will see later that analogy is often used in argument: children *should* be fully protected from various hazards because they are tender plants. The argument will stand or fall depending on how convinced we are of the similarities and of the unimportance of the differences.

Analogy is often used in explanations of scientific ideas. One of the most famous is Fred Hoyle's analogy between the moving apart of the galaxies in the universe and an expanding raisin cake:

> Suppose the cake swells uniformly as it cooks, but the raisins themselves remain of the same size. Let each raisin represent a cluster of galaxies, and imagine yourself inside one of them. As the cake swells, you will observe that all the other raisins move away from you. Moreover, the farther away the raisin, the faster it will seem to move. When the cake has swollen to twice its initial dimensions, the distance between all the raisins will have doubled itself—two raisins that were initially an inch apart will now be two inches apart; two raisins that were a foot apart will have moved two feet apart. Since the entire action takes place within the same time interval, obviously the more distant raisins must move apart faster than those close at hand. So it happens with the clusters of galaxies.

And Hoyle draws a further conclusion from his analogy:

> No matter which raisin you happen to be inside, the others will always move away from you. Hence the fact that we observe all the

199

other galaxies to be moving away from us does not mean that we are situated at the center of the universe. Indeed, it seems certain that the universe has no center. A cake may be said to have a center only because it has a boundary. We must imagine the cake to extend outward without any boundary, an infinite cake, so to speak, which means that however much cake we care to consider there is always more.—"When Time Began"

Hoyle points out the limits of the analogy in these final sentences. One advantage of the raisin analogy is the disparity of size between a raisin and a galaxy—a system of sometimes billions of stars occupying an enormous amount of space. The disparity in size provides a relative estimate of size in the universe.

PAUL DAVIES

Paul Davies *is a professor of mathematical physics at the University of Adelaide in Australia and the author of* Other Worlds *(1980),* Superforce *(1984), and other books that explain the new physics to the general reader. In* Other Worlds *Davies uses an analogy to explain how, according to the Big Bang theory of the origin of the universe, matter expanded in all directions from an "initial singularity" or original compact mass of energy. This expansion slowed down after the initial explosion. Davies asks the following question: "Out of all the unremarkable chaotic motions with which the universe could have emerged from the big bang, why has it chosen such a disciplined and specialized pattern of expansion?"*

The Expanding Universe

There is a helpful analogy to the expanding universe which should clarify the issue. Consider a large group of people in a tight huddle. Each person represents a region of space enclosed within its own horizon—a "bubble" of space—so to represent the fact that there is no communication between bubbles we equip everyone with blindfolds. Thus, each person is ignorant of the behavior of his fellows. The compact group represents the initial singularity, and when a whistle is blown, the people all start to run in straight lines away from the center of the huddle: the universe expands. The group spreads out in a sort of ring. The runners have instructions that they must adjust their stride so that the ring remains as circular as possible as it expands, but none of the runners knows how fast his neighbors are running, so each picks a random speed. The result is, almost certainly, a ragged, distorted line, very far from circular. There is, of course, a small chance that purely by accident all the runners will match their strides, but it is obviously pretty unlikely. What is observed of the universe today corresponds to a ring of runners so nearly circular that there is no detectable distortion in its shape. How can this have happened: is it a miracle? About ten years ago an ingenious suggestion was made to try and explain this curious symmetry. In the language of the runners it amounts to the following. When the group explodes outwards, some runners will inevitably run faster than their neighbors. However, after a while, fatigue will set in and they will slow down. Their colleagues, on the other hand, will not have dissipated their energy so rapidly and will have enough stamina to catch up. The end result will be, after a long enough time, an approximately circular ring of rather exhausted runners, plodding doggedly outwards at a considerably reduced rate.

Translated into cosmological language, the idea is this. In the primeval universe, some regions of space expanded rather more energetically (i.e. faster) than others, and some directions were vigorously stretched while others spread out more sluggishly. Dissipative effects began to sap the energy of the more vigorous motions and slow them down, enabling the sluggish motions to catch up. In the end the turbulent and chaotic early state is damped down and reduced to a rather slow and quiescent motion, with a high degree of uniformity, precisely as observed.

VOCABULARY

paragraph 1: symmetry, dissipated
paragraph 2: cosmological, primeval, turbulent, quiescent

QUESTIONS

1. Each runner in the analogy represents a portion of the compact energy that expands in the Big Bang. To explain the Big Bang, why does Davies blindfold each runner?
2. Why was the ring of runners not a perfect circle in earlier stages of the expansion?
3. How does Davies explain the nearly circular ring observable today by astronomers?
4. What questions about the Big Bang does the analogy not explain for you?

SUGGESTION FOR WRITING

Compare the analogy of Davies with that of Hoyle (p. 199), noting both similarities and differences and the advantages of each in explaining the Big Bang. Is one analogy more effective than the other, or are the analogies equally effective?

LOREN EISELEY

Loren Eiseley (*1907–1977*) *was Benjamin Franklin Professor of Anthropology at the University of Pennsylvania. His many books on human beings, their society, and their origins include* The Immense Journey (*1969*), The Unexpected Universe (*1969*), *and* The Night Country (*1971*). *Eiseley had the gift of making highly complex ideas clear to readers who know little about science. In this section from* The Invisible Pyramid (*1972*), *he uses brief, revealing analogies to help the reader to imagine one such idea.*

The Cosmic Prison

This, then, is the secret nature of the universe over which the   1
ebullient senator so recklessly proclaimed our absolute mastery. Time in that universe is in excess of ten billion years. It
recedes backward into a narrowing funnel where, at some
inconceivable point of concentration, the monobloc containing all the matter that composes the galaxies exploded in the
one gigantic instant of creation.

Along with that explosion space itself is rushing out-   2
ward. Stars and the great island galaxies in which they
cluster are more numerous than the blades of grass upon a
plain. To speak of man as "mastering" such a cosmos is
about the equivalent of installing a grasshopper as Secretary
General of the United Nations. Worse, in fact, for no matter
what system of propulsion man may invent in the future, the
galaxies on the outer rim of visibility are fleeing faster than
he can approach them. Moreover, the light that he is
receiving from them left its source in the early history of the
planet earth. There is no possible way of even establishing
their present existence. As the British astronomer Sir Bernard Lovell has so appropriately remarked, "At the limit of
present-day observations our information is a few billion
years out of date."

Light travels at a little over one hundred and eighty-six   3
thousand miles a second, far beyond the conceivable speed
of any spaceship devised by man, yet it takes light something
like one hundred thousand years just to travel across the star
field of our own galaxy, the Milky Way. It has been estimated
that to reach the nearest star to our own, four light-years
away, would require, at the present speed of our spaceships,
a time equivalent to more than the whole of written history,
indeed one hundred thousand earthly years would be a
closer estimate—a time as long, perhaps, as the whole existence of *Homo sapiens* upon earth. And the return, needless
to state, would consume just as long a period.

Even if our present rocket speeds were stepped up by a   4
factor of one hundred, human generations would pass on
the voyage. An unmanned probe into the nearer galactic
realms would be gone so long that its intended mission, in

fact the country which sent it forth, might both have vanished into the mists of history before its messages began to be received. All this, be it noted, does not begin to involve us in those intergalactic distances across which a radio message from a cruising spaceship might take hundreds of years to be received and a wait of other hundreds before a reply would filter back.

We are, in other words, truly in the position of the blood 5
cell exploring our body. We are limited in time, by analogy a miniature replica of the cosmos, since we too individually ascend from a primordial atom, exist, and grow in space, only to fall back in dissolution. We cannot, in terms of the time dimension as we presently know it, either travel or survive the interstellar distances.

Two years ago I chanced to wander with a group of 6
visiting scholars into a small planetarium in a nearby city. In the dark in a remote back seat, I grew tired and fell asleep while a lecture was progressing. My eyes had closed upon a present-day starry night as represented in the northern latitudes. After what seemed in my uneasy slumber the passage of a long period of time, I started awake in the dark, my eyes fixed in amazement upon the star vault overhead. All was quiet in the neighboring highbacked seats. I could see no one. Suddenly I seemed adrift under a vast and unfamiliar sky. Constellations with which I was familiar had shifted, grown minute, or vanished. I rubbed my eyes. This was not the universe in which I had fallen asleep. It seemed more still, more remote, more enormous, and inconceivably more solitary. A queer sense of panic struck me, as though I had been transported out of time.

Only after some attempt to orient myself by a dimin- 7
ished pole star did the answer come to me by murmurs from without. I was not the last man on the planet, far in the dying future. My companions had arisen and left, while the lecturer had terminated his address by setting the planetarium lights forward to show the conformation of the heavens as they might exist in the remote future of the expanding universe. Distances had lengthened. All was poised, chill, and alone.

I sat for a moment experiencing the sensation all the 8
more intensely because of the slumber which left me feeling

as though ages had elapsed. The sky gave little sign of movement. It seemed drifting in a slow indeterminate swirl, as though the forces of expansion were equaled at last by some monstrous tug of gravity at the heart of things. In this remote night sky of the far future I felt myself waiting upon the inevitable, the great drama and surrender of the inward fall, the heart contraction of the cosmos.

I was still sitting when, like the slightest leaf movement on a flooding stream, I saw the first faint galaxy of a billion suns race like a silverfish across the night and vanish. It was enough: the fall was equal to the flash of creation. I had sensed it waiting there under the star vault of the planetarium. Now it was cascading like a torrent through the ages in my head. I had experienced, by chance, the farthest reach of the star prison. I had similarly lived to see the beginning descent into the maelstrom. 9

VOCABULARY

paragraph 1: ebullient, monobloc
paragraph 4: intergalactic
paragraph 5: primordial, interstellar
paragraph 7: orient
paragraph 9: maelstrom

QUESTIONS

1. In paragraph 2 Eiseley depends on the simple comparison or analogy of blades of grass to suggest how many stars and galaxies exist. What other such analogies does he use in paragraph 1 and paragraph 9 for explanation?

2. What are the points of similarity in the analogy in paragraph 5? Does the difference in size between humankind and the cosmos increase the effectiveness of the analogy or diminish it?

3. What point is Eiseley making through the experience described in paragraphs 6–9? How is the experience analogous to that of the space traveler as well as to the human being on Earth?

4. Eiseley is arguing against the view that humans have attained or will attain "absolute mastery" over the universe. Is he also

implying that exploration of far space is a useless enterprise, given the enormous space between stars and galaxies?

SUGGESTION FOR WRITING

Eiseley states in a later section of *The Invisible Pyramid* that "there are other confinements . . . than that imposed by the enormous distances of the cosmos." Our senses, he suggests, confine us through their limitations. Write an essay developing this point through your own experiences. Focus on one or two of the senses.

PROCESS

❦ ❦ ❦

A process is a series of connected actions, each developing from the preceding one and leading to a result of some kind: a product, an effect, even a decision. Mechanical processes are probably the kind we deal with the most, and two of the examples in this section are of these—one the process of sharpening a knife, the other that of cooking over an outdoor fire. A mechanical process is one that we create. By contrast, a natural process such as Bronowski (p. 177) describes in his description of the athlete is one we may initiate but do not create:

> He seems all animal in action. The heartbeat goes up; when he sprints at top speed the heart is pumping five times as much blood as normal, and ninety per cent of it is for the muscles.

Both mechanical and natural processes are repeatable. A particular historical process—the events that led to Pearl Harbor or produce an economic depression or ecological disaster—is not, though the general circumstances may repeat themselves at another time.

Though we are committed in describing a process to present the steps chronologically—in the order they occur—we may interrupt the account to discuss the implications or details of a particular state. In describing a complex process, we need to distinguish the main stages and the steps and procedures each of these contain. Process and causal analysis, discussed in the next section, are closely related and are often combined.

FLORENCE H. PETTIT

A designer and professional craftswoman, FLORENCE H. PETTIT *has written much about the craft arts. Her description of how to sharpen a knife, from her book* How To Make Whirligigs and Whimmy Diddles *(1972), shows how im-*

portant the consideration of audience is in exposition: Pettit selects her details with beginners in mind, and is careful to define her tools and equipment, focusing on the difficult steps of the process.

How to Sharpen Your Knife

If you have never done any whittling or wood carving before, the first skill to learn is how to sharpen your knife. You may be surprised to learn that even a brand-new knife needs sharpening. Knives are never sold honed (finely sharpened), although some gouges and chisels are. It is essential to learn the firm stroke on the stone that will keep your blades sharp. The sharpening stone must be fixed in place on the table, so that it will not move around. You can do this by placing a piece of rubber inner tube or a thin piece of foam rubber under it. Or you can tack four strips of wood, if you have a rough worktable, to frame the stone and hold it in place. Put a generous puddle of oil on the stone—this will soon disappear into the surface of a new stone, and you will need to keep adding more oil. Press the knife blade flat against the stone in the puddle of oil, using your index finger. Whichever way the cutting edge of the knife faces is the side of the blade that should get a little more pressure. Move the blade around three or four times in a narrow oval about the size of your fingernail, going *counterclockwise* when the sharp edge is facing right. Now turn the blade over in the same spot on the stone, press hard, and move it around the small oval *clockwise*, with more pressure on the cutting edge that faces left. Repeat the ovals, flipping the knife blade over six or seven times, and applying lighter pressure to the blade the last two times. Wipe the blade clean with a piece of rag or tissue and rub it flat on the piece of leather strop at least twice on each side. Stroke *away* from the cutting edge to remove the little burr of metal that may be left on the blade.

QUESTIONS

1. What details help the reader to visualize the mechanical process described in the paragraph?

2. Are the stages of the process presented chronologically? If not, why not?

3. Are any terms defined in context—that is, in the description of how to sharpen a knife?

SUGGESTIONS FOR WRITING

1. Describe a mechanical process comparable to sharpening a knife—for example, sharpening the blades of a hand mower or pruning a tree or painting the exterior of a house.

2. Rewrite the paragraph on how to sharpen a knife, explaining the process to a child who is just beginning to learn how to carve wood.

JOHN RICHARDS

Trained as an engineer, the English nature writer JOHN RICHARDS *brings a keen eye to his description of the workings of nature—in the excerpt reprinted here from* The Hidden Country (1973), *the intricate natural process of spinning orb-webs. Richards is describing the web-spinning of the Diadem spider, a brown spider with a large white cross on its abdomen. Richards states: "These web-building spiders have eight eyes, yet in spite of this their sight is not good. Unlike the spiders which hunt and catch their prey by watching for them or by chasing, they do not need to see well; what is much more important is their ability to interpret the meaning of the various tensions in the threads of their webs."*

How the Spider Spins Its Web

I have shown the garden spider in the center of its web, but you will rarely find one there during the daytime. This would be a dangerous situation for the spider when birds are about, and it would be unlikely to stay there for long. Instead, it spends the day in a lair by the side of the web, coming out to the center only in the evening, and staying there for the night, unless otherwise engaged.

The orb-webs, as they are called, from their circular shape, are masterpieces of construction, and yet are relatively short-lived. They are usually built in the late evening, and may in some cases be virtually demolished and rebuilt each night. The webs vary considerably in size, and the one which I have drawn, for the sake of convenience, is one of the smallest.* 2

The spider constructs these webs using two different kinds of silk, which it produces from spinnerets at the end of the abdomen. A more or less horizontal thread is needed as a start for the web, and the spider produces this in one of several ways, depending on the circumstances. 3

If the wind direction is right, it may be enough to stand on one point and to put out a long thread into the wind, so that this eventually becomes fouled on a twig or other projection on the far side of the chosen gap. The spider can walk across this thread, anchor the other end firmly, and then reinforce the thread with one or more additional strands. 4

In other cases, as for example when the web is to be made across a window frame, it may be possible for the spider to walk from one point to the other, trailing a line as it goes, which can subsequently be tightened as necessary. Yet again, it will sometimes drop on a thread to the bottom of the window, and then walk up to the required spot, taking the thread with it. 5

Once this starting line is established, the rest of the outer frame of the web is built in much the same way, until the size and basic outline has been settled. A couple of radii can now be dropped from points along the top thread, and when these are crossed over, they locate the point which is to be the center of the web. 6

The rest of the radii are now laid in, so that when finished they are all at very nearly the same angle to their neighbors. The spider does this by walking along one thread as it spins the adjacent one, and it appears to be able to determine the appropriate distance at which to keep it with considerable accuracy. This is quite surprising, because as 7

---

* Drawing has been omitted. [Ed.]

the web does not have a circular outline, the radii cannot be evenly spaced along the outer threads.

Once the radii are in position, the spider constructs a flat 8 non-sticky platform at the center of the web, and then uses this same kind of silk to lay down a spiral, starting from the center and working outwards until it comes to the outer frame.

This thread serves only as a form of scaffolding, to 9 establish finally how the spiral will go, and to secure the radial threads firmly at the correct distances apart, ready for the next stage. In this last step, the sticky spiral will be placed in position.

Starting at the outer end of the scaffolding spiral, the 10 spider begins to work inwards, spinning a new sticky thread, anchoring this firmly to the radii, and destroying the temporary thread as it goes. The real purpose of the temporary spiral now becomes apparent. The sticky thread, when it first comes from the spinnerets, is smooth, and the spider tenses and relaxes it repeatedly as it is laid down. In doing this, it breaks up the gummy material on the silk from a continuous film into strings of small droplets at intervals along the silk thread. Had the spider not first fixed the radial threads firmly in the required position with the temporary spiral thread, this stretching and relaxing would pull them badly out of line.

VOCABULARY

paragraph 1: lair
paragraph 2: orb-webs
paragraph 3: spinnerets
paragraph 6: radii
paragraph 9: scaffolding

QUESTIONS

1. When must the spider take account of the place or setting and the weather in spinning the web?
2. How does the spider spin a temporary spiral, and what is its purpose?

3. What details does Richards stress to show that the orb-webs are "masterpieces of constructions"?

4. At which points in his description does Richards pause to give additional information or comment on the process?

SUGGESTION FOR WRITING

Make several observations of a natural process similar to the one Richards describes—for example, a bird building a nest, a grasshopper leaping through the grass, a dog swimming, or an ant moving a grain of sand. Then write a description of the process, explaining your terms and the steps of the process for readers unfamiliar with it.

JEARL WALKER

Jearl Walker, *Professor of Physics at Cleveland State University, writes about physics and other topics of science for the readers of* Scientific American, *in his column "The Amateur Scientist." Walker is also the author of* The Flying Circus of Physics (1977) *and* Roundabout: The Physics of Rotation in the Everyday World (1985). *In this excerpt from an article on outdoor cooking, he explains the physical basis of various mechanical cooking processes in nontechnical language understandable to the general reader. Later in the article, Walker describes other baking rigs. Through a careful selection of detail, Walker allows us to visualize each of the processes, and he is careful also to describe the necessary implements.*

Outdoor Cooking

Outdoor cooking can be a pleasant part of camping or a key to survival in an emergency. It can also provide a study in thermal physics: how heat can be transferred from a heat source to a food. This month I analyze several ways of cooking food with flames, coals or charcoal briquettes. The techniques require little or no equipment.

A few fundamental concepts of thermal physics underlie 2 all cooking procedures. One concept involves what is meant by heat and temperature. The atoms and molecules of a substance move randomly at any temperature above absolute zero. In a solid the motion consists in rotation and vibration. In a gas or a liquid the phenomenon also includes the random motion of atoms and molecules that are traveling in straight lines, colliding and then again traveling in straight lines.

When a substance is heated, the heat represents the 3 additional energy imparted to the random motion. Temperature is a measure of the amount of energy in the random motion. Thus when the substance is heated, its temperature increases and the substance is said to be hotter. The heat of cooking increases the energy of the random motion of the atoms and molecules in the food, and the food thereupon cooks by undergoing certain chemical and physical changes.

Conduction, convection and radiation are the three 4 primary ways of transferring heat energy. In conduction the heat is conveyed through some intermediate material such as a metal pan or foil by means of atomic collisions. As the outside surface of the metal warms, the energy in the random motion of the atoms there increases. They collide with atoms somewhat deeper in the metal, giving those atoms some of the kinetic energy derived from the heat source. Eventually atoms on the inside surface receive the energy and collide with atoms on the surface of the food, heating the food. Conduction continues for as long as the temperature of the heat source is above the temperature of the food.

Convection involves the ascent of a heated fluid, either 5 air or a liquid. Heat increases the energy in the random motion of the fluid and decreases the density of the fluid. The surrounding cooler and denser fluid then pushes the heated fluid upward. As the hot fluid passes the food, the atoms and molecules in the fluid collide with those on the surface of the food and transfer energy to them.

Radiation involves the emission and absorption of elec- 6 tromagnetic waves. In cooking the source is light. The surface of a heat source such as burning coal emits light in the infrared and visible parts of the electromagnetic spectrum. Since light has energy, this emission is a radiation of energy. When the light is absorbed by atoms and molecules on the surface of the food, the energy of their random motion increases, as does the temperature of the surface. Heating by radiation therefore requires that the food absorb some of the light (primarily the infrared) emitted by the heat source.

Many campfire-cooking techniques draw on more than one of these primary means of transferring heat. For example, a fire might heat a metal pan by both convection of hot air and radiation of light. As the metal warms, energy is conducted through it to the food. As the surface of the food then heats up, conduction brings the heat into the food. 7

One of the easiest ways to cook food such as meat is to spear it with a stick or wrap it around the stick and then suspend it over the fire or coals. The food is heated by the convection of rising hot air and by the radiation from the heated surfaces of the wood and from the hot regions in the flame. You can save work by propping the stick over the fire or suspending it across the fire by means of two forked sticks driven into the ground on opposite sides of the campfire. 8

A large piece of meat suspended over the fire must be turned frequently, because only the side toward the fire gets the effect of the rising hot air and the radiation. The rig known as a dingle fan, probably from the logging-camp shed called a dingle, is helpful in this task. To make the apparatus attach a short chain to the upper end of a stick that is angled upward over the perimeter of the campfire. Suspend the meat from the chain by a string attached to a hook in one end of the meat. Tie a short stick to the string. One end of the stick holds a fan made of wire or branches wrapped in aluminum foil or leaves. To the other end attach a small rock to serve as a counterweight to the fan. Orient the plane of the fan somewhat off the vertical and arrange the entire assembly so that the fan is in the hot air rising from the campfire. The meat is not in that convection current but is exposed to the radiation from the fire. 9

The rising hot air pushes against the underside of the 10

fan. The force moves the fan to one side, twisting the chain and rotating the meat. Once the fan is out of the convection current the chain untwists, rotating the meat in the opposite direction. It overshoots the original position, again twisting the chain. The cycle continues indefinitely, exposing about half of the meat to the radiation. After a while invert the roast and hang it from a hook on the other end to expose the other half of the meat to the radiation.

To fry food you can make a stove from an empty No. 10 can. Remove one end plate of the can and cut a flap at the open end. Bend the flap outward. Push the loose end plate into the can and against the other end plate. With a can opener (the kind that punches triangular holes) or a knife, cut flaps in the can in several places near the closed end. Push the flaps into the can and against the loose end plate to hold it near the fixed end one. Place the open end of the can over a heat source. The upper end plate serves as a surface on which eggs, bacon and other items can be fried. 11

The can functions as a chimney because cool air is sucked in through the open flap at the bottom to replace the hot air rising to the top and out through the holes there. The strong flow of air through the can fans the fire and keeps it burning briskly. 12

You could make the stove without the loose end plate held near the top. That plate, however, helps to produce a nearly uniform temperature over the entire cooking surface. Without this plate the part of that surface directly above the heat source would be hotter than the rest of the surface because it receives more radiation from the source. The loose plate is intended to heat the small layer of air above it, transferring heat to the cooking surface evenly by the conduction and convection through the air. 13

A popular heat source for the stove is a "buddy burner," a small can filled with corrugated cardboard over which hot paraffin has been poured. When the can is brought out for cooking, the paraffin is solid. A match melts and vaporizes some of it, and thereafter the vapor burns. The flame melts more paraffin, which is drawn to the top of the cardboard, where it vaporizes and burns. The cardboard also burns, but slowly, like the wick of a candle. A damper can be placed 14 over part of the burner to slow things down if the stove gets too hot. Make the damper by folding the lid from the can over a doubled piece of wire.

Charcoal briquettes also serve well as a heat source, but 15 it is hard to light them. One easy solution is to put them in a can that works like a chimney. Cut both ends off a large can and punch flaps into the side near one end. Fold the flaps inward. Push large wads of newspaper against them so that they hold the paper in place. Prop the can against a rock with the paper downward. Leave an air space between that end and the ground. Put the briquettes in the can and ignite the newspaper. The flame pulls air into the bottom of the can to replace the hot air rising through the briquettes and out of the can. The strong flow of air makes the flames ignite the briquettes. When the newspaper has burned up and the briquettes begin to fall to the ground, lift the can off them. You now have your cooking fire.

The can stove can be converted into a small oven by 16 means of two more cans and several flat rocks. One of the cans should be larger than the other but no wider than the top of the stove. Remove one end of the smaller can and both ends of the other one. Wrap transparent plastic around an open end of the larger can, holding it in place with a piece of wire. Tuck the ends of another piece of wire under the first one to form a handle. The plastic, commonly called oven wrap, is designed for oven cooking; it will not melt at typical oven temperatures.

Lay the flat rocks on top of the stove. Position the 17 smaller can on them with its open end upward. Put the larger can over that with the plastic upward. This assembly is an oven. Food can be baked in the smaller can. The plastic serves as the oven window.

VOCABULARY

paragraph 3: atoms, molecule
paragraph 4: kinetic energy
paragraph 5: ascent, density
paragraph 6: infrared spectrum, electromagnetic spectrum

paragraph 9: vertical

paragraph 10: paraffin

paragraph 15: briquette

QUESTIONS

1. What are the differences between conduction, convection, and radiation? How do the three sometimes work together in the process described in paragraph 7?

2. In the process described in paragraphs 8–10, what aspects does Walker describe in the most detail? How do his earlier definitions help him in explaining the process?

3. What devices used in the same process does Walker describe? Does he give a full description of each device, or does he describe only those parts needed in cooking?

4. What devices used in frying food does Walker describe in paragraphs 11–17? How detailed is his description of each device?

5. Is Walker writing to readers unfamiliar with laws of physics and cooking techniques? Or does he assume that his readers vary in knowledge and experience?

SUGGESTIONS FOR WRITING

Describe one of the following processes or another that you have performed often enough to explain thoroughly. Explain your terms and steps of the process in nontechnical language that readers unfamiliar with it will understand:

a. seeding and tending a lawn or garden

b. growing tomatoes or another fruit or vegetable

c. cutting down a dead tree

d. carving a turkey

e. mastering a difficult technique in learning to play a musical instrument or to draw or paint

f. repairing a small motor or other equipment

Cause and Effect

❦ ❦ ❦

There is not just one kind of causal analysis. In explaining why you missed an exam, you may say that you overslept without tracing the prior events that made you so tired. In explaining an event like a steep decline in stock prices, a market analyst may cite an event occurring immediately before the decline—for example, a rise in unemployment—and then consider earlier events that led to the rise. These *immediate* (or *proximate*) and *remote* (or *mediate*) events are possible "causes" in different senses of the word; on one occasion you may stress the immediate cause; on another the remote, as Norman Cousins does in his essay on the death of Benny Paret (p. 272). What you point to as the "cause" depends on the purpose of your analysis. In the analysis of an event like a market crash or a head cold, often an explanation that satisfies a person untrained in economics or medicine will usually not satisfy the economist or physician. Later in this book we will consider another, more technical kind of causal explanation.

Objects, too, have more than one cause. One traditional kind of analysis distinguishes four related ones. Consider a dictionary. Its *material cause* is the paper, ink, and other materials used in its manufacture. The *formal cause* is its shape—the alphabetic arrangement of words, and the arrangement of definitions according to a plan. The *efficient cause* is the dictionary writer, and the *final cause*, the use intended for the dictionary. The analysis of a chemical compound is more rigorous, requiring an account of substances that form the compound as well as the process by which the formation occurs. Process analysis is often an essential part of causal analysis because we want to understand both the how and the why of objects and events.

JOHN BROOKS

JOHN BROOKS *has written about American business for* The New Yorker *since 1949. His books include* The Go-Go Years (1973) *and* The Telephone (1976), *a history of AT&T. More recent are* The Games Players (1980), Showing Off in America (1981), *and* The Takeover Game (1987). *In the following paragraph from* The Telephone, *Brooks refers to the idea of Marshall McLuhan that the telephone is a "cool" medium—one requiring full participation because, unlike print, it is empty of content. The user supplies this content, unlike the reader of a book. Brooks says later in his book: "In the uneasy postwar world, people seemed to be coming to associate the telephone with their frustrations, their fears, and their sense of powerlessness against technology."*

The Telephone

What has the telephone done to us, or for us, in the hundred   1
years of its existence? A few effects suggest themselves at once. It has saved lives by getting rapid word of illness, injury, or famine from remote places. By joining with the elevator to make possible the multistory residence or office building, it has made possible—for better or worse—the modern city. By bringing about a quantum leap in the speed and ease with which information moves from place to place, it has greatly accelerated the rate of scientific and technological change and growth in industry. Beyond doubt it has crippled if not killed the ancient art of letter writing. It has made living alone possible for persons with normal social impulses; by so doing, it has played a role in one of the greatest social changes of this century, the breakup of the multigenerational household. It has made the waging of war chillingly more efficient than formerly. Perhaps (though not provably) it has prevented wars that might have arisen out of international misunderstanding caused by written communication. Or perhaps—again not provably—by magnifying and extending irrational personal conflicts based on voice contact, it has caused wars. Certainly it has extended the scope of human conflicts, since it impartially disseminates

the useful knowledge of scientists and the babble of bores, the affection of the affectionate and the malice of the malicious.

But the question remains unanswered. The obvious 2 effects just cited seem inadequate, mechanistic; they only scratch the surface. Perhaps the crucial effects are evanescent and unmeasurable. Use of the telephone involves personal risk because it involves exposure; for some, to be "hung up on" is among the worst of fears; others dream of a ringing telephone and wake up with a pounding heart. The telephone's actual ring—more, perhaps, than any other sound in our daily lives—evokes hope, relief, fear, anxiety, joy, according to our expectations. The telephone is our nerve-end to society.

In some ways it is in itself a thing of paradox. In one 3 sense a metaphor for the times it helped create, in another sense the telephone is their polar opposite. It is small and gentle—relying on low voltages and miniature parts—in times of hugeness and violence. It is basically simple in times of complexity. It is so nearly human, recreating voices so faithfully that friends or lovers need not identify themselves by name even when talking across oceans, that to ask its effects on human life may seem hardly more fruitful than to ask the effect of the hand or the foot. The Canadian philosopher Marshall McLuhan—one of the few who have addressed themselves to these questions—was perhaps not far from the mark when he spoke of the telephone as creating "a kind of extra-sensory perception."

QUESTIONS

1. Why does Brooks consider the effects he discusses in paragraph 1 less significant than those in paragraph 2? What does he mean by the statement, "Perhaps the crucial effects are evanescent and unmeasurable"?

2. In what ways is the telephone a paradox? Does the author show it to be a paradox in paragraphs 1 and 2?

3. Has Brooks stated all the effects of the telephone, or has he identified only a few? What central point is he making?

SUGGESTIONS FOR WRITING

1. Develop one of the ideas in the essay from your personal experience. You might discuss your own positive and negative attitudes toward the telephone, and the reasons for them, or you might develop the statement, "In some ways it is in itself a thing of paradox."

2. Write an essay describing what it would be like to live without a telephone, or discuss the impact of the telephone on life in your home. Distinguish the various uses and effects of the telephone for various members of your family.

MARVIN HARRIS

> MARVIN HARRIS, *Graduate Research Professor of Anthropology at the University of Florida, writes about American life from the point of view of the anthropologist in* Cannibals and Kings: The Origins of Culture *(1977) and* America Now: The Anthropology of a Changing Culture *(1981), from which the excerpt reprinted below is taken. Recent books include* Good to Eat *(1986) and* The Sacred Cow and the Abominable Pig *(1987), both concerned with "riddles of food and culture." Harris gives in this excerpt from* America Now *an interesting illustration of Murphy's Law. Notice that he combines many of the types of exposition discussed in this section of the book, including definition, process, and example. Later in this book, Edward Tenner gives another explanation for similar happenings (p. 241).*

Why Nothing Works

According to a law attributed to the savant known only as   1
Murphy, "if anything can go wrong, it will." Corollaries to Murphy's Law suggest themselves as clues to the shoddy goods problem: If anything can break down, it will; if anything can fall apart, it will; if anything can stop running,

it will. While Murphy's Law can never be wholly defeated, its effects can usually be postponed. Much of human existence consists of efforts aimed at making sure that things don't go wrong, fall apart, break down, or stop running until a decent interval has elapsed after their manufacture. Forestalling Murphy's Law as applied to products demands intelligence, skill, and commitment. If these human inputs are assisted by special quality-control instruments, machines, and scientific sampling procedures, so much the better. But gadgets and sampling alone will never do the trick since these items are also subject to Murphy's Law. Quality-control instruments need maintenance; gauges go out of order; X rays and laser beams need adjustments. No matter how advanced the technology, quality demands intelligent, motivated human thought and action.

Some reflection about the material culture of prehistoric 2 and preindustrial peoples may help to show what I mean. A single visit to a museum which displays artifacts used by simple preindustrial societies is sufficient to dispel the notion that quality is dependent on technology. Artifacts may be of simple, even primitive design, and yet be built to serve their intended purpose in a reliable manner during a lifetime of use. We acknowledge this when we honor the label "handmade" and pay extra for the jewelry, sweaters, and handbags turned out by the dwindling breeds of modern-day craftspeople.

What is the source of quality that one finds, let us say, in 3 a Pomo Indian basket so tightly woven that it was used to hold boiling water and never leaked a drop, or in an Eskimo skin boat with its matchless combination of lightness, strength, and seaworthiness? Was it merely the fact that these items were handmade? I don't think so. In unskilled or uncaring hands a handmade basket or boat can fall apart as quickly as baskets or boats made by machines. I rather think that the reason we honor the label "handmade" is because it evokes not a technological relationship between producer and product but a social relationship between producer and consumer. Throughout prehistory it was the fact that producers and consumers were either one and the same individuals or close kin that guaranteed the highest degree of reliability and durability in manufactured items. Men made their own spears, bows and arrows, and projectile points; women wove their own baskets and carrying nets, fashioned their own clothing from animal skins, bark, or fiber. Later, as technology advanced and material culture grew more complex, different members of the band or village adopted craft specialties such as pottery-making, basket-weaving, or canoe-building. Although many items were obtained through barter and trade, the connection between producer and consumer still remained intimate, permanent, and caring.

A man is not likely to fashion a spear for himself whose   4
point will fall off in midflight; nor is a woman who weaves her own basket likely to make it out of rotted straw. Similarly, if one is sewing a parka for a husband who is about to go hunting for the family with the temperature at sixty below, all stitches will be perfect. And when the men who make boats are the uncles and fathers of those who sail them, they will be as seaworthy as the state of the art permits.

In contrast, it is very hard for people to care about   5
strangers or about products to be used by strangers. In our era of industrial mass production and mass marketing, quality is a constant problem because the intimate sentimental and personal bonds which once made us responsible to each other and to our products have withered away and been replaced by money relationships. Not only are the producers and consumers strangers but the women and men involved in various stages of production and distribution— management, the worker on the factory floor, the office help, the salespeople—are also strangers to each other. In larger companies there may be hundreds of thousands of people all working on the same product who can never meet face-to-face or learn one another's names. The larger the company and the more complex its division of labor, the greater the sum of uncaring relationships and hence the greater the effect of Murphy's Law. Growth adds layer on layer of executives, foremen, engineers, production workers, and sales specialists to the payroll. Since each new employee contributes a diminished share to the overall production

process, alienation from the company and its product are likely to increase along with the neglect or even purposeful sabotage of quality standards.

QUESTIONS

1. What role does Murphy's Law play in Harris's explanation of why nothing works? Does he say or imply that the law is irreversible and that things inevitably break down?

2. How does Harris prove that quality is not dependent on technology? Has he provided enough evidence to establish this point?

3. Does Harris provide the same kind of evidence for his explanation of the source of quality in the handmade products he discusses in paragraphs 3–5?

4. We can test the evidence Harris presents in paragraph 2 by examining the museum objects discussed. Can you think of a way to test the explanation in paragraphs 3–5 if the evidence cannot be tested directly? How convincing do you find his explanation in these paragraphs?

SUGGESTIONS FOR WRITING

1. Write your own explanation of why something you own does not work. In the course of your analysis, discuss the extent to which the ideas of Harris offer an explanation.

2. Write an essay on succeeding in a sport or another topic of your choosing, using causal analysis and examples to develop a thesis. The more limited your focus and discussion, the stronger your thesis will be.

CATHERINE CAUFIELD

CATHERINE CAUFIELD *has written articles for* New Scientist *and other periodicals. Her books are* The Emperor of the United States of America and Other Magnificent Eccentrics *(1981),* Multiple Exposures: Chronicles of the Radiation Age *(1989), and* In the Rainforest *(1985)—a report on the destruction of rain forest in Brazil, Costa Rica, Indonesia, and other rain-forest countries. Caufield states her purpose of her report in these words:*

> Will the forest be so disturbed it can no longer protect wildlife, soils, and watersheds? Will the forest be squeezed dry in a few years or can the farming, mining, or whatever go on forever? Who will benefit from the new use—the people of the forest? the poor of the country? a domestic elite? foreign consumers? Although we may not live in rain forest countries, we have a right to ask these questions because millions of our fellow creatures—humans, animals, and plants—depend directly upon the health of the rain forests; because hundreds of millions more, including those in the industrialized countries, rely upon them indirectly; and because so much rain forest is destroyed in our names and with our money.

In the following excerpt, Caufield discusses the causes of this deforestation. Note also her use of definition, division, and examples.

The Rain Forest

"Its lands are high; there are in it many sierras and very lofty mountains. . . . All are most beautiful, of a thousand shapes; all are accessible and are filled with trees of a thousand kinds and tall, so that they seem to touch the sky. I am told that they never lose their foliage, and this I can believe, for I saw them as green and lovely as they are in Spain in May, and some of them were flowering, some bearing fruit, and some at another stage, according to their nature." This is how Columbus described to Ferdinand and Isabella the forests of Hispaniola—the island that is now divided into Haiti and the Dominican Republic. The description contains the seeds of two different but not incompatible views of the rain forest— the romantic and the scientific, each of which still has its adherents.

For four centuries after Columbus's discoveries, travellers and scientists had no special name for tropical rain forests. They contented themselves with calling them forests or tropical forests. The great Victorian naturalist Alfred

Russel Wallace, in his 1878 book "Tropical Nature," wrote of them, more precisely, as "the primeval forests of the equatorial zone." In 1898, the German botanist A. F. W. Schimper coined the phrase *"tropische Regenwald"*—"tropical rain forest." Schimper defined such a forest as "evergreen, hygrophilous in character [growing in wet places], at least 100 feet high, but usually much taller, rich in thick-stemmed lianas and in woody as well as herbaceous epiphytes." Botanists now distinguish, or try to, among thirty or forty types of rain forest, including evergreen lowland forest, evergreen mountain forest (subdivided into broad-leaved and needle-leaved), tropical evergreen alluvial forest (subdivided according to the degree of flooding), semi-deciduous forest (lowland and mountain), and so on. Because nature is continuous and science seeks clear-cut categories, these definitions are rarely wholly satisfactory, and each brave attempt to impose order on a complex and poorly understood ecosystem leads to revisions and adjustments and new tries.

The defining characteristics of tropical rain forests are temperature and rainfall. At one end of the spectrum are forests with high rainfall (a hundred and sixty to four hundred inches a year) and a high average temperature (eighty degrees), and without pronounced cold or dry spells. These are the equatorial evergreen rain forests. North and south of the equator, the climate gradually becomes more seasonal, with increasingly pronounced cold and dry spells. The second main group of tropical rain forests (more properly called tropical moist forests or tropical semi-deciduous forests) is marked by this seasonality. These forests get less rain (forty to a hundred and sixty inches a year), their temperature varies more, and during their dry season many or all of the trees lose their leaves. Generally, these seasonal forests are not as rich in species as the equatorial forests, but because for at least part of the year their canopies are more open they have a more luxuriant understory. Two-thirds of the world's rain forest is the wetter, richer, equatorial type. Its major concentrations are in lowland Amazonia, the Congo Basin, Sumatra, Kalimantan (on Borneo), and Papua New Guinea. Burma, Thailand, Kampuchea, Java and Sulawesi, northeast Australia, and parts of West Africa and

South America all have important areas of seasonal rain forest.

Throughout the wet tropics, rain forests are the natural 4 vegetation. All along the equator, from the Tropic of Cancer to the Tropic of Capricorn, wherever the temperature is high enough and the rain is heavy and regular enough, there is—or once was—rain forest. A few thousand years ago, the rain-forest belt covered five billion acres—twelve per cent of the earth's land surface. Man has already destroyed half of that. Most of the damage has been done in the last two hundred years—especially since the end of the Second World War. Now Latin America has fifty-seven per cent of the remaining rain forests. Southeast Asia and the Pacific islands have twenty-five per cent. Africa has eighteen per cent. Thirty-seven countries have significant areas of tropical rain forest, though three have half the total: Brazil, with a third, has by far the biggest share; Zaire and Indonesia have a tenth each.

Tropical rain forests are being destroyed faster than any 5 other natural community. A United Nations study published in 1979 offers the most optimistic assessment of forest loss. It found that of the twenty-four hundred million acres of rain forest left in the world fourteen million were permanently destroyed each year—almost thirty acres every minute of every day. In 1980, the National Academy of Sciences, in Washington, D.C., announced a worse figure: more than fifty million acres—an area the size of England and Scotland—destroyed or seriously degraded each year. The most comprehensive study to date was published in 1981 by the Food and Agriculture Organization of the United Nations; it says that at present rates almost a fifth of the world's remaining tropical rain forest will be destroyed or severely degraded by the end of the century. By that time, according to the F.A.O. study, even if there is no increase in current rates of deforestation Indonesia will have lost ten per cent of the forest it had remaining in 1981, the Philippines will have lost twenty per cent, Malaysia will have lost twenty-four per cent, and Thailand will have lost sixty per cent. In Africa, Nigeria and the Ivory Coast will have been completely deforested by 2000, and Guinea will have lost a third of its remaining rain forest, Madagascar thirty per cent, and Ghana twenty-six per cent. In Latin America, Costa Rica will have lost eighty per cent of its 1981 rain forest; Honduras, Nicaragua, and Ecuador will lose more than half of theirs; and Guatemala, Colombia, and Mexico will have lost a third.

Mainland India, Bangladesh, Haiti, and Sri Lanka have 6 already lost all their primary rain forests. By 1990, the lowland rain forests—the richest in terms of plant and animal species—of peninsular Malaysia, Thailand, the Philippines, Guatemala, Panama, Sierra Leone, and the Ivory Coast will have been reduced to a few remnant patches. And the United Nations says, in its 1978 state-of-knowledge report on tropical forest ecosystems, "At the present rate of forest destruction, all accessible tropical forests will have disappeared by the end of this century." Some large blocks—in Amazonia and Zaire, for example—may survive, provided that no new roads are built to open them to loggers, miners, and settlers. At the present rate, Brazil will lose eight per cent of its existing forest by the year 2000, and though that loss may sound small, it amounts to sixty-three million acres—an area almost three times the size of Portugal. But the rate of deforestation in the world's remaining rain forests is likely to increase. In Brazil, satellite studies carried out by the Brazilian Forestry Development Institute show that sixty per cent of the area deforested by 1978 had been cut between 1975 and 1978. The pressures to open these areas will intensify sharply in the near future. The logging industry is already turning its attention from the nearly depleted forests of Southeast Asia to the relatively untouched riches of Amazonia. And vast industrial developments are under way in or being planned for many of the few remaining unspoiled areas.

Why are these forests—the richest, oldest, most complex 7 ecosystems on earth—being cut down at such a rate? Why destroy a forest? To sell its timber, to get at the gold and iron underneath, to get more land for agriculture. There are psychological motives, too: the wish to conquer nature; fear of the unknown; nationalistic and strategic desires to occupy uncontrolled regions. Overpopulation is usually cited as the main cause of deforestation. Rain forests are often used as safety valves by governments to defuse pressure for land reform. The safety-valve theory is misguided. Rain forests are not empty; small groups of people are already living wherever the forest can support human life. Nor is the intact forest idle. It conditions the soil, regulates rainfall, and maintains the water cycle far beyond its own borders. Most attempts to turn rain forest into farmland have failed disastrously, damaging the forest, disrupting the soil and water balance for other farmers, and leaving the settlers even more desperate for land.

The true cause of agricultural settlement in rain forests is often inequitable land distribution rather than simple overpopulation. Among the rain-forest countries, only Haiti, India, Sri Lanka, Puerto Rico, Jamaica, and El Salvador have a population density higher than four hundred people per square mile; Japan, Great Britain, Belgium, the Netherlands, and West Germany all have more than six hundred. Brazil, which has had a policy of moving settlers into the Amazonian rain forest, does not need that land for agriculture. Leaving aside the Amazonian forest, it has roughly the same population density as the United States—about sixty-two people per square mile, compared with sixty-five in America. Western Europe averages more than four hundred people per square mile. The Netherlands is prosperous with more than a thousand people per square mile. Brazil has two and three-tenths acres of farmland per person—more than the United States, which is the world's greatest exporter of food. Taking potential farmland into account but still leaving aside Amazonia, each family in Brazil could have ten acres. Instead, four and a half per cent of Brazil's landowners own eighty-one per cent of the country's farmland, and seventy per cent of the country's rural households are landless. In Java, eighty-five per cent of the families have no land at all, but of the island's landowners just one per cent own a third of the land. In India, more than half the arable land is owned by eight per cent of the rural population. In El Salvador, whose population is five million, fewer than two thousand families own forty per cent of the land. And, when it comes to farmers who rent land from others, the picture isn't much better. In most developing countries, less than ten per cent of the rural population farms more than half the land. In

Peru, one per cent of the population farms more than eighty per cent of the land.

Common though it is for government officials, business- 9 men, and international agencies, like the United Nations and the World Bank, to attribute deforestation to masses of poor people searching for land, there are many areas in which that pressure is not the main cause of forest destruction. Land hunger is not even the prime motivation in many government-sponsored settlement schemes. Some of the largest ones—in Indonesia and Brazil, for example—are intended mainly to secure national sovereignty by establishing a civilian presence in frontier regions. In the words of one member of the Brazilian junta, "When we are certain that every corner of the Amazon is inhabited by genuine Brazilians, and not by Indians, only then will we be able to say that the Amazon is ours."

In Latin America, cattle ranching for the export trade is 10 the chief culprit in rain-forest destruction. According to Brazilian government figures, thirty-eight per cent of all deforestation in the Brazilian Amazon between 1966 and 1975 is attributable to large-scale cattle ranching, thirty-one per cent to agricultural colonization, and twenty-seven per cent to highway construction. The government gave fiscal incentives to ninety per cent of the ranches, and more than half the agricultural clearing was done under a government-sponsored peasant-colonization program. That program has now ended, in favor of investment in large-scale logging operations, hydroelectric dams, mines, and industrial development—activities that do not result from population pressure. "Those countries in which current forest harvesting is of greatest concern (Indonesia, Brazil, Malaysia, and Colombia) also have *relatively* low population densities," a 1982 State Department survey said. Nevertheless, industrial development and settlement often go hand in hand, because the roads enable settlers to reach previously inaccessible forests, and because settlers prefer to plant on the conveniently pre-cleared land that loggers and others leave behind them.

In Southeast Asia, Oceania, and Africa, logging vies 11 with peasant agriculture as the main cause of deforestation. According to figures from the F.A.O., peasant agriculture in

Indonesia affects half a million acres of rain forest a year, but that is only a quarter of the area annually affected by logging. Some heavily logged countries are now reaching the point of no return. Since 1960, more than half of peninsular Malaysia's rain forests have been logged, and the official forecast of that country's Federal Department of Forestry is that the remaining forest resources will be exhausted by 1990. One-quarter of the Ivory Coast's foreign earnings comes from timber, but with more than a million acres being cut by loggers each year the timber will run out well before the end of this decade. Sixty per cent of Africa's rain forest is in the Congo, and the Congolese government has scheduled logging of sixty-eight per cent of it.

In spite of claims that rain forests must be sacrificed for 12 the betterment of the poor and the landless, the effect of most rain-forest exploitation is to redistribute wealth upward. The permanent, wide-reaching benefits of the intact forest—the protection of wildlife, water catchments, and soil, and the provision of food, medicines, and building materials—are sacrificed for short-term profits for a small group of investors and consumers.

VOCABULARY

paragraph 1: sierras, adherents

paragraph 2: primeval, lianas, herbaceous, epiphytes, ecosystem

paragraph 3: spectrum, understory

paragraph 6: satellite

paragraph 9: junta

paragraph 10: fiscal incentives

paragraph 12: catchments

QUESTIONS

1. What is the basis of division of the four types of rain forest named in paragraph 2? What is the principle of division of rain forest into two main groups in paragraph 3? Does Caufield state this principle, or must you infer it?

2. To understand why rain forests are disappearing, is it necessary

to understand the existing types? Is the division of rain forests necessary to the causal analysis?

3. Why does Caufield stress the "*relatively* low population densities" of Indonesia, Brazil, Malaysia, and Colombia? What does the word *relatively* mean?

4. What are the effects of deforestation, and where in the essay does Caufield discuss them?

5. What causes does Caufield reject for deforestation? What alternate explanation does she give?

SUGGESTIONS FOR WRITING

Each of the following events has produced conflicting explanations and predictions in newspapers, popular magazines, and professional journals. Compare the evidence presented in two recent contrasting articles, noting important similarities and differences in the evidence presented and its interpretation. From your analysis, draw a conclusion about the controversy or the state of current knowledge about the subject:

a. the 1991–92 recession

b. destruction of the ozone layer

c. the greenhouse effect

d. the safety of nuclear reactors

e. the safety of household pesticides

f. disintegration of the Soviet Union

g. decline in the American manufacture of steel or textiles

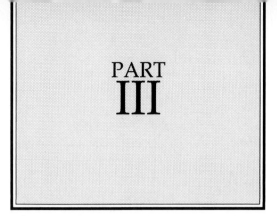

PART
III

ARGUMENT AND
PERSUASION

INDUCTIVE REASONING
❦ ❦ ❦

The previous section focused on expository writing—writing that defines, or that explains or illustrates or traces causes and effects, and so on. The essays that follow show how we reason from various kinds of evidence. The process by which we reason from experience and observation is called *induction*. It is a kind of reasoning we engage in daily, for example, in drawing the conclusion that a red and swollen finger is probably infected or that numerous car accidents will probably follow a heavy snowfall.

Inductive reasoning often makes generalizations or predictions about classes of things or people. An example is the generalization that drivers in a particular age group will probably have a higher than average number of car accidents, or the broader generalization that as a class another group of people are safe drivers. The prediction may be based on various kinds of evidence—for example, observation of drivers during a ten-month period, or statistical knowledge of the accident history of this group statewide or nationwide. No prediction can be made about any single member of the group, however, nor can the prediction be made with absolute certainty.

The problem in inductive reasoning is to choose particular instances that truly represent the group or class about which we are generalizing or making predictions. But, as in the sample precincts that pollsters use to predict the outcome of elections, it is impossible to guarantee that the limited number of people sampled are actually typical or representative. We also may be unaware of special circumstances that, if known, would weaken the generalization. These are important reasons for not claiming certainty for the generalization.

A "hasty generalization" is a judgment made on the basis of insufficient evidence or on the basis of special cases. Thus someone might argue that, because a large number of drivers seventy years of age or older had car accidents during a three-month period, all drivers seventy or older will have a higher than average number of accidents in the future, and therefore should pay higher insurance premiums. The argument might be worth considering if the behavior of sample drivers and the conditions under which they were driving could be shown to be typical. It might have been the case, however, that some of the drivers in these accidents proved to have impaired vision (by no means a characteristic of older people) or that the accidents occurred in a harsh winter month. The generalization in question would then have been based both on special cases and on special circumstances.

Many beliefs arise from hasty generalizations like the one just cited: small towns are safer than large cities; redheaded people have short tempers; New Yorkers are rude. Consider the last of these generalizations: the New Yorkers who prompted the statement may have been observed on a crowded, stalled bus on the hottest day of the year. We will consider some special forms of inductive reasoning in the discussions that follow.

Experience and Observation

The process of reasoning from experience and observation requires careful qualification and repeated testing. The scientist engages in a continuous process of testing promising explanations or hypotheses derived from previous experiments and observations in the laboratory and in the field and tests anew conclusions that seem well established. New hypotheses arise that require testing; if confirmed, these may lead to a questioning of earlier conclusions.

Reasoning from everyday experience and observation requires the same care taken in reasoning from scientific evidence. But this process of reasoning is perhaps even more difficult, for many ideas originate in attitudes and prejudices that we adopt unknowingly. The more deep-rooted the idea, the less likely we are to test it by experience. Indeed, we are more likely to seek in our experience confirmation of ideas we are certain are true. So the advice to think "objectively" about people and the world is not easily followed. We can, however, learn to treat with caution the ideas that we derive from what we hear and read. In writing about ideas, we do best to pause and ask where an idea came from before committing it to paper.

ALVIN TOFFLER

For many years the Washington correspondent and an editor of Fortune *magazine,* ALVIN TOFFLER *is the author of numerous articles and books on social change, including* Future Shock *(1970). In his book* The Third Wave *(1980), Toffler explores the changes that new technologies are bringing about in our lives. Previously, he argues, people's dual roles as producers and consumers split their personalities. As producers they were taught to develop restraint and defer pleasure; as consumers they were taught to seek immediate gratification and abandon restraint. But modern technology is increasingly bringing the consumer into manufacture—producing a new class of what Toffler calls "prosumers," that is, people who produce what they consume, like the "do-it-yourselfers" described in the section of the book reprinted here. Though he does*

> *not predict the exact changes to come, Toffler asks whether it is possible for a society "to attain a high material standard of living without obsessively focusing all its energies on production for exchange."*

The Do-It-Yourselfers

In 1956 the American Telephone & Telegraph Company, creaking under the burden of exploding communications demand, began introducing new electronic technology that made it possible for callers to direct-dial their long-distance calls. Today it is even possible to direct-dial many overseas calls. By punching in the appropriate numbers, the consumer took on a task previously done for him by the operator.

In 1973–74 the oil squeeze triggered by the Arab embargo sent gasoline prices soaring. Giant oil companies reaped bonanza profits, but local filling-station operators had to fight a desperate battle for economic survival. To cut costs many introduced self-service fuel pumps. At first these were an oddity. Newspapers wrote funny feature stories about the motorist who tried to put the fuel hose into the car radiator. Soon, however, the sight of consumers pumping their own gas became a commonplace.

Only 8 percent of U.S. gas stations were on a self-service basis in 1974. By 1977 the number reached nearly 50 percent. In West Germany, of 33,500 service stations some 15 percent had shifted to self-service by 1976, and this 15 percent accounted for 35 percent of all the gasoline sold. Industry experts say that it will soon be 70 percent of the total. Once more the consumer is replacing a producer and becoming a prosumer.

The same period saw the introduction of electronic banking, which not only began to break down the pattern of "banker's hours" but also increasingly eliminated the teller, leaving the customer to perform operations previously done by the banking staff.

Getting the customer to do part of the job—known to economists as "externalizing labor cost"—is scarcely new. That's what self-service supermarkets are all about. The smiling clerk who knew the stock and went and got it for you was replaced by the push-it-yourself shopping cart. While some customers lamented the good old days of personal service, many liked the new system. They could do their own searching and they wound up paying a few cents less. In effect, they were paying themselves to do the work the clerk had previously done.

6 Today this same form of externalization is occurring in many other fields. The rise of discount stores, for example, represents a partial step in the same direction. Clerks are few and far between; the customer pays a bit less but works a bit harder. Even shoe stores, in which a supposedly skilled clerk was long regarded as a necessity, are moving to self-service, shifting work to the consumer.

7 The same principle can be found elsewhere, too. As Caroline Bird has written in her perceptive book, *The Crowding Syndrome,* "More things come knocked down for supposedly easy assembly at home . . . and during the Christmas season shoppers in some of the proudest old New York stores have to make out sales slips for clerks unable or unwilling to write."

8 In January 1978 a thirty-year-old government worker in Washington, D.C., heard strange noises emanating from his refrigerator. The customary thing to do in the past was to call in a mechanic and pay him to fix it. Given the high cost and the difficulty of getting a repairman at a convenient hour, Barry Nussbaum read the instructions that came with his refrigerator. On it he discovered an 800 telephone number that he could use to call the manufacturer—Whirlpool Corporation of Benton Harbor, Michigan—free of charge.

9 This was the "Cool-Line" set up by Whirlpool to help customers deal with service problems. Nussbaum called. The man at the other end then "talked him through" a repair, explaining to Nussbaum exactly which bolts to remove, which sounds to listen for and—later—what part would be needed. "That guy," says Nussbaum, "was super-helpful. He not only knew what I needed to do, he was a great confidence builder." The refrigerator was fixed in no time.

10 Whirlpool has a bank of nine full-time and several part-time advisers, some of them former service field men, who wear headsets and take such calls. A screen in front of

them instantly displays for them a diagram of whatever product is involved (Whirlpool makes freezers, dishwashers, air-conditioners, and other appliances in addition to refrigerators) and permits them to guide the customer. In 1978 alone Whirlpool handled 150,000 such calls.

The Cool-Line is a rudimentary model for a future 11 system of maintenance that permits the homeowner to do much of what a paid outside mechanic or specialist once did. Made possible by advances that have driven down the cost of long-distance telephoning, it suggests future systems that might actually display step-by-step fix-it-yourself instructions on the home television screen as the adviser speaks. The spread of such systems would reserve the repair mechanic only for major tasks, or turn the mechanic (like the doctor or social worker) into a teacher, guide, and guru for prosumers.

What we see is a pattern that cuts across many indus- 12 tries—increasing externalization, increasing involvement of the consumer in tasks once done for her or him by others—and once again, therefore, a transfer of activity from Sector B of the economy to Sector A, from the exchange sector to the prosumption sector.

VOCABULARY

paragraph 6: externalization
paragraph 8: emanating
paragraph 11: rudimentary, guru

QUESTIONS

1. Toffler builds through a series of examples to a generalization supported by them. We call this order of ideas or method of organizing an essay—moving from the specific to the general, from particulars of experience to conclusions based on them—*inductive.* Would the generalization be unclear or difficult to understand if Toffler had begun with it?
2. How various are the examples Toffler presents? Has he chosen examples from a single area or from several?
3. How do Toffler's examples suggest the meaning of the terms *prosumer* and *prosumption?*

4. Does Toffler say or imply that the changes he describes are an improvement in any way, or is he merely presenting the facts?

5. What other conclusions about American society or the American economy can be drawn from these facts? Do your experiences and observations support Toffler's?

SUGGESTIONS FOR WRITING

1. Present a series of observations of your own about how people today behave as consumers. Build these observations to one or more conclusions they support. Be careful not to generalize more broadly than the evidence you have presented allows.

2. Discuss the extent to which your own experience and observation support the conclusion Toffler reaches. If you believe his conclusion needs qualification, explain why it does.

EDWARD TENNER

> EDWARD TENNER *attended Princeton University and received his Ph.D. in European history from the University of Chicago. He has been a junior fellow in the Harvard Society of Fellows, has worked in scientific and trade publishing, and has held visiting positions at Princeton and the Institute for Advanced Study. Tenner's description of how mechanical devices take revenge upon the user deserves comparison with Marvin Harris's explanation of "why nothing works" (p. 221).*

Revenge Theory

Why are the lines at automatic cash dispensers longer in the evening than those at tellers' windows used to be during banking hours? Why do helmets and other protective gear help make football more dangerous than rugby? Why do filter-tip cigarettes usually fail to reduce nicotine intake? Why are today's paperback prices starting to overtake yesterday's cloth-bound prices? Why has the leisure society gone the way of the leisure suit?

The world we have created seems to be getting even, ²
twisting our cleverness against us. Or we may be the ones
who are unconsciously twisting. Either way, wherever we
turn we face the ironic unintended consequences of mechanical, chemical, medical, social, and financial ingenuity—
revenge effects, they might be called.

Revenge effects don't require space-age technology. As ³
the humorist Will Cuppy observed of the first pyramids,
"Imhotep the Wise originated the idea of concealing the
royal corpse and his treasure in a monument so conspicuous
that it could not possibly be missed by body snatchers and
other thieves." At Elizabethan hangings of cutpurses, their
surviving colleagues worked the distracted throngs.

Cognizance of revenge effects is much more recent. ⁴
Craftworkers and farmers before the nineteenth century, as
far as I can tell, didn't seem to blame their tools or materials
when things went wrong. They recognized providence and
luck, and some of them (notably miners) discerned malicious
spirits, but not ornery ordinary *things*. For all the prophecy of
Mary Shelley and the insight of Henry David Thoreau, the
critic Friedrich Theodor Vischer (1807–1887) probably deserves the honor of propelling revenge theory into common
speech in a novel, *Auch Einer* (*Another*), published in 1867.
His eccentric—critics say, autobiographical—hero is convinced that everyday objects, like pencils, pens, inkwells,
and cigars, harbor a perverse and demonic spirit. Although
not quite in today's literary canon even in his native Germany, Vischer did achieve immortality through the phrase
die Tücke des Objekts—the malice of things.

In 1878 Thomas Edison, possibly echoing telegraphers' ⁵
slang, first wrote of a *bug* as a hidden problem to be removed
from a design. According to a later article in *The Pall Mall
Gazette*, he was implying "that some imaginary insect has
secreted itself inside and is causing all the trouble." It
appears that by the mid-1930s, "ironing the bugs out" had
become American engineering slang.

By the 1940s the complexity of technological systems ⁶
raised the consciousness of troops and civilians alike about
how many things could go wrong. The London *Observer*
acknowledged in 1942 that the behavior of machines
"couldn't always be explained by . . . laws of aerodynamics.

And so, lacking a Devil, the young fliers . . . invented a whole hierarchy of devils. They called them Gremlins. . . ."

In 1949 revenge theory took a giant step when Col. P. J. 7 Stapp of Edwards Air Force Base referred to (his colleague Captain Ed) Murphy's Law—that if something can go wrong, it will—in a press conference. Aeronautical manufacturers soon were exploiting it in their advertising, and it passed into folklaw, that vast body of free-form theorizing. Only a year later the British humorist Paul Jennings published, as a parody of the Paris avant-garde, an essay on "Resistential-ism," a movement supposedly sweeping the Left Bank with the watchword, *"Les choses sont contre nous."* Our growing "illusory domination over Things," the Resistentialists believed, "has been matched . . . by the increasing hostility (and greater force) or the Things arrayed against [us]."

In 1955 C. Northcote Parkinson (an expatriate historian 8 then as obscure as Murphy himself) began an article in *The Economist* with the "commonplace observation that work expands so as to fill the time available for its completion. Thus, an elderly lady of leisure can spend the entire day in writing and dispatching a postcard to her niece at Bognor Regis." He pointed out that there were nearly 68 percent fewer ships in the Royal Navy in 1928 than in 1914, but more than 78 percent more Admiralty officials.

What all this speculation had in common was a sense that 9 technology and the bureaucracies that sustained it had sometimes amusing and sometimes troubling sides. There probably is no single way to classify the tendencies that these and others have seen—whole books of folklaw principles have been compiled—but at least five are noteworthy. They might be called *repeating, recomplicating, recongesting, regenerating,* and *rearranging.*

Repeating is the most universal. When a chore becomes 10 easier or faster, people assume they will be able to spend less time on it and more on important matters. Instead, they may have to or want to do it more often, or to do new things. The historian of technology Ruth Schwartz Cowan has shown in *More Work for Mother* that while vacuum cleaners, washing machines, and other "labor-saving" appliances did gradually improve the working-class standard of living, they saved no time for middle-class housewives. Women who had sent soiled clothing to a commercial laundry began to do more and more loads of washing. And as laundries and other services went out of business, fewer choices remained.

Much computing is information housekeeping. The billions of dollars of microcomputers installed in the 1980s replaced batch processing and mainframes, just as home appliances had defeated the laundries. If this unprecedented power had performed as advertised, productivity in services should have soared. Instead, it increased only 1.3 percent a year between 1982 and 1986. In 1989–90 it grew by only 0.5 percent. The largely precomputer postwar average growth had been fully 2.3 percent.   11

Experts disagree about the reasons for what *Fortune* called "the puny payoff from office computers," but repeating effects are surely involved. When spreadsheets were laborious, people did them as seldom and as cautiously as possible. Now recalculations can be done much more easily, but at the cost of having to do them much more often, and of learning to use the software. Meanwhile, competitors have their own spreadsheets (and faxes and cellular telephones), so there isn't even a relative advantage. Likewise, the time spent revising a computerized letter or memo may cancel the advantage of not having to retype. And of course mass-produced "personal" letters and memos eat into the time of the recipients.   12

Computers also force repeating, because often at least some essential data aren't on line. Patrons at libraries with electronic catalogues usually have to search the old printed catalogue too, probably increasing total search time. And they may discover that precious data are almost inaccessible in tapes in obsolete formats.   13

Even the body rebels against repeating. According to the U.S. Bureau of Labor Statistics, repetitive motion disorders (including hand injuries related to computer keyboards) accounted for fully 147,000 of 284,000 occupational illnesses in 1989.   14

Recomplicating is another ironic consequence of the simplifying abilities of computers. Wands, bar codes, on-screen displays, have failed to demystify the operations of video cassette recorders. Touch-tone telephones began as a small   15 saving in dialing time for gadget-minded subscribers. By now the time savings of punching rather than dialing has been more than consumed by the elaborate systems built to take advantage of it. When the carrier access code and credit card number are added to the number itself, a single call may require thirty digits. And a voice mail system may then take over, demanding still more digits and waiting.

Powerful mainframes have allowed airlines to maximize   16
income with fare structures that are ever more difficult to understand. A single carrier routinely makes tens of thousands of fare changes each day. The Airline Tariff Publishing Company, the industry cooperative, has processed as many as 600,000 changes in 24 hours. Dozens of fares may apply on the same route. The system may benefit the airlines or the public, but it makes it almost impossible for either to understand without tying into the computer networks that make it possible.

Even safety devices can recomplicate fatally. In *Normal*   17
Accidents the sociologist Charles Perrow mentions, among other merchant marine perils, "radar-assisted collisions" caused in part by difficulties of plotting multiple and moving targets. One study even determined that as many vessels changed course *toward* a radar-detected target as went in the other direction.

Recomplicating may be political rather than technologi-   18
cal or economic. The 1986 tax code, introduced as fairer and simpler, has relieved some taxpayers of itemizing, but the cost of preparing a tax return may now be as much as 2 percent of a small company's revenue. *The Wall Street Journal* points out that the rules on passive-loss deductions alone take 196 pages to define *activity*. In 1988 the Business Council on the Reduction of Paperwork estimated an average time of 18.6 hours to complete Form 1040, as opposed to the 2.6 hours claimed by the Internal Revenue Service.

In *recongesting*, the system doesn't necessarily become   19
harder to understand. It's just slower and less comfortable. Technological change opens new frontiers but soon clogs them up again.

The automobile-based suburb once seemed to show that   20
new machines could break the stranglehold of grasping railroads and monopolistic center-city landlords. Only de-

cades later did rapid traffic flow turn out to be a mirage. As Parkinson observed of bureaucrats and budgets, cars and car trips have multiplied to saturate the roads built for them, and even the hours of the day. The lunchtime rush hour in the Washington, D.C., area is now as congested as those in the morning and evening. Traffic approaching New York City between 4 and 7 A.M. grew 60 percent from 1967 to 1987. Average travel speed in Los Angeles is projected to slow from 35 miles per hour to under twenty in the next twenty years. Daniel Patrick Moynihan predicts that at present rates, Interstate 95 between Fort Lauderdale and Miami will need 44 lanes in another thirty years.

21 The historian and critic Ivan Illich estimates that the average American now spends a combined 1,600 hours either driving or earning the money to support automotive costs "to cover a year total of 6,000 miles, four miles per hour. This is just as fast as a pedestrian and slower than a bicycle."

22 It's no longer unusual to spend more time on transportation to and from airports, waiting and connection times, and flight delays, than on actual time in the air. Congestion continues even within the aircraft cabin, as coach seats have shrunk from the formerly standard 22 inches to nineteen inches, and pitch (front-to-back spacing) from 34 to 31 inches.

23 Space itself is not immune. Between 30,000 and 70,000 pieces of space debris, each measuring a centimeter or more in diameter and capable of shattering a spacecraft, now clutter the earth's orbit, endangering future missions. Over 6,600 pieces are the size of a softball, or larger. Donald Kessler of the Johnson Space Center in Houston told *The Washington Post* that by 2050, space junk might reach "critical density" and "grind itself to dust," making low earth orbit unusable.

24 *Regenerating*, unlike recongesting, usually appears after a problem seems to have been solved. Instead, the solution turns out to have revived or amplified the problem. Some teachers reinforce the traditional European preference for pencils with plain, painted ends, banning built-in rubber tips as encouragements to sloppy work—a revenge hypothesis,

of course. Their pupils respond by finding great big erasers that can rub out entire lines with ease.

More seriously, pest control regenerates pests. In the 25 1950s and 1960s the pesticides heptachlor and later Mirex devastated wildlife and endangered human health when the U.S. Department of Agriculture deployed them over more than 130 million acres of the South. These tragic costs were tradeoffs, not revenge effects. The revenge effect was that the chemicals also killed the natural ant predators of the targets of the spraying, fire ants, which were able to move into their rivals' territory. Likewise in the 1950s, application of DDT wiped out natural wasp predators of Malaysian caterpillars, bringing defoliation until spraying was stopped. And it should hardly be news that anti-rattlesnake drives in the United States are leading to a surge in reported rattle-snake bites—after a period when there where so few that the Red Cross had discontinued snakebite courses.

Bacteria have a hydralike way of multiplying in response 26 to bathing and even surgical scrubbing; possibly because heat and moisture split large colonies into smaller ones. Michael Andrews reports in *The Life That Lives on Man* that "tests on volunteers who have showered and soaped for ten minutes showed a marked increase in the number of bacteria floating in the air on their rafts of shed skin when they were dressing."

Insects and bacteria that resist pesticides and drugs are 27 an even more alarming regenerating effect, the products of nature's own genetic engineering. Excessive use of antibiot-ics in livestock feed and over-the-counter drugs has made the problem urgent in the Third World, where resistant strains of bacteria causing ear infections, pneumonia, tuber-culosis, and gonorrhea are now common. Even in the United States, antimicrobials in animal feed have helped select and promote resistant strains of salmonella. In 1987 the Univer-sity of Illinois entomologist Robert Metcalf declared that "we may be rushing headlong back into the agricultural and medical dark ages that existed before the discovery of modern insecticides and antibiotics."

Finally, *rearranging* is the revenge effect that shifts a 28 problem in time or space. To be a true revenge effect it must, of course, fall on the same population. For example, if air conditioning raises the ambient temperature of city dwellers who lack it, the result may be uncomfortable and possibly unjust, but it is no revenge effect. But air conditioning in subway systems may be a different story. A spokesman for the New York Transit Authority recently acknowledged that air-conditioned subway cars may provide a cooler ride, "but the stations and the tunnels themselves have become a lot hotter. We seem to be averaging about ten degrees warmer than the outside temperature, so on a day when it's 92 outside, it can be over 100 inside the stations." In fact, heat can actually damage the train air-conditioning units them-selves. Then the train windows can't be opened, or opened much—a form of compound revenge.

As heat is pushed around beneath the cities, disaster is 29 deferred in the countryside and suburbs. The Caltech geolo-gist W. Barclay Kamb, in John McPhee's *The Control of Nature*, describes efforts to channel debris flow from the San Gabriel Mountains with crib structures. "You're not changing the source of the sediment," says Kamb. "Those cribworks are less strong than nature's own constructs. . . . Sooner or later, a flood will wipe out those small dams and scatter the debris. Everything you store might come out in one event."

The environmental historian Stephen J. Pyne points out 30 in *Fire in America* that suppressing forest fires may promote long-term accumulation of combustible materials, leading to even larger conflagrations, just as water control projects may make still heavier flooding possible by blocking off a river's normal channels. And of course all forms of disaster control and relief (including deposit insurance) risk increasing the casualties of disaster by encouraging people to move into and remain in risk-prone areas.

Problems are rearranged above the earth as well as in 31 and on it. The 1970 Clean Air Act, by requiring high smokestacks to protect the surroundings of Midwestern coal-burning plants, ensured the windborne transport of sulfur dioxide, spreading acid rain to woodlands and waters hundreds of miles away.

Do revenge effects teach a political and social lesson? Schol- 32 ars of unintended consequences draw different conclusions.

The historian William H. McNeill points out that Chinese engineers managing the Yellow River in 600 B.C. faced the same cycle as the Army Corps of Engineers does today on the lower Mississippi: levees concentrating sediment and raising water levels, requiring higher levees. The prosperity of the industrial West after World War II, he says, has depended in part on its ability to transfer much of the cost of fluctuations in the business cycle to the loosely organized raw materials producers and immigrant workers of less developed countries. He suggests that "every gain in precision in the coordinating of human activity and every heightening of efficiency in production" may be matched by "a new vulnerability to breakdown," and (while rejecting fatalism) wonders whether "the conservation of catastrophe may indeed be a law of nature like the conservation of energy."

The economist Albert O. Hirschman suggests in his new book, *The Rhetoric of Reaction* (Harvard University Press), that right-wing critics of social and economic reforms exaggerate the seriousness of unintended consequences. He labels the argument that change is counterproductive the "perversity thesis," the assertion that it is useless the "futility thesis," and the claim that it endangers already achieved reforms the "jeopardy thesis." And he shows how closely related the neoconservative critique of the welfare state is to the earlier conservative polemics against the French Revolution and, later, against the spread of the right to vote. 33

While McNeill sees what I call revenge effects as serious consequences probably fated by increasing economic and technological scale, Hirschman regards them as second-order problems magnified by the smug and self-interested. But the fact that all reactionaries invoke unintended consequences doesn't mean that all who take them seriously have been friends of the status quo ante or even the status quo. Consider George Orwell's observation in *The Road to Wigan Pier* (1937): "If the unemployed learned to be better managers they would be visibly better off, and I fancy it would not be long before the dole was docked correspondingly." 34

Fifty years later, liberals are as likely as conservatives to invoke revenge effects. Some cite them in arguing that new road construction may increase traffic congestion, others in 35 insisting that increasing police and prisons actually promotes criminality, and still others in arguing that advanced medical technology may be unhealthy, that pesticides and fertilizers endanger food production in the long run, and that new weapons systems make nations less secure. As the Right took over technological optimism from the Left in the 1970s and 1980s, liberal social critics (Hirschman does not deny this) countered with perversity and futility theories of their own. It is Ivan Illich who first suggested the tormented mythological figure of Tantalus as a symbol of the frustrations of modern life in his book *Medical Nemesis*.

Can there be a strategy against revenge effects? Observers of 36 ironies have been better at posing paradoxes than at resolving them. But that might be because they haven't paid enough attention to how revenge effects have been overcome or at least managed successfully. Think back to the gremlins of World War II aviation. Human ingenuity overcame them. The very jokes about gremlins must have done wonders for morale. And the Axis had gremlins (or Vischerian treacherous objects) of its own.

After the war, Murphy's Law entered the dictionary 37 only because Captain Murphy and his technician finally managed to get the strain gauge bridges wired to assure operation of the balky strap transducer that inspired his law in the first place. Despite tragic episodes, both aircraft design and air traffic control show how engineering practice is able to ensure a remarkably high level of safety in apparently fragile and complex systems. Entire textbooks deal with reliability engineering, though Charles Perrow has argued that nuclear weapons and nuclear power have risks that are inherently and unacceptably high.

Clarity about our expectations also helps. There's noth- 38 ing wrong with wanting to use higher productivity to repeat some activities, like washing clothing, instead of having more free time. Nor is it wicked or foolish to print out three or four drafts of a document or to withdraw cash at all hours from bank accounts. The pleasure of a cool ride, especially for longer-distance subway travelers, may more than offset the discomfort of a hotter platform. The point is to understand choices.

Manufacturers and programmers probably should think 39 more about designing products that can be switched easily among different levels of difficulty. There would be nothing wrong with a complex airline fare system if computer interfaces gave travel agents and eventually the public a clearer overview of alternatives. And individuals could learn to avoid revenge effects by developing their abilities to work without technology. People who can do rapid mental and back-of-the-envelope calculations are most likely to catch costly spreadsheet errors. Those who can write fluently with pencil and paper are best able to use the computer's powers of revision. People who can work with constraint are able to get the most out of power.

Revenge theory doesn't oppose change. It just favors 40 preventive pessimism. As the computer pioneer John Presper Eckert wrote: "If you have a radical idea . . . for God's sake don't be a radical in how you carry it out. . . . Become a right-wing conservative in carrying out a left-wing idea."

VOCABULARY

paragraph 4: cognizance, discerned, malicious, perverse

paragraph 6: aerodynamics, hierarchy

paragraph 7: avant-garde

paragraph 8: expatriate

paragraph 11: batch processing, mainframe, unprecedented, productivity

paragraph 12: spreadsheet, fax, cellular phone

paragraph 13: obsolete, format

paragraph 23: immune, debris, critical density

paragraph 26: hydralike

paragraph 27: genetic engineering, resistant

paragraph 28: ambient

paragraph 29: cribwork

paragraph 30: conflagration, casualty

paragraph 32: levee, fluctuations, coordinating

paragraph 33: neoconservative, polemics

paragraph 34: reactionary, status quo, ante

paragraph 35: Tantalus
paragraph 36: paradox
paragraph 39: interface, constraint

QUESTIONS

1. In what order does Tenner present the five "folklaw principles" discussed?
2. What is "repeating," and what kind of evidence does Tenner present for it?
3. How is "recomplicating" different from "recongesting," and what evidence does Tenner present for these?
4. What evidence does Tenner present for "regenerating," and how is this process different from "recongesting"?
5. How is "rearranging" different from the other folklaws, and what evidence does Tenner present for it?
6. What kinds of inductive evidence—personal experience, observation, statistical studies, for example—does Tenner present in support of his thesis?
7. What thesis concerning technological progress does Tenner develop, and where does he first state it? Does he argue that technological progress is a myth? Does he accept the view of the Left or the Right toward technological progress, or does he reject both views?

SUGGESTIONS FOR WRITING

1. Present personal experiences and observations that lead you to agree with Tenner's analysis about one of the five folklaws, or lead you to doubt or qualify his analysis.
2. State your own view of technological progress, and explain why you hold it. In the course of the discussion, explain why your view of technological progress is the same as or different from Tenner's.

WILLIAM ZINSSER

WILLIAM ZINSSER *has had wide opportunity to study American culture as a journalist and teacher. His long career includes experience as a film critic, a feature writer for* The New York Herald Tribune, *and a columnist for* Life *magazine and* The New York Times. *He has published several collections of essays on life in America, including* The Lunacy Boom (1970). *Zinsser also taught writing at Yale for a number of years and gives valuable advice on the subject in his book* On Writing Well, *a section from which appears later in this book (p. 561).*

The Right to Fail

I like "dropout" as an addition to the American language   1
because it's brief and it's clear. What I don't like is that we
use it almost entirely as a dirty word.

We only apply it to people under twenty-one. Yet an   2
adult who spends his days and nights watching mindless TV
programs is more of a dropout than an eighteen-year-old
who quits college, with its frequently mindless courses, to
become, say, a VISTA volunteer. For the young, dropping
out is often a way of dropping in.

To hold this opinion, however, is little short of treason   3
in America. A boy or girl who leaves college is branded a
failure—and the right to fail is one of the few freedoms that
this country does not grant its citizens. The American dream
is a dream of "getting ahead," painted in strokes of gold
wherever we look. Our advertisements and TV commercials
are a hymn to material success, our magazine articles a toast
to people who made it to the top. Smoke the right cigarette
or drive the right car—so the ads imply—and girls will be
swooning into your deodorized arms and caressing your
expensive lapels. Happiness goes to the man who has the
sweet smell of achievement. He is our national idol, and
everybody else is our national fink.

I want to put in a word for the fink, especially the   4
teen-age fink, because if we give him time to get through his
finkdom—if we release him from the pressure of attaining

certain goals by a certain age—he has a good chance of becoming our national idol, a Jefferson or a Thoreau, a Buckminster Fuller or an Adlai Stevenson, a man with a mind of his own. We need mavericks and dissenters and dreamers far more than we need junior vice-presidents, but we paralyze them by insisting that every step be a step up to the next rung of the ladder. Yet in the fluid years of youth, the only way for boys and girls to find their proper road is often to take a hundred side trips, poking out in different directions, faltering, drawing back, and starting again.

"But what if we fail?" they ask, whispering the dreadful word across the Generation Gap to their parents, who are back home at the Establishment, nursing their "middle-class values" and cultivating their "goal-oriented society." The parents whisper back: "Don't!" 5

What they should say is "Don't be afraid to fail!" Failure isn't fatal. Countless people have had a bout with it and come out stronger as a result. Many have even come out famous. History is strewn with eminent dropouts, "loners" who followed their own trail, not worrying about its odd twists and turns because they had faith in their own sense of direction. To read their biographies is always exhilarating, not only because they beat the system, but because their system was better than the one that they beat. 6

Luckily, such rebels still turn up often enough to prove that individualism, though badly threatened, is not extinct. Much has been written, for instance, about the fitful scholastic career of Thomas P. F. Hoving, New York's former Parks Commissioner and now director of the Metropolitan Museum of Art. Hoving was a dropout's dropout, entering and leaving schools as if they were motels, often at the request of the management. Still, he must have learned something during those unorthodox years, for he dropped in again at the top of his profession. 7

His case reminds me of another boyhood—that of Holden Caulfield in J. D. Salinger's *The Catcher in the Rye*, the most popular literary hero of the postwar period. There is nothing accidental about the grip that this dropout continues to hold on the affections of an entire American generation. Nobody else, real or invented, has made such an engaging shambles of our "goal-oriented society," so gratified our 8 secret belief that the "phonies" are in power and the good guys up the creek. Whether Holden has also reached the top of his chosen field today is one of those speculations that delight fanciers of good fiction. I speculate that he has. Holden Caulfield, incidentally, is now thirty-six.

I'm not urging everyone to go out and fail just for the sheer therapy of it, or to quit college just to coddle some vague discontent. Obviously it's better to succeed than to flop, and in general a long education is more helpful than a short one. (Thanks to my own education, for example, I can tell George Eliot from T. S. Eliot, I can handle the pluperfect tense in French, and I know that Caesar beat the Helvetii because he had enough frumentum.) I only mean that failure isn't bad in itself, or success automatically good. 9

Fred Zinnemann, who has directed some of Hollywood's most honored movies, was asked by a reporter, when *A Man for All Seasons* won every prize, about his previous film *Behold a Pale Horse,* which was a box-office disaster. "I don't feel any obligation to be successful," Zinnemann replied. "Success can be dangerous—you feel you know it all. I've learned a great deal from my failures." A similar point was made by Richard Brooks about his ambitious money loser, *Lord Jim.* Recalling the three years of his life that went into it, talking almost with elation about the troubles that befell his unit in Cambodia, Brooks told me that he learned more about his craft from this considerable failure than from his many earlier hits. 10

It's a point, of course, that applies throughout the arts. Writers, playwrights, painters, and composers work in the expectation of periodic defeat, but they wouldn't keep going back into the arena if they thought it was the end of the world. It isn't the end of the world. For an artist—and perhaps for anybody—it is the only way to grow. 11

Today's younger generation seems to know that this is true, seems willing to take the risks in life that artists take in art. "Society," needlessly to say, still has the upper hand—it sets the goals and condemns as a failure everybody who won't play. But the dropouts and the hippies are not as afraid of failure as their parents and grandparents. This could mean, as their elders might say, that they are just plumb lazy, secure in the comforts of an affluent state. It 12 could also mean, however, that they just don't buy the old standards of success and are rapidly writing new ones.

Recently it was announced, for instance, that more than 13 two hundred thousand Americans have inquired about service in VISTA (the domestic Peace Corps) and that, according to a Gallup survey, "more than three million American college students would serve VISTA in some capacity if given the opportunity." This is hardly the road to riches or to an executive suite. Yet I have met many of these young volunteers, and they are not pining for traditional success. On the contrary, they appear more fulfilled than the average vice-president with a swimming pool.

Who is to say, then, if there is any right path to the top, 14 or even to say what the top consists of? Obviously the colleges don't have more than a partial answer—otherwise the young would not be so disaffected with an education that they consider vapid. Obviously business does not have the answer—otherwise the young would not be so scornful of its call to be an organization man.

The fact is, nobody has the answer, and the dawning 15 awareness of this fact seems to me one of the best things happening in America today. Success and failure are again becoming individual visions, as they were when the country was younger, not rigid categories. Maybe we are learning again to cherish this right of every person to succeed on his own terms and to fail as often as necessary along the way.

VOCABULARY

paragraph 3: swooning, fink
paragraph 4: mavericks, dissenters
paragraph 6: exhilarating
paragraph 7: extinct, unorthodox
paragraph 8: shambles, fanciers
paragraph 9: coddle, frumentum
paragraph 12: affluent
paragraph 13: pining
paragraph 14: vapid

QUESTIONS

1. Zinsser develops his thesis in paragraphs 1–4. What is his thesis, and where does he state it? What kinds of evidence support it?

2. Paragraphs 5–8 provide support for the thesis by *defending* the right to fail. What form does this defense take? What does Zinsser gain by citing the hero of *The Catcher in the Rye?*

3. Paragraphs 9–12 *qualify* what has been said earlier: Zinsser tells us what he does not mean by "the right to fail." What does he not mean, and how does he qualify his idea of failure through discussion of success and failure in the arts, the film art specifically?

4. Paragraphs 13–15 provide additional supporting evidence that the maverick has a role to play in American society (Zinsser's point in paragraphs 6 and 7) and restate the thesis to conclude the essay. What is that evidence, and how is the thesis restated?

5. Do you agree with Zinsser that parents and society provide teenagers with rigid standards of success? Do you agree with his belief that failure is a means to growth?

6. Find information on Henry David Thoreau, Buckminster Fuller, and Adlai Stevenson in your own college library. What details of their lives suggest qualities Zinsser admires?

SUGGESTIONS FOR WRITING

1. Discuss your agreement or disagreement with Zinsser about the demands made on teenagers today, drawing on your own experiences and ideas of success and failure. Do not try to speak for all teenagers. Limit yourself to your experience and personal goals.

2. Discuss the value of two or three different courses you took in high school, with attention to their effect on your choice of a college or a college major, or on the development of long-term goals (or all of these).

3. Write an essay on one of the following topics. In the course of your essay, state a thesis and explain it, defend it with supporting evidence, qualify it (explaining what you do not mean and limiting your generalizations), provide additional evidence for

one or more of your supporting ideas, and restate your thesis in conclusion:

a. unintended lessons taught in high school classes

b. lessons that cannot be taught in school

c. discovering the nature of prejudice

d. "rules" that work at home or at school

e. "rules" that do not work

Analogy

We discussed earlier the use of analogy, or point-by-point comparison of two things, for the purpose of illustration (p. 199). In reasoning about everyday decisions and choices you often use analogy, as in deciding to buy a book similar in subject and setting to an author's earlier book you enjoyed. Since arguments from analogy make predictions only, the fact that you enjoyed the earlier book does not guarantee that you will enjoy the author's new one. But you can increase the probability by noting similarities with other enjoyable books of the same author.

The greater the number of relevant similarities, the stronger the argument. A candidate for governor may argue that she has the same record and personal characteristics as a much admired former governor; her case becomes stronger if she cites several similarities and not just one, and it becomes even stronger if she makes the comparison with several former governors instead of one. Thus she may point out that, like them, she was a mayor of a large city, held office in years of economic hardship, had a successful career as a state legislator, and served for several years in Congress.

Dissimilarities between the candidate and former governors cited must not be significant enough to weaken the argument. Differences in height or in color of hair are obviously insignificant and irrelevant to the conclusion. But the candidate may have to persuade some members of her audience that her being a woman is an insignificant difference, too. She may even use dissimilarities to strengthen her case. If the governors cited have the same record of service as she yet are different in gender, race, or background—some coming from small towns and some from large cities—the probability increases that the similarities she has cited support her claim to be qualified, despite these differences.

The points of similarity must be relevant to the conclusion: the similarities noted do support the claim of the candidate that she has the experience needed to deal intelligently with unemployment and the state budget deficit. However, they would not support the claim that she had the same kind of education as previous governors. A limited conclusion may be drawn from a limited analogy if the points of similarity are clearly specified or agreed upon, if these points are relevant to the conclusion, and if inferences are drawn from these points only.

BROOKS ATKINSON

BROOKS ATKINSON (1894–1984) was associated throughout his long career as a journalist with the New York Times, *as war correspondent, dramatic critic, and essayist. In 1947 he received the Pulitzer Prize for Foreign Correspondence. His books include* Henry Thoreau: The Cosmic Yankee *(1927),* East of the Hudson *(1931), and* Brief Chronicles *(1966). Atkinson wrote often about environmental issues. The essay reprinted here first appeared in the* New York Times *on November 23, 1968. The essay, one of Atkinson's finest on this subject, is particularly effective in its use of analogy.*

The Warfare in the Forest Is Not Wanton

After thirty-five years the forest in Spruce Notch is tall and 1 sturdy. It began during the Depression when work gangs planted thousands of tiny seedlings in abandoned pastures on Richmond Peak in the northern Catskills. Nothing spectacular has happened there since; the forest has been left undisturbed.

But now we have a large spread of Norway spruces a 2 foot thick at the butt and 40 or 50 feet high. Their crowns look like thousands of dark crosses reaching into the sky.

The forest is a good place in which to prowl in search of 3 wildlife. But also in search of ideas. For the inescapable fact is that the world of civilized America does not have such a clean record. Since the seedlings were planted the nation has fought three catastrophic wars, in one of which the killing of combatants and the innocent continues. During the lifetime of the forest 350,000 Americans have died on foreign battlefields.

Inside America civilized life is no finer. A President, a 4 Senator, a man of God have been assassinated. Citizens are murdered in the streets. Riots, armed assaults, looting, burning, outbursts of hatred have increased to the point where they have become commonplace.

Life in civilized America is out of control. Nothing is out 5 of control in the forest. Everything complies with the instinct for survival—which is the law and order of the woods.

Although the forest looks peaceful it supports incessant warfare, most of which is hidden and silent. For thirty-five years the strong have been subduing the weak. The blueberries that once flourished on the mountain have been destroyed. All the trees are individuals, as all human beings are individuals; and every tree poses a threat to every other tree. The competition is so fierce that you can hardly penetrate some of the thickets where the lower branches of neighboring trees are interlocked in a blind competition for survival.

Nor is the wildlife benign. A red-tailed hawk lived there last summer—slowly circling in the sky and occasionally drawing attention to himself by screaming. He survived on mice, squirrels, chipmunks and small birds. A barred owl lives somewhere in the depth of the woods. He hoots in midmorning as well as at sunrise to register his authority. He also is a killer. Killing is a fundamental part of the process. The nuthatches kill insects in the bark. The woodpeckers dig insects out. The thrushes eat beetles and caterpillars.

But in the forest, killing is not wanton or malicious. It is for survival. Among birds of equal size most of the warfare consists of sham battles in which they go through the motions of warfare until one withdraws. Usually neither bird gets hurt.

Nor is the warfare between trees vindictive. Although the spruces predominate they do not practice segregation. On both sides of Lost Lane, which used to be a dirt road, maples, beeches, ashes, aspens and a few red oaks live, and green curtains of wild grapes cover the wild cherry trees. In the depths of the forest there are a few glades where the spruces stand aside and birches stretch and grow. The forest is a web of intangible tensions. But they are never out of control. Although they are wild they are not savage as they are in civilized life.

For the tensions are absorbed in the process of growth, and the clusters of large cones on the Norway spruces are certificates to a good future. The forest gives an external impression of discipline and pleasure. Occasionally the pleasure is rapturously stated. Soon after sunrise one morning last summer when the period of bird song was nearly over, a solitary rose-breasted grosbeak sat on the top of a tall spruce and sang with great resonance and beauty. He flew a few rods to another tree and continued singing: then to another tree where he poured out his matin again, and so on for a half hour. There was no practical motive that I was aware of.

After thirty-five uneventful years the spruces have cre- 11 ated an environment in which a grosbeak is content, and this one said so gloriously. It was a better sound than the explosion of bombs, the scream of the wounded, the crash of broken glass, the crackle of burning buildings, the shriek of the police siren.

The forest conducts its affairs with less rancor and 12 malevolence than civilized America.

VOCABULARY

paragraph 8: wanton, malicious
paragraph 9: segregation, intangible
paragraph 10: discipline, resonance, matin
paragraph 12: rancor, malevolence

QUESTIONS

1. One sometimes hears the argument that violence is natural to human beings, since we are a part of a warring world. How does Atkinson implicitly reject this analogy? More specifically, what are the points of dissimilarity between the world of the forest and the world of humans?
2. How might the world of the forest be used to argue that competition in the world of humans need not be destructive of some of those competing—as the argument that only the "fit" survive in the world of business implies?
3. How does Atkinson increase the probability of his argument through the details he marshals in support of it?

SUGGESTIONS FOR WRITING

Each of the following statements suggests analogy. Write on one of them, discussing points of similarity and dissimilarity and using this discussion to argue a thesis.

a. The family is a small nation.
b. The nation is a large family.
c. College examinations are sporting events.
d. Choosing a college is like buying a car.

LIANE ELLISON NORMAN

LIANE ELLISON NORMAN, who has written on a range of subjects, founded the Pittsburgh Peace Institute and has had wide teaching experience. As her essay on college students shows, Norman uses the personal essay to write about important issues—with humor and insight. The unusual analogy that develops the essay is particularly worth study.

Pedestrian Students and High-Flying Squirrels

The squirrel is curious. He darts and edges, profile first, one
bright black eye on me, the other alert for enemies on the
other side. Like a fencer, he faces both ways, for every
impulse toward me, an impulse away. His tail is airy. He
flicks and flourishes it, taking readings of some subtle kind.

    I am enjoying a reprieve of warm sun in a season of rain
and impending frost. Around me today is the wine of the
garden's final ripening. On the zucchini, planted late, the
flagrant blossoms flare and decline in a day's time.

    I am sitting on the front porch thinking about my
students. Many of them earnestly and ardently want me to
teach them to be hacks. Give us ten tricks, they plead, ten
nifty fail-safe ways to write a news story. Don't make us
think our way through these problems, they storm (and
when I am insistent that thinking *is* the trick, "You never
listen to us," they complain.) Who cares about the First
Amendment? they sneer. What are John Peter Zenger and
Hugo Black to us? Teach us how to earn a living. They will be
content, they explain, with know-how and jobs, satisfied to

do no more than cover the tedium of school board and weather.

Under the rebellion, there is a plaintive panic. What if, on the job—assuming there is a job to be on—they fearlessly defend the free press against government, grand jury, and media monopoly, but don't know how to write an obituary. Shouldn't obituaries come first? 4

I hope not, but even obituaries need good information and firm prose, and both, I say, require clear thought. 5

The squirrel does not share my meditation. He grows tired of inquiring into me. His dismissive tail floats out behind as he takes a running leap into the tree. Up the bark he goes and onto a branch, where he crashes through the leaves. He soars from slender perch to slender perch, shaking up the tree as if he were the west wind. What a madcap he is, to go racing from one twig that dips under him to another at those heights! 6

His acrobatic clamor loosens buckeyes in their prickly armor. They drop, break open, and he is down the tree in a twinkling, picking, choosing. He finds what he wants and carries it, an outsize nut which is burnished like a fine cello, across the lawn, up a pole, and across the tightrope telephone line to the other side, where he disappears in maple foliage. 7

Some inner clock or calendar tells him to stock his larder against the deep snows and hard times that are coming. I have heard that squirrels are fuzzy-minded, that they collect their winter groceries and store them, and then forget where they are cached. But this squirrel is purposeful; he appears to know he'd better look ahead. Faced with necessity, he is prudent, but not fearful. He prances and flies as he goes about his task of preparation, and he never fails to look into whatever startles his attention. 8

Though he is not an ordinary pedestrian, crossing the street far above, I sometimes see the mangled fur of a squirrel on the street with no flirtation left. Even a highflying squirrel may zap himself on an aerial live wire. His days are dangerous and his winters are lean, but still he lays in provisions the way a trapeze artist goes about his work, with daring and dash. 9

For the squirrel, there is no work but living. He gathers 10 food, reproduces, tends the children for a while, and stays out of danger. Doing these things with style is what distinguishes him. But for my students, unemployment looms as large as the horizon itself. Their anxiety has cause. And yet, what good is it? Ten tricks or no ten tricks, there are not enough jobs. The well-trained, well-educated stand in line for unemployment checks with the unfortunates and the drifters. Neither skill nor virtue holds certain promise. This being so, I wonder, why should these students not demand, for the well-being of their souls, the liberation of their minds?

It grieves me that they want to be pedestrians, earth- 11
bound and always careful. You ask too much, they say. What you want is painful and unfair. There are a multitude of pressures that instruct them to train, not free, themselves.

Many of them are the first generation to go to college; 12
family aspirations are in their trust. Advisers and models tell them to be doctors, lawyers, engineers, cops, and public-relations people; no one ever tells them they can be poets, philosophers, farmers, inventors, or wizards. Their elders are anxious too; they reject the eccentric and the novel. And, realism notwithstanding, they cling to talismanic determination; play it safe and do things right and I, each one thinks, will get a job even though others won't.

I tell them fondly of my college days, which were a dizzy 13
time (as I think the squirrel's time must be), as I let loose and pitched from fairly firm stands into the space of intellect and imagination, never quite sure what solid branch I would light on. That was the most useful thing I learned, the practical advantage (not to mention the exhilaration) of launching out to find where my propellant mind could take me.

A luxury? one student ponders, a little wistfully. 14

Yes, luxury, and yet necessity, and it aroused that flight, 15
a fierce unappeasable appetite to know and to essay. The luxury I speak of is not like other privileges of wealth and power that must be hoarded to be had. If jobs are scarce, the heady regions of treetop adventure are not. Flight and gaiety cost nothing, though of course they may cost everything.

The squirrel, my frisky analogue, is not perfectly free. 16
He must go on all fours, however nimbly he does it. Dogs are

always after him, and when he barely escapes, they rant up the tree as he dodges among the branches that give under his small weight. He feeds on summer's plenty and pays the price of strontium in his bones. He is no freer of industrial ordure than I am. He lives, mates, and dies (no obituary, first or last, for him), but still he plunges and balances, risking his neck because it is his nature.

I like the little squirrel for his simplicity and bravery. He 17 will never get ahead in life, never find a good job, never settle down, never be safe. There are no sure-fire tricks to make it as a squirrel.

VOCABULARY

paragraph 2: reprieve, flagrant
paragraph 3: hacks
paragraph 4: plaintive
paragraph 11: pedestrians
paragraph 16: strontium

QUESTIONS

1. What are the dissimilarities between the squirrel and Norman's students?
2. In what ways does the writer resemble the squirrel? How does she establish these points of resemblance?
3. What point is the writer making in her final sentence, "There are no sure-fire tricks to make it as a squirrel"? Could this sentence be taken as the central idea or thesis of the essay and the central analogy?
4. Do you agree with Norman's characterization of college students today? Are the students you know different from the journalism students she is describing?

SUGGESTION FOR WRITING

Discuss your own goals in life, what you hope to gain from a college education, and what experiences and circumstances have shaped you as a student. In the course of your essay, discuss the extent to which you fit the characterization of college students in the essay.

MARK H. MOORE

Analogies with past historical events are popular in dealing with current issues. The Munich Pact, signed by Great Britain, Germany, Italy, and France in September of 1938, is commonly cited in discussions on dealing with dictatorial regimes; but, as Peter McGrath points out, "It is not at all clear that the 'lessons of Munich' are easily translated to other contexts" (Newsweek, October 3, 1988). To cite Munich, McGrath warns, "is inevitably to suggest that nothing has really changed since the world of the late 1930s, that if it was proper to risk war then, it is proper to do so now." MARK H. MOORE, Professor of Criminal Justice at Harvard University's Kennedy School of Government, warns against another popular analogy in discussions of the current drug war. His article appeared in The New York Times *on October 16, 1989.*

Prohibition and Drugs

History has valuable lessons to teach policy makers but it reveals its lessons only grudgingly. Close analyses of the facts and their relevance is required lest policy makers fall victim to the persuasive power of false analogies and are misled into imprudent judgments. Just such a danger is posed by those who casually invoke the "lessons of Prohibition" to argue for the legalization of drugs.

What everyone "knows" about Prohibition is that it was a failure. It did not eliminate drinking; it did create a black market. That in turn spawned criminal syndicates and random violence. Corruption and widespread disrespect for law were incubated and, most tellingly, Prohibition was repealed only 14 years after it was enshrined in the Constitution.

The lesson drawn by commentators is that it is fruitless to allow moralists to use criminal law to control intoxicating substances. Many now say it is equally unwise to rely on the law to solve the nation's drug problem.

But the conventional view of Prohibition is not supported by the facts.

First, the regime created in 1919 by the 18th Amendment and the Volstead Act, which charged the Treasury Department with enforcement of the new restrictions, was far from all-embracing. The amendment prohibited the commercial manufacture and distribution of alcoholic beverages; it did not prohibit its use, nor production for one's own consumption. Moreover, the provisions did not take effect until a year after passage—plenty of time for people to stockpile supplies.

Second, alcohol consumption declined dramatically dur- 6 ing Prohibition. Cirrhosis death rates for men were 29.5 per 100,000 in 1911 and 10.7 in 1929. Admissions to state mental hospitals for alcoholic psychosis declined from 10.1 per 100,000 in 1919 to 4.7 in 1928.

Arrests for public drunkenness and disorderly conduct 7 declined 50 percent between 1916 and 1922. For the population as a whole, the best estimates are that consumption of alcohol declined by 30 percent to 50 percent.

Third, violent crime did not increase dramatically during 8 Prohibition. Homicide rates rose dramatically from 1900 to 1910 but remained roughly constant during Prohibition's 14 year rule. Organized crime may have become more visible and lurid during Prohibition, but it existed before and after.

Fourth, following the repeal of Prohibition, alcohol 9 consumption increased. Today, alcohol is estimated to be the cause of more than 23,000 motor vehicle deaths and is implicated in more than half of the nation's 20,000 homicides. In contrast, drugs have not yet been persuasively linked to highway fatalities and are believed to account for 10 percent to 20 percent of homocides.

Prohibition did not end alcohol use. What is remarkable, 10 however, is that a relatively narrow political movement, relying on a relatively weak set of statutes, succeeded in reducing, by one-third, the consumption of a drug that had wide historical and popular sanction.

This is not to say that society was wrong to repeal 11 Prohibition. A democratic society may decide that recreational drinking is worth the price in traffic fatalities and other consequences. But the common claim that laws backed by morally motivated political movements cannot reduce drug use is wrong.

Not only are the facts of Prohibition misunderstood, but 12 the lessons are misapplied to the current situation.

The U.S. is in the early to middle stages of a potentially 13
widespread cocaine epidemic. If the line is held now, we can
prevent new users and increasing casualties. So this is
exactly *not* the time to be considering a liberalization of our
laws on cocaine. We need a firm stand by society against
cocaine use to extend and reinforce the messages that are
being learned through painful personal experience and testimony.

The real lesson of Prohibition is that the society can, 14
indeed, make a dent in the consumption of drugs through
laws. There is a price to be paid for such restrictions, of
course. But for drugs such as heroin and cocaine, which are
dangerous but currently largely unpopular, that price is
small relative to the benefits.

VOCABULARY

paragraph 2: spawned, syndicates, random, incubated
paragraph 3: moralist
paragraph 6: psychosis
paragraph 8: lurid
paragraph 13: epidemic, liberalization

QUESTIONS

1. Moore warns against "persuasive power of false analogies" in
   discussing legalization of drugs and other issues. What analogy
   is often cited in favor of legalization of drugs, and why does
   Moore consider it false?
2. What kind of evidence does Moore present to show that the
   analogy is false?
3. Does Moore believe that society was right to repeal Prohibition?
   How do you know?
4. What is the thesis of the essay, and where does Moore state it?

SUGGESTIONS FOR WRITING

1. Explain why, in your view, society was right or wrong to repeal
   Prohibition or is right or wrong to prohibit heroin and cocaine.

2. Moore states that, contrary to popular opinion, restrictions on alcohol and drugs can work, but "there is a price to be paid for such restrictions." Explain what price would be paid for restrictions on the use of alcohol, tobacco, or firearms. Then explain why, in your opinion, the price would or would not be too high for society to pay.

Cause and Effect

Earlier we discussed some ways of analyzing cause and effect in paragraphs and essays. These include tracing an effect to its recent or immediate cause (death because of famine) and to its more distant or remote causes (drought, soil erosion, ignorance, indifference, neglect). We also discussed the "four causes" of an object—the materials of its manufacture (material cause), the shape given it (formal cause), its maker (efficient cause), and use (final cause).

Cause may also be analyzed through the words *necessary* and *sufficient*, as when we say that getting an "A" on the final exam is necessary but not sufficient for an "A" in the course: an "A" on the final would be sufficient only if the exam solely determined the course grade. Notice what the words *necessary* and *sufficient* imply: they refer to the conditions or circumstances in which this event *might* occur. When scientists say that a necessary condition of getting a cold is exposure to a virus, they mean that a virus of some kind must be present—not that the virus always produces a cold. Other conditions obviously need to be present, but scientists do not now claim to know what all of these are. If all necessary conditions of the cold were known, we would consider their joining sufficient to produce the cold.

In reasoning about cause in this way, we implicitly recognize that events, like the reasons for our actions, are complex and not simple. Yet this is not what some of our statements show. Statements that generalize about *the* cause of a cold, or some other complex physical or social or political ill, often mistakenly assume that a single cause can be identified. Another hasty generalization arises from the idea that one event must be the cause of another because it precedes it: I caught the cold "because" I was soaked in a rainstorm. Temporal sequence does not necessarily make one event the cause of the next. Clearly we might have caught the cold even if we had not been soaked, and we cannot know whether getting soaked will always give one a cold—even if it has always in the past. This kind of reasoning (discussed by George F. Will, "The Not-So-Mighty Tube") is given a Latin name—the *post hoc* fallacy, from the expression "post hoc, ergo propter hoc" ("after this, therefore because of this").

NORMAN COUSINS

> NORMAN COUSINS *is inseparably linked with the* Saturday
> Review, *which he edited from 1940 to 1977. Cousins won
> numerous awards for his journalism and his work on behalf of
> world peace, including the Peace Medal of the United Nations
> in 1971. His columns, collected in a number of books, provide
> a continuous political commentary on postwar America and
> the world. His essay on Benny Paret, whose fatal knockout in
> the ring Norman Mailer describes earlier in this book (p. 115),
> raises important questions about boxing and spectator sports
> generally—and also about the responsibility of the public for
> the violence encouraged in them. The essay first appeared in*
> Saturday Review *on May 5, 1961.*

Who Killed Benny Paret?

Sometime about 1935 or 1936 I had an interview with Mike 1
Jacobs, the prize-fight promoter. I was a fledgling newspaper
reporter at that time; my beat was education, but during the
vacation season I found myself on varied assignments, all
the way from ship news to sports reporting. In this way I
found myself sitting opposite the most powerful figure in the
boxing world.

There was nothing spectacular in Mr. Jacobs's manner 2
or appearance; but when he spoke about prize fights, he was
no longer a bland little man but a colossus who sounded the
way Napoleon must have sounded when he reviewed a
battle. You knew you were listening to Number One. His
saying something made it true.

We discussed what to him was the only important 3
element in successful promoting—how to please the crowd.
So far as he was concerned, there was no mystery to it. You
put killers in the ring and the people filled your arena. You
hire boxing artists—men who are adroit at feinting, parrying,
weaving, jabbing, and dancing, but who don't pack dyna-
mite in their fists—and you wind up counting your empty
seats. So you searched for the killers and sluggers and
maulers—fellows who could hit with the force of a baseball
bat.

I asked Mr. Jacobs if he was speaking literally when he 4 said people came out to see the killer.

"They don't come out to see a tea party," he said evenly. 5 "They come out to see the knockout. They come out to see a man hurt. If they think anything else, they're kidding themselves."

Recently a young man by the name of Benny Paret was 6 killed in the ring. The killing was seen by millions; it was on television. In the twelfth round he was hit hard in the head several times, went down, was counted out, and never came out of the coma.

The Paret fight produced a flurry of investigations. 7 Governor Rockefeller was shocked by what happened and appointed a committee to assess the responsibility. The New York State Boxing Commission decided to find out what was wrong. The District Attorney's office expressed its concern. One question that was solemnly studied in all three probes concerned the action of the referee. Did he act in time to stop the fight? Another question had to do with the role of the examining doctors who certified the physical fitness of the fighters before the bout. Still another question involved Mr. Paret's manager; did he rush his boy into the fight without adequate time to recuperate from the previous one?

In short, the investigators looked into every possible 8 cause except the real one. Benny Paret was killed because the human fist delivers enough impact, when directed against the head, to produce a massive hemorrhage in the brain. The human brain is the most delicate and complex mechanism in all creation. It has a lacework of millions of highly fragile nerve connections. Nature attempts to protect this exquisitely intricate machinery by encasing it in a hard shell. Fortunately, the shell is thick enough to withstand a great deal of pounding. Nature, however, can protect man against everything except man himself. Not every blow to the head will kill a man—but there is always the risk of concussion and damage to the brain. A prize fighter may be able to survive even repeated brain concussions and go on fighting, but the damage to his brain may be permanent.

In any event, it is futile to investigate the referee's role 9 and seek to determine whether he should have intervened to stop the fight earlier. This is not where the primary responsibility lies. The primary responsibility lies with the people who pay to see a man hurt. The referee who stops a fight too soon from the crowd's viewpoint can expect to be booed. The crowd wants the knockout; it wants to see a man stretched out on the canvas. This is the supreme moment in boxing. It is nonsense to talk about prize fighting as a test of boxing skills. No crowd was ever brought to its feet screaming and cheering at the sight of two men beautifully dodging and weaving out of each other's jabs. The time the crowd comes alive is when a man is hit hard over the heart or the head, when his mouthpiece flies out, when blood squirts out of his nose or eyes, when he wobbles under the attack and his pursuer continues to smash at him with poleax impact.

Don't blame it on the referee. Don't even blame it on the fight managers. Put the blame where it belongs—on the prevailing mores that regard prize fighting as a perfectly proper enterprise and vehicle of entertainment. No one doubts that many people enjoy prize fighting and will miss it if it should be thrown out. And that is precisely the point. 10

VOCABULARY

paragraph 1: fledgling
paragraph 2: colossus
paragraph 3: adroit, feinting, parrying
paragraph 8: hemorrhage
paragraph 9: poleax

QUESTIONS

1. Cousins distinguishes between the immediate and the remote causes of Paret's death (see p. 218). What does he show to be the immediate cause, and why can this cause be stated with near certainty?

2. Cousins is concerned chiefly with the remote cause of Paret's death. How is this concern basic to his purpose in writing the essay? What are the chief indications of that purpose?

3. How would a different purpose have required Cousins to focus instead on the immediate cause?

4. How does Cousins establish the remote cause? Is his evidence statistical—based on a sample of statements of boxing fans? Is it theoretical—based on a discussion of "human nature"? Is he concerned with the psychology of the crowd or the sociology of boxing? Is his analysis of the event intended to offer a complete explanation?

SUGGESTIONS FOR WRITING

1. Analyze two or more pro football or hockey games to determine the extent of their appeal to violent emotions.
2. Contrast Cousins' view of the causes of Paret's death with Mailer's view in "The Death of Benny Paret" (p. 115).

GEORGE F. WILL

GEORGE F. WILL *taught political science and served as a senatorial aide before turning to journalism. From 1972 to 1976, Will served as Washington editor of the* National Review *and began his political column for* Newsweek *in 1975. Will is also a columnist for* The Washington Post *and appears regularly on ABC news programs. His numerous books include* Soulcraft as Statecraft (1983) *and* The Morning After (1986), *one of several collections of his newspaper and magazine columns. In 1977 Will received the Pulitzer Prize for Commentary. In the following essay Will discusses an interesting example of "post hoc" reasoning about the effects of television.*

The Not-So-Mighty Tube

In simpler days it was said that the hand that rocked the cradle ruled the world. Today, says Professor Michael J. Robinson of Catholic University (in *The Public Interest*), the rule of television rocks the world: "In the 1950s television was a *reflection* of our social and political opinions, but by the

1960s it was an important *cause* of them." He insists that television journalism did "engender" fundamental changes, "moving us" toward conservatism, and entertainment programming is a "fomenter" of social liberalism, "fostering" and "pushing us toward" change.

"Mary Tyler Moore and 'Mary Tyler Mooreism' seem to have been unusually effective in 'consciousness raising.' Between 1958 and 1969, the percentage of women accepting the idea that a woman could serve effectively as President actually *declined* by 3 percent. But between 1969 and 1972, the proportion of women who came to accept the idea of a female President *increased* by 19 percent. . . . During those first two seasons in which Mary Richards and Rhoda Morgenstern came to television, the level of public support among women for a female President increased more than among any other two-year—or ten-year—period since the 1930s." 2

The *post hoc, ergo propter hoc* fallacy involves mistaking mere antecedents for causes: the cock crows and then the sun rises, so the crowing caused the sunrise. Did prim Mary cause consciousness to rise? Does the water wheel move the river? Television conforms entertainment to market research, struggling to paddle as fast as the current. Robinson finds it ironic that entertainment programing, the servant of commerce, is supportive of "social liberalism," which he identifies with "hedonism and libertarianism" (and "Maude"). But commerce, which profits from the sovereignty of appetites, has never been a conservative force. 3

Television is not always benign or even innocuous. When vacuous or violent it is enervating and desensitizing; and it has influenced, often unfortunately, the way Americans campaign for office and for change. But it is more mirror than lever. 4

Robinson believes the "audio-visual orgy of the 1960s" shifted "power" upward toward the President and downward toward "have-nots" such as the civil-rights movement, and other "groups wretched or angry or clever enough to do what was needed to become photogenic." But Kennedy, constantly on television and consistently stymied by Congress, learned that conspicuousness is not power. Jimmy Carter, who uses television even more assiduously than 5

Kennedy did, is learning that television does not make governing easier. Americans have developed fine filters for what they consider static, commercial and political, so Carter's media blitz about the energy crisis was like water thrown on sand: it left little trace. Thanks in part to broadcasting, political rhetoric has become like advertising, audible wallpaper, always there but rarely noticed.

Robinson notes that the 1963 "March on Washington" 6 ("the greatest public-relations gambit ever staged") capped five months of intense civil-rights coverage, during which the percentage of Americans regarding civil rights as "the most important problem facing America" soared from 4 to 52. But it is unhistorical to say that this means the networks had begun "to define our political agenda."

Television did not give civil rights leaders the idea of a 7 March on Washington or make the idea effective. In 1941 the mere threat (by A. Philip Randolph) of a march frightened FDR into important policy changes. The civil rights movement did not start with television, but with the moral and social changes wrought by the Second World War. The movement's first great victory was the Supreme Court's 1954 desegregation decision, when television was in its infancy. (During the two television decades the least "photogenic" branch of government, the judiciary, has grown in importance relative to the other branches.) The movement had on its side great leaders, centuries of grievances, the Constitution, and justice. It benefited from television, but did not depend upon it. Television hastened change a bit, but probably did not determine the direction or extent of change. What television did on its own (for example, manufacturing Stokely Carmichael as a "black leader") was as evanescent as most shoddy fiction.

When Robinson says, "Nixon would have lost in 1968 8 had it not been for network news coverage of politics between 1964 and his election," he must mean either that LBJ would have been re-elected but for disintegration at home and defeat abroad; or that without television Americans would not have minded disintegration and defeat; or that without television there would not have been disintegration and defeat. The first idea is true but trivial; the last two are false.

The United States has never had national newspapers, so the focus of news was local. But network news is "national news." So, Robinson says, television has shifted frustrations toward the national government. But the centralization of power in Washington began well before television and would have "nationalized" news, and frustrations, with no help from television. Robinson believes that television journalism, although accused of liberal bias, has recently stimulated political conservatism. But the limitations of government would have become apparent, and the conservative impulse would have had its day, even if television had developed only as an entertainment industry.

To represent situation-comedy shows as shapers of the nation's consciousness is to portray the public as more passive and plastic than it is. To represent television journalism as a fundamentally transforming force is to make the nation's politics seem less purposeful, more mindless, more a matter of random causes than is the case. The contours of history are not determined by communications technology, however much it pleases people to think that history is what, and only what, can be seen at home. To see the rise of blacks, or the fall of LBJ, as primarily a consequence of television is to hollow out history. It discounts the noble and ignoble ideas and passions, heroes and villains and common people who make history.

In the silly movie *Network*, millions of Americans are prompted by a deranged anchor man to sprint to their windows to shout, "We're mad as hell and we won't take it any more." Modern man, proudly sovereign beneath a blank heaven, is prone to believe that "they" (evil persons, irresistible impulses, impersonal forces) control the world. Astrology, vulgar Marxism and Freudianism, and other doctrines nourish this need. So does the exaggeration of media influence. Journalists and perhaps even serious scholars, such as Robinson, who study television, are prone to believe that it turns the world. But the world is not that easy to turn.

VOCABULARY

paragraph 1: engender, fomenter
paragraph 3: antecedents, ironic, hedonism, libertarianism
paragraph 4: benign, innocuous, vacuous, enervating
paragraph 5: orgy, rhetoric
paragraph 10: plastic, contours, ignoble
paragraph 11: deranged

QUESTIONS

1. What in the reasoning that Will disputes illustrates the *post hoc* fallacy?
2. What evidence does Will present to show that television may not have created the civil rights movement and other social movements or influenced national politics to the extent that some people believe?
3. What alternative influences does he propose?
4. Does Will say or imply that television exerts no influence on our society and political life and thinking or that the media in general exert greater influence than they should?
5. Where does Will first state his thesis, and where does he restate it?
6. Do you agree with Will that media blitzes, like the one discussed in paragraph 5, exert less influence than some believe? On what evidence do you base your opinion?

SUGGESTIONS FOR WRITING

1. Trace an idea you hold about energy conservation or drug testing or nuclear power or a similar social or political issue today to its sources—family, friends, school, church, the media, or your own thinking on the issue. State which of these influences was the greatest, and present evidence for your reasons.
2. Discuss the extent to which television influences your attitude toward thinking about a current social or political issue—the power of the presidency or the Supreme Court, for example. Build your discussion to a general assessment of the influence of television on your thinking on social and political issues.

ALAN WERTHEIMER

Alan Wertheimer, *Professor of Political Science at the University of Vermont, writes often on issues of public policy. His essay, reprinted here, first published in the* New York Times *on April 25, 1980, explores the dilemma that he believes underlies much discussion today about government spending—the choice between "helping identifiable lives and saving statistical lives." Knowing that a large segment of his audience supports what he refers to as "welfare-state humanitarianism," Wertheimer uses the dilemma to force these people to recognize that the issue is complex, does not present a simple choice between right and wrong, and demands an examination of basic assumptions.*

Statistical Lives

Suppose the following were true: 1

At least some money spent on open-heart surgery could 2 be used to prevent heart disease. True, patients in need of such surgery might die, but many more lives would be saved.

Some money spent treating tooth decay among low- 3 income children might be used on fluoridation and dental hygiene. True, some decay would go untreated, but fewer children would ever need such treatment.

We could prohibit ransom payments to kidnappers. 4 True, kidnapped children might die, but by lowering the incentive to kidnap, fewer children would be taken.

We could drastically reduce unemployment compensa- 5 tion. True, the unemployed would suffer, but by converting the money saved to private investment and by lowering the incentive to stay jobless, there would be substantially less unemployment.

These cases exhibit a similar structure. All involve 6 choosing between a policy designed to help specific persons and one that seeks to prevent the need for such help. These choices are especially difficult because we know who needs help. The patient requiring open-heart surgery, the kidnapped child, the unemployed auto worker—they have names and faces; they are "identifiable" lives. On the other hand, we do not know whose lives will be saved or who will benefit from the prevention of heart disease, tooth decay, kidnappings, or creation of new jobs. Some people will, and we may be able to estimate their numbers with precision. These are real lives, but they are only "statistical" lives.

We might say we do not have to choose between 7 helping those in need and preventing future needs. After all, we could do both. But resources are scarce, and even when resources are not at issue (as in the kidnapping case), we often must choose between competing persons or goals. We cannot do everything we might like to the extent we might like. We must often choose between helping identifiable lives and saving statistical lives.

I wish to make three points about these dilemmas. First, 8 we do seem to favor the interests of identifiable lives (saving the kidnapped child) and it may not be irrational to do so. Second, we nevertheless do see the need to attend to the interests of statistical lives, even if this injures identifiable lives. Thus it is now common to hear people advocating directing more medical resources to primary prevention of disease and fewer to treatment. Israel's policy of refusing to negotiate with terrorists may risk the lives of some hostages, but we do see the point. Third, welfare-state policies focus on identifiable lives, whereas conservative economists prefer to focus on statistical lives.

Monetary theory and other technical issues aside, the 9 new Adam Smith tells us that however well-intentioned, welfare-state policies have not (always) worked—on the policies' own terms. Minimum-wage laws, unemployment compensation, consumer protection, occupational safety, Medicaid, Social Security—by interfering with market efficiency, by discouraging individual initiative, by impeding private-capital formation, by incurring large-scale expenditures on governmental bureaucracies—all these policies (and others) have been self-defeating. They argue that liberal economics, filled with concern for the genuine needs of identifiable lives, has swelled the future ranks of statistical lives in need. Welfare-state humanitarianism is short-sighted, they say, and is thus less humanitarian than we may believe.

We need not dwell on the accuracy of this account. 10 Conservative economists may be wrong about the facts. We certainly need not assume that market choices and private-capital formation always serve the interests of all social groups, that regulation always does more harm than good. But suppose conservative economists are (sometimes) right about the facts. Suppose that attempts to serve the needs of identifiable lives do end up harming future statistical lives. Should we turn our back on the needs that we see in order to prevent those that we cannot see? Regrettably, the answer may sometimes be yes.

VOCABULARY

paragraph 4: incentive
paragraph 6: statistical
paragraph 8: dilemmas
paragraph 9: impeding, incurring, humanitarianism

QUESTIONS

1. Wertheimer's argument is in part inductive: he shows that well-established facts and expert testimony make the dilemma real, not fictitious. What are these facts and testimony? What in the wording of paragraphs 9–10 shows that Wertheimer considers this evidence highly probable and not certain?

2. If we choose to save specific persons, what would be the consequences? What would they be if we choose to save "statistical" lives?

3. One way of refuting a dilemma is to "grasp the horns" and show that at least one of the alternatives is false or would not lead to the alleged consequences. Another way is to "go between the horns" and show that a third alternative exists—a policy that would save specific persons and "statistical" lives both. In paragraphs 7–8, how does Wertheimer anticipate refutation of the dilemma and answer it?

4. Do you agree with Wertheimer's response to the dilemma in paragraph 10? On what evidence do you base your agreement or disagreement—facts, expert testimony, or assumptions that you regard as self-evident?

SUGGESTIONS FOR WRITING

1. Present examples of your own of the dilemma Wertheimer presents, and use them to explore their implications for your own beliefs and conclusions.

2. Present a dilemma that you believe should concern Americans today. Introduce facts or expert testimony to show that the dilemma is a real one, anticipate a refutation of your dilemma and answer it, and state your own views on what can or should be done.

ROGER D. STONE

ROGER D. STONE *worked for* Time *magazine from 1955 to 1970, serving in the 1960s as bureau chief in San Francisco, Rio de Janeiro, and Paris from 1962 to 1970. He was vice-president of Chase Manhattan Bank until 1975, and in 1976 he joined the World Wildlife Fund—becoming vice-president in 1982. Stone is author of* Dreams of Amazonia *(1985), a history of the Brazilian rain forest. His argument on the benefits of rain forests may be compared with Catherine Caufield's essay on the causes of deforestation (p. 224). Stone's article appeared in* The New York Times *on November 11, 1986.*

Why Save Tropical Forests?

Many Americans feel that saving the world's tropical forests warrant about as much concern as the snail darter. In Europe and the United States, they say, deforestation was the inevitable and desirable consequence of economic progress; why, therefore, should it be any different in the largely underdeveloped nations where the world's tropical forests are to be found?

It *is* different, and our failure to appreciate the difference stems largely from our inability to distinguish between temperate and tropical conditions. The rich soils and relative biological simplicity of the temperate world enhances forest conversion and eventual reforestation. In tropical forest regions, soils tend to be poor. Life supporting nutrients are stored not in soils but in the trees. Remove them and the whole fragile system collapses. History is littered with examples of failed efforts to convert large areas of tropical forest to agriculture, cattle ranching or other "modern" uses.

People and nature both end up losers when the tropical forest is clumsily invaded. To begin with, such forests supply the world with goods—hardwoods, rubber, fruits and nuts, drugs and medicines and fragrances and spices— that often cannot be successfully raised in any but natural conditions. Harvesting beyond sustainable limits has already brought some of the tropical forests' best hardwoods— Brazilian rosewood for example—close to extinction. 3

The tropical forest is also a biological warehouse. Estimates of the total number of species on the planet range up to 30 million, of which only 1.6 million have been identified. It is further estimated that tropical forests, while occupying only 7 percent of the earth's surface, may contain as many as half of all the earth's forms of life. This means that only a tiny fraction of all tropical forest species has so far been studied, and despite the drug industry's increasing reliance on computer modeling, genetic engineering and other laboratory devices, concerned biologists regard the heedless squandering of the tropical forests' known and unknown resources as a major tragedy. 4

Similarly, we depend on a small group of plants—corn, rice, wheat and the like—for a large part of our sustenance. From time to time, plant pathologists have found, the commonly used strains of these plants require genetic fortification from the wild to protect them from blight and disease. Since many such plants originated in tropical areas and only later were cultivated elsewhere, the primeval forests of the tropics represent a vast genetic storehouse of great potential value to everyone. 5

Left untouched, tropical forests also contribute to the stability of the world's climate. But when the forests are burned, the carbon released plays an important role in the buildup of atmospheric gases producing the "greenhouse effect," which is causing a warming trend on the planet. The 6 consequences of this trend could be profound. America's corn belt could become a subtropical region, while the melting of the polar ice cap could cause sea levels to rise and lead to drastic losses of coastal land.

In view of all these factors, one might ask why the attack 7 against the tropical forest continues so relentlessly. The answer is that even the infertile tropical forest is often capable of providing short-term economic benefits to individuals and corporations. Given the human propensity to enjoy one last meal if the alternative seems to be no meal at all, the present defoliation will probably continue unless a revolution in public and official attitudes—equivalent to the dramatic change of the 1980's in how smoking is perceived and handled—comes to the rescue at the 11th hour.

VOCABULARY

paragraph 1: deforestation
paragraph 4: computer modeling, genetic engineering, squandering
paragraph 5: plant pathologists, blight
paragraph 6: "greenhouse effect"
paragraph 7: defoliation

QUESTIONS

1. Why must we distinguish between temperate and tropical conditions in discussing deforestation and its consequences for the planet? What argument in defense of tropical deforestation is Stone refuting in making this distinction?
2. What causes of tropical deforestation does Stone cite? Does he claim to have cited all of them?
3. What would be the short-range effects of tropical deforestation—those that would immediately change our lives? What would be the remote or long-range effects that would change our lives in the future or speed a process now occurring? In what order does Stone present these effects?
4. Is Stone addressing a general audience—some of whom are unfamiliar with the issues and the scientific facts of tropical deforestation? Or is he addressing a special audience—all of

whom are familiar with the issues and the facts? In addressing a different audience, would he need to argue in a different way?

SUGGESTION FOR WRITING

Analyze the causal arguments for and against a current policy that affects the environment—for example, allowing fires in national forests to burn out of control. In the course of your analysis, discuss how people who are for or against an issue distinguish these effects and use them in making their case.

HERBERT HENDIN

> HERBERT HENDIN, *Professor of Psychiatry at New York Medical College, practices in New York City and is director of psychosocial studies at the Center for Policy Research. His books include* Black Suicide *(1969),* The Age of Sensation *(1975), and* Wounds of War: The Psychological Aftermath of Combat in Vietnam *(1984). Hendin states the basic assumptions of his study of drug users in his preface to* The Age of Sensation: *"Social facts are empty numbers unless translated into psychosocial facts that reflect the dynamism of life, the emotion behind the fact, the cause for the statistic. Culture is a two-way street, a flow between individuals and institutions, single minds and collective forces." In this section from the book, Hendin identifies conditions present in the lives of particular users, without trying to suggest that these are necessary—that is, are always present.*

Students and Drugs

No more dramatic expression of the dissatisfaction students 1 feel with themselves can be found than students abusing drugs. Students often become drug abusers, that is, heavy and habitual users, in an attempt to alter their emotional lives, to transform themselves into the people they wish they could be, but feel they never could be without drugs. What they crave is to restructure their own emotions, not to be themselves, but to live as some "other." What this "other" is like and how it can be achieved cut to the center of the changing American psyche.

The turmoil over performance, achievement, and success, the increasing terror of becoming "too" involved with anyone; the attempt to find in fragmentation the means of effecting a pervasive change in one's total relation to life—all these are everywhere prevalent on campus. Students abusing drugs are often attempting to cure themselves of the malaise they see everywhere around them and in themselves. 2

Why do some students take LSD or heroin while others take marijuana or amphetamines? Why do still others take anything and everything? Students who are intrigued by drugs can learn through trial and error and from other students to find and favor the drugs which most satisfy their particular emotional needs. They rapidly become expert psychopharmacologists, able to locate the specific drug cure for what disturbs them. One student who by seventeen had tried just about everything and had become a daily, intravenous heroin user, had rejected LSD early in his drug career, explaining, "I can't see what anyone gets out of it. It just sort of makes you schizy—quiet one minute and freaked out the next." 3

Some students were initially drawn to the "cops-and-robbers" quality of drug abuse. While they were clearly out to defy their parents and the whole structure of authority, they were often unaware that their abuse had anything to do with their families, so profoundly had they pushed their rage at them out of their consciousness. Such students were invariably unable to deal with their parents directly and were bound in a need to defy them and a simultaneous need to punish themselves for their rebellion. 4

Drugs provided these students with both crime and punishment, while removing their defiance out of the direct presence of their parents. One student would "let his mind float away" and concentrate on music he liked whenever his father berated him. Afterward he went out and took whatever drugs he could buy. While he never connected his drug abuse with his anger toward his father, he often dreamed of 5 it as a crime for which he would be punished. He had a dream in which a riot was going on in another part of town while he was shooting heroin. He was afraid that somehow he would be arrested along with the rioters. Drugs were clearly his way of rioting, of diverting the crime of rebellion to the crime of drug abuse and focusing his destructive potential on himself. The expectation this student had that he would be arrested was typical, and revelatory of the appeal of drugs for him. Jail signified to such students a concrete way of locking up their rage. Drugs permitted them to both contain their rage and to express it in a way that gave them a sense of defiance, however self-damaging that defiance may be. Often, students who are most in trouble with the police over drugs are those for whom the need for crime and punishment was more significant than the need for drugs.

For most of the students who abused them, drugs also 6 provided the illusion of pleasurable connection to other people while serving to detach them from the emotions real involvement would arouse. Drugs were, for these students, the best available means of social relations. Heroin abusers found in the junkie underworld a sense of security, belonging, and acceptance derived from the acknowledgement and the shared need for heroin. LSD abusers felt their most intimate experiences involved tripping with another person. Marijuana abusers felt that drugs "took the edge off their personality" enough to permit them to be gentle and to empathize with other people. Amphetamine abusers were pushed into the social round on amphetamine energy, often being enabled to go through sexual experience they would otherwise have found unendurable.

For many students drug abuse is the means to a life 7 without drugs. Such students take drugs to support the adaptation they are struggling to make. Once it is established, they are often able to maintain it without drugs. The period of heavy drug abuse often marks the crisis in their lives when they are trying to establish a tolerable relation to the world and themselves. Appealing, tumultuous, sometimes frighteningly empty, the lives of students who turn to drugs are an intense, dramatic revelation of the way students feel today, what they are forced to grapple with not only in the culture, but in themselves.

VOCABULARY

paragraph 1: psyche
paragraph 2: fragmentation, malaise
paragraph 3: amphetamines, psychopharmacologists, intravenous
paragraph 5: berated, revelatory
paragraph 6: illusion, empathize
paragraph 7: tumultuous

QUESTIONS

1. Does Hendin single out a sufficient cause of drug use among students, or instead identify a number of related (or unrelated) necessary causes?
2. Does he distinguish psychological from social causes, or does he assume these are one and the same?
3. Is Hendin generalizing about all students today—even those who do not use drugs—or is he commenting merely on student drug users?
4. How does drug use foster "fragmentation" in the drug user? How can "fragmentation" provide a solution to the problems Hendin identifies in paragraph 2?
5. What does Hendin mean by the statement, "For many students drug abuse is the means to a life without drugs"?

SUGGESTION FOR WRITING

Describe tensions you have observed in yourself or in fellow students, and discuss the extent to which these tensions resemble those that Hendin identifies. Suggest some of the causes for those you have experienced or observed.

Deductive Reasoning
❦ ❦ ❦

Induction, as we saw, sometimes reasons from particular instances to a general conclusion or truth:

> I studied the equations but didn't do the practice problems, and I failed algebra. I studied French but skipped the language lab and did poorly on the exam. I studied the formulas and performed the experiments carefully and passed Chemistry [*three particular instances*]. Learning seems to depend on practice as well as study [*probable truth*].

Deduction, by contrast, is the process of inference—of reasoning from a general truth to another general truth or a particular instance:

> The act of learning is an act that depends on study and practice.
> The mastery of French is an act of learning.
> Therefore, the mastery of French is an act that depends on study and practice.

Often the argument is shortened and worded less formally:

> Learning depends on study and practice, and therefore so does mastery of French.

In shortened arguments such as this, the major premise, or minor premise (as in the example), or conclusion may be implied. A shortened argument is called an *enthymeme*. In ordinary conversation we may say, in different words, "I passed French because I studied and went to the language lab."

Where inductive arguments depend on the weight of factual evidence beyond the premises, deductive arguments depend on the premises alone as evidence for the conclusion. No other evidence is required because the premises are regarded to be true—as in the *Declaration of Independence:*

> We hold these truths to be self-evident: that all men are created equal; that they are endowed by their creator with certain unalien-

able rights; that among these are life, liberty, and the pursuit of happiness.

From truths such as these, or long-held beliefs, or generalizations well-supported by long experience, we make inferences as in our original example. Thus, if it is true that learning depends on study and practice and true also that mastery of French is an act of learning, it must be true that mastering French depends on study and practice. Though no other evidence but the premises *need* be provided, I may decide to illustrate or defend one or both. For a true statement is not always obvious to everyone.

The argument must satisfy two requirements: the propositions that form the premises must be true, and the process of reasoning must be correct, or to use the technical term, must be valid.

Note that "valid" does not mean "true": an argument may be false in its premises, but still be valid if the process of inference from these premises is correct. Here is a valid argument, both of whose premises are false:

> All Texans are taxpayers.
> All property owners are Texans.
> Therefore, all property owners are taxpayers.

We ask of an argument that it be valid in its reasoning and true in its premises. A valid argument whose premises are true is called sound. The argument just cited would be sound, if, in fact, all Texans do pay taxes, and all property owners (everywhere) are Texans. The argument is, of course, unsound. Logicians have complex techniques for testing the validity of the many kinds of syllogism; we cannot review them here. But we need to keep in mind a few characteristics that invalidate deductive arguments:

Someone says to us: "My neighbors must all be property owners because they all pay taxes." Something strikes us as wrong here, but what is it? We can construct the whole argument as follows:

> All property owners are taxpayers.
> My neighbors are taxpayers.
> Therefore, my neighbors are property owners.

The trouble is with the middle term, taxpayers. The major term of a syllogism is the predicate term of its conclusion; the minor term is the subject. The term that appears in the premises but not in the conclusion is called the middle term.

All	A	is	B
	middle		MAJOR
All	C	is	A
	MINOR		middle
All	C	is	B
	MINOR		MAJOR

Note that the argument may not have more than these three terms. For the argument to be valid, the middle term must be "distributed" in at least one of the premises; that is, it must refer to—that is, be distributed among—all members of the class named. In the argument above, the middle term, *taxpayers,* is undistributed in both premises—referring in each to some members of the class taxpayers, but not necessarily to all:

> All property owners are taxpayers.
> My neighbors are taxpayers.

Though all property owners are taxpayers, not all taxpayers may own property. And though all my neighbors are taxpayers, not all taxpayers may be my neighbors. But that is exactly what the conclusion asserts. The argument is thus invalid because the conclusion says more than the premises do.

Other invalid arguments can be analyzed more easily. The middle term must not be ambiguous, as in the following argument:

> Whoever helps himself is helped by God.
> A thief helps himself.
> Therefore, a thief is helped by God.

And both premises must be affirmative if the conclusion is so: if one of the premises is negative, so must be the conclusion. And, if both premises are negative, no conclusion follows. The following argument is invalid for this reason:

> No dogs are welcome visitors.
> Children are not dogs.
> Therefore, children are welcome visitors.

In developing arguments of our own, we need to remember that an argument may seem "logical" because the process of reasoning is correct, and yet be unsound because the premises are questionable or false. In reading arguments, we need to consider both the premises that form it and the way the writer reasons from them.

H. L. MENCKEN

HENRY LOUIS MENCKEN *(1880–1956) wrote for Baltimore newspapers and other periodicals most of his life and was one of the founders and editors of the* American Mercury *magazine. His satirical essays on American life and politics were collected in six volumes under the title* Prejudices. *His three volumes of autobiography describe his youth in Baltimore and his later career in journalism. Mencken's interests were wide, and he wrote extensively about American democracy and the American language, whose characteristics he describes in a classic book on the subject. His ironic, and often sarcastic, style is well illustrated by these reflections, published in* Minority Report *(1956).*

Reflections on War

The thing constantly overlooked by those hopefuls who talk   1
of abolishing war is that it is by no means an evidence of decay but rather a proof of health and vigor. To fight seems to be as natural to man as to eat. Civilization limits and wars upon the impulse but it can never quite eliminate it. Whenever the effort seems to be most successful—that is, whenever man seems to be submitting most willingly to discipline, the spark is nearest to the powder barrel. Here repression achieves its inevitable work. The most warlike people under civilization are precisely those who submit most docilely to the rigid inhibitions of peace. Once they break through the bounds of their repressed but steadily accumulating pugnacity, their destructiveness runs to great lengths. Throwing off the chains of order, they leap into the air and kick their legs. Of all the nations engaged in the two World Wars the Germans, who were the most rigidly girded by conceptions

of renunciation and duty, showed the most gusto for war for its own sake.

The powerful emotional stimulus of war, its evocation of motives and ideals which, whatever their error, are at least more stimulating than those which impel a man to get and keep a safe job—that is too obvious to need laboring. The effect on the individual soldier of its very horror, filling him with a sense of the heroic, increases enormously his self-respect. This increase in self-respect reacts upon the nation, and tends to save it from the deteriorating effects of industrial discipline. In the main, soldiers are men of humble position and talents—laborers, petty mechanics, young fellows without definite occupation. Yet no one can deny that the veteran shows a certain superiority in dignity to the average man of his age and experience. He has played his part in significant events; he has been a citizen in a far more profound sense than any mere workman can ever be. The effects of all this are plainly seen in his bearing and his whole attitude of mind. War may make a fool of man, but it by no means degrades him; on the contrary, it tends to exalt him, and its net effects are much like those of motherhood on women.

That war is a natural revolt against the necessary but extremely irksome discipline of civilization is shown by the difficulty with which men on returning from it re-adapt themselves to a round of petty duties and responsibilities. This was notably apparent after the Civil War. It took three or four years for the young men engaged in that conflict to steel themselves to the depressing routine of everyday endeavor. Many of them, in fact, found it quite impossible. They could not go back to shovelling coal or tending a machine without intolerable pain. Such men flocked to the West, where adventure still awaited them and discipline was still slack. In the same way, after the Franco-Prussian War, thousands of young German veterans came to the United States, which seemed to them one vast Wild West. True enough, they soon found that discipline was necessary here as well as at home, but it was a slacker discipline and they themselves exaggerated its slackness in their imagination. At all events, it had the charm of the unaccustomed.

We commonly look upon the discipline of war as vastly   4
more rigid than any discipline necessary in time of peace, but
this is an error. The strictest military discipline imaginable is
still looser than that prevailing in the average assembly-line.
The soldier, at worst, is still able to exercise the highest
conceivable functions of freedom—that is, he is permitted to
steal and to kill. No discipline prevailing in peace gives him
anything even remotely resembling this. He is, in war, in the
position of a free adult; in peace he is almost always in the
position of a child. In war all things are excused by success,
even violations of discipline. In peace, speaking generally,
success is inconceivable except as a function of discipline.

The hope of abolishing war is largely based upon the   5
fact that men have long since abandoned the appeal to arms
in their private disputes and submitted themselves to the
jurisdiction of courts. Starting from this fact, it is contended
that disputes between nations should be settled in the same
manner, and that the adoption of the reform would greatly
promote the happiness of the world.

Unluckily, there are three flaws in the argument. The   6
first, which is obvious, lies in the circumstances that a
system of legal remedies is of no value if it is not backed by
sufficient force to impose its decisions upon even the most
powerful litigants—a sheer impossibility in international
affairs, for even if one powerful litigant might be coerced, it
would be plainly impossible to coerce a combination, and it
is precisely a combination of the powerful that is most to be
feared. The second lies in the fact that any legal system, to be
worthy of credit, must be administered by judges who have
no personal interest in the litigation before them—another
impossibility, for all the judges in the international court, in
the case of disputes between first-class powers, would either
be appointees of those powers, or appointees of inferior
powers that were under their direct influence, or obliged to
consider the effects of their enmity. The third objection lies
in the fact, frequently forgotten, that the courts of justice
which now exist do not actually dispense justice, but only
law, and that this law is frequently in direct conflict, not only
with what one litigant honestly believes to be his rights, but

also with what he believes to be his honor. Practically every litigation, in truth, ends with either one litigant or the other nursing what appears to him as an outrage upon him. For both litigants to go away satisfied that justice has been done is almost unheard of.

In disputes between man and man this dissatisfaction is 7 not of serious consequence. The aggrieved party has no feasible remedy; if he doesn't like it, he must lump it. In particular, he has no feasible remedy against a judge or a juryman who, in his view, has treated him ill; if he essayed vengeance, the whole strength of the unbiased masses of men would be exerted to destroy him, and that strength is so enormous, compared to his own puny might, that it would swiftly and certainly overwhelm him. But in the case of first-class nations there would be no such overwhelming force in restraint. In a few cases the general opinion of the world might be so largely against them that it would force them to acquiesce in the judgment rendered, but in perhaps a majority of important cases there would be sharply divided sympathies, and it would constantly encourage resistance. Against that resistance there would be nothing save the counter-resistance of the opposition—*i.e.,* the judge against the aggrieved litigant, the twelve jurymen against the aggrieved litigant's friends, with no vast and impersonal force of neutral public opinion behind the former.

VOCABULARY

paragraph 1: repression, docilely, inhibitions, pugnacity, girded, gusto

paragraph 2: stimulus, evocation, impel, deteriorating, profound

paragraph 3: endeavor

paragraph 6: litigants, coerced

paragraph 7: feasible, aggrieved, essayed, puny

QUESTIONS

1. In paragraphs 1–4, Mencken argues that war will not be easily abolished, and he states his major premise explicitly: "To fight seems to be as natural to man as to eat." How do the wording of his statement and the wording of others in these paragraphs

show that Mencken regards these premises as certain and decisive evidence for his conclusions? What conclusions does he reach based on these premises?

2. Though he regards his premises as certain, Mencken explains and illustrates them. What examples does he present? Does he discuss one civilization or instead generalize about "warlike people" on the basis of observations made over a period of time?

3. Paragraph 1 of the Mencken essay contains the making of several syllogisms. In the first of these, the major premise may be stated in these words: "The expression of a natural instinct is evidence of health and vigor." What are the minor premise and conclusion?

4. In paragraph 1 Mencken argues that repression of a natural instinct leads to increased destructiveness. What are the minor premise and the conclusion?

5. L. A. White, in *Science of Culture*, argues that the need for military conscription refutes the assumption that people are naturally warlike. Given his assumptions and evidence, how might Mencken answer this objection? What do paragraphs 5–7 suggest?

6. In paragraphs 5–7 Mencken challenges "the hope of abolishing war," a hope based on the assumption that people have long since "submitted themselves to the jurisdiction of courts." What flaws does Mencken find in the argument, and what kind of evidence does he present in refutation? Does he deal with particular instances or instead generalize from observations made over a period of time?

7. Decide whether the following arguments are sound (review p. 291). It may be necessary to reword the premises:
   a. Since all voters are citizens and I am a voter, I am a citizen.
   b. Since all voters are citizens and I am a citizen, I am a voter.
   c. Since the Irish are vegetarians and Bernard Shaw was Irish, Shaw was a vegetarian.
   d. Those who made 93 or better on the exam will receive an A in the course. Seven of us received an A in the course and therefore must have made 93 or better on the exam.
   e. Since beneficent acts are virtuous and losing at poker benefits others, losing at poker is virtuous.

8. An *enthymeme* is a condensed syllogism (see p. 290). In the following enthymemes, reconstruct the original syllogism by supplying the missing premise, and then evaluate the argument. The premises and conclusion may need rewording:

    a. John F. Kennedy was a good President because he supported the space program and other kinds of scientific research.

    b. Capital punishment protects society from depraved individuals.

    c. I am successful at business because I once had a paper route.

    d. I am an independent voter, just as my father and grandfather were.

SUGGESTION FOR WRITING

Write an argument for or against one of the following. In an additional paragraph identify one or more assumptions that underlie your argument, and explain why you hold these assumptions:

a. setting the drinking age at 21
b. a ban on smoking in public transportation
c. retaining the 55-mile-per-hour speed limit
d. periodic examination of licensed drivers
e. required attendance in college classes

KENNETH B. CLARK

> Kenneth B. Clark, *Distinguished Professor of Psychology at City College of New York from 1970 to 1975, began teaching at City College in 1942, and has taught at other universities, including Columbia and Harvard. His writings on black life in America have exerted wide influence on social legislation and judicial thinking about civil rights. Among his many influential books are* Dark Ghetto *(1965) and* Pathos of Power *(1974), from which this section on the idea of "relevance" in education is taken.*

The Limits of Relevance

As one who began himself to use the term "relevant" and to   1
insist on its primacy years ago, I feel an obligation to protest the limits of relevance or to propose a redefinition of it to embrace wider terms.

Definitions of education that depend on immediate   2
relevance ignore a small but critical percentage of human
beings, the individuals who for some perverse reason are in
search of an education that is not dominated by the important, socially and economically required pragmatic needs of a
capitalist or a communist or a socialist society. Such an
individual is not certain what he wants to be; he may not
even be sure that he wants to be successful. He may be
burdened with that perverse intelligence that finds the
excitement of life in a continuous involvement with ideas.

For this student, education may be a lonely and tortuous   3
process not definable in terms of the limits of course requirements or of departmental boundaries, or the four- or six-year
span of time required for the bachelor's or graduate degree.
This student seems unable to seek or to define or to discuss
relevance in terms of externals. He seems somehow trapped
by the need to seek the dimensions of relevance in relation to
an examination and re-examination of his own internal
values. He may have no choice but to assume the burden of
seeking to define the relevance of the human experience as a
reflection of the validity of his own existence as a value-
seeking, socially sensitive, and responsive human being. He
is required to deny himself the protective, supporting crutch
of accepting and clutching uncritically the prevailing dogmatisms, slogans, and intellectual fashions.

If such a human being is to survive the inherent and   4
probably inevitable aloneness of intellectual integrity, he
must balance it by the courage to face and accept the risks of
his individuality; by compassion and empathetic identification with the frailties of his fellow human beings as a reflection of his own; by an intellectual and personal discipline
which prevents him from wallowing in introspective amorphousness and childlike self-indulgence. And, certainly, he
must demonstrate the breadth of perspective and human
sensitivity and depth of affirmation inherent in the sense of
humor which does not laugh at others but laughs with man
and with the God of Paradox who inflicted upon man the
perpetual practical joke of the human predicament.

American colleges, with few notable exceptions, provide   5
little room for this type of student, just as American society
provides little room for such citizens. Perhaps it is enough to

see that institutions of higher education do not destroy such potential. One could hope wistfully that our colleges and even our multiuniversities could spare space and facilities to serve and to protect those students who want to experiment without being required to be practical, pragmatic, or even relevant.

Is it possible within the complexity and cacophony of 6 our dynamic, power-related, and tentatively socially sensitive institutions for some few to have the opportunity to look within, to read, to think critically, to communicate, to make mistakes, to seek validity, and to accept and enjoy this process as valid in itself? Is there still some place where relevance can be defined in terms of the quest—where respect for self and others can be taken for granted as one admits not knowing and is therefore challenged to seek?

May one dare to hope for a definition of education 7 which makes it possible for man to accept the totality of his humanity without embarrassment? This would be valuable for its own sake, but it might also paradoxically be the most pragmatic form of education—because it is from these perverse, alone-educated persons that a practical society receives antidotes to a terrifying sense of inner emptiness and despair. They are the font of the continued quest for meaning in the face of the mocking chorus of meaninglessness. They offer the saving reaffirmation of stabilizing values in place of the acceptance of the disintegration inherent in valuelessness. They provide the basis for faith in humanity and life rather than surrender to dehumanization and destruction. From these impracticals come our poets, our artists, our novelists, our satirists, our humorists. They are our models of the positives, the potentials, the awe and wonder of man. They make the life of the thinking human being more endurable and the thought of a future tolerable.

VOCABULARY

paragraph 2: relevance, pragmatic, perverse
paragraph 3: dimensions, dogmatisms
paragraph 4: empathetic, introspective, amorphousness, paradox
paragraph 5: wistfully

paragraph 6: cacophony, validity

paragraph 7: antidotes, font, reaffirmation, dehumanization, satirists, humorists

QUESTIONS

1. How does Clark explain the meanings of the term *relevant?* Why does he briefly review these meanings?
2. What assumptions does Clark make about the educational needs of people?
3. What conclusions does he derive from his assumptions?
4. Do you agree that American colleges have little room for the kind of student described in paragraph 4? What is your answer to the questions Clark asks in paragraph 6?
5. Does Clark seek to refute those who argue the "pragmatic needs" of education? Or does he present confirming arguments only?
6. To what extent does Clark describe your goals in seeking an education?

SUGGESTION FOR WRITING

Evaluate one of the following statements on the basis of your experience and observation:

a. "American colleges, with few notable exceptions, provide little room for this type of student, just as American society provides little room for such citizens."
b. ". . . it is from these perverse, alone-educated persons that a practical society receives antidotes to a terrifying sense of inner emptiness and despair."

ELLEN GOODMAN

> Ellen Goodman, *another of the excellent writers of the journalistic essay in America today, was on the staff of* Newsweek *and the* Detroit Free Press *before joining the*

Boston Globe in 1967 as feature writer and columnist. Her commentary, for which she won the Pulitzer Prize in 1980, appears regularly in the Globe *and other newspapers in the United States. Goodman's statement on pornography was first published in January of 1984. The proposed ordinance was vetoed by the mayor of Minneapolis; in 1985 a similar Indianapolis ordinance was ruled invalid by the United States Court of Appeals in Chicago. On February 27, 1992, the Supreme Court of Canada ruled that materials harmful to women may be curbed, despite the restriction on freedom of expression (New York Times, February 28, 1992). Catharine A. MacKinnon is now a professor of law at the University of Michigan.*

When Pornography and Free Speech Collide

Just a couple of months before the pool-table gang rape in New Bedford, Massachusetts, *Hustler* magazine printed a photo feature that reads like a blueprint for the actual crime. There were just two differences between *Hustler* and real life. In *Hustler*, the woman enjoyed it. In real life, the woman charged rape. 1

There is no evidence that the four men charged with this crime had actually read the magazine. Nor is there evidence that the spectators who yelled encouragement for two hours had held previous ringside seats at pornographic events. 2

But there is a growing sense that the violent pornography being peddled in this country helps to create an atmosphere in which such events occur. As recently as last month, a study done by two University of Wisconsin researchers suggested that even "normal" men, prescreened college students, were changed by their exposure to violent pornography. 3

After just ten hours of viewing, reported researcher Edward Donnerstein, "the men were less likely to convict in a rape trial, less likely to see injury to a victim, more likely to see the victim as responsible." Pornography may not cause rape directly, he said, "but it maintains a lot of very callous attitudes. It justifies aggression. It even says you are doing a favor to the victim." 4

If we can prove that pornography is harmful, then 5

shouldn't the victims have legal rights? This, in any case, is the theory behind a city ordinance that recently passed the Minneapolis City Council. Vetoed by the mayor last week, it is likely to be back at the council for an overriding vote, likely to appear in other cities, other towns.

What is unique about the Minneapolis approach is that 6 for the first time it attacks pornography, not because of nudity or sexual explicitness, but because it degrades and harms women. It opposes pornography on the basis of sex discrimination.

University of Minnesota law professor Catharine Mac- 7 Kinnon, who coauthored the ordinance with feminist writer Andrea Dworkin, says that they chose this tactic because they believe that pornography is central to "creating and maintaining the inequality of the sexes. . . . Just being a woman means you are injured by pornography."

They defined pornography carefully as, "the sexually 8 explicit subordination of women, graphically depicted, whether in pictures or in words." To fit their legal definition it must also include one of nine conditions that show this subordination, like presenting women who "experience sexual pleasure in being raped or . . . mutilated. . . ."

Under this law, it would be possible for a pool-table rape 9 victim to sue *Hustler*. It would be possible for a woman to sue if she were forced to act in a pornographic movie. Indeed, since the law describes pornography as oppressive to all women, it would be possible for any woman to sue those who traffic in the stuff for violating her civil rights.

In many ways, the Minneapolis ordinance is an appeal- 10 ing attack on an appalling problem. The authors have tried to resolve a long and bubbling conflict among those who have both a deep aversion to pornography and a deep loyalty to the value of free speech.

"To date," says Professor MacKinnon, "people have 11 identified the pornographer's freedom with everybody's freedom. But we're saying that the freedom of the pornographer is the subordination of women. It means one has to take a side."

But the sides are not quite as clear as Professor MacKin- 12 non describes them. Nor is the ordinance.

Even if we accept the argument that pornography is 13

harmful to women—and I do—then we must also recognize that anti-Semitic literature is harmful to Jews and racist literature is harmful to blacks. For that matter, Marxist literature may be harmful to government policy.

It isn't just women versus pornographers. If women win 14 the right to sue publishers and producers, then so could Jews, blacks, a long list of people who may be able to prove they have been harmed by books, movies, speeches, or even records. The Manson murders, you may recall, were reportedly inspired by the Beatles.

We might prefer a library or bookstore or lecture hall 15 without *Mein Kampf* or the Grand Whoever of the Ku Klux Klan. But a growing list of harmful expressions would inevitably strangle freedom of speech.

This ordinance was carefully written to avoid problems 16 of banning and prior restraint, but the right of any woman to claim damages from pornography is just too broad. It seems destined to lead to censorship.

What the Minneapolis City Council has before it is a 17 very attractive theory. What MacKinnon and Dworkin have written is a very persuasive and useful definition of pornography. But they haven't yet resolved the conflict between the harm of pornography and the value of free speech. In its present form, this is still a shaky piece of law.

QUESTIONS

1. What distinguishes the Minneapolis definition of pornography from earlier definitions?

2. If the major premise of the definition is that whatever harms people violates their legal rights, what is the minor premise? What is the conclusion?

3. What does Goodman mean by "freedom of speech"? And what conclusion does she draw about the Minneapolis ordinance from her belief?

4. If Goodman opposes banning or censorship of magazines and books and opposes the prior restraint of speech that banning and censorship entail, is she therefore in favor of unrestrained expression of ideas? Or is it impossible to know from the essay?

5. Do you agree or disagree with Goodman that the Minnesota ordinance is flawed? Do you believe censorship is ever justified?

SUGGESTIONS FOR WRITING

1. Write a letter to the Minneapolis City Council, supporting the ordinance or opposing it. In the course of your letter, summarize Goodman's argument against the ordinance and explain why you agree or disagree with Goodman. State your own beliefs and defend them.

2. Goodman agrees with the Minneapolis City Council's definition of pornography but disagrees with the ordinance. Discuss an ordinance with which you similarly disagree and explain why you do. State whether or not a need exists for the ordinance and whether you would favor a better ordinance or none at all.

JANE GOODALL

JANE GOODALL began her studies of animal behavior as assistant and secretary to the distinguished paleontologist Dr. Louis Leakey, curator of the National Museum of Natural History in Nairobi, Kenya. Goodall began her study of chimpanzees under natural conditions in 1960 at Gombe Stream Research Centre, Tanzania, East Africa. Her numerous books and articles include In the Shadow of Man *(1971),* The Chimpanzees of Gombe *(1986), and* Through a Window *(1990), in which the essay reprinted here appears. Goodall discusses an issue under fierce debate in Great Britain and the United States—the use of animals in biomedical research, product testing, and other experimental studies. From beliefs that she holds, Goodall draws inferences or conclusions pertinent to the debate.*

Some Thoughts on the Exploitation of Non-Human Animals

The more we learn of the true nature of non-human animals, especially those with complex brains and correspondingly complex social behavior, the more ethical concerns are raised regarding their use in the service of man—whether this be in entertainment, as "pets," for food, in research laboratories or any of the other uses to which we subject them. This concern is sharpened when the usage in question leads to intense physical or mental suffering—as is so often true with regard to vivisection.

Biomedical research involving the use of living animals 2 began in an era when the man in the street, while believing that animals felt pain (and other emotions) was not, for the most part, much concerned by their suffering. Subsequently, scientists were much influenced by the Behaviorists, a school of psychologists which maintained that animals were little more than machines, incapable of feeling pain or any human-like feelings or emotions. Thus it was not considered important, or even necessary, to cater to the wants and needs of experimental animals. There was, at that time, no understanding of the effect of stress on the endocrine and nervous systems, no inkling of the fact that the use of a stressed animal could affect the results of an experiment. Thus the conditions in which animals were kept—size and furnishings of cage, solitary versus social confinement—were designed to make the life of the caretaker and experimenter as easy as possible. The smaller the cage the cheaper it was to make, the easier to clean, and the simpler the task of handling its inmate. Thus it was hardly surprising that research animals were kept in tiny sterile cages, stacked one on top of the other, usually one animal per cage. And ethical concern for the animal subjects was kept firmly outside the (locked) doors.

As time went on, the use of non-human animals in the 3 laboratories increased, particularly as certain kinds of clinical research and testing on *human* animals became, for ethical reasons, more difficult to carry out legally. Animal research was increasingly perceived, by scientists and the general public, as being crucial to all medical progress. Today it is, by and large, taken for granted—the accepted way of gaining new knowledge about disease, its treatment and prevention. And, too, the accepted way of testing all manner of products, destined for human use, before they go on the market.

At the same time, thanks to a growing number of 4 studies into the nature and mechanisms of animals' perceptions and intelligence, most people now believe that all except the most primitive of non-human animals experience pain, and that the "higher" animals have emotions similar to the human emotions that we label pleasure or sadness, fear or despair. How is it, then, that scientists, at least when they put on their white coats and close the lab doors behind them, can continue to treat experimental animals as mere "things"? How can we, the citizens of civilized, western countries, tolerate laboratories which—from the point of view of animal inmates—are not unlike concentration camps? I think it is mainly because most people, even in these enlightened times, have little idea as to what goes on behind the closed doors of the laboratories, down in the basements. And even those who do have some knowledge, or those who are disturbed by the reports of cruelty that are occasionally released by animal rights organizations, believe that *all* animal research is essential to human health and progress in medicine and that the suffering so often involved is a *necessary* part of the research.

This is not true. Sadly, while some research is under- 5 taken with a clearly defined objective that could lead to a medical breakthrough, a good many projects, some of which cause extreme suffering to the animals used, are of absolutely no value to human (or animal) health. Additionally, many experiments simply duplicate previous experiments. Finally, some research is carried out for the sake of gaining knowledge for its own sake. And while this is one of our more sophisticated intellectual abilities, should we be pursuing this goal at the expense of other living beings whom, unfortunately for them, we are able to dominate and control? It is not an arrogant assumption that we have the *right* to (for example) cut up, probe, inject, drug and implant electrodes into animals of all species simply in our attempt to learn more about what makes them tick? Or what effect certain chemicals might have on them? And so on.

We may agree that the general public is largely ignorant 6 of what is going on in the labs, and the reasons behind the research there, rather as the German people were mostly uninformed about the Nazi concentration camps. But what about the animal technicians, the veterinarians and the research scientists, those who are actually working in the labs and who know exactly what is going on? Are all those who use living animals as part of standard laboratory apparatus, heartless monsters?

Of course not. There may be some—there are occasional 7 sadists in all walks of life. But they must be in the minority. The problem, as I see it, lies in the way we train young people in our society. They are victims of a kind of brainwashing that starts, only too often, in school and is intensified, in all but a few pioneering colleges and universities, throughout higher science education courses. By and large, students are taught that it is ethically acceptable to perpetrate, in the name of science, what, from the point of view of the animals, would certainly qualify as torture. They are encouraged to suppress their natural empathy for animals, and persuaded that animal pain and feelings are utterly different from our own—if, indeed, they exist at all. By the time they arrive in the labs these young people have been programed to accept the suffering around them. And it is only too easy for them to justify this suffering on the grounds that the work being done is for the good of humanity. For the good of one animal species which has evolved a sophisticated capacity for empathy, compassion and understanding, attributes which we proudly acclaim as the hallmarks of humanity.

I have been described as a "rabid anti-vivisectionist." 8 But my own mother is alive today because her clogged aortic valve was removed and replaced by that of a pig. The valve in question—a "bioplasticized" one, apparently—came, we were told, from a commercially slaughtered hog. In other words, the pig would have died anyway. This, however, does not eliminate my feelings of concern for that particular pig—I have always had a special fondness for pigs. The suffering of laboratory pigs and those who are raised in intensive farming units has become a special concern of mine. I am writing a book, *An Anthology of the Pig*, which, I hope, will help to raise public awareness regarding the plight of those intelligent animals.

Of course I should like to see the lab cages standing 9 empty. So would every caring, compassionate human, including most of those who work with animals in biomedical research. But if all use of animals in the laboratory was *abruptly* stopped there would probably, for a while anyway, be a great deal of confusion, and many lines of inquiry would be brought to a sudden halt. This would inevitably lead to an increase in human suffering. This means that, until alternatives to the use of live animals in the research labs are widely available and, moreover, researchers and drug companies are legally compelled to use them, society will demand—and accept—the continued abuse of animals on its behalf.

Already, in many fields of research and testing, the 10 growing concern for animal suffering has led to major advances in the development of techniques such as tissue culture, *in vitro* testing, computer simulation and so on. The day will eventually come when it will no longer be necessary to use animals at all. It must. But much more pressure should be brought to bear for the speedy development of additional techniques. We should put far more money into the research, and give due acknowledgement and acclaim to those who make new breakthroughs—at the very least a series of Nobel prizes. It is necessary to attract the brightest in the field. Moreover, steps should be taken to insist on the use of techniques already developed and proven. In the meantime, it is imperative that the numbers of animals used be reduced drastically. Unnecessary duplication of research must be avoided. There should be more stringent rules regarding what animals may and may not be used for. They should be used only for the most pressing projects that have clear-cut health benefits for many people, and contribute significantly to the alleviation of human suffering. Other uses of animals in the labs should be stopped *immediately*, including the testing of cosmetics and household products. Finally, so long as animals are used in our labs, for any reason whatsoever, they should be given the most humane treatment possible, and the best possible living conditions.

Why is it that only relatively few scientists are prepared 11 to back those who are insisting on better, more humane conditions for laboratory animals? The usual answer is that changes of this sort would cost so much that all progress in medical knowledge would come to an end. This is not true. Essential research would continue—the cost of building new cages and instigating better care-giving programmes would be considerable, but negligible, I am assured, when compared with the cost of sophisticated equipment used by research scientists today. Unfortunately, though, many projects are poorly conceived and often totally unnecessary. They might indeed suffer if the costs of maintaining the research animals are increased. People making their living from them would lose their jobs.

When people complain about the cost of introducing 12 humane living conditions, my response is: "Look at your life-style, your house, your car, your clothes. Think of the administrative buildings in which you work, your salary, your expenses, the holidays you take. And, after thinking about those things, *then* tell me that we should begrudge the extra dollars spent in making a little less grim the lives of the animals used to reduce human suffering."

Surely it should be a matter of moral responsibility that 13 we humans, differing from other animals mainly by virtue of our more highly developed intellect and, with it, our greater capacity for understanding and compassion, ensure that medical progress speedily detaches its roots from the manure of non-human animal suffering and despair. Particularly when this involves the servitude of our closest relatives.

In the United States, federal law still requires that every 14 batch of hepatitis B vaccine be tested on a chimpanzee before it is released for human use. In addition, chimpanzees are still used in some highly inappropriate research—such as the effect on them of certain addictive drugs. There are no chimpanzees in the labs in Britain—British scientists use chimpanzees in the United States, or at the TNO Primate Centre in Holland where EEC funding has recently gone into a new chimpanzee facility. (British scientists do, of course, make massive use of other non-human primates and thousands of dogs, cats, rodents, and so forth.)

The chimpanzee is more like us than any other living 15 being. Physiological similarities have been enthusiastically described by scientists for many years, and have led to the use of chimpanzees as "models" for the study of certain infectious diseases to which most non-human animals are resistant. There are, of course, equally striking similarities between humans and chimpanzees in the anatomy of the brain and nervous system, and—although many have been reluctant to admit to these—in social behavior, cognition and emotionality. Because chimpanzees show intellectual abilities once thought unique to our own species, the line between humans and the rest of the animal kingdom, once thought to be so clear, has become blurred. Chimpanzees bridge the gap between "us" and "them."

Let us hope that this new understanding of the chim- 16 panzees' place in nature will bring some relief to the hundreds who presently live out their lives as prisoners, in bondage to Man. Let us hope that our knowledge of their capacity for affection and enjoyment and fun, for fear and sadness and suffering, will lead us to treat them with the same compassion that we would show towards fellow humans. Let us hope that while medical science continues to use chimpanzees for painful or psychologically distressing experiments, we shall have the honesty to label such research for what, from the chimpanzees' point of view, it certainly is—the infliction of torture on innocent victims.

And let us hope that our understanding of the chimpan- 17 zee will lead also to a better understanding of the nature of other non-human animals, a new attitude towards the other species with which we share this planet. For, as Albert Schweitzer said, "We need a boundless ethic that includes animals too." And at the present time our ethic, where non-human animals are concerned, is limited and confused.

If we, in the western world, see a peasant beating an 18 emaciated old donkey, forcing it to pull an oversize load, almost beyond its strength, we are shocked and outraged. That is cruelty. But taking an infant chimpanzee from his mother's arms, locking him into the bleak world of the laboratory, injecting him with human diseases—this, if done in the name of Science, is not regarded as cruelty. Yet in the final analysis, both donkey and chimpanzee are being exploited and misused for the benefit of humans. Why is one any more cruel than the other? Only because science has come to be venerated, and because scientists are assumed to be acting for the good of mankind, while the peasant is selfishly punishing a poor animal for his own gain. In fact, much animal research is self-serving too—many experiments are designed in order to keep the grant money coming in.

And let us not forget that we, in the west, incarcerate 19

millions of domestic animals in intensive farm units in order to turn vegetable protein into animal protein for the table. While this is usually excused on grounds of economic necessity, or even regarded by some as sound animal husbandry, it is just as cruel as the beating of the donkey, the imprisonment of the chimpanzee. So are the fur farms. So is the abandonment of pets. And the illegal puppy farms. And fox hunting. And much that goes on behind the scenes when animals are trained to perform for our entertainment. The list could get very long.

Often I am asked whether I do not feel that it is unethical 20 to devote time to the welfare of "animals" when so many human beings are suffering. Would it not be more appropriate to help starving children, battered wives, the homeless? Fortunately, there are hundreds of people addressing their considerable talents, humanitarian principles and fund-raising abilities to such causes. My own particular energies are not needed there. Cruelty is surely the very worst of human sins. To fight cruelty, in any shape or form—whether it be towards other human beings or non-human beings—brings us into direct conflict with that unfortunate streak of *inhumanity* that lurks in all of us. If only we could overcome cruelty with compassion we should be well on the way to creating a new and boundless ethic—one that would respect all living beings. We should stand at the threshold of a new era in human evolution—the realization, at last, of our most unique quality: humanity.

VOCABULARY

paragraph 2: biomedical, endocrine

paragraph 3: clinical

paragraph 4: mechanism

paragraph 5: arrogant, assumption

paragraph 7: sadist, empathy, hallmark

paragraph 8: rabid

paragraph 10: in vitro, simulation, stringent

paragraph 11: sophisticated, negligible

paragraph 13: servitude
paragraph 15: cognition, emotionality
paragraph 18: venerated
paragraph 19: incarcerate, husbandry
paragraph 20: threshold, evolution

QUESTIONS

1. According to paragraph 1, what is the central moral issue in the debate over the use of non-human animals in biomedical research?
2. What misconceptions about the use of animals in biomedical research does Goodall discuss in her review of the issue in paragraphs 2–7?
3. What personal experiences, attitudes, and ideas does Goodall discuss in paragraphs 8 and 9?
4. How does Goodall use her opening review in paragraphs 2–7 and the discussion that follows in paragraphs 8 and 9 to develop her point about biochemical research?
5. What objections to humane treatment of animals does Goodall answer in paragraphs 11–13? How does Goodall use chimpanzees to confirm the need for humane treatment?
6. What use does Goodall make of analogy in further supporting her thesis in paragraph 18?
7. Goodall states that "cruelty is surely the very worst of human sins" (paragraph 20). What conclusions does she draw from this belief about the use of animals in biomedical research? Where does she first refer to the ethic that should govern such research and policy decisions generally?
8. Goodall states that "until alternatives to the use of live animals in the research labs are widely available and, moreover, researchers and drug companies are legally compelled to use them, society will demand—and accept—the continued abuse of animals on its behalf" (paragraph 9). Does she believe that the use of animals in biomedical research has been ethical in the absence of alternatives? Would the use of animals be ethical if no other alternatives were to be found?
9. In your view, what policy should govern the use of animals in research of any kind? What beliefs govern your thinking on the issue?

SUGGESTIONS FOR WRITING

1. Though many will agree with Goodall that "cruelty is surely the very worst of human sins," they may not agree on how to define cruelty. For example, those who agree with the constitutional ban on "cruel and unusual punishment" may disagree on whether capital punishment is in fact cruel. Using the *New York Times Index* and other indexes available in your college library, discuss the role the word *cruelty* played in the public and judicial debate over capital punishment in 1973 and since. Focus on two or three judicial opinions issued in a single court case or articles prompted by the case or a particular event.

2. Discuss which of the definitions of cruelty in the judicial opinions or articles you compared best agrees with your own conception. Explain how your conception guides your thinking on capital punishment or another issue of concern to you.

Interpretation of Evidence

In explaining your ideas or beliefs, or in debating an issue, you usually draw on personal experience and observation for illustration and evidence. And sometimes you must turn to other sources of information. Opinions need the support of facts.

In investigating an event, you may find evidence in primary sources—firsthand accounts by participants and observers—and in secondary sources—reports and interpretations by those not present. An eyewitness account is a different kind of evidence from the reconstruction of the event by a historian in later years. Though primary evidence might seem the more reliable, it may be contradictory in itself or be contradicted by other eyewitnesses. At the time of the killing of President John F. Kennedy, eyewitnesses disagreed on what they saw and heard. More than twenty-five years after the event, researchers continue to disagree on what evidence to consider and how to interpret the evidence they do accept.

Secondary sources are often indispensable in deciding how to use primary sources and in determining their reliability. But establishing the reliability of secondary sources can also be difficult. For evidence seldom speaks for itself, and no presentation can be totally neutral or objective, even when the writer seeks to present the evidence fairly; all interpretations are shaped by personal and cultural attitudes. In judging a secondary source, the researcher must consider the weight given to various kinds of evidence, and must be alert to special circumstances or biases that limit the usefulness of the source or make it unreliable. Primary and secondary sources both are necessary in the search for facts, and both must be used with care.

PETER H. ROSSI

Peter H. Rossi *is Professor of Sociology at the University of Massachusetts in Amherst.* In his book Down and Out in America: The Origins of Homelessness (1989) *he gives a history of homelessness in America, describes sampling methods he and associates used to determine the number of homeless in Chicago, and reaches some conclusions about causes. Rossi states:*

> *The social welfare system has never been very attentive to unattached, disaffiliated men, and now it appears to be as unresponsive to unattached females. Likewise, the social welfare system does little to help families support their dependent adult members. Many of the homeless of the 1950s and early 1960s were pushed out or thrown away by their families when they passed the peak of adulthood; many of the new homeless are products of a similar process.*

In the following section from Down and Out in America, *Rossi describes the homeless of the 1970s and the 1980s. In his account he draws on authoritative studies by other sociologists and demographers, among them Donald B. Bogue (see list of references) who recommended that scattered housing and social services for the disabled and alcoholics replace flophouses in the Chicago central business district—to be subsidized by the city.*

The New Homeless of the 1970s and 1980s

By the middle of the seventies, striking changes had taken place in city after city. Indeed, it looked as if at least part of Bogue's advice to Chicago had been followed in every large city. Many of the flophouse cubicle hotels had been demolished, replaced initially by parking lots and later by office buildings and apartment complexes for young professionals. The collection of cheap SRO hotels, where the more prosperous of the old homeless had lived, also had been seriously diminished.

Although the long-established Skid Rows had shrunk 2
and in some cases had been almost obliterated, urban Skid
Rows did not disappear altogether: in most places the
missions still remained,[1] and smaller Skid Rows sprouted in
several places throughout the cities where the remaining
SRO hotels and rooming houses still stood.

In the 1960s and 1970s the need for very cheap accom- 3
modations for old age pensioners documented by Bogue and
by Caplow and Bahr diminished. The number of elderly
extremely poor had declined as the coverage of the Social
Security old age pension system increased to include more of
the labor force and Congress in the 1960s voted more
generous benefits for those who had been working all their
lives under its coverage. In 1974 Social Security old age
benefits were pegged to the cost-of-living index, ensuring
that the high inflation rates of the 1970s would not wipe out
their value. In addition, subsidized senior citizens' housing,
our most popular public housing program, began to provide
affordable accommodations to the elderly. This increase in
the economic well-being of the aged is most dramatically
shown in the remarkable decline in the proportion of those
sixty-five and over who were below the poverty line: from
25% in 1968 to less than 13% in 1985, with the most
precipitous decline of 9% in the three-year period between
1970 and 1973. The consequence of these changes was that a
large portion of those who might otherwise have been
residents of the 1950s-style Skid Row disappeared in the
1970s into the more general housing stock.[2] Higher benefits
and subsidized housing made it possible for the aged pensioners successfully to obtain modest housing. In addition,
more generous benefits were available for the physically
disabled and the chronic mentally ill through an expanded

---

[1] Pacific Garden Mission, one of Chicago's oldest and largest missions, is still at the
same address as in 1958. When studied by Bogue, it was surrounded by exceedingly
shabby buildings housing cubicle hotels, pawnshops, and cheap restaurants and
bars. When I visited there in 1987, it was in the midst of a considerably upgraded
neighborhood with only one of the SROs still functioning.

[2] The age structure of the 1950s and 1960s Skid Rows made changes rapidly evident.
The elderly residents of those times were mostly dead by the end of the 1970s. The
changes in the Social Security system primarily benefited those who retired after
1970.

Supplemental Security Income (SSI) and Social Security Disability Insurance (SSDI) program, enabling this group to move up in the housing market.

The "old" homeless may have blighted some sections 4 of the central cities, but from the perspective of urbanites they had the virtue of being concentrated on Skid Row, which one could avoid and hence ignore. Also, most of the old homeless had some shelter, although inadequate by any standards, and very few were literally sleeping on the streets.

Indeed, in those earlier years, if people had tried to bed 5 down on steam grates or in doorways and vestibules anywhere in the city, police patrols would have bundled them off to jail. The subsequent decriminalization of many status crimes, such as public inebriation and vagrancy—and the decreased emphasis on charges such as loitering has enlarged the turf homeless persons can claim.

Homelessness began to take on new forms by the end of 6 the 1970s. Although all the researchers found some homeless people sleeping out on the streets or in public places in the 1950s and 1960s, the homeless by and large were familyless persons living in very inexpensive (and often inadequate) housing, mainly cubicle and SRO hotels. Toward the end of the next decade, what had been a minor form of homelessness became more prevalent: literal homelessness began to grow and at the same time to become more visible to the public. It became more and more difficult to ignore the evidence that some people had no shelter and lived on the streets. The "new" homeless could be found resting or sleeping in public places such as bus or railroad stations, on steam grates, in doorways and vestibules, in cardboard boxes, in abandoned cars, or in other places where they could be seen by the public.

With the decriminalization of public drunkenness and 7 relaxed enforcement of ordinances concerning many status crimes, police patrols no longer picked up people sleeping out on the streets or warned them away from downtown streets or places with nighttime public access. In addition, whatever bizarre behavior may have characterized the old homeless of the 1950s and 1960s, that behavior was acted out on Skid Row.[3] Now the public could observe first-hand shabbily dressed persons acting in bizarre ways, muttering, shouting, and carrying bulky packages or pushing supermarket carts filled with junk and old clothes.

Even more striking was the appearance of significant 8 numbers of women among the homeless. Shabby and untidy women could now be seen shuffling along the streets with their proverbial shopping bags or nodding sleepily in bus stations. What few homeless women there were in the 1950s and 1960s must have kept out of sight.

Although homeless families rarely were seen walking 9 streets, they started to appear at welfare offices asking for help in obtaining shelter. When homeless families began to come to the attention of the mass media and to show up in television clips and news articles, public attention grew even stronger and sharper.

Reminiscent of the Dust Bowl migration of the Great 10 Depression, stories began appearing in the newspapers about families migrating from the Rust Belt cities to the Sun Belt. The resemblances were striking. The family bread-winner has lost his job in a factory and, after weeks of fruitless search for employment in one or another mid-American city, had loaded household possessions and family into an old car, driving to Houston or Phoenix in search of the employment reputed to be found in the booming Sun Belt.

Popular response to the new homeless grew with the 11 evidence of homelessness. In a celebrated 1979 New York case,[4] public interest lawyers sued the city, claiming that New York had an obligation to provide shelter to homeless men. Their victory in New York led to an expansion of a

---

[3] Bahr and Caplow mention that 1960s bus tours of New York advertised as visiting New York's famous "sights" regularly included a visit to the Bowery, with the tour guide pointing out the "scenes of depravity" that could be viewed safely from the bus.

[4] The case in question, *Callahan v. Carey*, was filed in the New York State Supreme Court in 1979 by Robert Hayes, then director of the New York Coalition for the Homeless. The suit claimed that the state constitution and municipal charter stated that shelter was an entitlement. Shortly after the case was filed, the court issued a temporary injunction requiring the city to expand the capacity of municipal shelters. When the case came to trial in 1981, it was settled by a consent decree in which the city agreed to provide shelter upon demand.

network of "emergency" municipal shelters in that city, which currently provides 6,000 beds nightly, almost entirely in dormitory quarters. Subsequent court decisions have extended New York City's shelter obligations to include homeless women.

The new "emergency shelters" that have been provided 12 in city after city are certainly better than having no roof at all over one's head, but a case can be made that in some respects the cubicle hotels were better. The men's shelters established in New York in the past decade resemble in physical layout the dormitory accommodations provided by the missions in the old Skid Row, which the homeless regarded as last-resort alternatives to sleeping outside. In social organization these shelters most closely resemble minimum-security prisons whose gates are open during the day.

As reported in a survey of New York shelter clients 13 (Crystal and Goldstein 1982), the shelter residents rated prisons *superior* to shelters in safety, cleanliness, and food quality. The shelters were regarded clearly superior only in freedom—meaning the right to leave at any time. The new homeless were clearly worse off in regard to shelter than the old homeless.

The housing for homeless single women was somewhat 14 better than that supplied to men. The single-women's shelters most closely resembled the cubicle flophouses with their cramped individual accommodations.

New York is exceptional in that the municipal govern- 15 ment has directly provided most of the shelters for the homeless. In most cities, private charities with government subsidies usually provide the shelters. The long-established religious missions—for example, the Salvation Army, the Volunteers of America, and the Society of Saint Vincent de Paul—expanded their existing shelters and in some instances undertook to run shelters under contract to municipalities or states. Other charities provided shelters for the first time.

In Bogue's 1958 study, the four or five mission shelters 16 provided only 975 beds for the homeless of Chicago, in contrast to the forty-five shelters we found in that city in the winter of 1985–86, providing a total of 2,000 beds. Several commentators have observed that the shelters provided by private charities are superior in many respects to those run by municipalities.[5]

To accommodate the influx of family groups into the homeless population, new types of shelter arrangements have come into being. Some specialize in quasi-private quarters for family groups, usually one or two rooms per family with shared bathrooms and cooking facilities. In many cities welfare departments have provided temporary housing for families by renting rooms in hotels and motels: for example, in 1986 New York City housed 3,500 homeless families a month in "welfare hotels" (Bach and Steinhagen 1987).[6]

On a scale that was inconceivable earlier, considerable funds for the new homeless have been allocated out of local, state, and federal funds. Private charity has also been generous; most of the "emergency" shelters for the homeless are organized and run by private groups with subsidies from public funds. Foundations have given generous grants. For example, the Robert Wood Johnson Foundation in association with the Pew Memorial Trust supports medical clinics for the homeless persons in nineteen cities. The states have provided funds through existing programs and special appropriations.

In the spring of 1987, after a prelude media event in which congressmen and advocates for the homeless slept overnight on the Capitol steps, Congress passed the McKinney Homeless Assistance Act, which appropriated $442 million for the homeless in fiscal 1987 and $616 million in 1988. The money was channeled through a group of agencies, providing some housing for the homeless, subsidies for existing shelters, and subsidies for a variety of rehabilitation programs including vocational training, medical care, and services for the chronically mentally ill. The funds authorized in the McKinney Act were in addition to those available from

17

18

19

---

[5] At least part of the difference in quality arises because most privately run shelters restrict whom they admit, usually excluding those who are drunk, appear aggressive or behave bizarrely. Municipal shelters ordinarily have to admit everyone and hence find it difficult to exclude anyone on such grounds.

[6] An ironic feature of the use of welfare hotels is that the rents paid by the welfare departments for these accommodations are clearly far greater than current rents at the lowest end of the housing market. Welfare payments are not enough to pay market rents for apartments, but the welfare departments find it possible to pay much higher hotel rents for homeless clients!

existing programs that have supported homeless persons through welfare benefit programs and federally supported medical services.

Reversing the decline discerned in the 1960s, there can [20] be little doubt that homelessness has increased over the past decade and that the composition of the homeless population has changed dramatically. There are ample signs of these changes. In the few cities where data over time exist, there is clear evidence that the number of homeless people is increasing in at least some localities. In New York City, shelter capacity has increased from 3,000 beds to 6,000 over a five-year period. In the same city, the number of families in the welfare hotels has increased from a few hundred to the 3,500 of today. In addition there are many homeless people who do not use the shelters, though the number is not known with any precision.

Nevertheless, for the country as a whole no one knows [21] for sure how much of an increase there has been over the past decade, let alone how many homeless people there are in the United States today. There are many obstacles to obtaining this knowledge. Some of the major obstacles are technical. For example, conventional census and surveys proceed on the assumption that nearly everyone in the United States can be reached through an address, an assumption that is clearly violated in the case of the homeless. Hence we cannot look to the 1980 census (or likely to the 1990 census)[7] or the Current Population Survey for credible estimates of homelessness. Other obstacles are more ideological, as discussed in chapter 1; a central one centers on whether the concept of homelessness should be restricted to those who are without conventional housing or extended to cover all who are inadequately housed. Depending on whether one adopts a narrow or a more inclusive definition, the number of homeless will differ by several magnitudes.

These difficulties notwithstanding, several estimates [22]

---

[7] Current plans for the 1990 census include enumerations late at night in public places, such as bus stations, where homeless persons are known to congregate, as well as full coverage of emergency shelters. If carried through as currently (1988) planned, the 1990 census will provide a better count of the literally homeless than now exists. Nevertheless, the improved tally will still not include homeless people in locations other than those best known to the local experts on whom the census will rely for information on where to count.

have been made of the size of the homeless population. The National Coalition for the Homeless, an advocacy group, "guesstimates" anywhere between 1.5 and 3 million. A much maligned report of the United States Department of Housing and Urban Development (1984), using four different estimation approaches, put the national figure at somewhere between 250,000 and 300,000 in 1983. A more recent estimate by Freeman and Hall (1986) comes closer to the HUD figures with an estimate of 350,000 in 1986. All the existing estimates are vulnerable to criticism, since they all rest on heroic assumptions that challenge credibility.

Although the issue of how many homeless people there 23 are in the United States is a contentious one, it does not really matter which of these estimates is most accurate: homelessness is obviously a major social problem. By any standards, all the estimates point to a national disgrace, clearly unacceptable in a rich, humane society.

Since 1980, there have been approximately forty reason- 24 ably well-conducted social science studies of the homeless whose results are available to the diligent and patient researcher.[8] As in the late 1950s and 1960s, the purpose of funding and carrying out these studies is to provide information on which to base policies and programs to alleviate the pitiful condition of the American homeless. Research funds have been provided by private foundations and government agencies, among which the National Institute of Mental Health has been a major contributor.

The cities studied range across all regions of the country, 25 including all the major metropolises as well as more than a score of smaller cities. One study even attempted to study the rural homeless but had little success in locating them. The cumulative knowledge about the new homeless that can be acquired through these studies is impressive and hardly contentious. Despite wide differences in the definitions of homelessness used,[9] approaches taken, methods, and degree of technical sophistication, there is considerable conver-

---

[8] Many of these studies are privately published in reports that are not circulated through the publications market.
[9] The definitional differences are mainly on the nominal level. Although many of the studies include the precariously housed as homeless in principle, in practice almost all deal with the literally homeless.

gence among their findings. A fairly clear understanding is now emerging concerning who the new homeless are, how they contrast with the general population, and how they differ from the homeless of the 1950s.

Some of the important ways the current homeless differ 26 from the old homeless have already been mentioned. Bogue estimated that in 1958 only about 100 homeless men slept out on the streets of Chicago. Caplow and Bahr make some passing mention of the Bowery homeless sleeping out on the streets or in public places in 1964, but their lack of attention to this feature implies that the number was small. Blumberg's study of Philadelphia uncovered only 64 homeless persons living on the streets in 1960. In contrast, my own studies of homelessness in Chicago found close to 1,400 homeless persons out on the streets in the fall of 1985 and 528 in that condition in the dead of winter in early 1986. Comparably large numbers of street homeless, proportionate to community size, have been found over the past five years in studies of, among other cities, Los Angeles, New York, Nashville, Austin, Detroit, Baltimore, and Washington, D.C. A major difference between the old and the new homeless is that the old homeless routinely managed somehow to find shelter indoors, while a majority of the new homeless in most studies are out on the streets. As far as shelter goes, the new homeless are clearly worse off. In short, *homelessness today means more severe basic shelter deprivation.*

There is also some evidence that those housed in emer- 27 gency shelters may be worse off than the homeless who lived in the cubicle hotels of the 1960s. Whatever the deficiencies of the cubicle hotels, they were a step above the dormitory arrangements of the 1980s and considerably better than sleeping on the streets or in public places.

Furthermore, the new homeless, sheltered or out on the 28 streets, are no longer concentrated in Skid Row. They can be encountered more widely throughout the downtown areas of our cities. Homelessness today cannot be easily ignored as in the past. In the expectation that homeless were on the decline, the traditional Skid Row areas were demolished and homelessness was decentralized. In addition, the liberalization of police patrol practices in many cities has meant that the homeless can wander more freely through our down-town areas. Thus the public receives more direct exposure to the sight of destitution.

A second major contrast is the presence of women among the homeless. In Chicago's Skid Row, Bogue estimated that women may have constituted up to 3% of the residents, and he thought that many were not homeless but were simply living in the Skid Row areas.[10] As reported by Bahr and Garrett (1976), homeless women on the Bowery in the 1960s constituted only a handful—64 over a period of a year—of alcoholics housed in a special shelter for homeless women.[11]

In contrast, we found that women constituted 25% of the 1985–86 Chicago homeless population, close to the average of 21% for studies of the homeless conducted during the 1980s. All the studies undertaken in the 1980s have found that women constitute a much larger proportion of the homeless than in research done before 1970. The proportion female among the homeless varies somewhat from place to place: if women living in the New York welfare hotels are counted as homeless, then women constitute close to one-third of the homeless population of New York. In contrast, a study of the homeless of Austin, Texas, found that only 7% were women, certainly a smaller proportion than in New York, but clearly greater than was found in any of the older Skid Row studies.

A third contrast with the old homeless is in age composition. There are very few persons over sixty among today's homeless and virtually no Social Security pensioners. Instead, today's homeless are concentrated in their twenties and thirties, the early years of adulthood. This is clearly shown in the median age of today's Chicago homeless,

---

[10] Bogue did not interview any women in his sample of cubicle hotel and SRO residents. His estimate of 3% comes from a special tabulation from the 1950 census of persons living outside households in Skid Row census tracts. Bogue believed some of the women were live-in employees of the hotels and others were simply renting rooms in households that lived in conventional dwellings in the Skid Row areas.

[11] In their study of homeless women, they took as subjects every person admitted to a Bowery treatment center for alcoholic women. It took an entire year's set of admissions to supply sixty-four subjects for their study.

29

30

31

thirty-nine, in comparison with the median age of fifty found in Bogue's study. In the forty studies of the homeless conducted in the past few years, the average median age recorded was thirty-six, with a range running from twenty-eight through forty-six. Among the homeless populations throughout the country, most people are in the middle and lower thirties. Where we have data over time, as in the New York City men's shelters, the median age has been dropping rapidly over the past decade.

A fourth contrast is in employment status and income: 32 except for aged pensioners, over half of the Chicago homeless studied in 1958 were employed in any given week, either full time (28%) or intermittently (25%), and almost all worked for some period during a year's time. In contrast, among the new Chicago homeless, only 3% reported having a steady job, and only 39% had worked for some time during the previous month.

Correspondingly, the new homeless have less income 33 than the old. Bogue estimated that the median annual income of the 1958 homeless was $1,058. Our Chicago finding was a median annual income of $1,198. Correcting for inflation, the income of the current homeless is equivalent to only $383 in 1958 dollars. The new homeless are clearly farther out on the fringe of the American economy: their income level is less than one-third that of the old homeless! Similar levels—average median was $1,127—were found in the nine other studies that attempted to measure income.

A final contrast is presented by the ethnic composition 34 of the old and new homeless populations. The old homeless were predominantly white—70% on the Bowery and 82% on Chicago's Skid Row. But the new homeless are recruited heavily from among ethnic minorities: in Chicago 54% were black, and in New York's shelters more than 75% were black, a proportion that has been increasing since the early 1980s. Similar patterns are shown in other American cities, with the minority group in question changing according to the ethnic mix of the general population. In short, we can generalize that minorities are consistently overrepresented among the new homeless in ratios that are some multiple of their presence in the community. The old homelessness was more blind to color and ethnicity than the new homelessness.[12]

There are also some continuities from the old to the new 35 homeless. First of all, they share the condition of extreme poverty. Although the new homeless are lower on the economic ladder, there can be little doubt that both groups' incomes are far too low to support any reasonable standard of living. In Chicago in 1985 and 1986, we found abysmally low incomes among the homeless. With median incomes of less than $100 per month or about $3.25 per day, even trivial expenditures loom as major expenses: for example, a round trip on Chicago's bus system in 1986 cost $1.80, more than half a day's income. A night's lodging at even the cheapest hotel costs $5.00 and up, more than a day's income. And of course, a median income figure simply marks the income received by persons right at the midpoint of the income distribution: half of the homeless live on less than the median, and close to one-fifth (18%) report no income at all. In addition, the income of the homeless is not a steady stream of $3.25 every day; it is intermittent and unpredictable, meaning that for many days in the week, weeks in the month, and months in the year many homeless people have no income at all.

Given these income levels, it is no mystery why the 36 homeless are without shelter; their incomes simply do not allow them to enter effectively into the housing market. Indeed, the only way they can get by is to look to the shelters for a place to sleep, to the food kitchens for meals, to the free clinics and emergency rooms for medical care, and to the clothing distribution depots for something to put on their backs.

The new and the old homeless also are alike in having 37 high levels of disability. The one change from the 1950s to the 1980s is that fewer have the disability of age. As I mentioned earlier, few of the new homeless are over sixty. The current homeless suffer from much the same levels of

---

[12] Blumberg speculated that the black homeless men in the Philadelphia of 1960 were kept out of Skid Row by the discriminatory practices of cubicle hotel landlords and had to be absorbed into the black ghetto areas in rented rooms and boarding-houses. He predicted that the proportion black would rise.

mental illness, alcoholism, and physical disability as the old homeless.

Much has been written asserting that the deinstitution- 38 alization of the chronically mentally ill during the 1960s and 1970s is a major cause of the recent rise in homelessness. Almost as much has been written denying it. At this time it is almost pointless to try to determine which side in this controversy is correct, largely or in part. The decanting of the mental hospital population occurred throughout the 1960s, so its current effects have in any event long since been diluted by time. What is important right now are the current admissions policies of our mental hospitals. Many of the chronically mentally ill homeless would have been admitted two decades ago under then-existing practices. The shelters and the streets now substitute in part for the hospitals of the past.[13]

Remember also that the old Skid Rows were not free of 39 the chronically mentally ill. All the researchers of the 1950s and 1960s remark on the presence of clearly psychotic persons in the flophouses of Chicago and New York. Bogue estimated that about 20% of Skid Row inhabitants were mentally ill. Blumberg found that among the 1960 Philadelphia homeless, 16% had been hospitalized at least once in a mental institution. Chronic mental illness seemingly has always been a significant presence among the homeless. Skid Row, with its easy acceptance of deviance of all sorts, certainly did not draw the line at chronic mental illness.

Because of the attention paid to deinstitutionalization as 40 a possible contributory factor in homelessness, research on the new homeless almost invariably attempts to estimate the prevalence of chronic mental illness among them. A variety of measures have been employed, with the surprising out-

---

[13] In 1958 the municipal court that had jurisdiction over Chicago's Skid Row area had a psychiatrist on its staff whose function was to recommend commitment to mental hospitals for Skid Row residents judged psychotic who were brought before the court. Bogue suggests that this screening process lowered the proportion of Skid Row residents he found to be psychotic. A 1934 study by Sutherland and Locke of emergency municipal shelters for homeless men describes a psychiatric screening process in admission that shunted the clearly psychotic men to mental hospitals. Shelters in Chicago now often refuse admission to persons who behave bizarrely. The clearly psychotic are left to sleep on the streets.

come that they tend to converge: a fair summary is represented by the following averages: 25% of the homeless report previous episodes as mental hospital patients, and 33% show signs of current psychosis or affective disorders. Although the reported current prevalence of chronic mental illness appears to be more than 50% higher among the new homeless than among the old, measurement procedures may account for that difference. In any event, compared with the general population both levels are extremely high.

Physical disabilities also are prevalent among the new 41 homeless. The best evidence on this score comes from the records of medical clinics for the homeless supported by the Robert Wood Johnson Foundation, which document high levels of both chronic conditions, such as hypertension, diabetes, and circulatory disorders, and acute conditions, some integrally related to homelessness, such as lice infestation, trauma, and leg ulcers. The few studies that looked into mortality rates among the new homeless reported rates ten to forty times those found in the general population. Unfortunately, none of the studies of the older homeless give comparable detail on medical conditions, although all the researchers remark on the presence of severe disabilities. Bogue did judge that close to half of the 1958 Skid Row inhabitants had moderate to severe disabilities that would substantially reduce their employability. His studies found much the same mortality levels as have been found among the new homeless—more than ten times higher than among comparable age groups in the domiciled population.

All the studies of the old homeless stress how wide- 42 spread alcoholism was. Bogue found that 30% were heavy drinkers, defined as persons spending 25% or more of their income on alcoholic beverages and drinking the equivalent or six or more pints of whiskey a week. Using a comparable measure, Bahr and Caplow found 36% to be heavy drinkers. Similar proportions were found in Minneapolis and Philadelphia about the same time.

Studies of the new homeless show similar degrees of 43 prevalence of alcoholism. In our Chicago study, 33% had been in a detoxification unit, indicating that one in three had had serious problems with alcohol. Studies in other cities produced estimates of current alcoholism averaging 33%, with a fairly wide range. The consensus of the studies is that about one in three of the new homeless are chronic alcoholics.

A new twist is drug abuse. None of the studies of the 1980 homeless has attempted to measure drug abuse in any satisfactory way, but all point to the significant presence of drug abuse, past and present, among the new homeless. Recent studies of the homeless in New York men's shelters claim that about 20% of the homeless men were current hard drug users or had been addicted in the past. 44

Although only large minorities of the new homeless are afflicted with any one of the disabilities of chronic mental illness, debilitating physical conditions, or chronic alcoholism, their effects are additive. A substantial majority have at least one and sometimes several disabling conditions. About two-thirds of the Chicago homeless had physical health problems, mental health problems, substance abuse problems, or some combination of them. 45

Another point of comparability between the old and the new homeless concerns the heterogeneity of both populations. Both comprised some persons who remained homeless for only short periods and others who were homeless for a long time. The Skid Rows were points of entry for poor migrants to urban centers, who rented cubicles until they had established themselves and could afford conventional dwellings. The short-term new homeless are somewhat different—poor persons whose fortunes have temporarily taken a turn for the worse and who find the shelters a good way to cut back on expenses until they can reestablish themselves.[14] A large portion of the temporary new homeless population consists of young female-headed households in transition from one household (often their parents') to another, using the shelters as a resting place until they can 46

---

[14] In many housing markets a prospective renter must have enough cash to put down a month's rent in advance plus a security deposit in order to rent an apartment. Thus one may need as much as $800 simply to make an offer for an apartment renting for $400 a month. If we also consider that some minimum of furniture is necessary, setting up a new household in a rental apartment may take more than $1,000 in cash. Although few researchers have provided any firm numbers, several have remarked on shelter dwellers who are employed full time and using the cheap accommodations while they accumulate the cash necessary to enter the conventional rental market.

establish a new home on their own, often while waiting for certification as AFDC recipients.

A final point of comparability between the old and the new homeless is that both are relatively isolated socially. The new homeless report few friends and intimates and little contact with relatives and family. There are also signs of some friction between the homeless and their relatives. So extensive was the absence of social ties with kin and friends among the old homeless that Caplow and Bahr define homelessness as essentially a state of *disaffiliation*, without enduring and supporting ties to family, friends, and kin. Disaffiliation also characterizes the new homeless, marking this group off from other extremely poor persons. 47

The contrasts between the homeless of the 1950s and 1960s and the homeless of the 1980s offer some strong clues to why homelessness has become defined as a social problem. First, there can be no doubt that more Americans are exposed to the sight of homelessness because homeless persons are less spatially concentrated today. Second, homelessness has shifted in meaning: the old homeless were sheltered in inadequate accommodations, but they were not sleeping out on the streets and in public places in great numbers. Literal on-the-street homelessness has increased from virtually negligible proportions to more than half of the homeless population. Third, homelessness now means greater deprivation. The homeless men living on Skid Row were surely poor, but their average income from casual and intermittent work was three to four times that of the current homeless. The emergency shelter housing now available is at best only marginally better than the cubicle rooms of the past. 48

Finally, the composition of the homeless has changed dramatically. Thirty years ago old men were the majority among the homeless, with only a handful of women in that condition and virtually no families. The current homeless are younger and include a significant proportion of women. Finally, advocate organizations and groups have arisen to speak on behalf of the homeless and to raise public consciousness of the problem. 49

This combination of changes helps explain why there is so much interest in the homeless today compared with a few decades ago. 50

References

Bach, Victor, and Renée Steinhagen. 1987. *Alternatives to the welfare hotel.* New York: Community Service Society.

Bahr, Howard M., and Theodore Caplow. 1974. *Old men: Drunk and sober.* New York: New York University Press.

Bahr, Howard M., and Gerald Garrett. 1976. *Women alone.* New York: New York University Press.

Blumberg, Leonard, Thomas E. Shipley, Jr., and Irving W. Shandler. 1973. *Skid Row and its alternatives.* Philadelphia: Temple University Press.

Bogue, Donald B. 1963. *Skid Row in American cities.* Chicago: Community and Family Study Center, University of Chicago.

Crystal, Stephen, and Merv Goldstein. 1982. *Chronic and situational dependency: Long-term residents in a shelter for men.* New York: Human Resources Administration.

Freeman, Richard B., and Brian Hall. 1986. "Permanent homelessness in America." Unpublished manuscript, National Bureau of Economic Research, Cambridge, Mass.

Sutherland, Edwin H., and Harvey J. Locke. 1936. *Twenty thousand homeless men: A study of unemployed men in Chicago shelters.* Chicago: J. B. Lippincott.

United States Department of Housing and Urban Development (HUD). 1984. A report to the secretary on the homeless and emergency shelters. Office of Policy Development and Research, Washington, D.C.

VOCABULARY

paragraph 1: flophouse, cubicle

paragraph 2: obliterated

paragraph 3: precipitous

paragraph 4: blighted, perspective, urbanite

paragraph 5: vestibule, decriminalization, inebriation, vagrancy

paragraph 17: influx, quasi-private

paragraph 19: subsidy

paragraph 22: heroic assumption

paragraph 25: cumulative, contentious, technical sophistication, convergence

paragraph 31: median age

paragraph 34: ethnic composition
paragraph 35: intermittent
paragraph 38: deinstitutionalization
paragraph 39: psychotic
paragraph 43: detoxification
paragraph 47: disaffiliation

QUESTIONS

1. What differences does Rossi cite between the new homeless of the 1970s and 1980s and the homeless of earlier times?
2. What characteristics or conditions do they share?
3. How does Rossi explain these differences? Does he explain all of them? Does he single out any cause as dominant?
4. Does Rossi base his conclusions on one kind of evidence—for example, interviews with the homeless, statistical studies, the testimony of social workers and psychologists—or does he base them on more than one kind?
5. What degree of probability does Rossi claim for his conclusions? Does he qualify his evidence or conclusion in any way?

SUGGESTIONS FOR WRITING

1. Drawing on the *New York Times Index, The Washington Post Index,* or the index to another metropolitan newspaper, compile a list of recent articles on homelessness in New York City, Washington, D.C., or another city. In reading the articles, note whether the authors state or imply any causes for homelessness or for its rise or decline. Then summarize your findings, noting similarities and differences in the evidence presented.
2. As an alternate topic, investigate action taken to deal with homelessness or a related social problem in the same city or area. Note differences of opinion on policies and their effects.

LEANNE G. RIVLIN

Leanne G. Rivlin *is Professor of Environmental Psychology at the Graduate School and University Center, University of New York. She is (with M. Wolfe) the author of* Institutional Settings in Children's Lives *(1985). Her essay on homelessness is a version of a paper presented to the Society for the Psychological Study of Social Issues, at the meeting of the American Psychological Association in Los Angeles in 1985. In discussing the causes of homelessness, Rivlin draws on her own research and that of other social psychologists.*

A New Look at the Homeless

The problem of homelessness has escalated into a critical contemporary social issue. Repeatedly, we hear the phrase, "not since the Great Depression of the 30s" have we faced such numbers of people without stable shelter, yet the efforts to deal with this tidal wave of miseries have been limited, at best.

In the last few years it has been difficult, if not impossible, to open the daily newspaper and fail to find at least one article on the homeless. Although attention to the problem declines in mild weather, it does not disappear. Accounts of suffering and deaths, reports of insufficient and brutal shelters, and deaths on the streets are commonplace. The problem is especially grave for homeless families who are housed in sleazy hotels in the Times Square area of New York City, where streets that are crowded with tourists, pimps, prostitutes, and drug pushers are the children's playgrounds.

Other homeless persons have been observed in public transportation stations such as Grand Central Terminal and the Port Authority Bus Terminal in New York. These are the homeless who find temporary havens in public places subject to the changing policies of the public officials who administer these sites and the private individuals who manage them. Open spaces such as parks, plazas, and the entrances of public buildings uncover other homeless persons who find a temporary perch in mild weather as these locations become public hotels for the needy.

By now most of us have had some contact with the 4
homeless, especially but not exclusively in cities. Even if we
have not seen or recognized homeless persons, we are
familiar with accounts of the problem. However, many may
not be aware of the extensiveness of homelessness and the
numbers of persons involved.

Incidences of Homelessness

Accurate statistics on homelessness are impossible to obtain 5
since the very nature of being homeless makes people difficult
to count, unless they come into contact with an official agency.
According to the U.S. Department of Housing and Urban
Development (1984), in the winter of 1983–1984, there were
between 250,000 and 350,000 homeless per night. These statistics have been criticized as inaccurate by many, among
them the research team of the Community Service Society of
New York, a group that has done some landmark work on
the homeless. They prefer to use an estimate of the *total
numbers* of people homeless over the course of a year (Hopper
and Hamburg, 1984), which might extend well beyond two
million. They also raise the question of the definition of a
homeless person, offering Caro's view—a person "without
an address which assures them of at least the following 30
days of sleeping quarters which meet minimal health and
safety standards" (Caro, 1981). While governmental guide-
lines are more restrictive, they are based largely on emergency
needs, although a month of assured residence does not constitute the security of a home. Since many of the homeless
persons today are children, especially minority children, this
criterion becomes even more questionable.

Homelessness exists in many different forms and de- 6
grees based on the time period involved, the alternative
shelter available, and the nature of the person's social
contacts. The stereotypic "Bowery bum" is a *chronic, marginal*
kind associated with alcoholism and drug abuse, with life on
the street most of the day, and with just enough money for
a "flophouse" bed. These people may have consistent social
contacts and many have a social network or support system
of persons like themselves. In some cases they form small
communities of persons with similar life styles.

Another kind is *periodic* homelessness—persons who ⁊
leave home when pressures become intense, leading them to
the shelter or the streets, but the home is still available when
the tensions subside. A form of periodic homelessness occurs
when migrant workers must move with or without their
families to the seasonal work that is the source of their live-
lihoods. This homelessness is time-limited and fairly predictable, with alternative shelter provided, however inadequate
it may be. Still, it does involve periodic uprooting and temporary loss of home-based social and emotional needs.

Temporary homelessness is more time-limited than the 8
other forms and is usually a response to a crisis that arises—a
fire, hospitalization, a move from one community to another.
The assumption here is that the ability to create a home has
not been threatened and that once the person leaves the
hospital, returns to the damaged home, or reaches a new one
the home-building will continue. Their roots are damaged
but not destroyed.

The most catastrophic form of homelessness may be the 9
total form involving the sudden and complete loss of home
and roots through natural, economic, industrial, or interper-
sonal disasters. Beds may be provided in city shelters, gym-
nasiums, or church basements, but there is no home left and
the physical and psychological process of home-building
must begin anew. Although the prospects for the future will
differ across individuals and families, the trauma of the total
devastation of social and physical supports seriously threatens the recuperative powers of the people involved. It is this
group that we see increasing in catastrophically huge numbers.

Sources of Homelessness

There are many assumptions as to why people are homeless, 10
which influence the ways they are perceived and dealt with,
ultimately shaping the policies of various levels of governmental agencies. This raises the question of how much we
really know about why people are homeless.

Most people move over the course of a lifetime, some- 11

times voluntarily, sometimes forced by circumstances over which they have little power. In fact, statistics indicate that one in five persons in the United States moves each year. But as Peter Rossi (1980) has described it, once the realization that one must move occurs, it is followed by a search for a new home, the assessment of an alternative or alternatives, and the selection of the place. Rossi has examined what he calls an "accounting scheme" that leads to the moving process. Although the scheme acknowledges that some families have very limited opportunities—in some cases a single alternative—the homeless have less than that one choice. Given the present housing market, all but the affluent have had their options seriously reduced, although usually not totally removed.

Studies such as those of the Community Service Society 12 of New York have laid to rest many unwarranted myths about the homeless (Baxter and Hopper, 1981). One such myth is that people are homeless by choice, that they prefer a nomadic existence. Thus, the term "urban nomad" that often is applied to them. This is a dangerous view, one that can give us license *not* to address the problems that lead to homelessness and fail to search out the root causes and take appropriate measures. Very few people choose to be homeless. Most are forced into this existence by poverty, the elimination of services, fires that demolish homes, and evictions that have resulted from the difficult economic circumstances in which people are finding themselves today.

Another myth relates to family responsibility: all home- 13 less persons have relatives who should take care of them. This view shifts the burden away from agencies and ordinary citizens, denying the needs that exist, and failing to recognize the devastation and pain that separate homeless persons from their families and friends, if, indeed, they exist.

Who are the homeless? In truth, many different kinds of 14 persons are affected: single men and women and poor elderly who have lost their marginal housing, ex-offenders, single-parent households, runaway youths, "throwaway" youths (abandoned by their families or victims of family abuse), young people who have moved out of foster care, women escaping from domestic violence, undocumented and legal immigrants, Native Americans leaving the reservation after federal cutbacks and unemployment, alcoholics and drug abusers, ex-psychiatric patients, and the so-called "new poor," who are victims of unemployment and changes in the job market (Hopper and Hamburg, 1984). Minorities are among the most affected groups (Mercado-Llorens and West, 1985), and there is persistent evidence that the homeless are getting younger and younger (Hopper and Hamburg, 1984; Salerno, Hopper and Baxter, 1984; U.S. Department of Housing and Urban Development, 1984).

Deinstitutionalization has been accused of being the 15 major contributor to the ranks of the homeless. In fact, many assume that *most* of the homeless are formerly hospitalized mental patients since they often are quite conspicuous. But this is another myth. Again, statistics are inadequate, but it is now estimated that the deinstitutionalized make up 20 to 30 percent of the total numbers of homeless. There is no question that emptying hospitals and failing to provide adequate back-up services led many ex-patients to the streets. Lacking the necessary skills for daily life after years of institutionalization, unable to maintain their fragile hold on housing and nourishment, many end up homeless. These victims of years of deprivation are likely to suffer in a situation where housing is costly and difficult to locate and maintain.

However, the major victims of homelessness are not 16 ex-patients but children, who are forced to live with their families under the most desperate conditions—in overcrowded shelters or welfare hotels. In some parts of the country families searching for employment have been living in their automobiles.

On an international scale the problem of homeless 17 children is remarkably widespread. Their numbers, estimated at 90 million in 1983, have been increasing—with a 90 percent increase anticipated for Brazil (Jupp, 1985). There are children without their families who roam the streets in many countries, but we hear most about them in South and Central America, Africa, India, Bangladesh, Thailand, and the Philippines.

A widely used typology makes the distinction among 18 "children *on* the street," "children *of* the street," and "abandoned" children (Jupp, 1985). Children on the street, over 60 percent of the total according to Felsman (1981; 1984), are children who work on the streets while still maintaining contacts with their families. Children of the streets (over 30 percent of the group) are those living independently with occasional contacts with families. The final group, perhaps 7 percent of the total, are "throwaway" children, abandoned by their families and lacking stable long-term housing and the security of a home.

Basic to most homelessness, in this country and else- 19 where, is the critical shortage of low-cost housing created by a combination of factors. One factor is the shrinking housing picture—each year about 2.5 million persons in this country lose the places where they live. Over half-a-million low-rental housing units are burned out, demolished, or upgraded and priced out of the market for low-income people. When this depressing loss of housing is placed against other changes—deindustrialization and loss of unskilled and semi-skilled jobs, a rise in the poorly paid service economy, the feminization of poverty and persistent unemployment, reduction of benefits due to tightened eligibility requirements (Hopper and Hamburg, 1984)—a disaster scenario emerges. The single-room occupancy hotels, rooming and boarding houses, and other inexpensive, marginal housing that were used by low-income people in the past have all but disappeared, leaving few alternatives. There is little doubt that housing policies and resulting housing shortages are at the base of much of the homelessness we see.

Most homeless persons do try to find places to live— 20 with families, friends, or housing offered by municipal agencies. In most cases these arrangements break down, in time, as families and friends become taxed by the additional burdens, forcing the extra members to leave. But there is no low-cost housing to turn to. Public housing has waiting lists years long. In many cities like New York, the homeless end up in shelters or hotels. Federal funds pay exorbitant monthly rates—generally well over $1,000 and often more than $2,000 for families—for a single substandard hotel room. Those going to municipal shelters find huge dormitories of hundreds of beds, impersonal service, unsanitary conditions, and threats to their person and belongings that may drive them back to the streets and total homelessness.

At a recent meeting on homelessness, a mother with 21 two young children described her shelter experiences—being shifted from one unfamiliar neighborhood to another while city agencies were trying to locate a replacement for her condemned apartment. She was appalled at the dirt, the closeness of the shelter beds, the mixture of people who, from her view, were threats to herself and her children. Coping with her four-year-old son's toileting needs made an ordinary activity into a major obstacle, since she had been warned against letting him use the men's room alone and the child was terrified of getting lost. It was a calamity every time the toilet had to be used.

Other homeless persons are victims of various kinds of 22 disasters that are as painful as fires, loss of income, or gentrification. Tidal waves and floods in Bangladesh is one such natural catastrophe, leaving thousands in a state of homelessness. The drought in Africa created another group of wanderers looking for food with many dying in the process, especially the children. In some cases the disaster is far from natural: the result of pollution, contamination, or nuclear accidents. The victims of Three Mile Island or Buffalo Creek are no less homeless than the tidal wave or drought survivor. So, too, the refugees of war, the boat people from Vietnam, the thousands of Central Americans who have fled their homes as a result of war, poverty, or political conflict are examples of the homeless. These victims share the fate of the burned-out or evicted families in their search for a haven, although the conditions and the needs may differ.

Although the homelessness that results from fire, 23 floods, famine, or political conditions that redefine national boundaries or wars that scatter populations can occur almost anywhere, there is evidence that in some societies the homeless are quickly absorbed, taken in and helped by friends, neighbors, and family. There are places and times in history where all participate in the reconstruction of the home. However, if the catastrophe affects a large enough area, rendering all residents victims, few resources or people may remain to provide help. The so-called "safety net" of the present Administration in Washington has great gashes that permit many to drop through.

We might suspect that some people are more vulnerable 24 than others for various reasons. For some, social or cultural supports may be strong, providing resources that others lack. Clearly, those with financial ability can find housing substitutes that are not available to the poor. Illness can exacerbate the condition of loss of home. Minority status offers both economic and social disadvantages in finding shelter and starting over. But we really know little about the contribution of people's past to their management of homelessness. Before decisions are made about what to do and where to direct resources, we need to know much more about homelessness.

The Homeless Existence

Wherever we find the homeless their days are filled with 25 constant battles to find places to rest or sleep, to keep clean, to find food, to be safe, to retain personal belongings, and, for some, to fill up the empty hours that stretch ahead. A woman describes the effort to find places where she can wash her hair. Men in a small voluntary shelter launder their clothing in a tiny washroom, drying garments over radiators. The hunger of the homeless is overwhelming as is their eagerness and gratitude for white bread and peanut butter, for hot coffee and oranges. The children play in huge armories around lines and lines of cots or in the plazas near welfare hotels dominated by drug pushers and alcoholics. This is the "life world" of homeless citizens:

> the taken-for-granted pattern and context of everyday life in which people routinely conduct their daily affairs without having to bring each gesture, behavior, and event to conscious attention (Seamon, 1984, p. 124).

For the homeless person, little can be taken for granted: 26 the lifeworld is threatened at the core. The struggle to satisfy the very basic needs taken for granted by most of us—for food, rest, protection from the elements, and safety—must be constantly and consciously negotiated. Life in the public shelters or welfare hotels can be as precarious and difficult as the streets. In the welfare hotels in New York, a parent must prepare meals on a limited daily food allowance in a room with no refrigerator and a single hotplate, difficult, indeed, when there are a number of persons to feed.

The public shelters for single persons and families are enormous barrack-like structures allowing no privacy and few comforts. The meals that are provided may be unfamiliar foods served at odd hours. The number of personal possessions that can be maintained is sorely limited since storage is non-existent and the loss of belongings persistent. These places share many of the qualities of other institutions—impersonality, routine, and lack of privacy and control (Rivlin, Bogert and Cirillo, 1981) 27

The challenges to daily life activities come from many sources—criminals who prey on the homeless, space managers who want them out of places, and others who find it uncomfortable to be around homeless persons. But the resourcefulness of many of the homeless is impressive. Some are able to "pass"—to cloak themselves in sufficiently ordinary ways so as to look like the people they are not. Others are able to find safe places for themselves, where there is warmth and some measure of security against the array of threats to their well-being. 28

There is also a great deal of supportiveness within homeless groups: the sharing of survival tips, of job possibilities, where to go to keep warm, as well as cigarettes, reading material, food, and clothing. It would be well to identify these strengths and build on them in the process of dealing with homelessness. There is cleverness and street-wisdom in the woman who found a place to shampoo her hair and clean herself or the man in Grand Central Terminal who converted an old wardrobe trunk into a portable earth station, neatly filled with an array of life-sustaining possessions—clothing, cleaning materials, and dishes. These are capable survivors, whose coping strategies and the competence that supports them need to be documented, rather than their weaknesses and needs alone. 29

Attitudes Toward the Homeless

Some of the challenges faced by homeless persons come 30 from the attitudes of those around them. Mobile people tend to be mistrusted by governments that want to count, tax, and control those living within their boundaries. Indeed, over the years there have been direct and indirect measures taken to sedentarize nomadic groups, to keep them in defined areas, often in the name of economic development. If governments have been unsympathetic toward mobile persons, there also is a long history of mixed reactions toward all kinds of strangers, especially destitute ones. Homeless strangers have been the object of pity, charity, and hospitality, but they also have been feared, rejected, and abused.

In literature the stranger is often the subject of suspicion, 31 at the very least. The Torah speaks of the "ger" (resident strangers), non-Israelites who were unable to rely on their tribes for protection (Union of American Hebrew Congregations, 1981). The kindness that was extended to these strangers derived from the Biblical injunction "You shall not wrong a stranger or oppress him for you were strangers in the land of Egypt" (Exodus 22,20). These were not homeless persons, in the sense that we have today. Our homeless were made strangers by their loss of permanent shelter and community connections. However, the concept of "resident stranger" is a useful one.

In many ways homeless people have become "resident 32 strangers," people who have lost their roles within society, along with their homes. Evidence for this can be found in the generic term "homeless": an undifferentiated form rather than mothers, children, fathers, sons, and daughters whose misfortunes and society's failures have led them to the streets, the welfare hotels, or the shelters. The label serves to obscure their heterogeneity. By depersonalizing them, the impact of their plight is blunted; we distance them from our own lives and fail to address the serious and complex social problems that have produced them in the numbers we see today. It is critical that the psychological, economic, and political dimensions of homelessness be understood and that the distorted, romantic, and inaccurate images of homeless life be disabused.

The current social context becomes apparent when we look *historically* at homelessness and how it defines a relationship between people and environments. There has been a long history of prejudice toward strangers, mobile people, and the poor. The most prevalent homeless persons were paupers, a term that included the indigent, sick or aged, widows and orphans, and also the insane. For example, in colonial times there was concern with the financial consequences of "all adverse conditions, not their idiosyncratic attributes" (Rothman, 1971, p. 5). Although there was some concern for "needy neighbors" there was none for "needy outsiders" (Rothman, 1971). The bases for these attitudes were the religious and social traditions of the colonists that reflected, in part, their English heritage. Almshouses and workhouses for the most "suspect" among the poor, a model adapted from English forms, along with various benevolent societies, became the means of dealing with poverty. The presence of the poor was seen as a way for people "to do good" (Rothman, 1971). 33

Paupers were some of this country's earliest homeless citizens and seen from afar the manner of dealing with them may seem to reflect different policies than we have today. However, there are some uncomfortable similarities in the generalizing, the victimization of children, and the ambivalence reflected in the attitudes of the community. 34

Today, our most powerful images of homelessness come from the media with their emphasis on the most visible homeless—usually the mentally disturbed—and from stereotypes of homeless life—gypsies, hoboes, and bag ladies, people who have been portrayed either as vagabonds with carefree lives or secret millionaires hoarding and hiding their affluence. But the homeless also have been greeted with suspicion and contempt and viewed as non-persons since they defy the largely middle-class moral order of the city, a moral order that frequently views homelessness as vagrancy (Duncan, 1975). 35

In his study of hoboes the British writer Kenneth Allsop (1967) looked for an explanation of mobility in this country and found considerable ambivalence in our attitudes. "My 36 starting point was not the belief that mobility is unique to America, only that America has a unique kind of mobility." He goes on to a broad, admittedly risky generalization:

> To the European impermanence and change are bad, restlessness reveals the flaw of instability; whereas to an American restlessness is pandemic; entrenchment means fossilization, a poor spirit (Allsop, 1967, p. 31).

He sees a prizing of "fluidity," mobile executives (as Toffler would later describe them in *Future Shock*, 1970) and millions on the road in automobiles, vans, trailers, and campers, using supermarket plazas, malls, drive-in banks, fast-food and open-air restaurants. Allsop suggests that there is a certain amount of official support for this migratory style especially for unemployed workers.

> Mobility is unarguably an indispensable component in an economy of the American character and in a nation of America's size, and so is justifiably prized and commended. But the idea itself has come to be qualified by a cluster of subordinate clauses. Mobility with money is, of course, laudable and desirable—you are then a tourist or envoy of business. Mobility between firms and cities is proof of a professional man's initiative and ambition. Mobility is also proof of a workless working man's grit, of his determination to hunt down the breach in the wall and find readmission to the commonwealth. Finally, mobility without these objectives or rationalizations—therefore, mobility for its own feckless sake—must be held to be bad, for it is the act of a renegade and puts in jeopardy the American declaration of intent (Allsop, 1967, p. 436).

Although there is ambivalence about mobility, in fact, we know little about specific attitudes toward homeless persons. It is clear, however, that people are not happy about having shelters in their neighborhoods. Public shelters tend to be concentrated in marginal areas, places where local residents have little political influence or the organization to resist.

A *Newsweek* article on the homeless in Arizona describes one kind of local resistance that seems to be working (Alter, 1984). A "fight back" campaign mounted by Phoenix community leaders to "wipe out the 'unacceptable behavior' of the area's 1,500 street-people" features an ad campaign that has an illustration of a man on a bench, sleeping. A red line is "drawn through it like an international traffic sign." Intended to discourage "outsiders" and abolish soup kitchens and other homeless hangouts, the effort to maintain an image of a clean and conventional community persists even as homelessness increases in the Southwest.

Significance of Homelessness

What does it mean to be homeless? On a practical level it means loss of the right to vote, to receive regular social services, to maintain contacts through mail and telephone. It includes loss of roles, loss of being a neighbor and having neighbors, of hosting visitors, of being a worker, a provider of shelter and nurturance. The homeless are perpetual guests and often unwelcome ones. 38

Loss of a home must be considered one of life's most profound traumas (Dohrenwend and Dohrenwend, 1974; Marris, 1975). Although residential mobility often is a response to stress (Shumaker and Stokols, 1982), it also is a producer of stress even when the decision to relocate is a voluntary one and a sign of upward mobility (Rossi, 1980). The slum clearance projects of the 50s and 60s have left us with vivid descriptions of "grieving for a lost home" (Fried, 1963), after the destruction of a neighborhood for urban renewal. 39

A home may be viewed as a slum by city officials and urban planners, but it is a place rich with social connections, familiar people, and deep personal meanings. When the uprooted residents of the West End of Boston were interviewed, the sadness that they felt for the loss of their old homes, and neighborhood was of major proportions. In fact, half of the 566 men and women studied described severe depression or other disturbances ("It was like a piece being taken from me." "Something of me went with the West End"). 40

This pattern also has been documented by Michael Young and Peter Willmott for the relocation of families from 41 the East End of London (1957; 1966), by Marris for Lagos, Nigeria (Marris, 1961; 1975), and Kai Erikson (1976) for the Buffalo Creek Dam disaster. In some cases grief can result from local changes that render a home geography unfamiliar. Nora Rubinstein's (1983) study of the Pine Barrens of New Jersey, a semi-rural area near Atlantic City, identified people deeply troubled by changes happening around them. A number of the residents could make enormous profits from the sale of their homes and property, but for many the transformation of the area is a painful reminder of a lost past and, most of all, their own limited power to control their immediate environment. Although the grief over the loss of a home and neighborhood, or profound changes to it, may subside over time and be replaced by attachment to the new setting (Willmott, 1963), it is useful to ask why the deep emotion over places exists and how it develops.

We are accustomed to discussions of attachment to 42 people—parents, families, friends—or even attachment to pets. In fact, the developmental literature from infancy through the later years defines growth largely in terms of social experiences. We are less likely to find the context, or setting, of this growth the subject of serious concern, although this is changing (Rivlin and Wolfe, 1985). The recognition that settings and objects within them are components of growth and development, in interactive participation with social experiences, provides a good deal of the answer of why people grieve for lost places and why homelessness is so profoundly painful. As we explore the meaning of home to people, we are learning about the attachments to place and the significance of change and loss (Marris, 1975).

We are beginning to appreciate the contribution of 43 environmental experiences to a person's identity (Proshansky, Fabian and Kaminoff, 1983), the power of enduring memories of home, and their effects on both the course of development and on the ability to make a home (see, for example, Cooper Marcus, 1978a;b; Hester, 1978; Horowitz and Klein, 1978; Horowitz and Tognoli, 1982; Rowles, 1978; 1980; 1981). The restorative qualities of a home as "a place to rest, whose familiarity and security permit the person to recuperate for future ventures away from home" (Seamon,

1984, p. 758) are being recognized. These are affective ties to place that the geographer Yi-Fu Tuan has described as *topophilia*, "love of place" (Tuan, 1974), giving people a sense of roots and a feeling of security (Tuan, 1980).

It is essential to question the impact of a homeless experience for anyone, but especially for children. Robert Coles (1970) has provided some powerful descriptions of periodic homelessness in the lives of migrant farm workers' children. Whether by accident, poverty, or corruption, larger numbers of urban children today lack permanent homes, live in temporary shelters and hotel rooms, in neighborhoods ill-equipped to support healthy childhood activities. Their education often is interrupted until emergency arrangements can be set up. In New York City, school buses now circulate among the welfare hotels and shelters, transporting children to schools. But it took a long time to set this system in place, and few children receive continuous schooling. [44]

There is recent evidence that homelessness has serious consequences for children. Some preliminary data from a study conducted by Dr. Ellen Bassuk, of Harvard University Medical School, found that 78 children (from 51 families) living in shelters had signs of anxiety, severe depression, and serious developmental lags (Bassuk, 1985). Some of the symptoms were severe enough to be considered a state of "acute psychiatric crisis." Emotional difficulties were only part of the problems—there were physical and learning disabilities, as well. [45]

Attachments to place are strongest when large portions of a person's life are laid down in an area (Rivlin, 1982). This occurs when a person resides in an area over an extended time and when a person uses the area for purposes central to life—working, shopping, raising children, playing, socializing, and attending religious services. The greater the *number* of domains of life that take place in an area and the more concentrated these domains are within an area, "the deeper the roots are likely to be in the place" (Rivlin, 1982, p. 89). Although it might be argued that the quality of life today does not encourage the development of roots, that people move widely over their geographies with few deep connections to place, the impact of each setting and the enduring memories of home that parallel these experiences must be [46] acknowledged. Home as an ideal image or a real place acts to anchor, shelter, and personally define an individual to herself or himself.

Rootedness and place attachment do not depend on the quality of a place, its amenities, its services, or the housing stock. Rootedness can occur in places defined as slums, as well as in modest and affluent areas. Although victims of urban homelessness are likely to come from poorer areas, their roots and attachments are as strong and their losses no less painful than victims of floods and fires. The young, disabled, and elderly are particularly vulnerable. For them uprooting means loss of familiar objects, possessions, people, and places and the need to adjust to a series of alternatives under difficult conditions over which they have little or no control. 47

Conclusion

Homelessness takes many forms, in terms of chronic, temporary, periodic and total types. They involve people who may be victims of poverty, many of them ill, or old, or very young, some alcoholic or with severe psychological problems. These are people caught in a reality in which programs developed to enable them to survive intact in their homes have been systematically dismantled by the current Administration, widening the possibility of who can become homeless. Homelessness itself creates a plethora of problems and personal risks, not the least of which is a severe threat to the person's identity and sense of self. 48

We can do something about this epidemic in personal, political, and professional ways and we must to do it soon, before the homeless become resigned to their state and other people become desensitized to the problems. We can identify the ecology of homelessness, how it happens, the series of stages that exist in the progress to the streets, in order to catch the problem before it escalates. We also need to know what happens to these people over time and determine how many are able to escape from the shelters, hotels, and streets and re-establish themselves. We can help to define the varied needs of the different types of homeless persons—for 49 housing, food, jobs, vocational training. We can recognize their capabilities and provide resources for self-help efforts wherever possible. We need to document coping strategies and competence, not just pathology. Most critically, we must recognize the most threatened among the group—the children.

We must work with communities to have them accept 50 shelters and other housing for the homeless, politic for affordable housing, and educate the public about the enormity of the problem. We have had emergency measures for dealing with acute homeless situations for some time. The Red Cross and Salvation Army have long histories of stepping in and offering assistance to victims of floods, fires, and the like. But there is a totally different condition today: an enormous pool of homeless persons largely created by contemporary social policies. We require new policies to deal with these numbers.

Temporary shelters are a small move toward resolving 51 the problem of homeless people. But unless people consider other alternatives to accommodate the homeless within their neighborhoods, we will end up with enormous shelter-institutions removed from communities and more and more families in hotels. Action research is needed to work with communities toward accepting diversity within their boundaries and to work with the homeless to provide housing and services.

In the end the images of homeless individuals, particu- 52 larly people that we see or read about, provide the strongest motivation to do something. I am reminded of a character in *The Street*, a novel by Israel Rabon, published in 1928 but recently translated from the Yiddish language. It describes the experiences of a veteran of World War I, a man without family who goes to the city of Lodz in Poland when discharged and ends up penniless and on the street. There is a brief passage that is the essence of the homeless experience:

> In the several weeks since I had been hanging around town, I had become acquainted with—and made only too much use of—the places where one could hope to get in out of the rain, or where one might run into somebody one knew. In the waiting rooms of the town's two train stations I was already

well known as a bad penny. To the women who kept the buffet counters and to the people at the newspaper kiosks, I was a suspicious character. I did not leave those places because anyone threatened me in any way but because I felt myself overwhelmed by pity—self-pity.

How could a healthy, vigorous person like me be down and out?

In those weeks of knocking about in Lodz, I had grown accustomed to the pathetic silence of my life. I felt my soul being swallowed up in the rhythms of idleness, of futility. There is something about wandering the strange streets of a large industrial city, trying to warm oneself by the light of a chilly sun, turning weaker and weaker with hunger—there is something in all this that separates, alienates one from the entire world.

Our efforts now must be directed toward preventing this alienation, and the bitter loss that goes with it. 53

References

K. Allsop, *Hard Travellin': The Hobo and his History* (New York: The New American Library, 1967).

J. Alter, "Homeless in America," *Newsweek* (Jan. 2, 1984), pp. 20–28.

E. L. Bassuk, *The Feminization of Homelessness: Homeless Families in Boston's Shelters.* Keynote address at the yearly benefit of Shelter, Inc. Cambridge, MA (July 11, 1985).

E. Baxter, and K. Hopper, *Private Lives/Public Spaces* (New York: Community Service Society of New York, 1981).

F. Caro, *Estimating Numbers of Homeless Families* (New York: Community Service Society of New York, 1981).

R. Coles, *Uprooted Children: The Early Life of Migrant Farmworkers* (Pittsburgh: University of Pittsburgh Press, 1970).

C. Cooper Marcus, "Remembrance of Landscapes Past," *Landscape*, vol. 22, no. 3 (1978), pp. 34–43.

———, "Environmental Autobiography," *Childhood City Newsletter* (Dec. 1978), pp. 3–5.

B. P. Dohrenwend, and B. S. Dohrenwend, *Stressful Life Events: Their Nature and Effects* (New York: John Wiley, 1974).

J. S. Duncan, *Men without Property: The Tramp's Classification and Uses of Urban Space.* Unpublished manuscript, Syracuse University, Department of Geography (1975).

K. T. Erikson, *Everything in its Path* (New York: Simon and Schuster, 1976).

J. K. Felsman, "Street Urchins of Colombia," *Natural History* (April 1981).

———, "Abandoned Children: A Reconsideration," *Children Today* (May–June 1984), pp. 13–18.

M. Fried, "Grieving for a Lost Home," in L. J. Duhl (ed.), *The Urban Condition* (New York: Basic Books, 1963).

R. Hester, "Favorite Spaces," *Childhood City Newsletter* (Dec. 1978), pp. 15–17.

K. Hopper and J. Hamburg, *The Making of America's Homeless: From Skid Row to New Poor* (New York: Community Service Society of New York, 1984).

J. Horwitz and S. Klein, "An Exercise in the Use of Environmental Autobiography for Programming and Design of a Day Care Center," *Childhood City Newsletter* (Dec. l984), pp. 18–19.

J. Horwitz and J. Tognoli, "The Role of Home in Adult Development," *Journal of Family Relations* (July 1982), pp. 134–140.

M. Jupp, "From Needs to Rights: Abandoned/Street Children," *Ideas Forum* (1985).

P. Marris, *Family and Social Change in an African City* (London: Routledge & Kegan Paul, 1961).

———, *Loss and Changes* (Garden City, NY: Anchor Books, 1975).

S. Mercado-Llorens and S. L. West, "The New Grapes of Wrath: Hispanic Homelessness in the Urban Highland," *U.S. Hispanic Affairs Magazine* (Summer 1985).

H. M. Proshansky, A. K. Fabian and R. Kaminoff, "Place Identity: Physical World Socialization of the Self," *Journal of Environmental Psychology* (1983), pp. 57–83.

I. Rabon, *The Street* (New York: Schocken, 1985).

L. G. Rivlin, "Group Membership and Place Meanings in an Urban Neighborhood," *Journal of Social Issues*, vol. 38 no. 3 (1982), pp. 75–93.

L. G. Rivlin, V. Bogert, and R. Cirillo, "Uncoupling Institutional Indicators," in A. E. Osterberg, C. P. Tiernan and R. A. Findlay (eds.), *Design Research Interactions: Proceedings of the Twelfth International Conference of the Environmental Design Research Association,* Ames, IA (1981).

L. G. Rivlin and M. Wolfe, *Institutional Settings in Children's Lives* (New York: John Wiley, 1985).

P. H. Rossi, *Why Families Move,* 2nd ed. (Beverly Hills, CA: Sage Publications, 1980).

D. Rothman, *The Discovery of the Asylum: Social Order and Disorder in the New Republic* (Boston: Little, Brown, 1971).

G. D. Rowles, *Prisoners of Space? Exploring the Geographical Experience of Older People* (Boulder, CO; Westview Press, 1978).

———, "Toward a Geography of Growing Old," in A. Buttimer and D. Seamon (eds.), *The Human Experience of Space and Place* (New York: St. Martin's Press, 1980).

———, "Geographical Perspectives on Human Development," *Human Development* (1981), pp. 67–76.

N. Rubinstein, *A Psycho-social Impact Analysis of Environmental Change in New Jersey's Pine Barrens.* Unpublished doctoral dissertation, City University of New York (1983).

D. Salerno, K. Hopper and E. Baxter, *Hardship in the Heartland: Homelessness in Eight American Cities* (New York: Community Service Society, 1984).

D. Seamon, "Emotional Experience of the Environment," *American Behavioral Scientist,* vol. 27, no. 6 (1984), pp. 757–770.

S. A. Shumaker and D. Stokols, "Residential Mobility as a Social Issue and Research Topic," *Journal of Social Issues,* vol. 38, no. 3 (1982), pp. 1–19.

A. Toffler, *Future Shock* (New York: Random House, 1970).

Y. Tuan, *Topophilia: A Study of Environmental Perceptions, Attitudes and Values* (Englewood Cliffs, NJ: Prentice Hall, 1974).

———, "Rootedness versus Sense of Place," *Landscape,* vol. 24, no. 1 (1980), pp. 3–8.

Union of American Hebrew Congregations, *The Torah: A Modern Commentary* (1985).

U. S. Department of Housing and Urban Development, *Report to the Secretary on the Homeless and Emergency Shelters* (1984).

P. Willmott, *Evolution of a Community* (London: Routledge & Kegan Paul, 1963).

P. Willmott and M. Young, *Family and Class in a London Suburb* (London: Routledge & Kegan Paul, 1966).

M. Young and P. Willmott, *Family and Kinship in East London* (London: Routledge & Kegan Paul, 1957).

VOCABULARY

paragraph 6: chronic

paragraph 9: trauma

paragraph 11: affluent

paragraph 12: nomadic

paragraph 15: deinstitutionalization

paragraph 18: typology

paragraph 19: deindustrialization, feminization

paragraph 22: gentrification

paragraph 24: exacerbate

paragraph 30: sedentarize

paragraph 32: heterogeneity, depersonalizing

paragraph 33: idiosyncratic

paragraph 36: ambivalence, pandemic, entrenchment, fossilization, feckless

paragraph 38: nurturance

paragraph 48: plethora

paragraph 49: ecology, pathology

QUESTIONS

1. By what principle does Rivlin distinguish types of homelessness in paragraphs 6–9? Why does she stress that there are different types?
2. Which type of homelessness is of most concern to Rivlin? In the remainder of the essay, does she discuss this type only, or does she give attention to other types?
3. Rivlin states that "Homelessness exists in many different forms and degrees based on the time period involved, the alternative shelter available, and the nature of the person's social contacts" (paragraph 6). What kind of evidence does she present to support this statement? To what extent does she depend on the testimony of the homeless? On statistical evidence? On studies by psychiatrists and sociologists?

4. What popular views of homelessness does Rivlin reject? How do these views impede a solution to the problem?

5. Why does Rivlin give particular attention to Kenneth Allsop's view of American life (paragraph 36)? Does she accept or reject his view? Does his view illuminate the causes of homelessness, or present a mistaken analysis, or suggest a solution?

6. Why does Rivlin give attention to "rootedness and place attachment" (paragraph 47)? Does her discussion bear on causes or solutions?

7. To what extent does the solution depend for Rivlin on a change in perception or understanding of the causes, or on sympathy for the homeless? How do you know?

8. Does Rivlin suggest a single social or political remedy—for example, restoration of government programs, increase in state and federal spending on the homeless? Or does she suggest various remedies?

SUGGESTIONS FOR WRITING

1. In seeking to persuade the audience, a writer may appeal to emotion as well to reason. The character of the writer displayed in the essay—in the reasoned judgment and the concern and sympathy shown—also makes an ethical appeal. What evidence do you find of these kinds of appeal in Rivlin's essay?

2. Rivlin discusses the condition of the homeless and causes of homelessness in the 1980s. Discuss an important recent development relating to one of the following topics or a related one. Include discussion of differing attitudes or alternate proposals. Base your discussion on newspapers, magazines, journal articles, and government publications available in your college library.

   a. "throwaway" children on American streets

   b. educating homeless children

   c. housing homeless families

   d. homeless women and their problems

   e. removing homeless people from public places

   f. medical care of the homeless

   g. improving homeless shelters

   h. public attitudes toward the homeless

> i. housing migrant workers
>
> j. a municipal, state, or federal program—new or proposed—to reduce homelessness

---

ANTONIA FRASER

The English historian ANTONIA FRASER *is the author of numerous historical and biographical studies, including* Mary, Queen of Scots *(1969), awarded the James Tait Black Prize for Biography in 1969, and* Cromwell, the Lord Protector *(1973). The* Warrior Queens *(1989) is a study of female military figures, prominent among them Boadicea, the British queen of the first century A.D., who is reputed to have led a revolt against the Roman occupiers of England, and, failing, died possibly by her own hand. In the excerpt reprinted here, Fraser analyzes attitudes toward women in combat, drawing upon primary and secondary sources. Her conclusions may be compared with those of David H. Hackworth and Elaine Tyler May in the section that follows.*

Unbecoming in a Woman?

At the heart of the matter lies the feeling, almost if not entirely universal in history, that war itself is "conduct unbecoming" in a woman. When George Buchanan attacked female government, especially in time of war, in the late sixteenth century, he explicitly contrasted the established roles of the two sexes. " 'Tis no less unbecoming [in] a Woman," he wrote, "to levy Forces, to conduct an Army, to give a Signal to the Battle, than it is for a Man to tease Wool, to handle the Distaff, to Spin or Card, and to perform the other Services of the Weaker Sex." When a woman did take part in such unnatural (to her sex) procedures, the effects were dire: for that which was reckoned "Fortitude and Severity" in a man, was liable to turn to "Madness and Cruelty" in a woman.[1]

It is not difficult to see why this philosophy should be

widely held. "The act of giving birth itself" has been considered throughout history to be "profoundly incompatible with the act of dealing death"; thus wrote Nancy Huston in a 1986 symposium of "contemporary perspectives" entitled *The Female Body in Western Culture.*[2] Biology alone—or by extension let us call it chivalry—provides an obvious explanation: if women, as the mothers of the race, need physical protection which they in turn extend to their young, then surely it is unreasonable, even unkind, to expect them to take part in war as well. From women's weaker physical strength, a more or less universal estimate, springs the concept of their tenderness, again an almost if not entirely universally held opinion; an extension of this is their timidity. (Why not be timid if physically so much weaker than a potential aggressor? It is a reasonable reaction.) And from their tenderness in one sense is derived another sense of their tenderness: woman the nurse, the nurturer, the succorer. . . .

The epitaph to Pocahontas in St. George's churchyard, Gravesend, on the outskirts of London, where she lies buried, is a perfect case in point: "Gentle and humane, she was the friend of the earliest struggling English colonists whom she boldly rescued, protected and helped." It was an early American feminist writer, Margaret Fuller, who commented on the universal appeal of the American Indian Princess: "All men love Pocahontas for the angelic impulse of tenderness and pity that impelled her to the rescue of Smith," she wrote in *The Great Lawsuit: Man v. Woman,* first published in *The Dial,* Boston, in 1843; while women pity her for "being thus made a main agent in the destruction of her own people."[3] Compared to Boadicea, with those threatening knives on the wheels of her chariot, Pocahontas is a heroine who fulfills the highest expectations concerning her sex in general.

The problems of "masculinity" in a woman—inevitable in some sense in a woman who leads in war—were argued by Helene Deutsch, one of the first four women to be analyzed by Freud. *The Psychology of Women* was a comprehensive study of the female life-cycle and emotional life, which extended and modified Freud's own postulates. In it, Helene Deutsch devoted considerable discussion to what she called "The Active Woman" and her "Masculinity Complex" which "originates in a surplus of aggressive forces that were not subjected to inhibition and that lack the possibility of an outlet such as is open to man. For this reason the masculine woman is also the aggressive woman." This view stretches back at least as far as the wild, untamed and basically anarchic conception of the female in Athenian drama, at a time when woman's physical nature was itself thought to be unstable (based on the demands of her reproductive system).[4]

Although *The Psychology of Women* was published in 1944 (in the United States whither Helene Deutsch had fled in 1933), time and political events have not diminished the strong perceived connection between "masculinity"—activity—in a woman and an "aggression" felt by many to be unsuitable in one of her sex.

It is the leading role upon the stage which is felt to be unnatural in a woman, as opposed to any role. Many men all through history have after all been content to accept and even approve the ambitions of Fulvia, wife to Antony, as described by Plutarch: "her desire was to govern those who governed or to command a commander-in-chief." Cleopatra the dominatrix (and the seducer) is another matter. Boadicea herself may have acted the Fulvia before the death of her husband Prasutagus: we cannot know, *pace* Judy Grahn's free-wheeling lesbian Celt.* When women have been compelled by circumstances to take a dominating role, they are expected to surrender it gracefully afterwards; the "natural" behavior is that of Spenser's Britomart, the chaste warrior–maid who finally dropped her shield when her purpose was fulfilled and became "a gentle courteous Dame." As for the unnatural Amazons whom Britomart subdued, "that liberty" being removed from them, which they as women had wrongfully usurped, they were returned to "men's subjection."[5]

The strong contention of many theorists of the Women's Movement that war itself is the product of aggressive *masculine* values, and might even be eliminated if "the whole

---

* The view of Boadicea developed by the poet Judy Grahn in an 1980 article. *Spare Rib*, referred to in the next paragraph, is a British feminist periodical—Ed.

wide world" were under "a woman's hand" (one of the Sibylline prophecies linked to Cleopatra), meshes of course with these more primitive feelings.[6] *Spare Rib*'s denunciation of Mrs. Thatcher following the Falklands War for promoting such values will be recalled, but the point is inclined to emerge whenever women, outraged by the depredations of war, manage to find a voice.

Militarism versus Feminism was written in 1915, the anguished product of feminist pacifism in response to the first terrible months of carnage in the First World War.[7] It was in effect a plea for internationalism—the Hague Women's Peace Conference of that year—in the cause of peace. The three authors, Mary Sargent Florence, Catherine E. Marshall and C. K. Ogden, argued not only that war was man's creation (as opposed to woman's) but also that man used war as a weapon in order to keep the other sex in perpetual subjection, since in time of war he was the manifest ruler. Catherine Marshall in particular, a prime mover behind the setting up of the conference, referred to the "deep horror of war" which had entered into the soul of the organized Women's Movement, adding her belief that "women's experience as mothers and heads of households" had given them "just the outlook on human affairs" which was needed in such a process of international and creative reconstruction. (This is the argument which Mrs. Thatcher, following the Falklands War, stood on its head by announcing that it was just her practical feminine abilities as a homemaker which had enabled her to keep going in the direction of military affairs.)

"But if woman climbed up to the clearer air above the battlefield," wrote Catherine Marshall in 1915, "and cried aloud in her anguish to her sisters afar off: 'These things must not be, they shall never be again!', would man indeed say, 'Down with her!' Would he not allow her prerogative? Would he not even wish to climb up, too?" Once again, the experience of women sixty or seventy years later protesting at Greenham Common against nuclear weapons in the cause of peace does not suggest that man necessarily allows woman her prerogative in this respect. Nor does it propose that all men (any more than all women) wish to climb up to the clearer air above the battlefield.

Nevertheless the sheer appalling magnitude of the di- 10 saster to humankind inherent in any actual use of nuclear weapons suggests an interesting possibility. John Keegan, at the end of *The Mask of Command* (1987), a study in heroic leadership, calls for a new "Post-heroic leadership"; he points out that the old inspiring "heroic" leader, at the forefront of the battle itself, has been rendered obsolete and even dangerous by the advent of nuclear weapons. "Today the best must find convictions to play the hero no more"; leaders should now be chosen for "intellectuality" and the capacity for making decisions.[8] Women might now make more suitable political leaders than men (being strong enough *not* to press the button), provided of course that the conventional view of woman the peacemaker is accepted.

Certainly for many feminists the connection between 11 women and peace remains "some sort of 'given' "—the phrase is that of the more skeptical Lynne Segal. As Petra Kelly for example wrote in 1984 in *Fighting for Hope:* "Woman must lead the efforts in education for peace awareness, because only she can . . . go back to her womb, her roots, her natural rhythms, her inner search for harmony and peace. . . ." Woman's pacific nature can however only be taken as some sort of given so long as any outstanding woman who does not seem to suffer from conspicuously peaceful inclinations is treated as an honorary male. According to this argument, which has a circular quality, Tomyris, issuing her plea to Cyrus of Persia, "Rule your own people, and try to bear the sight of me ruling mine," is acting in accordance with her true feminist nature, whereas the same Queen Tomyris who had Cyrus put bloodily to death was acting as a man.[9] In the absence of an all-female-ruled state (with all-female-ruled neighbors) the thesis must remain unproved. But the importance of the argument from the point of view of a study of Warrior Queens is that it represents the meeting point of visionary feminism and its direct opposite: war is an unnatural occupation for a woman.

Notes

1. Cit. Phillips, James E., Jr, "The Woman Ruler in Spenser's *Faerie Queen*," *Huntington Library Quarterly* (1941–2), p. 220.

2. Huston, Nancy, "The Matrix of War: Mothers and Heroes" in *The Female Body in Western Culture: Contemporary Perspectives*, edited by Susan Rubin Suleiman (1986); pp. 119–38.

3. Mossiker, Frances, *Pocahontas: The Life and the Legend* (1977), p. 225; Fuller Ossoli, Margaret, *Women in the Nineteenth Century*, edited by Arthur B. Fuller (Boston 1874), p. 307.

4. Deutsch, Helene, MD, *The Psychology of Women: A Psychoanalytic Interpretation*, 2 vols. (New York 1944), Vol. I, Ch. 8, pp. 279–324; see Foley, Helene B., "The Conception of Women in Athenian Drama" in *Reflections of Women in Antiquity* (New York, 1981), p. 134.

5. *Nine Lives by Plutarch*, "Makers of Rome," translated and with an Introduction by Ian Scott-Kilvert (1972 pbk reprint), p. 280.

6. Grant, Michael, *Cleopatra* (revised edn 1974 pbk), p. 84.

7. Marshall, Catherine, Ogden, C. K. and Florence, Mary Sargent, *Militarism versus Feminism*, edited by Margaret Kamester and Jo Vellacott (1987 pbk reprint), pp. 40, 47, 96, 140.

8. Keegan, John, *The Mask of Command* (New York 1987), pp. 345–6, 351.

9. Segal, Lynne, *Is the Future Female? Troubled Thoughts on Contemporary Feminism* (1987 pbk), p. 198; Kelly, Petra, *Fighting for Hope* (1984), p. 104; Herodotus, *The Histories*, translated by Aubrey de Sélincourt, revised by A. R. Burn (1972 pbk), p. 123; Boccaccio, Giovanni, *Concerning Famous Women*, translated with an Introduction by Guido A. Guarmio (1964), p. 104.

VOCABULARY

paragraph 1: explicitly, distaff, card, dire

paragraph 2: perspective, nurturer, succorer

paragraph 3: epitaph

paragraph 4: inhibition, anarchic

paragraph 6: dominatrix

paragraph 7: Sibylline

QUESTIONS

1. What biological evidence is sometimes presented for the view that war is unbecoming conduct to women? How does Fraser explain the reasoning of those who consider this evidence credible?

2. Does the historical evidence presented in paragraph 3 support the same view? Or is Fraser illustrating another view?

3. What psychological explanation does Fraser cite in paragraph 4 for female aggressiveness? Does Fraser accept this explanation?

4. Does the historical evidence cited in paragraph 6 further support the psychological explanation discussed earlier? Does the political evidence cited in paragraph 10?

5. How do the feminist views discussed in paragraphs 7–9 mesh or agree with the "more primitive feelings" cited in paragraph 6?

6. What "interesting possibility" or thesis does Fraser discuss in paragraphs 10 and 11? How does this thesis represent "the meeting point of visionary feminism and its direct opposite: war is an unnatural occupation for a woman"?

SUGGESTIONS FOR WRITING

1. Fraser discusses attitudes toward women in traditional male roles in literature of the past. Discuss what recent movies and television comedy and drama show to be conduct becoming or unbecoming to women in jobs they perform—for example, as police officers, private detectives, newscasters, teachers, or office workers. Explain how the movies or television programs make an explicit or implied judgment about one or more female characters.

2. Analyze a series of advertisements in one or more issues of a magazine published in the 1930s or 1940s to discover what conduct advertisers and editors assumed was becoming to women. Draw a limited conclusion on the stated or implied attitudes from the evidence you present. Describe the ads in sufficient detail to support your thesis.

CONTROVERSY
❦ ❦ ❦

Inductive and deductive reasoning often work together, depending on the particular argument and the point at issue. Proponents of nuclear power plants may, for example, insist that the issue in making the decision to build a plant in a particular region is economic—the increasing power needs of industry. Opponents may argue that the issue is the danger of an accident or the difficulty of disposing of nuclear waste. The argument in such a debate probably will be inductive: statistical information on productivity and nuclear fuel, eyewitness accounts of nuclear plant operations, scientific reports on waste disposal, and the like. The argument will also be deductive in the inferences drawn from certain assumptions: that a high standard of living is a desirable goal in the community; that risk must be taken into account in making a decision about nuclear power; that high productivity depends on a dependable source of electrical power.

Sometimes both assumptions and conclusions are debated; sometimes the assumptions are accepted as "givens" and not debated. In all debate, fairness and sound argument ideally should prevail. It hardly needs to be said that they often do not. Here are a few important "logical fallacies" that a good argument avoids:

> *Arguing in a circle* is closely related to begging the question, where we assume as true what we are trying to prove. "No person who cares about jobs would oppose the bill because it is one that those who care about jobs in Ohio can support." The speaker has not given a reason to support the bill, but has merely restated the opening assertion, arguing in a circle.
>
> *Non sequitur* ("it does not follow"): The assertion, "I oppose nuclear power because my father does," contains a hidden premise or assumption—that father knows best. Since this assumption is hidden, the second part of the statement does not follow from the first part clearly. Assumptions of this sort may be hidden because, once stated, the assumption shows the statement to be questionable or absurd.
>
> *Irrelevant conclusion:* If the point at issue is whether nuclear plants present a risk, the argument that they are needed is an irrelevant argument. It may, of course, be relevant later in the debate.

Ad hominem argument ("to the person"): I may attack my opponents rather than the issue—for example, by arguing that proponents of nuclear power are selfish and greedy. Even if they were people of bad character, their proposals must be judged on their merits. In other circumstances, such as an election campaign, the character of a person may be the issue.

Ad populum argument ("to the people"): I may also appeal to popular feeling or prejudice to gain support—suggesting that Lincoln or some other revered and usually long-dead person would have favored (or opposed) nuclear power. Appeals to authority may also depend on fear. But note that an appeal to authority is legitimate when the person cited is a recognized expert and has stated an opinion directly on the subject.

Either–or hypothesis: I may set up two alternatives—nuclear power or economic depression—without allowing for other solutions.

Complex question asks two questions in the guise of asking one. "Are you in favor of closing nuclear plants to remove an uncontrollable source of radiation?" The person answering no is forced to admit that nuclear power is in fact uncontrollable—a question that deserves to be debated separately.

Hasty generalization draws on a conclusion from an insufficient number of facts, sometimes even from a single fact (see p. 235). Even if one or more nuclear power plants have operated without an accident, we cannot draw the conclusion that all nuclear power plants are necessarily safe. Conversely, a large number of accidents, even a major one like that at Three Mile Island and at Chernobyl in the 1980s, does not prove conclusively that nuclear power plants cannot be operated safely. Numerous facts and possibilities including human and mechanical error need to be considered. Usually the greater number of instances cited, the more probable the generalization. But the probability may be qualified by unstated or unknown facts—for example, the risk presented by aging equipment. And, as in the example of Three Mile Island and Chernobyl, a single serious instance or fact may have great force in argument.

Argument from ignorance: We cannot draw the conclusion that something *must* exist because no evidence has been found to prove it does not. We cannot assert that nuclear power is not a threat to the environment or is not the cause of increasing cancer on the ground that no evidence exists to prove it is a threat. Judgment on such questions must remain open in light of possible new evidence. However, we can make qualified judgments and recommendations on the basis of available scientific evidence.

JONATHAN KOZOL

JONATHAN KOZOL's *experience as a teacher in Boston-area schools was the basis of his influential book on children in school,* Death at an Early Age—*given the National Book Award in 1967. Kozol's other books on education include* On Being a Teacher *(1981),* Illiterate America *(1985), and* Savage Inequalities: Children in America's Schools *(1991). Children of the homeless are the subject of* Rachel and Her Children *(1988), from which the following selection is taken. Many of the homeless whom Kozol interviewed in New York City were victims of economic hardship—many of them families given rooms by the city in welfare hotels—and not long-time street dwellers. Kozol states that "small children have become the fastest-growing sector of the homeless. At the time of writing there are 28,000 homeless people in emergency shelters in the city of New York. An additional 40,000 are believed to be unsheltered citywide. Of those who are sheltered, about 10,000 are homeless individuals. The remaining 18,000 are parents and children in almost 5,000 families. The average homeless family includes a parent with two or three children. The average child is six years old, the average parent twenty-seven." The essay draws on eyewitness evidence as well as interviews in drawing conclusions about the life of the homeless and attitudes toward them.*

The Homeless

Many homeless people, unable to get into shelters, or frightened of disease or violence, or intimidated by the regulations, look for refuge in such public places as train stations and church doorways. Scores of people sleep in the active subway tunnels of Manhattan, inches from six-hundred-volt live rails. Many more sleep on the ramps and the station platforms. Go into the subway station under Herald Square on a December night at twelve o'clock and you will see what scarce accommodations can mean. Emerging from the subway, walk along Thirty-third Street to Eighth Avenue. There you will see another form of scarce accommodations: hot-air grates outside the buildings on Eighth Avenue are highly prized. Homeless people who arrive late often find there is no vacancy, even for a cardboard box over a grate.

A man who has taken shelter from the wind that sweeps 2 Fifth Avenue by sleeping beneath the outstretched arms of Jesus on the bronze doors of St. Patrick's Cathedral tells a reporter he can't sleep there anymore, because shopkeepers feel that he is hurting business. He moves to the south side of the church, where he will be less visible.

Stories like this are heard in every state and every city of 3 the nation. In Florida, a twenty-year-old man tells me that he ran away from a juvenile-detention home in Michigan when he was nine years old. He found that he was small enough to slip his body through the deposit slot of a Goodwill box next to a Salvation Army building. Getting in was easy, he explains, and it was warm, because of the clothes and quilts and other gifts that people had dropped into the box. "Getting out was not so easy," he says. "I had to reach my arms above my head, grab hold of the metal edge, twist my body into an S, and pull myself slowly out through the slot. When I was fourteen, I was too big to fit into the slot. I believe I am the only person in America who lived for five years in a Goodwill box."

Many homeless people sleep in trash compactors and in 4 dumpsters behind restaurants. These offer perhaps the ultimate concealment, and the heat generated by the rotting food may protect a homeless person against freezing weather. In Chicago some years ago, a news report told of a man who had been sleeping in a broken trash compactor. One night, not knowing that in his absence the trash compactor had been repaired, he fell asleep, the engine was turned on, and he was compressed into a cube of refuse.

People in many cities speak of spending nights in phone 5 booths. I have seen this only in New York in 1986. Public telephones in Grand Central are aligned in recessed areas outside the main concourse. On almost any night, before one-thirty, visitors could see a score of people stuffed into these booths with their belongings. Even phone-booth vacancies are scarce in New York City: as in public housing, people are sometimes obliged to double up. One night, I saw three people—a man, a woman, and a child—jammed into a single booth. All three were asleep.

Officials have tried a number of times to drive the 6
homeless from Grand Central. In order to make conditions
less attractive, nearly all the benches have been removed
from the terminal. One set of benches has been left there, I
am told, because they have been judged "historic land-
marks." The terminal's three hundred lockers, used in
former times by homeless people to secure their few belongings, were removed in 1986. The authorities were forced to
justify this action by declaring the homeless "a threat to
public safety," according to the City Council. Shaving,
washing clothes, and other forms of hygiene are prohibited
in the men's room of Grand Central. A fast-food chain that
wanted to distribute unsold doughnuts in the terminal was
denied the right to do so, on the ground that it would draw
more hungry people.

At one-thirty every morning, homeless people are ejected 7
from Grand Central. Many initially took refuge on a ramp that
leads to Forty-second Street. The ramp provides a degree of
warmth, because it was protected from the street by wooden
doors. The station management—Grand Central is run by
Metro North—responded to this challenge in three ways.
First, the ramp was mopped with a strong mixture of ammonia
to produce a noxious smell. Then, when the people sleeping
there brought cardboard boxes and newspapers to protect
them from the fumes, the entrance doors were chained wide
open. Temperatures dropped some nights to ten degrees.
Finally, in early 1987, Metro North fenced off the ramp entirely.

In a case that won brief press attention in December of 8
1985, an elderly woman who had been living in Grand
Central, on one of the few remaining benches, was removed
night after night during the weeks preceding Christmas. On
Christmas Eve, it became evident that she was ill, but no one
called an ambulance. At one-thirty, the police compelled her
to move outside. At dawn, she came inside and climbed back
on a bench to sleep; she died during the morning of
pneumonia.

In 1988, homeless people will not often be found sleep- 9
ing on the benches in Grand Central. The benches now are
cordoned off with yellow tape at 9 P.M. Police patrol the area
with a dog.

At Penn Station in 1986, homeless women congregated 10
near the entrance to the bathroom. Each hour on the hour,
Amtrak police came by and herded them away. In June of
1985, Amtrak officials had issued this directive to all officers:
"It is the policy of Amtrak to not allow the homeless and
undesirables to remain. . . . Officers are encouraged to eject
all undesirables. . . . Now is the time to train and educate
them that their presence will not be tolerated as cold weather
sets in." In an internal memo, an Amtrak official later went
beyond this language and asked, "Can't we get rid of this
trash?"

In a surprising action, the American Federation of 11
Railroad Police, representing the station's police employees,
resisted the directive, and, in 1986, brought suit against
Penn Station's management. Nonetheless, as temperatures
plunged during the nights after Thanksgiving, homeless
men and women were ejected from the station. At two one
morning that November, I watched a man who was perhaps
fifty years old, about my age, carry a cardboard box outside
the station and try to construct a barricade against the wind
that tore across Eighth Avenue. The man was so cold his
fingers shook, and when I spoke to him he tried to answer
but could not.

Driving women from the toilets in a railroad station 12
raises questions that go far beyond the issue of "deterrence."
Some people may find it surprising to learn that many of the
women driven out are quite young. Few are dressed in the
rags that are suggested by the term "bag ladies." Some are
dressed so neatly and conceal their packages and bags so
skillfully that one finds it hard to differentiate them from
commuters waiting for a train. Given the denial of hygienic
opportunities, it is difficult to know how they are able to
remain presentable. The sight of clusters of police officials,
mostly male, guarding a women's toilet from being used by
homeless women does not speak well for the public conscience of New York.

Several cities have devised unusual measures to make 13
sure that homeless people will learn quickly that they are not
welcome. In Laramie, Wyoming, in recent years, homeless
people were given one night's shelter; the next morning, an
organization called the Good Samaritan Fund gave them

one-way tickets to another town. In 1986, the college town of Lancaster, Ohio, offered homeless families one-way tickets to Columbus.

In a number of states and cities, homeless people have 14 been knifed or set on fire. Two high-school students in California have been tried for the knife murder of a homeless man they found sleeping in a park. The man, an unemployed housepainter, was stabbed seventeen times, and then his throat was slashed.

In Chicago, a man was set ablaze while he slept on a 15 bench early in the morning, opposite a popular restaurant. Rush-hour commuters passed him and his charred possessions for hours. At noon, someone called the police. A man who reportedly had watched him burning from a third-floor apartment above the bench had refused to notify the police. The purpose of setting fire to him was "to get him out," according to a local record-store employee. The homeless man survived, according to the *Wall Street Journal*, because the fire did not penetrate his many layers of clothing. A local resident told reporters that his neighbors viewed the homeless as akin to "nuclear waste."

In Tucson, where police have used German shepherds 16 to hunt for the homeless in the skid-row neighborhoods, a mayor was reelected in 1983 on the promise that he would drive the homeless out of town. In Phoenix, a woman who leads an anti-homeless lobby known as Fight Back told reporters, "We're tired of it. Tired of feeling guilty about these people."

In several cities, it is a crime to sleep in public; in some, 17 armrests have been installed in the middle of park benches to make it impossible for people to lie down. In others, trash has been defined as "public property," to make it a felony for the poor to forage in the rotted food.

Some grocers in Santa Barbara have sprinkled bleach on 18 food that they discarded in their dumpsters. In Portland, Oregon, owners of some shops in the redeveloped Old Town have designed slow-dripping gutters (they are known as "drip lines") to prevent the homeless from attempting to take shelter under their awnings.

In Fort Lauderdale, harsher tactics have been recom- 19 mended. A member of the City Council offered a proposal to spray trash containers with rat poison to discourage foraging by homeless families. The way to get rid of vermin, he remarked, is to cut their food supply. Some of these policies have been defeated, but the inclination to sequester, punish, and conceal the homeless has attracted wide support.

"We are the rejected waste of the society," Richard 20 Lazarus told me.* "They use us if they think we have some use—maybe for sweeping leaves or scrubbing off graffiti in the subway stations. They don't object if we donate our blood. I've given plasma. That's one way that even worthless people can do something for democracy. We may serve another function, too. Perhaps we help to scare the people who still have a home—even a place that's got no heat, that's rat-infested, filthy. If they see us in the streets, maybe they are scared enough so they will learn not to complain. If they were thinking about asking for a better heater or a better stove, they're going to think twice. It's like farmers posting scarecrows in the fields. People see these terrifying figures in Penn Station, and they know that with one false step they could be here, too. They think, 'I better not complain.'

"The problem comes, however, when a city tries to find 21 a place to hide us. It comes to be an engineering question: waste disposal. Store owners certainly regard us in that way. We ruin business and lower the value of good buildings. People fear that we are carriers of illness. Many times, we are. So they wear those plastic gloves if they are forced to touch us. It reminds me of the workers in the nuclear reactors—they have to wear protective clothing if they come in contact with the waste. Then, you have state governors all over the United States refusing to allow this stuff to be deposited within their borders. Now you hear them talking about dumping toxic waste into the ocean in steel cans. Could they find an island someplace for the homeless?"

Lazarus's question brings back a strange memory for 22 me. In Boston, for years before the homeless were identified

---

* Richard Lazarus is the name given to a homeless man by Kozol. Lazarus, "an educated, thirty-six-year-old Vietnam veteran I met two days after Thanksgiving in the subway underneath Grand Central Station, tells me he had never been without a job until the recent summer. In July he underwent the loss of job, children and wife, all in a single stroke. As in almost all these situations, it was the simultaneous occurrence of a number of emergencies, any one of which he might sustain alone but not all at the same time, that suddenly removed him from his home." [Ed.]

as a distinguishable category of the dispossessed, a de-facto caste of homeless people dwelt in a vast public-housing project, called Columbia Point, built on a virtual island that was linked only by one access road to the United States. The project, infested with rats because it was constructed on a former garbage dump, was so crowded, violent, and ugly that social workers were reluctant to pay visits there, few shop owners would operate a business there, and even activists and organizers were afraid to venture there at night. From the highway to Cape Cod one could see the distant profile of those high-rise structures. A friend from California asked me if it was a prison. He told me that it looked like Alcatraz. I answered that it was a housing project. The notion of shoving these people as far out into the ocean as possible does bring to mind the way that waste-disposal problems are sometimes resolved.

New York has many habitable islands. One of them has 23 already earned a place in history as the initial stopping point for millions of European refugees who came to the United States in search of freedom. One reason for their temporary isolation was the fear that they might carry dangerous infections. New York's permanent refugees are carriers of every possible infection; most, moreover, have no prospering relatives to vouch for them, as earlier generations sometimes did, in order to assure that they will not become a burden to the state. They are already regarded as a burden. An island that once served as quarantine for aliens who crowded to our shore might serve now as quarantine for those who huddle in train stations and in Herald Square.

Richard Lazarus may not be paranoid in speaking of 24 himself as human waste; he may simply be reading the headlines in the press. "I just can't accommodate them," the owner of a building in midtown Manhattan says. The mayor of Newark, where a number of homeless families have been sent from New York City, speaks of his fear that displaced families from New York might be "permanently dumped in Newark." He announces a deadline after which they will presumably be dumped back in New York.

New Yorkers, according to the *Times*, "are increasingly 25 opposing the city's attempts to open jails, shelters for the homeless, garbage incinerators" in their neighborhoods. The

Times reports that the city has to reassure communities that they are not being singled out when they are chosen as sites "for homeless shelters and garbage-burning generating plants."

What startles most observers of the homeless is not simply that such tragedies persist in the United States but that almost all have been well documented and that even the most solid documentation does not bring about corrective action. Instead of action, a common response to this kind of problem in New York, as elsewhere, has been the appointment of a "task force" to investigate it. This is frequently the last we hear of the problem. Another substitute for action is a press event at which a city official seems to overleap immediate concerns by the unveiling of a plan to build a thousand, or a hundred thousand, homes over the next ten or twenty years at a cost of several billion dollars. The sweep of these announcements tends to dwarf the urgency of the initial issue. When, after a year or so, we learn that little has been done and the problem has grown worse, we tend to feel not outrage but exhaustion. Exhaustion, however, turns easily to a less generous reaction.

"I am about to be heartless," a columnist wrote in *Newsweek* in December of 1986. "There are people living on the streets of most American cities, turning sidewalks into dormitories. They are called the homeless, street people, vagrants, beggars, vent men, bag ladies, bums. Often they are called worse. They are America's living nightmare— tattered human bundles. They have got to go." The writer noted that it was his taxes that paid for the paving and the cleaning of the streets where some of the homeless lived. "That makes me their landlord," he wrote. "I want to evict them."

A senior at Boston University sees homeless people on the streets not far from where he goes to class. He complains to his college newspaper that measures taken recently to drive them from the area have not been sufficiently aggressive. "I would very much like to see actions more severe," he writes. Perhaps, he admits, it isn't possible to have them all arrested, though this notion seems to hold appeal for him; perhaps "a more suitable middle ground" may be arrived at to prevent this "nauseating and often criminal element" from being permitted to "run free so close to my home."

Another Bostonian says, in the weekly Boston *Phoenix,* 29 "Our response to these street people . . . has gone from indifference to pitying . . . to hatred." I think that this is coming to be true and that it marks an incremental stage in our preparedness to view the frail, the ill, the dispossessed, the unsuccessful not as people who have certain human qualities we share but as untouchables. From harsh deterrence to punitive incarceration and then to the willful cutting off of life supports is an increasingly short journey. "I am proposing triage of a sort, triage by self-selection," Charles Murray writes in "Losing Ground." "The patient always has the right to fail. Society always has the right to let him."

Why is it that writings that present such hardened 30 attitudes seem to prevail so easily in public policy? It may be that generous voices are more readily derided; callous attitudes are never subject to the charge of being sentimental. It is a recurrent theme in "King Lear," Michael Ignatieff writes, that "there is a truth in the brutal simplicities of the merciless which the more complicated truth of the merciful is helpless to refute. . . ." A rich man "never lacks for arguments to deny the poor his charity. 'Basest beggars' can always be found to be 'in the poorest things superfluous.' " So from pity we graduate to weariness, from weariness to impatience, from impatience to annoyance, from annoyance to dislike, and sometimes to contempt.

"No excuses are good enough," the *Times* observed in 31 reference to the Holland Hotel in 1985, a year before I spoke with Sarah Andrews of her stay there. But excuses did suffice. The city did, and does, continue to send children to the Holland and to many similar hotels. Nearly two hundred families, with over four hundred children, were still living in the Holland last September. Can it be that these children have by now become not simply noxious or unclean in our imagination but something like an ulcer to society?

Richard Lazarus said to me, "If the point is to dispose of 32 us most economically, why do they need to go to all this trouble and expense? Why not end this misery efficiently? Why not a lethal injection?" This question, voiced in panic and despair, is perhaps one that he would not have posed if he had been in a less tormented state of mind. The answer is that we have failed in many ways to do what conscience and American ideals demand, but we have yet to fall so far as to wish to engineer anyone's demise. Despite the grave injustices that we allow, or lack the power to confront, we do not in fact want to "dispose" of any people, or "compact" them into concentration camps or other institutions of internment. The truth is that we do not know what we want to do with these poor people. We leave them, therefore, in a limbo, and while waiting in that limbo many who are very young do cease to be a burden to society.

But the question asked by this shaken man emerging 33 from the underground of New York's subway system to gaze up at the Grand Hyatt may suggest a slightly different question: Might a day come in the not too distant future when a notion of this sort may be proposed and not regarded as abhorrent? It has happened in other advanced societies. We know this, and we also know that no society is totally exempt from entertaining "rational" solutions of this kind. State terrorism as social-welfare policy—that, I think, is a fair description of how Lazarus, a credible witness of life at the bottom in Manhattan, has come to see things. True, it has not yet achieved acceptance in our social order, but it may no longer be regarded as beyond imagining.

VOCABULARY

paragraph 7: noxious
paragraph 17: felony, forage
paragraph 19: sequester
paragraph 22: de facto, caste
paragraph 24: paranoid
paragraph 29: incremental, incarceration
paragraph 32: limbo

QUESTIONS

1. What kind of inductive evidence does Kozol present in support of his thesis? At what point in the discussion does he make an "inductive leap" from his evidence to his thesis or conclusion?

2. Is Kozol writing to an audience concerned with the plight of the homeless, or to an indifferent or a hostile audience? How do you know?

3. Kozol quotes the statement of one observer: "I am proposing triage of a sort, triage by self-selection. . . ." (paragraph 29) What does the word *triage* mean? Does "triage by self-selection" mean suicide?

4. Do you believe that Kozol makes an unfair appeal to our emotions through his graphic description of the New York homeless? How powerful do you find this appeal? Does his discussion persuade you that the situation is a desperate one?

SUGGESTIONS FOR WRITING

1. Discuss what solutions you believe Kozol would and would not favor, given what he says in this essay.

2. The observer who proposes "triage by self-selection" adds the following: "The patient always has the right to fail. Society always has the right to let him." Do you agree with this statement? In your view, how much responsibility should society assume for failure in the personal lives of its citizens? Does society have a responsibility for the care of homeless "throwaway" children?

3. Kozol states: "The truth is that we do not know what we want to do with these poor people." Does this statement describe your own attitude and feelings about the homeless? What experiences and beliefs help to explain your attitude and feelings?

HILARY DeVRIES

HILARY DeVRIES *graduated from Ohio Wesleyan University in 1976. In 1981 she received an M.A. in creative writing from Boston University. In 1983, she was named Magazine Writer of the Year by the New England Women's Press Association. Her essay describing a visit to a Boston shelter for the homeless was published in* The Christian Science Monitor *on September 17, 1987. Like Kozol, DeVries gives a face to the homeless and in this way urges the reader to reject a stereotype.*

"I Think I Will Not Forget This"

I never learned her name. But she spotted me across the room—the common area of the shelter for the homeless which served as her living room. If I wasn't exactly a guest in her house, then I was just another reporter doing another story on the homeless. She was the one who lived here. She was the one with a story to tell.

I arrived at the shelter in the early evening. Just before supper. Just in time to catch the nightly intake of the hundreds of men and women who, through alcoholism, or mental illness, or just plain hard times, had nowhere to call home but this shelter. It was one of a dozen in dozens of cities, tucked away in a commercial part of town where warehouses and loading docks didn't form neighborhood coalitions against the housing of the homeless.

I was here to put a face on what I thought was an all-too-faceless social problem. I had stepped around my share of breathing bodies lying on the sidewalk in front of department stores. I had argued with myself over whether to feel anger or pity or simply gratitude that it wasn't me lying there gloveless and filthy. Mostly, I wondered how people could live like that.

That's where the woman came in. The woman with neatly filed nails and beautiful skin who didn't wait for me but simply walked across the room and asked me if I was from a newspaper. Her breath smelled faintly of mint and she wore a yellow sweater. I thought at first she was a staff member, and told her I was touring the facility. Come back and talk to me, she said. I'll tell you what it's like to live here.

I was taken first to the men's side of the shelter, to their front door where I watched them being frisked, a man in a black baseball jacket running his hands lightly down their sides as the men stood silently in the first of many lines—a line for admittance, a line for supper, a line for bed. Here, there are only two rules: no guns, no violence. The men had only to get across the threshold to get a bed for the night. If they came late, they joined the 200 others lying on benches or the floor of the day room or the lobby. Every night it was the same. No one was turned away.

One man was lying in the doorway with a pink electric

blanket wrapped around him, cradling a boom box. The man next to him was snoring. His coat was greasy with dirt and served as a pillow for both of them. Neither of them noticed me stepping over them, or the officer who stood a few feet away. A policeman was posted here 24 hours. Just in case. Overhead fluorescent lights blazed. They stay on all night, I am told. All night someone will be awake—awake and walking, awake and talking to someone or to themselves. All night the phone will ring.

Upstairs in the painted cement block rooms, I walk by 7 rows of twin beds with rounded edges—nothing sharp here—and plastic-covered mattresses. Three hundred men on secondhand designer sheets and under donated blankets. Each bed is made up for the night. Outside in the hall, someone's heels click by, and the low rumble from the men standing downstairs, crowded and jostling, rises up the stairwell.

It must be easier to be a woman here, I think. It is less 8 crowded for them. They are neater. No torn bread crusts and spilled cups of soup in the corners. No loud bursts of laughter.

When I am taken to their side of the shelter, a woman 9 pushes open the door wearing a rabbit fur coat and suede boots. For a minute I think she works here, until I am told that the donations here are good ones, that the bulging sacks under the stairwell belong to the bag ladies, that the women do not steal from one another, that some of them do arts and crafts here. There are homemade paintings hanging on the wall.

Now, it is dinner time for the women. They sit on 10 benches alongside a wall waiting for an empty chair. It is almost like a restaurant, I think, but not quite. Women from a local church are serving the meal, cafeteria-style. The handwritten menu is posted at the head of the line: three kinds of sandwiches, pea soup, and fruit. At the plastic-covered picnic tables, the women eat neatly. They do not talk, only peel back the wax paper from the sandwiches and take small bites. They do not look at one another or anyone else.

Soon it will be time for bed. Lights here go out at 9 p.m. 11 No exceptions. The women will go upstairs, stand in line, put their clothes in a bin, put a rubberized band around their wrist. The band has a metal tab with a number on it. It is the number for their bed. In the middle of the night, if someone should call, the woman can be located by number. Next, a woman staff member takes their clothes, hands them a nightgown and a towel. Both are clean and folded. There is some lace on one of the nightgowns. The women's own clothes are put into the "oven," where they bake all night. This is to dry them and to kill lice. Then they take a shower. No exceptions. The women's showers are stalls fitted with curtains, not like the men's, a bare room with a guard posted. "No more than 5 minutes in the shower," says a sign taped to the wall. It is almost like being back in gym class, I think. But it isn't. It isn't a school. It isn't even a home. And I still wonder how people can live like this.

I make my way down the stairs, under the cold fluores-   12
cent lights and with the smell of antiseptic all around me. Now the woman in the yellow sweater finds me again, corners me here in the common room. She doesn't wait for my questions, but starts to tell me that all the women here are unique, that it is not easy or right to categorize them. That is her word, categorize. She tells me that the women are divorced or displaced or just couldn't deal with the life they were dealt. She tells me that it is hard to get stabilized when you do not have a job. She has lived here 3½ weeks; this is her address. She tells me she is going back to school, that she is working on her secretarial skills. She tells me she is from Cleveland, has a job here now but not the $600 a month for an apartment. "You know they give foot soaks here every night," she says. "Some of the women really need them."

Outside it has begun to snow. I would like to go home.   13
Or sit down, just for a minute. But the woman hasn't finished. She hands me a scrap of paper she took from the bulletin board that morning. "This says it for a lot of us," she says, looking right at me. She is not smiling. Someone yells for her to come pick up her things from the floor. I look down at the paper. The handwriting is in faint blue ink: "These times remind me of a situation I never want to realize again."

I look up at the woman. She is not smiling. Remember, she 14
says, everyone here is different, everyone here is an individual. I think I will not forget this, when I am out walking and
see a woman pulling bottles from a trash can with dirty,
ungloved hands and I start to wonder how can people live
like this.

I think I will remember this when I am tired and want to 15
go home or sit down, just for a minute. I will remember the
woman with no home, the woman with the neatly filed nails
practicing her typing skills. I think I will remember that
persistence does not have any particular address or wear any
specific outfit; that courage can be found in a gnarled hand
gripping the lip of a garbage can.

But mostly I think I will remember that compassion is 16
not limited to those who can write checks or their representative or articles for newspapers, that empathy might be
most easily found among those with their heads bowed over
bowls of donated soup, and that concern for one's fellow
human beings, as in the case of this one woman, does not
even have to come with a name.

QUESTIONS

1. DeVries says of the woman who showed her the shelter: "I
   never learned her name." Why does she stress this fact at the
   beginning of the essay and return to it at the end?
2. What details does she give us about the woman? What point is
   she making through these details? Is she arguing a thesis?
3. Does the visit to the shelter change her image of homeless
   people or of how they live? Does the visit change her attitude
   and feelings toward them?
4. Is DeVries contrasting the men's shelter with the women's or
   merely giving us a picture of both? What does she gain by
   focusing on a single shelter and homeless person?
5. A writer may appeal to our reason, our feelings, and our respect
   for qualities of the writer's character evident in the essay (ethical
   appeal). What appeals does DeVries make in her essay? How
   similar are these appeals to those of Kozol in his report on the
   homeless? How successful do you find the appeal that DeVries
   makes to you?

SUGGESTIONS FOR WRITING

1. Report an experience that changed your thinking and feelings about a group of people or a current social problem. Build your discussion to a judgment or a comment, as Kozol and DeVries do in their essays.

2. To what extent would Kozol and DeVries approve of measures taken in your city or town to deal with homelessness?

ROBERT C. ELLICKSON

Robert C. Ellickson, *Walter E. Meyer Professor of Property and Urban Law at Yale Law School, served on the President's Committee on Urban Housing in 1967–68 and taught at the University of California Law Center and Stanford Law School. At Yale he teaches a course on the homeless and the law. In the opening sections of his essay on homelessness, Ellickson argues that "semantic imprecision" marks current debate; the term* homeless *covers the "street homeless," those who sleep in vehicles and public areas, and the "sheltered homeless," those who are housed by friends and relatives or by welfare agencies and charities. This "bundled definition" distorts the problem by exaggerating the number of homeless people and therefore the need for public shelters, thereby discouraging solutions fitted to very different problems. Public shelters must be available to serve victims of fire and similar emergencies, Ellickson argues; but wide availability encourages "sheltered" families and individuals to use them and discourages them from seeking permanent solutions. An employed addict might, for example, move from rented housing to a shelter to have additional money for drugs. In the concluding sections of the essay reprinted here, Ellickson challenges "fatally flawed" assumptions about homelessness and proposes solutions. Ellickson cites James R. Knickman and Beth C. Weitzman, "A Study of Homeless Families in New York City" (NYU Graduate School of Public Administration, 1989), and Irving Piliavin and Michael Sosin, "Tracking the Homeless," Focus, vol. 10, no. 4 (1987–1988), p. 20.*

The Homelessness Muddle

The National Numbers Debate

In light of the political volatility of the homelessness issue, it 1
is hardly surprising that estimates of the growth and size of
the homeless population have varied widely. Predictably,
those who advocate spending more on homelessness programs have produced some of the most inflated estimates.
For example, Mitch Snyder's advocacy organization, the
Community for Creative Nonviolence (CCNV), currently
asserts that America has three to four million homeless
people. As scholars of homelessness have often pointed out,
the CCNV's national estimates have never rested on any
credible factual foundation. Indeed, Snyder himself has
never seriously tried to defend the CCNV figures, and for
good reason.

In 1984 the Department of Housing and Urban De- 2
velopment (HUD) made the first systematic attempt to count
the national homeless population, and arrived at a figure of
250,000 to 350,000—about one-tenth the CCNV's number.
The most careful recent field studies, such as Rossi's, Burt
and Cohen's,* and Georges Vernez's, indicate that HUD was
not far from the mark. Estimating the homeless population is
obviously a Herculean task, particularly because of the
difficulty of counting the street homeless. To overcome this
problem, Rossi pioneered the use of intensive field sweeps,
while Burt and Cohen interviewed patrons of soup kitchens
about where they had recently slept.

These scholars' findings suggest that the national home- 3
less population—both street and sheltered—on any given
night is between 0.1 percent and 0.2 percent of the total
population. Thus their counts correspond closely with
HUD's 1984 estimate. Rossi, for example, estimated the total
Chicago homeless at around 2,300 per night during the fall of
1985, or a bit under 0.1 percent of the city's population. In his

---

* Peter H. Rossi, *Down and Out in America* (University of Chicago Press, 1989);
Martha R. Burt and Barbara E. Cohen, "Feeding the Homeless" (Urban Institute,
1988); cited earlier in Ellickson's article.—Ed.

1989 book, Rossi indicated that his "best estimate" of the national homeless population was 250,000 to 350,000—the same estimate that HUD had made five years earlier.

By 1989, however, HUD officials had begun to rely on a national estimate of 600,000, a number derived from calculations made by Martha Burt in a memorandum dated September 11, 1988. Burt herself has made clear that this figure is probably too generous. Most of Burt's estimates aim at fixing the number of different people who would be on the street or in a shelter on at least one night during a one-week period. Previously, HUD had estimated the homeless population for a single night; given the fluidity of the homeless population, this number is considerably smaller. Burt did make some one-day estimates as well, but she based them on a street-shelter ratio of two to one. This ratio is almost certainly too high for several reasons. First, Burt applied the ratio to families, who are almost all sheltered, as well as to individuals. Second, there were far more shelter beds in 1987, the year of Burt's estimate, than in 1984, when HUD judged the street-shelter ratio to be less than two to one; by 1987 a one-to-one ratio was more realistic. Lastly, Burt assumed without explanation that the rate of homelessness in suburban and rural areas is about three times higher than her supporting studies would indicate. Stripped of all these upward biases, Burt's one-day estimates of the 1987 homeless population probably would have come out only slightly above HUD's 1984 estimate of 250,000 to 350,000.

Why Latent Homelessness Is on the Rise

Although most of the advocates' figures appear to be inflated, the nation's homeless population undoubtedly did grow during the 1980s. Even if we account for the fact that the addition of some 177,000 shelter beds between 1983 and 1988 pulled significant numbers of people out of housing and institutions, most observers believe that latent homelessness has been increasing.

The rise nevertheless has been smaller than most people who frequent downtowns might think. Such observers fail to reckon with the near demise of skid rows, where many destitute people used to live in relative isolation. In 1986 the *New York Times* reported, for example, that there were only one-fourth as many flophouse beds in New York's Bowery section as there had been twenty years earlier. Significantly, in most cities new skid rows have not arisen to replace the ones that have been gentrified. The dispersion of skid-row populations has done much to increase public awareness of the destitute and homeless.

One reason for the continuing decline of skid rows is 7 that Social Security and federal disability benefits have increased greatly over the past two decades. Many older people who would otherwise have spent their autumn years in skid-row neighborhoods can now afford to live elsewhere. In addition, since the 1960s the legal system has extended much more protection to down-and-out people. Before these reforms, an unspoken mission of the police in many cities was to keep "bums" out of the nicer parts of town. A police officer could perform this task with vagrancy arrests, mass roundups of street drunks, and commands—backed by a night-stick—to move along. Such tactics have now been blocked. Judicial decisions have struck down vagrancy laws, curbed the mass arrests of drunks, and assessed damages against police departments that have been too aggressive with street people. These legal innovations, coupled with greater police and citizen solicitude for the down and out, have allowed skid-row residents to escape their old confines. Advocates also seem to have learned that situating soup kitchens in conspicuous locations yields political benefits. The rise in homelessness, although real, is thus less than meets the middle-class eye.

Homeless advocates such as Jonathan Kozol offer a 8 simple explanation for the increase in latent homelessness during the 1980s: Reagan administration cuts in the federal housing budget. But the premise of this argument is false. During the late 1970s the Carter administration's HUD mapped out an ambitious expansion of federally subsidized housing projects, concentrating on public-housing projects built and managed by local authorities. Beginning in 1981, Reagan's HUD drastically cut back on these plans for future projects and instead redirected new federal spending to Section 8 housing allowances, which help low-income householders pay the rent due private landlords. Under federal accounting rules, Congress must provide forty years of "budget authority" when it approves a new public-housing dwelling unit, but only five years when it approves a new Section 8 allowance. This discrepancy arises because the unavoidable federal financial commitment is more long-lived in the case of public housing. As a result, the Reagan administration's decision to shift future initiatives from public housing to Section 8 assistance reduced by 87.5 percent the budget authority that HUD needed to aid an additional low-income household. When the specialists involved in the production of subsidized housing projects bemoan federal cuts, they usually trot out figures based on these paper cuts in budget authority, a highly misleading measure.

Much more relevant to low-income families are the 9 trends in how much HUD is spending and how many households it is aiding. Federal spending on low-income housing programs actually increased sharply during the 1980s. According to computations by University of Virginia economist Edgar Olsen, federal housing subsidies for low-income families went from $5.8 billion in fiscal 1980 to $13.8 billion in fiscal 1988. Adjusting for rent inflation, this represented a real spending increase of over 50 percent. Between 1980 and 1987 (the last year reported in the *Statistical Abstract*), the stock of public-housing units increased from 1.2 million to 1.4 million, as projects that Carter's HUD had put into the production pipeline were completed. More significantly, during the same years the number of low-income households receiving Section 8 assistance doubled to 2.2 million. Thus from 1980 to 1987, the federal government came to provide housing aid to an additional 1.3 million low-income households—more households than the entire public-housing program had assisted in 1980.

Advocates also frequently assert that decreases in the 10 number of single-room occupancy units (SROs) have reduced vacancies, raised rents, and spurred latent homelessness. This is plausible in some cities, notably New York, where municipal housing codes, rent controls, and slum-clearance programs have often impeded the creation and maintenance of these low-cost forms of housing. Still, the connection between homelessness and changes in housing markets is uncertain. Because most anti-SRO policies pre-dated the 1980s, it is unclear why the SRO market would suddenly have started to function poorly in that decade. Although many SROs have been demolished in recent years, many replacement dwelling units may also have been sup-plied by landlords who reconfigured their buildings to meet the demand for cheap rooms. Little is known about these matters, because in most cities data on abandonments and conversions are poor. Information on trends in rent levels *is* available, and it shows that during the 1980s residential rents generally did rise appreciably faster than inflation in the Northeast and West. If real rent increases were an important cause of the rise in latent homelessness, however, the South and Midwest, where real rents have not risen, should be relatively free of street people. Significant regional variations in homelessness have yet to be detected.

Other explanations for the recent increase in latent 11 homelessness are more compelling. First, most homeless in-dividuals are between twenty-five and forty-five. This age cohort, the baby-boom generation, is currently unusually large; in addition, it came of age when norms against sub-stance abuse were unusually weak. The crack and cocaine epidemics of the 1980s undoubtedly boosted latent homeless-ness. Addictions lessen capacities to pay rent and to keep a job; in addition, primary tenants are no doubt more likely to evict addicted housemates than unaddicted ones.

It is furthermore well known that many of the most 12 forlorn of the homeless are on the streets because of the emptying of mental hospitals, prompted in part by changes in treatment policies and in part by a sharp increase in the constitutional and statutory rights of the mentally ill. Today, a person cannot be committed involuntarily without a judi-cial finding—reached through protective procedures that include a right to counsel—that the person is dangerous to self or others. A physician, hospital, or police officer who violates these legal protections can be held liable for substan-tial damages to the wrongly confined patient. Half a million fewer people are in institutions today than would be the case if the rate of institutionalization were what it was in the 1950s. Indeed, between 1960 and 1975 the average daily population of state and county mental hospitals dropped by 60 percent. And, despite continuing increases in the adult population, the number of patients in state and county mental hospitals has continued to drop, going from 193,000 to 107,000 between 1975 and 1987. Because the last people to be released would tend to be least able to take care of themselves, the emptying of hospitals explains much of the rise in homelessness. There are now many more troubled people on the streets; in New York City between 1980 and 1988, for example, the number of emergency calls reporting emotionally disturbed people rose from 21,000 to 47,000.

Finally, the rise in latent homelessness seems linked to 13 the increasing social isolation of the underclass—that is, poor people who grew up in poor neighborhoods in single-parent or no-parent households that were highly dependent on public assistance. During the 1970s the central-city poor became more and more concentrated in poor neighborhoods. The connection between homelessness and the deepening of underclass cultures remains somewhat speculative, however, because interviewers have rarely asked homeless individuals about their cultural backgrounds. Nevertheless, the evidence does suggest that the homeless have disproportionately grown up in underclass households. In 1985 Harvard psychiatrist Ellen Bassuk conducted detailed interviews of families in Massachusetts shelters;[1] she found that one-third of homeless mothers never knew their own fathers. Similarly, Piliavin and Sosin reported that 38 percent of homeless individuals had received out-of-home care during childhood. The increasing fragility of poor families heightens susceptibility to homelessness in a number of ways. People without appropriate family role models have more difficulty entering the world of work; children who grow up in fragile families (not to mention foster homes) typically have fewer helpers to fall back on when adversity strikes them as adults.

---

[1] Bassuk reports her findings in "Characteristics of Sheltered Homeless Families," *American Journal of Public Health,* vol. 76 (1986), p. 1097.

Realism about the Homeless

These explanations for the rise in latent homelessness high- 14
light a key issue in the current policy debate. Activists for the
homeless often suggest that the only thing that distinguishes
the homeless from the rest of the population is the lack of a
home. For example, Kozol begins *Rachel and Her Children*, a
book on the plight of homeless families in a squalid and
dispiriting welfare hotel in New York, with a chapter entitled
"Ordinary People." But the families that he describes are far
from ordinary in important respects. For example, Kozol
profiles Laura, a young unmarried mother who, partly
because she is illiterate, fails to obtain medical treatment for
an infant with scabies and later abandons her children to
become a prostitute.

Most homeless families are not random victims of a 15
recent run of bad luck, and it is highly misleading to suggest
otherwise. In their study of New York, Knickman and
Weitzman found that a major cause of family homelessness
was the relative inability of heads of homeless families to
function independently—a theme missing in the *New York
Times* story on the study, which focused instead on the city's
tight housing market. Similarly, Bassuk found that the
homeless families she interviewed were overwhelmingly
headed by young unmarried women, a majority of whom
had never had a job and more than half of whom had first
given birth in their teens. Some 91 percent of these families
were currently receiving AFDC payments; a majority had
been receiving them for over two years. One-third of these
mothers had never known their own fathers and one-third
had been physically abused as children.

Like homeless families, few homeless individuals were 16
leading ordinary lives before slipping into homelessness.
Most homeless individuals suffer from either mental illness
or substance abuse, or from both. Findings from dozens of
careful field studies suggest that about 25 percent of homeless individuals have been patients in mental hospitals and
that an overlapping one-third currently show signs of a
psychosis or an affective disorder. Georges Vernez, who
supervised a far-flung field study in California, reported that

69 percent of homeless individuals interviewed were abusing either drugs or alcohol; over half of this subgroup abused both substances. Even more distressingly, Vernez found that three-quarters of the homeless with serious mental illnesses were also substance abusers. Only 23 percent of the homeless individuals in Vernez's sample were free from both major mental illness and substance abuse.[2]

Many homeless individuals have histories of multiple stays in institutions other than mental hospitals. Rossi found that one-third of the Chicago homeless had been in a detoxification unit for alcohol or drug abuse. Average findings in a dozen studies indicate that 21 percent of the homeless have served time in prison and an additional 21 percent have spent time in jail.   17

The claim made by some advocates of the homeless— that the stress of being on the streets *causes* the high incidence of mental illness and substance abuse—is unsupportable. Thus Piliavin and Sosin found in their study of Minneapolis that 70 percent of the homeless who had been patients in mental hospitals had been there before their first episode of homelessness.   18

What Is to Be Done?

No magic sword will slay homelessness. In a society committed to individual liberty, the ravages of substance abuse and mental illness cannot and should not always be hidden from view. Social-service programs designed to put down-and-out people back on their feet are of course appropriate in many contexts, but they are unlikely to enjoy high rates of success. Nonetheless, while my main purpose has been to describe the present situation, it is appropriate to close with a few suggestions.   19

First, all involved—particularly the media—should work to dispel the fog of misinformation that surrounds the homelessness issue. Hayes, Kozol, Snyder, and other advocates for the homeless have misled the public by exaggerating   20

---

[2] See Georges Vernez, *et al.*, "Review of California's Program for the Homeless Mentally Disabled" (Rand Corporation, 1988).

the size of the homeless population, asserting the ordinariness of homeless people, and misrepresenting recent trends in spending on low-income housing. If not corrected, these distortions may result in ill-advised policies.

Second and relatedly, policymakers should reject the 21 policy proposals that stem from the assumption that the homeless are ordinary people down on their luck. Many advocates refer to the housing market as a game of musical chairs. This invalid assumption underlies Robert Hayes's frequent assertion that the solution to homelessness can be stated in three words: "Housing, housing, housing."

Hayes's view is flawed because homelessness is not 22 mainly attributable to breakdowns on the supply side of the housing market, any more than hunger in the United States can be blamed on inadequacies in food production. Instead, homelessness in most cities stems primarily (if not entirely) from the demand side of the market—that is, from the condition of homeless people themselves. The great majority of homeless people are not random victims of a housing-market squeeze, but rather deeply troubled individuals and families who, when deserving of government aid, should be given tailored financial assistance and help in managing their lives more successfully. The construction of nonprofit and public housing projects is a slow and highly roundabout way of serving those ends.

Opening more all-purpose shelters also makes no sense. 23 As officials in New York City have learned, mass shelters that serve all comers not only make it difficult to deliver social services, but also foster a subculture of dependence and deviance. A faster, more economical, and less destructive way to house homeless people is to give them vouchers. Voucher programs, however, must be narrowly and carefully designed. Connecticut's experience with RAPs shows that a poorly structured program may induce households to get themselves into jams in order to receive vouchers.

Vouchers hold particular promise for the one-third of 24 homeless individuals with serious mental problems. Once identified, individuals with such problems could be given specialized housing vouchers that could be cashed only in small board-and-care facilities equipped to serve people with their ailments. Rossi's proposal for in-home cash assistance to families with dependent adults is even more decentralized and family-oriented.

Perhaps as many as a third of homeless singles are 25 presently employable (or indeed already employed), and more could work if they were to take appropriate medication. Many of these people are in their thirties (a prime working age) and must be encouraged to enter the job market. A policy that New York City recently adopted may help to achieve this goal. New York now "segments" homeless individuals among specialty shelters, such as facilities for the elderly and the mentally ill. This innovation will make it easier for the city to encourage those staying in its general shelters to reenter the labor and housing markets. Many nonprofit shelters have found it desirable to set a ceiling on the period during which able-bodied people can receive their services. Some limit maximum stays to perhaps two weeks at a time; others intentionally close during daylight hours, rather than staying open around the clock. To adopt policies along these lines, New York City would have to succeed in modifying the consent decrees that it signed to settle lawsuits brought by Hayes and others. If the city could implement these policies, it would both interrupt dependencies and signal that it expects able-bodied persons to reenter the work force.

For homeless families, another sort of reform seems 26 promising. About 90 percent of the heads of homeless families are already receiving AFDC benefits when they apply for emergency housing aid; Knickman and Weitzman found that these mothers are much less able than other AFDC mothers to manage an independent household, and that many of them turn repeatedly to emergency shelters within the course of a year. A paternalistic concern for the welfare of the children in these chaotic families should override the mothers' claims to autonomy. For the sake of these children, legislatures should amend welfare laws to let state agencies pay rent directly to the landlord of a family that has previously made significant use of emergency shelters. Both by deterring the repeat use of emergency shelters and by encouraging lasting post-shelter placements, this reform could bring a bit more stability to the lives of children growing up under the most trying of circumstances.

In sum, governments and charities should make distinc- 27
tions among the homeless instead of muddling together a
highly diverse group of people. Such distinctions would
enable service providers to extend aid to, say, the casualties
of deinstitutionalization, and to cease providing unlimited
and unconditional aid to the able-bodied. The current shelter
policies of many cities mire young adults in the dependent
and antisocial culture of the underclass. By now we should
know better than to provide cures that simply make things
worse.

VOCABULARY

paragraph 1: volatility, advocate
paragraph 2: Herculean
paragraph 4: fluidity
paragraph 6: gentrified, dispersion
paragraph 7: vagrancy, innovation
paragraph 8: discrepancy
paragraph 10: latent
paragraph 11: cohort
paragraph 16: psychosis, affective disorder
paragraph 17: detoxification
paragraph 23: deviance, voucher
paragraph 25: segments, innovation
paragraph 26: paternalistic, autonomy

QUESTIONS

1. Ellickson discusses three "misrepresentations" of homelessness
   in America—exaggeration of the numbers of homeless people,
   stress on the "ordinariness" of the homeless, and misstatement
   of government spending on housing for low-income people in
   the 1980s. What evidence does Ellickson present to dispute the
   exaggeration of numbers? Why is this exaggeration crucial in
   the debate over homelessness?
2. On what evidence does Ellickson dispute the ordinariness of the
   homeless? Why is this misrepresentation crucial to the debate?

3. How does Ellickson correct the misrepresentation of government spending for low-income people in the 1980s? In correcting
this misrepresentation, what view of governmental policy and
attitude toward the homeless is he also correcting?

4. How do the facts presented by Ellickson support his recommendations on policy toward the homeless?

SUGGESTIONS FOR WRITING

1. Compare Ellickson's analysis of homelessness with that of
Rivlin (p. 334) or Kozol (p. 365), noting differences and similarities in the facts presented and in policies or remedies.

2. Find letters to the editor of a newspaper that take opposing
positions on a current issue. Compare the reasoning in each
letter as well as the factual evidence presented by each
writer.

DAVID H. HACKWORTH

COLONEL DAVID H. HACKWORTH *served with the U.S.
Army in Korea and Vietnam, retiring in 1971. In his memoir*
About Face *(1989), he describes his eight years of combat
experience. A contributing editor to* Newsweek, *Hackworth
wrote an account of women in combat in the Persian Gulf War
for the issue of August 5, 1991. The point at issue in the debate
over women in combat, Hackworth states in* Newsweek, *is
not courage or heroism:*

> *Equality and opportunity are noble ideals, but they have
> little to do with the battlefield, where the issues are living
> and dying. The question is: what if it turns out that
> equality and opportunity hurt combat readiness? The
> issue is not female bravery; the gulf war proved that
> patriotism and heroism are not gender-dependent. It
> isn't professionalism. The women troops I met during
> and after the war are smart, dedicated and technically
> competent. They are also better educated than their male
> counterparts.*

Hackworth raises the same concern in his article in The Washington Post, *reprinted here. In the article Hackworth raises other concerns and makes a recommendation to legislators considering a revision of the federal Combat Exclusion Act of 1948 and army policies that exclude women from combat aircraft and ships and from infantry and armored combat.*

Women and Combat

Congress will decide very soon whether to set up a commission on women in combat.

I believe such a commission is essential. It is needed to determine whether women could be drafted and whether combat assignments for women could be kept voluntary when they aren't voluntary for men. More than that, though, the commission is needed to take stock of what we've learned so far about women in the military, and to look ahead.

As a *Newsweek* reporter assigned to the Persian Gulf during the war, I watched firsthand as American servicewomen performed splendidly there. A few years before that, I was a proud papa when my own daughter received three commendations for valor for her work on Coast Guard choppers plucking people from the sea. I understand America's sense of gratitude to its women warriors, and I know how important our nation's ideals, such as equality and opportunity, are to the whole sense of why we fight.

But as an experienced combat soldier, I have to say that in direct combat there's something more important than gratitude, more important even than equality and opportunity. It's life and death. Often, life and death for dozens of soldiers can come down to how fast a pace you can maintain with a hundred-pound pack on your back, to a split-second command to the fighter aircraft at your wingtip, to whether the grunt next to you is strong enough to carry you off the battlefield if your leg's been blown apart, to whether your platoon is operating at full fighting strength or is three soldiers short, and to whether your unit is moving faster than the enemy. Under modern conditions of fast-maneuver warfare, stamina and speed matter even more than they did a generation ago.

It's not that "women can't do it." It's rather that our information isn't good enough yet to risk lives on. Double standards for judging the physical strength and stamina of service men and women have become pervasive.

At West Point, for example, women practice handling an M-14 rifle whose spring has been modified to make it easier for them. The obstacle course has been eased for them. Running shoes are used because female cadets were getting too many foot injuries running in Army boots. Army physical fitness standards call for men to be able to do 80 pushups; women must do 56. Men 17 to 25 years of age must run two miles in 17 minutes, 55 seconds, or better; women are allowed 22 minutes, 14 seconds. Marine men must climb 20 feet of rope in 30 seconds; Marine women are given 50 seconds.

In the thousand-plus interviews of service men and women that I did for a *Newsweek* story on women in combat, these double standards were the No. 1 complaint. With women excluded from combat, such double standards were "only" morale-busters; in battle, they'll cost women and men their lives.

We need to know the truth about how many women would be capable and qualified under genuinely equal standards—and we need to know before we start assigning women to combat specialties and before bullets start flying.

A commission should also help the military accurately project how many soldiers would be available for combat in a future conflict.

How many soldiers deployed to the gulf were out of action—and for how long—because of noncombat-related accidents and pregnancies? What percentage of the men and women called up had custody of young children they couldn't leave? Such information tells us a lot about how many active and reserve personnel we'll need, and how fast, to keep the front lines at full strength. If we don't know or we're seriously wrong, we're going to lose battles and lives.

The biggest unknown, though, is what the soldiers who will be most affected by the proposed changes think.

The soldiers I interviewed, from buck privates to generals, raised detailed concerns that no one in Washington seems to be publicly discussing. And the closer one gets to the soldiers who will do the bleeding and dying, the more concerns they raise. Our country's leaders have a high moral responsibility to talk to these soldiers, to hear them out and to consider their views carefully.

Incidentally, these issues have not been "studied to 13 death." I asked senators and representatives, Pentagon officials, think tanks, service medical and training commands, and 45 years' worth of military contacts for any studies they had. What I got was anecdotes, opinions about what the facts show and random statistics. But no studies.

The achievements women have made in the armed 14 services will not be lost or forgotten if we reserve judgment on women's roles in the military until all the facts are in. Women themselves will see to that.

The greater danger is that mistakes made now, in a 15 haste to get women into combat, could lead to needless fatalities. If that happens, there will be hell to pay politically and militarily. The backlash could set military women back decades.

Let a commission of civilian and military leaders bring as 16 much expertise as possible to these decisions. Now is not the time for our political leaders to duck and weave, but to look this issue dead in the eye and act responsibly.

QUESTIONS

1. Does Hackworth support or oppose women in combat? Or does he reserve judgment on the issue?
2. Is there a single overriding issue for Hackworth in the debate? How do you know?
3. Do you support or oppose women in combat? What beliefs and experiences guide your thinking on the issue?

SUGGESTION FOR WRITING

Write an argumentative essay on a current issue of concern to you. Assume you are addressing an audience unfamiliar with the issue and therefore in need of facts. You might begin your essay by introducing the issue and then presenting the facts or background and stating your thesis—your position on the issue.

Next, you might argue in support of your position, then introduce and answer objections or counterarguments (see p. 399). An alternate method is to begin with these objections and state your position in answering them. To conclude your essay, you might restate your arguments and affirm your thesis.

ELAINE TYLER MAY

ELAINE TYLER MAY, *Professor of History at the University of Minnesota, is the author of* Great Expectations: Marriage and Divorce in Post-Victorian America (*1983*) *and* Homeward Bound: American Families in the Cold War Era (*1988*). *In examining the issue of women in combat, May employs the popular form of debate described on p. 399, using her narrative or background of the case to present the opposing arguments. May is particularly interested in assumptions that guide thinking on the issue, for example, the assumption that "the only good fighting force is one in which heterosexual men pursue their mission free from sexual temptation."*

Women in the Wild Blue Yonder

Now that Congress has opened the door for women to enter the ranks of combat pilots, many Americans find themselves uncomfortable with the idea. Why do so many people cringe at the thought of women in combat? Full access to the military is a logical next step on the road to equal opportunity for women. Perhaps the real question is why it has taken so long for women to enter battle.

The combat barrier somehow seems different, more ominous than other rights gained by women. Not because it marks the invasion of women into one of the few remaining bastions of masculinity, but because it threatens what is perhaps the sole surviving gender myth of the twentieth century: that women are the world's nurturers. Can a nurturer also be a destroyer?

Those opposed to sending women into combat sidestep 3
the issue. Some claim that women are not physically strong
enough to serve as fighter pilots. That argument collapses at
a time when strength and endurance are as readily developed in women as in men. Besides, these women would be
flying planes, not lifting them. And with sophisticated
weaponry, women can push the buttons to drop the bombs
as easily as men can.

Others argue that men should protect women, not the 4
other way around. That chivalry might make some sense if it
operated anywhere else in our society. But women are at risk
in other occupations, where hazards to their safety abound.
It is disingenuous to hear calls for their protection in battle
when they are not even protected at home, where domestic
abuse and violence against women are widespread.

Still, maybe war is different. Since our War of Indepen- 5
dence, women have participated in warfare. They have
provided supplies and medical care, even on the front lines.
During World War I, men were urged to fight for mothers,
wives and sweethearts back home.

In World War II, sentimental views of women were 6
replaced by other images. Rosie the Riveter became a national icon, doing "men's work" in war industries. These
female workers were glorified, though they were expected to
relinquish their well-paying, physically demanding jobs after
the war. At the same time, symbols of female sexuality
entered the iconography of war. Pinups appeared in military
barracks; the noses of thousands of bombers were decorated
with erotic portraits.

If the U.S. hires women as professional killers, allowing 7
them into the cockpit, what remains of the sentimental ideal
of women as pure and gentle creatures might vanish. It is not
so much that women might get killed; it is that they might
kill.

The ability to kill is the ultimate equalizer. Indeed, the 8
integration of combat units after World War II signaled a
major change in the nation's racial relations. The symbolic
impact of women fighting in combat cannot be overlooked.

Power, of course, is intimately connected to sex. It is no 9
accident that another policy under discussion bans homo-

sexuals from the armed forces. In World War II and the cold war, women and gays were barred from combat, in part because they were believed to be security risks.

We now know that in spite of the ban, many gay men and women served heroically in World War II. Still, military policies are based on the theory that the only good fighting force is one in which heterosexual men pursue their mission free from sexual temptation. Since no such force has ever existed, it is difficult to know if there is any truth to the myth. 10

There are those on the other side of the debate who argue that women are really less warlike than men and that bringing them fully into the military would humanize the armed services. Perhaps. But we won't know, at least not until women fill the leadership ranks of the military establishment—from running major defense industries and the Pentagon to serving as the Commander in Chief herself. 11

VOCABULARY

paragraph 2: ominous, bastion, nurturer

paragraph 3: sophisticated

paragraph 4: chivalry

paragraph 6: sentimental, icon, iconography

paragraph 8: symbolic

QUESTIONS

1. Is May addressing a general audience that varies in knowledge and interest in the controversy over women in combat, or is she addressing a special audience that knows the facts, is interested, and perhaps has special concerns? How do you know?

2. What is a "gender myth," and what gender myth does May challenge? How do the objections to women in combat discussed in paragraphs 3 and 4 illustrate this myth, and how does May answer them?

3. What additional answer does May give to the gender myth in paragraphs 5–7?

4. What explanation does May present in paragraphs 9 and 10 for male opposition to women in combat? What supporting evidence does she present?

5. Why does she conclude the essay by considering the argument that women are "really less warlike than men"?

6. Where does May first state her thesis? Where does she restate it?

7. Is the point at issue over women in combat the same for May and Hackworth, or are they concerned with different issues?

SUGGESTIONS FOR WRITING

1. Discuss the extent to which Antonia Fraser's survey of attitudes and opinions (p. 356) supports May's analysis of male opposition to women in combat.

2. Using magazine and newspaper articles and editorials, analyze other opinions on women in combat, focusing on contrasting statements or exchanges that vary sharply on problems and solutions. Don't try to cover all opinions on the issue. Focus on ones that represent major positions and disagreements.

ORDER OF IDEAS IN PERSUASIVE ESSAYS

Argumentative essays have a traditional organization that is easy to learn and to put to use. This organization, derived from the oration of the law courts and legislatures of ancient Greece and Rome, shaped the varieties of essay that we have been considering—in particular the division of the essay into an introduction that states the purpose and gives pertinent background, the main discussion or body, and the conclusion. The persuasive essay today, like the oration of ancient times, often contains these divisions but expands them to meet the needs of the argument. These divisions can be summarized:

> *introduction*, or what was called the exordium or exhortation to the audience, appealing to the interest and good will of the audience, and stating the subject of the oration or essay (Hackworth: paragraphs 1–2);
>
> *narration* or background, stating the facts of the case (paragraphs 3–4);
>
> *division of proofs*, stating the thesis partly or fully, and summarizing the evidence and arguments to be presented (paragraph 5: Hackworth's statement of thesis; summary of evidence and proof omitted);

confirmation or proof, arguing the thesis (paragraphs 6–12);

refutation, answering opponents (paragraph 13);

conclusion, reinforcing and summarizing the main argument, and reinforcing the original appeal to the audience (paragraphs 14–16, restating the thesis and calling for study of the issue).

These parts of the essay may be combined or arranged in a different order—the narration or background perhaps combined with the confirming arguments, or the refutation coming before the confirmation. Often the division or outline of the arguments is omitted, and instead of coming early in the argument, the thesis may be delayed until the conclusion for reasons discussed earlier. David H. Hackworth's essay illustrates this form, as the paragraph numbers given above show. Jane Goodall, earlier in this book (p. 305), follows the same plan but omits a summary of her evidence and main arguments and reverses her confirming arguments and her refutation.

METHODS OF PERSUASION

❦ ❦ ❦

How you develop an essay depends on your purpose and audience. The demands of exposition and persuasion are not the same. Your major concern in exposition is to be clear; clarity is important in a persuasive essay, but your major concern is to present your ideas in an honest and convincing way. In describing how to conserve fuel by driving properly, for example, your concern is to make the process clear; if your purpose is also to persuade drivers to change their driving habits, you consider the best means of doing so. These means depend on the nature of your audience. If the audience is hostile or indifferent to the idea of conservation, you might discuss conservation of fuel and make various appeals—for example, to conscience, public spirit, practical concerns—before turning to the matter of driving. If the audience is friendly to the idea, you probably need only remind them of the importance of conservation.

Persuasive arguments present additional challenges. You must construct a sound argument, arouse the interest of the audience through a legitimate appeal to their emotions, and show that you are well informed on the issue and honest in your presentation and therefore deserve a hearing. Though some writers seek to avoid all emotional appeals in the belief that the soundness of the argument guarantees its persuasiveness, few arguments are entirely free of emotion. The problem is not how to rid the argument of emotion but how to balance emotion and reason so that the aroused reader considers the argument fully, gives rational assent to it, and is free to disagree with it in whole or in part.

ANONYMOUS

The anonymous writer of this essay makes many of the same points that Edward Simmen does in his essay on the origin and meaning of the word Chicano. *But this writer has another purpose in mind and uses other means to achieve it. The essay was first published in 1970.*

Who Am I?

After I tell you who I am you may not know me. You may 1
not recognize me. You may deny that I exist. Who am I?
I'm a product of myself. I'm a product of you and of my
ancestors.

Now, one half of my ancestors were the Spanish who 2
were Western European, but who were also part African and
part Middle Eastern. They came to this country and met with
the other side of my family—the Indians. The Indians also
were a great race—people of a great culture. There were
many kinds of Indians, as there were many kinds of Spaniards. They mixed, they married, they had children. Their
children were called Mestizos, and this is what I am.

We came to California long before the Pilgrims landed at 3
Plymouth Rock. We settled California and all of the southwestern part of the United States, including the states of
Arizona, New Mexico, Colorado, and Texas. We built the
missions, and we cultivated the ranches. We were at the
Alamo in Texas, both inside and outside. You know, we
owned California—that is, until gold was found there.

I think it was a mistake to let you into the southwestern 4
states, because eventually you took away our lands. When
we fought to retain what was ours, you used the vigilantes to
scare us away, to hang us, and to take away our lands. We
became your slaves. Now we cook your food, we build your
railroads, we harvest your crops, we dig your ditches, we
stand in your unemployment lines—and we receive more
than 20 percent of your welfare. But we've done some good
things, too: We won more Medals of Honor during World
War II than any other ethnic group. We've never had a
turncoat, even during the Korean War. Yes we have had
outstanding war records. But, you know, we don't complain.
By the same token, we don't get much attention, either.

We don't live in your neighborhoods unless we let you 5
call us Spanish, French, or something else, but not what we

are. We usually attend our own schools at the elementary or junior high level; and if we get to high school, we may go to school with you. However, even before we finish high school, more than 50 percent of us drop out, and you know we don't go to college. We make up less than 1 percent of the college students, yet we are 12 percent of the total school population. We don't use government agencies because our experiences with them have been rather poor; they haven't been very friendly or helpful. The Immigration Department has never really been our friend. The land offices help to take away our lands—we couldn't exactly call them friendly. The Farm Labor Bureau has never truly served us. The schools haven't really lifted us educationally. The police—well, they haven't been the most cooperative agency in the government either. You accept our Spanish words as long as we don't speak them, because if we do, you say they're "poor" Spanish—not Castilian; so our language can't be very good— it's almost like swearing. We are usually Catholics and sometimes Protestants, but in either case we have our own churches. You say we can leave our *barrios* to live near you—that is, only if we stay in our own place. When we attend your parties to meet your friends, you usually intro- duce us as being Spanish or something else that we are not. You are ashamed of what we are, and your attitude makes us feel that we, too, should be ashamed of what we are. When we go to school, we don't take part in your school activities; we don't think we're wanted. We seldom participate in sports; we don't run for student offices; we don't go to your school dances; we aren't valedictorians at graduations; we seldom win recognition as students, even in Spanish; we seldom receive scholarships; we are seldom given consider- ation in school plans; we are seldom given lead parts in school plays. The higher in education we go, the more obvious are the double standards; yet, we haven't given up.

Who are we? Some call us the forgotten people; others 6 call us chili snappers, tacos, spics, mexs, or greasers. Some ignore us and pretend that we don't exist. Some just wish that we would go away. The late U.S. Senator Chavez from New Mexico once said, "At the time of war we are called 'the great patriotic Americans,' and during elections politicians call us 'the great Spanish-speaking community of America.' When we ask for jobs, we are called 'those damn Mexicans.' "

Who am I? I'm a human being. I have the same hopes ⁊ that you have, the same fears, same drives, same desires, same concerns, and same abilities. I want the same chance that you have to be an individual. Who am I? In reality, I am who you want me to be.

VOCABULARY

paragraph 5: Castilian, barrios, valedictorians

QUESTIONS

1. How does the author create an image of the class of people described? What defining qualities or facts does the author delay in presenting, and why?
2. What is the purpose of the essay, and what audience is the author addressing? Is the author seeking to persuade readers to change their thinking and possibly take action on discrimination or federal policies?
3. How do the persuasive means employed serve this purpose?
4. What does the author gain in persuasiveness by remaining anonymous?
5. How persuasive do you find the essay, and why?
6. How is the essay different in purpose and means from that of Edward Simmen, in his definition of the Chicano (p. 168)?

SUGGESTIONS FOR WRITING

1. Compare and contrast this essay with that of Simmen, noting similarities and differences in purpose, methods of development, and the nature and use of definition.
2. Write your own persuasive essay on who you are. Use the information you give about yourself and your ethnic, racial, religious, professional, or age group to persuade your readers to change their image of the group and possibly take action on a related issue.

WENDELL BERRY

WENDELL BERRY, *long associated with the environmental movement in the United States, has written much about the need to preserve wilderness and eliminate pollution. Berry has also written about his native Kentucky in poems, essays, and novels. His novels include* Nathan Coulter *(1960) and* The Memory of Old Jack *(1969). His essays have been collected in* The Long–Legged House *(1969),* The Unsettling of America *(1977),* Home Economics *(1987),* What Are People For? *(1990), and other volumes. In another essay, "The Rise," Berry comments on the pollution of the American continent:*

> *We haven't accepted—we can't really believe—that the most characteristic product of our age of scientific miracles is junk, but that is so. And we still think and behave as though we face an unspoiled continent, with thousands of acres of living space for every man. We still sing "America the Beautiful" as though we had not created in it, by strenuous effort, at great expense, and with dauntless self-praise, an unprecedented ugliness.*

Waste

As a country person, I often feel that I am on the bottom end of the waste problem. I live on the Kentucky River about ten miles from its entrance into the Ohio. The Kentucky, in many ways a lovely river, receives an abundance of pollution from the Eastern Kentucky coal mines and the central Kentucky cities. When the river rises, it carries a continuous raft of cans, bottles, plastic jugs, chunks of styrofoam, and other imperishable trash. After the floods subside, I, like many other farmers, must pick up the trash before I can use my bottomland fields. I have seen the Ohio, whose name (*Oyo* in Iroquois) means "beautiful river," so choked with this manufactured filth that an ant could crawl dryfooted from Kentucky to Indiana. The air of both river valleys is seriously polluted. Our roadsides and roadside fields lie under a constant precipitation of cans, bottles, the plastic-ware of fast food joints, soiled plastic diapers, and sometimes whole bags of garbage. In our county we now have a "sanitary landfill" which daily receives, in addition to our local production, fifty to sixty large truckloads of garbage from Pennsylvania, New Jersey, and New York.

Moreover, a close inspection of our countryside would 2 reveal, strewn over it from one end to the other, thousands of derelict and worthless automobiles, house trailers, refrigerators, stoves, freezers, washing machines, and dryers; as well as thousands of unregulated dumps in hollows and sink holes, on streambanks and roadsides, filled not only with "disposable" containers but also with broken toasters, television sets, toys of all kinds, furniture, lamps, stereos, radios, scales, coffee makers, mixers, blenders, corn poppers, hair dryers, and microwave ovens. Much of our waste problem is to be accounted for by the intentional flimsiness and unrepairability of the labor-savers and gadgets that we have become addicted to.

Of course, my sometime impression that I live on the 3 receiving end of this problem is false, for country people contribute their full share. The truth is that we Americans, all of us, have become a kind of human trash, living our lives in the midst of a ubiquitous damned mess of which we are at once the victims and the perpetrators. We are all unwilling victims, perhaps; and some of us even are unwilling perpetrators, but we must count ourselves among the guilty nonetheless. In my household we produce much of our own food and try to do without as many frivolous "necessities" as possible—and yet, like everyone else, we must shop, and when we shop we must bring home a load of plastic, aluminum, and glass containers designed to be thrown away, and "appliances" designed to wear out quickly and be thrown away.

I confess that I am angry at the manufacturers who make 4 these things. There are days when I would be delighted if certain corporation executives could somehow be obliged to eat their products. I know of no good reason why these containers and all other forms of manufactured "waste"— solid, liquid, toxic, or whatever—should not be outlawed. There is no sense and no sanity in objecting to the desecration of the flag while tolerating and justifying and encouraging as a daily business the desecration of the country for which it stands.

But our waste problem is not the fault only of producers. 5 It is the fault of an economy that is wasteful from top to bottom—a symbiosis of an unlimited greed at the top and a lazy, passive, and self-indulgent consumptiveness at the bottom—and all of us are involved in it. If we wish to correct this economy, we must be careful to understand and to demonstrate how much waste of human life is involved in our waste of the material goods of Creation. For example, much of the litter that now defaces our country is fairly directly caused by the massive secession or exclusion of most of our people from active participation in the food economy. We have made a social ideal of minimal involvement in the growing and cooking of food. This is one of the dearest "liberations" of our affluence. Nevertheless, the more dependent we become on the *industries* of eating and drinking, the more waste we are going to produce. The mess that surrounds us, then, must be understood not just as a problem in itself but as a symptom of a greater and graver problem: the centralization of our economy, the gathering of the productive property and power into fewer and fewer hands, and the consequent destruction, everywhere, of the local economies of household, neighborhood, and community.

This is the source of our unemployment problem, and I 6 am not talking just about the unemployment of eligible members of the "labor force." I mean also the unemployment of children and old people, who, in viable household and local economies, would have work to do by which they would be useful to themselves and to others. The ecological damage of centralization and waste is thus inextricably involved with human damage. For we have, as a result, not only a desecrated, ugly, and dangerous country in which to live until we are in some manner poisoned by it, and a constant and now generally accepted problem of unemployed or unemployable workers, but also classrooms full of children who lack the experience and discipline of fundamental human tasks, and various institutions full of still capable old people who are useless and lonely.

I think that we must learn to see the trash on our streets 7 and roadsides, in our rivers, and in our woods and fields, not as the side effects of "more jobs" as its manufacturers invariably insist that it is, but as evidence of good work *not* done by people able to do it.

VOCABULARY

paragraph 1: styrofoam, precipitation
paragraph 2: derelict
paragraph 3: ubiquitous, perpetrator
paragraph 5: symbiosis, affluence
paragraph 6: viable, desecrated

QUESTIONS

1. How does Berry try to persuade us that waste is an environmental problem? What other damage does waste create?
2. What causes of waste does Berry identify? Which cause does he discuss in most detail?
3. What is Berry's central point or thesis, and where does he state it? Where does he restate it? What does he gain by stating the idea where he does?
4. How persuasive do you find the essay?

SUGGESTIONS FOR WRITING

1. Discuss your own habits of consumption. Then state whether they give support to Berry's charge that consumption in America is "self-indulgent."
2. State your agreement or disagreement with the following statement or another in the essay, supporting your discussion from your own experience and observation:

   > We have made a social ideal of minimal involvement in the growing and cooking of food.

W. S. MERWIN

W. S. MERWIN *is a poet, playwright, translator, and essayist. His collections of poetry include* The Moving Target *(1963),* The Compass Flower *(1977), and* The Carrier of Ladders *(1970)—awarded the Pulitzer Prize in 1971. "Unchopping a Tree" is reprinted from* The Miner's Pale Children *(1970), a collection of essays. In the essay, Merwin chooses an unusual and even surprising means to arouse our concern over a commonplace event.*

Unchopping a Tree

Start with the leaves, the small twigs, and the nests that have   1
been shaken, ripped, or broken off by the fall; these must be gathered and attached once again to their respective places. It is not arduous work, unless major limbs have been smashed or mutilated. If the fall was carefully and correctly planned, the chances of anything of the kind happening will have been reduced. Again, much depends upon the size, age, shape, and species of the tree. Still, you will be lucky if you can get through this stage without having to use machinery. Even in the best of circumstances it is a labor that will make you wish often that you had won the favor of the universe of ants, the empire of mice, or at least a local tribe of squirrels, and could enlist their labors and their talents. But no, they leave you to it. They have learned, with time. This is men's work. It goes without saying that if the tree was hollow in whole or in part, and contained old nests of bird or mammal or insect, or hoards of nuts or such structures as wasps or bees build for their survival, the contents will have to be repaired where necessary, and reassembled, insofar as possible, in their original order, including the shells of nuts already opened. With spiders' webs you must simply do the best you can. We do not have the spider's weaving equipment, nor any substitute for the leaf's living bond with its point of attachment and nourishment. It is even harder to simulate the latter when the leaves have once become dry—as they are bound to do, for this is not the labor of a

moment. Also it hardly needs saying that this is the time for repairing any neighboring trees or bushes or other growth that may have been damaged by the fall. The same rules apply. Where neighboring trees were of the same species it is difficult not to waste time conveying a detached leaf back to the wrong tree. Practice, practice. Put your hope in that.

Now the tackle must be put into place or the scaffolding, 2 depending on the surroundings and the dimensions of the tree. It is ticklish work. Almost always it involves, in itself, further damage to the area, which will have to be corrected later. But as you've heard, it can't be helped. And care now is likely to save you considerable trouble later. Be careful to grind nothing into the ground.

At last the time comes for the erecting of the trunk. By 3 now it will scarcely be necessary to remind you of the delicacy of this huge skeleton. Every motion of the tackle, every slight upward heave of the trunk, the branches, their elaborately reassembled panoply of leaves (now dead) will draw from you an involuntary gasp. You will watch for a leaf or a twig to be snapped off yet again. You will listen for the nuts to shift in the hollow limb and you will hear whether they are indeed falling into place or are spilling in disorder—in which case, or in the event of anything else of the kind—operations will have to cease, of course, while you correct the matter. The raising itself is no small enterprise, from the moment when the chains tighten around the old bandages until the bole hangs vertical above the stump, splinter above splinter. Now the final straightening of the splinters themselves can take place (the preliminary work is best done while the wood is still green and soft, but at times when the splinters are not badly twisted most of the straightening is left until now, when the torn ends are face to face with each other). When the splinters are perfectly complementary the appropriate fixture is applied. Again we have no duplicate of the original substance. Ours is extremely strong, but it is rigid. It is limited to surfaces, and there is no play in it. However the core is not the part of the trunk that conducted life from the roots up into the branches and back again. It was relatively inert. The fixative for this part is not the same as the one for the outer layers and the bark, and if either of these is involved in the splintered section they must receive applications of the appropriate adhesives. Apart from being incorrect and probably ineffective, the core fixative would leave a scar on the bark.

When all is ready the splintered trunk is lowered onto the splinters of the stump. This, one might say, is only the skeleton of the resurrection. Now the chips must be gathered, and the sawdust, and returned to their former positions. The fixative for the wood layers will be applied to chips and sawdust consisting only of wood. Chips and sawdust consisting of several substances will receive applications of the correct adhesives. It is as well, where possible, to shelter the materials from the elements while working. Weathering makes it harder to identify the smaller fragments. Bark sawdust in particular the earth lays claim to very quickly. You must find your own ways of coping with this problem. There is a certain beauty, you will notice at moments, in the pattern of the chips as they are fitted back into place. You will wonder to what extent it should be described as natural, to what extent man-made. It will lead you on to speculations about the parentage of beauty itself, to which you will return.

The adhesive for the chips is translucent, and not so rigid as that for the splinters. That for bark and its subcutaneous layers is transparent and runs into the fibers on either side, partially dissolving them into each other. It does not set the sap flowing again but it does pay a kind of tribute to the preoccupations of the ancient thoroughfares. You could not roll an egg over the joints but some of the mineshafts would still be passable, no doubt. For the first exploring insect who raises its head in the tight echoless passages. The day comes when it is all restored, even to the moss (now dead) over the wound. You will sleep badly, thinking of the removal of the scaffolding that must begin the next morning. How you will hope for sun and a still day!

The removal of the scaffolding or tackle is not so dangerous, perhaps, to the surroundings, as its installation, but it presents problems. It should be taken from the spot piece by piece as it is detached, and stored at a distance. You have come to accept it there, around the tree. The sky begins to look naked as the chains and struts one by one vacate their positions. Finally the moment arrives when the last sustaining piece is removed and the tree stands again on its own. It is as though its weight for a moment stood on your heart. You listen for a thud of settlement, a warning creak deep in the intricate joinery. You cannot believe it will hold. How like something dreamed it is, standing there all by itself. How long will it stand there now? The first breeze that touches its dead leaves all seems to flow into your mouth. You are afraid the motion of the clouds will be enough to push it over. What more can you do? What more can you do?

But there is nothing more you can do.   7

Others are waiting.   8

Everything is going to have to be put back.   9

VOCABULARY

paragraph 1: simulate

paragraph 2: tackle

paragraph 3: panoply, bole, complementary, fixative

paragraph 5: translucent, subcutaneous, thoroughfares

paragraph 6: struts, joinery

QUESTIONS

1. What are the chief indications of Merwin's purpose in his essay? Does he state that purpose directly?

2. Examine the following statement from paragraph 4 carefully: "You will wonder to what extent it should be described as natural, to what extent man-made. It will lead you on to speculations about the parentage of beauty itself, to which you will return." What is the tone of the statement—that is, what seems to be the writer's attitude toward his reader as well as toward the act of unchopping a tree? Is an attitude *implied* in the whole essay that no single statement expresses? Could you accept an implication as embodying the thesis?

3. The writer has chosen a strategy to deal with his idea—that is, he approaches his reader in a particular way to achieve a particular effect. What does he want his reader to think and feel at the end of the essay, and what is his strategy in realizing these aims?

4. The essay ends with three single-sentence paragraphs. To what effect? What is Merwin saying?

5. How well does the writer achieve his purpose?

SUGGESTION FOR WRITING

Write an essay on a similar topic, for example, undoing an insult. Be consistent in conveying a tone and in building to your conclusion. Do not state your thesis directly; let the reader discover it in your tone and details.

BARBARA WARD

The British economist, teacher, and writer BARBARA WARD *(1914–1981) wrote much about the growing gap between rich and poor nations and the increasing scarcity of food and natural resources. Her books include* Faith and Freedom *(1954),* Spaceship Earth *(1966), and* The Home of Man *(1976). The term* triage *refers to the practice, in war and other catastrophes, of giving treatment first to the injured who have the greatest chance of surviving. In the early 1970s,* triage *became a term for the allocation of food to people, not on the basis of need but rather of worth to society. In an essay published in* The New York Times *on November 15, 1976, Ward responded to the argument that a policy of triage is necessary and inevitable, given the enormous rise of population, worldwide and particularly in poor countries.*

"Triage"

Now that the House of Representatives has bravely passed   1
its resolution on the "right to food"—the basic human right without which, indeed, all other rights are meaningless—it is perhaps a good moment to try to clear up one or two points of confusion that appear to have been troubling the American mind on the question of food supplies, hunger, and Amer-

ica's moral obligation, particularly to those who are not America's own citizens.

The United States, with Canada and marginal help from Australia, are the only producers of surplus grain. It follows that if any part of the world comes up short or approaches starvation, there is at present only one remedy and it is in Americans' hands. Either they do the emergency feeding or people starve. 2

It is a heavy moral responsibility. Is it one that has to be accepted? 3

This is where the moral confusions begin. A strong school of thought argues that it is the flood tide of babies, irresponsibly produced in Asia, Africa, and Latin America, that is creating the certainty of malnutrition and risk of famine. If these countries insist on having babies, they must feed them themselves. If hard times set in, food aid from North America—if any—must go strictly to those who can prove they are reducing the baby flood. Otherwise, the responsible suffer. The poor go on increasing. 4

This is a distinctly Victorian replay of Malthus.* He first suggested that population would go on rising to absorb all available supplies and that the poor must be left to starve if they would be incontinent. The British Poor Law was based on this principle. It has now been given a new descriptive analogy in America. The planet is compared to a battlefield. There are not enough medical skills and supplies to go round. So what must the doctors do? Obviously, concentrate on those who can hope to recover. The rest must die. This is the meaning of "triage." 5

Abandon the unsavable and by so doing concentrate the supplies—in the battlefield, medical skills; in the world at large, surplus food—on those who still have a chance to survive. 6

Thus the people with stable or stabilizing populations will be able to hold on. The human experiment will continue. 7

It is a very simple argument. It has been persuasively supported by noted business leaders, trade-unionists, aca- 8

---

* Thomas Malthus (1766–1834), in his *Essay on the Principle of Population* (1798), argued that population growth would have to be controlled, because population increases faster than the food supply. He opposed relief for the poor and higher wages on the ground that these encouraged idleness and early marriage.—Ed.

demics and presumed Presidential advisers. But "triage" is, in fact, so shot through with half truths as to be almost a lie, and so irrelevant to real world issues as to be not much more than an aberration.

Take the half truths first. In the last ten years, at least 9 one-third of the increased world demand for food has come from North Americans, Europeans and Russians eating steadily more high-protein food. Grain is fed to animals and poultry, and eaten as steak and eggs.

In real energy terms, this is about five times more 10 wasteful than eating grain itself. The result is an average American diet of nearly 2,000 pounds of grain a year—and epidemics of cardiac trouble—and 400 pounds for the average Indian.

It follows that for those worrying about available sup- 11 plies on the "Battlefield," one American equals five Indians in the claims on basic food. And this figure masks the fact that much of the North American eating—and drinking—is pure waste. For instance, the American Medical Association would like to see meat-eating cut by a third to produce a healthier nation.

The second distortion is to suggest that direct food aid is 12 what the world is chiefly seeking from the United States. True, if there were a failed monsoon and the normal Soviet agricultural muddle next year, the need for an actual transfer of grain would have to be faced.

That is why the world food plan, worked out at Secretary 13 of State Henry A. Kissinger's earlier prompting, asks for a modest reserve of grain to be set aside—on the old biblical plan of Joseph's "fat years" being used to prepare for the "lean."

But no conceivable American surplus could deal with 14 the third world's food needs of the 1980's and 1990's. They can be met only by a sustained advance in food production where productivity is still so low that quadrupling and quintupling of crops is possible, provided investments begin now.

A recent Japanese study has shown that rice responds 15 with copybook reliability to higher irrigation and improved seed. This is why the same world food plan is stressing a steady capital input of $30 billion a year in third-world farms, with perhaps $5 billion contributed by the old rich and the "oil" rich.

(What irony that this figure is barely a third of what 16 West Germany has to spend each year to offset the health effects of overeating and overdrinking.)

To exclaim and complain about the impossibility of 17 giving away enough American surplus grain (which could not be rice anyway), when the real issue is a sustained effort by all the nations in long-term agricultural investment, simply takes the citizens' minds off the real issue—where they can be of certain assistance—and impresses on them a nonissue that confuses them and helps nobody else.

Happily, the House's food resolution puts long-term 18 international investment in food production firmly back into the center of the picture.

And this investment in the long run is the true answer to 19 the stabilizing of family size. People do not learn restraint from "give-aways." (The arms industry's bribes are proof enough of that.) But the whole experience of the last century is that if parents are given work, responsibility, enough food and safe water, they have the sense to see they do not need endless children as insurance against calamity.

Because of food from the Great Plains and the reform of 20 sanitation, Malthusian fears vanished as an issue in Europe and North America in the 1880's. China is below 2 percent population growth today on the basis of intensive agriculture and popular health measures.

Go to the root of the matter—investment in people, in 21 food, in water—and the Malthus myth will fade in the third world as it has done already in many parts of it and entirely in the so-called first and second worlds.

It may be that this positive strategy of stabilizing popu- 22 lation by sustained, skilled and well-directed investment in food production, and in clean water suggests less drama than the hair-raising images of inexorably rising tides of children eating like locusts the core out of the whole world's food supplies.

But perhaps we should be wise to prefer relevance to 23 drama. In "triage," there is, after all, a suggestion of the battlefield. If this is how we see the world, are we absolutely certain who deserves to win—the minority of guzzlers who eat 2,000 pounds of grain, or the majority of despairing men of hunger who eat 400 pounds?

History gives uncomfortable answers. No doubt as they 24 left their hot baths and massage parlors for the joys of dining, vomiting and redining, Roman senators must have muttered and complained about the "awkwardness of the barbarians." But the barbarians won. Is this the battlefield we want? And who will "triage" whom?

VOCABULARY

paragraph 8: aberration

paragraph 12: monsoon

paragraph 14: quadrupling, quintupling

paragraph 16: irony

QUESTIONS

1. The general issue of Ward's essay is the feeding of the poor throughout the world: the point at issue is stated in paragraph 3: "It is a heavy moral responsibility. Is it one that has to be accepted?" What are the real issues that Ward identifies later, in dealing with the point at issue?
2. What background or narration does Ward provide? How does she use this narration to state the assumptions of those who argue for triage?
3. What assumptions does she present in opposition to those she is criticizing? How does she explain these assumptions?
4. Notice that Ward has put a deductive argument to the use of persuasion: this is why she must explain and defend her own assumptions. In doing so, what appeal to experience does she make, particularly in the concluding paragraph?
5. In the course of the essay, Ward poses a dilemma: either we select certain people to feed, or we all eventually starve and die. How does she deal with this dilemma?

SUGGESTION FOR WRITING

Discuss the extent of your agreement with Ward's assumptions and conclusions. If you agree with her conclusions for different reasons, explain what these are and defend them.

JONATHAN SWIFT

JONATHAN SWIFT *(1667–1745), the son of English Protestant parents, was born and educated in Ireland. In 1688 he went to England to seek a career in literature. Swift wrote satirical poems, essays, pamphlets, and tracts on the major issues of the day and became involved in many of its political and religious controversies. During his stay, Swift was ordained in the Church of England. In 1713 he became Dean of St. Patrick's Cathedral in Dublin and in the succeeding years wrote widely on various questions bearing on Ireland and England. His most famous satirical work,* Gulliver's Travels, *was published in 1726. Swift was deeply concerned about the sufferings that he had observed in his country from boyhood. Ireland, under the control of the British government, was an impoverished country—restricted in selling its goods and incapable of producing enough food to feed the population. Most of the poor were Catholic, a point that Swift emphasizes in his "modest proposal"—written in 1729 to suggest a remedy for the widespread starvation and misery of the country. Swift writes as a disinterested observer, anxious to perform a service to both the English and the Irish with his proposal. The persuasive means that Swift uses deserves the closest study.*

A Modest Proposal

*For Preventing the Children of
Poor People in Ireland from
Being a Burden to Their
Parents or Country, and for
Making Them Beneficial to the
Public*

It is a melancholy object to those who walk through this great town, or travel in the country, when they see the streets, the roads, and cabin-doors crowded with beggars of the female sex, followed by three, four, or six children, all in rags, and importuning every passenger for an alms. These mothers, instead of being able to work for their honest livelihood, are forced to employ all their time in strolling to beg sustenance for their helpless infants: who, as they grow up, either turn thieves for want of work, or leave their dear native country to fight for the Pretender in Spain, or sell themselves to the Barbadoes.

I think it is agreed by all parties, that this prodigious 2 number of children in the arms, or on the backs, or at the heels of their mothers, and frequently of their fathers, is in the present deplorable state of the kingdom, a very great additional grievance; and, therefore, whoever could find out a fair, cheap, and easy method of making these children sound and useful members of the commonwealth, would deserve so well of the public, as to have his statue set up for a preserver of the nation.

But my intention is very far from being confined to 3 provide only for the children of professed beggars; it is of a much greater extent, and shall take in the whole number of infants at a certain age, who are born of parents in effect as little able to support them as those who demand our charity in the streets.

As to my own part, having turned my thoughts for 4 many years upon this important subject, and maturely weighed the several schemes of other projectors, I have always found them grossly mistaken in their computation. It is true, a child, just dropped from its dam, may be supported by her milk for a solar year with little other nourishment; at most, not above the value of two shillings, which the mother may certainly get, or the value in scraps, by her lawful occupation of begging; and it is exactly at one year old that I propose to provide for them in such a manner, as, instead of being a charge upon their parents or the parish, or wanting food and raiment for the rest of their lives, they shall, on the contrary, contribute to the feeding, and partly to the cloth- ing, of many thousands.

There is likewise another great advantage in my scheme, 5 that it will prevent those voluntary abortions, and that horrid practice of women murdering their bastard children, alas, too frequent among us, sacrificing the poor innocent babes, I doubt more to avoid the expense than the shame, which would move tears and pity in the savage and inhuman breast.

The number of souls in this kingdom being usually 6

reckoned one million and a half, of these I calculate there may be about two hundred thousand couple whose wives are breeders; from which number I subtract thirty thousand couple, who are able to maintain their own children (although I apprehend there cannot be so many, under the present distresses of the kingdom); but this being granted, there will remain an hundred and seventy thousand breeders. I again subtract fifty thousand for those women who miscarry, or whose children die by accident or disease within the year. There only remain a hundred and twenty thousand children of poor parents annually born. The question therefore is how this number shall be reared and provided for? which, as I have already said, under the present situation of affairs, is utterly impossible by all the methods hitherto proposed. For we can neither employ them in handicraft or agriculture; we neither build houses (I mean in the country) nor cultivate land: they can very seldom pick up a livelihood by stealing until they arrive at six years old, except where they are of towardly parts; although I confess they learn the rudiments much earlier; during which time they can, however, be properly looked upon only as probationers; as I have been informed by a principal gentleman in the county of Cavan, who protested to me, that he never knew above one or two instances under the age of six, even in a part of the kingdom so renowned for the quickest proficiency in that art.

I am assured by our merchants that a boy or a girl before twelve years old is no salable commodity; and even when they come to this age they will not yield above three pounds or three pounds and half-a-crown at most, on the exchange; which cannot turn to account either to the parents or kingdom, the charge of nutriment and rags having been at least four times that value. 7

I shall now, therefore, humbly propose my own thoughts, which I hope will not be liable to the least objection. 8

I have been assured by a very knowing American of my acquaintance in London, that a young healthy child, well nursed, is, at a year old, a most delicious, nourishing, and wholesome food, whether stewed, roasted, baked, or boiled; and I make no doubt that it will equally serve in a fricassee or a ragout. 9

I do therefore humbly offer it to public consideration, 10
that of the hundred and twenty thousand children already
computed, twenty thousand may be reserved for breed,
whereof only one-fourth part to be males; which is more
than we allow to sheep, black cattle, or swine; and my reason
is, that these children are seldom the fruits of marriage, a
circumstance not much regarded by our savages, therefore
one male will be sufficient to serve four females. That the
remaining hundred thousand may, at a year old, be offered
in sale to the persons of quality and fortune through the
kingdom; always advising the mother to let them suck
plentifully in the last month, so as to render them plump and
fat for a good table. A child will make two dishes at an
entertainment for friends; and when the family dines alone,
the fore or hind quarter will make a reasonable dish, and,
seasoned with a little pepper or salt, will be very good boiled
on the fourth day, especially in winter.

I have reckoned, upon a medium, that a child just born 11
will weigh twelve pounds, and in a solar year, if tolerably
nursed, increaseth to twenty-eight pounds.

I grant this food will be somewhat dear, and therefore 12
very proper for landlords, who, as they have already devoured most of the parents, seem to have the best title to the
children.

Infants' flesh will be in season throughout the year, but 13
more plentifully in March, and a little before and after: for we
are told by a grave author, an eminent French physician, that
fish being a prolific diet, there are more children born in
Roman Catholic countries about nine months after Lent than
at any other season; therefore, reckoning a year after Lent,
the markets will be more glutted than usual, because the
number of popish infants is at least three to one in this
kingdom; and therefore, it will have one other collateral
advantage, by lessening the number of papists among us.

I have already computed the charge of nursing a beg- 14
gar's child (in which list I reckon all cottagers, labourers, and
four-fifths of the farmers) to be about two shillings per
annum, rags included; and I believe no gentleman would
repine to give ten shillings for the carcass of a good fat child,
which, as I have said, will make four dishes of excellent
nutritive meat, when he has only some particular friend, or

his own family, to dine with him. Thus, the squire will learn to be a good landlord, and grow popular among his tenants; the mother will have eight shillings net profit, and be fit for work till she produces another child.

Those who are more thrifty (as I must confess the times 15 require) may flay the carcass; the skin of which artificially dressed, will make admirable gloves for ladies, and summer-boots for fine gentlemen.

As to our city of Dublin, shambles[1] may be appointed 16 for this purpose in the most convenient parts of it, and butchers we may be assured will not be wanting; although I rather recommend buying the children alive, and dressing them hot from the knife, as we do roasting pigs.

A very worthy person, a true lover of this country, and 17 whose virtues I highly esteem, was lately pleased, in discoursing on this matter, to offer a refinement upon my scheme. He said, that many gentlemen of this kingdom, having of late destroyed their deer, he conceived that the want of venison might be well supplied by the bodies of young lads and maidens, not exceeding fourteen years of age, nor under twelve; so great a number of both sexes in every county being now ready to starve for want of work and service; and these to be disposed of by their parents, if alive, or otherwise by their nearest relations. But, with due deference to so excellent a friend, and so deserving a patriot, I cannot be altogether in his sentiments; for as to the males, my American acquaintance assured me from frequent experience, that their flesh was generally tough and lean, like that of our schoolboys, by continual exercise, and their taste disagreeable; and to flatten them would not answer the charge. Then as to the females, it would, I think, with humble submission, be a loss to the public, because they soon would become breeders themselves: and besides, it is not improbable that some scrupulous people might be apt to censure such a practice (although indeed very unjustly) as a little bordering upon cruelty; which, I confess hath always been with me the strongest objection against any project, how well soever intended.

---

[1] Butcher shops. (All notes in this section are the editor's.)

But in order to justify my friend, he confessed that this 18 expedient was put into his head by the famous Psalmanazar,[2] a native of the island Formosa, who came from thence to London above twenty years ago; and in conversation told my friend, that in his country, when any young person happened to be put to death, the executioner sold the carcass to persons of quality as a prime dainty; and that in his time the body of a plump girl of fifteen, who was crucified for an attempt to poison the emperor, was sold to his Imperial Majesty's prime minister of state, and other great mandarins of the court, in joints from the gibbet, at four hundred crowns. Neither indeed can I deny, that if the same use were made of several plump young girls in this town, who, without one single groat to their fortunes, cannot stir abroad without a chair, and appear at playhouse and assemblies in foreign fineries which they never will pay for, the kingdom would not be the worse.

Some persons of a desponding spirit are in great concern 19 about that vast number of poor people who are aged, diseased, or maimed; and I have been desired to employ my thoughts what course may be taken to ease the nation of so grievous an encumbrance. But I am not in the least pain upon that matter, because it is very well known, that they are every day dying, and rotting, by cold and famine, and filth and vermin, as fast as can be reasonably expected. And so to the younger labourers, they are now in almost as hopeful a condition: they cannot get work, and consequently pine away for want of nourishment, to a degree, that if at any time they are accidentally hired to common labour, they have not strength to perform it; and thus the country and themselves are happily delivered from the evils to come.

I have too long digressed, and therefore shall return to 20 my subject. I think the advantages by the proposal which I have made are obvious and many, as well as of the highest importance.

For first, as I have already observed, it would greatly 21 lessen the number of papists, with whom we are yearly

---

[2] A French writer, George Psalmanazar, who posed as a native of Formosa in a fake book he published about that country in 1704, in England.

overrun, being the principal breeders of the nation as well as our most dangerous enemies; and who stay at home on purpose with a design to deliver the kingdom to the Pretender, hoping to take their advantage by the absence of so many good Protestants, who have chosen rather to leave their country than stay at home and pay tithes against their conscience to an idolatrous Episcopal curate.[3]

Secondly, the poorer tenants will have something valu- 22 able of their own, which by law may be made liable to distress, and help to pay their landlord's rent; their corn and cattle being already seized, and money a thing unknown.

Thirdly, whereas the maintenance of an hundred thou- 23 sand children, from two years old and upwards, cannot be computed at less than ten shillings a piece per annum, the nation's stock will be thereby increased fifty thousand pounds per annum; besides the profit of a new dish introduced to the tables of all gentlemen of fortune in the kingdom who have any refinement in taste. And the money will circulate among ourselves, the goods being entirely of our own growth and manufacture.

Fourthly, the constant breeders, besides the gain of 24 eight shillings sterling per annum by the sale of their children, will be rid of the charge of maintaining them after the first year.

Fifthly, this food would otherwise bring great custom to 25 taverns; where the vintners will certainly be so prudent as to procure the best receipts for dressing it to perfection, and, consequently, have their houses frequented by all the fine gentlemen, who justly value themselves upon their knowledge in good eating: and a skillful cook, who understands how to oblige his guests, will contrive to make it as expensive as they please.

Sixthly, this would be a great inducement to marriage, 26 which all wise nations have either encouraged by rewards, or enforced by laws and penalties. It would increase the care and tenderness of mothers towards their children, when they were sure of a settlement for life to the poor babes,

---

[3] Swift is attacking the prejudice against Irish Catholics in his time, and also the motives of a number of Protestant dissenters from the Church of England.

provided in some sort by the public, to their annual profit instead of expense. We should soon see an honest emulation among the married women, which of them could bring the fattest child to the market. Men would become as fond of their wives during the time of their pregnancy, as they are now of their mares in foal, their cows in calf, or sows when they are ready to farrow; nor offer to beat or kick them (as is too frequent a practice) for fear of a miscarriage.

Many other advantages might be enumerated. For in- 27 stance, the addition of some thousand carcasses in our exportation of barrelled beef; the propagation of swine's flesh, and improvement in the art of making good bacon, so much wanted among us by the great destruction of pigs, too frequent at our tables, which are no way comparable in taste or magnificence to a well-grown, fat yearling child, which, roasted whole, will make a considerable figure at a Lord Mayor's feast, or any other public entertainment. But this, and many others, I omit, being studious of brevity.

Supposing that one thousand families in this city would 28 be constant customers for infants' flesh, besides others who might have it at merry meetings, particularly weddings and christenings, I compute that Dublin would take off annually about twenty thousand carcasses; and the rest of the kingdom (where probably they will be sold somewhat cheaper) the remaining eighty thousand.

I can think of no one objection that will possibly be 29 raised against this proposal, unless it should be urged, that the number of people will be thereby much lessened in the kingdom. This I freely own, and it was indeed one principal design in offering it to the world. I desire the reader will observe that I calculate my remedy for this one individual kingdom of Ireland, and for no other that ever was, is, or I think ever can be, upon earth. Therefore let no man talk to me of other expedients: of taxing our absentees at five shillings a pound: of using neither clothes nor household-furniture except what is of our own growth and manufacture: of utterly rejecting the materials and instruments that promote foreign luxury: of curing the expensiveness of pride, vanity, idleness, and gaming in our women; of introducing a vein of parsimony, prudence, and temperance:

of learning to love our country, wherein we differ even from Laplanders, and the inhabitants of Topinamboo:[4] of quitting our animosities and factions, nor act any longer like the Jews, who were murdering one another at the very moment their city was taken:[5] of being a little cautious not to sell our country and consciences for nothing: of teaching landlords to have at least one degree of mercy towards their tenants: lastly, of putting a spirit of honesty, industry, and skill into our shop-keepers; who, if a resolution could now be taken to buy only our native goods, would immediately unite to cheat and exact upon us in the price, the measure, and the goodness, nor could ever yet be brought to make one fair proposal of just dealing, though often and earnestly invited to it.

Therefore I repeat, let no man talk to me of these and the like expedients, till he hath at least some glimpse of hope that there will ever be some hearty and sincere attempt to put them in practice.   30

But, as to myself, having been wearied out for many years with offering vain, visionary thoughts, and at length utterly despairing of success, I fortunately fell upon this proposal; which, as it is wholly new, so it hath something solid and real, of no expense and little trouble, full in our own power, and whereby we can incur no danger in disobliging England. For this kind of commodity will not bear exportation, the flesh being of too tender a consistence to admit a long continuance in salt, although perhaps I could name a country which would be glad to eat up our whole nation without it.   31

After all, I am not so violently bent upon my own opinion as to reject any offer proposed by wise men which shall be found equally innocent, cheap, easy, and effectual. But before something of that kind shall be advanced in contradiction to my scheme, and offering a better, I desire the author, or authors, will be pleased maturely to consider two points. First, as things now stand, how they will be able to find food and raiment for a hundred thousand useless mouths and backs? And, secondly, there being a round million of creatures in human figure throughout this king-   32

---

[4] A district of Brazil notorious for its barbarism and ignorance.
[5] Swift is referring to the fall of Jerusalem to the Romans in 70 A.D.

dom, whose whole subsistence put into a common stock would leave them in debt two millions of pounds sterling, adding those who are beggars by profession, to the bulk of farmers, cottagers, and labourers, with the wives and children who are beggars in effect; I desire those politicians who dislike my overture, and may perhaps be so bold as to attempt an answer, that they will first ask the parents of these mortals, whether they would not at this day think it a great happiness to have been sold for food at a year old, in the manner I prescribe, and thereby have avoided such a perpetual scene of misfortunes as they have since gone through, by the oppression of landlords, the impossibility of paying rent without money or trade, the want of common sustenance, with neither house nor clothes to cover them from the inclemencies of weather, and the most inevitable prospect of entailing the like, or greater miseries, upon their breed for ever.

I profess, in the sincerity of my heart, that I have not the 33 least personal interest in endeavouring to promote this necessary work, having no other motive than the public good of my country, by advancing our trade, providing for infants, relieving the poor, and giving some pleasure to the rich. I have no children by which I can propose to get a single penny; the youngest being nine years old, and my wife past child-bearing.

VOCABULARY

paragraph 1: importuning
paragraph 2: prodigious
paragraph 4: schemes, projectors, raiment
paragraph 5: bastard
paragraph 6: apprehend, rudiments, probationers, renowned
paragraph 9: fricassee, ragout
paragraph 13: prolific, papists
paragraph 14: squire
paragraph 15: flay
paragraph 17: venison
paragraph 18: mandarins, gibbet

paragraph 19: encumbrance

paragraph 20: digressed

paragraph 21: tithes, idolatrous, Episcopal curate

paragraph 25: vintners

paragraph 26: emulation, foal, farrow

paragraph 27: yearling

paragraph 29: expedients, parsimony, animosities

paragraph 31: consistence

paragraph 32: effectual, entailing

QUESTIONS

1. How does Swift establish the basic character and motives of his proposer in the opening paragraphs?

2. How does Swift reveal his attitude toward the proposer? Is he in accord with his general view of the English and of absentee landlords? Are their motives stated directly or implied?

3. Is the proposer—and perhaps Swift himself—critical of the Irish, or does he exonerate them entirely?

4. Short of adopting the actual "modest proposal," is there another way of remedying the evils exposed in the course of the essay? In other words, does Swift suggest other policies that would reduce poverty and starvation in Ireland?

5. In general, what strategy does Swift employ to deal with English policies and motives and perhaps Irish attitudes too?

6. How persuasive do you find the essay? Is it an essay of historical interest or literary interest only, or does it have something to say to people today?

SUGGESTIONS FOR WRITING

1. Write your own "modest proposal" for dealing with a current social or political evil. You may wish to write as yourself or, like Swift, impersonate someone who wishes to make a modest proposal. Maintain a consistent tone throughout your essay, or at least make any shifts in tone consistent with the character of your speaker and his or her motives in writing.

2. Contrast Swift's attack on the English with Ward's attack on the idea of "triage." Distinguish the various persuasive means that they employ.

PART IV

MATTERS OF STYLE—DICTION

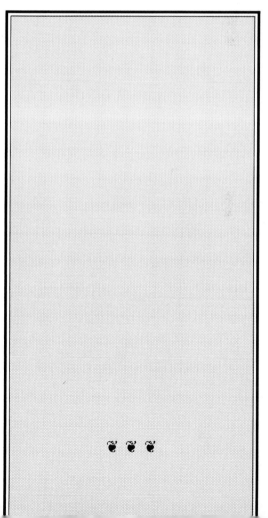

INTRODUCTION

The word *diction* refers to your choice of words in speaking and writing. The choice may be a matter of vocabulary—as in exposition, when you name a specific tool in performing a job, and in descriptive writing, when you choose concrete words or phrases and vivid images and suggestive metaphors to create a mental picture. In persuasive writing, you look for words that are exact but also move the reader to accept an idea or take action. Diction concerns both the use and the misuse of words. In all kinds of writing, you want to use words that have appropriate connotations and also to avoid words that have misleading ones.

The first two sections of Part IV discuss the matter of usage or appropriateness of words and phrases and show how writers control the tone of their essays to express their attitude toward the subject and audience. The sections that follow define and illustrate various kinds of images and common figurative language, such as simile, metaphor, and personification. The concluding section, on faulty diction, deals with inappropriate or inexpressive uses of words and singles out words that are meaningless and ugly.

Like earlier discussions and readings, those in this part of the book can serve you well as you draft and revise your papers. Finding the right tone and "level" of usage for an essay is a major concern in starting to write.

USAGE

❦ ❦ ❦

None of us speaks or writes in the same way on all occasions: the differences depend on how formal the occasion is. A letter of application for a job will be more formal than a letter to a friend; a graduation speech will sound different from a locker-room conversation.

Each of us has a formal and an informal language—and standards for judging their effectiveness. These standards come from the different groups we belong to—each group with its special idioms and vocabulary. Teenagers of a particular ethnic background share a special dialect or spoken language. So do teenagers of a particular city or region of the country. They may also share a special dialect with their families and with their friends. And at school they may share with their teachers a language different from the dialect they speak at home. Even a family may have its own private language—special words and expressions to describe acts and feelings.

Cutting across these differences is a standardized English we hear on television and read in newspapers—a language sometimes less colorful and personal than these other languages, but serving as a medium for communication among diverse groups of people, not only in the United States but in other English-speaking countries. This standard is of long growth, and it changes less than the informal language and slang of particular groups. This standard, represented in the readings in this book, falls between two extremes—one formal and abstract in its content and sentences, the other informal and concrete:

> [*Formal*] Of the influences that shape man's actions, none is more powerful than the images we carry in our heads. Every subject is apt to invoke in our minds a specific image, made up of concrete information, misinformation, folklore, desire and prejudice. Thus, how people see themselves as a nation determines to a large extent how they will respond to any new challenge. The roles we play in our family life, particularly with respect to our children, depend greatly on what roles we assign ourselves in the society around us.—Gerald Holton, "The False Images of Science"

[*Informal*] Bryant's specializes in barbecued spareribs and barbecued beef—the beef sliced from briskets of steer that have been cooked over a hickory fire for thirteen hours. When I'm away from Kansas City and depressed, I try to envision someone walking up to the counterman at Bryant's and ordering a beef sandwich to go—for me. The counterman tosses a couple of pieces of bread onto the counter, grabs a half-pound of beef from the pile next to him, slaps it onto the bread, brushes on some sauce in almost the same motion, and then wraps it all up in two thicknesses of butcher paper in a futile attempt to keep the customer's hand dry as he carries off his prize.—Calvin Trillin, *American Fried*

The abstract ideas of Holton could be stated less formally. But usage is a matter of convention and occasion as well as personal choice, and if we would not be surprised to find his ideas stated informally, we probably would be surprised to find barbecue described in formal language.

As a rule, informal writing is closer to the patterns of everyday speech; formal writing seems impersonal if it departs widely from these patterns. Much standard writing today has both formal and informal features: we find colloquialisms (*grabs a half-pound of beef, slaps it onto*) in company with abstract or less familiar words (*envision*). We also find striking balance and antithesis—a feature of formal sentences—in company with looser, more familiar phrasing and expressions:

What I would like to know is: how should I feel about the earth, these days? Where has all the old nature gone? What became of the wild, writhing, unapproachable mass of the life of the world, and what happened to our old, panicky excitement about it? Just in fifty years, since I was a small boy in a suburban town, the world has become a structure of steel and plastic, intelligible and diminished.—Lewis Thomas, "A Trip Abroad"

WILLIAM LEAST HEAT MOON

WILLIAM LEAST HEAT MOON *has had various names. He states that the name "Least Heat Moon" is Sioux in origin: "My father calls himself Heat Moon, my elder brother Little Heat Moon. I, coming last, am therefore Least." In 1978, he packed a 1975 Ford van that he called Ghost Dancing and began a search for his ancestors in rural America. Heat Moon traveled east from Columbia, Missouri, to the Atlantic and then clockwise around the United States, on backroads marked blue on roadmaps. In* Blue Highways: A Journey into America *(1982), he tells us that he sought places where "change did not mean ruin and where time and men and deeds connected." In his recent book* PrairyErth *(1991), Heat Moon describes later travels. The restaurant described in the following section from* Blue Highways *tells us much about the people and customs of rural Georgia.*

In the Land of "Coke-Cola"

In the land of "Coke-Cola" it was hot and dry. The artesian water was finished. Along route 72, an hour west of Ninety-Six, I tried not to look for a spring; I knew I wouldn't find one, but I kept looking. The Savannah River, dammed to an unnatural wideness, lay below, wet and cool. I'd come into Georgia. The sun seemed to press on the roadway, and inside the truck, hot light bounced off chrome, flickering like a torch. Then I saw what I was trying not to look for: in a coppice, a long-handled pump.

I stopped and took my bottles to the well. A small sign: WATER UNSAFE FOR DRINKING. I drooped like warm tallow. What fungicide, herbicide, nematicide, fumigant, or growth regulant—potions that rebuilt Southern agriculture—had seeped into the ground water? In the old movie Westerns there is commonly a scene where a dehydrated man, crossing the barren waste, at last comes to a water hole; he lies flat to drink the tepid stuff. Just as lips touch water, he sees on the other side a steer skull. I drove off thirsty but feeling a part of mythic history.

The thirst subsided when hunger took over. I hadn't eaten since morning. Sunset arrived west of Oglesby, and the air cooled. Then a roadsign:

SWAMP GUINEA'S FISH LODGE
ALL YOU CAN EAT!

An arrow pointed down a county highway. I would gorge myself. A record would be set. They'd ask me to leave. An embarrassment to all.

The road through the orange earth of north Georgia 4
passed an old, three-story house with a thin black child
hanging out of every window like an illustration for "The
Old Woman Who Lived in a Shoe"; on into hills and finally
to Swamp Guinea's, a conglomerate of plywood and two-
by-fours laid over with the smell of damp pine woods.

Inside, wherever an oddity or natural phenomenon 5
could hang, one hung: stuffed rump of a deer, snowshoe,
flintlock, hornet's nest. The place looked as if a Boy Scout
troop had decorated it. Thirty or so people, black and white,
sat around tables almost foundering under piled platters of
food. I took a seat by the reproduction of a seventeenth-
century woodcut depicting some Rabelaisian banquet at the
groaning board.

The diners were mostly Oglethorpe County red-dirt 6
farmers. In Georgia tones they talked about their husbandry
in terms of rain and nitrogen and hope. An immense woman
with a glossy picture of a hooked bass leaping the front of
her shirt said, "I'm gonna be sick from how much I've ate."

I was watching everyone else and didn't see the waitress 7
standing quietly by. Her voice was deep and soft like water
moving in a cavern. I ordered the $4.50 special. In a few
minutes she wheeled up a cart and began offloading dinner:
ham and eggs, fried catfish, fried perch fingerlings, fried
shrimp, chunks of barbecued beef, fried chicken, French
fries, hush puppies, a broad bowl of cole slaw, another of
lemon, a quart of ice tea, a quart of ice, and an entire loaf of
factory-wrapped white bread. The table was covered.

"Call me if y'all want any more." She wasn't joking. I 8
quenched the thirst and then—slowly—went to the eating. I
had to stand to reach plates across the table, but I intended
to do the supper in. It was all Southern fried and good,
except the Southern-style sweetened ice tea; still I took care
of a quart of it. As I ate, making up for meals lost, the
Old-Woman-in-the-Shoe house flashed before me, lightning
in darkness. I had no moral right to eat so much. But I did.
Headline: STOMACH PUMP FAILS TO REVIVE TRAVELER.

The loaf of bread lay unopened when I finally abandoned the meal. At the register, I paid a man who looked as
if he'd been chipped out of Georgia chert. The Swamp

Guinea. I asked about the name. He spoke of himself in the third person like the Wizard of Oz. "The Swamp Guinea only tells regulars."

"I'd be one, Mr. Guinea, if I didn't live in Missouri." 10

"Y'all from the North? Here, I got somethin' for you." 11 He went to the office and returned with a 45 rpm record. "It's my daughter singin'. A little promotion we did. Take it along." Later, I heard a husky north Georgia voice let go a down-home lyric rendering of Swamp Guinea's menu:

> That's all you can eat
> For a dollar fifty,
> Hey! The barbecue's nifty!

And so on through the fried chicken and potatoes.

As I left, the Swamp Guinea, a former antique dealer 12 whose name was Rudell Burroughs, said, "The nickname don't mean anything. Just made it up. Tried to figure a good one so we can franchise someday."

The frogs, high and low, shrilled and bellowed from the 13 trees and ponds. It was cool going into Athens, a city suffering from a nasty case of the sprawls. On the University of Georgia campus, I tried to walk down Swamp Guinea's supper. Everywhere couples entwined like moonflower vines, each waiting for the blossom that opens only once.

VOCABULARY

paragraph 1: artesian water, coppice

paragraph 2: fungicide, herbicide, nematicide, fumigant, tepid, mythic

paragraph 4: conglomerate

paragraph 5: phenomenon, Rabelaisian

paragraph 6: husbandry

paragraph 7: fingerlings

paragraph 9: chert

QUESTIONS

1. What expressions or grammatical characteristics mark the speech of the diner, the waitress, and the restaurant owner as regional or dialectal?

2. To what extent does Heat Moon depend on colloquial or everyday spoken expressions in writing about his experience? Is his sentence construction loose, or is he writing at a general or formal level?

3. Is he merely describing rural Georgia and the fish restaurant, or is he making a judgment about this world and developing a thesis?

4. Why does he conclude with the description of the couples on the Georgia campus?

SUGGESTION FOR WRITING

Describe a restaurant through its appearance, the food it serves, and the speech of its employees and possibly its owner. Let your details express a judgment or make a point about the restaurant. Don't state the judgment or the point explicitly.

NEWSWEEK

> *In its special fiftieth anniversary issue,* Newsweek *magazine traced the history of five families in Springfield, Ohio—typical of the life of Americans from 1933 to 1983. The description here is of Dick Hatfield, the "guru of cool" in Springfield in the 1950s. Hatfield illustrates an attitude and style that require concrete detail to be understood.*

Being Cool

The time then ending had been one in which quietude had   1
been elevated to national policy and a certain insouciance called *cool* became a personal style among the trendier young. The guru of cool in Springfield was Dick Hatfield, Catholic Central High class of '53, known as the Imperial Debubba of the Hort Club in tribute to two of the nonsense words he contributed to the nearly universal vocabulary of the city's cooler youth. Hatfield had been a precocious

student, a high-school graduate at 15, which gave him a long run on the street—he hung out with the classes of '53 through '57—and a recognized seniority in the world of cool. When local advertisers dropped his word "hort" into their copy or bought little blocks of space that said DIGGEDY DIGGEDY DA BUSH BUSH, nothing more, it was a homage to Hatfield, his gift of unintelligible gab and his authority as an arbiter of cool taste.

Being cool, Hatfield remembers now, had to do first 2 with how you looked and what you wore. Cool guys did not wear leather jackets or chinos and sweat socks, either. Cool guys wore pleated gray-flannel pants, custom pegged by a needlewoman named Ma Weiner for 75 cents a pair, with a skinny belt buckled on the side and a shirt with the billowing Mr. B collar popularized by the singer Billy Eckstine, who was *very* cool. Cool guys had cool walks, too, working at them till they had just the right hunch to the shoulders, just the right swing to the arms. "Sometimes," Hatfield recalls, "you would just *stand* there and be cool. Some chick would come by and say, 'He's cool,' just by the way you stood."

Cool guys did not sit home watching family sitcoms or 3 the Mouseketeers. When they were home at all, cool guys watched "77 Sunset Strip" mostly for Kookie, the eighth avatar of cool, or Dick Clark's "American Bandstand"; it was the constant intention of Hatfield's crowd to go to Philly, where the Bandstand was produced, and really show them how to dance, but somehow they never saved up enough money. They did their stepping inside at El Som (for sombrero) dances at the Y on football and basketball Friday nights, or later, when they came of drinking age, at upscale clubs like the Melody Showbar—the Four Freshmen played there once—or funkier joints like the Frolics out on Lagonda Avenue. Hatfield, ultracool, preferred the Frolics for its ambience, which included a bouncer with a .357 magnum and featured a rhythm-and-blues band presided over by a large black man named H-Bomb Ferguson. You could do the dirty boogie at the Frolics, "a modified jitterbug," as Hatfield remembered it, "with like more hips," and find out quickly which guys and chicks were truly cool.

Cool guys hung out, at Frisch's Big Boy for the burgers, 4 or under the clock at Woolworth's for the girl-watching, or at

East High Billiards for the action; Hatfield was taking tickets there one March day in 1954 when the great Willie Mosconi came in and sank 526 straight balls for a world's record. But mostly cool guys cruised, customizing their cars and living an automotive life later imitated by art in the film "American Graffiti." Hatfield's wheels supported a mink-white Chevy with scallops in three colors, regatta blue, Bahama blue and Inca gray, and the what-me-worry likeness of Alfred E. Neuman hand-done on the gas cap by a local painter. For a final touch of style, he installed a dummy telephone with a real-sounding Ma Bell ring, activated by a push button under the dashboard. Sometimes he would set it off with his knee at Frisch's just as one of the carhop girls came over to take his order. "Hold on a second, will you, honey," he would say, picking up the receiver. "I got an important call here."

The cruising route favored by the cool guys was down- 5 town when it still *was* downtown, its streets alive with life; Hatfield figured he spent very nearly every evening for four years going around the core block in the heart of the city, so many times he imagined that his tire tracks must have been indelibly imprinted in the left-hand lane. You cruised for a while, checking out the happenings; then you did the joints, O'Brien's Tavern at 9, then the Savoy, and then, at 1 A.M., the Alibi or the Shady Lane Saloon.

But suddenly everything began changing, and the cool 6 life began to chill. Hatfield noticed it around the time he was called up into the Reserves in 1960, at 22. Guys were getting restless, itchy for something new; some were disappearing into the military, some into marriages. The music was changing; five white guys named the Beach Boys were bleaching out Chuck Berry's black sound, and the dirty boogie was washed under by the twist, the pony and the mashed potato. "It was like everybody knew how to do *our* dance," Hatfield recalls. "The dirty boogie was no longer new." Downtown was changing, too, emptying out and beginning to go seedy. The difference struck Hatfield one day in the early '60s when he pulled up at East High Billiards and found a parking space right across the street. There was nobody around; being cool wasn't cool anymore.

Hatfield grew up when he came home from the Re- 7 serves; he went back to work with the railroad for a while, then spun records for Station WBLY for a while more and now sells steel for the Benjamin Steel Co. He sold the '53 Chevy with the tricolor scallops before he went away and bought a 1960 Plymouth Valiant when he came back, a car so square that it couldn't be customized. He restocked his record library with Percy Faith and retooled his nights out to consist of taking a nice girl to a nice dinner at the Holiday Inn.

But some of the cool guys of his day could never let go 8
of the rites of coolness. The world had changed under them; Kennedy had died, with all that diamond-bright promise; new tribes of the young had divided American politics, morals and popular culture across a void that came to be known as the generation gap; Chuck Berry's records were golden oldies, and Kookie was the answer to a trivia tease. Nothing remains now of the age of cool in Springfield except its last few survivors, baldish men in their middle and late 40s with two or three divorces behind them, still driving the old cruising routes as if in familiar motion they could catch up with the past and recover the last innocent time.

VOCABULARY

paragraph 1: quietude, insouciance, guru, arbiter
paragraph 3: magnum
paragraph 4: regatta
paragraph 8: trivia

QUESTIONS

1. How do the details help to explain what the phrase "being cool" meant to teenagers in the late 1950s? Does *Newsweek* state the meaning directly?

2. What other slang does *Newsweek* identify? How do you discover the meaning of these words or expressions?

3. What does the language of these teenagers tell you about their world and values? Is the *Newsweek* account a sympathetic one? Or is *Newsweek* merely reporting what happened to teenagers in the 1950s?

4. How different is the voice of *Newsweek* from the voice of Hatfield and the other teenagers described? What words and sentences tell you that the voices are different?

5. How different are Hatfield's world and values from your own? What language expresses the values of teenagers today? What influence does popular music have on current teenager slang and values?

SUGGESTIONS FOR WRITING

1. Analyze the language of two sports columnists, noting the degree of formality or informality in each and the extent to which each depends on sports jargon. Use your analysis to define the difference in the voice of each writer.

2. Describe a special jargon or slang that you share with friends or your family. Discuss the special meanings of these words and the values they express.

3. Every profession and trade has a special language or jargon that provides a "shorthand" or concise means of communicating. Examine a trade journal or popular magazine directed to a particular audience—*Popular Mechanics, Field and Stream, Stereo Review*—and identify particular words and phrases of this kind. Discuss the special meanings conveyed by several of these words or phrases.

4. Examine an issue of a professional journal in political science, sociology, medicine, or a similar field to find out how alike the various articles are in style. Consider the level of the writing as well as the choice of words. Note especially any special language or jargon.

Tone

❦ ❦ ❦

By the tone of a piece of writing, we mean the reflection of the writer's attitude toward the subject or reader. The possibilities are many: a piece of writing may be sarcastic, bitter, angry, mocking, whimsical, facetious, joyful, admiring, or indifferent. And we can reveal this attitude in numerous ways—most commonly by stating it directly:

> There should be more sympathy for school children. The idea that they are happy is of a piece with the idea that the lobster in the pot is happy.—H. L. Mencken, "Travail"

Or we can express our attitude indirectly—perhaps by exaggerating, sometimes to the point of absurdity, for a humorous or satirical effect, as in this parody of a course description in a college bulletin:

> Rapid Reading—This course will increase reading speed a little each day until the end of the term, by which time the student will be required to read *The Brothers Karamazov* in fifteen minutes.—Woody Allen, "Spring Bulletin"

Or we can write sarcastically or with a lighter irony that tells the reader we mean the opposite of what our words say:

> It has been known for years that prisons have been accepting a very low-class type of inmate, some without any education, others who are unstable, and some who are just plain anti-social.—Art Buchwald, "Upping Prison Requirements"

Irony arises from an obvious discrepancy between what we show and what we say. A common form of irony is understatement:

> It is, indeed, one of the capital tragedies of youth—and youth is the time of real tragedy—that the young are thrown mainly with adults they do not quite respect.—H. L. Mencken, "Travail"

Paradoxical statements also can be ironic:

Trash has given us an appetite for art.—Pauline Kael, *Going Steady*

And so can statements that prepare us for one conclusion and then turn around and surprise us with another:

> A little sincerity is a dangerous thing, and a great deal of it is absolutely fatal.—Oscar Wilde, *The Critic as Artist*

As these examples suggest, the tone of a sentence, a paragraph, or an essay is conveyed by the *voice* we try to express in writing. Voice depends on the rhythms and nuances of speech, carried into the modulations and rhythms of the sentences and paragraphs. False starts in writing are often failures to discover the right voice or tone. Too formal a sentence or choice of words may create the impression of distance or unconcern; a highly informal style may suggest lack of seriousness or flippancy. Not surprisingly, we often find as we write that we need to adjust the tone. An essay need not express a single dominant tone; however, the expression of our attitude often changes as we turn to new ideas and details.

MARK SINGER

> **MARK SINGER** *has written a number of talk pieces and profiles for* The New Yorker *magazine. He is also the author of* Funny Money *(1985) and* Mr. Personality *(1988). Singer's account of a karate birthday party in a New York suburb appeared in "The Talk of the Town"—a collection of short commentaries, profiles, and sketches in each issue of* THE NEW YORKER. *The observer in the account at no point makes a personal reference or states an opinion about the party. The tone of the essay is therefore crucial in deciding whether the observer is satirizing the birthday party or sharing in the fun.*

Osu!

The karate-birthday-party concept occurred to Howard Frydman because Howard Frydman is an acutely aware person. To begin with, it was obvious to Howard and his partner, 1

Tokey Hill, who run the Karate Center of Champions, a martial-arts academy that sits right next to the Long Island Rail Road station in Douglaston, Queens, that kids love karate. Then the mother of one of the many fine eight-year-old boys in Nassau County remarked to Howard that virtually every variety of kid's-birthday-party idea you could think of had been done to death. That was about three years ago. Since then, Howard and Tokey—Howard was the captain of the American karate team and a silver-medal winner at the 1981 Maccabiah Games, in Israel, and Tokey has won even more medals than Howard, and they both recently joined the Budweiser National Karate Team and appeared on the cover of the première issue of the magazine *American Karate*—have developed and refined the karate-birthday-party concept. By now, they've done hundreds of parties. For the basic fee—a hundred dollars—you get a thirty-minute karate class for the entire party, plus fifteen minutes of professional kicking, punching, blocking, and board-breaking. Maybe, for a little extra money, Howard and Tokey will arrange for a ninja to come out and terrify the guests with one of the magnificent steel-and-chrome ninja swords that you see advertised in all the martial-arts magazines. After the kicking, punching, blocking, and board-breaking (and the ninja appearance, if that's in the package) come the pizza and cake and ice cream and birthday presents. Howard and Tokey will stage a karate birthday party either way—at your home or at the Karate Center of Champions. They'll even do it in a restaurant; Howard has done a couple of karate birthday parties at Benihana. Another time, he went to New Jersey. For a karate birthday party in Jersey, though, he charges a pretty penny, because of all the travel.

The Karate Center of Champions has about two thousand square feet of classroom space, plywood floors, white walls, some broad mirrors along the walls, and, just inside the front door, a desk, plenty of framed and mounted photographs and martial-arts-magazine covers, and a Karate Master video game. Howard Frydman has dark hair, a trim, muscular build, a thin, bony face, and twenty years of seniority over this particular Saturday's birthday boy—Joshua Feldman, son of Geoff and Jill, of Great Neck. Joshua has the standard dimensions of an eight-year-old, curly blond hair, freckles, and pouchy cheeks. He wears a white karate robe with a blue belt. The blue belt signifies that Joshua knows how to execute fifteen basic karate movements—low block, chest block, head block, knife-hand block, several kicks, and some other stuff. If you are going to execute any of the fifteen basic karate movements, you first have to spit out your bubble gum. Then you line up and do whatever the sensei (that's an honorific term accorded a senior martial-arts instructor; Tokey Hill is out of town, so Howard is the principal sensei today) tells you to do.

Always—*always*—Sensei Frydman starts things off with 3 a formal Oriental bow and the Japanese greeting "*Osu!*"— which sounds more like "Oos!" There are very few gestures in karate that do not seem nicer with a heartfelt "*Osu!*" tacked on at the end.

Sensei Frydman (bowing): *Osu!* 4

Joshua and Invited Guests (Adam, Jason, Jeremy, 5 Michael, etc., in chorus, bowing): *Osu!*

S.F.: O.K., spread the feet a little bit. Hands on the hips. 6 Left ear to the left shoulder. Now right ear to the right shoulder. And rotate. Rotate. O.K., rotate the entire head. That's it. Roll it around. Anybody tired yet?

I.G.s (faint chorus): No, Sensei. 7

S.F. (loud enough to intimidate I.G.s): I CAN'T HEAR YOU! 8

I.G.s (loud enough to compete with passing train): NO, 9 SENSEI!

S.F.: Good. O.K., shake it out. Now, as part of this 10 demonstration, we demand that Josh cut Adam in half with the sword. Are you ready? Hmm. All right, we'll do that later, after we cut the cake. Now I need some hips. Let's loosen it up. Come on, Feldman. All right, everybody sit down. Heels together, head to toes. Loosen up the back, hold your breath. O.K. Legs apart. Nose to the knee. Come on, Blue Belts, lock those knees. Close it up, Silverman. Good. Shake it out. All right, who knows what "karate" means? (Silence.) The word "karate"—nobody knows what it means?

I.G. in back row: "Self-defense"? 11

S.F.: No, that's what karate *is*. What does it mean? 12

I.G. in front row (wearing white robe and blue belt): 13 "Empty hand."

S.F.: Empty hand. Right. Now, what is the main pur- 14
pose of karate?

A different Blue Belt: Self-defense. 15

S.F.: Good. So what does that mean? It means that after 16
class there will be no running around punching and kicking
each other. When you leave here and go home and are
playing with your friends, there will be no punching and
kicking. If you want to punch or kick the air, that's fine. But
otherwise no punching or kicking. Does everybody understand?

I.G.s: Yes, Sensei. 17

S.F. (painful to eardrums): I CAN'T HEAR YOU! 18

I.G.s (loud enough to compete with passing train plus 19
low-flying aircraft): YES, SENSEI!

S.F.: O.K., another thing. What is it you can't do if you 20
can't stand up? Come on, Blue Belts—Feldman, Teppel,
Stock—you know the answer.

A Blue Belt: Fight. 21

S.F.: Right. Because if you're down, your opponent can 22
do *this* to you. (Demonstrates incapacitating maneuvers that
opponent might, if provoked, consider doing.) O.K., stand
up. Up! Too slow. Down again. Now up! Stand straight.
Stand strong. Silverman, what happened to you? You're like
chopped liver today. You— Stop smiling. You don't have
any teeth. Your opponent sees that, you're open to attack.
Nice suntan, Levy. O.K., punch-and-twist exercise. That's it,
full speed, full power. We're all gonna count in Japanese.
Count with me.

S.F. and I.G.s count together in Japanese. 23

S.F.: O.K. Anybody tired yet? Hey, Silverman, what 24
you got there? A gun? Give me that gun. Oh, a toy gun.
Control yourself, Silverman. Relax.

At the conclusion of one exercise, Sensei Frydman says, 25
"What, no '*Osu*'? Down. Everyone. Ten pushups." Ten
pushups ensue. Next, the sensei demonstrates a U-punch
and an elbow strike. Then he announces that Joshua Feldman will demonstrate a flying front kick, whereupon he lifts
Joshua by the lapels of his white robe and Joshua incapaci-
tates the air with his bare feet.

Any minute now, thumping sounds will come from the 26
stairway that leads to the basement, and then the door will

burst open and one of the other Karate Center of Champions instructors, Sensei David Gonzalez, will appear wearing the sort of black ninja uniform that you see advertised in all the karate magazines: black jacket with hidden pocket, black pants with leg ties, black hood, black hand wraps, the magnificent sword—the works. After Sensei Frydman has vanquished the ninja, he will say, "All right, who wants to see the ninja break a board?" Then Sensei Frydman will hold an inch-thick board at eye level, and Sensei Gonzalez will try to break it with his left foot, using a spinning-jump-hook kick. On the fifth attempt, he will get it right. Everyone— the twenty birthday celebrators, Sensei Frydman, Sensei Gonzalez—will pose for a group picture, and then it will be time to go downstairs for pizza and soft drinks and cake and ice cream. During the pizza course, Joshua Feldman and some of the other Blue Belts will get tomato-sauce stains on their white robes. After the pizza and before the cake and ice cream (there's a drawing of Hulk Hogan on the cake), the invited guests will suffer a collective mental lapse and get up from the table and run around and kick and punch and scream—all in self-defense. There will be a crucial moment during which Joshua Feldman pauses to catch his breath and to contemplate what he might like to do at his ninth-birthday party: "Go bowling. *Osu!*"

QUESTIONS

1. Is the reporter chiefly concerned with Howard Frydman and the idea of the karate birthday party, or with the party itself and Howard's friends? How do you know?

2. What is the attitude of the reporter toward Howard Frydman and the karate party? Is he admiring, or critical, or amused, or is his account wholly neutral and objective?

3. Does the reporter hold the same attitude toward Joshua Feldman and the other eight-year-old boys? How do you know?

4. Does the tone of the report change?

5. Is the reporter making a point or arguing a thesis? Or is the reporter merely describing a party?

SUGGESTIONS FOR WRITING

1. Describe an event like the karate party from two points of view—from that of a neutral observer and from that of an angry or critical or amused one. Make the tone of each description clear and consistent.

2. Analyze a speech in a recent issue of *Vital Speeches* or another periodical to discover the tone of the speaker. Does the speech have a single, dominant tone, or does it change in tone? Explain how you know.

PHYLLIS ROSE

> Phyllis Rose, *Professor of English at Wesleyan University in Middletown, Connecticut, has written a number of books about nineteenth and twentieth century women. These include* Women of Letters: A Life of Virginia Woolf *(1977),* Parallel Lives: Five Victorian Marriages *(1983), and* Jazz Cleopatra *(1989), a life of the Afro-American singer Josephine Baker. "Of Shopping," an account of her experiences in Middletown stores, appears in her collection of essays,* Never Say Goodbye *(1991).*

Of Shopping

Last year a new Waldbaum's Food Mart opened in the   1
shopping mall on Route 66. It belongs to a new generation of superdupermarkets that have computerized checkouts and operate twenty-four hours a day. I went to see the place as soon as it opened and I was impressed. There was trail mix in Lucite bins. There was freshly made pasta. There were coffee beans, four kinds of tahini, ten kinds of herb teas, raw shrimp in shells and cooked shelled shrimp, fresh-squeezed orange juice. Every sophistication known to the big city, even goat's cheese covered with ash, was now available in Middletown, Connecticut. People raced from the warehouse aisle to the bagel bin to the coffee beans to the fresh fish

market, exclaiming at all the new things. Many of us felt
elevated, graced, complimented by the presence of this food
palace in our town.

This is the wonderful egalitarianism of American busi- 2
ness. Was it Andy Warhol who said that the nice thing about
Coke is, no can is any better or worse than any other? Some
people may find it dull to cross the country and find the
same chain stores with the same merchandise from coast to
coast, but it means that my town is as good as yours, my
shopping mall as important as yours, equally filled with
wonders.

Imagine what people ate during the winter as little as 3
seventy-five years ago. They ate food that was local, long-
lasting, and dull, like acorn squash, turnips, and cabbage.
Walk into an American supermarket in February and the
world lies before you: grapes, melons, artichokes, fennel,
lettuce, peppers, pistachios, dates, even strawberries, to say
nothing of ice cream. Have you ever considered what a
triumph of civilization it is to be able to buy a pound of
chicken livers? If you lived on a farm and had to kill a chicken
when you wanted to eat one, you wouldn't ever accumulate
a pound of chicken livers.

Another wonder of Middletown is Caldor, the discount 4
department store. Here is man's plenty: tennis racquets,
pantyhose, luggage, glassware, records, toothpaste, Timex
watches, Cadbury's chocolate, corn poppers, hair dryers,
warm-up suits, car wax, light bulbs, television sets. All good
quality at low prices with exchanges cheerfully made on
defective goods. There are worse rules to live by. I feel good
about America whenever I walk into this store, which is
almost every midwinter Sunday afternoon, when life elsewhere has closed down. I go to Caldor the way English
people go to pubs: out of sociability. To get away from my
house. To widen my horizons. For culture's sake. Caldor
provides me too with a welcome sense of seasonal change.
When the first outdoor grills and lawn furniture appear
there, it's as exciting a sign of spring as the first crocus or
robin.

Someone told me about a Soviet émigré who practices 5
English by declaiming, at random, sentences that catch his
fancy. One of his favorites is "Fifty percent off all items today

only." Refugees from Communist countries appreciate our supermarkets and discount department stores for the wonders they are. An Eastern European scientist visiting Middletown wept when she first saw the meat counter at Waldbaum's. On the other hand, before her year in America was up, her pleasure turned sour. She wanted everything she saw. Her approach to consumer goods was insufficiently abstract, too materialistic. We Americans are beyond a simple, possessive materialism. We're used to abundance and the possibility of possessing things. The things, and the possibility of possessing them, will still be there next week, next year. So today we can walk the aisles calmly.

It is a misunderstanding of the American retail store to think we go there necessarily to buy. Some of us shop. There's a difference. Shopping has many purposes, the least interesting of which is to acquire new articles. We shop to cheer ourselves up. We shop to practice decision making. We shop to be useful and productive members of our class and society. We shop to remind ourselves how much is available to us. We shop to remind ourselves how much is to be striven for. We shop to assert our superiority to the material objects that spread themselves before us. 6

Shopping's function as a form of therapy is widely appreciated. You don't really need, let's say, another sweater. You need the feeling of power that comes with buying it or not buying it. You need the feeling that someone wants something you have—even if it's just your money. To get the benefit of shopping, you needn't actually purchase the sweater, any more than you have to marry every man you flirt with. In fact, window shopping, like flirting, can be more rewarding, the same high without the distressing commitment, the material encumbrance. The purest form of shopping is provided by garage sales. A connoisseur goes out with no goal in mind, open to whatever may come his way, secure that it will cost very little. Minimum expense, maximum experience. Perfect shopping. 7

I try to think of the opposite, a kind of shopping in which the object is all-important, the pleasure of shopping at a minimum. For example, the purchase of blue jeans. I buy new blue jeans as seldom as possible because the experience is so humiliating. For every pair that looks good on me, 8 fifteen look grotesque. But even shopping for blue jeans at Bob's Surplus on Main Street—no-frills, bare-bones shopping—is an event in the life of the spirit. Once again I have to come to terms with the fact that I will never look good in Levi's. Much as I want to be mainstream, I will never be.

In fact, I'm doubly an oddball, neither Misses nor Junior, but Misses Petite. I look in the mirror, I acknowledge the disparity between myself and the ideal, I resign myself to making the best of it: I will buy the Lee's Misses Petite. Shopping is a time of reflection, assessment, spiritual self-discipline.

It is appropriate, I think, that Bob's has a communal dressing room. I used to shop only in places where I could count on a private dressing room with a mirror inside. My impulse was to hide my weaknesses. Now I believe in sharing them. There are other women in the dressing room at Bob's trying on blue jeans who look as bad as I do. We take comfort in one another. Sometimes a woman will ask me which of two items looks better. I always give a definite answer. It's the least I can do. I figure we are all in this together, and I emerge from the dressing room not only with a new pair of jeans, but with a renewed sense of belonging to a human community.

When a Solzhenitsyn* rants about American materialism, I have to look at my digital Timex and check what year this is. Materialism? Like conformism, a hot moral issue of the 1950s, but not now. How to spread the goods, maybe. Whether the goods are the Good, no. Solzhenitsyn, like the visiting scientist who wept at the beauty of the Waldbaum's meat counter but came to covet everything she saw, takes American materialism too materialistically. He doesn't see its spiritual side. Caldor, Waldbaum's, Bob's—these, perhaps, are our cathedrals.

---

* The Russian novelist Alexandr Solzhenitsyn, now living in the United States, criticized American consumerism and material values in a Harvard commencement address.—Ed.

VOCABULARY

paragraph 2: egalitarianism
paragraph 4: pub
paragraph 5: émigré, declaiming, abstract
paragraph 7: encumbrance, connoisseur
paragraph 11: rant

QUESTIONS

1. Do you hear a single tone of voice throughout the essay, or does the tone change, as Rose describes different kinds of stores and different experiences?

2. What personal view of life or personal qualities do the content and the tone of the essay convey?

3. Is the statement on materialism in paragraph 11 the central idea or thesis of the essay, or is it an afterthought or final reflection on shopping? If the latter, what is the thesis?

4. How different are the attitudes toward materialism expressed by Rose and Wendell Berry (p. 405)?

SUGGESTIONS FOR WRITING

1. Write your own essay on a similar topic, drawing on your personal experience as Rose does. Give particular attention to the tone of your essay. Write as you would talk about the subject to a friend.

2. Write on one of the following topics or another of your choosing, drawing on your personal experience. On completing a first draft of your essay, reread it to make needed adjustments in tone. You may discover that you have written in a tone inappropriate to the subject or one needlessly formal or stuffy.

   a. on the first day of class

   b. on the first day of a new job

   c. on learning to drive

   d. on riding the bus or subway

   e. on buying presents for friends

IMAGERY

❦ ❦ ❦

Images convey sensory impressions: impressions of sight, hearing, smell, taste, or touch. The following passage from a story by James Joyce illustrates most of these:

> The cold air stung us and we played till our bodies glowed. Our shouts echoed in the silent street. The career of our play brought us through the dark muddy lanes behind the houses where we ran the gauntlet of the rough tribes from the cottages, to the back doors of the dark dripping gardens where odors arose from the ashpits, to the dark odorous stables where a coachman smoothed and combed the horse or shook music from the buckled harness.—"Araby"

We think in images constantly. Joyce could not have expressed his sense of a particular street on a particular night in abstract language. The more evocative our imagery when the situation calls for vivid impressions, the more directly will our words express experience. A passage will seem overwritten if a vivid representation of experience is not needed; so-called fine writing tries to be too evocative of sense experience. In the passage quoted above, Joyce selects only those details that will give the reader an impression of the physical sensations experienced in the darkness. The imagery suggests the vitality of imagination, a theme of the story; Joyce probably could not have conveyed that vitality without it.

ANNIE DILLARD

The essayist ANNIE DILLARD *describes herself as "a poet and a walker with a background in theology and a penchant for quirky facts." Dillard writes about her life in the Roanoke Valley in Virginia in* Pilgrim at Tinker Creek (1974)— *awarded the Pulitzer Prize in 1975. A selection from this book appears on p. 521. Dillard later lived in the Pacific Northwest*

and wrote about Puget Sound *in* Teaching a Stone to Talk
*(1982), from which the following essay is taken. Writing of the
earlier book, a critic says of Dillard: "She has the rare ability
to recreate the emotional tone of experience without abandoning
accuracy or specificity of detail."*

Total Eclipse

The hill was five hundred feet high. Long winter-killed grass   1
covered it, as high as our knees. We climbed and rested,
sweating in the cold; we passed clumps of bundled people
on the hillside who were setting up telescopes and fiddling
with cameras. The top of the hill stuck up in the middle of
the sky. We tightened our scarves and looked around.

East of us rose another hill like ours. Between the hills,   2
far below, was the highway which threaded south into the
valley. This was the Yakima valley; I had never seen it
before. It is justly famous for its beauty, like every planted
valley. It extended south into the horizon, a distant dream of
a valley, a Shangri-la. All its hundreds of low, golden slopes
bore orchards. Among the orchards were towns, and roads,
and plowed and fallow fields. Through the valley wandered
a thin, shining river; from the river extended fine, frozen
irrigation ditches. Distance blurred and blued the sight, so
that the whole valley looked like a thickness or sediment at
the bottom of the sky. Directly behind us was more sky, and
empty lowlands blued by distance, and Mount Adams.
Mount Adams was an enormous, snow-covered volcanic
cone rising flat, like so much scenery.

Now the sun was up. We could not see it; but the sky   3
behind the band of clouds was yellow, and, far down the
valley, some hillside orchards had lighted up. More people
were parking near the highway and climbing the hills. It was
the West. All of us rugged individualists were wearing knit
caps and blue nylon parkas. People were climbing the
nearby hills and setting up shop in clumps among the dead
grasses. It looked as though we had all gathered on hilltops
to pray for the world on its last day. It looked as though we
had all crawled out of spaceships and were preparing to
assault the valley below. It looked as though we were

scattered on hilltops at dawn to sacrifice virgins, make rain, set stone stelae in a ring. There was no place out of the wind. The straw grasses banged our legs.

Up in the sky where we stood the air was lusterless 4 yellow. To the west the sky was blue. Now the sun cleared the clouds. We cast rough shadows on the blowing grass; freezing, we waved our arms. Near the sun, the sky was bright and colorless. There was nothing to see.

It began with no ado. It was odd that such a well- 5 advertised public event should have no starting gun, no overture, no introductory speaker. I should have known right then that I was out of my depth. Without pause or preamble, silent as orbits, a piece of the sun went away. We looked at it through welders' goggles. A piece of the sun was missing; in its place we saw empty sky.

I had seen a partial eclipse in 1970. A partial eclipse is 6 very interesting. It bears almost no relation to a total eclipse. Seeing a partial eclipse bears the same relation to seeing a total eclipse as kissing a man does to marrying him, or as flying in an airplane does to falling out of an airplane. Although the one experience precedes the other, it in no way prepares you for it. During a partial eclipse the sky does not darken—not even when 94 percent of the sun is hidden. Nor does the sun, seen colorless through protective devices, seem terribly strange. We have all seen a sliver of light in the sky; we have all seen the crescent moon by day. However, during a partial eclipse the air does indeed get cold, precisely as if someone were standing between you and the fire. And blackbirds do fly back to their roosts. I had seen a partial eclipse before, and here was another.

What you see in an eclipse is entirely different from 7 what you know. It is especially different for those of us whose grasp of astronomy is so frail that, given a flashlight, a grapefruit, two oranges, and fifteen years, we still could not figure out which way to set the clocks for Daylight Saving Time. Usually it is a bit of a trick to keep your knowledge from blinding you. But during an eclipse it is easy. What you see is much more convincing than any wild-eyed theory you may know.

You may read that the moon has something to do with 8

eclipses. I have never seen the moon yet. You do not see the moon. So near the sun, it is as completely invisible as the stars are by day. What you see before your eyes is the sun going through phases. It gets narrower and narrower, as the waning moon does, and, like the ordinary moon, it travels alone in the simple sky. The sky is of course background. It does not appear to eat the sun; it is far behind the sun. The sun simply shaves away; gradually, you see less sun and more sky.

The sky's blue was deepening, but there was no dark- 9 ness. The sun was a wide crescent, like a segment of tangerine. The wind freshened and blew steadily over the hill. The eastern hill across the highway grew dusky and sharp. The towns and orchards in the valley to the south were dissolving into the blue light. Only the thin river held a trickle of sun.

Now the sky to the west deepened to indigo, a color 10 never seen. A dark sky usually loses color. This was a saturated, deep indigo, up in the air. Stuck up into that unworldly sky was the cone of Mount Adams, and the alpenglow was upon it. The alpenglow is that red light of sunset which holds out on snowy mountaintops long after the valleys and tablelands are dimmed. "Look at Mount Adams," I said, and that was the last sane moment I remember.

I turned back to the sun. It was going. The sun was 11 going, and the world was wrong. The grasses were wrong; they were platinum. Their every detail of stem, head, and blade shone lightless and artificially distinct as an art photographer's platinum print. This color has never been seen on earth. The hues were metallic; their finish was matte. The hillside was a nineteenth-century tinted photograph from which the tints had faded. All the people you see in the photograph, distinct and detailed as their faces look, are now dead. The sky was navy blue. My hands were silver. All the distant hills' grasses were finespun metal which the wind laid down. I was watching a faded color print of a movie filmed in the Middle Ages; I was standing in it, by some mistake. I was standing in a movie of hillside grasses filmed in the Middle Ages. I missed my own century, the people I knew, and the real light of day.

I looked at Gary. He was in the film. Everything was 12 lost. He was a platinum print, a dead artist's version of life. I saw on his skull the darkness of night mixed with the colors of day. My mind was going out; my eyes were receding the way galaxies recede to the rim of space. Gary was light-years away, gesturing inside a circle of darkness, down the wrong end of a telescope. He smiled as if he saw me; the stringy crinkles around his eyes moved. The sight of him, familiar and wrong, was something I was remembering from centuries hence, from the other side of death: yes, *that* is the way he used to look, when we were living. When it was our generation's turn to be alive. I could not hear him; the wind was too loud. Behind him the sun was going. We had all started down a chute of time. At first it was pleasant; now there was no stopping it. Gary was chuting away across space, moving and talking and catching my eye, chuting down the long corridor of separation. The skin on his face moved like thin bronze plating that would peel.

The grass at our feet was wild barley. It was the wild 13 einkorn wheat which grew on the hilly flanks of the Zagros Mountains, above the Euphrates valley, above the valley of the river we called *River*. We harvested the grass with stone sickles, I remember. We found the grasses on the hillsides; we built our shelter beside them and cut them down. That is how he used to look then, that one, moving and living and catching my eye, with the sky so dark behind him, and the wind blowing. God save our life.

From all the hills came screams. A piece of sky beside 14 the crescent sun was detaching. It was a loosened circle of evening sky, suddenly lighted from the back. It was an abrupt black body out of nowhere; it was a flat disk; it was almost over the sun. That is when there were screams. At once this disk of sky slid over the sun like a lid. The sky snapped over the sun like a lens cover. The hatch in the brain slammed. Abruptly it was dark night, on the land and in the sky. In the night sky was a tiny ring of light. The hole where the sun belongs is very small. A thin ring of light marked its place. There was no sound. The eyes dried, the arteries drained, the lungs hushed. There was no world. We were the world's dead people rotating and orbiting around and around, embedded in the planet's crust, while the earth rolled down. Our minds were light-years distant, forgetful of almost everything. Only an extraordinary act of will could recall to us our former, living selves and our contexts in matter and time. We had, it seems, loved the planet and loved our lives, but could no longer remember the way of them. We got the light wrong. In the sky was something that should not be there. In the black sky was a ring of light. It was a thin ring, an old, thin silver wedding band, an old, worn ring. It was an old wedding band in the sky, or a morsel of bone. There were stars. It was all over.

VOCABULARY

paragraph 2: Shangri-la, fallow, sediment

paragraph 3: stela (*plural:* stelae)

paragraph 4: lusterless

paragraph 5: preamble

paragraph 6: crescent

paragraph 10: indigo

paragraph 11: matte

paragraph 12: galaxy

QUESTIONS

1. How does Dillard establish a place of observation or physical point of view in paragraphs 1 and 2? Does this point of view change in the course of the essay? Is this information essential to our understanding what the eclipse meant to her?

2. What images in paragraphs 4, 5, 7, and 8 suggest the change from the familiar to the unfamiliar in what Dillard saw and felt?

3. How is a partial eclipse different from a total eclipse? What comparisons does Dillard make to explain the difference in paragraph 6?

4. What comparisons help to convey the experience of the eclipse

in paragraph 12? What is Dillard led to imagine in paragraph 13?

5. How does the eclipse lead Dillard to see the world in a new way? What feelings does Dillard experience during the eclipse? Does Dillard name these feelings, or express them through images?

6. Does Dillard develop a thesis, or is her essay only descriptive and expressive?

SUGGESTIONS FOR WRITING

1. Analyze Dillard's use of imagery in her description of the eclipse. Explain how the imagery allows her to express the truths and the feelings she experienced.

2. Describe a suspenseful experience that gave you an unexpected picture of the world or revealed a truth about it. Make your details specific enough so that your reader sees the picture or understands the truth.

CONCRETENESS

❦ ❦ ❦

Writing is *concrete* when it makes an observation or impression perceptible to the senses. Eric Sevareid makes concrete the changes that occurred in his hometown in North Dakota:

> Sounds have changed; I heard not once the clopping of a horse's hoof, nor the mourn of a coyote. I heard instead the shriek of brakes, the heavy throbbing of the once-a-day Braniff airliner into Minot, the shattering sirens born of war, the honk of a diesel locomotive which surely cannot call to faraway places the heart of a wakeful boy like the old steam whistle in the night.—"Velva, North Dakota"

Complex ideas can be made concrete with vivid examples; indeed, examples are essential to our understanding:

> I have described the hand when it uses a tool as an instrument of discovery. . . . We see this every time a child learns to couple hand and tool together—to lace its shoes, to thread a needle, to fly a kite or to play a penny whistle. With the practical action there goes another, namely finding pleasure in the action for its own sake—in the skill that one perfects, and perfects by being pleased with it. This at bottom is responsible for every work of art, and science too: our poetic delight in what human beings do because they can do it.—J. Bronowski, *The Ascent of Man*

Imagery and figurative language can increase the vividness of specific details.

Whatever the purpose of the writer, excessive detail will blur the focus and perhaps make the writing incoherent. Voltaire said, "The secret of being a bore is to tell everything." A boring movie may show everything in what seems like an endless stream of detail; a boring paragraph or essay does the same thing. To develop an idea or impression effectively, we must *select* the detail. Good writing is economical.

LILLIAN ROSS

A staff writer for The New Yorker, LILLIAN Ross *has written numerous profiles and sketches for the "Talk of the Town" column and as reporter at large. Some of these writings are collected in* Reporting (*1952*), Portrait of Hemingway (*1961*), Talk Stories (*1963*), *and* Reporting Two (*1969*). Vertical and Horizontal (*1963*) *is a collection of stories. The humorous essay reprinted here establishes its tone and point of view through a parody of "The Night Before Christmas." Ross saturates the reader in sounds, colors, sights. She does not merely give us impressions.*

The Vinyl Santa

Our lighted fireproof plastic Christmas bells are strung all 1 through the house, not a creature is stirring, and our mail-order catalogues—now piled high on the back porch— have been under surveillance since August, when they started coming in from Atlantic City, New Jersey; Oshkosh, Wisconsin; Evanston, Illinois; Chicago, Illinois; Falls Church, Virginia; Omaha, Nebraska; Vineland, New Jersey; North- port, New York; New York, New York; and elsewhere, including points across the seas. We did our shopping during Indian summer, without leaving our chair. Our house is full. Our task is completed. We are ready.

On our front door is a "Deck the Door Knob of red-and- 2 green felt with touches of glittering gold that has three jingly bells to say 'Hi! and Merry Christmas!' to all comers." On our windows are "Press-On Window Scenes" of snowmen and reindeer, and the windows are further ornamented with "Giant, 29-inch by 20-inch Personal Balls Artistically Hand- Lettered with the Family Name." Mounted outside on the wall of the house are "The Three Wise Men in Full Color in a Procession of Heavy Weatherproof Methyl-methacrylate Plastic." Each Wise Man is three feet tall and illuminated. A "Life-Size Climbing Vinyl Santa" is on the rooftop, and on the front lawn we have "3-D Thirty-Inch High Full Color Carollers of Strong Vinylite Carolling 'Oh, Come All Ye Faithful!'" In place of our regular doorbell we have a "glowing, jingling Santa stamped with the family name with a cord that visitors pull that raises Santa's arms in welcome, jingling bright brass bells." The garage door is covered with a "Giant Door Greeter Five Feet High and Six Feet Wide, Reading 'Merry Christmas.' " Indoors, all our rooms have been sprayed either with "Bayberry Mist, the forest-fresh scent-of-Christmas" or with the "pungent, spicy, exotic, sweet and rare frankincense-and-myrrh spray—gift of the Magi to the newborn Babe." Each light switch is covered with a "Switchplate-Santa made of white felt with red bell-bedecked cap—the switch comes through his open mouth, the sight of which will make you feel jolly." The towels on the bathroom racks are hand-printed with designs of sleighs and candy canes. The rug next to the tub has "Jolly Old Santa centered in deep, soft, plushy, white pile, and he's wreathed in smiles and in cherries, too, for 'round his head is a gay, cherry wreath." All the mirrors in the house are plastered with red, green, and white pleated tissue cutouts of angels with self-adhesive backs. In the dining room, "Full Size Santa Mugs of Bright Red-and-White Glazed Ceramic are 'Ready' for a 'Spot' of Holiday Cheer." In the living room, we have a "giant holiday chandelier of metallic foil discs reflecting a rainbow of colors," and "giant four-foot electric candles in festive red-and-white candy stripes are glowing cheerfully from their rock-steady base to their dripping wax 'flame.' " On the hall table stands our "Electric Musical Church, five inches high, with inspirational strains of 'Silent Night' pealing reverently from behind lighted, colorfully stained windows."

The tree is trimmed, all the way from a "Perforated 3 Golden Star Making the Sun Envious of Its Brilliance, as though the Blazing Star of Bethlehem Were Pausing in Its Orbit at Your Home," down to the "Christmas Tree Bib Covered with a Profusion of Christmas Designs and Colors" on the floor. Reflecting the light of the Perforated Golden Star, which is made of anodized aluminum with "Hundreds of Holes through which the Light Twinkles just like a Real Star," hang dozens of "Personalized Tree Balls with Names of the Family Nicely Applied in Shimmering, Non-Tarnishing Glitter." Bare spots on the tree are filled in with "Luminous Tree Icicles of Plastic," "Luminous, Plastic,

Heavenly Angel Babes Who Have Left the Milky Way," "Handcarved Wooden Angels Holding Hymnals on Gilded Hanging Strings," "Frosty White Pine Cones Lit with Colored Bulbs," "Miniature Felt Money Bags Gayly Trimmed in Assorted Designs of Yuletide," and "Yummy-Yum-Yum Santa Sweetest Holiday Lollipops."

On Christmas morning, there will be plenty of laughs 4 when everybody gets dressed. Dad will be wearing his "Personalized Holiday Ringing Bell Shorts of White Sanforized Cotton with Santa Claus Handpainted in All His Glory on One Side with a Tinkling Bell on the Tassel of His Cap and Dad's name embroidered in Contrasting Red on the Other." Big Sister will have on "Bright Red Holiday Stretch Socks of Bright Red Nylon Embossed with Contrasting White Holiday Motif." Little Sister and Mom will have on matching "Candy Striped Flannelette Housecoats." Brother will have on a "Clip-On Bow Tie of Red Felt in a Holly Pattern" and also "The Host with the Most Bright Red Felt Vest with Colorful Christmas Accent." Auntie will have on "Ringing Bell Panties Boasting a Ribbon Bedecked Candy Cane Handpainted in Brilliant Yuletide Colors with a Real Tinkling Bell for Extra Cheer." And Shep will have on his own "Personalized Dog Galoshes Embossed with Dog Claus on the Toes." Odds and ends under the tree will include a "Jingle Bell Apron that Plays a Merry Tune with Every Movement," "Donner and Blitzen Salt and Pepper Shakers," a set of "Holly Jewelry for the Holly-Days," a "Ten Commandments Bookmark of Ten Radiant Gold-Plated Squares that Look Like Ancient Scrolled Pages of the Old Testament with the Commandments Etched Upon Them," and "Hi-Fi Bible Stories on a Personalized Record." And our Christmas dinner will be prepared with the help of the "No Cooking Cookbook, with a Collection of Easy-To-Fix Recipes for Busy Mothers that Turns Canned and Frozen Foods into a Banquet of Gourmet Dishes."

QUESTIONS

1. What does the inventory of objects show about the meaning of Christmas to people? What people does Ross have in mind?

2. Is Ross ridiculing practices and attitudes through her details, or is she merely deriving humor from them?

3. How does Ross organize these details? Does she build them to a climax, or does she present them at random?

SUGGESTION FOR WRITING

Write a description of the objects and slogans associated with another holiday, perhaps Thanksgiving or the Fourth of July. Let your point of view and tone emerge through your details. Be as specific as you can in describing these objects and slogans.

Figurative Language

❦ ❦ ❦

A simile is an explicit comparison (using *like* or *as*) that usually develops or implies one or more simple points of resemblance:

> Will Brangwen ducked his head and looked at his uncle with swift, mistrustful eyes, like a caged hawk.—D. H. Lawrence, *The Rainbow*

A metaphor is an implicit comparison in which an object is presented as if it were something else:

> Constant use had not worn ragged the fabric of their friendship.— Dorothy Parker, *The Standard of Living*

Personification is the attribution of human qualities to abstract ideas or objects. Simile, metaphor, and personification unite in the following passage:

> Then Sunday light raced over the farm as fast as the chickens were flying. Immediately the first straight shaft of heat, solid as a hickory stick, was laid on the ridge.—Eudora Welty, *Losing Battles*

One purpose of figures of speech is to evoke the qualities of experience and give shape or substance to an emotion or awareness that up to the moment of its expression may be indefinite. In exposition a writer will depend on metaphor because of its property of expressing an attitude as well as representing an idea:

> My parents' house had an attic, the darkest and strangest part of the building, reachable only by placing a stepladder beneath the trapdoor and filled with unidentifiable articles too important to be thrown out with the trash but no longer suitable to have at hand. This mysterious space was the memory of the place. After many years all the things deposited in it became, one by one, lost to consciousness. But they were there, we knew, safely and comfortably stored in the tissues of the house.—Lewis Thomas, "The Attic of the Brain"

Figurative writing is particularly important in descriptive writing, as in the following paragraph which conveys an unusual experience and sensation through metaphor and other figures:

Although I was still miles from the ocean, a heavy sea fog came in to muffle the obscure woods and lie over the land like a sheet of dirty muslin. I saw no cars or people, few lights in the houses. The windshield wipers, brushing at the fog, switched back and forth like cats' tails. I lost myself to the monotonous rhythm and darkness as past and present fused and dim things came and went in a staccato of moments separated by miles of darkness. On the road, where change is continuous and visible, time is not; rather it is something the rider only infers. Time is not the traveler's fourth dimension—change is.—William Least Heat Moon, *Blue Highways*

K. C. COLE

A former editor of Saturday Review *and* Newsday, *K. C.* COLE *has written articles for numerous periodicals, including the* New York Times *and* Psychology Today. *Her book* Between the Lines *(1982) discusses contemporary issues of feminism. Cole has also written about physics as a profession in* Sympathetic Vibrations: Reflections on Physics as a Way of Life *(1985). She draws on her knowledge of physics in this unusual essay on the literal and metaphorical meanings of resonance.*

Resonance

Metaphor is truly a marvelous thing. We speak of being in 1 tune with the times or out of tune with each other. We speak of sympathetic vibrations and being on the same wavelength. We speak of going through phases, of ideas that resonate and descriptions that ring true. I wonder how many of us know that all the time we are talking physics?

Resonance is the physics lesson all children learn the 2 first time they try to pump themselves on a swing. Pushing forward or leaning backward at the wrong place or time in the swing gets them nowhere. But pushing and pulling precisely in tune with the natural period of swing will get them as high as they want to go. Being in tune means pushing in the same direction that the swing naturally wants to go. It means going with the flow. Pushing at any other time goes against the swing and bucks the current. It saps energy instead of adding it. Eventually, it will bring the highest swinger to a halt.

Resonance is music to our ears. A violin bow slips along the string, imperceptibly catching it at precise intervals that push it at the proper time to keep it vibrating. The air in a flute resonates at many different frequencies, depending on how far the vibration can travel between lips and mouthpiece. But the stops in a flute are not spaced just anywhere. Beware the flute player who sets the air vibrating at a frequency not natural to the flute; the sound is not a note at all, only an amorphous, irritating hiss. 3

Being out of tune is always irritating because the energy we put into our efforts doesn't seem to get us anywhere. It goes against our grain instead of with it. It steals our harmony and leaves us noise. We can be in or out of tune with ourselves—like the flute and the violin—or in or out of tune with others. Two flutes played beautifully but slightly out of tune with each other can be just as unpleasant as one played badly. Partners in a marriage who are perfectly in tune with their professional or personal lives can be badly out of tune with each other too. 4

To resonate means to sound again, to echo. The trick is to have something that resounds again and again. Two can play this game much better than one because one can feed energy to the other. That's what sympathetic vibrations are all about. 5

Though almost everything—and everyone—can resonate to many different frequencies, it is rare to find ourselves exactly in resonance with something or someone else. When we do, it is the click of recognition that comes with finding a friend who laughs at your jokes and whose understanding goes without saying, who reads correctly the exact meaning of the tilt of your slightly raised eyebrow and who provides the ingredients that make the occasion. 6

It's like the car with the unbalanced wheel that starts to shimmy at exactly 62 miles per hour. At other speeds the wheel still wobbles but the springs of the car can't respond; 7

only at 62 miles an hour do the two frequencies coincide and the two vibrations become completely sympathetic. Then the car shakes like mad. It's all a matter of timing.

With resonance, a small unnoticed vibration can add up 8 to large, often lovely effects. Lasers are the result of sympathetic vibrations of light. The opera singer's aria is an ode to resonance. Each pure tone that fills the opera house is the tiny vibration of a vocal cord amplified by the shape of chest and throat. The same pure tone can shatter a crystal glass. Resonance can be dangerous. Soldiers marching in step across a bridge can cause it to start swinging at its natural frequency, straining its supports and making it collapse. A lot of little pushes in an angry crowd can add up to a full-scale riot. A lot of little digs over the dinner table can lead to a divorce.

Resonance can also be deceiving: a politician who senses 9 dissatisfaction over inflation and taxes can get a large resonant response with a very small input of energy or new ideas—and winds up playing in a vacuum, with no result. A woman who comes into a man's life at the moment he happens to be looking for a wife (or vice versa) may find herself quickly, but in the long run unhappily, married. Being in tune can easily be a matter of superficial coincidence, not lasting harmony.

It is not easy, that is, to stay in tune even when we start 10 up that way. I am always unprepared for the precipitate ups and downs in my marriage and my relations with friends. One week we seem never to be together enough, seem never to have enough time to say what we want to say, seem so closely attuned to each other's needs and fancies that we are irrevocably inseparable. A week or month later the feelings of being in tune evaporate as invisibly—but surely—as water from a dry stream. Suddenly we seem to have nothing to say to each other and everything we do say is misunderstood. Arguments and hurt feelings lie beneath the surface like spikes, waiting to trip us up.

Anything that resonates necessarily oscillates; it swings 11 or vibrates back and forth. Just because you start out swinging in the same direction doesn't mean you will reverse direction at the same time. Each part of the swing has its phases: ups and downs, stops and starts. If your timing is not right you will soon find yourself up when your partner is down, just starting when your partner has already stopped. Even flutes get out of tune as they warm up. People or things that make beautiful music together must continually be adjusted, fine-tuned. Resonance is a delicate thing.

Still, it is amazing how much of the world around us is 12 colored by resonance. Each atom resonates with one or, often, seven natural frequencies. Sodium light is yellow because the sodium atom resonates with the frequency of radiation we see as the color yellow. Grass is green because all the colors of sunlight except green resonate within the grass and become stuck; green is the only color left to reflect to our eyes. Ultraviolet wavelengths of light become stuck within the molecules of a windowpane and prevent us from getting a suntan indoors. The ozone layer of the atmosphere, like suntan lotion, also absorbs resonant ultraviolet rays and protects us from potentially damaging light.

Resonance determines what is transparent, what is 13 invisible, what we see and hear. Tuning into a radio or television station merely means putting your receiver on the same wavelength as the station's transmitter. In the process of tuning into one channel, of course, we ignore all the others. We do the same thing when we tune in to certain people or ideas. When a woman becomes pregnant she focuses on her condition and sometimes ceases to pay attention to anything else. Teen-agers tune into teen-agers; kids into other kids.

It's important to have something around that responds 14 when you push against it, of course; a resounding board, so to speak. I never felt so lonely as when I was bringing up my son and all my friends, childless, were bringing up their careers. I'd throw out experiences and insights only to have them land with a thud. My friends had nothing to give back, nothing to reinforce my joys or help to lessen the sting of my sorrows. On the other hand, I felt just as isolated when I was surrounded by women whose lives were exclusively submerged in homes and children. They could not have commiserated with my conflicts even if they had wanted to.

My friend Alice, who is 73, joked that I would never find 15 a compatible neighborhood because I would never find neighbors who shared my eclectic collection of experiences.

It reminded me of a middle-aged woman who was visiting a museum I work in and complained that people like herself probably couldn't relate to our teen-age guides. She had a good point. And yet I wonder how many teen-agers have been permanently put off museums by middle-aged guides like myself. And how much nicer it would be if we could vibrate to a large collection of resonances. How sad it would be if we could relate only to people exactly like ourselves.

Resonance determines what goes right through and 16 what sinks in. It even determines what we are. Particles of matter, it turns out, are really just resonances of energy. A certain frequency of vibration and presto! a proton. Change the frequency and presto! you have something else.

Fortunately, in addition to the sharp focus of single 17 resonance, we can have a rich spectrum of resonances called harmonics. Harmonics sounds the difference between a twanging string and a violin. Changing our tunes every now and then may not be such a bad idea.

VOCABULARY

paragraph 3: amorphous
paragraph 8: lasers
paragraph 10: precipitate
paragraph 14: commiserated
paragraph 15: eclectic

QUESTIONS

1. What is resonance, and where does Cole first define it? How does she develop this definition in the course of the essay?
2. Cole concludes with the statement that "changing our tunes every now and then may not be such a bad idea." How does she develop this metaphorical statement through the physical resonance of music?
3. What other metaphorical meanings of resonance does Cole discuss? How does she illustrate them?
4. Is the essay an account of the many uses of a single metaphor, or is Cole making a point about people or life through the metaphor of resonance?

SUGGESTIONS FOR WRITING

1. Through experiences and observations of your own, illustrate one of the points Cole makes about resonance. You might begin your essay by restating her definition of resonance and commenting on it.

2. Give the dictionary meaning of each of the following words, then discuss the various metaphorical meanings of one of the words in your own experience:

   a. resilience

   b. flexibility

   c. toughness

   d. tenacity

DIANE ACKERMAN

DIANE ACKERMAN *is a poet, an essayist, and a staff writer for* The New Yorker *magazine. She has written numerous articles on natural history, some of which are collected in* The Moon by Whale Light *(1991); she has also written literary criticism and essays on travel. Her books of poetry include* Wife of Light *(1978),* Lady Faustus *(1983), and* Reverse Thunder *(1988).* On Extended Wings: An Adventure in Flight *(1985) is a memoir. Her essay on a night launching of the space shuttle appears in* A Natural History of the Senses *(1990). Ackerman writes: "We live on the leash of our senses. Although they enlarge us, they also limit and restrain us, but how beautifully." Figurative language is one means by which Ackerman helps the reader experience the sensations of the launch.*

Watching a Night Launch of the Space Shuttle

A huge glittering tower sparkles across the Florida marshlands. Floodlights reach into the heavens all around it, rolling out carpets of light. Helicopters and jets blink around the launch pad like insects drawn to flame. Oz never filled the sky with such diamond-studded improbability. Inside the cascading lights, a giant trellis holds a slender rocket to its heart, on each side a tall thermos bottle filled with solid fuel the color and feel of a hard eraser, and on its back a sharp-nosed space shuttle, clinging like the young of some exotic mammal. A full moon bulges low in the sky, its face turned toward the launch pad, its mouth open.

On the sober consoles of launch control, numbers count backward toward zero. When numbers vanish, and reverse time ends, something will disappear. Not the shuttle—that will stay with us through eyesight and radar, and be on the minds of dozens of tracking dishes worldwide, rolling their heads as if to relieve the anguish. For hours we have been standing on these Floridian bogs, longing for the blazing rapture of the moment ahead, longing to be jettisoned free from routine, and lifted, like the obelisk we launch, that much nearer the infinite. On the fog-wreathed banks of the Banana River, and by the roadside lookouts, we are waiting: 55,000 people are expected at the Space Center alone.

When floodlights die on the launch pad, camera shutters and mental shutters all open in the same instant. The air feels loose and damp. A hundred thousand eyes rush to one spot, where a glint below the booster rocket flares into a pinwheel of fire, a sparkler held by hand on the Fourth of July. White clouds shoot out in all directions, in a dust storm of flame, a gritty, swirling Sahara, burning from gray-white to an incandescent platinum so raw it makes your eyes squint, to a radiant gold so narcotic you forget how to blink. The air is full of bee stings, prickly and electric. Your pores start to itch. Hair stands up stiff on the back of your neck. It used to be that the launch pad would melt at lift-off, but now 300,000 gallons of water crash from aloft, burst from below. Steam clouds scent the air with a mineral ash. Crazed by reflection, the waterways turn the color of pounded brass. Thick cumulus clouds shimmy and build at ground level, where you don't expect to see thunderheads.

Seconds into the launch, an apricot *whoosh* pours out in spasms, like the rippling quarters of a palomino, and now outbleaches the sun, as clouds rise and pile like a Creation scene. Birds leap into the air along with moths and dragon-flies and gnats and other winged creatures, all driven to panic by the clamor: booming, crackling, howling down-wind. What is flight, that it can take place in the fragile wings of a moth, whose power station is a heart small as a computer chip? What is flight, that it can groan upward through 4.5 million pounds of dead weight on a colossal gantry? Close your eyes, and you hear the deafening *rat-a-tat-tat* of firecrackers, feel them arcing against your chest. Open your eyes, and you see a huge steel muscle dripping fire, as seven million pounds of thrust pauses a moment on a silver haunch, and then the bedlam clouds let rip. Iron struts blow over the launch pad like newspapers, and shock waves roll out, pounding their giant fists, pounding the marshes where birds shriek and fly, pounding against your chest, where a heart already rapid begins running clean away from you. The air feels tight as a drum, the mole-cules bouncing. Suddenly the space shuttle leaps high over the marshlands, away from the now frantic laughter of the loons, away from the reedy delirium of the insects and the open-mouthed awe of the spectators, many of whom are crying, as it rises on a waterfall of flame 700 feet long, shooting colossal sparks as it climbs in a golden halo that burns deep into memory.

Only ten minutes from lift-off, it will leave the security 5 blanket of our atmosphere, and enter an orbit 184 miles up. This is not miraculous. After all, we humans began in an early tantrum of the universe, when our chemical makeup first took form. We evolved through accidents, happen-stance, near misses, and good luck. We developed language, forged cities, mustered nations. Now we change the course of rivers and move mountains; we hold back trillions of tons of water with cement dams. We break into human chests and heads; operate on beating hearts and thinking brains. What is defying gravity compared to that? In orbit, there will be no night and day, no up and down. No one will have their "feet on the ground." No joke will be "earthy." No point will be "timely." No thrill will be "out of this world." In orbit, the sun will rise every hour and a half, and there will be 112 days to each week. But then time has always been one of our boldest and most ingenious inventions, and, when you think about it, one of the least plausible of our fictions.

Lunging to the east out over the water, the shuttle rolls slowly onto its back, climbing at three g's, an upshooting torch, twisting an umbilical of white cloud beneath it. When the two solid rockets fall free, they hover to one side like bright red quotation marks, beginning an utterance it will take four days to finish. For over six minutes of seismic wonder it is still visible, this star we hurl up at the star-studded sky. What is a neighborhood? one wonders. Is it the clump of wild daisies beside the Banana River, in which moths hover and dive without the aid of rockets? For large minds, the Earth is a small place. Not small enough to exhaust in one lifetime, but a compact home, cozy, buoyant, a place to cherish, the spectral center of our life. But how could we stay at home forever? 6

VOCABULARY

paragraph 1: Oz, trellis

paragraph 2: console, obelisk

paragraph 3: incandescent

paragraph 4: palomino, gantry, arcing, haunch, bedlam, reedy

paragraph 5: tantrum, happenstance, plausible

paragraph 6: umbilical, seismic

QUESTIONS

1. What similes and metaphors help to describe the launch pad in paragraph 1? What use does Ackerman make of personification?

2. What similes, metaphors, and personifications help her describe the launch in paragraphs 3 and 4?

3. How do these and other figures help Ackerman express her feelings about the launch?

4. What central idea or thesis does she develop? Where does she first state it? What images and figures help her to express it?

SUGGESTIONS FOR WRITING

1. Write several paragraphs describing an exciting event you once witnessed. Rewrite your description, heightening it through similes, metaphors, and other figures. Keep your audience in mind as you write.

2. Analyze the use Annie Dillard makes of figurative language in one or two paragraphs of her description of the partial eclipse (p. 453).

3. Analyze the figurative language in a series of automobile or cosmetic ads, or those for another product. Comment on the effectiveness of the language.

Faulty Diction

❦ ❦ ❦

We hear much today about the abuse of language—particularly about euphemism and equivocation like that cited by George Orwell in his classic essay on language and politics included in this section:

> Defenseless villages are bombarded from the air, the inhabitants driven out into the countryside, the cattle machine-gunned, the huts set on fire with incendiary bullets: this is called *pacification*. Millions of peasants are robbed of their farms and sent trudging along the roads with no more than they can carry: this is called *transfer of population* or *rectification of frontiers*.

Writing in 1946, Orwell bluntly tells his readers that "In our time, political speech and writing are largely the defense of the indefensible," and he adds that this language "has to consist largely of euphemism, question-begging, and sheer cloudy vagueness." We can guess what Orwell would have said about political language in our own time—about such phrases as "credibility gap" and "positive reference input" to describe the reputations of office holders and candidates, and in nonpolitical discourse, "learning resource centers" and "interfaces between student and teacher" to describe libraries and conferences. Such vague and pretentious language can be comical, as Russell Baker shows in his retelling of "Little Red Riding Hood," but as Orwell explains, the abuses of language have consequences: ". . . if thought corrupts language, language can also corrupt thought."

The two essays in this section offer an opportunity to consider many of these abuses and their possible causes.

GEORGE ORWELL

In 1946 GEORGE ORWELL (p. 13) wrote his classic essay on the political uses of language. The recently ended Second World War provided ample illustration of his statement in the essay, *"In our time, political speech and writing are largely the defense of the indefensible."* But Orwell drew his examples also from events prior to the war—from such totalitarian acts as the starving and deportation of Russian farmers in the late 1920s and the imprisonment and execution of millions more in the Purge Trials of 1936–38. Totalitarianism is not only a kind of political organization, but also a general way of thinking, speaking, and writing. Orwell was to develop this idea in his most famous novel Nineteen Eighty-Four *(1949).*

Politics and the English Language

Most people who bother with the matter at all would admit that the English language is in a bad way, but it is generally assumed that we cannot by conscious action do anything about it. Our civilization is decadent and our language—so the argument runs—must inevitably share in the general collapse. It follows that any struggle against the abuse of language is a sentimental archaism, like preferring candles to electric light or hansom cabs to airplanes. Underneath this lies the half-conscious belief that language is a natural growth and not an instrument which we shape for our own purposes. 1

Now, it is clear that the decline of a language must ultimately have political and economic causes: it is not due simply to the bad influence of this or that individual writer. But an effect can become a cause, reinforcing the original cause and producing the same effect in an intensified form, and so on indefinitely. A man may take to drink because he feels himself to be a failure, and then fail all the more completely because he drinks. It is rather the same thing that is happening to the English language. It becomes ugly and inaccurate because our thoughts are foolish, but the slovenliness of our language makes it easier for us to have foolish thoughts. The point is that the process is reversible. Modern English, especially written English, is full of bad habits which spread by imitation and which can be avoided if one is willing to take the necessary trouble. If one gets rid of these habits one can think more clearly, and to think clearly is a necessary first step toward political regeneration: so that 2 the fight against bad English is not frivolous and is not the exclusive concern of professional writers. I will come back to this presently, and I hope that by that time the meaning of what I have said here will have become clearer. Meanwhile, here are five specimens of the English language as it is now habitually written.

These five passages have not been picked out because they are especially bad—I could have quoted far worse if I had chosen—but because they illustrate various of the mental vices from which we now suffer. They are a little below the average, but are fairly representative samples. I number them so that I can refer back to them when necessary:

> (1) I am not, indeed, sure whether it is not true to say that the Milton who once seemed not unlike a seventeenth-century Shelley had not become, out of an experience ever more bitter in each year, more alien [*sic*] to the founder of that Jesuit sect which nothing could induce him to tolerate.
>
> Professor Harold Laski (Essay in *Freedom of Expression*)

> (2) Above all, we cannot play ducks and drakes with a native battery of idioms which prescribes such egregious collocations of vocables as the Basic *put up with* for *tolerate* or *put at a loss* for *bewilder*.
>
> Professor Lancelot Hogben (*Interglossa*)

> (3) On the one side we have the free personality: by definition it is not neurotic, for it has neither conflict nor dream. Its desires, such as they are, are transparent, for they are just what institutional approval keeps in the forefront of consciousness; another institutional pattern would alter their number and intensity; there is little in them that is natural, irreducible, or culturally dangerous. But *on the other side,* the social bond itself is nothing but the mutual reflection of these self-secure integrities. Recall the definition of love. Is not this the very picture of a small academic? Where is there a place in this hall of mirrors for either personality or fraternity?
>
> Essay on psychology in *Politics* (New York)

> (4) All the "best people" from the gentlemen's clubs, and all the frantic fascist captains, united in common hatred of Socialism and bestial horror of the rising tide of the mass revolutionary movement, have turned to acts of provocation, to foul incendiarism, to medieval legends of poisoned wells, to legalize their own destruction of proletarian organizations,

3

and rouse the agitated petty-bourgeoisie to chauvinistic fervor on behalf of the fight against the revolutionary way out of the crisis.

Communist pamphlet

(5) If a new spirit *is* to be infused into this old country, there is one thorny and contentious reform which must be tackled, and that is the humanization and galvanization of the B.B.C. Timidity here will bespeak canker and atrophy of the soul. The heart of Britain may be sound and of strong beat, for instance, but the British lion's roar at present is like that of Bottom in Shakespeare's *Midsummer Night's Dream*—as gentle as any sucking dove. A virile new Britain cannot continue indefinitely to be traduced in the eyes or rather ears, of the world by the effete languors of Langham Place, brazenly masquerading as "standard English." When the Voice of Britain is heard at nine o'clock, better far and infinitely less ludicrous to hear aitches honestly dropped than the present priggish, inflated, inhibited, school-ma'amish arch braying of blameless bashful mewing maidens!

Letter in *Tribune*

Each of these passages has faults of its own, but, quite apart from avoidable ugliness, two qualities are common to all of them. The first is staleness of imagery; the other is lack of precision. The writer either has a meaning and cannot express it, or he inadvertently says something else, or he is almost indifferent as to whether his words mean anything or not. This mixture of vagueness and sheer incompetence is the most marked characteristic of modern English prose, and especially of any kind of political writing. As soon as certain topics are raised, the concrete melts into the abstract and no one seems able to think of turns of speech that are not hackneyed: prose consists less and less of *words* chosen for the sake of their meaning, and more and more of *phrases* tacked together like the sections of a prefabricated henhouse. I list below, with notes and examples, various of the tricks by means of which the work of prose-construction is habitually dodged:

Dying metaphors. A newly invented metaphor assists thought by evoking a visual image, while on the other hand a metaphor which is technically "dead" (e.g., *iron resolution*) has in effect reverted to being an ordinary word and can generally be used without loss of vividness. But in between these two classes there is a huge dump of worn-out metaphors which have lost all evocative power and are merely used because they save people the trouble of inventing phrases for themselves. Examples are: *Ring the changes on, take up the cudgels for, toe the line, ride roughshod over, stand shoulder to shoulder with, play into the hands of, no axe to grind, grist to the mill, fishing in troubled waters, rift within the lute, on the order of the day, Achilles' heel, swan song, hotbed.* Many of these are used without knowledge of their meaning (what is a "rift" for instance?), and incompatible metaphors are frequently mixed, a sure sign that the writer is not interested in what he is saying. Some metaphors now current have been twisted out of their original meaning without those who use them even being aware of the fact. For example, *toe the line* is sometimes written *tow the line.* Another example is *the hammer and the anvil,* now always used with the implication that the anvil gets the worst of it. In real life it is always the anvil that breaks the hammer, never the other way about: a writer who stopped to think what he was saying would be aware of this, and would avoid perverting the original phrase.

Operators or *verbal false limbs.* These save the trouble of picking out appropriate verbs and nouns, and at the same time pad each sentence with extra syllables which give it an appearance of symmetry. Characteristic phrases are *render inoperative, militate against, make contact with, be subjected to, give rise to, give grounds for, have the effect of, play a leading part (role) in, make itself felt, take effect, exhibit a tendency to, serve the purpose of, etc., etc.* The keynote is the elimination of simple verbs. Instead of being a single word, such as *break, stop, spoil, mend, kill,* a verb becomes a *phrase,* made up of a noun or adjective tacked on to some general-purpose verb such as *prove, serve, form, play, render.* In addition, the passive voice is wherever possible used in preference to the active, and noun constructions are used instead of gerunds (*by examination of* instead of *by examining*). The range of verbs is further cut down by means of the *-ize* and *de-* formations, and the banal statements are given an appearance of profundity by means of the *not un-* formation. Simple conjunctions and prepositions are replaced by such phrases as *with respect to,* *having regard to, the fact that, by dint of, in view of, in the interests of, on the hypothesis that;* and the ends of sentences are saved from anticlimax by such resounding commonplaces as *greatly to be desired, cannot be left out of account, a development to be expected in the near future, deserving of serious consideration, brought to a satisfactory conclusion,* and so on and so forth.

Pretentious diction. Words like *phenomenon, element, 7 individual* (as noun), *objective, categorical, effective, virtual, basic, primary, promote, constitute, exhibit, exploit, utilize, eliminate, liquidate,* are used to dress up simple statements and give an air of scientific impartiality to biased judgments. Adjectives like *epoch-making, epic, historic, unforgettable, triumphant, age-old, inevitable, inexorable, veritable,* are used to dignify the sordid processes of international politics, while writing that aims at glorifying war usually takes on an archaic color, its characteristic words being: *realm, throne, chariot, mailed fist, trident, sword, shield, buckler, banner, jackboot, clarion.* Foreign words and expressions such as *cul de sac, ancien régime, deus ex machina, mutatis mutandis, status quo, gleichschaltung, weltanschauung,* are used to give an air of culture and elegance. Except for the useful abbreviations *i.e., e.g.,* and *etc.,* there is no real need for any of the hundreds of foreign phrases now current in English. Bad writers, and especially scientific, political, and sociological writers, are nearly always haunted by the notion that Latin or Greek words are grander than Saxon ones, and unnecessary words like *expedite, ameliorate, predict, extraneous, deracinated, clandestine, subaqueous,* and hundreds of others constantly gain ground from their Anglo-Saxon opposite numbers.[1] The jargon peculiar to Marxist writing (*hyena, hangman, cannibal, petty bourgeois, these gentry, lackey, flunkey, mad dog, White Guard,* etc.) consists largely of words and phrases translated from Russian, German, or French; but the normal way of coining a new word is to use a Latin or Greek root with the appropriate affix and, where necessary, the *-ize* formation. It

---

[1] An interesting illustration of this is the way in which the English flower names which were in use till very recently are being ousted by Greek ones, *snapdragon* becoming *antirrhinum, forget-me-not* becoming *myosotis,* etc. It is hard to see any practical reason for this change of fashion: it is probably due to an instinctive turning away from the more homely word and a vague feeling that the Greek word is scientific.

is often easier to make up words of this kind (*deregionalize, impermissible, extramarital, nonfragmentary* and so forth) than to think up the English words that will cover one's meaning. The result, in general, is an increase in slovenliness and vagueness.

Meaningless words. In certain kinds of writing, particu- 8 larly in art criticism and literary criticism, it is normal to come across long passages which are almost completely lacking in meaning.[2] Words like *romantic, plastic, values, human, dead, sentimental, natural, vitality,* as used in art criticism, are strictly meaningless, in the sense that they not only do not point to any discoverable object, but are hardly ever expected to do so by the reader. When one critic writes, "The outstanding feature of Mr. X's work is its living quality," while another writes, "The immediately striking thing about Mr. X's work is its peculiar deadness," the reader accepts this as a simple difference of opinion. If words like *black* and *white* were involved, instead of the jargon words *dead* and *living,* he would see at once that language was being used in an improper way. Many political words are similarly abused. The word *Fascism* has now no meaning except in so far as it signifies "something not desirable." The words *democracy, socialism, freedom, patriotic, realistic, justice,* have each of them several different meanings which cannot be reconciled with one another. In the case of a word like *democracy,* not only is there no agreed definition, but the attempt to make one is resisted from all sides. It is almost universally felt that when we call a country democratic we are praising it: consequently the defenders of every kind of régime claim that it is a democracy, and fear that they might have to stop using the word if it were tied down to any one meaning. Words of this kind are often used in a consciously dishonest way. That is, the person who uses them has his own private definition, but allows his hearer to think he means something quite different. Statements like *Marshal Pétain was a true patriot, The*

---

[2] Example: "Comfort's catholicity of perception and image, strangely Whitmanesque in range, almost the opposite in aesthetic compulsion, continues to evoke that trembling atmospheric accumulative hinting at a cruel, an inexorably serene time-lessness. . . . Wrey Gardiner scores by aiming at simple bull's-eyes with precision. Only they are not so simple, and through this contented sadness runs more than the surface bittersweet of resignation." (*Poetry Quarterly.*)

Soviet press is the freest in the world, The Catholic Church is opposed to persecution, are almost always made with intent to deceive. Other words used in variable meanings, in most cases more or less dishonestly, are: *class, totalitarian, science, progressive, reactionary, bourgeois, equality.*

Now that I have made this catalog of swindles and 9 perversions, let me give another example of the kind of writing that they lead to. This time it must of its nature be an imaginary one. I am going to translate a passage of good English into modern English of the worst sort. Here is a well-known verse from *Ecclesiastes:*

> I returned and saw under the sun, that the race is not to the swift, nor the battle to the strong, neither yet bread to the wise, nor yet riches to men of understanding, not yet favour to men of skill; but time and chance happeneth to them all.

Here it is in modern English:

> Objective consideration of contemporary phenomenon compels the conclusion that success or failure in competitive activities exhibits no tendency to be commensurate with innate capacity, but that a considerable element of the unpredictable must invariably be taken into account.

This is a parody, but not a very gross one. Exhibit (3), 10 above, for instance, contains several patches of the same kind of English. It will be seen that I have not made a full translation. The beginning and ending of the sentence follow the original meaning fairly closely, but in the middle the concrete illustrations—race, battle, bread—dissolve into the vague phrase "success or failure in competitive activities." This had to be so, because no modern writer of the kind I am discussing—no one capable of using phrases like "objective consideration of contemporary phenomena"—would ever tabulate his thoughts in that precise and detailed way. The whole tendency of modern prose is away from concreteness. Now analyze these two sentences a little more closely. The first contains forty-nine words but only sixty syllables, and all its words are those of everyday life. The second contains thirty-eight words of ninety syllables: eighteen of its words are from Latin roots, and one from Greek. The first sentence contains six vivid images, and only one phrase ("time and chance") that could be called vague. The second contains not a single fresh, arresting phrase, and in spite of its ninety syllables it gives only a shortened version of the meaning contained in the first. Yet without a doubt it is the second kind of sentence that is gaining ground in modern English. I do not want to exaggerate. This kind of writing is not yet universal, and outcrops of simplicity will occur here and there in the worst-written page. Still, if you or I were told to write a few lines on the uncertainty of human fortunes, we should probably come much nearer to my imaginary sentence than to the one from *Ecclesiastes*.

As I have tried to show, modern writing at its worst 11 does not consist in picking out words for the sake of their meaning and inventing images in order to make the meaning clearer. It consists in gumming together long strips of words which have already been set in order by someone else, and making the results presentable by sheer humbug. The attraction of this way of writing is that it is easy. It is easier—even quicker, once you have the habit—to say *In my opinion it is not an unjustifiable assumption that* than to say *I think.* If you use ready-made phrases, you not only don't have to hunt about for words; you also don't have to bother with the rhythms of your sentences, since these phrases are generally so arranged as to be more or less euphonious. When you are composing in a hurry—when you are dictating to a stenographer, for instance, or making a public speech—it is natural to fall into a pretentious, Latinized style. Tags like *a consideration which we should do well to bear in mind* or *a conclusion to which all of us would readily assent* will save many a sentence from coming down with a bump. By using stale metaphors, similes, and idioms, you save much mental effort, at the cost of leaving your meaning vague, not only for your reader but for yourself. This is the significance of mixed metaphors. The sole aim of a metaphor is to call up a visual image. When these images clash—as in *The Fascist octopus has sung its swan song, the jackboot is thrown into the melting pot*—it can be taken as certain that the writer is not seeing a mental image of the objects he is naming; in other words he is not really thinking. Look again at the examples I gave at the beginning of this essay. Professor Laski (1) uses five negatives in fifty-three words. One of these is superfluous, making nonsense of the whole passage, and in addition there is the slip—*alien* for akin—making further nonsense, and several avoidable pieces of clumsiness which increase the general vagueness. Professor Hogben (2) plays ducks and drakes with a battery which is able to write prescriptions, and, while disapproving of the everyday phrase *put up with,* is unwilling to look *egregious* up in the dictionary and see what it means; (3) if one takes an uncharitable attitude towards it, is simply meaningless: probably one could work out its intended meaning by reading the whole of the article in which it occurs. In (4), the writer knows more or less what he wants to say, but an accumulation of stale phrases chokes him like tea leaves blocking a sink. In (5), words and meaning have almost parted company. People who write in this manner usually have a general emotional meaning—they dislike one thing and want to express solidarity with another—but they are not interested in the detail of what they are saying. A scrupulous writer, in every sentence that he writes, will ask himself at least four questions, thus: What am I trying to say? What words will express it? What image or idiom will make it clearer? Is this image fresh enough to have an effect? And he will probably ask himself two more: Could I put it more shortly? Have I said anything that is avoidably ugly? But you are not obliged to go to all this trouble. You can shirk it by simply throwing your mind open and letting the ready-made phrases come crowding in. They will construct your sentences for you—even think your thoughts for you, to a certain extent—and at need they will perform the important service of partially concealing your meaning even from yourself. It is at this point that the special connection between politics and the debasement of language becomes clear.

In our time it is broadly true that political writing is bad 12 writing. Where it is not true, it will generally be found that the writer is some kind of rebel, expressing his private opinions and not a "party line." Orthodoxy, of whatever color, seems to demand a lifeless, imitative style. The political dialects to be found in pamphlets, leading articles, manifestoes, White Papers and the speeches of undersecretaries do, of course, vary from party to party, but they are all alike in that one almost never finds in them a fresh, vivid, homemade turn of speech. When one watches some tired hack on the platform mechanically repeating the familiar phrases—*bestial atrocities, iron heel, bloodstained tyranny, free peoples of the world, stand shoulder to shoulder*—one often has a curious feeling that one is not watching a live human being but some kind of dummy: a feeling which suddenly becomes stronger at moments when the light catches the speaker's spectacles and turns them into blank discs which seem to have no eyes behind them. And this is not altogether fanciful. A speaker who uses that kind of phraseology has gone some distance toward turning himself into a machine. The appropriate noises are coming out of his larynx, but his brain is not involved as it would be if he were choosing his words for himself. If the speech he is making is one that he is accustomed to make over and over again, he may be almost unconscious of what he is saying, as one is when one utters the responses in church. And this reduced state of consciousness, if not indispensable, is at any rate favorable to political conformity.

In our time, political speech and writing are largely the defense of the indefensible. Things like the continuance of British rule in India, the Russian purges and deportations, the dropping of the atom bombs on Japan, can indeed be defended, but only by arguments which are too brutal for most people to face, and which do not square with the professed aims of political parties. Thus political language has to consist largely of euphemism, question-begging and sheer cloudy vagueness. Defenseless villages are bombarded from the air, the inhabitants driven out into the countryside, the cattle machine-gunned, the huts set on fire with incendiary bullets: this is called *pacification*. Millions of peasants are robbed of their farms and sent trudging along the roads with no more than they can carry: this is called *transfer of population* or *rectification of frontiers*. People are imprisoned for years without trial, or shot in the back of the neck or sent to die of scurvy in Arctic lumber camps: this is called *elimination of unreliable elements*. Such phraseology is needed if one wants to name things without calling up mental pictures of them. Consider for instance some comfortable English professor defending Russian totalitarianism. He cannot say outright, "I believe in killing off your opponents when you can get good results by doing so." Probably, therefore, he will say something like this:

"While freely conceding that the Soviet régime exhibits 14 certain features which the humanitarian may be inclined to deplore, we must, I think, agree that a certain curtailment of the right to political opposition is an unavoidable concomitant of transitional periods, and that the rigors which the Russian people have been called upon to undergo have been amply justified in the sphere of concrete achievement."

The inflated style is itself a kind of euphemism. A mass 15 of Latin words fall upon the facts like soft snow, blurring the outlines and covering up all the details. The great enemy of clear language is insincerity. When there is a gap between one's real and one's declared aims, one turns as it were instinctively to long words and exhausted idioms, like a cuttlefish squirting out ink. In our age there is no such thing as "keeping out of politics." All issues are political issues, and politics itself is a mass of lies, evasions, folly, hatred, and schizophrenia. When the general atmosphere is bad, language must suffer. I should expect to find—this is a guess which I have not sufficient knowledge to verify—that the German, Russian, and Italian languages have all deteriorated in the last ten or fifteen years, as a result of dictatorship.

But if thought corrupts language, language can also 16 corrupt thought. A bad usage can spread by tradition and imitation, even among people who should and do know better. The debased language that I have been discussing is in some ways very convenient. Phrases like *a not unjustifiable assumption, leaves much to be desired, would serve no good purpose, a consideration which we should do well to bear in mind,* are a continuous temptation, a packet of aspirins always at one's elbow. Look back through this essay, and for certain you will find that I have again and again committed the very faults I am protesting against. By this morning's post I have received a pamphlet dealing with conditions in Germany. The author tells me that he "felt impelled" to write it. I open it at random, and here is almost the first sentence that I see: "[The Allies] have an opportunity not only of achieving a radical transformation of Germany's social and political structure in such a way as to avoid a nationalistic reaction in Germany itself, but at the same time of laying the foundations of a co-operative and unified Europe." You see, he "feels impelled" to write—feels, presumably, that he has something new to say—and yet his words, like cavalry horses answering the bugle, group themselves automatically into the familiar dreary pattern. This invasion of one's mind by ready-made phrases (*lay the foundations, achieve a radical transformation*) can only be prevented if one is constantly on guard against them, and every such phrase anaesthetizes a portion of one's brain.

I said earlier that the decadence of our language is 17 probably curable. Those who deny this would argue, if they produced an argument at all, that language merely reflects existing social conditions, and that we cannot influence its development by any direct tinkering with words and con-structions. So far as the general tone or spirit of a language goes, this may be true, but it is not true in detail. Silly words and expressions have often disappeared, not through any evolutionary process but owing to the conscious action of a minority. Two recent examples were *explore every avenue* and *leave no stone unturned,* which were killed by the jeers of a few journalists. There is a long list of flyblown metaphors which could similarly be got rid of if enough people would interest themselves in the job; and it should also be possible to laugh the *not un-* formation out of existence,[3] to reduce the amount of Latin and Greek in the average sentence, to drive out foreign phrases and strayed scientific words, and, in general, to make pretentiousness unfashionable. But all these are minor points. The defense of the English language implies more than this, and perhaps it is best to start by saying what it does *not* imply.

To begin with it has nothing to do with archaism, with 18 the salvaging of obsolete words and turns of speech, or with the setting up of a "standard English" which must never be departed from. On the contrary, it is especially concerned with the scrapping of every word or idiom which has outworn its usefulness. It has nothing to do with correct grammar and syntax, which are of no importance so long as one makes one's meaning clear, or with the avoidance of

---

[3] One can cure oneself of the *not un-* formation by memorizing this sentence: *A not unblack dog was chasing a not unsmall rabbit across a not ungreen field.*

Americanisms, or with having what is called a "good prose style." On the other hand it is not concerned with fake simplicity and the attempt to make written English colloquial. Nor does it even imply in every case preferring the Saxon word to the Latin one, though it does imply using the fewest and shortest words that will cover one's meaning. What is above all needed is to let the meaning choose the word, and not the other way about. In prose, the worst thing one can do with words is to surrender to them. When you think of a concrete object, you think wordlessly, and then, if you want to describe the thing you have been visualizing you probably hunt about till you find the exact words that seem to fit it. When you think of something abstract you are more inclined to use words from the start, and unless you make a conscious effort to prevent it, the existing dialect will come rushing in and do the job for you, at the expense of blurring or even changing your meaning. Probably it is better to put off using words as long as possible and get one's meaning as clear as one can through pictures or sensations. Afterward one can choose—not simply *accept*—the phrases that will best cover the meaning, and then switch round and decide what impression one's words are likely to make on another person. This last effort of the mind cuts out all stale or mixed images, all prefabricated phrases, needless repetitions, and humbug and vagueness generally. But one can often be in doubt about the effect of a word or a phrase, and one needs rules that one can rely on when instinct fails. I think the following rules will cover most cases:

(i) Never use a metaphor, simile, or other figure of speech which you are used to seeing in print.

(ii) Never use a long word where a short one will do.

(iii) If it is possible to cut a word out, always cut it out.

(iv) Never use the passive where you can use the active.

(v) Never use a foreign phrase, a scientific word, or a jargon word if you can think of an everyday English equivalent.

(vi) Break any of these rules sooner than say anything outright barbarous.

These rules sound elementary, and so they are, but they demand a deep change of attitude in anyone who has grown used to writing in the style now fashionable. One could keep all of them and still write bad English, but one could not write the kind of stuff that I quoted in those five specimens at the beginning of this article.

I have not here been considering the literary use of language, but merely language as an instrument for expressing and not for concealing or preventing thought. Stuart Chase and others have come near to claiming that all abstract words are meaningless, and have used this as a pretext for advocating a kind of political quietism. Since you don't know what Fascism is, how can you struggle against Fascism? One need not swallow such absurdities as this, but one ought to recognize that the present political chaos is connected with the decay of language, and that one can probably bring about some improvement by starting at the verbal end. If you simplify your English, you are freed from the worst follies of orthodoxy. You cannot speak any of the necessary dialects, and when you make a stupid remark its stupidity will be obvious, even to yourself. Political language—and with variations this is true of all political parties, from Conservatives to Anarchists—is designed to make lies sound truthful and murder respectable, and to give an appearance of solidity to pure wind. One cannot change this all in a moment, but one can at least change one's own habits, and from time to time one can even, if one jeers loudly enough, send some worn-out and useless phrase—some *jackboot, Achilles' heel, hotbed, melting pot, acid test, veritable inferno,* or other lump of verbal refuse—into the dustbin where it belongs.

VOCABULARY

paragraph 1: decadent, archaism, hansom cabs

paragraph 3: ducks and drakes, idioms, egregious, collocations, vocables, integrities, humanization, galvanization, canker, atrophy, virile, effete, languors, brazenly, mewing

paragraph 5: evocative, perverting

paragraph 6: symmetry, keynote, banal

paragraph 7: categorical, virtual, inexorable, expedite, ameliorate, extraneous, deracinated, clandestine, subaqueous, Anglo-Saxon, jargon, slovenliness

paragraph 8: totalitarian, reactionary, bourgeois

paragraph 9: commensurate

paragraph 10: parody

paragraph 11: humbug, euphonious, superfluous, scrupulous, debasement

paragraph 12: orthodoxy, phraseology

paragraph 13: euphemism, pacification, rectification

paragraph 15: inflated, cuttlefish, schizophrenia

paragraph 16: anaesthetizes

paragraph 18: Americanisms, colloquial, dialect

paragraph 19: quietism

QUESTIONS

1. How does the third example in Orwell's paragraph 3 help to explain the statement in paragraph 4 that "the concrete melts into the abstract"?

2. What visual image did *iron resolution* in paragraph 5 originally convey? What other dead metaphors can you cite, and what was the original significance?

3. Why is the passage cited in the footnote to paragraph 8 "almost completely lacking in meaning"? Given Orwell's criticisms in paragraph 8, what would be the proper use of language in art criticism?

4. Compare the passage from Ecclesiastes quoted in paragraph 9 (King James version) with modern renderings of it. Do you think these modern renderings are superior to Orwell's parody or to the King James version? Why?

5. "If you or I were to write a few lines on the uncertainty of human fortunes," why would the writing come nearer to Orwell's parody than to the sentence from Ecclesiastes?

6. Why are all issues "political issues" for Orwell?

7. Orwell says in paragraph 18 that his concern has not been to promote a "standard English" or "to make written English colloquial." Explain what he means here. Has he not recommended the use of plain English words? What exceptions would he allow?

SUGGESTIONS FOR WRITING

1. Analyze a paragraph from the catalog of your college or university to discover its tone and judge the writing according to the criteria Orwell proposes.

2. Analyze a letter to the editor of a newspaper or magazine and indicate the self-impression the writer wishes to create, the qualities of the prose, and the virtues or defects of the letter.

3. Analyze three paragraphs from a current textbook in one of your courses to determine how much needless jargon is employed and how well the writing meets the standard of good writing Orwell proposes.

4. Analyze a published speech of a major political figure (see the *New York Times, Vital Speeches,* or *Congressional Record*). How honest is the use of language? Compare this speech with another by the same person. How consistent is he or she in use of language?

RUSSELL BAKER

> RUSSELL BAKER *began his career in journalism as a reporter for the* Baltimore Sun, *and in 1954 began his long association with the* New York Times. *His column for the* Times *began in 1962. Baker is a keen observer of life in America and, as the essay reprinted here shows, a satirist of the pretentious language we often speak and write. His essays are collected in a number of books, including* All Things Considered *(1965) and* So This Is Depravity *(1980), and he has written about his life in* Growing Up *(1983) and* The Good Times *(1989). In 1979 he was awarded the Pulitzer Prize for Journalism.*

Little Red Riding Hood Revisited

In an effort to make the classics accessible to contemporary readers, I am translating them into the modern American language. Here is the translation of "Little Red Riding Hood": 1

Once upon a point in time, a small person named Little 2
Red Riding Hood initiated plans for the preparation, delivery
and transportation of foodstuffs to her grandmother, a
senior citizen residing at a place of residence in a forest of
indeterminate dimension.

In the process of implementing this program, her incur- 3
sion into the forest was in mid-transportation process when
it attained interface with an alleged perpetrator. This individual, a wolf, made inquiry as to the whereabouts of Little
Red Riding Hood's goal as well as inferring that he was
desirous of ascertaining the contents of Little Red Riding
Hood's foodstuffs basket, and all that.

"It would be inappropriate to lie to me," the wolf said, 4
displaying his huge jaw capability. Sensing that he was a
mass of repressed hostility intertwined with acute alienation,
she indicated.

"I see you indicating," the wolf said, "but what I don't 5
see is whatever it is you're indicating at, you dig?"

Little Red Riding Hood indicated more fully, making 6
one thing perfectly clear—to wit, that it was to her grandmother's residence and with a consignment of foodstuffs
that her mission consisted of taking her to and with.

At this point in time the wolf moderated his rhetoric and 7
proceeded to grandmother's residence. The elderly person
was then subjected to the disadvantages of total consumption
and transferred to residence in the perpetrator's stomach.

"That will raise the old woman's consciousness," the 8
wolf said to himself. He was not a bad wolf, but only a victim
of an oppressive society, a society that not only denied
wolves' rights, but actually boasted of its capacity for keeping
the wolf from the door. An interior malaise made itself
manifest inside the wolf.

"Is that the national malaise I sense within my digestive 9
tract?" wondered the wolf. "Or is it the old person seeking to
retaliate for her consumption by telling wolf jokes to my
duodenum?" It was time to make a judgment. The time was
now, the hour had struck, the body lupine cried out for
decision. The wolf was up to the challenge. He took two
stomach powders right away and got into bed.

The wolf had adopted the abdominal-distress recovery 10
posture when Little Red Riding Hood achieved his presence.

"Grandmother," she said, "your ocular implements are 11 of an extraordinary order of magnitude."

"The purpose of this enlarged viewing capability," said 12 the wolf, "is to enable your image to register a more precise impression upon my sight systems."

"In reference to your ears," said Little Red Riding Hood, 13 "it is noted with the deepest respect that far from being underprivileged, their elongation and enlargement appear to qualify you for unparalleled distinction."

"I hear you loud and clear, kid," said the wolf, "but 14 what about these new choppers?"

"If it is not inappropriate," said Little Red Riding Hood, 15 "it might be observed that with your new miracle masticating products you may even be able to chew taffy again."

This observation was followed by the adoption of an 16 aggressive posture on the part of the wolf and the assertion that it was also possible for him, due to the high efficiency ratio of his jaw, to consume little persons, plus, as he stated, his firm determination to do so at once without delay and with all due process and propriety, notwithstanding the fact that the ingestion of one entire grandmother had already provided twice his daily recommended cholesterol intake.

There ensued flight by Little Red Riding Hood accom- 17 panied by pursuit in respect to the wolf and a subsequent intervention on the part of a third party, heretofore unnoted in the record.

Due to the firmness of the intervention, the wolf's 18 stomach underwent ax-assisted aperture with the result that Red Riding Hood's grandmother was enabled to be removed with only minor discomfort.

The wolf's indigestion was immediately alleviated with 19 such effectiveness that he signed a contract with the intervening third party to perform with grandmother in a television commercial demonstrating the swiftness of this dramatic relief for stomach discontent.

"I'm going to be on television," cried grandmother. 20

And they all joined her happily in crying, "What a 21 phenomena!"

VOCABULARY

paragraph 2: initiated, indeterminate, dimension

paragraph 3: implementing, incursion, interface, alleged, perpetrator, ascertaining

paragraph 4: intertwined, alienation

paragraph 6: consignment

paragraph 7: rhetoric

paragraph 8: interior, malaise, manifest

paragraph 9: lupine

paragraph 11: ocular, implements

paragraph 13: elongation

paragraph 15: masticating

paragraph 16: posture, propriety, ingestion, cholesterol

paragraph 18: aperture

paragraph 19: alleviated

paragraph 21: phenomena

QUESTIONS

1. The faddish language Baker parodies reflects faddish ideas. Here is one example: "An interior malaise made itself manifest inside the wolf." What current attitude toward human predators is Baker satirizing? How does the language help him to satirize the idea?

2. Red Riding Hood prefers the farfetched to the simple, as in the expression "ocular implements." What others examples can you find of euphemism, circumlocution, and other faults of diction?

3. What examples of repetitious phrasing and sentence padding do you find?

4. What kind of advertising language is Baker satirizing toward the end of his version?

5. What is the difference between the wolf's language and Red Riding Hood's? What does the wolf's language tell you about his personality and view of the world?

6. What other ideas is Baker satirizing in the course of his telling of the story?

SUGGESTION FOR WRITING

Rewrite another fairy tale in the modish language of advertising or other contemporary jargons and styles. Let your choice of jargon and style make a point—or several points—as Baker's telling of "Little Red Riding Hood" does.

MORE ON FAULTY DICTION

The following suggestions supplement those of Orwell in his essay, and will help you identify the faults in diction that Russell Baker is satirizing in the essay on pages 492–94.

1. Using the same word more than once in a sentence can be confusing if the senses are different:

   We were present for the presentation of the award.

   However, we need not avoid repeating a word if the senses are the same. Indeed, substitution can also be confusing:

   The person who entered was not the individual I was expecting.

   Though *individual* is a popular synonym for *person*, it has other meanings. The substitution may confuse the reader.

2. Needless repetition can make sentences hard to understand:

   There are necessary skills that writers need to make their ideas easy to understand and comprehensible.

3. Words that overlap in meaning can have the same effect:

   The result of the survey should produce a change in policy.

   The words *result* and *produce* mean the same thing here. Better:

   The survey should produce a change in policy.

4. Euphemism—providing a mild or pleasant substitute for a blunt term—can be a source of ambiguity. The euphemism *delinquent* to describe a juvenile criminal or the words *slow* and *retarded* to describe children who have trouble learning or are crippled mentally help us avoid giving pain. What words should we use in speaking about children who have trouble learning or have broken the law? We know the price of speaking bluntly, but also the price of hiding facts.

5. Equivocal terms are also a source of ambiguity because they have double meanings. The word *exceptional* is widely used to describe bright children as well as crippled ones or children who

have broken the law. We need to know what children we are talking about.

6. A cliché is a phrase or saying that has become trite through overuse: *sweet as sugar, conspicuous by his absence, outwore his welcome.* Clichés rob prose of conviction and vigor.

7. Mixed metaphors cause confusion and can be unintentionally funny:

   Blows to one's pride stick in the craw.

8. Technical words or jargon can also have the same effect. The words *interface* (to describe the boundary between two independent machines) and *software* (to describe accessory equipment) are useful words in computer language. They become jargon in a different sense of the word—to quote H. W. Fowler, "talk that is considered both ugly-sounding and hard to understand"— when borrowed to describe other things. A conference is not an "interface," and referring to a book as "software" suggests something mechanical or perhaps dispensable.

9. Circumlocution means taking the long way around—in other words, saying something in inflated language: saying "he has difficulty distinguishing the real from the imagined" when we mean "he lies." Euphemisms often depend on inflation of this kind.

MATTERS OF STYLE— THE SENTENCE

INTRODUCTION

This part of the book will show you how to make your sentences more effective as you draft and revise your paragraphs and essays. Unity and proper emphasis are just as important in sentences as they are in paragraphs. In fact, sentences can be loosely viewed as miniature paragraphs. For example, in the same way that the topic sentence of a paragraph states the core idea that the remainder of the paragraph develops, the main clause of a simple or complex sentence states the core idea that the rest of the sentence develops through its modifiers:

> I *heard* instead the shriek of brakes, the heavy throbbing of the once-a-day Braniff airliner into Minot, the shattering sirens born of war, the honk of a diesel locomotive which surely cannot call to faraway places the heart of a wakeful boy like the old steam whistle in the night.—Eric Sevareid, "Velva, North Dakota" [italics added]

The core subject and verb of this complex sentence (*I heard*) is completed by a series of modified objects—the final object further modified by a lengthy subordinate clause beginning with the word *which*.

Just as a series of main ideas combine in a single paragraph, so can simple and compound sentences join to form larger, single sentences:

> You can walk down the streets of my town now and hear from open windows the intimate voices of the Washington commentators in casual converse on the great affairs of state [*simple sentence: main clause with compound predicate*]; but you cannot hear on Sunday morning the singing in Norwegian of the Lutheran hymns [*simple sentence: main clause with simple predicate*]; the old country seems now part of a world left long behind and the old-country accents grow fainter in the speech of my Velva neighbors [*compound sentence: two main clauses with simple predicates*].—Sevareid

And so can main and subordinate ideas, expressed in main and subordinate clauses and their modifiers, combine to form larger sentences:

> Attic and screen porch are slowly vanishing [*main clause*] and lovely shades of pastel are painted upon new houses [*main clause*], tints that once would have embarrassed farmer and merchant alike [*subordinate clause modifying the appositive "tints"*].—Sevareid

Though the parallel between paragraphs and sentences suggested here is not exact (main clauses do not always contain the most important idea of a sentence), it does suggest that, like paragraphs, sentences build from cores to which subordinate ideas and details must relate. And sentences, like paragraphs, also can contain two or more core ideas.

We write as we speak—stressing the core idea of a simple sentence and joining several core ideas into compound ones. We also place modifying words, phrases, and clauses in different positions in writing, as in speech, to gain different kinds of emphasis. In addition, we frequently make special use of the beginning and ending of the simple sentence for emphasis. We can, however, achieve emphasis in other ways. The following sections illustrate these possibilities.

Addition and Modification

❦ ❦ ❦

As a paragraph usually begins with a topic sentence that states the subject or central idea, so the sentence may begin with a main clause that performs a similar job. Here is a sentence from Jane Jacobs' description of a New York street scene in the essay that follows:

> *Character dancers come on,*
>> *a strange old man* with strings of old shoes over his shoulders,
>> *motor-scooter riders* with big beards and girl friends who bounce on the back of the scooters and wear their hair long in front of their faces as well as behind,
>> *drunks* who follow the advice of the Hat Council and are always turned out in hats,
>>> but not hats the Council would approve.

The three additions—*strange old man, motor-scooter riders,* and *drunks*—make the main clause specific: they name the character dancers. Notice that these *appositives* (adjacent words or phrases that explain or identify another word) are considerably longer than the main clause. Notice, too, that the third appositive is itself modified. English sentences can be modified endlessly. They are not, however, because the reader would soon lose sight of the central idea. The length of a sentence often depends on how many ideas and details a reader can grasp.

JANE JACOBS

JANE JACOBS *has influenced current ideas on city architecture through her many articles and books. After completing high school in Scranton, Pennsylvania, Jacobs worked for a year as a newspaper reporter, then moved to New York City where she worked at various jobs and wrote articles about the city's*

503

working-class neighborhoods. In 1952 she became an associate editor of Architectural Forum. *Jacobs has long been critical of city planning that breaks up close-knit neighborhoods like Hudson Street with housing projects and "cultural centers" that disperse people. "These thin dispersions lack any reasonable degree of innate vitality, staying power, or inherent usefulness as settlements," she writes in her book,* The Death and Life of Great American Cities (1961), *which contains her description of Hudson Street. Jacobs is as effective a stylist as she is a thinker; her sentences, as this description shows, let us hear a personal voice—as if she were talking to us informally about the everyday world.*

Hudson Street

Under the seeming disorder of the old city, wherever the old city is working successfully, is a marvelous order for maintaining the safety of the streets and the freedom of the city. It is a complex order. Its essence is intricacy of sidewalk use, bringing with it a constant succession of eyes. This order is all composed of movement and change, and although it is life, not art, we may fancifully call it the art form of the city and liken it to the dance—not to a simple-minded precision dance with everyone kicking up at the same time, twirling in unison and bowing off en masse, but to an intricate ballet in which the individual dancers and ensembles all have distinctive parts which miraculously reinforce each other and compose an orderly whole. The ballet of the good city sidewalk never repeats itself from place to place, and in any one place is always replete with new improvisations. 1

The stretch of Hudson Street where I live is each day the scene of an intricate sidewalk ballet. I make my own first entrance into it a little after eight when I put out the garbage can, surely a prosaic occupation, but I enjoy my part, my little clang, as the droves of junior high school students walk by the center of the stage dropping candy wrappers. (How do they eat so much candy so early in the morning?) 2

While I sweep up the wrappers I watch the other rituals of morning: Mr. Halpert unlocking the laundry's handcart from its mooring to a cellar door, Joe Cornacchia's son-in-law 3 stacking out the empty crates from the delicatessen, the barber bringing out his sidewalk folding chair, Mr. Goldstein arranging the coils of wire which proclaim the hardware store is open, the wife of the tenement's superintendent depositing her chunky three-year-old with a toy mandolin on the stoop, the vantage point from which he is learning the English his mother cannot speak. Now the primary children, heading for St. Luke's, dribble through to the south; the children for St. Veronica's Cross, heading to the west, and the children for P.S. 41, heading toward the east. Two new entrances are being made from the wings: well-dressed and even elegant women and men with brief cases emerge from doorways and side streets. Most of these are heading for the bus and subways, but some hover on the curbs, stopping taxis which have miraculously appeared at the right moment, for the taxis are part of a wider morning ritual: having dropped passengers from midtown in the downtown finan-cial district, they are now bringing downtowners up to midtown. Simultaneously, numbers of women in house-dresses have emerged and as they crisscross with one another they pause for quick conversations that sound with either laughter or joint indignation, never, it seems, anything between. It is time for me to hurry to work too, and I exchange my ritual farewell with Mr. Lofaro, the short, thick-bodied, white-aproned fruit man who stands outside his doorway a little up the street, his arms folded, his feet planted, looking solid as earth itself. We nod; we each glance quickly up and down the street, then look back to each other and smile. We have done this many a morning for more than ten years, and we both know what it means: All is well.

The heart-of-the-day ballet I seldom see, because part of [4] the nature of it is that working people who live there, like me, are mostly gone, filling the roles of strangers on other sidewalks. But from days off, I know enough of it to know that it becomes more and more intricate. Longshoremen who are not working that day gather at the White Horse or the Ideal or the International for beer and conversation. The executives and business lunchers from the industries just to the west throng the Dorgene restaurant and the Lion's Head coffee house; meat-market workers and communications scientists fill the bakery lunchroom. Character dancers come on, a strange old man with strings of old shoes over his shoulders, motor-scooter riders with big beards and girl friends who bounce on the back of the scooters and wear their hair long in front of their faces as well as behind, drunks who follow the advice of the Hat Council and are always turned out in hats, but not hats the Council would approve. Mr. Lacey, the locksmith, shuts up his shop for a while and goes to exchange the time of day with Mr. Slube at the cigar store. Mr. Koochagian, the tailor, waters the luxuriant jungle of plants in his window, gives them a critical look from the outside, accepts a compliment on them from two passers-by, fingers the leaves on the plane tree in front of our house with a thoughtful gardener's appraisal, and crosses the street for a bite at the Ideal where he can keep an eye on customers and wigwag across the message that he is coming. The baby carriages come out, and clusters of everyone from toddlers with dolls to teenagers with homework gather at the stoops.

When I get home after work, the ballet is reaching its 5 crescendo. This is the time of roller skates and stilts and tricycles, and games in the lee of the stoop with bottletops and plastic cowboys; this is the time of bundles and packages, zigzagging from the drug store to the fruit stand and back over to the butcher's; this is the time when teenagers, all dressed up, are pausing to ask if their slips show or their collars look right; this is the time when beautiful girls get out of MG's; this is the time when the fire engines go through; this is the time when anybody you know around Hudson Street will go by.

As darkness thickens and Mr. Halpert moors the laun- 6 dry cart to the cellar door again, the ballet goes on under lights, eddying back and forth but intensifying at the bright spotlight pools of Joe's sidewalk pizza dispensary, the bars, the delicatessen, the restaurant and the drug store. The night workers stop now at the delicatessen, to pick up salami and a container of milk. Things have settled down for the evening but the street and its ballet have not come to a stop.

I know the deep night ballet and its season best from 7 waking long after midnight to tend a baby and, sitting in the dark, seeing the shadows and hearing the sounds of the sidewalk. Mostly it is a sound like infinitely pattering

ADDITION AND MODIFICATION **507**

snatches of party conversation and, about three in the morning, singing, very good singing. Sometimes there is sharpness and anger or sad, sad weeping, or a flurry of search for a string of beads broken. One night a young man came roaring along, bellowing terrible language at two girls whom he had apparently picked up and who were disappointing him. Doors opened, a wary semicircle formed around him, not too close, until the police came. Out came the heads, too, along Hudson Street, offering opinion, "Drunk . . . Crazy . . . A wild kid from the suburbs."*

Deep in the night, I am almost unaware how many **8** people are on the street unless something calls them together, like the bagpipe. Who the piper was and why he favored our street I have no idea. The bagpipe just skirled out in the February night, and as if it were a signal the random, dwindled movements of the sidewalk took on direction. Swiftly, quietly, almost magically a little crowd was there, a crowd that evolved into a circle with a Highland fling inside it. The crowd could be seen on the shadowy sidewalk, the dancers could be seen, but the bagpiper himself was almost invisible because his bravura was all in his music. He was a very little man in a plain brown overcoat. When he finished and vanished, the dancers and watchers applauded, and applause came from the galleries too, half a dozen of the hundred windows on Hudson Street. Then the windows closed, and the little crowd dissolved into the random movements of the night street.

The strangers on Hudson Street, the allies whose eyes **9** help us natives keep the peace of the street, are so many that they always seem to be different people from one day to the next. That does not matter. Whether they are so many always-different people as they seem to be, I do not know. Likely they are. When Jimmy Rogan fell through a plate-glass window (he was separating some scuffling friends) and almost lost his arm, a stranger in an old T shirt emerged from the Ideal bar, swiftly applied an expert tourniquet and, according to the hospital's emergency staff, saved Jimmy's life. Nobody remembered seeing the man before and no one

---

* He turned out to be a wild kid from the suburbs. Sometimes, on Hudson Street, we are tempted to believe the suburbs must be a difficult place to bring up children.

has seen him since. The hospital was called in this way: a woman sitting on the steps next to the accident ran over to the bus stop, wordlessly snatched the dime from the hand of a stranger who was waiting with his fifteen-cent fare ready, and raced into the Ideal's phone booth. The stranger raced after her to offer the nickel too. Nobody remembered seeing him before, and no one has seen him since. When you see the same stranger three or four times on Hudson Street, you begin to nod. This is almost getting to be an acquaintance, a public acquaintance, of course.

I have made the daily ballet of Hudson Street sound 10 more frenetic than it is, because writing it telescopes it. In real life, it is not that way. In real life, to be sure, something is always going on, the ballet is never at a halt, but the general effect is peaceful and the general tenor even leisurely. People who know well such animated city streets will know how it is. I am afraid people who do not will always have it a little wrong in their heads—like the old prints of rhinoceroses made from travelers' descriptions of rhinoceroses.

On Hudson Street, the same as in the North End of 11 Boston or in any other animated neighborhoods of great cities, we are not innately more competent at keeping the sidewalks safe than are the people who try to live off the hostile truce of Turf in a blind-eyed city. We are the lucky possessors of a city order that makes it relatively simple to keep the peace because there are plenty of eyes on the street. But there is nothing simple about that order itself, or the bewildering number of components that go into it. Most of those components are specialized in one way or another. They unite in their joint effect upon the sidewalk, which is not specialized in the least. That is its strength.

QUESTIONS

1. The main clause in the first sentence of paragraph 3 is followed by a series of appositives explaining the *rituals of morning.* How many appositives do you find? Which of them is modified?

2. The colon in the following sentence introduces an addition that explains the main clause:

Two new entrances are being made from the wings: well-dressed and even elegant women and men with brief cases emerge from doorways and side streets.

Does the colon in the succeeding sentence, in paragraph 3, serve the same purpose? What about the colon in the concluding sentence of the paragraph?

3. The second sentence of paragraph 5 might have been divided into four separate sentences. What does the author gain by joining the main clauses through semicolons? Are the semicolons in paragraph 3 used in the same way?

4. Notice that the main clause of the first sentence of paragraph 6 is modified by the opening subordinate clause and by the phrases that follow, beginning with *eddying*. Try rewriting the sentence, beginning with *eddying*. Try rewriting the sentence, beginning with the main clause. Can you put the opening subordinate clause elsewhere in the sentence without obscuring the meaning?

5. What point is Jacobs making about the "daily ballet" of Hudson Street? How do the various details illustrate her point?

6. Jacobs is defining what makes a New York street a neighborhood. How different is this neighborhood from yours?

SUGGESTIONS FOR WRITING

1. Explain why the specialization in each of the "bewildering number of components" that make up the street is the source of its strength. Show how Jacobs illustrates this strength.

2. Develop the following main clauses through addition of your own details. Use colons and semicolons if you wish:

   a. "Deep in the night, I am almost unaware how many people are on the street . . ."

   b. "The crowd could be seen on the shadowy sidewalk . . ."

   c. "People who know well such animated city streets will know how it is . . ."

EMPHASIS

❦ ❦ ❦

The speaker of the following sentence, a witness before a congressional committee, repeats certain phrases and qualifies his ideas in a typical way:

> My experience is that we hold people sometimes in jail, young people in jail, for days at a time with a complete lack of concern of the parents, if they do live in homes where parents live together, a complete lack of concern in many instances on the part of the community or other agencies as to where these young people are or what they are doing.

Sentences as complex and disjointed as this one seems when transcribed are understood easily when spoken. In speaking, we often interrupt the flow of ideas to emphasize a word or phrase or to repeat an idea. Written punctuation sometimes clarifies the points of emphasis, but in a limited way. We cannot depend directly on vocal inflection for clarity and emphasis in writing; we can suggest these inflections by shaping the sentence in accord with ordinary speech patterns. Clearly written sentences stay close to these patterns.

The core of English sentences, we saw, can be expanded, and at length, if each modifier is clearly connected to what precedes it. To achieve special emphasis the writer may vary the sentence even more, perhaps by making special use of the end of the sentence— the position that in English tends to be the most emphatic:

> The cold passed reluctantly from the earth, and the retiring fogs revealed an army stretched out on the hills, *resting.*—Stephen Crane, *The Red Badge of Courage* [italics added]

Or the writer may break up the sentence so that individual ideas and experiences receive separate emphasis:

> The youth stopped. He was transfixed by this terrific medley of all noises. It was as if worlds were being rended. There was the ripping sound of musketry and the breaking crash of the artillery.—Stephen Crane

English word order largely controls the relation of subordinate clauses to other elements in a sentence. The position of subordinate clauses that serve as nouns or adjectives (sometimes called noun clauses and adjective clauses) is rather fixed; the position of subordinate clauses that serve as adverbs (sometimes called adverb clauses) is not. The position of the adverb clause depends on its importance as an idea and on its length:

I majored in zoology *because I like working with animals.*

Because I like working with animals, I majored in zoology.

The position of the subordinate clause determines what information is stressed. In the first sentence, the subordinate clause seems to express the more important idea because it follows the main clause. In the second sentence, the main clause receives the emphasis. But the end of the sentence will not take the thrust of meaning if ideas appearing toward the beginning are given special emphasis.

Our informal spoken sentences show the least variation and depend heavily on coordination. The *stringy sentence* in writing—a series of ideas joined loosely with *and* and other conjunctions—is a heavily coordinated sentence without the usual vocal markers. The sentence *fragment*—a detached phrase or clause, or a sentence missing either a subject or a verb—sometimes derives from the clipped sentences and phrases common in speech.

MARK TWAIN

Born and reared in Hannibal, Missouri, on the Mississippi River, SAMUEL CLEMENS *(1835–1910) worked as a river pilot from 1857 to 1861. He wrote about these experiences in* Life on the Mississippi, *published in 1883. Like the boy described in the passage reprinted here, Twain ran away to go on the river, but without immediate success: "Months afterward the hope within me struggled to a reluctant death, and I found myself without an ambition. But I was ashamed to go home." Eventually he did become a cub pilot on a river boat. Later, working as a newspaper reporter, he adopted the pen name "Mark Twain," the term of leadsmen on river boats for "two fathoms deep."*

The Steamboatman

[1]When I was a boy, there was but one permanent ambition among my comrades in our village on the west bank of the Mississippi River. [2]That was, to be a steamboatman. [3]We had transient ambitions of other sorts, but they were only transient. [4]When a circus came and went, it left us all burning to become clowns; the first negro minstrel show that ever came to our section left us all suffering to try that kind of life; now and then we had a hope that, if we lived and were good, God would permit us to be pirates. [5]These ambitions faded out, each in its turn; but the ambition to be a steamboatman always remained.

[6]Once a day a cheap, gaudy packet arrived upward from St. Louis, and another downward from Keokuk. [7]Before these events, the day was glorious with expectancy; after them, the day was a dead and empty thing. [8]Not only the boys, but the whole village, felt this. [9]After all these years I can picture that old time to myself now, just as it was then: the white town drowsing in the sunshine of a summer's morning; the streets empty, or pretty nearly so; one or two clerks sitting in front of the Water Street stores, with their splint-bottomed chairs tilted back against the walls, chins on breasts, hats slouched over their faces, asleep—with shingle-shavings enough around to show what broke them down; a sow and a litter of pigs loafing along the sidewalk, doing a good business in watermelon rinds and seeds; two or three lonely little freight piles scattered about the "levee"; a pile of "skids" on the slope of the stone-paved wharf, and the fragrant town drunkard asleep in the shadow of them; two or three wood flats at the head of the wharf, but nobody to listen to the peaceful lapping of the wavelets against them; the great Mississippi, the majestic, the magnificent Mississippi, rolling its mile-wide tide along, shining in the sun; the dense forest away on the other side; the "point" above the town, and the "point" below, bounding the river-glimpse and turning it into a sort of sea, and withal a very still and brilliant and lonely one. [10]Presently a film of dark smoke appears above one of those remote "points"; instantly a negro drayman, famous for his quick eye and prodigious voice, lifts up the cry, "S-t-e-a-m-boat a-comin'!" and the

scene changes! [11]The town drunkard stirs, the clerks wake up, a furious clatter of drays follows, every house and store pours out a human contribution, and all in a twinkling the dead town is alive and moving. [12]Drays, carts, men, boys, all go hurrying from many quarters to a common center, the wharf. [13]Assembled there, the people fasten their eyes upon the coming boat as upon a wonder they are seeing for the first time. [14]And the boat *is* rather a handsome sight, too. [15]She is long and sharp and trim and pretty; she has two tall, fancy-topped chimneys, with a gilded device of some kind swung between them; a fanciful pilot-house, all glass and "gingerbread," perched on top of the "texas" deck[1] behind them; the paddleboxes are gorgeous with a picture or with gilded rays above the boat's name; the boiler-deck, the hurricane-deck, and the texas deck are fenced and orna- mented with clean white railings; there is a flag gallantly flying from the jack-staff; the furnace doors are open and the fires glaring bravely; the upper decks are black with passen- gers; the captain stands by the big bell, calm, imposing, the envy of all; great volumes of the blackest smoke are rolling and tumbling out of the chimneys—a husbanded grandeur created with a bit of pitch-pine just before arriving at a town; the crew are grouped on the forecastle; the broad stage is run far out over the port bow, and an envied deck-hand stands picturesquely on the end of it with a coil of rope in his hand; the pent steam is screaming through the gaugecocks; the captain lifts his hand, a bell rings, the wheels stop; then they turn back, churning the water to foam, and the steamer is at rest. [16]Then such a scramble as there is to get aboard, and to get ashore, and to take in freight and to discharge freight, all at one and the same time; and such a yelling and cursing as the mates facilitate it all with! [17]Ten minutes later the steamer is under way again, with no flag on the jack-staff and no black smoke issuing from the chimneys.[18] After ten more minutes the town is dead again, and the town drunkard asleep by the skids once more.

[19]My father was a justice of the peace, and I supposed he possessed the power of life and death over all men, and

---

[1] The deck above the officers' quarters.—Ed.

could hang anybody that offended him. [20]This was distinction enough for me as a general thing; but the desire to be a steamboatman kept intruding, nevertheless. [21]I first wanted to be a cabin-boy, so that I could come out with a white apron on and shake a tablecloth over the side, where all my old comrades could see me; later I thought I would rather be the deck-hand who stood on the end of the stage-plank with the coil of rope in his hand, because he was particularly conspicuous. [22]But these were only daydreams—they were too heavenly to be contemplated as real possibilities. [23]By and by one of our boys went away. [24]He was not heard of for a long time. [25]At last he turned up as apprentice engineer or "striker" on a steamboat. [26]This thing shook the bottom out of all my Sunday-school teachings. [27]That boy had been notoriously worldly, and I just the reverse; yet he was exalted to this eminence, and I left in obscurity and misery. [28]There was nothing generous about this fellow in his greatness. [29]He would always manage to have a rusty bolt to scrub while his boat tarried at our town, and he would sit on the inside guard and scrub it where we all could see him and envy him and loathe him. [30]And whenever his boat was laid up he would come home and swell around the town in his blackest and greasiest clothes, so that nobody could help remembering that he was a steamboatman; and he used all sorts of steamboat technicalities in his talk, as if he were so used to them that he forgot common people could not understand them. [31]He would speak of the "labboard" side of a horse in an easy, natural way that would make one wish he was dead. [32]And he was always talking about "St. Looy" like an old citizen; he would refer casually to occasions when he was "coming down Fourth Street," or when he was "passing by the Planter's House," or when there was a fire and he took a turn on the brakes of "the old Big Missouri"; and then he would go on and lie about how many towns the size of ours were burned down there that day. [33]Two or three of the boys had long been persons of consideration among us because they had been to St. Louis once and had a vague general knowledge of its wonders, but the day of their glory was over now. [34]They lapsed into a humble silence, and learned to disappear when the ruthless "cub"-engineer approached. [35]This fellow had money, too, and hair-oil. [36]Also an ignorant silver watch and a showy brass watch-chain. [37]He wore a leather belt and used no suspenders. [38]If ever a youth was cordially admired and hated by his comrades, this one was. [39]No girl could withstand his charms. [40]He "cut out" every boy in the village. [41]When his boat blew up at last, it diffused a tranquil contentment among us such as we had not known for months. [42]But when he came home the next week, alive, renowned, and appeared in church all battered up and bandaged, a shining hero, stared at and wondered over by everybody, it seemed to us that the partiality of Providence for an undeserving reptile had reached a point where it was open to criticism.

[43]This creature's career could produce but one result, and it speedily followed. [44]Boy after boy managed to get on the river. [45]The minister's son became an engineer. [46]The doctor's and the postmaster's sons became "mud clerks"[2]; the wholesale liquor dealer's son became a barkeeper on a boat; four sons of the chief merchant, and two sons of the county judge, became pilots. [47]Pilot was the grandest position of all. [48]The pilot, even in those days of trivial wages, had a princely salary—from a hundred and fifty to two hundred and fifty dollars a month, and no board to pay. [49]Two months of his wages would pay a preacher's salary for a year. [50]Now some of us were left disconsolate. [51]We could not get on the river—at least our parents would not let us.

[52]So, by and by, I ran away. [53]I said I would never come home again till I was a pilot and could come in glory. [54]But somehow I could not manage it. [55]I went meekly aboard a few of the boats that lay packed together like sardines at the long St. Louis wharf, and humbly inquired for the pilots, but got only a cold shoulder and short words from mates and clerks. [56]I had to make the best of this sort of treatment for the time being, but I had comforting day-dreams of a future when I should be a great and honored pilot, with plenty of money, and could kill some of these mates and clerks and pay for them.

---

[2] The second clerk on river steamers who went ashore to take account of freight.—Ed.

QUESTIONS

1. How does Twain give equal emphasis to the many sights described in sentence 9? How do sentences 15 and 46 resemble sentence 9 in structure and emphasis?

2. How does sentence 11 build in emphasis? How does sentence 16?

3. Rewrite sentence 19, subordinating one of the clauses. How does your revision affect the emphasis of ideas in the original sentence?

4. Combine sentences 35, 36, and 37 into a single sentence. What does your revision gain or lose in emphasis?

5. How does Twain build sentences 41 and 42 to give the end of the sentences the greatest emphasis?

6. Where does Twain mix short and long sentences to emphasize certain perceptions and feelings?

7. What emotions does Twain convey, and what examples can you cite of how sentence construction conveys these emotions and creates a mood?

8. How well does Twain convey the sense of childhood aspiration and frustration?

SUGGESTIONS FOR WRITING

1. Rewrite several of Twain's sentences, giving different emphasis to his ideas through a different coordination and subordination of sentence elements.

2. Twain says in his autobiography: "The truth is, a person's memory has no more sense than his conscience and no appreciation whatever of values and proportions." Discuss how his picture of the Missouri town and the coming of the steamboat illustrates this statement. Then develop the same idea from your own personal experience and observation.

3. Write a characterization of Mark Twain, the man and the humorist, through the details and other revealing features of his essay. Stress the qualities that most stand out.

LOOSE AND PERIODIC SENTENCES

❦ ❦ ❦

Sentences are sometimes classified as loose or periodic to distinguish two important kinds of emphasis: the use made of the beginning or the end of the sentence. The loose sentence begins with the core idea, explanatory and qualifying phrases and clauses trailing behind:

> It was not a screeching noise, only an intermittent hump-hump as if the bird had to recall his grievance each time before he repeated it.—Flannery O'Connor, *The Violent Bear It Away*

If the ideas that follow the core are afterthoughts, or inessential details, the sentence will seem "loose"—easy and relaxed in its movement, perhaps even plodding if the content of the sentence permits:

> His eyes glittered like open pits of light as he moved across the sand, dragging his crushed shadow behind him.—Flannery O'Connor

A subordinate element will not seem unemphatic or plodding, however, if it expresses a strong action or idea and the details cumulate:

> He beat louder and louder, bamming at the same time with his free fist until he felt he was shaking the house.—Flannery O'Connor

Opening with modifiers or with a series of appositives, the periodic sentence ends with the core:

> Living this way by the creek, where the light appears and vanishes on the water, where muskrats surface and dive, and redwings scatter, I have come to know a special side of nature.—Annie Dillard, *Pilgrim at Tinker Creek*

The strongly periodic sentence is usually reserved for moderate or unusually strong emphasis:

> Partway down the long, very steep slop of Loma Vista Drive, descending through Beverly Hills, with the city of Los Angeles spread out far below the houses of sparkling opulence on either side, there is a sign warning "Use Lowest Gear" and, shortly after that, a sign that says "Runaway Vehicle Escape Lane 600 Feet Ahead."—James Stevenson, "Loma Vista Drive"

> To believe your own thought, to believe that what is true for you in your private heart is true for all men—that is *genius.*—Ralph Waldo Emerson, "Self-Reliance"

Most contemporary English sentences fall between the extremely loose and the extremely periodic. Compound sentences seem loose when succeeding clauses serve as afterthoughts or qualifications rather than as ideas equal in importance to the opening idea:

> I was very conscious of the crowds at first, almost despairing to have to perform in front of them, and I never got used to it.—George Plimpton, *Paper Lion*

Periodic sentences are used sparingly, with emphasis distributed more often throughout the whole sentence, as in Dillard's sentence above. Sometimes two moderately periodic sentences will be coordinated, with a corresponding distribution of emphasis:

> Though reliable narration is by no means the only way of conveying to the audience the facts on which dramatic irony is based, it is a useful way, and in some works, works in which no one but the author can conceivably know what needs to be known, it may be indispensable.—Wayne C. Booth, *The Rhetoric of Fiction*

JOHN STEINBECK

John Steinbeck *(1902–1968) was born in the Salinas Valley of California, the setting of many of his stories and novels. In 1962 he received the Nobel Prize for Literature—a testimony to the great reputation of his fiction throughout the world. His greatest work is undoubtedly* The Grapes of Wrath*—an account of the Joads, a family who, dispossessed of their Oklahoma farm during the Great Depression, make an arduous journey to California. Steinbeck's account of Depression poverty and the exploitation of migrant workers—awarded the*

Pulitzer Prize in 1939—remains a powerful one. Toward the beginning of the novel, Steinbeck describes a turtle making its own difficult journey—a hint of what is to follow. Steinbeck's sentences are notable for the various ways they convey the movement of the turtle up the embankment.

The Turtle

[1]The sun lay on the grass and warmed it, and in the shade under the grass the insects moved, ants and ant lions to set traps for them, grasshoppers to jump into the air and flick their yellow wings for a second, sow bugs like little armadillos, plodding restlessly on many tender feet. [2]And over the grass at the roadside a land turtle crawled, turning aside for nothing, dragging his high-domed shell over the grass. [3]His hard legs and yellow-nailed feet threshed slowly through the grass, not really walking, but boosting and dragging his shell along. [4]The barley beards slid off his shell, and the clover burrs fell on him and rolled to the ground. [5]His horny beak was partly open, and his fierce, humorous eyes, under brows like fingernails, stared straight ahead. [6]He came over the grass leaving a beaten trail behind him, and the hill, which was the highway embankment, reared up ahead of him. [7]For a moment he stopped, his head held high. [8]He blinked and looked up and down. [9]At last he started to climb the embankment. [10]Front clawed feet reached forward but did not touch. [11]The hind feet kicked his shell along, and it scraped on the grass, and on the gravel. [12]As the embankment grew steeper and steeper, the more frantic were the efforts of the land turtle. [13]Pushing hind legs strained and slipped, boosting the shell along, and the horny head protruded as far as the neck could stretch. [14]Little by little the shell slid up the embankment until at last a parapet cut straight across its line of march, the shoulder of the road, a concrete wall four inches high. [15]As though they worked independently the hind legs pushed the shell against the wall. [16]The head upraised and peered over the wall to the broad smooth plain of cement. [17]Now the hands, braced on top of the wall, strained and lifted, and the shell came slowly up and rested its front end on the wall. [18]For a moment the

turtle rested. [19]A red ant ran into the shell, into the soft skin inside the shell, and suddenly head and legs snapped in, and the armored tail clamped in sideways. [20]The red ant was crushed between body and legs. [21]And one head of wild oats was clamped into the shell by a front leg. [22]For a long moment the turtle lay still, and then the neck crept out and the old humorous frowning eyes looked about and the legs and tail came out. [23]The back legs went to work, straining like elephant legs, and the shell tipped to an angle so that the front legs could not reach the level cement plain. [24]But higher and higher the hind legs boosted it, until at last the center of balance was reached, the front tipped down, the front legs scratched at the pavement, and it was up. [25]But the head of wild oats was held by its stem around the front legs.

QUESTIONS

1. The base idea in sentence 2 is *a land turtle crawled.* If this clause were moved to the end of the sentence, what change would occur in focus or meaning?

2. How does the structure of sentence 3 help us visualize the movement of the turtle? Is the sentence loose or periodic?

3. Consider this revision of sentence 7:

   His head held high, he stopped for a moment.

   Is the meaning of the original sentence changed?

4. Combine sentences 7, 8, and 9 into one sentence. What change in meaning, focus, or emphasis occurs?

5. Consider this revision of sentence 11:

   The hind feet kicking his shell along, it scraped on the grass and on the gravel.

   What is gained or lost in meaning or effect by the revision?

6. Sentences 11 and 12 both describe the action of the turtle— moving on the grass at the edge of the embankment, then moving up the steep part. What difference do you see in the structure of these sentences? How does each structure convey the action in a different way?

7. How does the coordinate structure of sentence 23 show that the movement of the legs and the tipping of the shell are not happening at the same time? How could Steinbeck change the

structure of the sentence to show the two actions occurring at the same time?

8. How does the structure of sentence 24 help us to visualize the action here?

SUGGESTION FOR WRITING

Steinbeck's turtle seems to many readers symbolic of the Joad family in *The Grapes of Wrath,* the novel in which this description of the turtle appears. Dispossessed of their Oklahoma farm during the Great Depression of the 1930s, they make an arduous journey to California. Discuss the qualities or attitudes that Steinbeck might be symbolizing in the turtle.

ANNIE DILLARD

In Pilgrim at Tinker Creek ANNIE DILLARD *(p. 453) says of the Virginia creeks in the Blue Ridge about which she writes: "It's a good place to live; there's a lot to think about. The creeks—Tinker and Carvin's—are an active mystery, fresh every minute." The following section is from the chapter "Seeing." "It's all a matter of keeping my eyes open," Dillard tells us. "Nature is like one of those line drawings of a tree that are puzzles for children. Can you find hidden in the leaves a duck, a house, a boy, a bucket, a zebra, and a boot? Specialists can find the most incredibly well-hidden things."*

At Tinker Creek

[1]Where Tinker Creek flows under the sycamore log bridge to the tear-shaped island, it is slow and shallow, fringed thinly in cattail marsh. [2]At this spot an astonishing bloom of life supports vast breeding populations of insects, fish, reptiles, birds, and mammals. [3]On windless summer evenings I stalk along the creek bank or straddle the sycamore log in absolute stillness, watching for muskrats. [4]The night I stayed too late

I was hunched on the log staring spellbound at spreading, reflected stains of lilac on the water. [5]A cloud in the sky suddenly lighted as if turned on by a switch; its reflection just as suddenly materialized on the water upstream, flat and floating, so that I couldn't see the creek bottom, or life in the water under the cloud. [6]Downstream, away from the cloud on the water, water turtles smooth as beans were gliding down with the current in a series of easy, weightless push-offs, as men bound on the moon. [7]I didn't know whether to trace the progress of one turtle I was sure of, risking sticking my face in one of the bridge's spider webs made invisible by the gathering dark, or take a chance on seeing the carp, or scan the mudbank in hope of seeing a muskrat, or follow the last of the swallows who caught at my heart and trailed it after them like streamers as they appeared from directly below, under the log, flying upstream with their tails forked, so fast.

[8]But shadows spread, and deepened, and stayed. [9]After thousands of years we're still strangers to darkness, fearful aliens in an enemy camp with our arms crossed over our chests. [10]I stirred. [11]A land turtle on the bank, startled, hissed the air from its lungs and withdrew into its shell. [12]An uneasy pink here, an unfathomable blue there, gave great suggestion of lurking beings. [13]Things were going on. [14]I couldn't see whether that sere rustle I heard was a distant rattlesnake, slit-eyed, or a nearby sparrow kicking in the dry flood debris slung at the foot of a willow. [15]Tremendous action roiled the water everywhere I looked, big action, inexplicable. [16]A tremor welled up beside a gaping muskrat burrow in the bank and I caught my breath, but no muskrat appeared. [17]The ripples continued to fan upstream with a steady, powerful thrust. [18]Night was knitting over my face an eyeless mask, and I still sat transfixed. [19]A distant airplane, a delta wing out of nightmare, made a gliding shadow on the creek's bottom that looked like a stingray cruising upstream. [20]At once a black fin slit the pink cloud on the water, shearing it in two. [21]The two halves merged together and seemed to dissolve before my eyes. [22]Darkness pooled in the cleft of the creek and rose, as water collects in a well. [23]Untamed, dreaming lights flickered over the sky. [24]I saw hints of hulking underwater shadows, two pale splashes

out of the water, and round ripples rolling close together from a blackened center.

[25]At last I stared upstream where only the deepest violet remained of the cloud, a cloud so high its underbelly still glowed feeble color reflected from a hidden sky lighted in turn by a sun halfway to China. [26]And out of that violet, a sudden enormous black body arced over the water. [27]I saw only a cylindrical sleekness. [28]Head and tail, if there was a head and tail, were both submerged in cloud. [29]I saw only one ebony fling, a headlong dive to darkness; then the waters closed, and the lights went out.

[30]I walked home in a shivering daze, up hill and down. [31]Later I lay open-mouthed in bed, my arms flung wide at my sides to steady the whirling darkness. [32]At this latitude I'm spinning 836 miles an hour round the earth's axis; I often fancy I feel my sweeping fall as a breakneck arc like the dive of dolphins, and the hollow rushing of wind raises hair on my neck and the side of my face. [33]In orbit around the sun I'm moving 64,800 miles an hour. [34]The solar system as a whole, like a merry-go-round unhinged, spins, bobs, and blinks at the speed of 43,200 miles an hour along a course set east of Hercules. [35]Someone has piped, and we are dancing a tarantella until the sweat pours. [36]I open my eyes and I see dark, muscled forms curl out of water, with flapping gills and flattened eyes. [37]I close my eyes and I see stars, deep stars giving way to deeper stars, deeper stars bowing to deepest stars at the crown of an infinite cone.

QUESTIONS

1. To make sentences 9 and 20 periodic sentences, open them with the modifying phrases that conclude them. Do these revisions change the meaning of the sentences or merely change the emphasis?

2. Revise sentences 23 and 33 to put the opening modifiers at the end. What is gained or lost in emphasis?

3. Break sentence 7 into its component parts and combine them into shorter sentences. Then discuss the differences in effect or meaning from the original sentence.

4. How do the following revisions of sentence 11 change the emphasis and effect:

    a. Startled, a land turtle on the bank hissed the air from its lungs and withdrew into its shell.

    b. Hissing the air from its lungs, a startled land turtle on the bank withdrew into its shell.

    c. A land turtle, hissing the air from its lungs, withdrew into its shell, startled.

Do the words *startled* and *hissing* refer clearly to the turtle in these revisions?

    d. How does the following revision change the effect of sentence 15?

Tremendous action—big action, inexplicable—roiled the water everywhere I looked.

5. How does sentence 37 build in emphasis?

6. What in the experience at Tinker Creek prompts the feelings Dillard describes in the final paragraph? What is the relationship between water and sky?

7. What implied thesis or idea is Dillard developing in the four paragraphs? What sentence comes closest to stating a thesis?

SUGGESTION FOR WRITING

Develop an implied thesis of your own through the details of an outdoor experience. You might build your description to the insight you reached into the world of nature as Dillard does.

CLIMAX

❦ ❦ ❦

Periodic sentences achieve climax by delaying the main idea or its completion until the end of the sentence. Even in loose or coordinated sentences, modifying or qualifying phrases and clauses following the main idea can be arranged in the order of rising importance—as in *I came, I saw, I conquered*. Here are sentences of Annie Dillard that do the same:

> But shadows spread, and deepened, and stayed.
>
> I close my eyes and I see stars, deep stars giving way to deeper stars, deeper stars bowing to deepest stars at the crown of an infinite cone.—*Pilgrim at Tinker Creek*

A sense of anticipation, promoted through the ideas themselves, is necessary to climax. Anticlimax will result if the culminating idea is less significant than what has gone before. The resulting letdown may be deliberately comic:

> If once a man indulges himself in murder, very soon he comes to think little of robbery; and from robbing he next comes to drinking and Sabbath-breaking, and from that to incivility and procrastination.—Thomas De Quincey, *Supplementary Papers*

JOHN UPDIKE

Born in Shillington, Pennsylvania, in 1932, JOHN UPDIKE *began his long association with* The New Yorker *early in his career and has published many of his poems, stories, and essays in that magazine. His collection of stories,* The Music School, *won the O. Henry Award in 1966. He received the National Book Award in 1963 for his novel* The Centaur *and the Pulitzer Prize and the American Book Award in 1981 for* Rabbit Is Rich. *The speaker in one of* JOHN UPDIKE's *stories is describing his grandmother as he remembers her from his youth. He says about her: "At the time I was married, she was in her late seventies, crippled and enfeebled. She had fought a long battle with Parkinson's disease; in my earliest memories of her she is touched with it. Her fingers and back are bent; there is a tremble about her as she moves about through the dark, odd-shaped rooms of our house in the town where I was born." His thoughts turn in this passage to happier days.*

My Grandmother

[1]When we were all still alive, the five of us in that kerosene-lit house, on Friday and Saturday nights, at an hour when in the spring and summer there was still abundant light in the air, I would set out in my father's car for town, where my friends lived. [2]I had, by moving ten miles away, at last acquired friends: an illustration of that strange law whereby, like Orpheus leading Eurydice, we achieve our desire by turning our back on it. [3]I had even gained a girl, so that the vibrations were as sexual as social that made me jangle with anticipation as I clowned in front of the mirror in our kitchen, shaving from a basin of stove-heated water, combing my hair with a dripping comb, adjusting my reflection in the mirror until I had achieved just that electric angle from which my face seemed beautiful and everlastingly, by the very volumes of air and sky and grass that lay mutely banked about our home, beloved. [4]My grandmother would hover near me, watching fearfully, as she had when I was a child, afraid that I would fall from a tree. [5]Delirious, humming, I would swoop and lift her, lift her like a child, crooking one arm under her knees and cupping the other behind her back. [6]Exultant in my height, my strength, I would lift that frail brittle body weighing perhaps a hundred pounds and twirl with it in my arms while the rest of the family watched with startled smiles of alarm. [7]Had I stumbled, or dropped her, I might have broken her back, but my joy always proved a secure cradle. [8]And whatever irony was in the impulse, whatever implicit contrast between this ancient husk, scarcely female, and the pliant, warm girl I would embrace before the evening was done, direct delight flooded away: I

was carrying her who had carried me, I was giving my past a dance, I had lifted the anxious caretaker of my childhood from the floor, I was bringing her with my boldness to the edge of danger, from which she had always sought to guard me.

QUESTIONS

1. How does Updike construct sentence 3 to take advantage of the strong terminal position? Does the context justify the double emphasis given to *beloved?*
2. Sentence 3 develops through an accumulation of detail. Does the sentence develop a single idea? Could Updike break it up without interrupting the meaning or disturbing the effect?
3. What technique aids in achieving the climax in sentences 5 and 8? Does the same kind of sentence construction achieve it?

SUGGESTIONS FOR WRITING

1. Describe an episode involving a close relative or friend that reveals a special relationship. Let your details reveal the relationship; do not state it directly.
2. Discuss how sentence climax conveys the sense of anticipation built into Updike's paragraph.

PARALLELISM

❦ ❦ ❦

The italicized words in the following sentence are parallel in structure; that is, they perform the same grammatical function in the sentence and, as infinitives, are the same in form:

> So long as I remain alive and well I shall continue *to feel* strongly about prose style, *to love* the surface of the earth, and *to take* a pleasure in solid objects and scraps of useless information.—George Orwell, *Why I Write* [italics added]

In speaking and writing, we make elements such as these infinitives parallel naturally. No matter how many words separate them, we continue the pattern we start. Indeed, our "sentence sense" tells us when a pattern has been interrupted. We know something is wrong when we read

> I shall continue to feel strongly about prose style, to love the surface of the earth, and taking pleasure in solid objects and scraps of useless information.

Parallelism is an important means to concision and focus in sentences. It also allows us to make additions to the sentence without loss of clarity.

A special use of parallelism is the balancing of similar ideas in a sentence for special emphasis:

> Violence ends by defeating itself. It creates bitterness in the survivors and brutality in the destroyers.—Martin Luther King, Jr., *Nonviolent Resistance*

Notice that the parallel phrases here are of the same weight and length. Writers can balance clauses and occasionally whole sentences in the same way:

> Every landscape in the world is full of these exact and beautiful adaptations, by which an animal fits into its environment like one cog-wheel into another. The sleeping hedgehog waits for the spring to burst its metabolism into life. The humming-bird beats the air and dips its needle-fine beak into hanging blossoms. Butterflies mimic

leaves and even noxious creatures to deceive their predators. The mole plods through the ground as if he had been designed as a mechanical shuttle.—J. Bronowski, *The Ascent of Man*

The marked rhythm of these sentences creates a highly formal effect by slowing the tempo. Such exact balance interrupts the natural flow of the sentence, giving emphasis to most or all of its parts. For this reason it is exceptional to find sentences as studied and formal as these in modern writing. But we do find a moderate balance used to give a greater emphasis to similar ideas than ordinary parallelism provides.

ERNESTO GALARZA

> ERNESTO GALARZA (1905–1984), *the American labor leader, teacher, and writer, was born in Jalcocotán, Nayarit, Mexico, and came to the United States when he was six. He went to school in Sacramento, and later studied at Occidental College and at Stanford and Columbia universities, receiving his Ph.D. in history and political science in 1947. Galarza's youthful experience as a farm and cannery worker prepared him for his life's work organizing agricultural workers. He taught at various universities and as Regents Professor at the University of California, San Diego. His books include the autobiography* Barrio Boy, *which describes his childhood in Mexico and California.*

Boyhood in a Sacramento Barrio

Our family conversations always occurred on our own 1 kitchen porch, away from the gringos. One or the other of the adults would begin: *Se han fijado?* Had we noticed—that the Americans do not ask permission to leave the room; that they had no respectful way of addressing an elderly person; that they spit brown over the railing of the porch into the yard; that when they laughed they roared; that they never brought *saludos* to everyone in your family from everyone in their family when they visited; that *General Delibree* was only a clerk; that *zopilotes* were not allowed on the streets to collect garbage; that the policemen did not carry lanterns at night; that Americans didn't keep their feet on the floor when they were sitting; that there was a special automobile for going to jail; that a rancho was not a rancho at all but a very small hacienda; that the saloons served their customers free eggs, pickles, and sandwiches; that instead of bullfighting, the gringos for sport tried to kill each other with gloves?

I did not have nearly the strong feelings on these   2
matters that Doña Henriqueta expressed. I felt a vague admiration for the way Mr. Brien could spit brown. Wayne, my classmate, laughed much better than the Mexicans, because he opened his big mouth wide and brayed like a donkey so he could be heard a block away. But it was the kind of laughter that made my mother tremble, and it was not permitted in our house.

Rules were laid down to keep me, as far as possible, *un*   3
muchacho bien educado. If I had to spit I was to do it privately, or if in public, by the curb, with my head down and my back to people. I was never to wear my cap in the house and I was to take it off even on the porch if ladies or elderly gentlemen were sitting. If I wanted to scratch, under no circumstances was I to do it right then and there, in company, like the Americans, but I was to excuse myself. If Catfish or Russell yelled to me from across the street I was not to shout back. I was never to ask for tips for my errands or other services to the tenants of 418 L, for these were *atenciones* expected of me.

Above all I was never to fail in *respeto* to grownups, no   4
matter who they were. It was an inflexible rule; I addressed myself to *Señor* Big Singh, *Señor* Big Ernie, *Señora* Dodson, *Señor* Cho-ree Lopez.

My standing in the family, but especially with my   5
mother, depended on my keeping these rules. I was not punished for breaking them. She simply reminded me that it gave her acute *vergüenza* to see me act thus, and that I would never grow up to be a correct *jefe de familia* if I did not know how to be a correct boy. I knew what *vergüenza* was from feeling it time and again; and the notion of growing up to keep a tight rein over a family of my own was somehow satisfying.

In our musty apartment in the basement of 418 L, ours   6

remained a Mexican family. I never lost the sense that we were the same, from Jalco to Sacramento. There was the polished cedar box, taken out now and then from the closet to display our heirlooms. I had lost the rifle shells of the revolution, and Tio Tonche, too, was gone. But there was the butterfly sarape, the one I had worn through the Battle of Puebla; a black lace mantilla Doña Henriqueta modeled for us; bits of embroidery and lace she had made; the tin pictures of my grandparents; my report card signed by Señorita Bustamante and Don Salvador; letters from Aunt Esther; and the card with the address of the lady who had kept the Ajax for us. When our mementos were laid out on the bed I plunged my head into the empty box and took deep breaths of the aroma of *puro cedro,* pure Jalcocotán mixed with camphor.

We could have hung on the door of our apartment a sign 7 like those we read in some store windows—*Aquí se habla español.* We not only spoke Spanish, we read it. From the *Librería Española,* two blocks up the street, Gustavo and I bought novels for my mother, like *Genoveva de Brabante,* a paperback with the poems of Amado Nervo and a handbook of the history of Mexico. The novels were never read aloud, the poems and the handbook were. Nervo was the famous poet from Tepic, close enough to Jalcocotán to make him our own. And in the history book I learned to read for myself, after many repetitions by my mother, about the deeds of the great Mexicans Don Salvador had recited so vividly to the class in Mazatlán. She refused to decide for me whether Abraham Lincoln was as great as Benito Juarez, or George Washington braver than the priest Don Miguel Hidalgo. At school there was no opportunity to settle these questions because nobody seemed to know about Juarez or Hidalgo; at least they were never mentioned and there were no pictures of them on the walls.

The family talk I listened to with the greatest interest 8 was about Jalco. Wherever the conversation began it always turned to the pueblo, our neighbors, anecdotes that were funny or sad, the folk tales and the witchcraft, and our kinfolk, who were still there. I usually lay on the floor those winter evenings, with my feet toward the kerosene heater, watching on the ceiling the flickering patterns of the light filtered through the scrollwork of the chimney. As I listened once again I chased the *zopilote* away from Coronel, or watched José take Nerón into the forest in a sack. Certain things became clear about the *rurales* and why the young men were taken away to kill Yaqui Indians, and about the Germans, the Englishmen, the Frenchmen, the Spaniards, and the Americans who owned the haciendas, the railroads, the ships, the big stores, the breweries. They owned Mexico because President Porfirio Díaz had let them steal it, José explained as I listened. Now Don Francisco Madero had been assassinated for trying to get it back. On such threads of family talk I followed my own recollection of the years from Jalco—the attack on Mazatlán, the captain of Acaponeta, the camp El Nanchi and the arrival at Nogales on the flatcar.

Only when we ventured uptown did we feel like aliens 9 in a foreign land. Within the *barrio* we heard Spanish on the streets and in the alleys. On the railroad tracks, in the canneries, and along the riverfront there were more Mexicans than any other nationality. And except for the foremen, the work talk was in our language. In the secondhand shops, where the *barrio* people sold and bought furniture and clothing, there were Mexican clerks who knew the Mexican ways of making a sale. Families doubled up in decaying houses, cramping themselves so they could rent an extra room to *chicano* boarders, who accented the brown quality of our Mexican *colonia*.

VOCABULARY

barrio: neighborhood
Se han fijado?: Did you notice?
saludos: greetings
zopilotes: vultures, buzzards
un muchacho bien educado: a well-bred boy
atenciones: duties
respeto: respect
vergüenza: shame, embarrassment
jefe de familia: head of the family

puro cedro: pure cedar
Aquí se habla español: Spanish spoken here
Librería Española: Spanish Bookstore
rurales: rural mounted police
chicano: American of Mexican descent
colonia: colony

QUESTIONS

1. How does the author use parallelism in the third sentence of paragraph 1 to give equal emphasis to the various ideas?
2. How is the same use made of parallelism in paragraph 6?
3. Whole sentences can be parallel to one another. How much parallelism of this kind do you find in paragraph 3?
4. In general, how loose or how strict do you find the parallelism of Galarza's sentences? How formal an effect do his sentences create?
5. How do you believe children are best taught to respect people who are different from them culturally? How different from Galarza's was your training in manners?

SUGGESTIONS FOR WRITING

1. Galarza uses his account to say something about Mexican and American folkways and the changes brought about in moving from one world to another. Discuss what Galarza is saying, and comment on his attitude toward the changes he experiences.
2. Discuss the increased importance manners have when you find yourself in a new environment, perhaps in a new school or neighborhood. You might want to discuss changes in speech habits as well as changes in behavior.

ANTITHESIS

❦ ❦ ❦

When contrasting ideas are balanced in sentences and paragraphs, they are said to be in antithesis:

> History proves that dictatorships do not grow out of strong and successful governments, but out of weak and helpless ones.—Franklin D. Roosevelt

> Shallow understanding from people of good will is more frustrating than absolute misunderstanding from people of ill will.—Martin Luther King, Jr., *Letter from Birmingham Jail*

> We can no longer afford to take that which was good in the past and simply call it our heritage, to discard the bad and simply think of it as a dead load which by itself time will bury in oblivion.—Hannah Arendt, *The Origins of Totalitarianism*

This moderate balancing to heighten the contrast of ideas is found often in modern writing, though usually in formal discussions. Like the exact balance of similar ideas, the balancing of sentences containing antithetical phrases is exceptional today. The following passage is the climax of a long book on the history of Roman society:

> Rome did not invent education, but she developed it on a scale unknown before, gave it state support, and formed the curriculum that persisted till our harassed youth. She did not invent the arch, the vault, or the dome, but she used them with such audacity and magnificence that in some fields her architecture has remained unequaled.—Will Durant, *Caesar and Christ*

MARTIN LUTHER KING, JR.

Born in 1929, MARTIN LUTHER KING, JR., was ordained in 1947 in the Atlanta church where his father was the minister. He graduated from Morehouse College the following year and received his Ph.D. from Boston University in 1953. In 1955 he rose to prominence in America and throughout the world as leader of the Montgomery, Alabama, bus boycott, and he continued as one of the leaders of the Civil Rights Movement until his assassination in Memphis on April 4, 1968. "From my Christian background I gained my ideals, and from Gandhi my technique," King said. It is the technique of passive resistance that he describes here. King's style of writing reflects the cadences of his speeches—influenced strongly by the style of the Old Testament prophetic books, to name just one of many sources.

Nonviolent Resistance

Oppressed people deal with their oppression in three characteristic ways. One way is acquiescence: the oppressed resign themselves to their doom. They tacitly adjust themselves to oppression, and thereby become conditioned to it. In every movement toward freedom some of the oppressed prefer to remain oppressed. Almost 2800 years ago Moses set out to lead the children of Israel from the slavery of Egypt to the freedom of the promised land. He soon discovered that slaves do not always welcome their deliverers. They became accustomed to being slaves. They would rather bear those ills they have, as Shakespeare pointed out, than flee to others that they know not of. They prefer the "fleshpots of Egypt" to the ordeals of emancipation. 1

There is such a thing as the freedom of exhaustion. Some people are so worn down by the yoke of oppression that they give up. A few years ago in the slum areas of Atlanta, a Negro guitarist used to sing almost daily: "Ben down so long that down don't bother me." This is the type of negative freedom and resignation that often engulfs the life of the oppressed. 2

But this is not the way out. To accept passively an unjust system is to cooperate with that system; thereby the oppressed become as evil as the oppressor. Noncooperation with evil is as much a moral obligation as is cooperation with good. The oppressed must never allow the conscience of the oppressor to slumber. Religion reminds every man that he is 3 his brother's keeper. To accept injustice or segregation passively is to say to the oppressor that his actions are morally right. It is a way of allowing his conscience to fall asleep. At this moment the oppressed fails to be his brother's keeper. So acquiescence—while often the easier way—is not the moral way. It is the way of the coward. The Negro cannot win the respect of his oppressor by acquiescing; he merely increases the oppressor's arrogance and contempt. Acquiescence is interpreted as proof of the Negro's inferiority. The Negro cannot win the respect of the white people of the South or the peoples of the world if he is willing to sell the future of his children for his personal and immediate comfort and safety.

A second way that oppressed people sometimes deal 4 with oppression is to resort to physical violence and corroding hatred. Violence often brings about momentary results. Nations have frequently won their independence in battle. But in spite of temporary victories, violence never brings permanent peace. It solves no social problem; it merely creates new and more complicated ones.

Violence as a way of achieving racial justice is both 5 impractical and immoral. It is impractical because it is a descending spiral ending in destruction for all. The old law of an eye for an eye leaves everybody blind. It is immoral because it seeks to humiliate the opponent rather than win his understanding; it seeks to annihilate rather than to convert. Violence is immoral because it thrives on hatred rather than love. It destroys community and makes brotherhood impossible. It leaves society in monologue rather than dialogue. Violence ends by defeating itself. It creates bitterness in the survivors and brutality in the destroyers. A voice echoes through time saying to every potential Peter, "Put up your sword." History is cluttered with the wreckage of nations that failed to follow this command.

If the American Negro and other victims of oppression 6 succumb to the temptation of using violence in the struggle for freedom, future generations will be the recipients of a desolate night of bitterness, and our chief legacy to them will be an endless reign of meaningless chaos. Violence is not the way.

The third way open to oppressed people in their quest 7 for freedom is the way of nonviolent resistance. Like the synthesis in Hegelian philosophy, the principle of nonviolent resistance seeks to reconcile the truths of two opposites— acquiescence and violence—while avoiding the extremes and immoralities of both. The nonviolent resister agrees with the person who acquiesces that one should not be physically aggressive toward his opponent; but he balances the equation by agreeing with the person of violence that evil must be resisted. He avoids the nonresistance of the former and the violent resistance of the latter. With nonviolent resistance, no individual or group need submit to any wrong, nor need anyone resort to violence in order to right a wrong.

It seems to me that this is the method that must guide 8 the actions of the Negro in the present crisis in race relations. Through nonviolent resistance the Negro will be able to rise to the noble height of opposing the unjust system while loving the perpetrators of the system. The Negro must work passionately and unrelentingly for full stature as a citizen, but he must not use inferior methods to gain it. He must never come to terms with falsehood, malice, hate, or destruction.

Nonviolent resistance makes it possible for the Negro to 9 remain in the South and struggle for his rights. The Negro's problem will not be solved by running away. He cannot listen to the glib suggestions of those who would urge him to migrate en masse to other sections of the country. By grasping his great opportunity in the South he can make a lasting contribution to the moral strength of the nation and set a sublime example of courage for generations yet unborn.

By nonviolent resistance, the Negro can also enlist all 10 men of good will in his struggle for equality. The problem is not a purely racial one, with Negroes set against whites. In the end, it is not a struggle between people at all, but a tension between justice and injustice. Nonviolent resistance is not aimed against oppressors but against oppression. Under its banner consciences, not racial groups, are enlisted.

If the Negro is to achieve the goal of integration, he must 11 organize himself into a militant and nonviolent mass movement. All three elements are indispensable. The movement for equality and justice can only be a success if it has both a mass and militant character; the barriers to be overcome require both. Nonviolence is an imperative in order to bring about ultimate community.

A mass movement of militant quality that is not at the same time committed to nonviolence tends to generate conflict, which in turn breeds anarchy. The support of the participants and the sympathy of the uncommitted are both inhibited by the threat that bloodshed will engulf the community. This reaction in turn encourages the opposition to threaten and resort to force. When, however, the mass movement repudiates violence while moving resolutely toward its goal, its opponents are revealed as the instigators and practitioners of violence if it occurs. Then public support is magnetically attracted to the advocates of nonviolence, while those who employ violence are literally disarmed by overwhelming sentiment against their stand. 12

QUESTIONS

1. Note the sentences that conclude paragraph 1:

   > They would rather *bear those ills they have,* as Shakespeare pointed out,
   >> than *flee to others that they know not of.*

   > They prefer the *"fleshpots of Egypt"*
   >> to the ordeals of emancipation.

   What sentences in paragraph 5 contain antithetical elements? How exact is the antithesis? How many of these sentences are balanced to emphasize similar ideas?

2. How exact is the antithesis of ideas in paragraphs 8 and 10?

3. One way to moderate the tension of a passage containing considerable balance and antithesis is to vary the length of clauses or sentences. To what extent are the sentences of paragraphs 5, 8, and 10 varied in their length?

4. What do balance and antithesis contribute to the tone of the passage? What kind of voice do you hear?

SUGGESTIONS FOR WRITING

1. Compare King's sentence style with that of another of his writings, for example, "Letter from Birmingham Jail." Discuss how the relative exactness of sentence balance and antithesis is used to moderate or increase the tension of the writing.

2. Compare a letter by Saint Paul in the King James version of the Bible with the rendering of the same letter in the Revised Standard Version. Comment on the differences you notice in the use of balance or antithesis.

LENGTH

❧ ❧ ❧

There is nothing inherently effective or ineffective, superior or inferior about short or long sentences, just as there is nothing inherently effective or ineffective in a single note of the scale. How effective a sentence is depends on what it does in a paragraph or essay. The very short, disconnected sentences in a story by Ernest Hemingway effectively express the monotony a young war veteran feels on his return home, but would probably also create a feeling of monotony in a piece of writing on another subject:

> He did not want any consequences. He did not want any consequences ever again. He wanted to live alone without consequences. Besides he did not really need a girl. The army had taught him that. It was all right to pose as though you had to have a girl. Nearly everybody did that. But it wasn't true. You did not need a girl. That was the funny thing.—"Soldier's Home"

A sentence, as we have seen, often starts with the main idea and then develops it:

> She was a spirited-looking young woman, with dark curly hair cropped and parted on the side, a short oval face with straight eyebrows, and a large curved mouth.—Katherine Anne Porter, "Old Mortality"

How much detail a writer can provide depends on how prominent the main ideas are—whether in a sentence consisting of a single core idea followed by a series of modifiers, as in Porter, or in one consisting of a series of connected core ideas or main clauses, modified as in this sentence:

> Morrall would duck his head in the huddle and if it was feasible he would call a play which took the ball laterally across the field—a pitchout, perhaps, and the play would eat up ground toward the girls, the ball carrier sprinting for the sidelines, with his running guards in front of him, running low, and behind them the linemen coming too, so that twenty-two men were converging on them at a fair clip.—George Plimpton, *Paper Lion*

BRUNO BETTELHEIM

BRUNO BETTELHEIM (1903–1990) *was Professor of Educational Psychology and Distinguished Service Professor of Psychology and Psychiatry at the University of Chicago. A refugee from Hitler's Germany, his imprisonment in Nazi concentration camps, described in* The Informed Heart (1960), *deepened his lifelong concern with people under extreme emotional stress. A pioneer in the education of autistic children, Bettelheim directed the Sonia Shankman Orthogenic School at the university. His work with children is the basis of numerous books including* Symbolic Wounds (1954), The Empty Fortress (1967), *and* The Uses of Enchantment, *a psychological study of fairy tales. The essay reprinted here is taken from* Freud's Vienna and Other Essays (1990).

Essential Books of One's Life

If we enjoy reading, books enrich our lives as nothing else can do. Some throw new light on vexing problems, others open up new vistas on the world or on man in general and—most important of all—on ourselves. Although many books can enlarge our horizons, and some may influence aspects of our life, only a very few will change its course.

At least so it was with me: while many books made a strong impression on my thinking, only a few changed my very being. On reading these books, I experienced what Edmund Wilson so aptly described as a "shock of recognition," because they enlightened me about what were (at the time) my most pressing problems in finding my way in life. And they did so despite the fact that I knew not all of them were great books while I was reading them, powerfully impressed by them as I was. Some were great books, but others were not, neither as works of literature, nor by virtue of their content. As it happened, becoming acquainted with these books at particular moments in my life took on the features of revelation—of new vision that put my inner world into some order, where before there had been great uncertainty and confusion, if not outright chaos.

The reading of a book could bring about this "shock of recognition" only because something had been going on in myself which, unbeknownst to me, had made me ready for and even needful of the message. Some inner process had been at work, something vague which suddenly attained form and concrete content through reading a book. Thus some books have made it possible for me to recognize what has been germinating in me, usually for quite some time, with no awareness on my part beyond a feeling that something was not quite right with me and my life, that something needed rectifying—and this without my having any idea what was wrong, or what needed to be done about it. In a different form, I encountered this experience in my own psychoanalysis, when a significant unconscious process suddenly became clear to me, and I realized, with a shock of recognition, "This is it!"—the "it" being something with which I had been struggling, perhaps even to the point of obsession, without knowing that this was going on in my mind. Years later, as a practitioner of psychoanalysis, I met with this shock of recognition again in my patients, when suddenly things fell into place for them and confusion was replaced by clarity.

Books that do this for the reader provide quite a different experience from that provided by other books which also make a strong impression. Luckily there are many books that can move one deeply, even though they do not produce the shock of recognition and do not reveal something of greatest personal significance.

At the time that I read books that helped me change my life, permitted it to attain greater meaning and some new direction, I also read many other books which were "great literature," masterpieces that I admired. But the world of these books, while fascinating, was too alien for me to feel that the books were in some ways also about me and my life. An example that comes to mind is the novels of Dostoevsky. They moved me deeply and opened up a world very different from my own. I could not put them down, and I read one after another, entranced by the world they showed me. But they were not about me and my pressing problems. While they added much to my life, they brought about no change in it. Perhaps the Russian ambience was too alien for that; but I think it was rather the deeply felt Russian religiosity permeating these novels which prevented me from feeling that they carried a personal message. However, it cannot only have been that the Russian "soul" was too strange to my experience, because the same was true for other novels that impressed me very much while depicting a world more familiar to me. For instance, I was very taken by Romain Rolland's *Jean Christophe.* I loved reading it, but I did not find myself in it. I can only conclude that nothing in me had prepared me for making significant changes sparked by the experience of reading these books.

For a book to change one's life, processes—as mentioned before—must have been going on within oneself to make one ready and eager to change. Other books may have an impact that carried one away for a time, without actually influencing one's life. For example, when I read Sinclair Lewis's *Arrowsmith,* and for a few days afterward, I was convinced that only becoming a medical researcher could fulfill my hopes in life. However, this did not last long, because even while reading *Arrowsmith* I felt that it was not quite up to my own literary standards as a great book; and although I was tempted for a time to think of myself as a future medical researcher, deep down I knew that this was not the right profession for me. Clearly, nothing in me had prepared me to respond to this reading with the lightning shock of recognition which would say, "This book answers questions, solves problems, that have deeply disturbed me, that I have been struggling with without my knowing that this was so; and through reading it, suddenly everything has fallen into place, all my unasked questions have been answered by it."

Whether or not a book will influence us depends on our mental state at the time we are reading it. The more finally our personality has been formed, the more set in our ways of thinking and living we are, the less will books be able to change us; also, the more our personality will determine both our choice of books and what we get out of reading them. Then we are likely to read those books which are in accordance with our values and preferences. Witness the fact that most people read chiefly those books and periodicals whose values conform to their own, thus reinforcing their point of view. A magazine or book or newspaper likely to present views opposite to those we cherish will have little appeal, if any. And even when we read them, our minds will be closed to their message. Hence most books are denied the chance to alter opinions already firmly held.

All through life we may read books for enjoyment and 8 for the information we gain, arousing and at the same time satisfying our curiosity; but only at certain periods in our lives will we read books in the hope that they will influence it, give it direction, solve pressing problems. This is especially true when we find ourselves in a crisis of life or when we are undergoing obscure inner developments. Then a book can influence our whole being, while the same book read at another, more settled period of life may impress us very little. Thus all depends on when in our development as persons we read a book. Very few books can be read with pleasure all our lives, and even when one can, the pleasure we experience is different at different ages.

One of the best ways to see how much we have changed 9 and, we hope, grown over the years is to reread books that at one time were very meaningful to us. This experience was so valuable in understanding my own development that, in teaching psychology to university students, I encouraged them to reread books they had loved at one time. Their task was to try to understand why this had been so, and why it often no longer was, or not to the same degree. They were usually amazed that in this way they were able to recognize change in themselves and to speculate about its causes. Thus how we react to what we read is always a function more of what is going on in us at the time than of a book's content.

VOCABULARY

paragraph 1: vexing, vista, horizon
paragraph 2: enlightened

paragraph 3: germinating, rectifying, psychoanalysis, obsession, practitioner

paragraph 5: entranced, ambience, religiosity

paragraph 8: obscure

QUESTIONS

1. In sentences containing semicolons in paragraphs 5, 7, and 8, the two parts of each might stand as separate sentences. What does Bettelheim gain by joining the two parts in each sentence? Could a colon substitute for the semicolon in each?

2. Why does Bettelheim set off phrases with dashes rather than parentheses in paragraph 1? Could dashes substitute for the parentheses in paragraph 2?

3. What is the function of the dash in sentences in paragraph 3?

4. Bettelheim might have broken the following sentence into a series of shorter ones instead of building the sentence by addition. What does Bettelheim gain in not doing so?

> In a different form, I encountered this experience in my own psychoanalysis, when a significant unconscious process suddenly became clear to me, and I realized, with a shock of recognition, "This is it!"—the "it" being something with which I had been struggling, perhaps even to the point of obsession, without knowing that this was going on in my mind. (paragraph 3)

5. What does Bettelheim gain by setting related ideas apart in the first of the following pair of sentences, and joining related ideas in the second?

> A magazine or book or newspaper likely to present views opposite to those we cherish will have little appeal, if any. And even when we read them, our minds will be closed to their message. (paragraph 7)

> Very few books can be read with pleasure all our lives, and even when one can, the pleasure we experience is different at different ages. (paragraph 8)

6. How does Bettelheim explain Edmund Wilson's phrase "shock of recognition," and how does the phrase help Bettelheim distinguish kinds of reading experience?

7. What central point or thesis is Bettelheim developing through his comparison of reading experiences?

SUGGESTIONS FOR WRITING

1. Rewrite paragraphs 3, 7, 8, or 9, breaking up or recasting Bettelheim's compound and complete sentences. Then discuss what your rewriting loses or gains in emphasis and coherence.
2. Discuss the extent to which Bettelheim's description of his reading experiences matches your own. Cite examples in the course of your comparison, giving details of particular reading experiences.
3. Discuss two or more essential books in your life, explaining why they are essential and noting similarities and differences in your reading experience.

PART
VI

ESSAYS ON
WRITING

INTRODUCTION

In the first essay that follows, Mark Twain stresses the unconscious powers of mind that come into play in the act of composition. Twain refers to "an automatically-working taste . . . which selects and rejects without asking you for any help, and patiently and steadily improves itself without troubling you to approve or applaud." But that taste has been shaped by what the writer has read; Twain takes note of the "model-chamber" in which writers store those effective sentences they find as they read. Though writers shape their sentences unconsciously, drawing upon these model sentences, the act of writing becomes conscious when they reject sentences that don't make sense and experiment with sentences that are different from the ones they usually write.

John Ciardi agrees with Twain that reading is essential to the writer: "No writer can produce good writing without a sure sense of what has been accomplished in the past within his form." But, Ciardi adds, the writer does not adhere to the past but rather innovates: "it is impossible to venture meaningful innovation unless one knows what he is *innovating from*." But more so than Twain, Ciardi stresses the conscious side of creativity, which he defines as "the imaginatively gifted recombination of known elements into something new." Practiced writers possess a power of mind akin to that described by Twain—in Ciardi's words, "a second attention lurking in the mind at the very moment [writers] have felt the need to be most indivisibly absorbed in what they are doing." The competent writer, like the competent reader, must possess "fluency," which Ciardi defines as "the ability to receive more than one impression at the same time."

In his essay on revision, William Zinsser focuses on what happens in the course of writing and afterwards, as we rethink and revise initial drafts. Zinsser gives the same advice that George Orwell does in his essay on political language. In his discussion of how to avoid ready-made words and phrases, Orwell suggests how these words and phrases find their way into a piece of writing: "When you think of something abstract you are more inclined to use words from the start, and unless you make a conscious effort to prevent it, the existing dialect will come rushing in and do the job for you, at the expense of blurring or even changing your meaning." Zinsser shows how to deal with this problem of ready-made words and ideas. "The secret of good writing is to strip every sentence to its cleanest components," he states, and he illustrates how to do so.

These three essays by no means suggest all the ways writers proceed. They agree, however, on one point—that the act of writing is not aimless or undirected. Writers give attention to what they have written—to its clarity and effectiveness—at some stage in the process and sometimes at all stages.

MARK TWAIN

Mark Twain's description of life in the Missouri river town where he grew up appears earlier in this book. His numerous stories, novels, sketches, and essays seem the work of a writer who lets a tale or comment develop leisurely, in the manner of the relaxed yarn spinner. This impression is deceptive, for Twain was attentive to the craft, as all good storytellers and writers must be. Yet, he tells us in this short statement on writing, he allowed his imagination to shape the work, without constant awareness of means and effects. Rather, he depended on the "model-chamber" he describes and on "an automatically-working taste" that came to him through wide reading. Twain suggests one way that writers develop their craft.

The Art of Composition

Your inquiry has set me thinking, but, so far, my thought fails to materialize. I mean that, upon consideration, I am not sure that I have methods in composition. I do suppose I have—I suppose I must have—but they somehow refuse to take shape in my mind; their details refuse to separate and submit to classification and description; they remain a jumble—visible, like the fragments of glass when you look in at the wrong end of a kaleidoscope, but still a jumble. If I could turn the whole thing around and look in at the other end, why then the figures would flash into form out of the chaos, and I shouldn't have any more trouble. But my head isn't right for that today, apparently. It might have been, maybe, if I had slept last night.

However, let us try guessing. Let us guess that when- 2
ever we read a sentence and like it, we unconsciously store
it away in our model-chamber; and it goes with the myriad of
its fellows to the building, brick by brick, of the eventful
edifice which we call our style. And let us guess that
whenever we run across other forms —bricks—whose color,
or some other defect, offends us, we unconsciously reject
these, and so one never finds them in our edifice. If I have
subjected myself to any training processes, and no doubt I
have, it must have been in this unconscious or half-conscious
fashion. I think it unlikely that deliberate and consciously
methodical training is usual with the craft. I think it likely
that the training most in use is of this unconscious sort, and
is guided and governed and made by-and-by unconsciously
systematic, by an automatically-working taste—a taste which
selects and rejects without asking you for any help, and
patiently and steadily improves itself without troubling you
to approve or applaud. Yes, and likely enough when the
structure is at last pretty well up, and attracts attention, *you*
feel complimented, whereas you didn't build it, and didn't
even consciously superintend. Yes; one notices, for instance,
that long, involved sentences confuse him, and that he is
obliged to re-read them to get the sense. Unconsciously,
then, he rejects that brick. Unconsciously he accustoms
himself to writing short sentences as a rule. At times he may
indulge himself with a long one, but he will make sure that
there are no folds in it, no vaguenesses, no parenthetical
interruptions of its view as a whole; when he is done with it,
it won't be a sea-serpent, with half of its arches under the
water, it will be a torchlight procession.

Well, also he will notice in the course of time, as his 3
reading goes on, that the difference between the *almost right*
word and the *right* word is really a large matter—'tis the
difference between the lightningbug and the lightning. After
that, of course, that exceedingly important brick, the *exact*
word—however, this is running into an essay, and I beg
pardon. So I seem to have arrived at this: doubtless I have
methods, but they begot themselves, in which case I am only
their proprietor, not their father.

JOHN CIARDI

The poet, editor, and translator John Ciardi *(1916–1986) is the author of forty books of poetry and criticism. He was poetry editor for* Saturday Review *from 1956 to 1972, writing a column "Manner of Speaking" for that magazine. These columns and other essays are collected in* Dialogue with an Audience *(1963) and* Manner of Speaking *(1972). His distinguished translation of Dante's* The Divine Comedy *was published in its full edition in 1977. Ciardi was director of the Bread Loaf Writers' Conference at Middlebury College from 1955 to 1972. The essay that follows was presented to the conference in its inaugural year.*

What Every Writer Must Learn

The teaching of writing has become practically a profession by now. There is hardly a college in the land that does not offer at least one course in "creative writing" (whatever that is) by some "teacher of writing" (whoever he is). There are, moreover, at least fifty annual writers' conferences now functioning among us with something like fifty degrees of competence. And there seems to be no way of counting the number of literary counselors, good and bad, who are prepared to promise that they can teach a writer what he needs to know.

I am myself a "teacher of writing," but though it be taken as a confession of fraud I must insist, in the face of all this "teaching" apparatus, that writing cannot in fact be taught. What a writer must have above all else is inventiveness. Dedication, commitment, passion—whatever one chooses to call the writer's human motivation—must be there, to be sure. But to require human motivation is only to assume that the writer is a human being—certainly not a very hard assumption to make. Art, however, is not humanity but the *expression* of humanity, and for enduring expression the one gift above all is inventiveness.

But where, in what curriculum ever, has there been, or can there be, a course in inventiveness—which is to say, in creativity? The truly creative—whether in art, in science, or in philosophy—is always, and precisely, that which cannot be taught. And yet, though it seem paradoxical, creativity cannot spring from the untaught. Creativity is the imaginatively gifted recombination of known elements into something new.

And so, it may seem, there is no real paradox. The 4 elements of an invention or of a creation can be taught, but the creativity must be self-discovered and self-disciplined. A good teacher—whether in a college classroom, a Parisian café, or a Greek market place—can marvelously assist the learning. But in writing, as in all creativity, it is the gift that must learn itself.

The good teacher will be able to itemize a tremendous 5 amount of essential lore. He can tell a would-be novelist that if an incidental character is given a name that character had best reappear in the later action, and that if he is not going to reappear he should be identified simply as "the supply sergeant," "the big blond," "the man in the red waistcoat," or whatever. He can point out that good dialogue avoids "he averred," "he bellowed," "he boomed," "he interpolated," and that it is wise to write simply "he said," indicating any important direction for the tone of voice in a separate sentence. He can demonstrate that in all fiction the action must be perceived by someone, and he can defend in theory and support by endless instances that in effective fiction one does not allow more than one means of perception within a single scene. He can point out to would-be poets that traditional rhyme and traditional metrics are not indispensable, but that once a pattern has been established the writer must respect it. And he can then point out that within the pattern established at the start of the student's poem certain lines are metrically deficient and certain rhymes forced.

He may "teach" (or preach) any number of such partic- 6 ulars. And if he is a good man for the job he will never forget that these particulars are simply rules of thumb, any one of which may be violated by a master, but none of which may be safely ignored by a writer who has not yet learned they exist.

Belaboring such particulars is a useful device to the 7 would-be writer, who under a competent teacher may save himself years of floundering trial-and-error. Writers are forever being produced by literary groups of one sort or another, and one of the most important things a writer acquires in the give-and-take of a good literary group is a headful of precisely such particulars. The most important thing a teacher of writing can do is to create a literary group in which he teaches minimums while the most talented of his students learn maximums—very largely from fighting with one another (rarely, if ever, from mutual admiration).

But if writing requires a starting talent that a man either   8 has or has not and which he cannot learn, and if the teachable elements are not enough to make a writer of him, what is it he must learn? What are the measures by which his gift comes to know itself?

The answers to that question must be given separately,   9 and if they are so given they must be put down one after the other with some sort of natural implication that the order in which they are given is keyed to their importance. Such mechanical necessity (and it is one of the most constant seductions of the classroom) must not be allowed to obscure the far greater likelihood that the answers all exist at the same time in the behavior of a good writer, and that all are equally important. That, too, is part of what must be learned. As is the fact that no one set of generalizations will ever suffice. But one must begin somewhere. I offer the following six points as the most meaningful and the most central I have been able to locate.

1. Something to Write About

"You have to give them something to write about," Robert   10 Frost once said in discussing his classroom principles. His own poems are full of stunning examples of the central truth that good writers deal in information, and that even the lofty (if they are lofty) acreages of poetry are sown to fact. Consider the opening lines of "Mending Wall":

> Something there is that doesn't love a wall,
> That sends the frozen-groundswell under it,
> And spills the upper boulders in the sun;
> And makes gaps even two can pass abreast.
> The work of hunters is another thing:

I have come after them and made repair
Where they have left not one stone on a stone,
But they would have the rabbit out of hiding,
To please the yelping dogs. The gaps I mean,
No one has seen them made or heard them made,
But at spring mending-time we find them there . . .

I intend no elaborate critique of this passage. I want simply
to make the point that it contains as much specific information about stone walls as one could hope to find in a
Department of Agriculture pamphlet.

Frost states his passion for the *things* of the world both in 11
example and in precept. "The fact is the sweetest dream the
labor knows," he writes in "The Mowing." One has only to
compare that line with R. P. T. Coffin's "Nothing so crude as
fact could enter here" to understand an important part of the
difference between a poet and something less than a poet.

Even so mystical a poet as Gerard Manley Hopkins (I 12
misuse the word "mystical" in order to save three paragraphs, but let me at least file an apology) is gorgeously
given to the fact of the thing. Consider: "And blue bleak
embers, ah my dear,/Fall, gall themselves, and gash gold-
vermilion." (I.e., "Coal embers in a grate, their outside
surfaces burned out and blue-bleak, sift down, fall through
the grate, strike the surface below, and are gashed open to
reveal the gold-vermilion fire still glowing at their core.")

The writer of fiction deals his facts in a different way, but 13
it will not do to say that he is more bound to fact than is the
poet: he simply is not required to keep his facts under poetic
compression; keep hard to them he still must. Consider
Melville's passion for the details of whaling; or Defoe's for
the details of criminality, of ransoming an English merchant
captured by a French ship, or of Robinson Crusoe's carpen-
try. The passion for fact was powerful enough in these
masters to lure them into shattering the pace of their own
best fiction, and to do so time and time again. And who is to
say that a man reading for more than amusement, a man
passionate to touch the writer's mind in his writing, has any
real objection to having the pace so shattered? All those
self-blooming, lovingly managed, chunky, touchable facts!

For a writer is a man who must know something better 14

than anyone else does, be it so little as his own goldfish or so much as himself. True, he is not required to know any one specific thing. Not at least until he begins to write about it. But once he has chosen to write about X then he is responsible for knowing everything the writing needs to know about X. I know of no writer of any consequence whatever who did not treasure the world enough to gather to himself a strange and wonderful headful and soulful of facts about its going and coming.

2. An Outside Eye

Nothing is more difficult than for the writer to ride his passion while still managing to observe it critically. The memoirs of good writers of every sort are studded with long thoughts on this essential duplicity, this sense of aesthetic detachment, of a second attention lurking in the mind at the very moment they have felt the need to be most indivisibly absorbed in what they are doing. 15

The writer absolutely must learn to develop that eye outside himself, for the last action every writer must perform for his writing is to become its reader. It is not easy to approach one's own output as if he were coming on it fresh. Yet unless the writer turns that trick any communication that happens will either be by accident or by such genius as transcends the possibility of discussion. 16

For the writer's relation to his writing is a developing relation. The writing starts as a conceptual buzz. Approaching the writing thus with the buzz loud in the head, one may easily believe that anything he sets down is actually full of that starting buzz. But one must remember that the buzz is there before the writing, and that should some accident interfere with the actual writing the buzz would still be there. A writer in a really heightened state could jot down telephone numbers and actually believe that he has set down a piece of writing that accurately conveys his original impulse. 17

The reader, however, is in a very different situation. He comes to the writing committed to no prior emotion. There is no starting buzz in his head, except by irrelevant accident. It 18 is the writer's job to make that reader buzz. Not, to be sure, to make every reader buzz—the world is full of the practically unbuzzable—but to make the competent reader buzz. Simply to say, "I buzz," is not enough. To make the reader experience the original buzz with nothing but the writing to create the buzz within him—that is the function of every sort of literature, the communication of experience in experience-able terms. The disciplines of any art form are among other things ways of estimating the amount of buzz the form is transmitting.

3. Fluency

As noted, one does not hope to reach all readers, but only 19 the competent. In one way the qualifications of a good reader are the same as those of a competent writer. Both must achieve fluency. By fluency I mean the ability to receive more than one impression at the same time. To create or to experience art one must be both technically and emotionally fluent.

A pun is a simple example of the necessity for technical 20 fluency. The two or more faces of a pun must be received at the same instant or all is lost. The news comes over the radio that the Communist leader of Pisa has been chastised by Moscow for making overtures to the left-center parties for a unified front, and the happy punster says, "Aha, a Lenin tower of a-Pisa-ment!" then settles back in his moment of personal splendor. This golden instant from my autobio-graphy—but what good is even glory if it has to be explained? "I don't get it," says the guest who will never be invited again, and the evening is ruined.

The pun, of course, is only the simplest example of the 21 need for technical fluency. Unless the writer and the reader have in common the necessary language of simultaneity in its millions of shadings, the best will die en route.

The need for emotional fluency is analogous. Good 22 writing constantly requires the writer to perceive and the reader to receive different sets of feelings at the same instant. Both the writer and the reader must be equal to the emotion of the subject dealt with. Shakespeare can put a world into

Hamlet, but where is that world when a five-year-old child or an emotionally-five-year-old adult attempts to read or to see the play? Whatever he may see, it is certainly not Shakespeare. A reader who is emotionally immature, or who is too psychically rigid (the same thing really) to enter into the simultaneity of the human experiences commonly portrayed in literature, is simply not capable of any sort of writing with the possible exception of the technical report, the statistical summary, or that semi-literate combination, the Ph.D. thesis.

4. A Sense of the Past

No painter can produce a good canvas without a broad 23 knowledge of what has been painted before him, no architect can plan a meaningful building except as he has pondered the architecture of the past, and no writer can produce good writing without a sure sense of what has been accomplished in the past within his form.

There are legions of poets today who are trying belatedly 24 to be Wordsworth, and legions of fictioneers who are trying to be Louisa May Alcott. I imply no attack here on either Wordsworth or Alcott. I simply make the point that it is too late to be either of them again. Both of them, moreover, did a better job of being themselves than any of their imitators can aspire to. As the Kitty-cat bird in Theodore Roethke's poem said: "Whoever you are, be sure it's you."

Nor does one learn the past of his form only to adhere to 25 it. Such an adherence, if overdedicated, would be a death in itself. I mean, rather, that it is impossible to venture meaningful innovation unless one knows what he is *innovating from*. With no exception I am able to think of, the best innovators in our literature have been those who best knew their past tradition.

I am saying simply that a writer must learn to read. He 26 must read widely and thoughtfully, and he must learn to read not as an amateur spectator but as an engaged professional. Just as the football coach sees more of the play than do the coeds, so the writer must learn to see more of what is happening under the surface of the illusion than does the reader who simply yields to the illusion. William Dean Howells, then editor of *The Atlantic*, paid what he intended as a supreme compliment to one of Mark Twain's books when he reported that he had begun the book and for the first time in many years had found himself reading as a reader rather than as an editor. A happy indulgence and a gracious compliment, but once the writer has allowed himself that much it becomes his duty to reread the book with his glasses on—not only to enter into the illusion of the writing, but to identify the devices (*i.e.*, the inventions) by which the illusion was created and made to work upon him. And here, too, he must experience his essential duplicity, for the best reading is exactly that reading in which the passion of the illusion and the awareness of its technical management arrive at the same time.

5. A Sense of the Age

The true writer, that is to say the writer who is something 27 more than a competent technician, has a yet more difficult thing to learn. He must not only know his human and artistic past; he must learn to read the mood of his world under its own names for itself. He must become an instrument, tuned by devices he can never wholly understand, to the reception of a sense of his age, its mood, its climate of ideas, its human position, and its potential of action. And he must not let himself be deceived into thinking that the world answers to the names it gives itself. Hitler's agencies once gave a great deal of attention to what they called "Strength-through-Joy." It was the product of this Strength-through-Joy that Lord Beaverbrook called at the time "the stalwart young Nazis of Germany." The names were "strength," "joy," and "stalwarts." Yet any man today can see that those who answered to these shining names contained within themselves possibilities for action that must answer to much darker names. Any man can see it—now. I think it is very much to the point that all of the best writers sensed it then, and that the better the German writers were, the earlier they left Germany.

Good writing must be of its times and must contain within itself—God knows how but the writer must learn for himself—a sense of what Hippolyte Taine called "the moral temperature of the times," what the Germans call "der Zeitgeist," and what English and American writers have come to call "the climate."

6. Art Is Artifice

And along with all else, as an essential part of his duplicity, 28 his commitment, his fluency, and his sense of past and present, the writer must learn beyond any flicker of doubt within himself that art is not life itself but a made representation of life. He must learn that it is no defense of a piece of fiction, for example, to argue, "But that's the way it happened." The fact that it happened that way in the world of the *Daily News* does not make it happen to the reader within the world of the writing.

The writer's subject is reality but his medium is illusion. 29 Only by illusory means can the sense of reality be transmitted in an art form. That complex of pigment-on-canvas is not four maidens dancing, but it is the managed illusion whereby Botticelli transmits his real vision of the four seasons. Those words on paper are not Emma Bovary, but they are the elements of the illusion whereby we experience her as a living creation. The writer, like every artist, deals in what I have come to call the AS-IF. AS-IF is the mode of all poetry and of all imaginative writing. IS is the mode of what passes for reality and of all information-prose. Is IS more real than AS-IF? One must ask: "More real for what purposes?" I have no argument with, for example, the research chemists. I mean rather to hold them in considerable admiration. But though many of them think of themselves as the IS-iest men in the world, which of them has ever determined a piece of truth except by setting up and pursuing a starting hypothesis (let me leave accident out of consideration)? And what is a starting hypothesis but an AS-IF? "Let us act AS-IF this hypothesis were true," says the researcher, "and then see how it checks out." At the end of ten, or a hundred, or ten thousand starting AS-IF's lurks the nailed-down IS of valence, or quanta, or transmutation of elements. Maybe. And then only until the next revolution in IS outdates the researcher's results.

At the far end of all the AS-IF's a man, and particularly 30 a writer, can summon from himself, there lurks that final IS (maybe) that will be a truth for him. But not all of the truth will be told at one time. Part of the truth, I think the most truth, a writer must learn is that writing is not a decorative act, but a specific, disciplined, and infinitely viable means of knowledge. Poetry and fiction, like all the arts, are ways of perceiving and of understanding the world. Good writing is as positive a search for truth as is any part of science, and it deals with kinds of truth that must forever be beyond science. The writer must learn, necessarily of himself and within himself, that his subject is the nature of reality, that good writing always increases the amount of human knowledge available, and that the one key to that knowledge of reality is AS-IF. His breadth and depth as a human being are measured by the number of AS-IF's he has managed to experience; his stature as a writer, by the number he has managed to bring to life in his work.

For no man in any one lifetime can hope to learn by 31 physical experience (IS) all that he must know and all that he must have experienced in order to be an adequate human being. No writer can hope to engage physically enough worlds of IS to make his imagination and his humanity pertinent. Only by his vicarious assumptions of AS-IF can the writer learn his real human dimension, and only as he dedicates his writing to the creation of a meaningful and experienceable new AS-IF can he hope to write well—to write as no school can teach him to write, but he must learn for himself if he cares enough, and if he has gift enough.

WILLIAM ZINSSER

WILLIAM ZINSSER, *whose essay "The Right to Fail" appears earlier in this book, has had a long and varied career as a journalist, critic, columnist, and teacher of writing. His*

numerous essays are collected in The Lunacy Boom (*1970*)
and other books. In this essay from his book On Writing Well
(*4th ed., 1990*), *Zinsser discusses the clutter that infects so
much American writing today, and he emphasizes the importance of revision and editing in the act of writing. In the
sample extract included in the essay, Zinsser gives an example
of his own revising and editing.*

Simplicity

Clutter is the disease of American writing. We are a society   1
strangling in unnecessary words, circular constructions,
pompous frills and meaningless jargon.

Who can understand the viscous language of everyday   2
American commerce and enterprise: the business letter, the
interoffice memo, the corporation report, the notice from the
bank explaining its latest "simplified" statement? What
member of an insurance or medical plan can decipher the
brochure that describes what the costs and benefits are?
What father or mother can put together a child's toy—on
Christmas eve or any other eve—from the instructions on the
box? Our national tendency is to inflate and thereby sound
important. The airline pilot who announces that he is presently anticipating experiencing considerable precipitation
wouldn't dream of saying that it may rain. The sentence is
too simple—there must be something wrong with it.

But the secret of good writing is to strip every sentence   3
to its cleanest components. Every word that serves no
function, every long word that could be a short word, every
adverb that carries the same meaning that's already in the
verb, every passive construction that leaves the reader
unsure of who is doing what—these are the thousand and
one adulterants that weaken the strength of a sentence. And
they usually occur, ironically, in proportion to education and
rank.

During the late 1960s the president of a major university   4
wrote a letter to mollify the alumni after a spell of campus
unrest. "You are probably aware," he began, "that we have
been experiencing very considerable potentially explosive
expressions of dissatisfaction on issues only partially re-

lated." He meant that the students had been hassling them about different things. I was far more upset by the president's English than by the students' potentially explosive expressions of dissatisfaction. I would have preferred the presidential approach taken by Franklin D. Roosevelt when he tried to convert into English his own government's memos, such as this blackout order of 1942:

> Such preparations shall be made as will completely obscure all Federal buildings and non-Federal buildings occupied by the Federal government during an air raid for any period of time from visibility by reason of internal or external illumination.

"Tell them," Roosevelt said, "that in buildings where 5
they have to keep the work going to put something across the windows."

Simplify, simplify. Thoreau said it, as we are so often 6
reminded, and no American writer more consistently practiced what he preached. Open *Walden* to any page and you will find a man saying in a plain and orderly way what is on his mind:

> I went to the woods because I wished to live deliberately, to front only the essential facts of life, and see if I could not learn what it had to teach, and not, when I came to die, discover that I had not lived. I did not wish to live what was not life, living is so dear; nor did I wish to practice resignation, unless it was quite necessary. I wanted to live deep and suck out all the marrow of life, to live so sturdily and Spartan-like as to put to rout all that was not life, to cut a broad swath and shave close, to drive life into a corner, and reduce it to its lowest terms, and, if it proved to be mean, why then to get the whole and genuine meanness of it, and publish its meanness to the world; or if it were sublime, to know it by experience, and be able to give a true account of it.

How can the rest of us achieve such enviable freedom 7
from clutter? The answer is to clear our heads of clutter. Clear thinking becomes clear writing; one can't exist without the other. It's impossible for a muddy thinker to write good English. You may get away with it for a paragraph or two, but soon the reader will be lost, and there's no sin so grave, for the reader will not easily be lured back.

is too dumb or too lazy to keep pace with the ~~writer's~~ train of thought. My sympathies are ~~entirely~~ with him. ⟩ ~~He's not so dumb.~~ (If the reader is lost, it is generally because the writer ~~of the article~~ has not been careful enough to keep him on the ~~proper~~ path.

(This carelessness can take any number of ~~different~~ forms. Perhaps a sentence is so excessively ~~long and~~ cluttered that the reader, hacking his way through ~~all~~ the verbiage, simply doesn't know what it ~~the writer~~ means. Perhaps a sentence has been so shoddily constructed that the reader could read it in any of several ~~two or three different~~ ways. ~~He thinks he knows what the writer is trying to say, but he's not sure.~~ Perhaps the writer has switched pronouns in mid-sentence, or ~~perhaps he~~ has switched tenses, so the reader loses track of who is talking ~~to whom,~~ or ~~exactly~~ when the action took place. Perhaps Sentence B is not a logical sequel to Sentence A -- the writer, in whose head the connection is ~~perfectly~~ clear, has not bothered to provide ~~given enough thought to providing~~ the missing link. Perhaps the writer has used an important word incorrectly by not taking the trouble to look it up ~~and make sure.~~ He may think that "sanguine" and "sanguinary" mean the same thing, but ⟩ ~~I can assure you that~~ (the difference is a bloody big one ~~to the reader.~~ The reader ~~He~~ can only ~~try to~~ infer ~~what~~ (speaking of big differences) what the writer is trying to imply.

(Faced with these ~~such a variety of~~ obstacles, the reader is at first a remarkably tenacious bird. He ~~tends to~~ blames himself, ~~He~~ obviously missed something, ~~he thinks,~~ and he goes back over the mystifying sentence, or over the whole paragraph,

piecing it out like an ancient rune, making guesses and moving
on. But he won't do this for long. ~~He will soon run out of~~
~~patience.~~ (The writer is making him work too hard ~~— harder~~
~~than he should have to work —~~ and the reader will look for
~~a writer~~ **one** who is better at his craft.

The writer must therefore constantly ask himself: What am
I trying to say? ~~in this sentence?~~ (Surprisingly often, he
doesn't know.) ~~And~~ then he must look at what he has ~~just~~
written and ask: Have I said it? Is it clear to someone
encountering ~~who is coming upon~~ the subject for the first time? If it's
not, ~~clear,~~ it is because some fuzz has worked its way into the
machinery. The clear writer is a person ~~who is~~ clear-headed
enough to see this stuff for what it is: fuzz.

I don't mean ~~to suggest~~ that some people are born
clear-headed and are therefore natural writers, whereas
others ~~other people~~ are naturally fuzzy and will ~~therefore~~ never write
well. Thinking clearly is ~~an entirely~~ conscious act that the
writer must **force** ~~keep forcing~~ upon himself, just as if he were
embarking ~~starting~~ out on any other ~~kind of~~ project that **requires** ~~calls for~~ logic:
adding up a laundry list or doing an algebra problem ~~or playing~~
~~chess.~~ Good writing doesn't ~~just~~ come naturally, though most
people obviously think **it does.** ~~it's as easy as walking.~~ The professional

Two pages of the final manuscript of this chapter from the First Edition
of *On Writing Well.* Although they look like a first draft, they had
already been rewritten and retyped—like almost every other page—
four or five times. With each rewrite I try to make what I have written
tighter, stronger and more precise, eliminating every element that is
not doing useful work. Then I go over it once more, reading it aloud,
and am always amazed at how much clutter can still be cut. In this
Fourth Edition I've eliminated the sexist pronoun "he" to denote "the
writer" and "the reader."

Who is this elusive creature, the reader? The reader is 8
someone with an attention span of about sixty seconds—a
person assailed by forces competing for the minutes that
might otherwise be spent on a magazine or a book. At one
time these forces weren't so numerous or so possessive:
newspapers, radio, spouse, home, children. Today they also
include a "home entertainment center" (TV, VCR, video
camera, tapes and CDs), pets, a fitness program, a lawn and
a garden and all the gadgets that have been bought to keep
them spruce, and that most potent of competitors, sleep. The
person snoozing in a chair, holding a magazine or a book, is
a person who was being given too much unnecessary trouble
by the writer.

It won't do to say that the reader is too dumb or too lazy 9
to keep pace with the train of thought. If the reader is lost,
it's usually because the writer hasn't been careful enough.
The carelessness can take any number of forms. Perhaps a
sentence is so excessively cluttered that the reader, hacking
through the verbiage, simply doesn't know what it means.
Perhaps a sentence has been so shoddily constructed that the
reader could read it in any of several ways. Perhaps the
writer has switched pronouns in mid-sentence, or has
switched tenses, so the reader loses track of who is talking or
when the action took place. Perhaps Sentence B is not a
logical sequel to Sentence A—the writer, in whose head the
connection is clear, hasn't bothered to provide the missing
link. Perhaps the writer has used an important word incorrectly by not taking the trouble to look it up. The writer may
think that "sanguine" and "sanguinary" mean the same
thing, but the difference is a bloody big one. The reader can
only infer (speaking of big differences) what the writer is
trying to imply.

Faced with such obstacles, readers are at first remarkably 10
tenacious. They blame themselves—they obviously missed
something, and they go back over the mystifying sentence,
or over the whole paragraph, piecing it out like an ancient
rune, making guesses and moving on. But they won't do this
for long. The writer is making them work too hard, and they
will look for one who is better at the craft.

Writers must therefore constantly ask: What am I trying 11
to say? Surprisingly often they don't know. Then they must

look at what they have written and ask: Have I said it? Is it clear to someone encountering the subject for the first time? If it's not, that's because some fuzz has worked its way into the machinery. The clear writer is someone clearheaded enough to see this stuff for what it is: fuzz.

I don't mean that some people are born clearheaded and 12 are therefore natural writers, whereas others are naturally fuzzy and will never write well. Thinking clearly is a conscious act that writers must force upon themselves, just as if they were embarking on any other project that requires logic: adding up a laundry list or doing an algebra problem. Good writing doesn't come naturally, though most people obviously think it does. The professional writer is constantly being bearded by strangers who say they'd like to "try a little writing sometime"—meaning when they retire from their real profession, like insurance or real estate. Or they say, "I could write a book about that." I doubt it.

Writing is hard work. A clear sentence is no accident. 13 Very few sentences come out right the first time, or even the third time. Remember this as a consolation in moments of despair. If you find that writing is hard, it's because it *is* hard. It's one of the hardest things that people do.

GLOSSARY

❦ ❦ ❦

allusion: An indirect reference to a presumably well-known literary work or an historical event or figure. The phrase "the Waterloo of his political career" is a reference to Napoleon's disastrous defeat at the Battle of Waterloo in 1815. The allusion implies that the career of the politician under discussion has come to a disastrous end.

analogy: A point-by-point comparison between two unlike things or activities (for example, comparing writing an essay to building a house) for the purpose of illustration or argument. Unlike a comparison (or contrast), in which the things compared are of equal importance, analogy exists for the purpose of illustrating or arguing the nature of one of the compared things, not both.

antithesis: The arrangement of contrasting ideas in grammatically similar phrases and clauses (*The world will little note, nor long remember, what we say here, but it can never forget what they did here*—Lincoln, *Gettysburg Address*). See *parallelism*.

argument: Proving the truth or falseness of a statement. Arguments are traditionally classified as *inductive* or *deductive*. See *deductive argument* and *inductive argument*. Argument can be used for different purposes in writing. See *purpose*.

autobiography: Writing about one's own experiences, often those of growing up and making one's way in the world. The autobiographical writings of Mary E. Mebane and Eudora Welty describe their childhood in the South.

balanced sentence: A sentence containing parallel phrases and clauses of approximately the same length and wording (*You can fool all the people some of the time, and some of the people all the time, but you cannot fool all the people all of the time.*—Lincoln).

cause and effect: Analysis of the conditions that must be present for an event to occur (*cause*) and of the results or consequences of the event (*effect*). An essay may deal with causes or with effects only.

classification and division: *Classification* arranges individual objects into groups or classes (GM cars, Chrysler cars, Ford cars). *Division* arranges a broad class into subclasses according to various principles (the broad class GM *cars* can be divided on the basis of their transmission or manufacturing unit).

cliché: A once-colorful expression made stale through overuse (*putting on the dog, mad as a wet hen*).

coherence: The sense, as we read, that the details and ideas of a work connect clearly. A paragraph or essay that does not hold together seems incoherent. Transitions are a means of coherence.

colloquialism: An everyday expression in speech and informal writing. Colloquialisms are not substandard or "illiterate" English. They are common in informal English and occur sometimes in formal English.

comparison and contrast: The analysis of similarities and differences between two or more persons, objects, or events (A and B) for the purpose of a relative estimate. The word *comparison* sometimes refers to the analysis of similarities and differences in both A and B. *Block comparison* presents each thing being compared as a whole (that is, if the comparison is between A and B, then features a, b, c of A are discussed as a block of information, then features a, b, c of B are compared to A in their own block of information). *Alternating comparison* presents the comparable features one by one (a, a, b, b, c, c).

complex sentence: A sentence consisting of one main or independent clause and one or more subordinate or dependent clauses (*The rain began when she stepped outside*).

compound sentence: A sentence consisting of coordinated independent clauses (*She stepped outside and then the rain began*).

compound-complex sentence: A sentence consisting of two or more main or independent clauses and at least one subordinate or dependent clause (*She stepped outside as the rain began, but she did not return to the house*).

concrete and abstract words: Concrete words refer to particular objects, people, and events (Valley Forge, Franklin Delano Roosevelt, the Rocky Mountains); abstract words refer to general shared qualities (heroism, courage, beauty). Concrete writing makes abstract ideas perceptible to the senses through details and images.

concreteness: Making an idea exist through the senses. Writing can be concrete at all three levels—informal, general, and formal. See *concrete and abstract words*.

connotation: Feelings, images, and ideas associated with a word. Connotations change from reader to reader, though some words probably have the same associations for everybody.

context: The surrounding words or sentences that suggest the meaning of a word or phrase. Writers may dispense with formal definition if the context clarifies the meaning of a word.

coordinate sentence: A sentence that joins clauses of the same weight and importance through the conjunctions *and, but, for, or, nor,* or *yet,* or through conjunctive adverbs and adverbial phrases (*however, therefore, nevertheless, in fact*).

deductive argument: Reasoning from statements assumed to be true or well established factually. These statements or assumptions are thought sufficient to guarantee the truth of the inferences or conclusions. In formal arguments they are called *premises*. A valid argument reasons correctly from the premises to the conclusion. A sound argument is true in its premises and valid in its reasoning. See *enthymeme, syllogism*.

definition: Explaining the current meaning of a word through its etymology or derivation, its denotation, or its connotations. Denotative or "real" definitions single out a word from all other words (or things) like it by giving *genus* and *specific difference*. Connotative definitions give the associations people make to the word. See *connotation*.

description: A picture in words of people, objects, and events. Description often combines with narration and it may serve exposition and persuasion.

division: See *classification and division*.

enthymeme: A deductive argument that does not state the conclusion or one of the premises directly. The following statement is an enthymeme: *Citizens in a democracy, who refuse to register for the draft, are not acting responsibly*. The implied premise is that the responsible citizen obeys all laws, even repugnant ones.

essay: A carefully organized composition that develops a single idea or impression or several related ideas or impressions. The word sometimes describes a beginning or trial attempt that explores the central idea or impression instead of developing it completely.

example: A picture or illustration of an idea, or one of many instances or occurrences that is typical of the rest.

exposition: An explanation or unfolding or setting forth of an idea, usually for the purpose of giving information. Exposition is usually an important part of persuasive writing. Example, process analysis, causal analysis, definition, classification and division, and comparison and contrast are forms of exposition.

expressive writing: Essays, diaries, journals, letters, and other kinds of writing that present personal feelings and beliefs for their own sake. The expressive writer is not primarily concerned with informing or persuading readers.

figure of speech: A word or phrase that departs from its usual meaning. Figures of speech make statements vivid and capture the attention of readers. The most common figures are based on similarity between things. See *metaphor, personification, simile*. Other figures are based on relationship. See *allusion*. *Metonymy* refers to a thing by one of its qualities (*the Hill* as a reference to the United States Congress). *Synecdoche* refers to a thing by one of its parts (*wheels* as a reference to racing cars). Other figures are based on contrast between statements and realities. See *irony*. Related to irony is *understatement*, or saying less than is appropriate (*Napoleon's career ended unhappily at Waterloo*). *Hyperbole* means deliberate exaggeration (*crazy about ice cream*). *Paradox* states an apparent contradiction (*All great truths begin as blasphemies*—G. B. Shaw). *Oxymoron*, a kind of paradox, joins opposite qualities into a single image (*lake of fire*).

focus: The limitation of subject in an essay. The focus may be broad, as in a panoramic view of the mountains, or it may be narrow, as in a view of a particular peak. For example, a writer may focus broadly on the contribution to scientific thought of scientists from various fields, or focus narrowly on the achievements of astronomers or chemists or medical researchers, or focus even more narrowly on the achievements of Albert Einstein as representative of twentieth-century science.

formal English: Spoken and written English, often abstract in content, with sentences tighter than colloquial ones and an abstract and sometimes technical vocabulary. See *general English* and *informal English*.

general English: A written standard that has features of informal and formal English. See *formal English* and *informal English*.

image: A picture in words of an object, a scene, or a person. Though visual images are common in writing, they are not the only kind. Images can also be auditory, tactile, gustatory, and olfactory. John Keats's line *With beaded bubbles winking at the brim* appeals to our hearing and taste as well as to our sight. His phrase *coming musk-rose* appeals to our sense of smell. Images help to make feelings concrete.

implied thesis: The central idea of the essay, suggested by the details and discussion rather than stated directly. See *thesis*.

inductive argument: Inductive arguments reason from particulars of experience to general ideas—from observation, personal experience, and experimental testing to probable conclusions. Inductive arguments make predictions on the basis of past and present experience. An argumentative analogy is a form of inductive argument because it is based on limited observation and experience and therefore can claim probability only. Analysis of causes and effects is inductive when used in argument.

"inductive leap":   Making the decision that sufficient inductive evidence (personal experience, observation, experimental testing) exists to draw a conclusion. Sometimes the writer of the argument makes the leap too quickly and bases conclusions on insufficient evidence.

informal English: Written English, usually concrete in content, tighter than the loose sentences of spoken English, but looser in sentence construction than formal English. The word *informal* refers to the occasion of its use. A letter to a friend is usually informal; a letter of application is usually formal. See *formal English* and *general English*.

irony: A term generally descriptive of statements and events. An ironic statement says the opposite of what the speaker or writer means, or implies that something more is meant than is stated, or says the unexpected (*He has a great future behind him*). An ironic event is unexpected or is so coincidental that it seems highly improbable (*The fireboat burned and sank*).

jargon: The technical words of a trade or profession (in computer jargon, the terms *input* and *word processor*). Unclear, clumsy, or repetitive words or phrasing, sometimes the result of misplaced technical words (*He gave his input into the decision process*).

loose sentence: A sentence that introduces the main idea close to the beginning and concludes with a series of modifiers (*The car left the* *expressway, slowing on the ramp and coming to a stop at the crossroad*). See *periodic sentence.*

metaphor: An implied comparison that attributes the qualities of one thing to another (the word *mainstream* to describe the opinions or activities of most people).

mixed metaphor: The incongruous use of two metaphors in the same context (*the roar of protest was stopped in its tracks*).

narration: The chronological presentation of events. Narration often combines with description and it may serve exposition or persuasion.

order of ideas: The presentation of ideas in a paragraph or an essay according to a plan. The order may be *spatial,* perhaps moving from background to foreground, or from top to bottom, or from side to side; or the order may be *temporal* or chronological (in the order of time). The presentation may be in the order of *importance,* or if the details build intensively, in the order of *climax.* The paragraph or essay may move from *problem* to *solution* or from the *specific* to the *general.* Some of these orders occur together—for example, a chronological presentation of details that builds to a climax.

parallelism: Grammatically similar words, phrases, and clauses arranged to highlight similar ideas (*There are streets where, on January nights, fires burn on every floor of every house, sending fragrant smoke through the cold black trees. There are meadows and fields, long rows of old oaks, bridges that sparkle from afar, ships about to leave for Asia, lakes, horses and islands in the marsh*—Mark Helprin). See *antithesis.*

paraphrase: A rendering of a passage in different words that retain the sense, the tone, and the order of ideas.

periodic sentence: A sentence that builds to the main idea (*Building speed as it curved down the ramp, the car raced into the crowded expressway*). See *loose sentence.*

personification: Giving animate or human qualities to something inanimate or inhuman (The sun *smiled* at the earth).

persuasion: The use of argument or satire or some other means to change an audience's thinking and feeling about an issue.

point of view: The place or vantage point from which an event is seen and described. The term sometimes refers to the mental attitude of the viewer in narration. Mark Twain's *Huckleberry Finn* narrates the adventures of a boy in slave-owning Missouri from the point of view of the boy, not of an adult.

premise: See *syllogism.*

process: An activity or operation containing steps usually performed in the same order. The process may be mechanical (changing a tire), natural (the circulation of the blood), or historical (the rise and spread of a specific epidemic disease, such as bubonic plague, at various times in history).

purpose: The aim of the essay as distinguished from the means used to develop it. The purposes or aims of writing are many; they include expressing personal feelings and ideas, giving information, persuading readers to change their thinking about an issue, inspiring readers to take action, giving pleasure. These purposes may be achieved through description, narration, exposition, or argument. These means may be used alone or in combination, and an essay may contain more than one purpose.

reflection: An essay that explores ideas without necessarily bringing the exploration to completion. The reflective essay can take the form of a loosely organized series of musings or a tightly organized argument.

satire: Ridicule of foolish or vicious behavior or ideas for the purpose of correcting them. *Social satire* concerns foolish but not dangerous behavior and ideas—for example, coarse table manners, pretentious talk, harmless gossip. George Bernard Shaw's *Arms and the Man* is a social satire. *Ethical satire* attacks vicious or dangerous behavior or ideas—religious or racial bigotry, greed, political corruption. Mark Twain's *Huckleberry Finn* is an ethical satire.

simile: A direct comparison between two things (*A growing child is like a young tree*). See *figure of speech, metaphor*.

simple sentence: A sentence consisting of a single main or independent clause and no subordinate or dependent clauses (*The rain started at nightfall*).

slang: Colorful and sometimes short-lived expressions peculiar to a group of people, usually informal in usage and almost always unacceptable in formal usage (*nerd, goof off*).

style: A distinctive manner of speaking and writing. A writing style may be plain in its lack of metaphor and other figures of speech. Another writing style may be highly colorful or ornate.

subordinate clause: A clause that completes a main clause or attaches to it as a modifier (She saw *that the rain had begun. When it rains,* it pours).

syllogism: The formal arrangement of premises and conclusion of a deductive argument. The premises are the general assumptions or truths (*All reptiles are cold-blooded vertebrates. All snakes are reptiles*) from which particular conclusions are drawn (*All snakes are cold-blooded vertebrates*). This formal arrangement helps to test the validity or correctness of the reasoning from premises to conclusion. See *deductive argument*.

symbol: An object that represents an abstract idea. The features of the symbol (the fifty stars and thirteen horizontal stripes of the American flag) suggest characteristics of the object symbolized (the fifty states of the Union, the original confederation of thirteen states). A *sign* need not have this representative quality: a green light signals "go" and a red light "stop" by conventional agreement.

thesis: The central idea that organizes the many smaller ideas and details of the essay.

tone: The phrasing or words that express the attitude or feeling of the speaker or writer. The tone of a statement ranges from the angry, exasperated, and sarcastic to the wondering or approving. An ironic tone suggests that the speaker or writer means more than the words actually state.

topic sentence: Usually the main or central idea of the paragraph that organizes details and subordinate ideas. Though it often opens the paragraph, the topic sentence can appear later—in the middle or at the end of the paragraph.

transition: A word or phrase (*however, thus, in fact*) that connects clauses and sentences. Parallel structure is an important means of transition.

unity: The connection of ideas and details to a central controlling idea of the essay. A unified essay deals with one idea at a time.

COPYRIGHTS AND ACKNOWLEDGMENTS

❧ ❧ ❧

Mary McCarthy, "UNCLE MYERS" from *Memories of a Catholic Girlhood.* Copyright 1951 and renewed 1979 by Mary McCarthy. Reprinted by permission of Harcourt Brace Jovanovich, Inc. Selection title by editor.

Margaret Mead and Rhoda Metraux, "DISCIPLINE—TO WHAT END?" from *A Way of Seeing.* Copyright © 1961, 62, 63, 64, 65, 66, 67, 68, 69, 70 by Margaret Mead and Rhoda Metraux. Reprinted by permission of William Morrow & Company, Inc.

Mary Mebane, "NONNIE" and "LIVING WITH SEGREGATION" from *Mary.* Copyright © 1981 by Mary Elizabeth Mebane. Used by permission of Viking Penguin, a division of Penguin Books USA Inc. Selection title by editor.

H. L. Mencken, "REFLECTIONS ON WAR" from *Minority Report: H. L. Mencken's Notebooks.* Copyright © 1956 by Alfred A. Knopf, Inc. Reprinted by permission of Alfred A. Knopf, Inc. Selection title by editor.

W. S. Merwin, "UNCHOPPING A TREE" from *The Miner's Pale Children,* published by Atheneum 1970. Copyright © 1969, 1970 by W. S. Merwin. Reprinted by permission of Georges Borchardt, Inc.

William Least Heat Moon, "IN THE LAND OF 'COKE-COLA'" from *Blue Highways: A Journey Into America.* Copyright © 1982 by William Least Heat Moon. Reprinted by permission of Little, Brown and Company. Selection title by editor.

John L. Moore, "BAD DAYS AT 'BIG DRY'" from *The New York Times,* August 14, 1988. Copyright © 1988 by The New York Times Company. Reprinted by permission.

Mark H. Moore, "ACTUALLY, PROHIBITION WAS A SUCCESS" from *The New York Times,* October 16, 1989 (OpEd). Copyright © 1989 by The New York Times Company. Reprinted by permission.

Allan Nevins, "THE NEWSPAPER" from *Allan Nevins on History.* Copyright © 1975 by Columbia University. Reprinted with permission of Charles Scribner's Sons, an imprint of Macmillan Publishing Company. Selection title by editor.

Newsweek, "BEING COOL" from Spring 1983 Special Issue of *Newsweek.* Copyright © 1983 Newsweek Inc. All rights reserved. Reprinted by permission. Selection title by editor.

Liane Ellison Norman, "PEDESTRIAN STUDENTS AND HIGH-FLYING SQUIRRELS" from *The Center* Magazine, January/February 1978. Reprinted by permission of the author.

George Orwell, "POLITICS AND THE ENGLISH LANGUAGE" from *Shooting an Elephant and Other Essays.* Copyright 1946 by Sonia Brownell Orwell and renewed 1974 by Sonia Orwell; and "SHOOTING AN ELEPHANT" from *Shooting an Elephant and Other Essays.* Copy-

of Viking Penguin, a division of Penguin Books USA Inc. Selection title by editor.

James Stevenson, "LOMA VISTA DRIVE" from "PEOPLE START RUNNING" in *The New Yorker,* January 20, 1980. Copyright © 1980 by *The New Yorker.* Reprinted by permission of The New Yorker Magazine. Selection title by editor.

Roger D. Stone, "WHY SAVE TROPICAL FORESTS?" from *The New York Times,* November 8, 1986 (OpEd). Copyright © 1986 by The New York Times Company. Reprinted by permission.

Lytton Strachey, "QUEEN VICTORIA AT THE END OF HER LIFE" from *Queen Victoria.* Copyright 1921 by Harcourt Brace Jovanovich, Inc. and renewed 1949 by James Strachey. Reprinted by permission of the publisher. Selection title by editor.

Pierre and Peggy Streit, "A WELL IN INDIA" from *The New York Times,* September 20, 1959. Copyright © 1959 by The New York Times Company. Reprinted by permission.

Kate Swift and Casey Miller, "MANLY" AND "WOMANLY" from *Words and Women,* Updated Edition by Kate Smith and Casey Miller. Copyright © 1976, 1991 by Kate Swift and Casey Miller. Reprinted by permission of HarperCollins Publishers Inc. Selection title by editor.

Edwin Way Teale, from *Wandering through Winter* (Dodd, Mead and Company, 1966). Reprinted by permission of the publisher.

Edward Tenner, "REVENGE THEORY" from *Harvard Magazine,* March–April 1991. Reprinted by permission of Edward Tenner.

Alvin Toffler, "THE DO-IT-YOURSELFERS" from *The Third Wave.* Copyright © 1980 by Alvin Toffler. Reprinted by permission of William Morrow & Company, Inc.

John Updike, "MY GRANDMOTHER" from *Pigeon Feathers.* Copyright © 1962 by John Updike. Reprinted by permission of Alfred A. Knopf, Inc. Originally appeared in *The New Yorker.* Selection title by editor.

Alice Walker, "IN SEARCH OF OUR MOTHERS' GARDENS" from *In Search of Our Mothers' Gardens.* Copyright © 1974 by Alice Walker; and the poem "Women" from *Revolutionary Petunias and Other Poems.* Copyright © 1970 by Alice Walker. Reprinted by permission of Harcourt Brace Jovanovich, Inc.

Jearl Walker, "OUTDOOR COOKING" from "The Amateur Scientist" in *Scientific American,* August 1985. Reprinted by permission of Jearl Walker. Selection title by editor.

Barbara Ward, "TRIAGE" from *The New York Times,* November 15,

INDEX

❦ ❦ ❦